THE WORKS OF JONATHAN EDWARDS

VOLUME 17

Harry S. Stout, General Editor

President Edwards' House, Northampton, Massachusetts.

A sketch of the Edwards parsonage in Northampton, Massachusetts, from Edwin M. Bacon, *Literary Pilgrimages in New England to the Homes of Famous Makers of American Literature* (1902)

JONATHAN EDWARDS

Sermons and Discourses 1730–1733

EDITED BY
MARK VALERI

ERNEST TRICE THOMPSON PROFESSOR OF CHURCH HISTORY
UNION THEOLOGICAL SEMINARY IN VIRGINIA

New Haven and London

YALE UNIVERSITY PRESS, 1999

Funds for editing The Works of Jonathan Edwards *have been provided by The Pew Charitable Trusts, Lilly Endowment, Inc., and The Henry Luce Foundation, Inc.*

Published with assistance from The Exxon Education Foundation.

Set in Baskerville type by The Composing Room of Michigan, Inc., Grand Rapids, Michigan. Printed in the United States of America by Vail-Ballou Press, Binghamton, New York.

Library of Congress Cataloging-in-Publication Data

Edwards, Jonathan, 1703–1758.
Sermons and discourses, 1730–1733 / Jonathan Edwards ; edited by Mark Valeri.
p. cm. — (The works of Jonathan Edwards ; v. 17)
Includes bibliographical references and index.
ISBN 0-300-07840-4 (cloth : alk. paper)
1. Congregational churches—Sermons. 2. Sermons, American. I. Valeri, Mark R. II. Title. III. Series: Edwards, Jonathan, 1703–1758. Works. 1957. vol 17.
BX7117.E3 1999
[BX7233.E3]
285.8 s—dc21
[252'.058] *98-51003*
CIP

A catalogue record for this book is available from the British Library.

The paper in this book meets the guidelines for permanence and durability of the Committee on Production Guidelines for Book Longevity of the Council on Library Resources

10 9 8 7 6 5 4 3 2 1

PREVIOUSLY PUBLISHED

PAUL RAMSEY, ed., *Freedom of the Will*
JOHN E. SMITH, ed., *Religious Affections*
CLYDE A. HOLBROOK, ed., *Original Sin*
C. C. GOEN, ed., *The Great Awakening*
STEPHEN J. STEIN, ed., *Apocalyptic Writings*
WALLACE E. ANDERSON, ed., *Scientific and Philosophical Writings*
NORMAN PETTIT, ed., *The Life of David Brainerd*
PAUL RAMSEY, ed., *Ethical Writings*
JOHN F. WILSON, ed., *A History of the Work of Redemption*
WILSON H. KIMNACH, ed., *Sermons and Discourses, 1720–1723*
WALLACE E. ANDERSON AND MASON I. LOWANCE, eds., *Typological Writings*
DAVID D. HALL, ed., *Ecclesiastical Writings*
THOMAS A. SCHAFER, ed., *The "Miscellanies," a–500*
KENNETH P. MINKEMA, ed., *Sermons and Discourses, 1723–1729*
STEPHEN J. STEIN, ed., *Notes on Scripture*
GEORGE S. CLAGHORN, ed., *Letters and Personal Writings*

CONTENTS

ILLUSTRATIONS

NOTE TO THE READER

The third volume of *Sermons and Discourses* covers a slightly briefer time span than the second but, like it, offers a representative selection of sermons, from a period of intense and voluminous composition. The sermons presented here were chosen to illuminate Edwards' personal development as a preacher and theologian, and they include works of historical, philosophical, and rhetorical significance. Thus, in addition to being the "best" sermons from this period, they attempt to cover, in a judicious and nonrepetitive manner, the various purposes and major themes found in Edwards' sermons and discourses, from scriptural exegesis to local politics.

Starting in 1723 other compositions of theological and literary substance, such as the "Miscellanies" and Scripture notebooks, began supplementing the sermons in documenting Edwards' creative life. To illustrate his homiletical activity, however, the volume appendix, "Dated Batches of Sermons and Dated Sermons," lists all extant sermons composed during the period covered by the volume, individually numbered and identified by Scripture text, and further identified by the doctrinal statement if unpublished, and by title if published in the Edition or previously. Throughout this volume, unpublished sermons are referred to by text and number as found in the appendix.

The reader of this volume may wish to consult the "General Introduction to the Sermons: Jonathan Edwards' Art of Prophesying" in *The Works of Jonathan Edwards, 10, Sermons and Discourses, 1720–1723* (1992) for an overview of the sermons and an examination of Edwards' practices as a homiletical author. Volume 10 also contains a preface to that early period which examines Edwards' early expressions of his personal religion in their biographical context; similarly, the second sermon volume, *The Works of Jonathan Edwards, 14, Sermons and Discourses, 1723–1729* (1997), contains a preface to its period, stressing Edwards' intellectual flowering during the years of his tutorship in Yale College and his apprentice pastorate in Northampton under his grandfather Solomon Stoddard. The preface below will continue this serial biography of Edwards' career as a preacher, focusing upon the first—and perhaps only—"conventional" New England pastorate in Edwards' complicated ministry. The period covered by this volume has hitherto appeared as a lull between Edwards' early personal struggles and his later emergence as a public figure of historic proportions, but, as the editor points out, it is evident that much of that later eminence is the direct result of Edwards' response to his "conventional" pastorate during these outwardly quiet years. His new role as pastor of an important colonial community, and his experience of the religious, social, political, and economic tensions and dislocations of the first third of the eighteenth century, are analyzed in the period preface and documented by the sermons selected.

Wilson H. Kimnach
Editor of Sermons

Preparation of the Text

The text of Jonathan Edwards is reproduced in this Edition as he wrote it in manuscript, or, if he published it himself, as it was printed in the first edition. In order to present this text to modern readers as practically readable, several technical adjustments have been made. Those which can be addressed categorically are as follows:

1. All spelling is regularized and conformed to that of *Webster's Third New International Dictionary*, a step that does not involve much more than removing the "u" from "colour" or "k" from "publick" since Edwards was a good speller, used relatively modern spelling, and generally avoided "y" contractions. His orthographic contractions and abbreviations, such as ampersands, "call'd," and "thems." are spelled out, though pronounced contractions, such as "han't" and "ben't," are retained.

2. There is no regular punctuation in most of Edwards' manuscripts and where it does exist, as in the earliest sermons, it tends to be highly erratic. Editors take into account Edwards' example in punctuation and related matters, but all punctuation is necessarily that of the editor, including paragraph divisions (especially in some notebooks such as the "Miscellanies") and the emphasizing devices of italics and capitalization. In reference to capitalization, it should be noted that pronouns referring to the deity are lower case except in passages where Edwards confusingly mixes "he's" referring to God and man: here capitalization of pronouns referring to the deity sorts out the references for the reader.

3. Numbered heads designate important structures of argument in Edwards' sermons, notebooks, and treatises. Numbering, including spelled-out numbers, has been regularized and corrected where neces-

sary. Particularly in the manuscript sermon texts, numbering has been clarified by the use of systematic schemes of heads and subheads in accordance with eighteenth-century homiletical form, a practice similar to modern analytical outline form. Thus the series of subordinated head number forms, 1, (1), *1*, a, (a), in the textual exegesis, and the series, I, *First,* 1, (1), *1*, a, (a), in Doctrine and Application divisions, make it possible to determine sermon head relationships at a glance.

4. Textual intervention to regularize Edwards' citation of Scripture includes the correction of erroneous citation, the regularizing of citation form (including the standardization of book abbreviations), and the completion of quotations which Edwards' textual markings indicate should be completed (as in preaching).

5. Omissions and lacunae in the manuscript text are filled by insertions in square brackets ([ ]); repeated phrases sometimes represented by Edwards with a long dash are inserted in curly brackets ({ }). In all cases of uncertain readings, annotation gives notice of the problem. Markings in the text designate whole word units even when only a few letters are at issue.

6. Minor slips of the pen or obvious typographical errors are corrected without annotation. Likewise, Edwards' corrections, deletions, and internal shifts of material are observed but not noted unless of substantive interest.

7. Quotations made by the editor from the Bible (AV) and other secondary sources are printed *verbatim ac literatim.* Edwards' quotations from such sources are often rather free but are not corrected and are not annotated as such unless significant omissions or distortions are involved.

Sermon texts in this volume were composed at the time of their delivery in Northampton and generally have not been as heavily revised for repreaching as those in the former sermon volumes. Nevertheless, any significant later modifications and additions have been published in textual footnotes. The prefaces to the two sermons published by Edwards during this period have been included as appendices to those sermons.

Acknowledgments

Scholars who work on Edwards' manuscripts frequently get caught up in the collaborative ethos of the project in New Haven. I am no exception. This volume has been shaped by discussions with Tom Schafer, Wilson Kimnach, and Ken Minkema, each of whom introduced me to the mysteries of the Edwards reading room in the Beinecke Library. I thank Ken and Wilson particularly for the ongoing conversation, which has ranged from deciphering Edwards' shorthand to pondering the effect of Edwards on American theology. In the *Works of Jonathan Edwards* offices, Ken, along with Ava Chamberlain and Doug Sweeney, deftly fielded my requests for background information. They also facilitated several visits to New Haven and helped with the mechanical aspects of the manuscript preparation. Max Lesser initially edited several of the sermons here and provided the title for *East of Eden.* Lynn MacKinnon Valeri proofed the introductory material and suggested ways to clarify it for the general reader. The general editor of this series, Harry S. Stout, has given sage advice and practical assistance throughout. The manuscripts published in this volume are housed at Yale University's Beinecke Rare Book and Manuscript Library, whose staff has been very helpful to the ongoing efforts of the Yale Edwards Edition.

I express my appreciation especially to John F. Wilson. Assisting him on Edwards' *History of the Work of Redemption* taught me much about Edwards. The invitation to join this project was not unrelated to his promptings—and he knows quite well the frustrations and satisfactions of accepting such an invitation.

The American Council of Learned Societies provided a grant for work on this project. I also acknowledge Union Theological Seminary in Virginia, which generously granted me a leave to complete this volume during the first semester of my appointment there. Funding for this volume and for the Edition as a whole has been provided by the Pew Charitable Trusts, Lilly Endowment, Inc., and the Henry Luce Foundation, Inc.

SERMONS AND DISCOURSES, 1730–1733

PREFACE TO THE PERIOD

JONATHAN Edwards was a philosopher-theologian who came to terms with the New Science; a revivalist who preached famous sermons throughout New England; a polemicist who wrote learned treatises in support of experimental Calvinism—and a pastor of the church in Northampton, Massachusetts. The sermons in this volume, dating from the beginning of 1730 through mid-September 1733,[1] show him particularly in the last of these vocations. They demonstrate how he shaped his preaching in reaction to the realities of day-to-day existence in his town. The more he turned his attention to the political, social, and economic activities of his congregation, the more he developed the theological themes that came to characterize his mature evangelical thinking: the viciousness of the unregenerate life, the importance of evangelical humiliation as a religious exercise, and the necessity of a radical conversion from worldliness to godliness.

Certainly, Edwards approached similar issues at other times in his life. But in keeping with the practice of the Yale Edition, which presents his sermons and discourses in terms of thematic focuses for different stages in his career, this volume concentrates on a period that was marked by Edwards' maturation as a local pastor. It was at this time that he consolidated his clerical position and addressed the relation between practical moral concerns and spiritual renewal. The present volume thus complements the one covering the period from 1720 to 1723, which highlights Edwards' spiritual sensibilities and personal religious growth, and the volume from 1723 through 1729, which reveals his intellectual flowering.[2]

In order to orient the reader to these themes, I shall describe, after a brief biographical background, the overall contours of Edwards' preach-

1. Though *A Divine and Supernatural Light*, included here, was published in 1734, it was first preached in Aug. 1733.

2. See *The Works of Jonathan Edwards, 10, Sermons and Discourses, 1720–1723*, ed. Wilson H. Kimnach (New Haven, Yale Univ. Press, 1992); and *The Works of Jonathan Edwards, 14, Sermons and Discourses, 1723–1729*, ed. Kenneth P. Minkema (New Haven, Yale Univ. Press, 1997).

ing, with some discussion of Puritan approaches to the question of the relation between moral agency and conversion. I shall then survey developments in Edwards' homiletical method in this period, as well as the setting for his sermons in corporate worship. Next, I shall summarize the political and social background, Edwards' reflections on it, and his moral critique and doctrine of sin. I shall conclude with a commentary on three of the dominant themes that recur in these sermons: the theological end of human depravity, evangelical humiliation as preparation for conversion, and the necessity of a divine and supernatural light for regeneration.

Biographical Background

Previous experiences as a practicing minister certainly influenced Edwards; but the years covered in this volume were quite unlike the traumatic period from 1723 through 1729.[3] In 1723 Edwards had resigned his pastorate in Bolton, Connecticut, and the next year he assumed a tutorship at Yale. In 1725, after undergoing some self-confessed spiritual despondency provoked (he surmised) by an undue attachment to his worldly career, he worked himself into a state of anxiety and exhaustion, and the following year moved to Northampton, Massachusetts, to assist his grandfather Solomon Stoddard. In July 1727 he married Sarah Pierpont. Stoddard died in February 1729, and Edwards assumed the pulpit of the Northampton church. In the summer of 1729 he had another breakdown, related to fatigue and mental stress. The year ended with the death of his sister Jerusha from diphtheria.

Edwards did not suffer such personal crises in the early 1730s. Nor did he undertake the widespread travel, accompanied by growing notoriety, that characterized his career from 1734 through 1743, when the revivals that began in the Connecticut River Valley thrust Edwards into a position of intercolonial prominence. His life from 1730 through 1733, though sparsely documented, appears to have been rather uneventful, except for the birth of his second and third daughters, Jerusha (b. April 26, 1730) and Esther (February 13, 1732). This is not to say that Edwards was idle. With Stoddard's death, and having exhausted his stock of previously written sermons, he increased his pace of sermon composition markedly. Yet Edwards' private affairs were basically stable. He remained for the

3. See *Works, 14*, 3–46, esp. 6–16. See also Sereno E. Dwight, *The Works of President Edwards* (10 vols. New York, 1830), *1*, 114–21 (hereafter Dwight ed.); and Ola E. Winslow, *Jonathan Edwards, 1703–1758* (New York, Macmillan, 1941), 118–19.

most part in Northampton, growing accustomed to the steady rhythms of pastoral life.[4]

Perhaps the relative tranquillity of these years afforded Edwards the opportunity to expend his energies on the routine responsibilities of his calling: getting acquainted with the people, finding his voice as the religious leader in the town, exercising moral and spiritual guidance, consulting with other pastors at the county-wide meeting of clergy (which became the Hampshire Association in 1731), and developing a mature preaching style. He had the opportunity to learn about his parishioners' interests and problems through commonplace socializing and various pastoral activities, such as catechizing children, teaching young converts, performing weddings, lending books, visiting the homes of distressed townspeople, and receiving prayer requests. He also had business dealings with his neighbors. He bought, raised, and sold sheep as a supplement to his professional income. He negotiated his salary and allotment of firewood from the lay leaders of the church. His sermons from the early 1730s, in fact, reveal a rather intimate knowledge of his people. He frequently refers to the common sentiments and behavior of the congregation—their private opinions and public gossip, affections for family and relationships with neighbors, business dealings and consumer tastes.[5]

Edwards did not always like what he encountered. This was perhaps the natural reaction of any young, idealistic pastor confronting the realities of social existence in a mid-eighteenth-century New England town. There was something more in Edwards' case, however, than the inevitable disappointments of his profession. Edwards might well have come to Northampton—one of the more prosperous settlements along the Connecticut River—with high hopes. His grandfather Stoddard had had a very successful ministry there, and the town was reputed to have undergone several periods of spiritual renewal. The people welcomed Edwards

4. There is little autobiographical evidence from 1730 through 1733: no entries in JE's "Diary" and no surviving letters from him.

5. For JE's pastoral and business activities, see Winslow, *Jonathan Edwards*, 118–33. Many of the pastors of the county met to discuss disciplinary cases and consult with each other; in 1731 they formalized their association by founding the Hampshire Association, which convened twice a year. Its minutes (MS, Forbes Library, Northampton, Massachusetts) show that JE attended their meetings on Oct. 6, 1731 at Westfield, on Apr. 1, 1732 at Hatfield, and on Oct. 3, 1732 at Springfield. JE performed four weddings in 1733, to cite one year. Among the books that he lent to parishioners were catechisms and treatises on moral issues. For mention of these weddings and books, see his MS "Diary and Account Book," pp. 1–2, Beinecke Library, Yale University, New Haven, Connecticut. Unless indicated otherwise, all MSS are in the Beinecke Library.

warmly, provided him with a large salary, and built a barn for him soon after he settled. Yet if Edwards had imagined that he was to be the pastor of a pious society, then his expectations were dashed during the early 1730s. He repeatedly found his people guilty of religious apathy, worldliness, selfishness, and a nearly constant habit of bickering and quarreling. Added to his previous, personal failures to maintain the godly fervor he had experienced before becoming a tutor at Yale, his disappointments with the people of Northampton and, indeed, with social and political affairs throughout New England, led him to dwell on sin as the essence of the human condition.[6]

We cannot draw certain conclusions about the acuity of Edwards' social analyses. He has been described as a critical observer of a new, socially fractious style: of the market-driven individual abetted by an Arminian theology that exalted the assertion of self. He has also been portrayed as somewhat aloof from his congregation, led by his theological agenda into misreading his people and his neighboring pastors as lax, heterodox, or materialistic. Certainly, other pastors in the Connecticut River Valley shared Edwards' perception that Arminianism, spiritual apathy, social schism, and economic ambition were genuine threats. Nor was he alone in promoting evangelical revival; Stoddard and other pastors in the area had been engaged in that task throughout the 1720s. But Edwards' evangelical theology grew out of his belief that the collective behavior of his people evidenced an urgent need for moral reformation and spiritual regeneration.[7]

Edwards' private writings from the period show that he had begun to experiment with different ways of formulating the relation between moral problems and evangelical solutions. In his more speculative moments he adopted the method of European and British moral philosophers who conceived of moral relationships in terms of natural law. Rationalist writers like Samuel Clarke, to cite but one important figure for Edwards, maintained that the human mind had innate faculties of

6. See James R. Trumbull, *History of Northampton, Massachusetts, From Its Settlement in 1654* (2 vols. Northampton, 1902), 2, 50. Perry Miller portrayed (in an overly dramatic but yet effective manner) the weight of Stoddard's mantle and the high expectations placed on JE as he assumed the pulpit in Northampton. See Miller, *Jonathan Edwards* (New York, 1949; rep. Cleveland, Ohio, World Publishing Co., 1959), pp. 3–40.

7. For JE as a trenchant social critic, see especially Miller, *Jonathan Edwards*; for the countervailing view, see *The Works of Jonathan Edwards, 12, Ecclesiastical Writings*, ed. David D. Hall (New Haven, Yale Univ. Press, 1994), pp. 1–89. For the observations and evangelistic efforts of neighboring pastors, see Kevin Michael Sweeney, "River Gods and Related Minor Deities: The Williams Family and the Connecticut River Valley, 1736–1790." Ph. D. diss., Yale University, 1986.

reason that could deduce fundamental virtues and vices from observation of society. Reason could also determine that there was a moral order to the universe, a natural and moral law according to which such virtues as benevolence were laudable or worthy of reward and such vices as inhumaneness shameful or worthy of punishment. Edwards mused on the connections between natural law and divine revelation and ruminated on the possibilities of a correlation between the two in terms of a universal ethical system that would lead humankind to acknowledge the true essences of virtue and vice, the moral depravity of people in light of a reasoned ethics, and the universal need for supernatural grace.[8]

In 1729 or 1730 Edwards drafted an outline for a new theological system, tentatively entitled "A Rational Account," which he intended as a full and systematic demonstration of how a rational moral philosophy could sustain Calvinism. He proposed "to show how all arts and sciences, the more they are perfected, the more they issue in divinity, and coincide with it." Edwards specifically was attracted to the notion of a theology in which the laws of nature were explained as congruent with the laws of God. He hoped to show, using the language of the Enlightenment, that a genuine ethics would demonstrate the reasonableness of the central truths of the gospel and the necessity for revelation. "Natural notions, as they are called, of God, natural notions of justice, of good and evil," Edwards wrote, are "certainly prejudices" if they do not issue in these conclusions. He never composed his "Rational Account," but there are bits and pieces of writing in this vein scattered throughout his "Miscellanies" and other notebooks from the period. They provide, as it were, Edwards' more philosophical, if incomplete, statements on the issue that framed his preaching: the moral limitations of natural existence.[9]

Edwards' Sermon Corpus and the Puritan Paradigm for Conversion

Whereas Edwards incorporated the idioms of contemporary moral philosophy into his notebooks and such later writings as *The Nature of True Virtue*, he employed the vocabulary of everyday experience, Puritan divinity, and biblical narrative in his sermons. In the selections that follow—eighteen sermons comprising some forty preaching units (the amount of text preached in a single service)—Edwards thus labored to translate his emerging theology into language that was accessible to his

8. See Norman Fiering, *Jonathan Edwards's Moral Thought and Its British Context* (Chapel Hill, Univ. of North Carolina Press, 1981).

9. "Outline of 'A Rational Account,'" in *Works of Jonathan Edwards, 6, Scientific and Philosophical Writings*, ed. Wallace E. Anderson (New Haven, Yale Univ. Press, 1980), 396–97.

congregation.[1] They represent a range of homiletical responses to the issues of his day: regular sermons, lectures, two sermons prepared for publication, and a variety of sermons for special occasions. There are two sacrament sermons, an election sermon, a fast-day sermon, a funeral sermon, and a sermon that was probably delivered on the occasion of a charitable contribution. Together, they illustrate Edwards' preaching as he reached his full powers as a homiletician, just before the revivals that made him famous.

Several motifs and doctrines appear in the sermon corpus. Edwards preached about more than social problems, sin, and the need for regeneration. He reworked many ideas common to the Anglo-American Reformed canon, drawing widely from his private notebooks of the period.[2] In *Honey from the Rock*, for example, one of his more intricate sermons from a literary standpoint, he gives a highly christocentric, typological reading of God's provision to the people of Israel in the wilderness. A sermon on Cant. 1:3 (288) from June 1733—which bears marked similarities to the sermon on Rev. 5:5–6 (405), published in 1738 as *The Excellency of Christ*—contains an unusually lengthy exposition of the nature of Christ in terms of his love for his people. *The True Christian's Life a Journey Towards Heaven* is pastoral in tone—an effort toward consolation and encouragement in light of death. The most frequently repeated and thoroughly developed themes, however, concerned the moral condition

1. See the Appendix for a complete list of sermons from this period. Sermons mentioned in this Preface to the Period but not published in this volume are cited by the biblical text on which JE preached and the Schafer number as given in the Appendix. For matters of sermon dating, see the "Editor's Introduction" to *The Works of Jonathan Edwards, 13, The "Miscellanies," a–500*, ed. Thomas A. Schafer (New Haven, Yale Univ. Press, 1994), 1–123. For a survey of JE's sermon corpus as a whole and a discussion of the literary techniques mentioned below, see the "General Introduction to the Sermons: Jonathan Edwards' Art of Prophesying," in *Works, 10*, 3–258.

2. JE's nonsermonic compositions from 1730 through 1733 include the following published materials: "Apocalypse" nos. 52 through 65 (*The Works of Jonathan Edwards, 5, Apocalyptic Writings*, ed. Stephen J. Stein [New Haven, Yale Univ. Press, 1977], 146–60); "Images" nos. 20–45 (*The Works of Jonathan Edwards, 11, Typological Writings*, eds. Wallace E. Anderson and Mason I. Lowance [New Haven, Yale Univ. Press, 1993], 56–63); "Notes on Scripture" no. 192 to *circa* no. 219 (see *The Works of Jonathan Edwards, 15, Notes on Scripture*, ed. Stephen J. Stein [New Haven, Yale Univ. Press, 1998], 106–54); and "Miscellanies" entries from the 460s through the 620s (see *Works, 13*, 501–41, and *The Works of Jonathan Edwards, "Miscellanies," 501–832*, ed. Ava Chamberlain, [New Haven, Yale Univ. Press, forthcoming]). See also the following unpublished notebooks: "Catalogue of Reading" from *circa* no. 339 to 372 (a large number of books that he recorded in this period dealt with either church history or natural religion); entries in the notebook on "Faith" from the low 60s through the high 70s; "Signs of Godliness," MS pp. 4–5, and scattered entries on MS pp. 6–19; and "Christ's Example," MS pp. 1–2. JE also acquired his MS "Blank Bible" in 1730. For full bibliographic information, see *Works, 13*, 91–109.

of Edwards' people and the problem—acute for a Calvinist like Edwards—of the relation between human efforts toward reform, which presuppose some natural moral capacity, and the doctrine of divine election, which implies human depravity and God's sovereignty.

This last issue presented Edwards with a theological conundrum. From a psychological standpoint, it appeared to be a contradiction to claim that people were inveterate sinners and yet free to choose to obey God.[3] From a doctrinal perspective, it was problematic to assert that God determined human destinies and yet was just in holding individuals accountable to moral law. As a preacher, however, Edwards faced the dilemma in more practical terms. How was he to urge people to repent and exhort them to obey God, while telling them that the one thing they most needed was to deny their moral competence and entrust themselves to God's mercy in Christ?

Individual sermons were not systematic theologies, and at times Edwards stressed one side of the equation (human responsibility) or the other (divine sovereignty). He could sound like an Arminian, demanding self-initiated moral reform and threatening God's punishment for unrepentance. In *The Duty of Charity to the Poor*, he tells his people that neglect of the needy will be punished with an eternity in hell; and in an unpublished sermon on Matt. 5:13 (151) from early in this period, he emphasizes the importance of visible moral behavior as the key to true religion. In his sermon on Eccles. 9:10 (307), he urges the unregenerate to do what they can to act rightly and religiously, even in their "natural power," as steps toward godliness. Edwards could also replicate the formula of Puritan federal theologians, who posited a common moral standard by which God judged earthly collectivities and an interior, spiritual dynamic by which he elected individuals to salvation apart from their human foibles. In *The Dangers of Decline*, for instance, Edwards turns to the necessity for public virtue and the collective duty to mitigate divine judgment through moral reformation. Edwards can also recommend a form of piety so focused on affective religious experience apart from moral reform that it verges on antinomianism. So in *The Pure in Heart Blessed*, he appears intent on disabusing his congregation of the belief that their moral efforts have any worth and urges them to chiefly seek their own happiness by delighting in the presence of God.

3. In *Freedom of the Will*, JE wrote a systematic analysis of the problem, in the language of moral psychology, as the relation between cognition, volition, and disposition. See, for example, *The Works of Jonathan Edwards, 1, Freedom of the Will*, ed. Paul Ramsey (New Haven, Yale Univ. Press, 1957), 297–301.

To be sure, none of these sermons is Arminian or antinomian in a technical sense. Taken together, they reveal the extent to which Edwards worked within the parameters of Reformed teaching to affirm the moral obligations of individuals and their dependence on grace. Indeed, Puritan teachings on the relation between human sinfulness, moral agency, and the process of conversion provided Edwards with a pattern for his ideas. Scholastic Calvinists of the post-Reformation era, whose formulations—such as the 1619 decrees of the Synod of Dort—influenced many New England divines, analyzed this relation by drawing a distinction between moral capacity and merit. They held that the unconverted, despite their sinfulness, retained a natural ability to will and to act in accordance with God's laws. To obey God, however, in no way merited the saving grace that effected faith in Christ, justified the sinner, and led to salvation. Nor did obedience provide an efficient cause for God to bestow such grace. Only God's sovereign and self-determined will caused grace to be instilled in particular persons. Reformed thinkers nonetheless contended that God ordinarily used natural acts of obedience as instruments, or secondary causes, through which he effectively called individuals to faith and regenerated their moral faculties.[4]

Orthodox Calvinists thus distinguished their teachings from antinomianism, the radical offshoot of Protestantism made infamous in Massachusetts in the case of Anne Hutchinson. Antinomians denied that natural moral effort had any efficacy in the process of conversion. Puritan preachers in England and New England claimed, in contrast, that one could properly use religious means (moral striving, prayer, Bible study, worship, and, as Stoddard held, attendance on the sacraments) as a prelude to conversion. God had chosen these measures—known as the means of preparation for salvation—to be the ordinary instruments through which he bestowed grace. From the perspective of covenant theology, God judged the worthiness of a church or civil order by the extent to which it instituted these means and promoted the diligent use of them.

4. The material in this and the following discussion of Puritan ideas of conversion draws on the different analyses provided in William K. B. Stoever, *'A Faire and Easie Way to Heaven': Covenant Theology and Antinomianism in Early Massachusetts* (Middletown, Conn., Wesleyan Univ. Press, 1978), esp. 110–18; Charles Lloyd Cohen, *God's Caress: The Psychology of Puritan Religious Experience* (New York, Oxford Univ. Press, 1986); and Norman Pettit, *The Heart Prepared: Grace and Conversion in Puritan Spiritual Life* (New Haven, Yale Univ. Press, 1966). Janice Knight, *Orthodoxies in Massachusetts: Rereading American Puritanism* (Cambridge, Mass., Harvard Univ. Press, 1994), shows how there were different strains of Puritan teaching on the subject and indicates some of the lines between Puritans and Edwards.

Subjectively experienced, preparatory activity ushered the elect through a sequence of spiritual conditions that resulted in salvation. There was, many divines explained, a predictable if not universal pattern, the *ordo salutis* ("order of salvation"), by which God turned sinners into saints. Over the course of the seventeenth century, Puritan commentators on the process of conversion came to center especially on "legal" humiliation. They often described the components of humiliation in elaborate detail, replete with analyses of various interior moral states. According to the typical scenario, converts initially underwent a period of legal humiliation in several stages. First, they learned of the evil of disobedience to God, then felt remorse for their sin. They next came to hate their sin and to attempt repentance under their natural faculties and powers (although the Holy Spirit, operating through the Word of God, provoked their consciences). Yet while this preparatory work of repentance or humiliation was crucial in producing a change of heart, it was ultimately unsuccessful. Sinners would therefore fall into despair over their inability to repent.

Here the process of legal humiliation ended, and God bestowed grace on the elect. This infusion of grace was the activity of the Holy Spirit. Out of despair the sinner began to perceive his or her faith in Christ as the sole means to salvation. Joy and peace ensued. The new love for God enabled individuals to evidence their regeneration by obedience to his commands as well as by a continued recognition of their sinfulness, which was called "evangelical" humiliation.

With its precise psychological commentary and its assertion of the imperative of using one's natural powers through preparatory means, the Puritan paradigm tended to emphasize the individual's understanding of, or even control over, the spiritual processes prior to the gift of grace. The most effective thing sinners could do to prepare themselves for regeneration (or that lapsed Christians could do to reinvigorate their spiritual and moral lives) was to attempt to obey God's law, discover how utterly vain were their efforts, and thereby appreciate the extent of their dependence on Christ. Strict Calvinists insisted, however, that there was no inherent relation between preparatory works and God's decision to give grace—no merit, no diminution of human depravity, no causation, no guarantee, no complete predictability. God freely chose to save some people through such means.

A thin line separated this doctrine from the non-Calvinist teaching that fallen humanity retained a moral capacity to act in such a way as to secure conversion. Calvinists labeled those who crossed the line Arminians. Although no respectable eighteenth-century congregationalist clergyman would have labeled himself an Arminian—the term had an odious association with the Church of England—many New Englanders in Edwards' day did affirm a version of Reformed teaching that provided an alternative to the Calvinist understanding of the relation between natural moral acts and saving grace; this doctrine bore some resemblance to the teachings of the seventeenth-century Dutch theologian who provoked the Synod of Dort, Jacob Arminius. Those of an Arminian bent taught that faith, as a natural and voluntary act in itself, effected saving grace. They held that there was an inherent connection between a human moral decision and the gift of salvation.

The difference between Calvinist and Arminian teachings at this point may appear slight in comparison with their mutual divergence from Roman Catholicism or even some forms of Anglican doctrine, which posit a correlation between the moral merit of obedience and how much saving grace God bestows. Neither Calvinists nor Arminians spoke of merit in such terms. In the balance, however, Calvinists stressed the priority of grace and therefore divine initiative. Arminians stressed the priority of faith and therefore the individual's moral decision. These different emphases implied variant religious sensibilities. Calvinists insisted on the radical nature of regeneration, while Arminians focused on religious teaching and moral training as the necessary antecedents to conversion. In the course of the eighteenth century, each side produced polemical caricatures of the other. Arminians like Boston's Charles Chauncy portrayed Calvinists as morally fatalistic, and holding to an oppressive view of human nature that implied that God was an arbitrary and despotic being. Calvinists like Edwards, in turn, described Arminians as naively optimistic about human nature, maintaining a doctrine that constrained God's sovereignty within the bounds of human agency.

Nowhere in his sermons from this period, however, did Edwards state the classical Calvinist scheme explicitly. Indeed, by 1730 so many permutations had been made to the scheme that it defied a single formulation. Yet the Calvinist paradigm, in contrast to the Arminian and the antinomian, definitively shaped Edwards' understanding of the dialectic between human act, or the use such means as moral obedience and proper worship, and the divine prerogative to bestow grace on those whom God had elected to salvation. Edwards' formulation was threefold. First, he maintained a moral critique of his society, asserting that human beings were utterly sinful. Morally incapable of doing anything to earn or effect grace, they needed to recognize their complete dependence on Christ. This is the burden of his first published sermon, *God Glorified in Man's Dependence,* as well as of his sermon on Rom. 9:18 (250). Second, he insisted that people must nonetheless strive to reform morally. For the regenerate, such striving was a means to sanctification; for the unregenerate, it was a means of self-humiliation and a preparation for genuine conversion. *God Makes Men Sensible of Their Misery Before He Reveals His Mercy and Love* contains an extended discussion on this point. Third, he contended that only an infusion of the Holy Spirit could regenerate fallen human beings and capacitate them for faith and genuine virtue. He fastened on divine light as a trope for this dynamic, as is evident not only in *A Divine and Supernatural Light* but also in *The Pure in Heart Blessed* and his unpublished sermon from 1731 on Luke 10:38–42 (196).

Edwards' Homiletical Method

As Edwards attempted to convey increasingly complex theological concepts to his congregation, he experimented with different ways of organizing his sermons. Wilson H. Kimnach has shown how Edwards adopted and modified various homiletical strategies throughout his career.[5] Puritan preaching in the seventeenth century tended toward doctrinal analysis organized by the definition of central concepts into several divisions; the elucidation of a doctrine might take several major points, each divided into many subheads—all of which were incorporated into a single sermon. In the early eighteenth century a simpler format emerged: one text, one doctrine with several points, and one application with several admonishments. Timothy Edwards adopted this format in part, although he continued to rely on multiple doctrines and many subheads. Solomon Stoddard also employed the new threefold division but further reduced the number of subheads. He relied instead on rhetorical dynamism: aphoristic phrasing, metaphor, and penetrating psychological analysis.

Edwards followed Stoddard's form closely, but from 1730 through 1733 he introduced organizational complexities. Five of the sermons in this volume retain the simpler format: a one-unit sermon that contains an explication of the biblical text, a single doctrine with two to three subheads, and an application with multiple uses. Five sermons here also contain single doctrines but are lengthier, from two to four preaching units. Yet there are many sermons from this period in which Edwards did

5. See *Works, 10,* 42–129.

not attempt to simplify his message into a single doctrinal proposition. He still devoted a single portion of the sermon to doctrine, but he often expanded this section and relied on multiple major divisions of the doctrine into discrete propositions of equal weight. Edwards' three-unit sermon on Luke 10:38–42 (196) contains three doctrines related to the topic of spiritual knowledge. His sermon on Matt. 7:21 (176) has two doctrines or propositions, as does *The State of Public Affairs* and his three-unit lecture, *The Pure in Heart Blessed.* His lengthiest sermon on a single text from the period, *Christians a Chosen Generation,* is a six-unit performance that also followed this pattern.

Edwards experimented in other ways. *Honey from the Rock* is a two-unit sermon with three doctrines: the first unit contains the text, the first proposition of the doctrine, an application, and the second proposition without any application. The second unit returns to the text for a brief further explication, then proceeds to the third doctrine and an application. In *Born Again,* possibly written for a private meeting, Edwards skips the text and its exposition altogether. And in *The Duty of Charity to the Poor,* he devotes less than one unit of the sermon to doctrine and the entirety of the remaining four units to application, the third major division of which had eleven subpoints in the form of objections and answers.

Such innovations reflect Edwards' attempts to make controversial theological issues intelligible. He wanted to persuade, not just to inform. The division of a complex doctrine into equal but discrete units allowed him to expand on one issue and employ such nonanalytical discursive techniques as metaphor, narrative, and vivid imagery. When he lectured to other clergy or prepared his sermons for publication, Edwards felt free to return to a single doctrine and develop it with a high degree of nuance and sophistication. So *God Glorified in Man's Dependence,* delivered to the Boston clergy and his first published sermon, shows a great deal of cutting between manuscript and print, as does *A Divine and Supernatural Light.* For the most part, however, Edwards moved toward creating a sermon series, as in *The Pure in Heart Blessed* and *Christians a Chosen Generation,* or a discourse that could carry the load of a sophisticated theological analysis by addressing the doctrine in several separate units. Comprising seven units altogether, his unpublished sermons on Rom. 3:13–18 (249) and Rom. 9:18 (250) were closely linked and in effect a contiguous exposition of the nature of fallen humanity, the sovereignty of God in salvation, and predestination. Edwards linked two sermons and doctrines from Eccles. 9:10 (307, 311) to deal with a single text and issue—the nature of unregenerate efforts toward conversion. By the end of 1733 Edwards had settled on this method to accommodate his more extensive theological efforts. He did not deviate much farther from the simple tripartite structure of the sermon; rather, he extended the length of his sermons into multiple units, or series. This resulted in his influential discourses from 1734 through 1738: *Justification by Faith Alone, Charity and Its Fruits,* and *A History of the Work of Redemption.*

The Setting for Preaching

Edwards searched for a lucid method to convey his ideas because he preached first and foremost to his congregation in the midst of regular worship. In his discourse on *The Perpetuity and Change of the Sabbath* he goes to great lengths to demonstrate the importance of sabbath observance as an expression of common religious identity and solidarity. In gathering for corporate worship, Christians are, by his account, withdrawn from the factious world of social affairs. They are caught up in the rhythms of biblical history, according to which believers position their lives in the pattern of creation, fall, and redemption.

In Northampton, as in most towns in colonial New England, the sermon was the central event of worship, and accordingly crucial to the corporate religious life of its people. The Puritan preacher, as William Perkins and other English divines described him, made the truths of the Bible alive by applying them to his auditors.[6] Since the Word of God had priority in the divine-human relationship, preaching surpassed other activities in worship, in which human beings addressed God through prayer and singing.

The Puritan form of service reflected this emphasis. We do not have a record of the order of worship in Edwards' church, but we can surmise that it replicated the general form used throughout New England's congregational churches.[7] The typical meeting, according to the Puritan

6. See David D. Hall, *The Faithful Shepherd: A History of the New England Ministry in the Seventeenth Century* (Chapel Hill, Univ. of North Carolina Press, 1972), esp. 48–71; and Harry S. Stout, *The New England Soul: Preaching and Religious Culture in Colonial New England* (New York, Oxford Univ. Press, 1986), 13–49.

7. The following discussion on worship relies on Horton Davies, *Worship and Theology in England, Vol. II: From Andrews to Baxter and Fox, 1603–1690* (Princeton, Princeton Univ. Press, 1975), 405–34; Davies, *Worship and Theology in England, Vol. III: From Watts and Wesley to Maurice, 1690–1850* (Princeton, Princeton Univ. Press, 1961), 19–39, 94–113, 184–209; Davies, *The Worship of the American Puritans* (New York, Peter Lang, 1990); Alice Morse Earle, *The Sabbath in Puritan New England* (New York, Charles Scribner's Sons, 1891), 202–29; Charles E. Hambrick-Stowe, *The Practice of Piety: Puritan Devotional Disciplines in Seventeenth-Century New England* (Chapel Hill, Univ. of North Carolina Press, 1982), 96–135. On the importance of the sabbath

"Directory for the Public Worship of God" of the Westminster Assembly, contained, with some local variations and emendations, the following elements: a call to worship (typically a quotation from Scripture), a prayer of adoration and supplication for illumination, a psalm (most likely, from the *Bay Psalm Book*),[8] a reading from the Old Testament,another psalm, a reading from the New Testament, a prayer of confession of sin on behalf of the whole congregation, the sermon, a general pastoral prayer (which included prayers of intercession for sick or otherwise distressed parishioners), another psalm, and a blessing or benediction by the pastor.

Corporate worship took place ordinarily on Sunday morning and Sunday afternoon. Many churches, including the one in Northampton, also conducted a Thursday lecture. Celebrations of the Lord's Supper, which were held in Northampton every eight weeks and to which only members were welcome, occupied a separate service following the regular Sunday morning meeting. Special occasions like a baptism, a funeral, or a charitable collection were typically observed on Sunday afternoons. Fast days were called twice a year by colonial decree, and public days of thanksgiving once a year, though local fasts and thanksgiving could be called as circumstances dictated.

Edwards assumed a position of immense authority in this form of worship. All parts of the Sunday morning meeting except the sermon might have lasted half an hour to an hour together (and even the prayers were offered solely by Edwards); one of his preaching units—the sermon for a service—probably took from an hour to an hour and a half to deliver. The gathered community, in other words, focused its attention on the preacher. He would speak of their moral and religious states, their concerns, and their prospects for salvation; and he was often the chief means of their intellectual as well as spiritual instruction. It was no won-

---

as a social and cultural institution, see Winton U. Solberg, *Redeem the Time: The Puritan Sabbath in Early America* (Cambridge, Mass., Harvard Univ. Press, 1977).

8. The old Puritan method was to line out the psalm in a simple melody. JE noted in 1734 that his congregation had learned to sing the psalms in meter and had begun to use four-part harmony—an indication of his willingness to accept innovations in worship. By the late 1730s some churches experimented with a choir of song leaders; the Northampton church may have followed suit. In 1742, under the influence of revivalistic practice, the Northampton congregation began using Isaac Watts' hymns in the Sunday afternoon service. Musical instruments were not used in New England's Congregational worship services until the 1790s. See *A Faithful Narrative*, in *The Works of Jonathan Edwards, 4, The Great Awakening*, ed. C. C. Goen (New Haven, Yale Univ. Press, 1972), 118, 151; and JE to Benjamin Colman, May 22, 1744, in *The Works of Jonathan Edwards, 16, Letters and Personal Writings*, ed. George S. Claghorn (New Haven, Yale Univ. Press, 1998), 144–45.

der that Edwards was jealous of his office. He concentrated on theological themes and rhetorical devices that were designed to evoke not just temporary awe and reverence but also a steady dedication to moral and religious performance in society.

Edwards' Response to Political and Social Affairs

That many of the sermons in this volume should address political and social affairs is unremarkable.[9] Edwards, like his pastoral colleagues, preached about government as a matter of professional and personal interest. He inherited Puritan aspirations for communal solidarity and viewed social concord as one of the chief ends of the civil order. Politics had a religious mandate in this tradition. Edwards was also an employee of a church that had been established by law. The government of Massachusetts enforced the payment of taxes for his salary and the maintenance of the local meetinghouse, legislated statutes in conformity with such moral conventions as sabbath observance, recognized the authority of the clerical association of which he was a member, and protected the status of the congregational order of which he was a part.[1] The Hampshire County court met periodically at Northampton, giving Edwards an audience of justices and other public officials. He was a public spokesman by his very position, and indebted to the political constitution of the colony. During the late 1720s and early 1730s, moreover, political contention and social disintegration reached alarming levels in Massachusetts, compelling Edwards to address public issues with a heightened sense of urgency and specificity.

Political and social issues appear sporadically throughout the sermons in this volume, moving to the foreground in many of them. Clearly such concerns were never far from Edwards' mind. His references to public events will not always be obvious to the modern reader, however. Edwards

9. Of the seventy sermons by JE published in the eighteenth and nineteenth centuries, none dealt explicitly with public affairs. Only recently, with attention to unpublished and especially occasional sermons, have historians begun to uncover the civic dimensions of JE's thought. For a general statement on the relation between occasional sermons and politics in New England preaching, with references to JE, see Stout, *The New England Soul.* For recent attempts to describe some of the political and economic themes in JE's MS sermons, see Gerald R. McDermott, *One Holy and Happy Society: The Public Theology of Jonathan Edwards* (University Park, Penn., Pennsylvania State Univ. Press, 1992); and Mark Valeri, "The Economic Thought of Jonathan Edwards," *Church History* 60 (1991), 37–54.

1. See George Lee Haskins, *Law and Authority in Early Massachusetts: A Study in Tradition and Design* (Hamden, Conn., Archon Books, 1960), esp. 85–93, for a discussion of the legal establishment of the churches.

rarely finished a sermon in this period, for example, without mentioning the vice of envy. As he employed it, the term was not an abstract, private, or merely interpersonal moral concept. It had a political valence. Edwards used "envy" to evoke a social dynamic that appeared to him especially characteristic of political and economic contests in Massachusetts in the early 1730s. At times Edwards specified his meaning. At others he left it to inference; he preached, in a technical sense, about the doctrine rather than the occasion. People in Northampton would nonetheless have heard many passages in Edwards' sermons as commentary on the month-to-month political developments in Boston and elsewhere. To grasp his references, an overview of the relevant events is required.

We can distinguish two overriding, interrelated concerns. First, disputes between the elected legislature of the colony and the governor appeared to threaten the charter, which secured the religious establishment. These disputes had been some four decades in the making and were much publicized.[2] The government of the colony rested on the charter of 1691. Negotiated between agents for the colony and the crown, it had succeeded the unpopular regime of Gov. Edmund Andros and represented the effects of the Glorious Revolution in provincial politics. This charter did not have the nearly mythic aura that surrounded the colony's original charter of 1629, but Edwards, like other provincials, viewed it with pride. It encoded some measure of self-rule. Each May towns elected representatives to the legislative assembly, or lower house. The 1691 charter ended the colony's practice of requiring full membership in the church for suffrage and imposed some measure of religious toleration; but it tacitly kept other measures of New England's congregational order in place. The assembly made laws, elected an upper house (or council), established the judiciary system, and issued money for the colony. Known as bills of credit, this money was denominated in pounds sterling; but since the treasury in Boston did not have a supply of sterling, bills of credit were basically promissory notes from the provincial government. They were intended chiefly as a medium of exchange and were backed by the colony's ability to raise funds (through taxes and duties) and pay them off at some future date.

2. The following account of Massachusetts politics relies on Henry Russell Spencer, *Constitutional Conflicts in Provincial Massachusetts: A Study of Some Phases of the Opposition Between the Massachusetts Government and General Court in the Early Eighteenth Century* (Columbus, Ohio, n. p., 1905); and William Pencak, *War, Politics, and Revolution in Provincial Massachusetts* (Boston, Northeastern Univ. Press, 1981), 61–113. For an influential statement on the importance of political contests in this period, see Bernard Bailyn, *The Origins of American Politics* (New York, Alfred A. Knopf, 1968).

Yet for all of the apparent power vested in the assembly, the charter gave an enormous amount of prerogative to the executive. The crown appointed a governor and lieutenant governor. Although the governor supposedly represented the interests of the colony to the court in London, his chief function was to fulfill the mandates of the monarchy. The governor could veto, on behalf of the crown and the Lords of Trade, any legislation and election to the upper house. The governor also appointed judges and decreed the amount of money to be issued by the colony. The system was a mélange of local power and royal privilege, in which executive appointment, administrative preferment, and patronage played a large role.

Long-standing tensions between the assembly and the governor erupted in highly publicized quarrels over fundamental political prerogatives in 1729, under the administration of William Burnet. First, the governor and assembly quarreled over the terms of his remuneration: whether it should be an annual stipend (as the representatives argued) or a fixed salary (as decreed by the king). Second, the governor attempted to enforce a royal mandate for the assembly to restrict the number of bills of credit in circulation. Bills of credit had depreciated in value, relative to sterling, more than 100 percent from 1710 to 1727. This provoked complaints from creditors and financiers who found their investments subject to deflation.[3]

The assembly spurned Burnet at every turn, rejecting his appeals on the salary issue, and continuing to issue new bills—prodded in part by poor citizens who needed cash to invest in land or to buy necessities. Demands for fiscal reform, which would have limited the amount of currency in circulation, sparked fears of a dearth of money and economic collapse. Burnet in turn threatened in 1729 to ask the crown to revoke Massachusetts' charter.

News of Burnet's death in early September raised hopes for some rapprochement between London and Boston. As Stephen Williams, Edwards' relative and colleague in nearby Longmeadow, observed, such relief was greatly needed since the country was "in an uproar." Williams expressed the anxiety shared by Edwards and other pastors. "What the event of our struggles will be," Williams confided to his diary, "God only knows." By May 1730, reports in Boston heralded the appointment of

3. Joseph B. Felt, *Historical Account of Massachusetts Currency* (Boston, 1839; rep. New York, Burt Franklin, n. d.), 64–109. For further discussion of the fiscal crisis, see Leslie V. Brock, *The Currency of the American Colonies, 1700–1764: A Study in Colonial Finance and Imperial Relations* (New York, Arno Press, 1975), 1–64, 130–51.

Jonathan Belcher, a native of Massachusetts who, according to the *Boston Gazette*, "fully" understood "the Constitution" of the "Colony, and how far their lawful Rights" extended. In August the assembly welcomed Belcher as a godsend.[4]

The crown nonetheless instructed Belcher to assert imperial prerogatives vigorously. Less than a month after he took office, he delivered a speech that raised all the familiar issues, including the need to legislate his salary and reform the bills of credit. Attempting to win support in the assembly, he temporized on some demands and applied his powers of patronage, especially judicial appointments, to his advantage. The effect was to factionalize the assembly. Debate between the governor and his opponents in the assembly soon became vicious; newspapers expressed a sense of impending crisis and reported anti-Belcher mobs in the streets.[5]

Mercantilist economic policies and imperial diplomatic measures further escalated the conflict. Belcher presented Massachusetts' fiscal problems in the most dire terms, arguing that the assembly's unwillingness to retire its bills of credit was tantamount to fraud and had destroyed the colony's fiscal credibility. With its treasury nearly empty, the assembly was in fact in arrears. To add to the sense of crisis, diplomatic hostilities between Britain and Spain brought rumors of impending war. Without funding for a strong militia, unnerved colonists faced hostile French colonies to the north and west, and Spanish colonies to the south and in the Caribbean.[6]

All parties recognized the instability of the colonial government, but some representatives continued to back Belcher. Controversy at the highest level manifested itself in regional and local affairs as a contest between what have been called "court" and "country" factions.[7] Those of the court party favored centralized authority and supported the prerogatives of

4. Stephen Williams, "Diary" (typescript), Apr. 19, 1730, Storrs Library, Longmeadow, Mass.; *Boston Gazette*, May 11, 1730. For the high expectations of Belcher, see the *Boston Gazette*, Aug. 17, 1730; and the election sermon of Samuel Fiske, *The Character of Candidates for Civil Government* (Boston, 1731), 39.

5. For popular outcries at Belcher's policies, see the *Boston Gazette*, Sept. 14, 1730; and Pencak, *War, Politics, and Revolution in Provincial Massachusetts*, 95.

6. *Boston Gazette*, Dec. 21, 1730; see also the *Boston Gazette*, Apr. 12, 1731. Stephen Williams again expressed the fears of a Hampshire county clergyman; his reflections on the possibility of war with Spain are in his "Diary," Aug. 4, 1730. Accounts of similar apprehensions were printed in the *Boston Gazette*, Jan. 4, 1731.

7. For court and country politics in Massachusetts, see Pencak, *War, Politics, and Revolution in Provincial Massachusetts*, 61–113; and Gregory H. Nobles, *Divisions Throughout the Whole: Politics and Society in Hampshire County, Massachusetts, 1740–1775* (New York, Cambridge Univ. Press, 1983), 12–35.

royal administration in the colony. They looked to an established and stable magistracy to solve the colony's problems in consort with the governor. Those of the country, or opposition, faction favored localized authority, resisted imperial claims, and generally regarded those in powerful positions with suspicion.

Debates between Belcher and his opponents turned to larger questions of political rights and self-determination, producing an ominous tone in late 1730 and 1731. Several members of the assembly made overtures to the House of Commons to have Belcher removed from office, which provoked the king himself to issue a warning against Massachusetts. In February 1731 Belcher delivered a censorious address on the "broils and confusions" going on; speaking of "the future peace and welfare of this people," he threatened "such consequences to this people as I am sure they will wish they had prevented," that is, the revocation of the charter.[8]

Some members of the assembly viewed the governor's overtures as an attack on "the very essentials of Government, to wit, the power of legislation." By 1733 many citizens were openly voicing a republican sentiment of opposition. They attributed the crisis to Belcher's attempts to manipulate the assembly, bribing Massachusetts' leading representatives and thereby corrupting the body politic for the sake of his own income. As one editorialist put it, borrowing rhetoric from court and country debates in England, "Our *Domestic* Affairs are all out of Order, the *Practices* of some *Men in Power* . . . [are] contrary to all the *Ancient Principals* [sic] of the *Whig* Party; Bribery! Corruption! Standing Armies! Dependent Parliaments! Places! Pensions!"[9]

Political conflicts in Boston were important to Edwards in part because they were mirrored in Hampshire County, of which Northampton was a part.[1] By 1730 a small group consisting chiefly of the Stoddard, Williams,

8. See Spencer, *Constitutional Conflict in Provincial Massachusetts*, [illegible]; Belcher's address is quoted in ibid., 91.

9. The opposition in the assembly is quoted in the *Boston Gazette*, Dec. 18, 1732; the editorialist is quoted in ibid., Jan. 22, 1733. Political and fiscal crises abated some in the late 1730s and 1740s. After unsuccessful measures to retire the deflated currency and issue new notes, the assembly considered and rejected a proposal for private "bankers" to issue notes based on land rather than silver. The British government then stepped in with a large loan and forced the colony to turn to silver in 1750. An immediate financial crisis and political uproar was temporarily averted thereafter by the Seven Years War; see Pencak, *War, Politics, and Revolution in Provincial Massachusetts*, 101–08.

1. The following account of political affairs and socio-economic relations in Hampshire County relies on Nobles, *Divisions Throughout the Whole*. For a general study of town politics in Massachusetts and their relation to provincial affairs, see Michael Zuckerman, *Peaceable Kingdoms: New England Towns in the Eighteenth Century* (New York, Alfred A. Knopf, 1970).

Pynchon, and Dwight families, had accumulated political power and much of the land in the county. Closely related to one another, these families monopolized elections to the assembly and appointments to such local offices as tax collector, clerk, and justice. They were also creditors to their neighbors.

The interest of these elites, known as the "[Connecticut] River gods," aligned them with court sensibilities. They lobbied the governor and worked in the assembly for policies favorable to their position, including currency reform. They were brokers between the colonial government and regional interests, benefiting from a relationship in which they received the perquisites of patronage in return for support of the governor. Col. John Stoddard, for example, an uncle of Jonathan Edwards' and one of his most consistent supporters, was one of the wealthier landowners in Hampshire County. A militia officer, he was frequently reelected to the assembly as the representative from Northampton and served on the governor's council. Loyal to Belcher, he criticized country agitation against the executive. Belcher, in turn, appointed him to the seat of local justice and appointed his nephew Israel Williams to the office of clerk of court. Against this group stood newer residents, would-be traders, and debtors, whose views coincided with the country faction in the assembly.

The second major development in this period, connected to the first, concerned the growth of social stratification, an increase in poverty, and the attendant strains on communal relations in towns like Northampton.[2] Most of the town's usable land had been parceled out by 1730, and what remained was of poor quality. There were few opportunities for newer settlers or younger families to make a good living from agricultural production. Many small farmers released what lands they had to well-to-do families and turned to trade. The town became a center for regional commerce. To invest in trade, however, entrepreneurs required cash, which they borrowed from the town's wealthier citizens. All of this exacerbated tensions between elite and common families, and re-created the colony-wide conflict between creditors and debtors, proponents and opponents of wholesale fiscal reform, long-term residents and newcomers, older citizens and the rising generation.

Northampton's oligarchy of wealthy, court-leaning landholders—Cols. John Stoddard and Timothy Dwight and Maj. Ebenezer Pomeroy—grad-

2. The following account is based on Patricia Tracy, *Jonathan Edwards, Pastor: Religion and Society in Eighteenth-Century Northampton* (New York, Hill and Wang, 1980), 38–46; and Trumbull, *History of Northampton*, 2, 33–51.

ually faced challenges from neighbors who had begun to accumulate wealth through trade. Townsmen with country sympathies criticized the old elite. They contested, sometimes successfully, the election to the assembly of long-term representatives like Stoddard.

Edwards often preached on the dynamics of provincial politics and local social divisions. Although his allusions were often oblique, his congregation would readily have grasped their specific meaning: struggles between the legislature of Massachusetts and the royal governorship, threats to the charter, contested elections, political factionalization, fiscal crises, the specter of war, and friction between economic elites and commoners. Political and economic commentary abound in his occasional sermons. Edwards had preached on political issues in the past, but he composed an unusually large number of such sermons from 1730 through 1733.[3] His election sermon from 1730, *The Dangers of Decline,* and his fast sermon from late 1731 or 1732, *The State of Public Affairs,* are good examples of these.

Besides those printed in this volume, Edwards delivered fast sermons on I Kgs. 8:35–36 (142) in 1730 and on Num. 14:21 (165) in 1731, as well as a thanksgiving sermon on II Chron. 32:25 (166) in 1730. Emphasis on social solidarity and criticism of economic vice also become major threads in Edwards' sacrament sermons, including his 1730 *Envious Men* and his 1731 *Self-Examination and the Lord's Supper.* Possibly delivered on the occasion of a contribution for a charitable project (most likely poor relief), *The Duty of Charity to the Poor,* written in 1733, is full of economic commentary.

More telling still, Edwards turned to civic matters frequently and with a great deal of intensity in his regular preaching during the early 1730s. He repeatedly linked his spiritual counsel and doctrinal reflection to the mundane workings of politics and economics. In his lengthy 1731 series *Christians a Chosen Generation,* he contrasted the concord of life in heaven with public contention on earth. *East of Eden* incorporated a political critique in a discussion of Adam's fall. We see the same trend throughout many of the unpublished sermons from this period. Edwards made his moral analyses concrete with reference to current issues, such as the plight of Northampton's growing number of indigents (Phil. 3:11 [158]), the dangers of political contests and bickering (Jas. 1:26 [258]), and even changing patterns of economic consumption (Eccles. 9:10 [307]).

3. See his 1729 *Sin and Wickedness Bring Calamity and Misery on a People,* in *Works, 14,* 485–505.

Edwards drew from a deep Puritan tradition in his civic preaching. New Englanders frequently, and with no small amount of self-consciousness, portrayed their public affairs as a vital part of the drama of providential history. Ministers employed various rhetorical strategies, evident in the annual election sermons from 1729 through 1734, which were delivered at the first meeting of the new assembly in Boston. In 1729 Jeremiah Wise expressed bewilderment at the hostilities between the governor and the people's representatives. He called on the executive to attend to the "Liberties and Privileges" of the people and urged the assembly to refrain from factional politics. He also emphasized the duty of citizens to pay their debts (hence alleviating the need for more currency) and to care for the poor. Wise thus provided a straightforward analysis of political conflict in the vocabulary of contemporary moral philosophy: the virtue of public-spiritedness as opposed to the vice of self-interestedness.[4]

The next year, Thomas Prince delivered a sermon in a different genre. He drew a typological "parallel," to use his word, between ancient Israel and the Bay Colony. The people of Massachusetts, he claimed, were "the particular Antitypes of that primitive People" whom God called as a nation and punished with servitude for its betrayals. Here Prince, an admirer of Edwards' who later arranged for the printing of *God Glorified in Man's Dependence*, placed the contemporary crisis in the scope of New England's covenantal history. By this account God established New England and allowed its citizens the "advantages" of the congregational establishment: the liberty to adopt their own creeds, choose their own ministers, and worship without deference to the English state church. If they were abused or neglected, these privileges were liable to revocation. Assaults on the socioreligious order, portended in threats issued against the charter by the likes of Burnet and Belcher, indicated divine warnings and a call for repentance. Clearly, by Prince's lights, the sins of the people lay beneath the colony's political quarrels.[5]

4. Jeremiah Wise, *Rulers the Ministers of God for the Good of their People* (Boston, 1729), 24, 53. For general background on preaching and politics, see Stout, *The New England Soul.*

5. Thomas Prince, *The People of New England Put in mind of the Righteous Acts of God* (Boston, 1730), 21. For covenant theology in general, see Perry Miller, *The New England Mind: The Seventeenth Century* (New York, Macmillan, 1939; rep. Boston, Beacon Press, 1961), 365–491; for the jeremiad, Sacvan Bercovitch, *The American Jeremiad* (Madison, Wis., Univ. of Wisconsin Press, 1978); and for typology, Mason I. Lowance, *The Language of Canaan: Metaphor and Symbol in New England from the Puritans to the Transcendentalists* (Cambridge, Mass., Harvard Univ. Press, 1980).

In 1731 Samuel Fiske refrained from such a jeremiad and preached, in a republican vein, on Belcher's responsibilities and the political dangers of venality, unjust judicial appointments, and patronage. The most explicitly political of the election sermons came from John Barnard in 1734. He chastised representatives who agitated against the government. He also called on them to legislate strict limits to the amount of bills of credit in circulation. At the same time he balanced these conservative opinions with a republican warning against the avarice of rulers—an implicit critique of Belcher's political tactics.[6]

Edwards wrote his election sermon of 1730, *The Dangers of Decline*, when antagonisms between court and country had reached critical levels. He must have had some sense of a wide public audience. Three weeks before he delivered this sermon the ministers of Hampshire County had met in Northampton; we can surmise that the political situation entered into their deliberations.[7]

The sermon incorporates many of the themes and rhetorical strategies reflected in the election sermons mentioned above. It was not an innovative effort. Although he was not as explicit as Prince in his use of typology, Edwards did bring covenantal motifs into his oration. He compared the "decay of strictness" and general degeneracy of the religious state of the land to what it had been in the more pure and fervent period of Massachusetts' original settlement. He recounted the "privileges" of religious liberty, secured by "a charter" that supported the "liberty to serve God according to our consciences without any [Anglican] molestation." He viewed contemporary threats to the charter as means of "God's threatening providence."

Edwards, however, did not place as much emphasis on the moral-philosophical dynamics of political corruption and responsibility as did Fiske and Bernard. He instead focused on the spiritual dynamics of social contention and economic aspiration. New Englanders, he argued, had pursued their worldly business to the neglect of religion. This lack of vital piety had kindled God's anger and occasioned political dangers as a

6. Fiske, *The Character of Candidates for Civil Government*; John Barnard, *The Throne Established in Righteousness* (Boston, 1734). John Swift urged a broad-based moral reformation as the means to corporate prosperity in 1732 in his *Sermon Preach'd at Boston* (Boston, 1732); Samuel Wigglesworth took an entirely different approach in 1733, pleading with the government to protect the churches (*An Essay for Reviving Religion* [Boston, 1733]). For republican language, see Bernard Bailyn, *The Ideological Origins of the American Revolution* (Cambridge, Mass., Harvard Univ. Press, 1967).

7. Williams, "Diary," May 5, 1730.

means of divine threat. Edwards' election sermon thus differed from others preached to the assembly in this singular respect: he prayed for a resolution to the public calamity through spiritual revival, for God to "pour out his Spirit upon us to revive our first love." Edwards' stress on the necessity of heartfelt, inner conversion, a hallmark of his mature theology, emerged in part out of the political turmoil of the early 1730s.

This is not to say that Edwards was silent on the explicitly political dynamics of the imperial-colonial struggle. In *The State of Public Affairs* he discusses the "secondary means," or natural causes, by which providence shapes political outcomes. Stability and a balance of powers are, to his mind, the keys to corporate longevity. External threats such as invasion by a foreign power or oppression by an imperial sovereign are calamitous enough (and real enough, given the state of affairs). Internal instabilities, however, are particularly dangerous to the commonweal. By Edwards' reading, political events in Massachusetts from 1729 through 1731 had been symptomatic of such instability: the change of administration from Burnet to Belcher, quarrels between the assembly and the governor, "debates long maintained about privilege and prerogative," the division of civic life into court and country loyalties (manifest within Northampton itself), and other layers of factionalization. An "unsettled state of public affairs," which Edwards perceived in his day, was threatening the foundational "privileges" of the colony, that is, the charter itself.

These events, however, are but secondary causes, used by God to warn the whole populace against their "evil ways and doings." Edwards avers that those who chafe, cavil, and agitate against civil rulers and the established elite are misguided; citizens ought to repent the sin that is theirs rather than criticize their rulers. God has appointed well-placed magistrates. Their demise—especially poignant in the death of a good ruler—is but a further sign of divine displeasure. Edwards also calls on magistrates to repent their ungodliness; yet he directs his admonitions particularly to restive members of the assembly, the opposition or country faction, and townsmen who speak ill of civic leaders.

In such terms Edwards propounded a rather conservative politics. He urged deference to political leaders and admonished those tempted to popular opposition. He detected, moreover, an unseemly ambition among local partisans of the country faction, a self-serving (and therefore corrupt) eagerness to censure Hampshire County's and Northampton's elite. The sermon *Envious Men* makes this clear. In it, he reprimands anyone who contests the prerogatives of his superiors, questions the appointment of others to civil office, or speaks ill of wealthier citizens. Such dissidents may have cried for justice, Edwards maintains, but they sought only their own advancement. They were motivated by factional interest and fueled by envy. They divided society and harmed the commonweal.

Some twenty-one years after his sermon on *Envious Men,* Edwards mused further on the moral dynamics underlying the political and social contests of the 1730s. "There has been," he wrote, "a sort of settled division of the people into two parties, somewhat like the *Court* and *Country party,* in England." The "chief men in the town, of chief authority and wealth, that have been great proprietors of their lands . . . have had one party with them. And the other party, which has commonly been the greatest, have been of those, who have been jealous of them, apt to envy them, and afraid of their having too much power and influence in town and church. This has been a foundation of innumerable contentions among the people," and "exceedingly grievous to me." Edwards considered it especially perverse that opponents of the local elite became increasingly belligerent as they themselves prospered. The more these dissidents achieved economic security, the more they envied the older oligarchy. Aspiring to public prominence and claiming such as their due, they quarreled and broke the solidarity that had been built on deference to customary patterns of leadership. Writing in 1751, after many of the town's elite had turned against him and participated in his dismissal, Edwards concluded that pride had infected the whole society, making all factions "difficult and unmanageable."[8]

In the early 1730s Edwards focused his critique against popular discontent and sanctioned the social values of stability and deference, as a defense of, *inter alia,* his own social location. He himself was a member of the town's elite by blood, education, profession, and temperament. He was related directly to the Stoddards; Col. John Stoddard was his uncle and a noted supporter. Edwards' wife, Sarah Pierpont, came from a wealthy and highly reputed New England family. He arrived in Northampton after a tutorship at Yale. He was also a leader, along with several of his cousins, in the Hampshire Association, which controlled clerical politics in the region. During his early years in Northampton he might well have been self-conscious enough of his pedigree to assert the prerogatives of the social class to which he belonged.

8. JE to Thomas Gillespie, July 1, 1751, in *Works, 4,* 564. In his *Faithful Narrative of the Surprising Work of God,* in ibid., 146, JE also attributed local political divisions to envy.

Edwards also recognized connections between popular social discontent and disrespect for the pastorate. Puritan divines had long held that godly ministers were ordained to their office and so gifted in order to administer God's word to their congregations through preaching, admonition, and the discipline of the sacraments. The laity's responsiblity was to honor and heed its pastors accordingly. Yet as fellow ministers in Hampshire County frequently complained during the 1730s, there was a growing disregard for clerical authority. Edwards joined the lament. In his sermon from late 1730 or early 1731, *Stupid as Stones*, he contrasted the dignity of the prophetic office and its message of salvation to the response of the congregation. "They come to meeting," he observed, "but it is only in conformity to custom," so that they "take no sort of pains to attend to and to apply it to themselves. . . . Their thoughts are intent upon something else; their hearts are in the ends of the earth. They are gazing about the assembly minding this and the other person . . . or they are thinking about their worldly business." Such a lack of deference to ministers, as Edwards viewed it, reflected a more pervasive resistance to God-ordained authorities.[9]

Yet it would be misleading to construe Edwards' social and political ideals as riveted solely on the maintenance of customary hierarchies. Although he was no populist, he inherited a Puritan wariness of king and Parliament. In the most general terms, Edwards also inherited a suspicion of the abuse of prerogative, employing some the motifs of classical republican ideology that pervaded political polemics in Britain.[1] As a provincial, he viewed Massachusetts as a divinely ordained society with peculiar privileges of self-rule. He portrayed the good ruler as concerned for the commonweal above any self-interest or factional politics. He idealized a cohesive society of New Englanders who secured their rights—their charter—through a sincere life of godliness and deference to fellow citizens and their pastors.

9. See *Stupid as Stones*, p. 179. On JE's view of the ministry and preaching, see *Works, 10*, 21–27. For the Hampshire Association and its concern for clerical authority, see Winslow, *Jonathan Edwards*, 123–24. In *Some Thoughts Concerning the Revival* (*Works, 4*, 484–88), JE lauded the revivals because, in part, they reversed this trend toward popular disrespect for authority, restoring social harmony and deference to pastors.

1. By "classical republicanism," I refer to a broad tradition of political thought as described by Gordon S. Wood in *The Creation of the American Republic, 1776–1787* (Chapel Hill, Univ. of North Carolina Press, 1969), 46–90. Eighteenth-century Americans drew on this tradition to assert either critical-opposition (country) rights or to affirm conservative-hierarchical (court) prerogatives.

Edwards' Moral Critique and Doctrine of Sin

The public discord of the early 1730s pushed Edwards to speak about the moral dynamics of social and economic tensions. He had inherited a Puritan conviction that God instituted social hierarchies as the means to social integration and solidarity. Commoners were to honor and defer to the elite, which was expected to serve the people in a spirit of self-sacrifice. The rich were to care for the poor. In theory (and, by Edwards' account, in New England's early history), such love and exchange of social responsibilities formed bonds of sociability and secured the commonweal.

Edwards thought that he saw the exact antithesis to this ideal in provincial politics and their manifestation in Northampton's social contests. Like many preachers, he may well have been prone to view local affairs through the lenses of events elsewhere, overstating parallels between his congregation and reports of political factions, economic dislocations, and the rise of religious infidelity in other parts of the Atlantic world. He preached as though his people mimicked the worst behaviors in Boston or London. The lower or rising social classes envied their superiors. The powerful displayed pride and arrogance. The rich were cruel. As much as he propounded a traditional notion of deference to civic and religious leaders, Edwards discovered a frightening depth of sin at every level of Northampton's social order. He was shocked at the moral and spiritual condition of his people.

In retrospect, he also was shocked at his own condition. He was not immune, he later recalled in his "Personal Narrative" (1739), from the worldly affectations, the pride of position, and the general spiritual apathy that affected Northampton as a whole in the early 1730s. "I have often since I lived in this town had very affecting views of my own sinfulness and vileness," that is, the "pride, hypocrisy, and deceit, left in my heart." He too evidenced a "proud and self-righteous spirit." He even found it difficult at times to attend to the concerns of parishioners who came to him with their "soul-concerns" about their "wickedness."[2]

Any number of vices caught Edwards' attention, but he especially targeted the worldliness engendered by the heated economic climate and competitiveness of Northampton. His unpublished 1730 sermon on Rom. 7:14 (154) is typical in this regard. "Love" to "profit," he writes, "is

2. "Personal Narrative," in *Works, 16,* 801–03.

First Meeting-House in West Springfield.

No depictions of Northampton's second meeting house (1662), in which Edwards preached during his early years, exist, but the photograph at the top of the page opposite shows the interior of the Hingham, Massachusetts, "Old Ship" church (1661), which probably bore some similarity to it (Courtesy Philip Davies, Wenham, Massachusetts). Below it is a sketch of the first meetinghouse in West Springfield, Massachusetts (1704), a typical example of Connecticut Valley church architecture for the period (Courtesy Connecticut Valley Historical Museum, Springfield, Massachusetts).

now become covetousness," from which stems the factious dispositions of "malice, envy, and revenge"; such depravity accounted for political disputes and social schisms. In *God Makes Men Sensible of Their Misery Before He Reveals His Mercy and Love* (1730), Edwards maintains that love of money has blinded people to a true conviction of right and wrong. It destroys all bases for religion. Throughout the early 1730s Edwards directed his sermons to a remarkable degree against the temptations of business—more so than to the sins of illicit sex, drunkenness, or adolescent rebellion against parents.[3]

In *The Duty of Charity to the Poor*, Edwards levels the charge of self-interestedness and avarice against members of the upper and middle social orders of society who fail to take responsibility for their neighbors of lesser means. Poverty was not severe, which is to say widespread and systemic, in Northampton. Yet it existed. The received wisdom among Anglo-American Protestants attributed poverty to two factors (granting, that is, the ultimate source of all social conditions in providence). First, a person could become impoverished by accidental means: the farmer whose goods were destroyed by a fire or who became physically incapacitated, the merchant who made an otherwise sound investment in goods that were sunk at sea by a storm, the aged widower, the orphan. For such cases there were civic institutions for poor relief. Towns could raise charitable funds by taxes or petition the government for provisions. Indeed, one of the hallmarks of Protestant societies in this period was the institutionalization of poor relief as a civic function. Second, one could fall into indigence by self-inflicted means: indolence, foolish business ventures, a reputation for fraud or dishonesty, drunkenness, gambling, or profligate spending. These cases deserved moral disapprobation and social discipline, ranging from ostracism and exclusion from the community to imprisonment.[4]

3. For similar statements, and a warning that it was foolish to envy the rich in light of the fact that they were to be subject to a strict divine judgment, see also JE's sermon on Eccles. 2:26 (170).

4. For a general survey of poor relief in English law, which New Englanders adapted to their situation, see Paul Slack, *The English Poor Law, 1531–1782* (London, Macmillan Press for the

By Edwards' account, the people of Northampton were so spiritually desiccated that they used such customary prescriptions to excuse themselves from the scriptural mandate to help those in need. Their excuses amounted to bad faith. He recollected the duty to give alms, that is, to provide voluntary, immediate relief to people customarily excluded from charity. These included people who were temporarily in arrears or on the fringe of subsistence but not legally destitute, those who had fallen into poverty by self-inflicted means but who were repentant, strangers and persons of ill-repute, the imprudent as well as the incompetent. Edwards reminded his people that all human beings bore the image of God. All residents of the town were in this sense "of one blood." To deny them alms was inhumane—and inhuman. Worse, an unforgiving spirit in economic matters, visible not only in uncharitableness but also in disputes between debtors and creditors, denigrated the value of forgiveness itself. It denied the worth of the free grace that Christ bestowed on sinners, betrayed the gospel, and therefore merited damnation. Economic competition and factionalization indicated to Edwards Northampton's lack of grace.

Edwards expanded his moral critique theologically in his lengthy 1731 discourse, *Christians a Chosen Generation.* He devotes this series to the doctrine of election and its relation to conversion and Christian existence. In the most general terms, God elects believers to a life of holiness, the signs of which stand in contrast to the common ills of earthly life. Asking his auditors to consider whether they exhibited the signs of holiness or reprobation, Edwards implicates them in nearly every form of sin, particularly the social vices of the day. "'Tis very unbecoming those that are God's offspring to entertain a spirit of hatred and ill will towards another. 'Tis very unbecoming thus to be backward in helping and assisting one another and supplying each other's wants, much more to contrive and seek one another's hurt, to be revengeful towards another."

Economic History Society, 1990; rep. New York, Cambridge Univ. Press, 1995). For Puritan attitudes toward almsgiving, see Christopher Hill, *Society and Puritanism in Pre-Revolutionary England* (New York, Schocken Books, 1964). For patterns of poor relief and policies toward the indigent in New England, see especially Christine Leigh Heyrman, "A Model of Christian Charity: The Rich and the Poor in New England, 1630–1730," Ph.D. diss., Yale University, 1977. See also Robert W. Kelso, *The History of Public Poor Relief in Massachusetts, 1620–1920* (Boston, Houghton Mifflin, 1922; rep. Montclair, N. J., Patterson Smith, 1969); and Stephen Foster, *Their Solitary Way: The Puritan Social Ethic in the First Century of Settlement in New England* (New Haven, Yale Univ. Press, 1971), 127–52.

NEW-ENGLAND, Numb. 58[illegible]

THE Boston Gazette

From *MONDAY* February 15, to *MONDAY* February 22. 1731.

BOSTON:

IN our last we gave an Account, that the Great and General Court or Assembly met here on Wednesday the 10th Instant: Here follows the Names of the Gentlemen who were return'd to serve for and represent the several Towns within this Province: (Those that have this (*) Mark, were not of the last Assembly.

The County of Suffolk.

Boston, { The Hon. Elisha Cooke Esq; Mr. Ezekiel Lewis, Mr. Thomas Cushing, * Mr. Samuel Welles

Roxbury, John Bowles, Esq;
Dorchester, Mr. Benja. Bird
Milton, * Mr. Ephra. Tucker
Braintree, The Hon. JOHN QUINCY, Esq; *Speaker.*
Weymouth, * Mr. Tho. White
Hingham, Mr. John Jacob
Dedham Mr. Joseph Ellis
Medfield, Mr. Ebenezer Mason
Mendon, * Mr. Seth Chapin, *Jun.*
Wrentham, Capt. Robert Blake
Brookline, * Mr. Samuel White
Woodstock, Maj. John Chandler
Needham, * Mr. Josiah Kingsbury
Medway Mr. Jonathan Adams
Sutton, Mr. Samuel Dudley
Oxford, * Capt. Eben. Learned
Bellingham, Hull, Walpole —
Kingston, * Mr. Moses Gill
Uxbridge, ——

The County of Essex

Salem, { Benjamin Lynde Esq; Mr. John Wolcott
Ipswich { * Mr. Jonath. Fellows, * Mr. John Choat
Newbury, { Joseph Gerrish Esq; Henry Rolfe, Esq;
Lynn, Capt. Ebenezer Burrel
Marblehead, Mr. Jer. Gatchel
Haverhill, Mr. Nathan Webster
Rowley, Mr. John Hobson
Salisbury, * Mr. William True
**Gloucester,* * Mr. Andr. Robinson
Andover, Mr. Joseph Parker
Topsfield, Capt. Joseph Gould
Beverly * Mr. William Eliot
Wenham * Capt. Wm. Rogers
Boxford, Capt. Joseph Hale
Bradford, * Mr. John Hardy[illegible]
Amesbury, * Mr. Thomas Hoyt
Manchester, Methuen, and *Middleton,* ——

The County of Middlesex

Cambridge, William Brattle, Esq;
Charlestown { Mr. Stephen Hall, Mr. Joseph Lemmon
Watertown, * Mr. Nathan Fisk
Concord, Mr. Samuel Chandler
Woburn, Mr. Richard Ward
[illegible]
Marlborough, * Capt. Nathan Brigham
Lancaster, Mr. Josiah White
Sherborn, Mr. John D'Eath
Groton, Mr. John Longley
Framingham, Capt. Ed. Goddard
Chelmsford, Mr. Wm Fletcher
Billerica, * Mr. Benja. Tompson
Woburn, Capt. John Fowle
Reading, Mr. Thomas Bancroft
Malden, Mr. Jacob Wilson
Lexington, * Mr. Benj. Willington

Weston, Francis Fullham, Esq;
Worcester, * Mr. Benjamin Flagg
Medford, Mr. Benjamin Willis
Stoneham, —— *Dunstable.* ——
Dracut, —— *Littleton,* ——
Stow, —— *Hopkinton,* ——
Shrewsbury, —— *Westborough,* ——
Leicester —— *Southborough,* ——
Westford, —— *Holliston,* ——
Bedford, —— *Wilmington,* ——

The County of Hampshire.

Springfield, { Wm Pynchon, Esq; * Mr. Wm Pynchon
Northampton, Mr. Eben. Wright
Hatfield, * Mr. Nath. Colman
Hadley, * Eleazer Porter, Esq;
Westfield, ——
Suffield, { Capt. John Kent, * Mr. Abra. Adams
Enfield, * Mr. Joseph Sexton
Deerfield, —— *Northfield,* ——
Brookfield, * Mr. Tho. Gilbert
Brimfield, —— *Sunderland,* ——

The County of Plymouth.

Plymouth, Mr. John Foster
Scituate * Mr. Thomas Bryant
Marshfield, John Little Esq;
Duxbury, Capt. John Alden
Bridgewater, * Mr. Neh. Washburn
Middleborough, Mr. Sam. Barrow
Rochester, Mr. Samuel Sprague
Plimpton, Mr. Samuel Bradford
Pembroke, Mr. Elisha Bisby
Kingston, —— *Abington,* ——
and *Hanover,* ——

The County of Barnstable.

Barnstable, Shubael Gorham Esq;
Yarmouth, * Mr. John Hedge
Sandwich, [illegible] Bourn Esq;
Eastham * Capt. John Knowles
Harwich, * Capt. Eden Freeman
Truro, —— *Chatham,* ——
Falmouth, —— *Province-Town.*

The County of Bristol.

Bristol, Charles Church Esq;
Taunton, Mr. Ezra Dean
Swanzey, Mr. Joseph Mason
Rehoboth, Mr. Jathniel Peck
Little Compton, * Thomas Church Esq;
Dighton, Mr. Edward Shove
Tiverton, Job Almy Esq;
Dartmouth, * Mr. John Akin
Attleborough, Capt. John Foster
[illegible]
Freetown — *Barrington* — *Easton.*

The County of York.

York, Mr. Samuel Sewall
Kittery, * Mr. Wyther Berry
Wells, * Mr. Joseph Hill
Berwick, Mr. Roger Plaisted
Falmouth, Mr. John Tyng
Scarborough, Biddeford, Arundel,

The County of Dukes County

Edgartown, — *Chilmark,* — *Tisbury.*

The County of Nantucket.

Sherburn, ——

The SPEECH of His Excellency

JONATHAN BELCHER, Esq;

Captain General and GOVERNOR in Chief in and over His Majesty's Province of the *Massachusetts-Bay* in *New-England.*

To the General Assembly of the said Province, Met at Boston *on* Wednesday *the* Tenth *Day of* February, 1730.

Gentlemen of the Council and House of Representatives,

AT my last meeting of the late Assembly, I suggested to them those things which I judg'd would most of all advance the publick Weal; But the unhappy Temper they manifested with respect to His Majesty's Royal Instruction for fixing a Salary on me and my Successors, brought me under an indispensible Necessity of Dissolving them, and so prevented their deliberating on those things, which I believe might lay a Foundation for some Laws that would greatly promote the Happiness of this People, and of which you will now have Opportunity to consider.

By the late Dissolution I have given the whole Country the Opportunity of sending such to Represent them, as may put an end to the Broils and Confusions in which you have been so long and so unhappily involved; and I hope you are now come together to be the happy Deliverers of your Country from the Troubles and Difficulties that still hang over it. I must desire you to look back on all I said to the last Assembly upon the King's easy and reasonable Demand for the Support of His Governour, & then your true Love to your Country will discover it self in nothing more, than by acting in this critical Juncture with great calmness and caution, for upon your present Determinations depends much of the future Peace and Welfare of this People. I can't help repeating how vast has been the Charge and what the Loss this Province has suffered in their Disputes with the Crown: It has been with Indignation that I have sometimes heard without Doors, That we must act as if we had a bad King, and a bad Governour. How great is such Ingratitude, while we are happy under the Government of the best Monarch upon Earth, in the full Enjoyment of all our Liberties religious and civil! And for the little time I have had the Honour to be the Representative of the King's Royal Person among you, I flatter my self the worst of my Enemies can't Tax me with the least Male Administration.

Again, consider the King's Grace and Favour to you in His Officers absolutely reserved to His own Appointment in the Royal Charter, and all those He has given you from among your selves. What could be more Kind and indulgent? Certainly then there must be some return of Duty and Obedience to so much Goodness.

I doubt not but you will act above the Insinuations of those, who would fill you with Fears of what may happen [illegible] get the recent Instance of speedy Redress [illegible] upon your humble Application.

As it is one of His Majesty's shining Characters to protect His Subjects in all their just Rights and Liberties, you may most sacredly depend, He will never suffer any of His Governours to prostitute His Authority and Honour by making their arbitrary Will and Pleasure a Rule of Government for His Subjects.

Should you Oblige me to put in practice that part of my Duty to the King, of making another Voyage to *Great Britain,* there to represent to His Majesty and His

Ministers

Page one from the *Boston Gazette* of February 22, 1731. The left column prints the list of delegates to the Massachusetts assembly for that year (with the name of Northampton's deputy, Ebenezer Wright, appearing near the upper right) and the right column the text of a speech by Gov. Jonathan Belcher berating the assembly for its uncooperativeness.

True members of the chosen, he reminds his parishioners, are so sure of their heavenly destiny that they forsake earthly ambitions. In contrast, he sees people governed by their "passions," which is to say, "overmuch concerned about earthly honor." This is apparent in the readiness of citizens to engage in contests for political power and to slander officeholders with charges of venality and bribery. As types of priests, the people of God participate in the self-sacrificial service of charity and generosity. Sinners are a selfish people, unwilling to help one another and even resentful of paying their ministers. As a godly nation, the church experiences the freedom of Christ's kingdom and the common happiness that derives from peace. Edwards discerns the opposite. "You," he charges, "are of a different company; you are one of those that are in slavish subjection to Satan," which is to say, "slaves to [your] lusts." This bondage showed itself in the "miserable" condition of public affairs, when the "nation" was "rent by civil wars or disturbed by intestine broils." Here Edwards' theological rhetoric reflects the specific political contexts of the early 1730s. Even the local elite, as well as imperial officials, fall short of a Christian character. "There are many great men of the world, noble men and kings and men of great power and policy . . . men of great wealth," who "are greatly honored and make a great figure," who "are wicked men and reprobates." Although New Englanders claimed to be the covenant people, Edwards describes them as "hypocrites" operating "from a principle of self-love."

This was to be the key refrain for the future in Edwards' analysis of moral freedom and original sin. People apart from regeneration operate out of a vicious self-love; and it is all too evident by the state of social and political affairs in New England that most people are unregenerate. Edwards thought that religious rationalism and certain forms of Arminianism abetted an increasingly popular belief that the natural human heart was good enough to cooperate with God. From his perspective, such a presumption was self-delusion. Social facts, as Edwards intimated in *East of Eden,* pointed to nothing but the evil inclinations of the will and the universality of original sin. Toward the end of *Christians a Chosen Generation,* Edwards reiterated his critique: the social dispositions of his people demonstrated their need for conversion; "There should be a great difference between their way of living and other men's, the way men commonly live," but there patently was not. There are too many people "affronted or injured by their neighbors" and ready to "entertain a spirit of revenge." Edwards concluded this sermon series with an extended discussion of regeneration, his prescription for all social ills.

The Theological End of Human Depravity

Edwards' sentiments about human sinfulness were thoroughly Calvinist. As the clerical sponsors of *God Glorified in Man's Dependence* suggested, many people in New England would have found his ideas "unfashionable." It was commonplace for preachers to say that people were sinners. Edwards appeared to be something of a throwback to the seventeenth century, however, in taking the doctrine to extremes. He asserted not only that people were sinners by nature but also that God judged them guilty and fit for damnation by the depth of depravity that kept them from turning away from sin. Edwards also illustrated this corruption in embarrassing detail. He was severe in his critique of the agitation that drove politics in Boston, of the economic competitiveness that made New Englanders prosperous, and of the petty jealousies and small-minded arrogance of local society. Edwards' parishioners might well have resented such criticism. Furthermore, opponents of strict Calvinism in New England had begun to question its theological premises. Drawing on English writers of an Arminian, if not rationalist and Latitudinarian bent, they charged that the Calvinist doctrine of sin cast an unbecoming shadow over God's beneficence and disregarded the natural moral faculties for good that God had implanted in created agents.[5]

Edwards' response to such criticism was not merely to reiterate his fundamental social critique—human depravity and therefore the ultimate futility of natural moral acts were evident for all to see—but also to provide a constructive theological answer. In *God Glorified in Man's Dependence*, Edwards suggests the form of this answer in the following terms: human sinfulness served God's purposes by glorifying God. Indeed, humanity's corruption and dependence on God led to a demonstration of the very nature of God as triune.

Edwards would later develop his doctrine of sin systematically in *Original Sin* (1758); the central theme of *God Glorified* is the dependence of fallen humanity on all three persons of the Trinity for salvation.[6] Humanity, he reasons, is dependent on God the Father because he provided grace in Jesus Christ, on God the Son because he was the mediator who

5. See *Works of Jonathan Edwards, 3, Original Sin*, ed. Clyde A. Holbrook (New Haven, Yale Univ. Press, 1970), 1–85. For religious rationalism, see Conrad Wright, *The Beginnings of Unitarianism in America* (Boston, Starr King Press, 1955).

6. For JE on the Trinity, see the commentary and notes in *Works, 14*, 42–45. See also Amy Plantinga-Pauw, "'The Supreme Harmony of All': Jonathan Edwards and the Trinity," Yale Univ. diss., 1990.

procured humanity's redemption, and on God the Spirit because he came to dwell in believers, instilling faith and conveying the "vital principle" of spiritual excellency. In each step of this argument, Edwards contends that such dependence was absolute because of the pervasiveness of sin. Humanity's "fallen and undone state," its "insufficiency and helplessness" to convert itself from corruption to holiness, is "apparent" and "conspicuous." One has only to read the newspapers or listen to the town gossip to discover this. One cannot, that is, choose any moral good, including faith, apart from God's prior decision to grant grace.

Those who judge human beings to be not completely depraved grant them independence from God, deny the need for either the Son or the Spirit, and therefore, by implication, reject the Godhead. Any concession to human ability, such as is made by Arminians, amounts to unbelief. Conversely, a doctrine of sin in Calvinist fashion affirms humanity's need for all persons of the Trinity and thereby glorifies God. Edwards' private religious experience informed his thoughts at this point. As he wrote in his "Personal Narrative," the sense of his own sinfulness, his "vile self-exaltation," led him in Northampton to an affective appreciation of his "universal, exceeding dependence on God's grace and strength," "a delight" in "the absolute sovereignty of God," a "sense of the glory of Christ, as a mediator," and "a sense of the glory of the third person of the Trinity, in his office of Sanctifier."[7] The admission of depravity is integral to genuine faith because faith implies a trust in Christ rather than in one's own moral abilities. So, Edwards concludes in *God Glorified*, "faith abases men, and exalts God."

Evangelical Humiliation as Preparation for Conversion

Edwards' view of sin did not preclude intense moral scrutiny and even efforts to obey God's law—the moral and religious precepts of the Bible. Rather, it reinforced them. He repeatedly urged his people to conduct themselves in a godly manner, to act correctly, and to pursue the standard religious devotions of Protestantism, chief among them Bible reading, prayer, and attendance at corporate worship.

Was it illogical to tell people that they were depraved while exhorting them to good deeds? Edwards did not think so. First, he held that God's laws were objectively right and true: certain acts were virtuous, others vicious. Caring for a neighbor was always preferable to harming one.

7. "Personal Narrative," in *Works, 16*, 801, 803.

Praying was always preferable to visiting the tavern. This was true even though the person who gave alms or prayed did so with a fickle and corrupt heart. Good deeds were good to the extent that they followed God's law, despite the fact that they came from impure motives and could never make the performer good. So the unregenerate, according to Edwards, had to strive to lessen their sin even as they admitted their damnable state. The regenerate likewise were to do good works and perform religious duties as a means of testimony to the truth of God's law and thereby to God's glory. It was an expression of their sanctification and evidence of God's work in their hearts.

Second, although the natural pursuit of virtue was inadequate in terms of the divine-human relationship, it served as a social good in the context of temporal and corporate affairs. Attempts to avoid immorality and behave charitably were, in effect, better than moral resignation. Self-interested antinomianism or libertinism were horrid specters from the standpoint of the common good.

Third, and most important, Edwards maintained that the performance (or, more properly, attempted performance) of religious and moral disciplines prepared people for regeneration by revealing to them the depth of their own iniquity, culpability, and need for grace. Here he appropriated and modified the standard Puritan paradigm of conversion, which located humiliation as a work of preparation. His approach may be seen clearly in *God Makes Men Sensible of Their Misery Before He Reveals His Mercy and Love.* The doctrine of this lengthy 1730 sermon on Hos. 5:15 is straightforward: "'Tis God's manner to make men sensible of their misery and unworthiness before he appears in his mercy and love to them." Such was common Puritan fare. Edwards, however, takes his argument from biblical history rather than from a morphology of individual conversion, recasting the analysis to emphasize divine sovereignty. The story of Israel, he argues, demonstrates that God restored a people to his favor only after allowing them to fall into sin, suffer punishment, and thereby recognize their unworthiness. God tends to work in this way in history. Individuals should make application to themselves; but it is God doing the work, shaping human affairs to glorify himself. By Edwards' lights, the process is discernible in the grand sweep of history. It is less precise and predictable in terms of the individual's story.

So Edwards reduced the manifold stages of the Puritan ordo salutis to a simple, twofold pattern of humiliation. First, God brought his people to a remorse for their sins, a recognition of the evil of their acts and dispositions. He did this by a variety of means—divinely revealed law, natural conscience, and threats of punishment. There was enough in the observation of everyday life, Edwards pointed out, to convince people of their corruption. "Their sinful natures appear by their sinful lives. There is sin enough that every man has committed to convince him that his is like a viper, that he is sold under sin."

Second, God's people then attempted to reform themselves, but failed; they reverted to their old ways or remained wicked in their affections. "'Tis usual with sinners when they are first made sensible of their danger," Edwards preached, "to try their own strength, hoping to help themselves. They are striving to make themselves better," but God makes "them sensible that they are utterly helpless in themselves; they are brought to despair." God thus destroyed all grounds for self-confidence and prepared sinners to receive the message of divine mercy and forgiveness.

Edwards makes two applications of the doctrine. First, he exhorts his people to seek convictions of their sin. They must prepare themselves by engaging in religious exercises that reveal their moral condition. Edwards' "Personal Narrative" again gives some clues to his meaning here. He recalled there how the key to his own revival and reformation had been his determination to plumb the depths of his sin, to fathom "the bottomless, infinite depths of wickedness" in his heart. Such an affective knowledge of his sinful state and his dependence on God came from desperate attempts to read and pray, "to lie low before God" and "ask for humility."[8] Edwards' task as a preacher, demonstrated in *God Makes Men Sensible of Their Misery Before He Reveals His Mercy and Love,* was accordingly to pierce people's hearts: to strip bare their corrupt affections, false ideas, and self-serving actions through psychological analysis, and to lay before the congregation the terrors of divine judgment in the rhetoric of sensation.

In the second application, Edwards urges people to strive to avoid sin and to live godly lives. Such attempts do not merit salvation, but they nonetheless sharpen the sinner's moral consciousness and direct him or her forward in the process of salvation. To sin willingly, "to return to your former careless way of living," in Edwards' words, is to revert to an even worse state than one occupied before falling under conviction. As a preparatory means, humiliation implies some measure of resistance to

8. Ibid., in *Works, 16,* 803. JE also preached on the importance of striving for conversion through pious exercises in his sermons on Ex. 20:24 (97), Matt. 7:21 (176), and Rom. 3:13–18 (249).

evils that would divert people from their conviction of sin. That his people would "be the better directed in taking care not to lose" their "convictions," Edwards specifies such evils: lusts, quarrels, "malice and revenge," "worldly enjoyments and entertainments," the preoccupations of "business," and the "worldly cares" of "growing richer." So Edwards circles back to the very vices that provoked his denunciations against Northampton. By his logic, preaching in such a vein was not mere moralism or legalism. It promoted an evangelical experience.

In his sacrament sermons Edwards argued that the Lord's Supper should be a particularly important context for humiliation and repentance. In the early 1730s he retained the practice of Solomon Stoddard, who had allowed people to attend communion without undergoing a strict test of conversion. They could commune according to the dictates of their consciences and their desire for conversion. Edwards nonetheless hesitated, unlike Stoddard, to embrace the sacrament as a converting ordinance. He presented it instead as an occasion to enforce the discipline of self-humiliation in a corporate context.[9]

Edwards was not yet at the point of barring the unregenerate from communion, but he mistrusted the private consciences of his parishioners—at least those (particularly younger ones) who had become caught up in newer social and economic mentalities. In *Envious Men* and *Self-Examination and the Lord's Supper*, he insisted that even members of the church reflect long and hard on the extent to which envy, avarice, or uncharitableness warped their social relationships. Evidence of such dispositions, he warned, should cause them to meditate on their sins and repent before they accepted their sacramental privileges. As he put it in

9. JE eventually rejected the Stoddardean pattern and contended for a restriction of communion to those previously determined to be regenerate. David Laurence has made the following argument to explain JE's change of mind: Stoddard's practice assumed that converting grace came precisely in the sequence of the *ordo salutis*. No preparatory works contained evidence of grace, which came in a single, unpredictable, yet unmistakable moment. Therefore, by Stoddard's reasoning, there was no basis to determine whether grace might or might not strike the communicant at any moment. Barring people from the sacrament was an obstruction of God's activity. JE found Stoddard's reasoning, by his own experience, false. The sequence of the *ordo salutis* was not clear and predictable. There were indeed tokens of grace in the process of humiliation and other preparatory works; therefore there were evidences, gleaned from Scripture, by which to determine who should and who should not presume to communicate. Although JE came to this conclusion in the 1740s, it reinforces the point here about his attitude in the early 1730s: he took the sacrament as an occasion for intense moral scrutiny, perhaps to a greater degree than did Stoddard. See David Laurence, "Jonathan Edwards, Solomon Stoddard, and the Preparationist Model of Conversion," *Harvard Theological Review* 72 (1979), 267–83. See also, for a different perspective, John F. Jamieson, "Jonathan Edwards's Change of Position on Stoddardeanism," *Harvard Theological Review* 74 (1981), 79–99.

his 1732 sermon on Ezek. 23:37–39 (222), attending ordinances in a state of known wickedness was a form of pollution and a damnable sin.[1]

The Necessity for a Divine and Supernatural Light

Edwards concluded during his early tenure as Northampton's pastor that even these preparations and humiliations could not secure a genuine moral conversion. The pervasiveness of his people's sin indicated their need for a radical transformation of their inner natures. This would come about, he believed, by "a divine and supernatural light"—the true and only means of the regeneration that he deemed crucial for his parishioners and for New England at large.

So Edwards' sermon by that name represented his ultimate response to the pastoral problems of the early 1730s. This is perhaps his most sophisticated, and certainly his most celebrated, sermon from the period. It is a lecture that Edwards revised only slightly for publication. In it he drew together themes and verbatim passages from more than a decade of preaching and reflection in his private notebooks. Some of its themes, such as a distinction between notional knowledge and a sensible apprehension of divine truths, appeared throughout the "Miscellanies," especially nos. 489, 540, 628, and 630. He worked on the image of spiritual light—a trope for the Holy Spirit and the sensible presence of divine truths—in his typological notebooks. Several of his sermons from the 1720s contained passages that adumbrated the central motifs of *A Divine and Supernatural Light.*[2] That Edwards should set out to incorporate so much of his previous work into a single statement was his own recognition of the signal importance of the sermon.

A Divine and Supernatural Light forms a bridge between the period of Edwards' career covered in this volume and the period from 1734 through 1742, when he emerged as the leading theologian of New England's evangelical revivals. Much has been written about the literary shape of this sermon—its composition, redaction for the press, and rhetorical

1. Full discussions of JE's sacramental theology with citations of the relevant literature are provided in *Works, 14*, 38–42, and *Works, 12*, 1–89. For a general introduction to Puritan sacramental theology, see E. Brooks Holifield, *The Covenant Sealed: The Development of Puritan Sacramental Theology in Old and New England, 1570–1720* (New Haven, Yale Univ. Press, 1974).

2. See "Images" nos. 52, 58, and 185, in *Works, 11*, 65, 67–69, 120; *Christ, the Light of the World*, in *Works, 10*, 287, 533–46; *A Spiritual Understanding of Divine Things Denied to the Unregenerate*, in *Works, 14*, 67–96; "Miscellanies" no. 498 in *Works, 13*, 533; and "Miscellanies" nos. 540, 628, and 630 in the forthcoming volume of *"Miscellanies," 501–832* in the Yale edition.

techniques—as well as its theological thrust.[3] Here I provide a brief analysis of this remarkable text and how it reflects Edwards' proposed remedy for the spiritual and moral malaise that he diagnosed among his congregation in the early 1730s.

Edwards begins the lecture with an exposition of Jesus' response to Peter's great confession (Matt. 16:17). Many people around Peter, Edwards observes, had an acquaintance with Christ and a naturally derived knowledge of Christ. Peter's knowledge transcended this notional recognition of Christ. He came to confess Christ and secure the blessings of faith because he had a direct revelation of Jesus' nature. Given by the Spirit of God, this knowledge or divine light eventuated in faith because it was sensible. Peter's soul, or faculty of spiritual sense, experienced divine light in a way that effected a change in Peter's affections, and thus his moral disposition toward spiritual things.

With his emphasis on "sense," Edwards took an idiom that was not central to the standard vocabulary of seventeenth-century Puritan dogmatics and made it a crucial part of his argument. The word was common currency in other forms of religious writing—so common, in fact, that Edwards employed it at times without bothering to be precise or to give a consistent definition. Puritan devotional writers like Thomas Hooker and Cambridge Platonists like John Smith and Henry More used the expression as a rhetorical device for feeling, apart from any technical or theoretical specificity in psychological terms. The epistemological works of the English empiricist John Locke, a highly influential source for the eighteenth-century world of letters, employed "sense" to refer to the mental effects of the immediate perception of physical objects (or, in a more complex fashion, of the immediate perception of one's own mental operations). A school of British moral philosophy known as the "Moral Sense," formulated by the third earl of Shaftesbury and Francis Hutcheson, treated the term in yet another

3. For the composition and redaction, see *Works, 10*, 111–15. For the rhetoric, see ibid., 6–9, 199–207; and Perry Miller, "The Rhetoric of Sensation," in *Errand Into the Wilderness* (Cambridge, Mass., Harvard Univ. Press, 1956), 167–83. On the relation of the rhetoric of sensation to JE's psychology of conversion and doctrine of salvation, see Roland André Delattre, *Beauty and Sensibility in the Thought of Jonathan Edwards: An Essay in Aesthetics and Theological Ethics* (New Haven, Yale Univ. Press, 1968); and Terrence Erdt, *Jonathan Edwards and the Sense of the Heart* (Amherst, Mass., Univ. of Massachusetts Press, 1980). And on JE's doctrine of conversion and its relation to divine revelation, see Conrad Cherry, *The Theology of Jonathan Edwards: A Reappraisal*, (New York, Anchor Books, 1966), 12–106; and Sang Hyun Lee, *The Philosophical Theology of Jonathan Edwards* (Princeton, N. J., Princeton Univ. Press, 1988), 115–69.

way: an innate awareness of moral qualities such as beauty or virtue. Here "moral sense" referred to both a mental faculty (also called conscience or taste or, more simply, the heart) and to the effects of moral relations on that faculty (as in to "have a moral sense" of the virtue of benevolence or the vice of cruelty).[4]

In the most general terms, Edwards used the language of sense throughout his writings to refer to the immediate perception of moral or spiritual, rather than physical, phenomena. To this extent his definition bore slim resemblance to Locke's empiricism and mirrored the Moral Sense school. Unlike seventeenth-century Puritans, who tended to assume that the mental faculty of understanding shaped the will, Edwards accepted the "Moral Sense" premise that the faculty of moral affection or taste shaped understanding and constituted, in effect, the will. Yet drawing on Puritan devotional writing, he often turned the language of sense to a theological purpose never embraced by the likes of Hutcheson. He thought that the natural faculty of moral sense was incapable of perceiving the primary or defining moral qualities that inhered in God, such as perfect loveliness and goodness. For this, one needed a spiritual sense. The ability to perceive spiritual realities, to put it bluntly, required regeneration. As real and palpable as physical perceptions or common moral judgments, true spiritual sensations were of a different order altogether. They came only by the infusion of the Holy Spirit.

In *A Divine and Supernatural Light*, Edwards reads this concept of sensation into the story of Peter's confession in several ways. First, it helps him to explain why so many people in New England have failed, by his judgment, to undergo a genuine moral revitalization. As much as the attempted performance of moral duties is crucial for the commonweal, and as much as the trials of humiliation prepare people for conversion, they cannot change the sinner's character. New England's vaunted tradition of religious practice, or Northampton's customary orthodoxy, for that matter, had not produced a truly godly society because both were, as commonly practiced, bereft of divine light. People's consciences might be wounded by "an apprehension of right and wrong." They might confess their sin. But their humiliations as yet derive from a merely natural knowledge—even if it is a principled knowledge. They know the Bible but they do not apprehend the glories of the divine character. They might say that they believe; but they cannot truly love God until they have

4. This and the following discussion of the concept of sense in British thought and its appropriation by JE relies on Fiering, *Jonathan Edwards's Moral Thought*, esp. 123–38.

an affective experience of God. They have the creed but not the Spirit. Metaphorically, as Edwards suggests, they have a certain indirect knowledge of what honey is like, but they have never tasted it.

Thus, according to Edwards, people remain unregenerate. Their attempted reformations are merely transitory and external. Only with an infusion of supernatural light would New Englanders be genuinely converted. Their moral recovery would be steady and continual if and only if the Spirit of God acted in them "as an indwelling vital principle." With this, their moral "principles," the dispositions to godliness, would be "restored that were utterly destroyed by the fall; and the mind thenceforward habitually [would exert] those acts that the dominion of sin had made it as wholly destitute of, as a dead body is of vital acts." Edwards thought that the evangelical experience of which he spoke might produce what New England so sorely lacked: "an universal holiness of life." Likewise, when the first wave of the Great Awakening washed over the Connecticut River Valley during the next two years, Edwards highlighted the social righteousness—love, deference, and mutual respect—that blessed Northampton as a result.[5]

Second, in *A Divine and Supernatural Light,* Edwards maintains that the possession of this light depends solely on divine initiative. Here Edwards affirms indirectly the Calvinist understanding of divine election. He is less intent on pursuing that doctrine, however, than on offering an alternative to the Arminianism that assumes human moral competence, and mitigates the need for supernatural conversion, by emphasizing moral training and education. Edwards defends his claim that "this knowledge should be given immediately by God." Sinners have access to notions of right and wrong, the natural knowledge gained "by the strength of natural reason." But it is quite apparent that their corrupt hearts incline away from the good and the true. Political contention, social schism, and private iniquity provide ample evidence in that regard. Mere reason cannot change their moral dispositions. People need a revelation from God "to see the beauty and loveliness of spiritual things," which "is not a speculative thing, but depends on the sense of the heart."

If only God can change hearts, then the best that New Englanders can do—what they should do—is to seek spiritual light, to cleave to "the revelation of Christ as our Savior" with "full inclination and affection." This is Edwards' concluding exhortation. They are to pray for revival.

5. *Works, 4,* 147–59.

Edwards intimated that it came as a surprise even to him when the prayer was answered and Northampton underwent a spiritual awakening in 1734 and 1735.[6] It is tempting to suggest that he eventually turned to revival—the collective manifestation of the conversion of individuals—as an avenue of escape from the political and economic affairs, even the pastoral encounters, that occasioned his denunciations of human nature. Edwards did promote evangelical humiliation and the necessity of conversion because he had become frustrated by what he believed was the pervasiveness of discord, faction, and sheer meanness in his society. Throughout his career, he displayed a prophetic high-mindedness and patrician sensibility that had the potential to distance him from his congregation.

Yet we should not underestimate the extent to which from 1730 through 1733 Edwards labored to build and sustain a pastoral relationship with his people. In no other period of his career was he so engaged in learning about his congregation and its social world. His sermons reveal a great deal of familiarity with his parishioners' concerns: relationships between neighbors, struggles for position in the community, economic matters, and personal ambitions. He did not wish to sever religious experience from these affairs. He focused on supernatural conversion as a means of regenerating individuals to a life of godliness, and thus of restoring human solidarity as well as securing individual salvation. Conversion, in effect, was his answer to, rather than a retreat from, social problems.

That Edwards led his congregation into a revival in 1734 suggests that he achieved a rapport with at least some of the citizens of Northampton. His homiletical powers grew in proportion to his ability to probe the psychological and social sensibilities of his people and to appropriate the language of ordinary experience. His promotion of and writings about the revival movement in the late 1730s and 1740s made him famous; but the evangelical theology that underpinned his more celebrated works emerged from the period 1730–1733, when he established himself as Northampton's pastor.

6. Ibid., 149.

PRACTICAL ATHEISM

WE might wonder whether atheism was really a danger to participants in New England's standing order, not to mention congregants in the Northampton church, who viewed themselves as genuinely Christian. Yet Edwards makes it clear in this sermon that by atheism he refers to more than the urbane skepticism of self-styled literati in America and the doctrine of radical philosophes and proponents of Enlightenment in Britain or France. Edwards brings the dangers of atheism to bear on Northampton by linking it to such common shortcomings as the neglect of private and corporate religious exercises. His statement of the Doctrine implies that there is an intimate connection between practical ungodliness and philosophical unbelief. From Edwards' perspective, any form of disobedience is a denial of God's existence.

The source of atheism, by Edwards' account, is not chiefly an epistemological problem. In the explication of the Doctrine, Edwards holds that sinners resent a God who judges their sin. Such an affective distaste for the Almighty makes them insensible to reasonable arguments in favor of God's existence. In several passages reminiscent of John Calvin's description of the fall—a descent into stupidity and laziness—Edwards portrays the intellectual negligence of those who are too preoccupied with their vices to contemplate the reality of the Creator.[1] Prone to deny God, they live as though there is none. The practical outcome, as well as origin, then, of atheism, is immorality. In the Application, Edwards can do little more than bemoan such folly and berate those who cloak their desire to serve their own sin with claims of a reasoned unbelief.

By distilling the philosophical issue to moral disposition, Edwards led his auditors to consider the immediate implication of a far-reaching debate. In the Anglo-American world of letters in Edwards' day, atheism was a frequent topic for formal and popular literary genres. Part of its currency stemmed from the fact that it was often connected, as in the

1. John Calvin, *Institutes of the Christian Religion* [1559], ed. John T. McNeill, trans. Ford Lewis Battles (2 vols. Philadelphia, Westminster Press, 1960), Bk. I, ch. 3; Bk. II, chs. 1–2.

case of Thomas Hobbes, to particular social and political positions. It had social and moral valence.[2] From Edwards' perspective, even the citizens of Northampton in early 1730, when this sermon was preached, might be subject to a European-wide current of popular disbelief, although such atheism expressed itself in the local idiom: the village atheist, the recalcitrant sinner, or the disdainful nonattender of church.

In many of his "Miscellanies" during the next few years, such as nos. 519 and 547, Edwards struggled to refute atheism in the same terms presented in *Practical Atheism.* He repeatedly joined the epistemological to the moral problem, contending that the existence of God, revelation, and a doctrine of reward and punishment were necessary to even the most basic moral assumptions. When Edwards preached again on Ps. 14:1, in a different sermon given to the Stockbridge Indians in 1752, he turned from his psychological critique and provided a simple argument from design to the existence of God.

* * *

The manuscript is a typical duodecimo booklet, consisting of nine leaves. The last leaf has one large corner missing. At the end of the third major head of the Doctrine and under the second inference of the second major head of the Application, Edwards resorted to short phrases rather than full sentences; otherwise, the text is relatively clean and clear, with few signs of reworking. The manuscript has no repreaching marks.

2. See John Redwood, *Reason, Ridicule and Religion: The Age of Enlightenment in England, 1660–1750* (Cambridge, Harvard Univ. Press, 1976). For a sustained, later critique of atheism by JE, see his sermon on Rom. 1:20, dated June 1743, with the doctrine: "The being and attributes of God are clearly to be seen by the works of creation."

PRACTICAL ATHEISM

PSALM 14:1.

The fool hath said in his heart, There is no God.

He who has infinite wisdom, who sits in heaven and from thence perfectly beholds all things as they are and knows better than any other what is wisdom and what is folly, has in his Holy Word stigmatized the wicked as the greatest fools. So that we find 'em there called fools, as though they were so in the most eminent manner. And so wisdom is used for holiness commonly in the Scriptures, as if the word were synonymous or exactly of the same signification.

The wicked are called fools in this verse:

1. As a general appellation that belonged to them, as they are called elsewhere; Ps. 107:17, "fools because of their transgressions"; and Prov. 13:19, "it is an abomination to fools to depart from evil"; and [v.] 20, "a companion of fools shall be destroyed"; and in many other places.

2. With a particular eye to that part of their folly here mentioned, viz. that they say in their hearts, "There is no God." This is a chief influence of the strong stupidity and sottishness of their minds.

Some do suppose that by the expression of "saying in their hearts, There is no God," is meant chiefly in their inclination. But by "heart" in the Scriptures is often very commonly meant the whole soul, including all the faculties. Thus we read of pondering things in the heart, by which is principally intended the act of the understanding. And it seems here to be meant of the whole soul. As sin has dominion over the whole soul, so atheism is what taints all the faculties.

DOCTRINE.

A principle of atheism possesses the hearts of all ungodly men.

By atheism is commonly meant the disbelieving or denying the being of a God, as extending no further than to the act of the understanding.

But by the word "atheism" in the doctrine, I would be understood in a sense something more extensive: for any kind of rejecting, renouncing, or opposing the divine existence or the being of a God with whatever faculty. Which sense we suppose to be parallel with the expression in the text of "saying in the heart, there is no God." And accordingly we shall show,

I. That there is an atheistical inclination.

II. There is a principle of speculative atheism or atheism of judgment in every ungodly man.

III. They have a disposition practically to deny God or to live as if there were no God.

I. There is an atheistical inclination that possesses the heart of every ungodly man; i. e. they have such an inclination and nature that it would suit them if there were no God. They have nothing in them that makes them incline that there should be a God, but they could be glad if there were none. It would mightily suit and please them if they could be assured that there was none.

There is such a spirit of enmity in their hearts against God; everything that is in God is disagreeable to 'em. Their natures are entirely contrary to the nature of God. In the first place they hate the holiness of God. And then they hate all the other attributes because his holiness does, as it were, influence and actuate all his other attributes, as his power, wisdom, and mercy.

They easily perceive that 'tis not for [their] interest as sinners that there should be a God. If there be a God, then they are sensible that he is their enemy, unless they take up a wrong opinion of themselves and think themselves to be God's friends.

This belief of the being of a God, they perceive would be a thing very much cross to their strongest inclinations and appetites. It would disturb them and create them a great deal of uneasiness in their pursuit of their pleasures, to think that there is an almighty Being that has them and all things in his[3] hands, and that perfectly hates sin, and will revenge it; that beholds them continually and sees their hearts and all their secret actions. They have no inclination that it should be thus. It is what they could heartily wish for, that they could be assured it were otherwise, that there was no supreme Being to take notice of their behavior and call them to an account. They have disposition enough to dethrone God or to kill him if it lay in their power.

3. MS: "their."

II. A principle of speculative atheism, or atheism of judgment, possesses the hearts of all ungodly men. The natural blindness of the children of men extends so far as to darken their understandings with respect to the very being of God.

Men's judgments are naturally so depraved. The principle of unbelief that is in the heart extends to everything that is divine; it respects the whole of religion. They have not only unbelief with relation to the sufficiency of Christ's righteousness to satisfy for their sins and recommend them to God, and with relation to those divine doctrines of the gospel about the incarnation and mediation of Christ that are so much above the light of nature, but they have in their hearts a principle of unbelief[4] of the very first principle of natural religion.

Here we shall take notice of the ways wherein this atheistical principle expresses itself. But I shall first observe that, however there is such a principle of atheism in all ungodly men, yet 'tis very questionable whether there ever was any man that ever was able to satisfy himself that there was no God.

There have been many that, finding that the belief of the being of a God would not suit with their sinful pursuits or agree with their carnal pleasures, have labored to free themselves from this encumbrance, and entirely to throw off the yoke of religion, and to get rid of all restraint from the apprehensions of a supreme judge to call them to an account. But 'tis very questionable whether any of them ever so far obtained their end, or by objecting and caviling to free themselves from all sense of the being of a God, so as to get rid of fears and jealousies and terrifying apprehensions of his being, and especially at times.

However perverse and depraved some men's reason is, being blinded and misled by their sinful prejudices and made headstrong by their pride, yet studying and reasoning is not the way to make men perfect atheists, though they set themselves about it for that very end, to ease their own minds of the burden of a jealousy of it.

But the likeliest way for men to bring themselves to it, or to come as near it as men can come, is not to consider at all: to exercise their reason as little as ever they can, and make haste and make themselves every way as much like beasts as lies in their power, to be as inconsiderate as beasts and stupefy their minds and darken their understandings with beastly lusts as fast as they can. That is the readiest way to arrive at atheism or to arrive at perfection in it.

4. The following phrase, excised by JE, specifies the first principle of natural religion: "of the very being of a God."

But if men set themselves to study, though it be on purpose to cavil and object, men can't that way so blind themselves but that the evidences of God's existence will discover themselves. The discoveries of it are so numerous and so obvious that 'tis difficult for a man to turn his eyes off from them, or so to blind himself that he shall not see them. And the evidences are so direct that it's difficult to reason so little or so wrong as not to see the dependence of the conclusion on the premises.

Though there be a principle of atheism in the heart of all ungodly men, yet there is also a natural faculty of reason, and the atheistical principle never can so far prevail against the principle of reason as so far to hinder its exercise or wholly to put out the light of nature in this particular.[5] God hath showed to every man his own existence by the light of nature; Rom. 1:19–20, "Because that which may be known of God is manifest in them; for God hath showed it unto them. For the invisible things of him from the creation of the world are clearly seen, being understood by the things that are made" (v. 18). So that the heathen held the truth in unrighteousness; Rom. 1:18, "For the wrath of God is revealed from heaven against all ungodliness and unrighteousness of men, who hold the truth in unrighteousness."

That natural conscience that is in every man will make him at least suspicious of a supreme judge. For that tells every man, when he has committed wickedness, that he deserves punishment, and makes it manifest to him that it is most fitting and suitable that there should be a supreme governor of the world and judge of men to assign to every one according to his works; and therefore men naturally expect it. And therefore it has been observed of some of the most atheistical and those that professed atheism, that they have at times been greatly terrified with apprehensions of God's being and vengeance, and especially on a death bed.

But this atheism that is in the hearts of ungodly men appears and expresses itself these ways.

First. The minds of ungodly men are not susceptive of a certain conviction and realizing apprehension of the being of God. They may give way to the arguments that they hear for it and give their consent to the thing, as being that which is upheld by arguments that they can't answer, but after all they are not completely convinced of it. It don't seem as a thing real to them. It don't make that impression upon them that things which they apprehend to be real do, but rather such as some fable. Things that

5. I.e. in this particular case: the existence of God.

they have seen with their eyes and conversed with by their bodily senses make another kind of impression upon their minds.

Wicked men don't thoroughly realize it, that there is an eternal, almighty Being that they "live and move and have their beings in" [Acts 17:28] and that sees them and takes notice of all their actions. It is a thing, it may be, that they have been taught from their childhood, and a thing they have heard many arguments for and that they can't answer, and so what they are wont to allow. But it is one thing to do so and another to have a realizing sense and conviction of it.

Second. Ungodly men have a principle in them that makes them very prone to call the being of God in question. They are ready to listen to objections and to imagine that there is much in them. A little objection will take much faster hold of 'em than arguments on the contrary of far greater strength.

They are ready to say with themselves oftentimes, "How do I know that there is any thing as a God? It may be there is nothing in it. It may be the Scriptures and the scheme about a creator and judge and a future state is only an invention of men. How do I know but that when I die I shall return to nothing; that there will be an end of 'em as there is of the beasts? Them that are gone before don't come back and tell us whether they find it true. It may be 'tis all a mere notion."

And there is a principle and nature that is very apt to fall in with such surmises. The corrupt nature of man is such as they very much suit with. Man is prone to infidelity and to catch at arguments for it.

And though sometimes they may seem to be convinced and silenced, yet when once those arguments are a little out of the mind, then that [thought] will return again: "How do I know but that the world is all this while deceived about the being of God and there is no such?" All the while there are many in the world that love to be caviling and objecting against it, and there have been some that have openly denied and renounced the being of God, and others that have not gone so far have denied a providence: denied that God has anything to do in governing the world, or that he takes any notice of the affairs of mankind, which is very much equivalent with denying the being of God itself.

Though it be a general thing to profess a belief of the existence of God, yet there is the same principle naturally in us as in them, the same proneness to unbelief of God's existence. These following things seem to be the causes of it.

1. The dullness and sloth of the minds of wicked men. Sin is a thing that is of a benumbing, stupefying nature. It renders the soul insensible

and indolent and restive; it exceedingly disposes it to sloth and inactivity. Atheism, as we observed before, is most firmly founded in inconsideration. Men are naturally exceedingly inclined to be inconsiderate and unthoughtful of things of a spiritual nature. It makes the mind exceeding inattentive to those clear and bright evidences that we have of the being of God in the works of God.

The minds of carnal men are so clogged and overcharged with the world and so immersed in senses that they are, as it were, lulled asleep thereby, and the understandings are held down and kept from soaring aloft to spiritual and divine objects.

2. It arises from their aversion to divine and spiritual things. The atheism of the understanding arises in great measure from the prejudices that possess the hearts of men against the belief of the being of a God. They hate that there should be a God. They wish that there was none, and so they are very ready to hearken to any objections against his being, because what is aimed at in those objections is what suits them, and the contrary way disagreeable to them.

And then their aversion to spiritual objects leads 'em to atheism another way, viz. as it indisposes them to think about them. If men thought more about God and his word and works, and if they dwelled upon such things with greater fixedness, they would be more likely to be convinced of the being of a God. But the objects being disagreeable to them, they seldom think of them. Many of them scarce ever think of God with any attention. Such thoughts ben't at all apt to stay in their mind; the ideas make no impression scarcely upon that that is of so contrary a nature, and resists them and endeavors to throw them out as soon as possible; Ps. 10:4, "God is not in all his thoughts."

3. It arises from an habitual dependence on their senses. Wicked men are so immersed in sense and so enslaved thereto that they've become habitually dependent upon them, so that they believe nothing, they realize nothing, but what is the object of sense.

Men having lost their relish for spiritual enjoyment, they seek their pleasure and happiness only in sensual enjoyment, and so are wont to employ and exercise their souls wholly about sensitive things, till what is sensible seems to be all to them. And that which is not the object of sense seems to be nothing; that which they can't see or feel don't seem real to them.

And this is the principal reason that men can give why they are apt to question the being of God: because they never saw him with their bodily eyes. They see this world, and the things of the world, and therefore they can realize them. Man has a nobler way of perception than that of sense, but it has been disused, and men have so devoted themselves to sense that it has taken the place of reason and the nobler powers. The souls of carnal men, the understandings as well as inclinations and wills, are become slaves to sense.

III. Ungodly men are prone practically to deny the being of God; that is, to live as if there was no God, to live without any respect or regard to him, as if he were not, or had nothing to do with them, or were any way concerned about the government and ordering of the world. They practically deny that God is their creator, in that they refuse to acknowledge him and to pay him those regards which are due to him as such. They violate those obligations that immediately result from the relation of a creature to a creator.

They deny God as their owner, in that they refuse to devote themselves to him. They deny God as their disposer, in that they refuse to submit to his disposal. They deny him as their lawgiver and judge, by showing no regard to his commands or threatenings.

They practically deny all the attributes of God and consequently his being. They deny his holiness, in that they live as if there were no superior Being that hated sin. They deny his wisdom, by living as though God did [not] behold them and see their secret actions and thoughts. They practically deny his power; they live as if God were not able to punish them and make them miserable for their sins. They deny his mercy, in that they have no regard to the offers and tenders of it.

But especially is there one sort of wickedness that is a practical denying the being of God, which is profaneness, or a behavior that shows a contempt or disregard to those things whereby God makes himself known or that relate to his more immediate worship.

Thus wicked men by living prayerless lives, they live like atheists. [They do not practice] secret prayer; [they] profane [the] sabbath; [they neglect gospel] ordinances; [and they do not attend] public worship.[6]

APPLICATION.

I. Hence we may see one cause why there is so much wickedness in places of light. It is mysterious how men dare go on in wickedness, and give themselves such a license as they do, where they are taught that there

6. As JE neared the end of the Doctrine, he sketched in only phrases, upon which he most likely would have expanded extemporaneously in preaching.

is a God that is infinitely holy, that will surely call them to an account, and that he will punish all the ungodly with eternal burnings. But this doctrine will do something towards explaining the mystery. They have a principle of atheism in their hearts: a principle of infidelity whereby they deny the reality of these things. They ben't really and thoroughly convinced, after all that is said, that there is any such thing as heaven or hell or any such being as God. There is none of all the talk about another world and a future judgment that seems real to them. And this is the reason why they can hear about the wrath of an almighty Being, about weeping and wailing and gnashing of teeth, about eternity, and about despair in hell without being much disturbed by it. This is the reason that they can hear such things on the sabbath and go right away and commit wickedness as they used to do, the same wickedness that they have been hearing so terribly threatened.

So if men were not in a considerable measure atheists, it would be utterly impossible that they should go on and live so peaceably and quietly in every wickedness and commit sin so boldly as they do under such warnings as they have. We may as well suppose that it is possible for man to love misery and hate happiness, that he can choose pain and torment, as foremost and for its own sake.

II. Hence we learn the dreadful wickedness and sottishness of the heart of man naturally.

[*First Inf.*] Hereby appears firstly the dreadful wickedness of the hearts of natural men. It shows the great enmity that is in man against God, that they are so prejudiced against his being.

[*Second Inf.*] It shows this exceeding stupidity, folly, and sottishness of the hearts of wicked men. Well might the Psalmist call them fools. The folly of it appears from these three considerations, viz. first, that the being of God is so exceeding manifest; and second, that our inquiring into the truth in this matter is that which so much concerns [us]; third, the weakness of their main objection.

1. The being of God is a thing abundantly manifest. God has so ordered that there is nothing whatever that is more manifest to reason than his own being. The evidences of his being are exceeding, plain, direct, obvious, and numerous. The being of a God is not only a thing that is discoverable by reason, by a long train of ratiocination, but the arguments are direct and immediate. There is no need of any long and intricate argumentations to argue the Creator from the creature.

Neither is [there] only one or two or a few things from whence the being of God is discoverable, but everything shows it.

I shall not pretend to particularly enumerate all the ways by which the being of God is evident, but the consideration of these two things may be sufficient to show what stupidity of mind it argues in a person endowed with the faculty of reason to question the being of a God.

(1) That men carry such abundant evidence of the being of God in their own beings. There is no need of going far for it. Every time we behold ourselves, look upon our own bodies, or exert any of our bodily powers, and exercise and find the benefit of our senses, or are so much as conscious of any thought in our souls, there is abundant demonstration that we may see of the being of God.

There is no part of our bodies, from the crown of our heads to the bottom of our feet, but that the being of God might be made exceeding evident. Nothing can be more evident, then, than that the wisdom and contrivance of some being had the formation of the human body. [Think of our] eyes, [which could] not [have been contrived by] the wisdom of [our] parents.[7]

[It is] not the less in evidence of the being and wisdom of God because we ben't immediately formed out of the dust of the earth but the wombs of our mothers, but more; for that is one instance of the wisdom and contrivance of God, that such a body of so wonderful a frame should be so propagated.

Or [what] if a man should make an inquiry [about what it is] to propagate others of like kind, from the consideration of our souls? Our souls are certainly more wonderful pieces of divine workmanship than our bodies. And how obvious is the argument, if we put the question to ourselves, "How came we into being? Who made our souls [and] gave us something that thinks and understands?" Men can't make such things as souls.

How sottish are men, that when they perceive their own beings, they can't argue their own author from thence; that they don't consider how they came to be.

(2) There is nothing else that we behold or converse with but that the being of God is evident from it. The very being of any of them [is evidence]: creation, daily providences, sun, moon, [and] stars. Their motion and why [they] move thus and not thus [is evidence]; if you say [that they move] from [the laws of] nature, [then you must ask], "Who gave them those laws?"

7. Bracketed phrases here and throughout the rest of the Application mark places where JE provided only a few words upon which he probably would have expanded extemporaneously in preaching.

The rain from heaven [is evidence], the growing of corn and grass, the self-evidency of one thing to another.

2. This folly appears from the vast importance of inquiring into the truth in this matter, and attending to the evidences we have of it. This shows their folly, that they do no more consider, and that they do no more diligently and impartially inquire. Atheism, as we have observed once and again, is founded in inconsideration. The evidences are such that the least degree of consideration without a sottish blindness would be sufficient to convince. So that if with consideration they are unbelieving, that argues the great stupidity and blindness of their minds; and if it be because they don't consider, that argues monstrous folly and imprudence, that they will say, "There is no God."

3. Their folly appears in the weakness of their main objection, that they can't see God, as if there were nothing but what they could see. Why don't they question the being of men? They don't see their souls. They don't see that he thinks and reasons; yet they believe there is something in men that they converse with, that doth so [exist]. And they see God as much [as they see men's souls].

[*Third*] *Inf.* The dismal waste that the fall has made in man's soul: that he should be so separated and removed from God that he should question his being, that the light of his mind should be so put out, that he should question the very being of that only being and author of all things, that he should be without that knowledge that is the main end of the faculty of reason.

THE PURE IN HEART BLESSED

IN *The Pure in Heart Blessed,* Edwards uses a familiar Beatitude to explore the nature of spiritual knowledge and its relation to human happiness. After an exegesis of the setting of Jesus' saying, a comparison with Moses' reception of the Law on Mount Sinai, and an excursus on the Transfiguration account, Edwards provides an extended discussion of the meaning of spiritual sight. He draws on the vocabulary of sensation, popular in eighteenth-century moral philosophy, to argue for an affective perception of God's glory. Spiritual sensation, he maintains, is the soul's perception of the divine attributes. An encounter with God's moral perfections yields joy and pleasure, so that a genuine sight of God yields happiness.

A lecture in three preaching units dating from early 1730, *The Pure in Heart Blessed* has two major propositions. The first proposition contains a slowly developed, occasionally repetitive analysis of perception. Edwards attempts to give a sensible cast to the notion of spiritual knowledge with a rumination on what the experience of God in heaven is like and the emotional disposition of those blessed enough to have it. In the second proposition the sermon reaches a high level of rhetorical intensity, displaying Edwards' use of earthy language, common metaphor, and even humor to convey, in compressed form, an erudite message. Only the pure in heart will see God, he insists, because "it would be most unsuitable for the glorious and most blessed God to embrace and caress in the arm of his love that that is infinitely more filthy than a toad or a serpent." A brief Application, nearly an afterthought, concludes the lecture.

The Pure in Heart Blessed clearly adumbrates Edwards' more celebrated sermon on spiritual knowledge, *A Divine and Supernatural Light.* Both lectures show his increasing interest in putting into concrete language the nature of spiritual experience. Yet there are some notable differences. Here, Edwards struggles to define the experience of seeing God, and thus draws on the image of the saints in heaven and their joy. Later, Edwards would focus on the theological significance of divine illumination in terms of the necessity for a divinely given regeneration on earth.

* * *

The manuscript is a duodecimo booklet consisting of twenty-five extant leaves. At least one final leaf has been lost, and two leaves are seriously damaged. These missing passages are provided from the Dwight edition. Edwards repreached the sermon twice, once at a neighboring parish, and once to the Stockbridge Indians. There are, however, no indications of reorganization or major revisions.

First published in the Dwight edition (*8*, 280–304), the sermon was edited in notable ways by its nineteenth-century handlers. Edwards' use of "ratiocination" to describe inadequate knowledge was changed to "speculative reasoning," perhaps to distance him from a denial of reason per se. Dwight also removed the adjective "immediate" from the description of the knowledge of God by the saints in heaven, perhaps to eliminate any hint of mysticism.

THE PURE IN HEART BLESSED

MATTHEW 5:8.

Blessed are the pure in heart: for they shall see God.

GOD formerly delivered his Law from a mountain, from Mount Sinai, by an audible voice, with the sound of a trumpet, with the appearance of devouring fire, with thunders and lightnings and earthquakes [Ex. 19: 16–21]. But the principal discoveries of God's mind and will to mankind were reserved to be given by Jesus Christ, his own Son and the Redeemer of men, who is the light of the world; Heb. 1:1–2, "God, who at sundry times and in divers manners spake in time past unto the fathers by the prophets, hath in these last days spoken unto us by his Son."

In this sermon of his, of which my text is a part, we have him delivering the mind of God also from a mountain. Here is God speaking as well as from Mount Sinai, and as immediately, but after a very different manner. There God spoke by a preternatural formation of sounds in the air. Here he becomes incarnate. He takes on him our nature and speaks and converses with us not in such a preternatural, awful, and terrible manner, but familiarly, as one of us. His face was beheld freely by all that were about him. His voice was heard without those terrors which made the children desire that God might speak to them immediately no more. And the revelation which he makes of God's mind is more clear and perfect and fuller of the discoveries of the spiritual duties, the spiritual nature of the command of God, and of our spiritual and true happiness, and of mercy and grace to mankind; John 1:17, "The law was given by Moses, but grace and truth came by Jesus Christ."

This discourse of Christ on the mountain is a compendium principally leveled against the false notions and carnal prejudices that were at that day embraced by the nation of the Jews. And those benedictions that we have in the beginning of his sermon were sayings that were paradoxes to 'em, were quite contrary to notions that they had received, as that he that was poor in spirit was blessed. It was contrary to the received opinion of the world, and especially of that nation who were exceeding ambitious of the praise of men, and highly conceited of their own righteousness. And that he was a blessed and happy man that mourned, that mourned for sin and lived mortified to the pleasures and vanities of the world, was contrary to their notions, who placed their highest happiness in worldly and carnal things. So that they that were meek were blessed, was another doctrine very contrary to their notion, who were an exceeding haughty, proud nation, and very revengeful, and held the lawfulness of private revenge, as you may see [in] v. 38. So that they that hunger and thirst after righteousness were happy [was contrary to their notion], for they placed their happiness not in having a great deal of righteousness but in having much of the world. They were wont to labor for the meat that perisheth; they had no notions of any such as spiritual riches or of a happiness in the satisfying of a spiritual appetite. The Jews were dreadfully in the dark at that day about spiritual things. The happiness they expected by the Messiah was a temporal and carnal, and not a spiritual, happiness.

Again, Christ tells them that they were blessed that were merciful and that were peacemakers, which was also a doctrine that the Jews especially stood in need of at that day. For they were generally of a cruel, unmerciful, persecuting, contentious spirit. So that they that were persecuted and reviled were blessed was [a] strange doctrine [to those who] sought [the] praise of men.

The doctrine Christ teaches them in our text, viz. that they were blessed that were pure in heart, was a thing that was beyond their divinity. The Jews had got into a way of placing almost the whole of religion in external things: in a conformity to the rites and ceremonies of the law of Moses. They placed a great deal of religion in tithing mint and anise and cumin, and in their tradition, as in washing hands before meat and the like, but neglected the weightier matters of the law [Matt. 23:23], and especially such as respected heart holiness. They took a great deal more care to have clean hands and a clean outside than a clean heart, as Christ tells them; Matt. 23:25, 27, "ye make clean the outside of the cup and of the platter but within they are full of extortion and excess . . . ye are like unto whited sepulchers, which indeed appear beautiful outward but within are full of dead men's bones, and of all uncleanness."

1. In our text Christ in the first place pronounces the pure in heart blessed. Christ, in this and the rest of these, accommodates his instructions to the human nature. Happiness, he knew, was what all mankind

were in the pursuit of. He here directs them in the true way to it, and tells them what they must be in order to be blessed, and happy.

2. He gives the reason why such are blessed, or shows wherein the blessedness of such consists: "for they shall see God." 'Tis probable the Jews had a notion that it was a great privilege to see God, from those passages in the Law where there is an account of Moses' earnest desiring to see God's glory, and God's showing him his back parts but refusing to show him his face because no man could see God and live, and from the account that is given of the seventy elders; Ex. 24:9–11, "Then went up Moses . . . and seventy of the elders of Israel; and they saw the God of Israel: and there was under his feet as it were a paved work of a sapphire stone, and as it were the body of heaven in its clearness. And upon the nobles of the children of Israel he laid not his hand; also they saw God, and did eat and drink."

Though 'tis also probable then that they had very poor notions of what the seeing of God was, and of the happiness that consisted in it, and that their notion of this matter, agreeably with the rest of their carnal, childish notions, was of some outwardly splendid and glorious sight, to please the eye of them and entertain their fancy. From these words I shall observe two propositions:

[DOCTRINE.]

[I.] *It is a thing truly happifying to the soul of men to see God.*
[II.] *The having a pure heart is the certain and only way to come to the blessedness of seeing God.*

Prop. I. *That is, a seeing of God is what will make the soul of men truly blessed and happy.* In the consideration of this point we shall, first, briefly show what is meant by seeing God; second, give the reasons why it is truly happifying to the soul.

First. Show what is meant by seeing God.[1]

1. 'Tis not any sight with the bodily eyes. [True] blessedness of the soul don't enter in at that door; [this] would be to make the blessedness of the soul depend [on] the body, or the happiness of men's superior [parts] be dependent on the inferior. [This] is to conform to the carnal and childish notions of the Jews.

God is a spirit and is not to be seen with bodily [eyes. There] is one thing we find attributed to God, that [he is invisible]; Heb. 11:27, "as

1. At this point the MS is damaged and partially missing; interpolated phrases, based partly on the Dwight edition, have been marked by brackets through the next five paragraphs.

seeing him who is invisible"; and Col. 1:15, "who is the image of the invisible God." 'Tis mentioned as part of God's glory; I Tim. 1:17, "to the King eternal, immortal, invisible, be honor and glory for ever and ever."

'Tis not any sight with the bodily eyes. For [the] souls of the saints [in heaven], they see God, and the angels [also, who are] spirits and never were united to bodies; Matt. 18:10, "their angels do always behold the face of my Father which is in heaven." 'Tis not any form or visible representation, not any shape or color or shining light that is seen, wherein this great happiness of the soul consists.

Indeed, God was wont to manifest himself of old in outward glorious appearances. There was a shining light that was called the glory of the Lord; thus the glory of the Lord was said to descend on the mount and on the tabernacle of the congregation [Ex. 19:17–19; 33:9–10]. There was an outward visible token of God's presence; and the seventy [elders], when they saw God in the [mount], they saw a visible shape [Ex. 24:9–11]. And it seems [that] when Moses desired to see God's glory, [he stood upon a rock] and he saw God's back parts when God passed by [and covered Moses] with his hand in the hole of the rock (Ex. 33:18–23); [Moses] saw some visible glory. But it was so God [might there] condescend to the infant state of the church and to the childish notions that were entertained [in] those days of lesser light; and Moses' request [seems to have been more clearly] answered by God's making his goodness to [pass before] him, and proclaiming his name, and giving [a clear sense] of mind of those things contained in that name, than in showing him [a form of outward] glory.

[The saints] in heaven will behold an outward glory as they [behold] the human nature of Christ, which is united to the Godhead, as it is the body of that person that is God. And there will doubtless be appearances of a divine and inimitable glory and beauty in Christ's glorified body, which it will indeed be a ravishing and blessed sight to see.

But the beauty of Christ's body that will be beheld with bodily eyes will be ravishing and delighting chiefly as it will express his spiritual glories. The majesty that will appear in Christ's body will express and show forth the spiritual greatness and majesty of the divine nature. The pureness and beauty of that light and glory will express the perfection of the divine holiness. The sweetness and ravishing mildness of his countenance will express his divine and spiritual love and grace.

Thus it was, when the three disciples beheld Christ at his transfiguration upon the mount. They beheld a wonderful, outward glory in Christ's body, an inexpressible beauty in his countenance; but that outward glory and beauty delighted them principally as it was an expression or signification of the divine excellencies of his mind, as we may see by their manner of speaking of it. It was the sweet mixture there was of majesty and grace in his countenance that ravished them; II Pet. 1:16–18, "We were eyewitnesses of his majesty. For he received from God the Father honor and glory, when there came such a voice to him from the excellent glory, This is my beloved Son, in whom I am well pleased. And this voice we heard when we were with him in the holy mount."

But especially by the account that John gives of it; John 1:14, "And the Word was made flesh and dwelt among us (and we beheld his glory, the glory as of the only begotten of the Father), full of grace and truth," where John very probably had in his mind what he had seen in the mount at the Transfiguration. Grace and truth are not outward but spiritual glories. But,

2. It is an intellectual view by which God is seen. God is a spiritual being, and he is beheld with the understanding. The soul has in itself those powers whereby it is capable of apprehending of objects, and especially spiritual objects, without looking through the windows of the outward senses.

This is a more perfect way of perception than by the eyes of the body. We are so accustomed and habituated to depend upon our senses, and our intellectual powers are so neglected and disused, that we are ready to conceive that seeing things with the bodily eye is the most perfect way of apprehending them. But it is not so; the eye of the soul is vastly nobler than the eye of the body.

But it is not every kind of apprehending God by the understanding that may be called seeing of [God].

(1) [The seeing of God is not] the having an apprehension of God merely by hearsay. If we hear of such a being as God and are educated and instructed that there is such a being, are told what sort of being he is and what he has done and are told right, and we give credit to what we hear, yet have no apprehension of God any other way than only [this], then we can't be said to see God in the sense of the text. This is not that beatific, happifying sight of God.

(2) Nor if we have an apprehension of God merely by speculative reasoning. If we come to some apprehension of God's being, and his being almighty and all-wise and good, by ratiocination, that is not what the Scripture calls seeing God. It is some more immediate way of understanding and viewing that is called sight. Nor will such an apprehension as this, merely, ever make the soul truly blessed.

(3) Nor is every immediate apprehension of God that seeing of him mentioned in the text, and that which is truly happifying to the soul. The wicked spirits in the other world, they doubtless [have] more immediate apprehensions of the being of God, and his power and wrath, than the wicked have in this world. They stand before God to be judged; they receive the sentence from him; they have a dreadful, amazing apprehension of his wrath and displeasure. But yet they are exceeding remote from seeing God in the sense of the text.

[3.] But to see God is this: it is to have an immediate and certain understanding of God's glorious excellency and love.

(1) There must be a direct and immediate sense of God's glory and excellency. I say direct and immediate to distinguish from a mere acknowledging that God is glorious and excellent by ratiocination, which is a more indirect and mediate way of apprehending things than intuitive knowledge.

A true sense of the glory of [God] is that which never can be got by ratiocination.[2] If men argue that God is holy, that never will give a sense of his amiable and glorious holiness. If they argue that he is very merciful, that won't give a sense of his glorious grace and mercy. It must be a more immediate discovery, that must give the mind a real sense of the excellency and beauty of God. He that sees God, he has an immediate view of God's great and awful majesty, of his pure and beauteous holiness, of his wonderful and enduring grace and mercy.

(2) There is a certain understanding of his love; there is a certain apprehension of his presence. He that views and beholds anything, 'tis as being present. And he that sees God, he don't only see him as present by his essence; for so he is present with all, both godly and ungodly. But he is more especially present with those whom he loves. He is graciously present with them, and when they see him they see him and know him to be so. They have an understanding of his love to them; they see him from love manifesting himself to them. He that has a blessed-making sight of God, he not only has a view of God's glory and excellency, but he views it as having a propriety in it. They also see God's love to them; they receive the testimonies and manifestations of that.

God's favor is sometimes in the Scriptures called "his face"; [in] Ps. 119:58, where it is translated, "I entreated thy favor with my whole heart," it is in the original, "thy face." And God's "hiding his face" is a very

2. JE here deleted the following aside: "nor indeed [can ratiocination give] a sense of any beauty and comeliness of anything."

common expression to signify the withholding the testimonies of his favor.

A seeing God in our text implies a seeing God glorious and seeing him gracious, a seeing the light of his countenance both as it is understood of the effulgence of his glory and the manifestation of his favor and love. Here it may be observed,

1. That the discoveries that the saints have in this world of the glory and love of God is often in the Scriptures called a seeing of them. It is said of Abraham that he saw "him who is invisible" (Heb. 11:27). So the saints are said "as in a glass to see the glory of the Lord" (II Cor. 3:18). Christ, speaking of the spiritual knowledge of God, [says], John 14:7, "If ye had known me, ye should have known my Father also: and from henceforth ye know him and have seen him." The saints in this world have an earnest of what is future; they have the dawnings of future light. But,

2. The more perfect views that the saints have of God's glory and love in another world is what is especially called seeing of God. Then they shall see him as he is. Their light, which now is but a glimmering, will be brought to clear sunshine; that which is here but the dawning, will become perfect day. Those intellectual views which will be granted in another world are called seeing God:

a. Because the view will be as immediate as when we see things with our bodily eyes. God will as immediately discover himself to their minds, so that the understanding shall as immediately behold the glory of God and his love as a man can behold the countenance of his friend that he looks in the face.

The discoveries that the saints have of God's excellency and grace here, they are immediate in a sense; that is, they don't depend on ratiocination. But yet in another sense they are mediate; that is, as they are by means of the gospel through a glass. But in heaven God will immediately excite apprehensions of himself without the use of any such means.

b. It is called seeing because it will be most certain. When a person sees a thing with their own eyes, it gives them the greatest certainty they can have of it, greater than they can have by any information of others; so the sight that they will have in heaven will exclude all doubting. The knowledge of God which the saints have in this world has certainty in it, but yet the certainty is liable to be interrupted with temptations and some degree of doubtings. But there is no such thing in heaven. The looking in the sun don't give a greater nor fuller certainty that it shines.

c. It is called seeing because the apprehension of God's glory and love is as clear and lively as when anything is seen with bodily eyes. When we are actually beholding anything with our eyes in the meridian light of the sun, it don't give a more lively idea and apprehension of it than the saints in heaven [have] of divine excellency and that love of God. When we are looking upon things, our idea is much more clear and perfect, and the impression stronger on the soul, than when we only think of a thing absent. But the intellectual views the saints in heaven will have of God will have far the advantage of bodily sight; it will be a much more perfect way of apprehending.

The saints in heaven, they will see the glory of the body of Christ after the resurrection with bodily [eyes], but they will have no more immediate or perfect way of seeing that visible glory than they will of beholding Christ's divine and spiritual glory. They won't want eyes to see that which is spiritual as well as we can see anything that is corporeal. They will behold God in an ineffable, and to us now inconceivable, manner.

d. The intellectual sight the saints will have of God will make them as sensible of his presence and give them as great advantage of conversing with him as the sight of the bodily eye doth an earthly friend; yea, and more too. For when we see our earthly friends with bodily eyes we don't immediately see their souls' principal part, even their souls. We see the qualities and dispositions and acts of their minds not immediately but only by outward signs of speech and behavior. We don't see the men in strictness, but only the vehicle or dwelling place.

But their souls will see the spiritual nature of God itself immediately. They shall behold his attributes and disposition towards them more immediately, and therefore with greater authority, than it is possible to see anything in the soul of an earthly friend by his speech and behavior. And therefore their spiritual sight will give 'em greater advantage for conversing with God than the sight of earthly friends with bodily eyes or hearing them with our ears gives us for conversing with them. We come now, in the

Second place, to give the reasons why a thus seeing God is that which will make the soul truly happy.

The following reasons may be given of it, viz. first, that it yields a delight suitable to the nature of an intelligent creature. Second, at the same time that [it] is the delight of the soul, it is also its highest excellency and perfection. Third, it not only gives pleasure but excludes everything of the contrary. Fourth, it is satisfying because the fountain that supplies it is equal to men's desires and capacity. [Fifth] and lastly, it hath an unfailing foundation.

[*Reason*] 1. The seeing of God yields a delight most suitable to the nature of an intelligent creature. God hath made man, and man only of all the creatures here below, an understanding creature; his reason and understanding is that by which he is distinguished from all inferior ranks of being. Man's reason is, as it were, an heavenly ray, or, as the wise man calls it, it is "the candle of the Lord" (Prov. 20:27); it is that wherein mainly consists the natural image of God. It is the noblest faculty of man; 'tis that which ought to bear rule over the other powers. It was given for that end, to govern in the soul.

And therefore those delights are most suitable to the nature of man that are intellectual or do result from the exercises of this noblest and distinguishing faculty. God, by giving man understanding, he made him capable of such delights, and fitted him for them, and designed that such pleasures as these should be his happiness.

Intellectual pleasure consists in beholding of spiritual excellencies and beauties; but the glorious excellency and beauty of God, they are far the greatest. God's excellence is the supreme excellence; when the understanding of the reasonable creature dwells here, it dwells at the fountain and swims in a boundless and bottomless ocean.

The love of God is also the most suitable entertainment of the soul of man, that naturally desires the happiness of society, or of union, with some other being. The love of so glorious a Being is infinitely valuable, and the discoveries of it are capable of ravishing the soul above all other loves.

It is suitable to the nature of an intelligent being also as it is that kind of delight that reason approves of. There are many other delights that men indulge themselves in, that although they are pleasing to the senses and inferior powers, yet they are contrary to reason. Reason opposes the enjoyment of them, so that unless reason be suppressed and stifled they can't be enjoyed without war in the soul. Reason, the noblest faculty, resists the inferior, rebellious powers; and the more reason is in exercise, the more will it resist and the greater will the inward war and opposition be.

But in this kind of delight in seeing of God, the understanding approves of it. It is a thing most agreeable to reason that the soul should delight itself in this, and the more reason is in exercise, the more it approves of it; so that when it is enjoyed, it is with inward peace and a sweet tranquillity of soul. There is nothing in human nature that is opposite to it, but everything agrees and consents to it. And therefore with what quickness does the soul [delight itself in the seeing of God.][3]

3. A corner of the leaf on which this passage occurs is cut off, making illegible a short phrase

[*Reason*] 2. The pleasure the soul has in seeing God is not only its pleasure, but it is at the same time its highest perfection and excellency.

That is man's true happiness: that is, not only his pleasure, but his perfection and true excellency. And such is the soul's seeing of God and that joy it has therein. When a man or any reasonable creature is once come to that, [that] his excellency and his joy are the same thing, then he is come to the right and real happiness, and not before.

If a man enjoys pleasure and lives in it, how much soever he may be taken with what he enjoys, if he be never the better for his pleasure, if he be not the more excellent for it, it is a certain sign that he is not a truly happy man. There are many pleasures that men are wont violently to pursue and to devote themselves very much to that are no part of their dignity or perfection; but on the contrary they debase the man and make him vile. There are such pleasures as instead of adding any beauty to 'em are indeed the filth of their minds; they don't excel their natures but make them more akin to beasts.

But it is quite the contrary with the pleasure that is to be enjoyed in seeing God. A seeing God is the highest honor and dignity that the human nature can come to; that intellectual beholding of him itself is the highest excellency of the understanding. That is one great part of the excellency of man, his knowledge and understanding, but the knowledge of God is the most excellent and noble knowledge.

And the delight and joy the soul has in that sight is the highest excellency of the other faculty, viz. the will. The heart of man cannot be brought to a higher excellency than to have delight in God and complacency in the divine excellency and glory. The soul, while it remains under the power of corruption and depravity, cannot have any delight in God's glory; and when it is brought to such a disposition that it is disposed to delight in it, it is most excellently disposed. And when it actually exercises delight in God, it is its most noble and exalted exercise that it's capable of.

So that the soul's seeing of God and having pleasure and joy in it is the greatest excellency of both the faculties.

[*Reason*] 3. The happiness of seeing God is a pure sweet without any mixture. That pleasure has the best claim to be called man's true happiness that comes unmixed, that has no alloy. But so doth the joy of seeing God; it neither brings any bitterness, neither will it suffer any.

---

that follows "quickness." The passage ends abruptly at "the soul" and is followed by a blank leaf. At the top of the next leaf, JE began a new preaching unit, repeating the text, the two doctrines, and the list of reasons under the first section of the first proposition.

(1) This pleasure brings no bitterness with it. This is not the case with other kind of delights, those that carnal men are wont to place their happiness in. They are bitter sweets; they afford a kind of pleasure for a moment in gratifying an appetite, but there is wormwood and gall mingled in the cup. Their roses grow upon thorns, and there is a sting with their honey. There is generally a bitterness that accompanies them, and a bitterness that follows them; if men place their happiness in them, reason and conscience gives them inward disturbance in their enjoyment.

And there will be the sting of continual disappointments. For carnal delights are of that nature, that they keep the soul that places happiness in them always big with expectation and in eager pursuit, but they are ever more like shadows, never yield what is hoped for. And they that give themselves up to them, they unavoidably bring upon themselves many heavy inconveniences; wherein they promote their pleasure one way, they destroy their comfort other ways. And there is this sting accompanies them every time there is any consideration exercised: that they are but short-lived. They will soon vanish and be no more.

And as to the pleasures that are to be had in the enjoyment of earthly friends, there is a bitterness goes with that. A dear love to any earthly object, though it afford comfort, yet it greatly multiplies cares and anxieties through the defects and blemishes, the calamities, the instability and changeableness of the object, and short-livedness of all such friendship, and the pleasures thence arising.

Some men take a great deal of pleasure in learning, in studying and increasing knowledge. But Solomon, who had great experience, long ago observed that this also is vanity, because he that increaseth knowledge increaseth sorrow; Eccles. 1:17–18, "I gave my heart to know wisdom, and to know madness and folly: I perceived that this also is vexation of spirit. For in much wisdom is much grief: and he that increaseth knowledge increaseth sorrow."

But the delight that the seeing God affords to the soul brings no bitterness with it; it has nothing to be a damp to it. There is no disappointment accompanies it. It promises not more than it yields; but on the contrary, the pleasure is greater than could be imagined before God was seen. It brings no sting of conscience along with it. It brings no vexing care or anxiety. It leaves no loathing or disrelish behind it.

There is nothing in God that gives uneasiness to him that has the vision of him. It all heightens the joy; the view of one attribute adds to the joy that is raised by another. The beholding the beautiful holiness of God gives unspeakable pleasure to the mind; the idea of that is immensely the most agreeable and amiable idea that can be in a created mind. And then the beholding of God's grace, it adds to the joy to consider that that Being that is so amiable in himself is so communicative, so disposed to love and benevolence.

The view of God's majesty and greatness again will greatly heighten the joy. To behold such grace and goodness, and such grace and goodness and majesty united together! And especially will the beholding of God's love to the person beholding increase the pleasure, to consider that He that is so great and so glorious a being loves him, and is his God and friend!

Again, the beholding of God's infinite power will still add to the pleasure, to think that He that is his friend, and loves him with so great a love, can do all things for him! So the beholding of His wisdom, because He thereby knows what is best for him and knows how so to order things as shall make him most blessed. So the consideration of his eternity and immutability: it will rejoice him to think that his friend and his portion is an eternal and unchangeable portion and friend.

The beholding of God's happiness will increase the joy, to consider that He is so happy that is so much the object of his love that beholds Him! The love of God in those that shall see God will cause them exceedingly to rejoice in God's happiness.

And even the sight of God's vindictive justice will add to their joy. The seeing of this will be no damp to their pleasure but will heighten it. This justice of God will appear glorious to them, and will make them to prize his love.

(2) This joy is without mixture not only as it brings no bitterness with it, but also as it will not suffer any. The seeing of God excludes everything that is of a nature different to joy and delight; this light is such as wholly excludes darkness.

This is not in the power of any earthly enjoyment or pleasure, to drive and shut out all trouble from the heart. If a man has some things that he takes comfort and pleasure in, there are others that yield him uneasiness and sorrow. If he have some things in the world that are sweet, there are others that are bitter, which it is not in the power of his pleasures to help him against. There never can anything be found here below that shall make a man so happy, but that he must have grief and pleasure mixed together. This world, let us make the best of it, will be spotted with black and white, varied with clouds and sunshine; and to them who yield their hearts to it, it will yield pain as well as pleasure, even to them that it deals best by. But this pleasure of seeing God won't suffer mixture, [for] these two reasons.[4]

1. The pleasure of seeing God is so great and strong that it takes the full possession of the heart; it fills it brimful, so that there shall be no room for any sorrow, no room in any corner for anything of an adverse nature from joy. There is no darkness can bear such powerful light. It is impossible that they that see God face to face, that behold his glory and love so immediately as they do in heaven, should have any such thing as grief or pain in their hearts.

When once the saints are thus come into God's presence, tears shall be wiped from their eyes and sorrow and sighing shall flee away [Rev. 21:4].

The pleasure will be so great as fully and perfectly to employ every faculty. The sight of God's glory and love will be so wonderful, so engaging to the mind, and shall keep all the powers of it in such strong attention, that the soul will be wholly possessed and taken up.

2. There will be in what they shall see a sufficient antidote against everything that would afford uneasiness or that can have any tendency thereto. If there was sin in the heart before, that used by its exercises to disturb the peace and quiet of it and was a seed and spring of trouble, the immediate and full sight of God's glory will immediately drive it all away. Sin can't remain in the heart that thus beholds God, for sin is a principle of enmity against God; but there can no enmity remain in one that after this manner sees God's glory. It must and will wholly drive away any such imperfect principle and change it[5] into love. The sight that the saints have of God's glory here transforms 'em in part into the same image, but that perfect sight will transform them perfectly.

If there be the hatred of enemies, the view of the love and power of God will be a sufficient antidote against it, so that it can give no uneasiness. If he is taken away from all earthly enjoyment, that will give no uneasiness to him that sees what a fullness there is in God. They will see that there is all in Him, so that he that possesses Him can lose nothing; or that whatever he is taken from, it is no loss. And whatsoever else there be that would otherwise afford grief and uneasiness to the soul, it cannot affect him that is in the presence of God and sees his face.

Therefore this pleasure may justly be looked upon as the true happiness of men, being such as is not consistent with any kind or degree of

4. MS: "won't suffer mixture; reasons these two."
5. MS: "him."

trouble or uneasiness. That pleasure has the best claim to be called men's happiness that is unmixed, and not only so but is of such a nature that it will not bear any mixture. But we now proceed to the

Reason 4. [Fourth reason] why this joy of seeing God is the true blessedness of man, viz. that it is satisfying, the fountain that supplies it being equal to man's desires and capacity.

When God gave man his capacity of happiness, he doubtless made provision for the filling of it. There was some good that God had in his eye when he made the vessel, and made it of such dimensions, that he knew to be sufficient to fill it and to contain which the vessel was prepared; and doubtless that, whatever it be, is man's true blessedness. And that good which is found not to be commensurate to men's capacity and natural cravings, and never can equal it, it certainly denotes it not to be that wherein men's happiness consists.

Men's desires and capacity are commensurate one with another. Till the capacity be filled, the appetite of the soul will not be filled; but when once the capacity is filled, the soul desires no more.

Now in order to judge how great his capacity is, we must consider the capacity of his principal and leading faculty, viz. his understanding. So great as the capacity of that faculty is, so great is man's capacity of enjoyment. So great a good as the soul is capable of understanding, so great a good is it capable of enjoying. So great a good as the soul is capable of receiving in its perception and idea, so great a good is it capable of receiving with the other faculty, the will, which keeps pace with the understanding. And that good which the soul can receive with both faculties, it is capable of being made the possessor and enjoyer of.

But it is easy to perceive that there is nothing here below that can give men such delight that shall be equal to their faculties. Let a man enjoy as great an affluence of creature comforts as he will, yet there is room; man's nature is capable of a great deal more. There are these and those things wanting that their understanding can extend itself to, that they could wish more added.

But the fountain that supplies that joy and delight which the soul has in seeing God is sufficient to fill the vessel, because it is infinite. He that sees the glory of God, he in his measure beholds that that there is no end of. The understanding may extend itself as far [as] it will; it doth but take its flight out into an endless expanse and dive into a bottomless ocean. It may discover more and more of the beauty and loveliness of God, but it never will exhaust the fountain. Man may as well swallow up the ocean as he can extend his faculties to the utmost of God's excellency.

So in like manner may it be said of the love of God. They can never by soaring and ascending come to the height of it, and never by descending come to the depth of it, or by measuring know the length and breadth of it; Eph. 3:18–19, "What is the breadth, and length, and depth, and height of the love of Christ which passeth knowledge." So then let the thoughts and desires extend themselves as much as they will, here is enough for them.

How blessed therefore are they that do see God, that are come to this exhaustless fountain! They have obtained that delight that gives full satisfaction; being come to this pleasure, they neither do nor can desire any more. They can sit down fully contented, and take up with this enjoyment forever and ever, and desire no change. After they have had the pleasures of beholding the face of God millions of ages, it won't grow a dull story; the relish of this delight will be as exquisite as ever. There is enough still for the utmost employment of every faculty.

[*Reason*] 5. And last, this delight in seeing of God hath an unfailing foundation. God made men to endure for ever, and therefore that which is men's true blessedness, we may conclude, has a sure and lasting foundation. As to worldly enjoyments, their foundation is a sandy one that is continually wearing away and certainly will at last let the building fall. If we take pleasure in riches, riches in a little while will be gone. If we take pleasure in gratifying our senses, both those things, whence we drew these gratifications, they'll perish with the using, and also our senses will be gone. The agent will be worn out and our whole outward frame will turn to dust. If we take pleasure in union and society with earthly friends, those unions must be broke; the bonds, they are not durable, but will soon wear asunder.

But he that has the immediate intellectual views of God's glory and love, and rejoices in that, his happiness is built upon an everlasting rock; Is. 26:4, "Trust ye in the Lord for ever: for in the Lord Jehovah is everlasting strength." In the Hebrew it is, "in the Lord Jehovah is the rock of ages."

The glory of God is a thing subject to no changes or vicissitudes. It will never cease to shine forth. History gives us accounts of the sun's light failing and being more faint and dim for many months together, but the glory of God never will be subject to fade. There never will be any eclipse or dimness, but it will shine eternally in its strength; Is. 60:19, "The Lord shall be unto thee thine everlasting light."

So the love of God, to [those] that see his face, it will never be subject to any coolings. He loves his saints with an everlasting love; Jer. 31:3, "I have loved thee with an everlasting love."

Those streams of pleasure that are at God's right hand, they are never dry, but ever flowing and ever full.

How much doth the sense of the sureness of this foundation confirm and heighten the joy! The soul enjoys its delight in a sense of this, free from all fears and jealousies, and with an unspeakable quietness and assurance; Is. 32:17, "And the works of righteousness shall be peace, and the effect of righteousness, quietness and assurance forever."

INFERENCES.

I. Here we may see one instance wherein the revelation of Jesus Christ excels all human wisdom. It was a thing that had been beyond the wisdom of the world, to tell wherein men's true happiness consisted. There was a vast variety of opinions about it amongst the wise men and philosophers of the heathen. There was scarcely anything that there was so great differences amongst them about. If I remember right, there were more than a hundred different opinions reckoned up about it, which shows that they were woefully in the dark, though there were many very wise men amongst them, men famed through all succeeding ages for their knowledge and wisdom. Yet their reason was not sufficient to find out men's true happiness.

We can give reasons for it now it is revealed, and it seems so rational, that one would think the light of nature sufficient to discover it. But we, having always lived in the enjoyment of gospel light and being accustomed to it, are hardly sensible how dependent we are upon it, and how much we should be in the blind and dark about things that now seem plain to us, if we never had had our reason assisted by revelation. "God hath made foolish the wisdom of this world" by the gospel (I Cor. 1:20), i.e. he hath shown the foolishness of their wisdom by the brighter light of his revelation. For all that philosophy and human wisdom could do, it was the gospel that first taught the world wherein mankind's true blessedness consisted, and told them the way to come to it. This brings me to the

II. [*Second Inf.*] Hence we learn one great privilege we enjoy, that are under such advantages to come to the blessedness of seeing God: we have the true God revealed to us in the Word of God, who is the Being in the sight of whom this happiness is to be enjoyed. The heathen world have not so much as that.

We have the glorious attributes and perfections of God declared to us; the glory of God in the face of Jesus Christ is discovered in the gospel which we enjoy. His beauties and glories are there by God himself, as it were pointed forth by God's own hand to our view, so that we have those means which God hath provided for our obtaining those beginnings of the sight of him which the saints have in this world, in the spiritual knowledge which they have of God, which is absolutely necessary in order to the coming to have it perfectly in another world.

The knowledge which believers have of God and his glory as appearing in the face of Christ is the imperfect beginning of this heavenly sight; 'tis an earnest of it. 'Tis the dawning of the heavenly light; and this beginning must ever more recede, or a perfect vision of God in heaven cannot be obtained. And all those that have these beginnings, they shall obtain the perfection also. Therefore great is our privilege, that we have the means of this spiritual knowledge. We may in this world see God as in a glass darkly in order to our hereafter [seeing him] face to face. And surely our privilege is very great, that he has given us that glass from whence God's glory is reflected.

And we han't only the discoveries of God's glory in the doctrines of his Word, but we have plenty of God's own directions how to do that, that we may be in the way to obtain a perfect and beatifical sight of God, which we have in our text, of which I may speak particularly under this next proposition:

III. This proposition or doctrine may lead us to a sense of the blessedness of the heavenly state and justly cause us to long after it.

In heaven the saints do see God; they enjoy that vision of him, that we have been speaking of, in its perfection. They han't only the beginnings, as the saints have here, but all clouds and darkness are removed. They there behold the glory and love of God more immediately, and with greater certainty, and a more strong and lively apprehension, than a man beholds his friend when he is with him and sees his face by the noon-day sun, and with far greater advantages for conversation and enjoyment. Well may this make the heavenly state appear a blessed state to us, and make us to breathe after it! Well may the consideration of these things make the saints wait for and desire their happy change! Well may it make them long for the appearing of Christ; for this they know, that "when he shall appear they shall see him as he is" (I John 3:2)!

This may well be comforting to the saints under apprehensions of death, and is a consideration sufficient to take away the sting of it, and uphold [them] while walking through the midst of that valley. This may well comfort and uphold them in all troubles and difficulties they meet with here, that after a little while they shall see God, which will immediately dry up all tears, and drive away all sorrow and sighing, and expel forever every darksome thought from the heart.

IV. Hence we learn that a life of holiness is the pleasantest life in this world, because in such a life men have the imperfect beginnings of a blessed-making sight of God. And so they have something of true happiness while here: they have the seeds of blessedness sown in their souls, and they begin to sprout forth.

As for all others, those that don't live a holy life, they have nothing at all of true happiness, because they have nothing of the knowledge of God.[6]

[DOCTRINE RESUMED.]

Prop. II. *To be pure in heart is the certain and only way to come to the blessedness of seeing God.*

We have shown what this seeing of God [is], and represented something [of] how great the blessedness is of so seeing of him; and if what we have heard concerning that be believed and entertained by us, it will be sufficient to awaken our attention to any instructions from the Word of God that are to point forth the way to us wherein we may come to this blessedness.

If men should hear of some vast estate or some rich, hid treasure, and also should hear at the same time of some very feasible way whereby they might come at it and make it all their own, how ready would they be to hear; with what eagerness would they listen to one that brought such news, and gave them such directions, provided they had reason to believe that what was told them was true!

We are here told of a much truer and greater blessedness than any treasure of silver, gold, and pearls can yield; and also are told of the way whereby we may assuredly come to be the possessors of it by him that certainly knows.

Here our work is, first, to inquire what it is to be pure in heart; second, to show that this is the sure way to come at this blessedness; [and] third, [to show that this is] the only way.[7]

First. And I would here observe, in order to make way for the better understanding of it, that purity of heart is here to be understood in distinction from a mere external purity, or a purity of the outward actions

6. This ends the second preaching unit; JE begins the third and final unit with a repetition of the text and the second proposition or doctrine.

7. JE inserted mention of this third head after the initial composition.

and behavior in those things that appear to men in an external morality and an outward attendance on ordinancy, and a profession of the true religion and pure doctrines, and a making an outward show and appearance of saintship.

Christ very probably in our text had an eye to the formality and hypocrisies of the scribes, and Pharisees, and other great saints, as they accounted themselves and were accounted amongst the Jews, that were exceeding exact in their observance of the ordinances of the ceremonial law. They were careful not to deviate from it in the least punctilio. For instance, how exact were they in observing the law of tithes: they were careful to bring the tenths even of the herbs in their gardens, as of mint, and anise, and cumin [Matt. 23:23]. They were exceeding careful to keep themselves from all ceremonial uncleanness. They even added to the law in this particular; they were for being stricter and purer than the law required, and therefore made conscience of washing their hands before every meal.

They were very strict to keep from conversing with the Samaritans; they would not eat with them nor have any dealings with them, lest they should be defiled. They used to say to other nations, "Stand by thyself; come not nigh, for I am holier than thou." They looked upon themselves only as pure because they were the children of Abraham, and because they were circumcised and attended the ceremonial law; thus they made clean the outside of the cup and the platter [Matt. 23:25]. And because of their external purity, they looked upon themselves as the peculiar favorites of heaven and expected to be admitted to see God, when all the uncircumcised and those that were not the children of Abraham should be excluded.

But Christ corrects this their mistake, and teaches that such an external purity will never give a man a title to this blessedness, though it was to the degree of the scribes and Pharisees, that were looked upon [as] the most pure of all—that fasted twice a week and gave tithes [Luke 18:12]. For it is purity of heart that is requisite in order to come to this blessedness; v. 20 of this chapter [Matt. 5], "for I say unto you, except your righteousness shall exceed the righteousness of the scribes and Pharisees, ye shall in no case enter into the kingdom of heaven."

However exact any man may be in the external observance of moral or instituted duties: if he be careful to wrong no man, and can say as the young Pharisee did, "All these have I kept from my youth" [Matt. 19:20], i.e. as to an external observance; if he be very strict in keeping the sabbath and in coming to meeting, attending family and closet prayer:

yet if he has not heart-holiness, he is never like to come to see God. 'Tis no reformation of manners that is sufficient, but there must be a new heart and a right spirit.

'Tis the heart that God requires; Prov. 23:26, "My son, give me thine heart." 'Tis the heart that God looks at. However fair and pure an outside there may be, that may be very pleasing and taking with men, yet if there be not purity of heart, the man is not at all the more acceptable to God; I Sam. 16:7, "For man looketh on the outward appearance, but the Lord looketh on the heart." If men outwardly behave well and speak well, yet it is not accepted without trying and weighing the heart; Prov. 16:2, "All the ways of man are clean in his own eyes, but the Lord weigheth the spirits."

It is the spirit [that] is the subject of this blessedness of seeing of God; and therefore the qualities of the spirit and not so much the outward man are what are looked at as those [things] in which are to consist the necessary qualifications fit for it.

Now the heart is said to be pure in the sense of the text, first, with respect to the spiritual filthiness that it is pure from, [and] second, with respect to certain positive qualities that it is endowed with.

The word "pure" in its common acceptation only signifies something negative, viz. the absence of all mixture or defilement; but in "pureness of heart," as it is used in the Scriptures, seems to be implied both that that is negative and positive: not only the absence or removal of filth, but also positive qualities that are called pure.

1. The heart is said to be pure with respect to that filth that it is pure from. Sin is the greatest filthiness. There is nothing that can so defile and render so abominable; it is that which has an infinite abominableness in it. And indeed, it is the only spiritual filthiness; there is nothing else that can defile a soul but sin.

Now, there are none in this life that are pure from sin in that sense, that there is no remainder, no mixture of sin; Prov. 20:9, "Who can say, I have made my heart clean, I am pure from my sin?" So that if this were the requisite qualification, there never would any of the children of men come to see God.

But the pureness of the heart with respect to sin, that may be obtained in this life, consists in the following things.

(1) It implies that the soul sees the filthiness that there is in sin and accordingly abhors it. Sin, that is so filthy in itself, is become so sensibly. He sees its odiousness and deformity, and it is become nauseous to him.

Those creatures that are of a filthy and impure nature, as swine, and dogs, and ravens, and vermin; those things that are filthy, that are nauseous to mankind, such as putrefying, dead carcasses, they don't seem at all filthy to them. They ben't disagreeable to 'em; they don't nauseate 'em at all. But, on the contrary, they love 'em; it is food that suits their appetite. 'Tis because they are of an impure and filthy nature: the nature of the creature is agreeable to such things.

So it is with men of impure hearts. They see no filthiness in sin. They don't nauseate it; it is no way uncomfortable to them to be amongst it, to have it hanging about them. They can wallow themselves in it without any reluctance; yea, they take pleasure in it. It is like meat and drink to them; it don't turn their stomachs, but suits their appetites. 'Tis because they are of an impure nature.

But he that is become pure in heart, he hates sin; he has an antipathy against it. He don't love to do with it. He don't love to be near it. If he sees any of it hanging about him, he abhors himself for it. He seems filthy to himself; he is a burden unto himself. He abhors the very sight of it, and shuns the appearance of it.

If he sees sin in others, it is a very unpleasant sight to him; and it is abominable to him as sin, as it is against God. It's grievous and uncomfortable to him wherever he discerns it. 'Tis because his heart is changed and God has given him a pure nature.

(2) It implies godly sorrow for sin. The pure heart han't only respect to that spiritual filthiness that is present, to abhor it and shun it, but it hath also respect to past sin. The consideration of that grieves it; it causes shame and sorrow to think that he ever did wallow in such defilement, that he ever was so abominable as to love it and feed upon it.

Every transgression leaves a filth behind it upon the soul. This remaining filth causes pain to the renewed and purified heart. By godly sorrow the heart exerts itself against the filthiness of past sins and does as it were endeavor to cast it off and purge itself from it.

(3) It implies that sin is mortified in the heart, so that it is free from the reigning power and dominion of it. Though the heart ben't perfectly free from all sin, yet a freedom is begun. Before, spiritual filth had the possession of the heart; corruption had the entire government of the soul. Every faculty was so wholly defiled by it that all its acts were filthy, and only filthy. The heart was entirely enslaved to sin.

But now the power of sin is broke. The strong bonds by which it was tied and fastened to the heart are in a great measure broke, so that corruption has no longer the possession and government of the heart as it used to have. The principal seat, the throne of the heart, that used to be possessed by corruption, is now purged, and filthiness does now as it were only possess the inferior and exterior parts of the soul; John 13:10, "He that is washed needeth not, save to wash his feet."

(4) The heart that is pure is of that nature that it will be continually exerting itself to cleanse itself from remainders of filthiness. Though there be remainders of filthiness, yet the nature is such, so contrary, that it will never rest or be quiet, but will always be purging and cleansing itself. Like a vessel of fermenting liquor, it will continue working till it has worked itself clear, and till it has cast off all the filthy and heterogeneous parts. Or, like a stream of good water: if the water be in itself sweet and good, however it may be defiled from the muddy banks, yet it will refine as it runs; it will run itself clear again. But if the fountain itself be bad, that yields water of an ill sort, then it will [not] purge itself as it runs.

He that is pure in heart, his heart never will suffer him to live in any sin. If he be ever taken in a fault, he will return, and be cleansing himself again by repentance, and reformation, and a more earnest care, and prayer, that he may avoid that sin for the future.

The remainders of corruption that are in his heart will be his great and continual burden, and he will be endeavoring to cleanse himself more and more. He won't rest in any supposed degree of purity as long as he sees any degree of impurity remaining, but will be striving after progress in the mortification of sin and increase of holiness.

(5) The heart is said to be pure especially with respect to its cleanness from and opposition to the lusts of uncleanness. This kind of wickedness we find to be more especially called uncleanness and filthiness in the Scriptures. This brings a peculiar turpitude upon the soul; these lusts "defile the temple of God" (I Cor. 3:17). Pureness in the Scriptures is sometimes meant only in this restrained sense, with respect to freedom from fleshly impurities; so it seems to be in Phil. 4:8, "Finally, brethren, whatsoever things are true, whatsoever things are pure, whatsoever things are lovely, whatsoever things are of good report . . . think on these things."

Now this sort of purity of heart is absolutely necessary in order to our coming to see God. There must be a detestation of all impure and lascivious practices and talk. They that live in the indulgences of such a lust in one kind of practice or another, or though it be only with their eyes or in their thoughts, they are of impure hearts and shall never come to see God unless they have new hearts given [them].

They that have pure hearts, they abhor and are afraid of such things; they hate "even the garment spotted with the flesh" (Jude 23). They take heed that they don't prostitute their souls to so much as imaginary impurities, much less to practical impurities and works of darkness.

2. The heart is said to be pure with respect to its endowment with positive qualities that are of a contrary nature to spiritual filthiness.

Though purity in strictness be only a freedom from filth, yet there are positive qualities and beauties of mind that seem to be implied in pureness of heart; they may be reckoned as part of the pureness of the heart because of their contrariety to filthiness. The heart by reason of them is still remoter from defilement, as a greater light may be said to be purer than a lesser light; for although the lesser light has no mixture of darkness, yet the greater light is still remoter from darkness. And here,

(1) He is pure in heart that delights in holy exercises. Those exercises that are holy are natural and pleasant to his heart; he sees the beauty that is in holiness, and that beauty has such strong influence upon his heart that it is captivated thereby. He delights in the pure and holy exercises of love to God, in the fear of God, in praising and glorifying God, and in pure and holy love to men.

He delights in holy thoughts and meditations. Those exercises of the understanding that are holy, in contemplating divine things, are most agreeable to him. And those exercises of the will, such inclinations, desires and affections, are most delightful that are spiritual and holy.

(2) He is pure in heart that chooses and takes the greatest delight in spiritual enjoyment. A spiritual appetite is that which governs in his soul, and carries him above the mean, base, and defiled enjoyments of this world, towards spiritual and heavenly objects.

The enjoyments which he chooses and chiefly desires, such as the seeing God and enjoying communion with him, they are enjoyments of the most refined and pure nature. He hungers and thirsts after the pure light of the new Jerusalem. They that have such appetites as these prevailing in them, they are pure in heart.

Second. To have a pure heart is a sure way to obtain the blessedness of seeing God. This is the direct road to the blissful and glorious presence of God, which if we take, it will infallibly lead us thither, as is evident by these two things:

1. God is the giver of the pure heart, and he gives it for this very end, that it may be prepared for the blessedness of seeing. Thus we are taught in the Word of God. The people of God are sanctified and their hearts are made pure, that they may be prepared for glory, as vessels are prepared by the potter for the use he designs. They are elected from all eternity to eternal life, and have purity of heart given them, on purpose to fit them for that which they are chosen to; Rom. 9:23, "And that he might make known the riches of his glory on the vessels of mercy, which he had afore

prepared to glory." We read of the church being arrayed in fine linen, clean and white, by which is signified the church's purity; and it was to prepare her for the enjoyment of Christ (Rev. 19:7–8). And in [Rev.] 21:2, the church thus purified is said to be "as a bride adorned for her husband."

Therefore, if it be so, that God gives the pure heart on purpose to fit and prepare for the seeing of himself, he will obtain his own end. For who can hinder him, that he should not do what he purposes?

2. God hath promised; he hath given his faithful word for it in our text. And to the same purpose again [is] Ps. 24:3–4, "Who shall ascend into the hill of the Lord? Who shall stand in this holy place? He that hath clean hands, and a pure heart." And again, Is. 33:14–17, "He that walketh righteousness and speaketh uprightly," that is, with sincerity of heart, "he shall dwell on high; his place of defense shall be the munitions of rocks; bread shall be given him; his waters shall be sure. Thine eyes shall see the King in his beauty."

Third. This is the only way to come to this blessedness. 'Tis impossible for any ever to come to this blessedness that are not pure in heart, and that for these reasons:

1. 'Tis no way fit or suitable that those that have not pure hearts should be admitted to this privilege. 'Twould be most unsuitable for those who are all over defiled with the most loathsome filth to be admitted into the glorious presence of the king of heaven and earth. 'Twould be no way becoming of the majesty of God for those that are so abominable to come into his blessed presence; nor is it at all becoming his holiness, whereby he is of purer eyes than to behold such filth.

It becomes persons, when they come into the presence of a king, so to attire themselves that they mayn't appear in a sordid habit; and it would be much more unsuitable still for any to come all over defiled with ordure. But sin is that which renders the soul much more loathsome in the sight of God. This spiritual filth is of a nature most different to that pure heavenly light. It would be a very unsuitable mixture to have the stench of sin and wickedness and the light of glory mixed together; and 'tis what God never will suffer.

It would be a most unbecoming thing for such to be the objects of God's favor, and to see the love of God, and [be] receiving the testimonies [of it]. It would be most unsuitable for the glorious and most blessed God to embrace and caress in the arm of his love that that is infinitely more filthy than a toad or a serpent.

2. 'Tis naturally impossible that the soul that is not pure should see God. The sight of God's glory and impurity of heart ben't compatible in the same subject. As long as spiritual impurity holds possession of the heart, it is impossible that the divine light that discovers God's glory should enter. How is it possible for him that is under the power of enmity against God, that only hates God, should see his beauty and loveliness at the same time? Sin, so long as it has the government and possession of the soul, will blind the mind and maintain darkness; as long as sin keeps possession, the heart will be blinded through its deceitfulness.

3. If it were possible for them to see God, they could not relish any sweetness in it; it would be not very agreeable or acceptable to 'em. What pleasure would it be to a soul that hates holiness, to see the holiness of God; what pleasure to them that are God's enemies, to see God's greatness and glory? Wicked men have no relish at all for such intellectual, pure, and holy delights and enjoyments as these. As we have observed already, to have an appetite to and relish for spiritual enjoyments is one part of the purity of heart spoken of in the text.

4. 'Tis impossible that such should be the objects of God's favor and complacence; and, therefore, they can't have this part of the blessed-making vision of God, viz. the seeing of his love. 'Tis impossible that God should take pleasure in wickedness or should have complacence in the wicked, those that have nothing but spiritual filthiness.

And, therefore, they can't have the blessed-making vision of God; for seeing the love of God is an essential part of it. If a man sees how glorious God is, and han't this consideration withal, that he has a propriety in this glory of God, can't consider that this glorious Being is his friend, that He takes pleasure in him, but on the contrary loathes and abhors him, it will not be a blessed-making sight.

APPLICATION

I. *Use* of *Instr.* Hence we learn how great a thing it is to be an upright and sincere Christian, for all such are pure in heart and stand entitled to the blessedness of seeing the most high God. The time is coming when they shall assuredly see him. They shall see him that is infinitely greater than all the kings of the earth; they shall see him face to face; shall see as much of his glory and beauty as the eyes of their souls are capable of beholding. They shall not only see for a few minutes or an hour, but they shall dwell in his presence; they shall sit down forever to drink in the rays of his glory. They shall see him invested, with all this majesty, with smiles and love in his countenance; they shall see him, and converse with [him] as their nearest and best friend.

Thus they shall see him in a little while. The time flies swiftly; the time is even at the door when they shall be admitted to this blessedness.

II. *Use* of *Exam.* Let this put us all upon inquiring whether or no we are pure in heart. Is our religion what has its seat chiefly in the heart, or doth it chiefly consist in what is outward, in morality and formality?

Have we ever experienced a change of heart? Have we a right spirit renewed within us? Have we ever seen the odiousness and filthiness that there is in sin? Is it what we hate wherever we see it, and do we especially hate it in ourselves, and loathe ourselves for it? Is it the object of our hatred as sin, and as it is against God? And in the mourning for sin, have our hearts been broken with the reflection on our own past filthiness?

Are we delivered from the reigning power [of sin], so that no lust has dominion over [us], to lead us captive? Is the power of every lust that we formerly used to be enslaved to now broken, so that we are no longer in bondage to it?

Are our souls now of such a nature that the remainders of sin are their continual burden; is sin that which we long to get rid of? Are we ready with the Apostle to cry out, "O wretched man that I am! Who shall deliver me from the body of this death" [Rom. 7:24]? Cannot we rest and be quiet in the beholding of any sin in us, but that we must be continually laboring to cleanse ourselves from it more and more? Is that what we thirst after, to have sin more and more mortified?

And are there any that now hear me, that think themselves to be godly, that do yet, either in their imaginations and thoughts or in any secret practice, allow and indulge the lust of uncleanness and live in such a way? If it be so, they had great need to bethink themselves whether or no they are not of that generation that are pure in their own eyes, and yet are not cleansed from their filthiness. If they imagine that they are pure in heart, and live in such wickedness, their confidence is vain presumption.[8]

Inquire whether holy exercises and holy employments are the delight of your soul, and what you take pleasure in above all other things in which you can be engaged. Are the enjoyments that you choose, and take the

8. The MS ends abruptly at this point. The version of this sermon published in the Dwight ed., *8*, 303–04, indicates that at least one leaf, now missing from the manuscript booklet, followed. The rest of the sermon printed here, then, is based entirely on the Dwight edition.

greatest delight in, spiritual and heavenly enjoyments? Is the seeing of God, and conversing with him, and dwelling in his presence for ever what you should of your own accord choose above all other things?

III. *Use* of *Exh.* I would earnestly exhort those who hear me, to make to themselves a pure heart. Though it be God's work to purify the heart, yet the actual, or rather the active, procuring of it is your act. All pure and holy exercises are man's acts, and they are his duty. Therefore we are commanded to make us a new heart; Ezek. 18:31, "Make you a new heart and a new spirit."

We must not think to excuse ourselves by saying that it is God's work, that we cannot purify our own hearts; for though it be God's work in one sense, yet it is equally our work in another; Jas. 4:8, "Cleanse your hands, ye sinners; and purify your hearts, ye double-minded." If you do not engage in this work yourselves, and purify your own hearts, they will never be pure. If you do not get a pure heart, the blame of it will be laid to your own backwardness. The unclean soul hates to be purified. It is opposite to its nature; there is a great deal of self-denial in it. But be content to contradict the nature and bent of your own heart, that it may be purified; however grating it may be to you at first, yet consider how blessed the issue will be. Though the road be a little rough in the beginning, yet it will grow pleasanter and pleasanter, till at last it will infallibly lead to that lightsome and glorious country, the inhabitants of which do see and converse with God; Prov. 4:18, "The path of the just is as the shining light that shineth more and more unto the perfect day."

If you would be in the way to have a pure heart:

First. Purify your hands. Cleanse yourself from every external impurity of speech and behavior; take heed that you never defile your hands in known wickedness. Break off all your sins by righteousness, and take heed that you do not give way to impure lusts that would entice to sinful actions. If you set about the work of cleansing yourself but when a temptation comes to plunge yourself into the mire again, you never will be likely to become pure. But you must be steady in your reformation and the amendment of your ways and doings.

Second. Take heed you do not rest in external purity, but seek purity of heart in the ways of God's appointment. Seek it in constant and diligent attendance on all God's ordinances.

Third. Be often searching your own heart, and seek and pray that you may see the filthiness of it. If ever you are made pure, you must be brought to see that you are filthy; you must see the plague and pollution of your own heart.

Fourth. Beg of God that he would give you his Holy Spirit. It is the Spirit of God that purifies the soul; therefore the Spirit of God is often compared to fire, and is said to baptize with fire. He cleanses the heart as fire cleanses the metals, and burns up the filth and pollution of the mind, and is therefore called the spirit of burning; Is. 4:4, "When the Lord shall have washed away the filth of the daughters of Zion, and shall have purged the blood of Jerusalem from the midst thereof by the spirit of judgment, and by the spirit of burning."

THE DANGERS OF DECLINE

Jonathan Edwards has not always been associated with election-day preaching in New England. By tradition and ordinance, congregational ministers used the occasion of election days to preach on the religious duties of government or, conversely, the political duties of Christians. During the eighteenth century, such performances often followed one or more strategies within a set script: assertion of the divine origin of civil government; affirmation of the providential origins and covenantal responsibilities of New England; rehearsal of New England's peculiar advantages or blessings, such as material prosperity or independence from the corruptions of the English church; warnings against current signs of divine judgment, such as political discord or economic crisis; and exhortations to repentance and reform on the part of magistrates, ministers, and citizens.

In *The Dangers of Decline* we have one of Edwards' few contributions to this genre.[1] It is, for him, an unusual sermon in its explicit adoption of covenantal motifs. He considers Christ's warning to the church at Ephesus to be applicable to the civil order in Massachusetts, as though the latter were itself a church. Probably delivered on the election day of May 27, 1730, *The Dangers of Decline* is closely allied to the following sermon in this volume, *Envious Men*, by its commentary on social contention. Whereas Edwards directed *Envious Men*, however, to social affairs in Northampton, he pointed *The Dangers of Decline* to colony-wide political controversy, which reached feverish proportions in Massachusetts in 1729 and 1730.

Edwards claims in the Application of the sermon that God has appointed the "ticklish posture" of the "privileges of this land," the "doubtful" state of "the government," and the "present difficult and doubtful circumstances" to chastise the town and colony for their religious apathy.

1. See also the sermon fragment (73) probably preached for the election day of May 29, 1728, and *The State of Public Affairs*, below, which may have been preached for an election day.

The crises to which he refers involved relations between the provincial government of Massachusetts (the elected legislators or assembly) and the governor, who was appointed by the crown. There appeared to be some instability in the governorship after the death of William Burnet in 1729: first came the temporary administration of William Dummer and then the appointment of Jonathan Belcher in August 1730. During these months there ensued a lengthy debate about the charter rights and obligations of the colony. The assembly repeatedly refused to fix and fund the governor's salary, against instructions from London. The governors, meanwhile, were charged with pressuring the assembly to remedy the depreciation of the colony's currency. Many of the proposed measures, such as restrictions on new currency issues, provoked controversy because they were seen to benefit London bankers at the expense of New Englanders.[2]

Friction between provincial and royal governments alarmed Edwards all the more because it threatened the colony's privileges of religious self-determination, particularly the powers of New Englanders to train and choose their own pastors. As he argues in the Doctrine, people have abused such privileges by their preoccupation with profit, neglect of piety, engagement in business fraud, contention, and inattentiveness to their need for spiritual conversion. This belief reflects Edwards' deepening sensitivity to social forces and problems in the town. His particular contribution here is to fasten on the work of the Spirit in revival as the key to corporate renewal. New England will pass through the crisis safely, he argues, if New Englanders seek the Spirit in prayer and reform their affections accordingly.[3]

* * *

The manuscript is a typical duodecimo booklet, consisting of ten leaves. The writing is clean and clear. The final extant leaf, however, which is fully used, ends in mid-illustration (of historical instances of the ill-effects of contention); this may indicate that a leaf is missing. There are no marks for editorial reorganization or repreaching. Edwards probably did not return to this sermon, set as it was in the peculiar context of Massachusetts' political controversies and economic trials of 1730.

2. See Spencer, *Constitutional Conflicts in Provincial Massachusetts.* For further information and citations, see Preface to the Period, above, pp. 17–28.

3. On the theme of reform, see *Impending Judgments Averted Only by Reformation, Works, 14,* 213–27.

THE DANGERS OF DECLINE

REVELATION 2:4–5.

Nevertheless I have somewhat against thee, because thou has left thy first love. Remember therefore from whence thou art fallen, and repent, and do the first works; or else I will come unto thee quickly and will remove thy candlestick out of its place, except thou repent.

THE apostle John in the latter part of his life had been principally conversant in Asia Minor, and especially in that part of it where were the seven cities mentioned in these two chapters—Ephesus, Smyrna, Pergamos, Thyatira, Sardis, Philadelphia, and Laodicea—which were cities that were in that part of Asia that was next to the sea that divided Asia from Greece, in which was the island called Patmos, where John now was living, banished "for the Word of God and for the testimony of Jesus Christ" (see ch. 1, v. 9).

The churches that were in these cities were churches in which he had much in the exercise of his ministry. They had been much under his care; he had been as a father to 'em. And therefore, being now confined in the place of his banishment, so that he could not preach to 'em as he had been used to do, he by the direction of Jesus Christ writes to 'em in Christ's name, severally and distinctly rehearsing to 'em the words of the Lord Jesus Christ, directing himself most immediately to the ministry of the churches because they had the instruction and oversight of the churches. [He] called [them] the angels of the churches.

First, Christ directs him to write to the church of Ephesus, one of the principal cities in Asia Minor. And here,

1. We hear Christ's commendation of the church: "I know thy works, and thy labor, and thy patience, and how thou canst not bear them which are evil: and thou hast tried them which say they are apostles, and are not, and hast found them liars: and hast borne, and hast patience, and for my

name's sake hast labored, and hast not fainted" [Rev. 2:3–4]. 'Tis a considerable commendation. But yet it seems the church was in a declining posture. And therefore,

2. Here is also Christ's reproof and warning.

(1) Here is a reproof; he reproves them, that they had left their first love. They were not so fervent in spirit, in the profession and service of Christ, nor so zealous in works of charity as they [once] were.

(2) Here is his warning.

1. He warns them of the evil they were in danger [of]: having their candlestick removed out of its place. We learn what is meant by the candlestick by Christ's own explication [in] v. 20 of the preceding chapter: "the seven candlesticks which thou sawest are the seven churches." Christ here has reference to the vision that John had of seven stars, representing the ministry of the churches, and the seven golden candlesticks, representing the churches. So, by "removing their candlestick out of its place" can be intended nothing else than the taking away of their ecclesiastical advantages: the means and ordinances that were administered and enjoyed in the church, by which a church subsists and flourishes.[4]

2. He directs them, what they must do to avoid such a punishment: "Remember therefore from whence thou art fallen, and repent, and do the first works." Their having left their first love appeared in that, that they had left their first works; therefore they are directed to make it appear that they had recovered their first love that way, viz. by doing their first works.

DOCTRINE.

When any visible people of God continue long cold and dead, and declining in the things of religion, there is danger that God will take away their religious advantages.

The church of Ephesus were threatened with this except they repented. They had of late been in a declining way; they were grown cool to what they used to be. And if they still continued, Christ threatened that he would come and "remove thy candlestick out of its place." If they continued so for any long time, he would execute this threatening upon them, as is implied in his threatening that he would "come unto 'em quickly," which implies if they did not repent quickly.

4. JE here deletes: "When God doth so to any church people, he forsakes as to his visible presence amongst them."

The Ephesian church had had great advantages. They had been blessed with the preaching of the apostle Paul, as we have an account in the Acts, and with the ministry of the evangelist Timothy, who was a bright light in the church of God [Acts 19]. And after that it was the place of the abode of the apostle John and was under his more immediate care, besides their having such for their stated elders as were appointed under the conduct and direction of the apostles.

And they had been fervent for religion. Their first love was warm, and their first works were very worthy and excellent. But they had declined and were already grown cold to what they were, and were declining more and more. And therefore Christ threatens them with the withdrawing of his visible presence amongst them. Their advantages had been great; their candlestick was a candlestick of gold; but this was in danger to be removed.

[I.] Inquire wherein the declension and deadness of a people in the things of religion appears. [I] answer,

First. When a people grow cold and dead with respect to religion, there generally is but little said about [it]. There will be but little said about it in families. And when neighbors meet, you shall hear but little talk about soul concerns; all the talk will be about the world. They'll be full of talk about their worldly business, about this and the other worldly design, about buying and selling. Or their tongues will be yet worse employed, in talking against their neighbor.

That which men's hearts do most abound with, that their tongues will be apt to [be] employed about. When men's hearts are taken up about the world, there will be little talk about anything [else]; but if men are full of concern about spiritual and eternal things, and they have the principal possession of their hearts, it will surely be agreeable to 'em sometimes to speak of them. And when there is a warm spirit in religion, it will oftentimes be the subject of conversation. Men will naturally fall into it: Matt 12:34, "of the abundance of the heart the mouth speaketh"; see Mal. 3:16, "They that feared the Lord spoke often one to another."

Second. When a people decline and grow cold in religion, there is a decay of outward strictness in religion. There is not that strictness in keeping the sabbath day; but it will be violated by people's encroaching upon holy time at its beginning, and by their talking [of] worldly and profane things, or by such light and diverting talk which don't show that reverence for the sabbath which is becoming. There is not that appearance of reverence and solemnity in public worship which is becoming.

There is great decay of family religion. There is great want of care and pains in instructing children and instilling principles of religion into 'em. There is not a strict care to keep up a constant attendance on family worship in the members of the family. There is want of care to keep God's ordinances pure, and to hear a testimony against scandalous iniquity.

Third. When a people grow cold and dead in religion, immoralities are wont to prevail. There is a near alliance between morality and grace; though morality don't include grace, yet grace includes morality. And when one flourishes amongst a people, the other will flourish; and when one decays, it is an argument that the other also decays. If immorality is suppressed, and outward religion and morality flourishes amongst a people, 'tis a sign that there are many have true grace. But [if] immorality increases, 'tis a sign that the power of godliness declines. 'Tis also a sign of carnal security, and want of convictions in men of their sin, and danger in a natural condition.

If men are cold in religion, their hearts will be warm about something else; if virtue and holiness be not pursued, vice and wickedness will. When a people grow cold and unconcerned about the things of religion, injustice, and fraud, and oppression will grow. There will be an increase of a spirit of sensuality; licentiousness will increase amongst young people.

Fourth. When religion declines there will be a decay of a spirit of love amongst neighbors and brethren. When religion flourishes it will cause a spirit of love and peace to prevail amongst a people, and that, several ways.

It cuts off the occasion of men's contending. When men contend it is generally about the world and worldly things; but when religion flourishes, men's minds are taken off from worldly things. They are not so much disposed to contend for their profit and for their honor, because they are more concerned that they may be saved. The world is the bone of contention, and their minds are more taken up about other things. Convictions and a concern about another world restrain men's lusts, and 'tis from men's lusts that comes contention; Jas. 4:1, "From whence come wars and fightings among you? Come they not hence, even of your lusts which war in your members?"

And then there will be many that will be truly gracious; and in times wherein the Spirit of God is poured out upon a people, grace is wont to be more lively in its exercises in the saints than at other times. And true grace confers a disposition to love and peace. It mortifies contrary dispositions; it disposes to pursue after peace and to be peacemakers. It makes men humble, and 'tis "only by pride," as Solomon says, "comes contention" [Prov. 13:10].

When religion therefore prevails among a people, there will be seen much of a spirit of love one towards another amongst them; but when a people are cold and dead in matters of religion, a contrary spirit will prevail. There will be a spirit of malice and revenge, a spirit of envy; and hence will come evil-speaking and backbitings, emulations, wrath, [and] strife. The prevalence of a spirit of contention amongst a people is a certain sign of deadness with respect to the things of religion. When men's spirits are hot with contention, they are cold to religion.

Fifth. When a people decline and grow cold in religion, there are but rare instances of a saving work of conversion. Ministers preach in vain; the wicked are not plucked away. 'Tis but seldom that they hear the joyful tidings from their hearers of a discovery of the glory of Christ, and of the redeeming mercy and love of God in him to the souls of [men].[5] Old converts die and new ones are not raised up in their room, so that the number of the saints is diminished, or at least it is less in proportion to the whole. The truly and sincerely righteous, the true fearers and servants of God, become more and more thin-sown.

II. When a people long continue thus, there is great danger that God will take away their religious advantages. When God takes any people to be his and gives 'em great advantages, and they, instead of improving under them, decline; and when he reproves and warns them, they yet continue to decline instead of repenting and doing the first works, they revolt more and more and are for a long time cold and dead in the things of religion, there is great danger of God's being provoked to remove their candlestick out of its place. This may appear from the following considerations:

First. When a people are cold and dead in the things of religion, they frustrate their religious advantages. The life and power of godliness is the end of outward advantages; they are in vain to a people if they can't thereby [be] rendered lively in religion, if they don't beget love in their hearts and cause good works in their lives. Religious advantages, they are no otherwise advantages than as a people thereby have advantage to live to God and to bring forth the fruits of righteousness.

They are frustrated, both as they are designed as a means to be improved by a people in God's service and to his glory, and as a means of a people's own good; for they are neither when a people are cold and

5. Illegible in the MS.

lifeless in the things of religion. The means are in vain; the end is not obtained.

Indeed, God can and will so order and dispose that he will obtain his own ends and glorify his own name, as he doth, in the heavier condemnation of a people; but so far as the people are active in the matter, the advantages they have are in vain, as the labor of the husbandman in cultivating his field or his vineyard is in vain when there is no fruit produced.

And how just is it, that a people should be deprived of their advantages if they make no use of 'em! Why should a husbandman continue with care and labor cultivating and manuring a piece of ground that he finds yields him no fruit? Why should advantages for glorifying God and obtaining salvation be continued to him that will not make improvement of em? That is the language of justice; Luke 13:7, "Then he said unto the dresser of his vineyard, Behold these three years I come seeking fruit on this fig tree and find none: cut it down; why cumbereth it the ground?"

Second. When it is so with a people, they abuse their advantages. They don't merely neglect 'em and not improve them to those purposes to which they are given, but they improve 'em to ill purpose. They were given to 'em to glorify God with, but they improve 'em to God's dishonor; for, as we observed, when a people are lifeless in religion, they will be lively in irreligion and wickedness.

The vineyard under divine cultivation is not only unfruitful as to good fruit, but it brings forth evil fruit: the grapes of Sodom and clusters of Gomorrah [Deut. 32:32]. The rain that descends upon it is to no other purpose than only to cause it to bear briars and thorns. The mercies that are enjoyed are improved in the service of Baal; the advantages and means of grace which they enjoy do but harden them in sin.

When God gives a people advantages for his glory and their own good, and they make use of 'em as means to provoke and dishonor God, how just is it that they should be taken away. Thus when the husbandmen to whom the householder let out his vineyard abused their advantage by evil-treating [6] the messengers that he sent to receive the fruits, and at last his son, the Jews themselves could not help owning {that it was just that the husbandmen be destroyed}; Matt. 21:33–41,

> There was a certain householder, which planted a vineyard, and hedged it round about, and digged a winepress in it, and built a tower, and let it out to husbandmen, and went into a far country: and when

6. MS: "Evil Intreating."

> the time of the fruit drew near, he sent his servants to the husbandmen, that they might receive the fruits of it. And the husbandmen took his servants, and beat one, and killed another, and stoned another. Again, he sent other servants more than the first: and they did unto them likewise. But last of all he sent unto them his son, saying, They will reverence my son. But when the husbandmen saw the son, they said among themselves, This is the heir; come let us kill him. . . . When the lord therefore of the vineyard cometh, what will he do unto these husbandmen? They say unto him, He will miserably destroy those wicked men, and let out his vineyard unto other husbandmen, which shall render him the fruits in their seasons.

Third. God hath declared that his "spirit shall not always strive with man" (Gen. 6:3). When God is waiting upon a people under means of grace, them that neglect and misimprove those means, his spirit may be said to be striving with them in two senses. His spirit strives with them; that is, he with longsuffering bears with; he restrains and keeps back his wrath. To speak after the manner of men, there is a strife in God's spirit to restrain his anger and to bear with their provocation. And therefore the apostle Peter expresses the striving of God's spirit with the old world by his longsuffering waiting; I Pet. 3:20, "when once the longsuffering of God waited in the days of Noah."

And God's spirit strives another way, viz. as the influences of his spirit upon men's minds accompany the means of grace, whereby God is, as it were, striving to bring 'em to repent. There is always a degree of the influences of the Spirit of God goes along with the administration of gospel ordinances among a visible people of God.

Now although God be longsuffering, yet his spirit will not always strive with men. When a people decline and grow cold {in religion}, 'tis his manner to warn them and to wait on them; but if they continue yet declining and don't reform, there is great danger that he will leave a people.

And thus it has been God's manner to do. Thus he did of old by Samaria and the ten tribes. We have an account how God waited long upon them, and often warned them, and when notwithstanding they continued dead {in the things of religion}, how he "removed them out of his sight" (II Kgs. 17:18). So he did with Judah and Jerusalem, as is represented in the parable of the vineyard in the beginning of the fifth chapter of Isaiah [vv. 5–6]: "I will tell you what I will do to my vineyard: I will take away the hedge thereof, and it shall be eaten up; and break down the wall thereof, and it shall be trodden down: and I will lay it waste." So he did with the Jews at their second destruction, signified by the parable of the barren fig tree in the vineyard (Luke 13:6–9). Justice called to have the tree cut down at the end of three years, but mercy and patience stepped in {to delay its destruction}. But then patience itself was at an end, presented by his cursing the barren fig tree (Matt. 21:19).

APPLICATION.

I. Let the consideration of the truth before us stir us up to reflect upon the present state of this land, and especially of this town, with respect to religion. Let it be considered by us whether we are fallen. The time when God first took us to be his people, when our fathers went after God into the wilderness, was a time of love on God's part and on ours; the land was then famous for religion. What a spirit for God and religion did then appear amongst rulers, and ministers, and heads of families![7]

And how much is the land degenerated. What a general coldness and deadness is there about the things of religion! How different a face is there upon the country, with respect to religion, from what there used to be. How rare are instances of remarkable pouring out of the Spirit of God in towns and congregations. How much less is there of religious conscience, and how much less is religion the subject of conversation, how much more seldom that inquiry, "What shall {I do to be saved}?" than it used to be. How does all the talk seem to be about the world. What a decay of strictness; {what} immorality; {what} decay of family government! Is not there less of a spirit of love? Has not there been a spirit of contention amongst our rulers? Has not the country to a great degree left its first love?

And how long have we been degenerating and waxing more lifeless and cold in the things of religion. And how many warnings has the country had; how many corrections? And how dead are we at this day! What a deadness does there seem to be in spiritual [things] in this town. This town has been greatly blessed of God in times past, both as to means and the successes of them; but how dead a time is it now, and how long has it been so?

II. Let it be considered how agreeable the late and present threatenings of God's providence towards this land are to the threatenings of his Holy Word. God in his Word declares that his "spirit shall not always strive

7. JE here deletes: "How much was religion the subject of conversation; how much more generally was there of good order and government in families."

with man" [Gen. 6:3], and that when a professing people continue cold {in religion, Christ will come and} remove [their] candlestick; and there we have instances of this nature. In how ticklish a posture have the privileges of this land stood in for this considerable time. And how doubtful does the government seem at this day. We ought to look at the present difficult and doubtful circumstances as being so of the ordering of God, whatever second causes are made use of. And if God is now about to punish the land by taking away the advantages that we have neglected and abused, we know not how much he will take from us, nor what we shall lose; it will be according as God sees meet to punish us, less or more for our backslidings and coldness in religion.

If we consider our deserts, the greatness and long-continuance and aggravatedness, by the mercies and warnings, of our declensions, can we have any reason to think that God will deal gently with us? Have we not deserved to have our candlestick removed out of its place?

III. Let us remember from whence we are fallen, and repent, and now draw up a resolution, everyone to reform what is amiss in us and do the first works, lest Christ come to us quickly and take away our religious advantages.

We have yet opportunity to repent. If the warnings of God's Word and providence shall now so affect our souls as to make us penitently to reflect on ourselves, and to lament our degeneracies and deadness in the things of religion, and those things in us that have been contrary to the life of godliness, and take up candor and sincere resolution of doing the first works, we may possibly do what shall be for the lengthening out of our tranquillity.

IV. Let us earnestly cry to God, that he would pour out his Spirit upon us to revive our first love and excite us to the doing of our first works: and particularly that God would pour out his Spirit on this part of the land, and in this town. Though we are so dead, God is able to revive us; he is able soon to make a great alteration amongst us. And God is wont to give his Holy Spirit in answer to prayer. Christ directs us to pray for the Holy Spirit, and gives us great encouragement of being successful; Luke 11:11–13, "If a son asks bread of any of you that is a father, will he give him a stone? or if he ask a fish, will he for a fish give a serpent? Or if he shall ask an egg, will he offer a scorpion? If ye then, being evil, know how to give good gifts unto your children: how much more shall your heavenly Father give the Holy Spirit to them that ask him?"

Though the Spirit of God be the choicest gift that he has to bestow, yet 'tis a gift that God delights to bestow in answer to prayer. The Spirit was sent down on the apostles and primitive church when they were convened together to prayer; they continued sustent[8] in prayer and supplication. The sincere and fervent prayers of God's people have that power to bring down spiritual showers; the prayers of God's people can call God down from heaven [and] cause him to "bow the heavens and come down" [Ps. 144:5].

Let everyone therefore that has anything of the spirit of grace and supplication now improve it.[9] If God gives his people a heart to cry mightily to him, and pours out his spirit upon us, it will be a happy omen that God is not as yet about to forsake us, and that he will not remove our candlestick out of its place. To stir us up to these duties at this time,

V. Let it be considered,

First. How great [are] our advantages. {We have} liberty to serve God according to our consciences without any molestation; {we are} not persecuted; we are not burdened with impositions and human inventions.

None of these burdens [are] laid upon us, as others of our principles and persuasion have in England, to maintain any other worship than that which we ourselves have benefit by. People are not obliged to support any other [ministers][1] but those they choose themselves. Our rulers give us no molestation in our worship, but are, most of them, of the same principles with ourselves; and we have liberty of choosing them ourselves, and such as shall support and encourage religion in the way that we profess it.

We may make what laws for the support of religion and divine worship according to our conscience, and for the suppressing of vice and immorality, we please. We may choose such men for our rulers as shall encourage and recommend religion by their example. We may choose such as we think will be most tenderly concerned for the good of the land, and of religion in it. If all or many in the highest posts should be sent us from abroad of different persuasion and loose morals, [they] want influence.

We have colleges amongst ourselves, where the country may educate children of their own to be teachers and pastors of our churches. And these seminaries are under our own care, under the oversight of such as are chosen from amongst ourselves. We have comparatively but few in the country of a different persuasion or way of worship in material things from that we are of. We are under great advantages to unite together as

8. I.e. to be sustained.

9. JE here deletes: "We have had many calls to it, but there seems to be a special call at this time."

1. It is clear from a deleted phrase immediately before this sentence that JE intends to mention ministers here.

one body to serve the Lord and promote the interest of his kingdom amongst us, and the interest of our own souls.

We at present enjoy a charter which secures these mentioned privileges to us, which if we should lose, 'tis doubtful whether any one of 'em should be retained. The charter of this province is to this part of the church of God as the walls and tower [are] to [the] vineyard, which if it should be lost, we should be, as is greatly to be feared, at once as a vineyard or garden that lies open and unfenced [Matt. 21:33–41].

God's threatening providence therefore should awaken us to turn to God, and earnestly to seek to him for the pouring out of his Spirit to revive his work, as we have any concern for our own good and the good of our children. If the country should lose these privileges mentioned, there would probably be a vast alteration in the face of things in a little time, and we should see cause to mourn with burning of bowels for our dear children when it will be too late.

Second. Our repentance and turning to God will be the best security to our spiritual advantages, much better than our own wisdom or skill. God may bring the country into such a case as that they shall not know what to do; God may leave us to be deceived, and infatuated, and not to understand the things that make for our peace.

God may leave us to be [the] means to destroy ourselves by our own folly. It frequently is, that before God destroys a people he leaves them to be infatuated so that they bring their own ruin upon themselves. So it was in Jerusalem's destruction in Zedekiah's time. The king of Babylon had taken the city, and he appointed Zedekiah to be king in Jerusalem under him. But Zedekiah rebelled, and the Jews with him; they would needs have their old privileges of being an independent kingdom, or run the venture of not having one at all. And though the prophet Jeremiah earnestly exhorted them to serve the king of Babylon, and told 'em if they did so they should live, the city should not be burnt with fire, and they should yet dwell in their own land, they were obstinate against it. And so the Chaldeans took the city, and burnt it with fire, and put out the king's eyes, and carried the people away to Babylon [II Kgs. 24:17–25:21; Jer. 52:1–11].

So it was in Jerusalem in its second destruction, by the Romans. Titus the Roman general, while he besieged the city from time to time, made 'em offers of peace, if they would submit; but they would by no means hearken to it. And though they were besieged so long that multitudes died with famine, so that they ate one another, they ate their own children, and dead bodies lay thick about in the city, unburied till they stank;

yet they would not submit. They would by no means give up their privilege of being a free and independent government, which they thought belonged to 'em as the children of Abraham and peculiar people of God. They were exceeding willful.

God sometimes leaves a people to bring ruin upon themselves by contentions, and a party spirit amongst themselves. So it was in Jerusalem at its second destruction. While the Romans besieged it without, there were three parties within, under three leaders at war, killing one another till the blood ran out under the gates of the city, which greatly affected Titus, the Roman general. He lifted up his hands to heaven, calling the gods to witness; and so they contended amongst themselves till the Romans took and burnt the city.[2]

2. JE may have drawn from Josephus, *The Wars of the Jews*, VI, for this anecdote. This work later appeared in JE's "Catalogue of Books."

ENVIOUS MEN

ALONG with *The Dangers of Decline* and *The State of Public Affairs, Envious Men* shows Edwards' increasing attention to political, social, and economic controversy in Northampton and in Massachusetts generally in the early 1730s.[1] His subject here, in a two-preaching-unit sermon delivered on Aug. 9, 1730, a sacrament day, is envy.[2] Whereas the text warns against envy as a source of contention chiefly in the church, Edwards also employs the term to refer to a peculiarly civil disaffection. By his definition, envy involves relative social positions, political prerogatives, and economic advantages. The Lord's Supper, he concludes, was an occasion for repentance of envy and thus for unity in all matters of corporate life. The sacrament brought the Christian mandate of love to bear on a multiplicity of social relationships.

Two specific developments informed the application of Edwards' moral analysis. First, the growth of Northampton's economy in the 1720s and early 1730s, which elevated land values and favored established citizens, heightened economic stratification in the town. It also enhanced competition between long-term residents and newer settlers, who aspired to wealth and positions of social influence. Second, these economic factions were mirrored in such political contests as election to the offices of selectman and representative to the assembly, as well as in appointments to the civic duties of clerk or treasurer. Both economic and political factors exacerbated longstanding party contentions within Northampton, to which Edwards refers in this sermon.[3]

Using the Moral Sense vocabulary of Anglo-American ethics, Edwards describes envy as a sort of psychological pain: grief at the prosperity of

1. For related earlier sermons, see *Living Peaceably One with Another*, preached at Bolton in 1723, and *Sin and Wickedness Bring Calamity and Misery on a People*, from late 1729, in *Works, 14*, 116–33, 484–505.

2. On the dating of this sermon, see *Works, 13*, 106–07.

3. For further discussion of relevant political and economic developments in Northampton and JE's commentary on them, see Tracy, *Jonathan Edwards, Pastor*, pp. 93–108, and Preface to the Period, above, pp. 17–28.

others and "an uncomfortable sort of passion." Much of *Envious Men* is taken up with a description, in common language, of the workings of this passion in the individual and in society. Once allowed to take root, Edwards preaches, envy comes to preoccupy people and expresses itself in socially destructive acts like gossip, slander, and quarreling—all of which drive Christ away from the community. With obvious reference to those who resent the wealth of the landed elite of the town or the prerogatives of elected or appointed officials, Edwards attempts to demonstrate that contentious persons operate out of a vicious passion rather than a sense of justice. They judge others as unworthy of their social status, yet they themselves destroy their own souls, as well as social concord, by their envy.

In the Application, Edwards calls on people to examine their motives, especially before they come to the Lord's table, a feast of love. The sacrament is not merely a means to salvation but also a location of Christian and communal solidarity. The Lord's Supper links individual piety to social identity. As Edwards continued to rethink and refine his sacramental theology in this period, he retained this highly social reading of the Lord's Supper.[4] So in a subsequent sacramental sermon in this volume, *Self-Examination and the Lord's Supper*, Edwards stresses envy and contention as two of the most dangerous and self-destructive vices in those who approach the Lord's Supper.

This sermon provides an engaging description of the dynamics of power and prerogative in an eighteenth-century New England town. Edwards appears as a spokesman for civil rulers and the social elite—or at least as a critic of those who chafe against authority. Perhaps the patronage afforded him by wealthy landowners and officials like Col. John Stoddard influenced Northampton's pastor before he reached his full stature. It would be some twenty years before his climactic falling-out with the town leaders alienated him from Northampton's social and political elite.

* * *

The manuscript is a duodecimo booklet of seventeen leaves. One marginal mark may indicate a single repreaching. Possibly reflecting the delicate nature of its subject, the manuscript shows signs of a nearly fretful composition: many emendations, sections redrafted, and several

4. For a discussion of JE on sacramental issues, see *Works, 14*, 38–42.

whole paragraphs deleted and rewritten nearly verbatim. At the end of the sermon Edwards jotted two words: "Baptism," presumably a reference to a sacramental occasion on the day of preaching, and "Fast," an announcement for the following week. On Aug. 16, Edwards did indeed preach a fast sermon, on I Kgs. 8:34–36 (142).

ENVIOUS MEN

JAMES 3:16.

For where envying and strife is, there is confusion and every evil work.

THE Apostle, in this chapter, is upon the duty of bridling the tongue,[5] and he has a special respect to that part of the government of the tongue which consists in refraining from talking against others and expressing with the tongue an ill-spirit towards our neighbors. He begins, "my brethren, be not many masters" [Jas. 3:1], i. e. don't set up for judges of others; let not every man take upon him to be his neighbor's judge; it is not fit you should be all masters, all judges. The apostle Paul informs us that if we talk against our neighbors and judge them, we take upon us to treat men as if they were our servants; Rom. 14:4, "Who art thou that judgest another man's servant? to his own master he standeth or falleth." And this Apostle, in the next chapter, [writes] that if we judge our neighbors we don't act like God's servants, or doers of the law, but as if we were the lawgivers and judges (Jas. 4:11–12).

The Apostle sets forth the great difficulty and importance of this duty of bridling the tongue. He compares an ungoverned tongue to a little fire that is sufficient to set a great matter in flames; as a coal or spark is sufficient to burn up a house or city, so an unruly tongue is sufficient to put a family or town into a fire of contention. It "setteth on fire the course of nature," says the Apostle, "and is set on fire of hell" (v. 6); and again, "it is an unruly evil, full of deadly poison" (v. 8).

In v. 9, the Apostle sets forth the poisonous nature of an unruly tongue in an instance. "Therewith," says he, "bless we God," and "therewith curse we men." I. e. men that seem to be religious, that will seem to pray to God devoutly, yet with the same tongue will show a malignant spirit against

5. See "Images" nos. 104 and 120, *Works, 11*, 90–91, 95; and "Signs of Godliness," MS p. 2, entry on "Bridling and well-using our tongues."

their neighbor. By cursing, here we are to understand not only imprecating a curse upon men, but speaking evil to or of men, or any way showing a desire of his hurt, or expressing an ill-will against him; so blessing and cursing seem often to be intended in Scripture-blessing for expressing good will.

The Apostle in v. 13 recommends a contrary disposition and behavior to an aptness to talk and show a spirit against our neighbor, from its becoming of a wise man.

But envying and strife, he shows to be contrary to true wisdom and goodness. Men that are of such a spirit and practice may think themselves to be wise men and good men, but the Apostle informs us that they lie against the truth in boasting of any such thing [v. 14]. He gives such a spirit as bad a character as any disposition need to have: it is "earthly, sensual, devilish" [v. 15]. What can be worse?

And in the text, the Apostle evidences the character he had given of it by the fruits: "for where envying and strife is, there is confusion and every evil work." He puts envying and strife together, as he had before in v. 14, probably for two reasons.

1. As being very near akin, and one arising from the other. Contention is the natural offspring of envy.

2. Because that sort of contention that is an envious contention is one of the worst sorts, and of most pernicious effects.

The effects he mentions are two, viz.

(1) Confusion, or a tumult and uproar and uneasiness, as the original word signifies. It turns everything upside down in men's own hearts and in societies.

(2) Every evil works when envying and contention enter into any society. It comes from hell; it is earthly, sensual, devilish, as the Apostle tells us, and it brings up its fruits with it, all sorts of wickedness.

DOCTRINE.

Envying and contention are things of exceeding pernicious consequences.

I. Show what envy is.
II. That it is of very pernicious tendency.
III. Especially so when it breaks out into contention.

Envy is a being grieved or uneasy of another's prosperity, as if the prosperity of another be the thing that hurts a man and makes him feel uneasy or unpleasantly. That is envy, of whatever kind that prosperity is, whether it be spiritual or temporal prosperity. The elder brother's envying the younger, who was the prodigal, when his father killed the fatted calf for him, signifies envy for spiritual prosperity [Luke 15:11–32]; and so, when those that were called to labor in the vineyard in the morning envied those that were called at the ninth and at the eleventh hour, because they had equal wages with them, it signified envy for spiritual prosperity [Matt. 20:1–16]. And if it be uneasiness at another's temporal prosperity, of whatever kind that be, whether they are uneasy at another's honor or wealth or pleasure, it is envy.

And whether the persons whose prosperity they are uneasy at are either good men or wicked men, it alters not the case. If a man's spirit be hurt at the honor or wealth of a wicked man, let him be never so wicked, that is envy. And therefore we are directed in Prov. 24:1, "Be not envious against evil men."

Indeed, the prosperity of a wicked man may be the occasion of grief in another, and yet that be not envy, because though the prosperity be the occasion of the unease, yet it is not the thing that they are uneasy of. For instance, the prosperity of Antichrist may be the cause of grief in a man; and the thing he is uneasy of may be not the prosperity any person enjoys, is not the thing they are uneasy with, but only the mischief that is the occasion to the church.

But whenever another's prosperity be the thing that is grievous, it is envy.

It may arise from various causes. If it arises from a spirit against a man's person, those that persons hate, they don't love to see in prosperity. It may arise from a grudge that one person has against another, from some injury received or some quarrel that there has been between them. Sometimes it arises from pride. Pride loves to be alone in prosperity; it loves neither superiors nor equals in prosperity. The nature of it is to aspire to be like God. God is alone; he has no superiors nor equals. That is the way the first pride that ever was worked, viz. the pride of the devils: they endeavored to get into the throne of God.

Envy evermore arises from self-love and a want of loving our neighbor as ourselves. Some envy others because their prosperity is greater than theirs; they can't bear to see others above 'em. And a man may envy another whose prosperity is not so great as his own. It may come too near an equality with it for him to be easy with it; though he is something above his neighbor, yet he loves to be more above him than he is. Thus the elder brother envied the younger because his father killed the fatted calf for him, though, as his father told him, he was always with him and all that he had was his [Luke 15:31].

II. This envy is a thing of a very pernicious tendency, when it only lurks in a man's heart and puts forth itself in inward exercises, if it don't break out into outward actions. All men have this principle of corruption in them, but some are much more in the exercise of it than others. Where there is much of the workings of an envious spirit in a man's heart, it is like poison to him. The prevalency of such lusts is like a viper at the heart of religion. Religion never will, never can, flourish in a heart where envy is indulged; it is exceeding contrary to Christianity.

And then it is an uncomfortable sort of passion. What we have said of the nature of it evidences this; the nature of it consists in grief and uneasiness. It destroys a man's comfort to be of an envious disposition. He goes about fretting himself and having pain and uneasiness at those things that he has no sort of occasion to be uneasy of. He can't enjoy himself because his neighbor prospers. If he would be easy and quiet about the condition of other men, he would be in far better condition himself; he would enjoy himself a great deal better.

And if he restrains himself and his envy don't break out into open contention, yet if there be a great deal of the exercises of it in a man's breast, it will show itself in some way or other. He won't perform those duties towards his neighbor that he should do, and he will not be forward to promote his good. He will inwardly rejoice at his misfortunes. It will be agreeable to him to hear him talked against; he'll hear it with pleasure. Many other pernicious consequences might be here mentioned which will be taken notice of under the next [head]. Therefore,

III. Especially is envy a thing of pernicious consequences when it breaks out into contention, that is, when men show the spirit that they have against others that they envy, in their words or in their outward behavior. When a man has not only enmity in his breast, but when he vents it in his talk to or of the persons that [he] envies, when it causes him to him to break out in a passion, or when he carries on any design against a man to endeavor any mischief to him or to lessen his property, such a practice as this is indeed of very pernicious consequences. Here,

First. It is of very pernicious consequence to the persons contending; it is especially pernicious unto them. The man that from envy contends with his neighbor and shows his ill will to him, and spirit against him, he don't hurt his neighbor one-tenth part so much as himself. He foolishly bites himself out of envy and spite to another. He endeavors to send his darts against his neighbor, when indeed he stabs them into himself. He gives himself abundantly the worst wounds.

1. He destroys his own peace and comfort. He disturbs the calm and repose of his own mind; by the heats of his spirit he is put into a tumult. There is as much difference between him whose spirit is disturbed by envy and malice and contention, and a man that is of a meek and quiet spirit, as there is at sea when it is calm, and the surface of the water is smooth, and the sky clear and the heavens serene, and when there is a storm, and the water and the winds are all in a rage, and the heavens covered with black clouds. The envious, contentious man's mind can't rest; Is. 57:20, "The wicked are like the troubled sea, when it cannot rest, whose waters cast up mire and dirt."

2. Envious contention contracts abundance of guilt; God exceedingly hates such things. 'Tis very contrary to the nature of true holiness and the nature of God; God is a God of love and of peace. And how much has he insisted upon the duties of love in his holy Word! 'Tis exceeding contrary to the nature of Christ, the Lamb of God. Men are not sensible how guilty they are before God by their strife and envy.

And, as it contracts guilt and provokes God, so it very much tends to the undoing of men; it tends to hinder their salvation. 'Tis very provoking to God to suffer the exercises of envy in a man's own breast, but exceedingly more so when men give way to it, and allow it so as to practice upon it for carrying on designs and maintaining strife against their neighbor. While men keep provoking God in such a manner, they ben't in a very fair way to salvation.

3. 'Tis a great enemy to the spiritual health of the soul. Envious strife is a dreadful enemy to all true religion; 'tis as contrary as is possible to the spirit of God, and nothing tends more to quench the Spirit. It will hinder all his kindly motions, not only the exercises of grace but the converting influence of the Spirit.

'Tis an enemy to all religious exercises. It hinders men's prayers; 'tis in a miserable manner men are like to pray to God, and lift up their souls to him, that come but out of contention into God's presence, and bring their envy and contentious spirit along with them. Such sacrifices are very poor things; such devotion is good for nothing. God nauseates and abominates such prayers; they stink in his nostrils. So it hinders men in attendance on ordinances. When men bring their envy, and their wrath, and their spite with them to God's house and to his table, what are their services good for? They ben't like to attend on any ordinance in an acceptable or a profitable manner.

There is nothing that is good is like to be promoted in a man's heart while he is going on in this way of envying and strife. All that grows is evil; there are no advantages like to be gained of a religious or spiritual nature. The times of the prevalence of such a spirit are the devil's times,[6] and all things of a religious nature and that tend to the good of a man's soul go to rack.

When such a spirit prevails, many lusts are in exercise. When a man's spirit is heated with envy and a spirit against others, all the whole gang of lusts, they rise. There is pride; men never show their pride so much as in contention. There is intemperate wrath. There is revenge. There is covetousness, for when they contend it is about the world generally, and raises and puts into exercise a covetous spirit. And there is injustice. So, when men's spirits are heated in contention, they han't regard to justice; they ben't wont to tie up themselves to rules. They han't coolness of spirit enough to consider [whether] what they do is just or unjust.

Contention puts the soul into an exceeding ill frame.

Second. Envy and strife are of exceeding pernicious consequences in any society. When any society are got into a contention, and there are envyings, emulation, wrath, strife in the society, or when there is such a spirit shown publicly and in the management of public business, 'tis of very pernicious consequences. Here,

1. It destroys the comfort of society. God has made man with such a nature that he is fitted and inclined to live in society, and he is of such a nature and circumstances that we are necessitated to dwell in society. And society, if well improved, tends much to the happiness of mankind. But the comfort of society very much consists in love and peace; Ps. 133:1, "Behold, how good and how pleasant it is for brethren to dwell together in unity!" Especially it should be accounted so amongst a Christian people.

The more any society is full of contentions, the more they are like the company of the damned; for great part of the misery of hell consists in the reign of malice and spite there. And the more there is of love and peace, the more are they like heaven.

2. It makes confusion in a society. As it is said in our text, "where there is envy and strife, there is confusion." Contention puts things in an uproar; it confounds that good order which is the beauty of society. It frequently occasions many indecencies. Men in the heat of their passion don't keep

6. Here JE excised the following sentence: "They are times wherein the devils hold their frolick in men's hearts."

themselves within the bounds of decency and good order; they'll vent their spirit and don't regard what becomes of decency.

It is said of love and charity in I Cor. 13:5 that it "behaveth not itself unseemly"; but the contrary may be said of its contrary, envy and strife: it behaveth itself very unseemly. When men's spirits are heated, oftentimes they don't mind what they say or do. They forget that respect which is due to superiors, or that honor which is due to all men, and oftentimes forget their own reputation.

It may be marked that those societies that are most contentious evermore have the least of good order.

3. 'Tis to a people's dishonor. Such things are soon famed abroad.

4. The prevailing of envy and contention exceedingly hinders the success of ordinances and the flourishing of religion amongst a people. When a people are contending, religion evermore runs very low.

Contention kills religion many ways. It greatly hinders it, as we have shown, in the hearts of those that exercise a spirit of contention; it drives away the Spirit of God and lets in the spirit of the devil. It hinders them in private.

So it keeps the presence and blessing of God from accompanying public worship and ordinances. When such a society meet together, Christ won't be in the midst of 'em. He has no pleasure in being amongst a quarreling, envious crew; their pretended public worship is nauseous to him. When there comes out of the same mouth blessing and cursing, when the same tongue blessed God that curses men, God won't have any pleasure in such blessing. That blessing which comes out of such a mouth is like to be dreadfully tainted; see vv. 10–11 of [the] context: "Out of the same mouth proceedeth blessing and cursing. My brethren, these things ought not to be so. Doth a fountain send forth at the same place sweet water and bitter?"

And it hinders religion in a place another way, viz. as it takes up men's thoughts. When there is contention in a place, person's minds are taken up about it, and all the talk is about it, and there is little said about the things of religion and another world.

5. In a society where there is contention, there is every evil work; that is, it has a tendency to promote every ill thing. There will be evil speaking, backbiting; men will get together and spend away their evenings in talking against their neighbor, setting forth his ill qualities and telling of the ill things he has done. They feed one another with such talk.

There will be a great deal of evil surmising and jealousies. They'll surmise this thing and the other, what mischiefs this man intends to do, what evil designs he has in his heart, when it may be 'tis but mere guesswork; they have very little foundation for their surmises. This is directly contrary to the spirit of charity which the Apostle describes; I Cor. 13:5, "thinketh no evil." Evil surmising is generally an attendant of envy and strife; I Tim. 6:4, we there find those things joined together: "envy, strifes, railings, evil surmisings." There is emulation, striving with others with respect to honor, [among the] works of flesh; Gal. 5:20–21, "Hatred, variance, emulations, wrath, strife, envyings." Where there is envious strife amongst a people, there will be plottings and contrivings against this and the other person, how to pull him down. Hypocrisy [and] flattering appear fair to a man's face when mischief [is] in [his own] heart.

Where there is envying and contention, ten to one but there will be misrepresentations of things and lying, carried on [without] end by one or other. There will be slandering; there will be abundance of false reports spread about that have been raised by one busybody or other.

Sometimes envy and contention is the occasion of abominable cheating. Men will take fraudulent, knavish, vile methods to accomplish their designs, and to get their wills, and to carry their purposes against those that they envy.

Some men get such a blot upon their names by what they do in contention that [it] shall not be soon wiped away.[7]

APPLICATION.

Use I. Of *Self-Exam.* In two branches.

First. Examine yourself, whether or no you don't harbor within yourself an envious spirit towards any of your neighbors. Be strict in examining yourself, as it greatly concerns you to know. Ben't you grieved at the prosperity of some of your neighbors? Ben't you uneasy, that they are in such prosperity? Don't it hurt your spirit and make you feel unpleasantly, that they are under such advantages to get money; that they get it so easily and grow rich so fast? Don't it make you feel unpleasantly, that they get wealth so much easier and faster than you? Or that such an one of your neighbors is advanced; he is put into offices; he grows great? Examine whether or no you don't indulge this vile temper and disposition in you to envy such. Ben't you hurt in your spirit, that such or such a man has so much power and influence, that he gets his will and has things as he

7. Here ends the first preaching unit; at the beginning of the second unit, JE cited the text and doctrine.

would; don't you find that you are concerned about it? When you hear of the advancement of one or another, is it not unpleasant news to you; is it ungrateful tidings? Could not you be glad it was otherwise? Would it not be pleasant tidings to you now to hear that such an one had lost his post, that he was deprived of such an advantage to get money? Would you not be the more easy if such an one was pulled down? Don't you indulge such an unchristian and abominable spirit as this is?

I know well enough that envious persons are full of their excuses. They are not wont to call their envy by any bad names; they will plead to themselves that they don't do amiss. Yea, sometimes they persuade themselves they do well; they call their envy by some good name or other.

Envious men hate to own that they do envy, for all the world knows that envy is a base disposition. Those that are bred up among Christians know that it is a devilish temper, and a man that indulges himself in it will hardly ever own it; no, not to himself. They'll call it something else. If they should own it was envy, it would take away much of that base kind of delight they have in indulging such a lust; for though envy be an uneasy passion, yet men love to indulge and gratify it, and therefore they are full of their excuses.

[1.] One thing it may be that you'll say in excuse for yourself, is that they whose advancement you are uneasy at ben't worthy of their advancements. Such a man is not fit to be chosen by a town. Such an one is not worthy of such a commission. They ben't worthy of such honor and advancement; there are other men that are as fit as they, and a great deal more that are overlooked. And it may be you think so of yourselves. And so you plead that that is not envy for you to be uneasy when those men are advanced that ben't fit for it; it is lawful for you to be uneasy, because it is not for the interest of the country for men to be advanced to posts that ben't worthy of 'em.

But here, pray consider whether or no you don't deceive yourself in this excuse that you make for yourself. Examine your own heart. Is it out of pure love to your country and tender concern for its welfare that you are concerned that such persons are in such and such honorable or profitable posts? Is that indeed the very thing; is it only that, or is it that chiefly? Or is not this the truth of the case: that 'tis the person's honor or prosperity that is the very spring of your concern and uneasiness? Would it not be agreeable to you, and what you would in your heart be glad of, if he should be deprived of it, though it should not be at all more for the interests and welfare of the country? Be plain and ingenuous in confessing the matter as it really is to your own conscience.

Do you verily think that your uneasiness at such and such man's advancement and profit, and others that are of the same spirit with you, is only or chiefly out of a public spirit and a peculiar love to your country and concern for its welfare that you are of, more than other men? Would you not be glad, though your country suffered as much another way? Or is it not envy; is not the prosperity of their persons the main thing with you? If you are a good man, you'll bear to be searched.

2. Again, it may be you'll say it is from love to justice. There are other men that deserve such posts it is but fitting they should have. And so you pretend that your uneasiness is only because you are concerned that other men may have their rights. Here again I desire you, see that you don't deceive yourself. Is not there many other things that are as much out of course as this, that don't give you a quarter of the uneasiness? Be you concerned for every man that suffers as much injustice, that you are as near to as you are to those, so as to make you so uneasy and concerned as you are about this matter? Or supposing the post should be taken away and given to another one that you are more friendly with and han't such a spirit against, though he should not be at all more deserving; would you not be glad? Is it not thus? Examine your own heart, if it be thus. Don't lay your uneasiness to your love of justice, but lay it to envy. The elder brother that envied the prodigal pretended that he did not deserve [Luke 15:30].

You pretend you are uneasy because the man has more honor or better advantages than he deserves. But why should you be so uneasy if he has? What need you vex yourself, if he has more honor than his share, and though he gets more money than he has goodness? If it was your own case, you would not be uneasy at it! If you had respect put upon you, rather more than you deserved, and if you have a great deal more money than you have virtue, you ben't concerned! If a man has a true Christian love to his neighbor, he won't be apt to break his rest about such things. One would think that men that have so much from God that they don't deserve, should not envy.

3. Again you'll say, it may be, in excuse for yourself, that such a man is a bad sort of man and don't make a good improvement of his honor and prosperity; he abuses it. But what if it be so? That is no excuse for your envy. He is to be pitied by you with hearty compassion, and not to be envied. Ben't you often warned against envying wicked men; Ps. 37:1, "Fret not thyself because of evildoers, neither be thou envious against the workers of iniquity"; Prov. 23:17, "Let not thine heart envy sinners"; and Prov. 24:1, "Be not thou envious against evil men"?

4. Again, it may be you'll say that their honor and prosperity hurts them. It makes 'em proud; they have too much sail; they are like to be overset with it. They advanced too high; they can't bear it; they grow so proud and assuming that there is no doing with them. And so you pretend that it is out of concern for them, for their good, that you are uneasy of their advancement. But is it so indeed? Is it really out of hearty and sincere love to 'em that you are concerned at their prosperity? Is not this a mere sham? Is it not the right reverse of love?

When will you ever find a man that envies another, but that he will have some such excuses and pleas for it? He'll say he is not fit, and he is proud, and it does him a great deal of hurt, and many things they'll say against those that they envy, as if they were worthy to be hated by everyone.

Second. Examine yourself, whether or no you don't suffer your envy to break out in your talk and behavior. Is it not the occasion of a great deal of evil speaking? Is it not a thing that you allow yourself, to vent your envy in reproaching and reviling the men you envy? Don't you love to go and sit and talk with some others of the same party and the same spirit with yours, and spend your time in judging and declaiming against your neighbor?

Is not this the root and spring of heats of spirit, and anger, and contention in you? Has not this been the occasion of contentious talk?

Is not this the occasion of your opposing your neighbor? Oftentimes, men that envy another and have a spirit against him will oppose another in anything that [he] endeavors to promote for no other cause but only that he loves to vent his spite. He'll endeavor to hinder and clog him in any of his designs and undertakings, for no other reason.

Han't your envy proceeded so far, that you have laid yourself out in contriving how you may pull your neighbor down: how you may bring it about that you may deprive him of his prosperity?

There is generally much of this envious spirit, and envious designs and actions, where there are parties in a place; there is generally a great deal of it on both sides. If one party has the advantage of the other as to power and influence, they'll be envied of the other party. If one party gets their wills in any public affair, the other party can't bear it; it sorely vexes 'em. They that are advanced[8] of either party are envied by the other party.

Generally there are some particular men that do the greatest part towards maintaining a party spirit. They are hottest with hatred, wrath, and strife, and envy, themselves; and they blow up the same flame in

8. Here JE excised the following phrase: "to honorable or profitable places."

others. They are the principal instruments of bringing contention into a society.

Sometimes there is so much of this spirit between parties in a place that there are many that regard the carrying on the particular designs of their party more than the greatest public good; it is very sorrowful when it is so.

Envy between parties is a passion that generally is not alone; there are others as bad as that, or at least much akin to it for badness, along with it. There is generally a spirit of revenge. There are old grudges. Men remember some old things that have passed long ago, some old affront they can't forget, and never will leave trying to come up with 'em for it.

Let every one examine how it has been with himself, whether or no he, in his heats, and debates, and party contention, and evil speakings, han't been influenced by this envious spirit we have been speaking of.

Use II. Of *Reproof* to those who do indulge an envious spirit and vent in envious talk and practices. Here,

First. Consider how exceeding contrary such a spirit and practice is to the spirit of Christianity. The spirit of Christianity is a spirit of love and peace; Christ is the Prince of Peace. He abundantly insisted upon it, that his disciples should love one another. That was his commandment; hereby, he told 'em, all men should know his disciples from others, that they loved one another [John 13:34–35]. This is the royal law, that we should love one another.

Christ himself, whose professed disciples we are, was meek and lowly, exceeding far from an envious and contentious spirit. He did not vex himself about this and that man's being promoted.

How full is the gospel of rules and precepts of love and peace! It would be well for men if they read and considered the New Testament more than they do. I shall mention a few places out of a thousand; Eph. 4:31–32, "Let all bitterness, and wrath, and anger, and clamor, and evil speaking, be put away from you, with all malice; and be ye kind one to another, tenderhearted, forgiving one another, even as God for Christ's sake hath forgiven you"; Phil. 2:3, "Let nothing be done through strife or vainglory; but in lowliness of mind let each esteem other better than themselves"; I Pet. 2:1–2, "Wherefore laying aside all malice, and all guile, and hypocrisies, and envies, and all evil speakings, as newborn babes desire the sincere milk of the word"; Matt. 18:3,[9] "Except ye be converted, and become as little children, ye shall not enter the kingdom of heaven"; Jas.

9. From here until the end of this paragraph, JE sketched short phrases that clued his recitation of the cited Scripture; the MS reads exactly as follows: "except converted; v. after text, wisdom from above; I Cor. 13, begin[ning], without charity, nothing."

3:17, "But the wisdom that is from above is first pure, then peaceable, gentle, and easy to be entreated, full of mercy and good fruits, without partiality"; I Cor. 13:2, 4–5, "though I have all faith . . . and have not charity, I am nothing. . . . Charity suffereth long, and is kind; charity envieth not; charity vaunteth not itself, is not puffed up, doth not behave itself unseemly, seeketh not her own, is not easily provoked, thinketh no evil."

This, it becomes Christians to do. Such a spirit as this becomes the members of Jesus Christ; such a spirit as this becomes the dear children of God. An envious spirit and practice is as different from the spirit of true Christianity as hell is unlike to the highest heaven.

Second. How contrary your envious practices are to that rule of doing to others as you would that they should do to you! When you endeavor to do your neighbor a displeasure, are trying to pull him [down], would you like it if it were your case, if you had the same advantages as he has and another should be so uneasy at it, and should be wishing and crying out himself to deprive you of what you had? Would you not take it hardly? Yea, though it was more than you deserved, though your advancements were beyond your virtue, and though there were others more fit for it than you, yet would not you find fault with him, that he should go to busy himself so much about it that he should concern himself in contriving to pull you down? Would not you be ready to think that it was none of his business, and wonder that he could not let you alone?

Would not you be ready to say with yourself, "I have done him no hurt; what need he concern himself about me, to do me a displeasure?" And why will you do that which is so contrary to what you would be willing to receive?

Third. Generally, those that are of an envious spirit and practice towards their neighbor are guilty of the very same things that they find fault with them for. Envious persons generally find fault with them they envy for their pride. They make that an excuse for their envy, that he is a proud man, and 'tis not fit that such a person should be advanced; it makes 'em still more proud and they want[1] to be humbled, whereas they are guilty of the very same thing: they are proud, and thence comes their envy. They would not concern themselves who is advanced and who has honor, were it not for their pride; but their proud hearts can't bear to see their neighbor above them or, it may be, not equal with them. They think their neighbor is proud, and intends to grow great, and to get above them, and

1. I.e. need.

they can't bear it; 'tis because of their pride. Otherwise, it would not hurt 'em at all. They would let him alone who would get honor; they would not concern themselves about it.

And hence comes their strife and contention; Prov. 13:10, "Only by pride cometh contention"; and Prov. 22:10, "Cast out the scorner, and contention shall go out; yea, strife and reproach shall cease."

Fourth. If you were concerned, as you ought to be, about your own soul and your eternal salvation, you would not be so concerned and uneasy at the temporal prosperity of others. You would be sensible, then, that you have concerns enough of your own to take up your thoughts. If you were sensible of the vanity of this world and of the vast importance of eternal things, you would find enough else to be concerned about. You would not vex your mind about this man's being advanced to honor, and to that man's getting money so fast. You would not concern yourself so much whether he was worthy of his temporal advantages; you would think more of your own unworthiness a great deal than of other persons.

It is a shame for[2] persons that have a hell of eternal misery to avoid and a heaven of eternal happiness, that are in a few days to be called before God to be judged for eternity, to grieve because their fellow worm gets more of this earth than they, and to be so engaged in their plotting and contriving how to pull down their neighbor, as if they had nothing else more worthy to be minded by 'em.

It is of infinitely greater concern to you that your soul may be saved, than who shall be in this or that profitable post. If men see the vanity of the world, they would envy not [a] man because he has more of it than he.

Fifth. It is a thing difficult enough to get to learn; you had not need to block up the way by indulging envy against your neighbor. You had need to lay aside every weight in order to your being successful in salvation. You desire to be saved? Why will you, then, go to block up your way by envy and contention? If you seek salvation, the living in envy and practicing according to it tends as much to hinder it as if you lived in a way of drunkenness. It exceedingly tends, as we have shown, to quench the Spirit. The Spirit of God is a spirit of love; there is no readier way to drive it away than by such lusts as malice and envy.[3]

Men that live in such a way, they dreadfully expose their own souls to ruin. What says the Apostle [in] Gal. 5:15? "If ye bite and devour one

2. MS: "that."

3. Here JE deleted the following sentence: "Persons are not like to have the influences of the Spirit of God, neither in convictions nor gracious influences, while they are in such a way."

another, take heed that ye be not consumed one of another"; men's souls perish and are consumed oftentimes by envying and contention. You talk of cutting down your neighbor; there is more danger of your cutting down your own soul; Prov. 26:27, "Whoso diggeth a pit shall fall therein."

There is danger that God will deal with you according to your envious designs towards others; "to the froward God will show himself froward" [Ps. 18:26]. You endeavor to pull down your neighbor; God may pull down your soul; Ezek. 35:11, "Therefore, as I live, saith the Lord God, I will even do according to thine anger, and according to thine envy which thou hast used out of thine hatred against them."

Sixth. While you continue in such a way, your prayer avails to no other purpose but only to enkindle God's anger against you. Your prayers in your families and closets are good for nothing if you are in such a way. Christ directs us, when we bring our gift to the altar, first to be reconciled to our brother before we offer our gift [Matt. 5:24].

With what face can we beg mercy of God, who have so provoked God all the while with evil in our hearts to our neighbor, that we have not a thousandth part so much reason to hate, as God has to hate us? Truly the prayers of such persons who indulge a spirit of envy against their neighbor, and allow themselves to go on in an agreeable practice, their prayers are abominable to God. You go to private meetings, it may be, to pray for the pouring out of the Spirit of God![4]

Seventh. An envious disposition is a devilish disposition. It is not only devilish as all sin may be said to be, but 'tis a temper that is peculiarly the temper of the devil, as the Apostle informs us in the two verses preceding the text: "if ye have bitter envying and strife in your hearts, glory not, and lie not against the truth. This wisdom descendeth not from above, but is earthly, sensual, devilish." It don't come from above; it comes from hell.

The devil is an exceeding envious spirit. He envied man in a state of innocency.[5]

Eighth. Consider how much it destroys your own comfort here in this world. Which do you think is the happiest man? He that minds his own concerns, seeking his own salvation and eternal happiness, and is not uneasy at others' prosperity, has not his own calm at all disturbed, let who will be advanced; he [that] is willing to leave it with providence to pro-

4. This sentence has been edited to convey a sarcastic tone, i.e. "How hypocritical for you to go to private prayer meetings when you are in a state of envy!" JE alternatively may have intended to expand on this phrase extemporaneously in a non-sarcastic tone, to the effect that it is necessary to lay aside envy while praying for revival.

5. A dash here indicates JE's possible intention to expand extemporaneously on this point.

mote whom God will to earthly honor and wealth? Or[6] he that frets himself about such a man's getting money easily, and about his growing great, and for fear he will think himself bigger than he; he frets himself, it may [be], about the honor that is put upon him, his being advanced to some post, or having a higher seat in the meeting house, or some such thing? "A sound heart is life of the flesh: but envy rottenness to the bones" (Prov. 14:30).

Ninth. This argues a littleness of soul. It's a poor, mean sort of a spirit to be so meddling in other men's affairs, and so concerned about their prospering, and for fear he'll be counted bigger than he. It is a foolish, silly sort of uneasiness; it is beneath a wise man to be concerned at such things; Job 5:2, "Wrath killeth the foolish man, and envy killeth the silly one."

A man of true wisdom and greatness of soul won't have the calm of his soul disturbed by such things. How impertinent is such a man that is hurt because another man prospers! What if there is one of his neighbors that gets money apace, and is called by such and such titles, a higher title than he; what is that to him? How silly it is in a man to distress himself about it! This is not the part of a wise man, as the apostle James teaches us in the context; v. 13, "Who is a wise man and endued with knowledge among you? let him show out of a good conversation his works with meekness of wisdom." And as it is concerning envy, so may it be said of contention: them are little souls that are easily ruffled, and that are apt to be snarling and contending.

Tenth. Consider how soon death will put an end to your envy and strife. You have but a little while here in this world; it is not worth the while to spend that in envying and quarreling.

If you are carrying on designs against your neighbor to pull him [down], consider how soon death may come, and thus all that you can do to asperse and revile and pull down your neighbor will be at end. Death at one stroke puts an end to all such things; Eccles. 9:5–6, "The living know that they must die: but the dead know not any thing . . . Also their love, and their hatred, and their envy, are now perished."

And what comfort do you think it will be to you when you come to die, to think that you have lived in envy, and that you have been a means of pulling down such and such men and depriving of 'em of an advantage to get money? Will this be any comfort to you when you come to look death in the face? Alas, you won't care who is in this or the other office; then you'll have something else to think of and be concerned about.

6. MS: "and."

Eleventh. How exceeding unbecoming is this of those that sit at the same table of the Lord! This feast is a feast of love; Christ instituted this ordinance partly that his disciples, by coming and sitting together at the same table, might testify and seal their charity and peace with all their brethren. Feasting together has been generally used in all ages and nations as a token and seal of love and friendship.

If a person indulges envy or malice towards any of his brethren, and is carrying on envious[7] designs against him, it will be in the Lord's Supper a leaven. A leaven was in the Passover, as the Apostle instructs us; I Cor. 5:8, "Therefore let us keep the feast not with old leaven, neither with the leaven of malice and wickedness." If a person kept the Passover with leaven, it made the feast void; and not only so, but it wrought for their condemnation; Ex. 12:15, "even the first day shall ye put away leaven out of your houses: for whosoever eateth leavened bread from the first day until the seventh day, that soul shall be cut off from Israel."

So he that partakes of the Lord's Supper indulging of envy and malice in his heart, he eats and drinks judgment to himself [I Cor. 11:29].[8]

How does it seem to see a company and family of the visible children of the Most High God, sitting together at God's table, feeding on the body and blood of Jesus Christ, God's own Son, who was from God's love to 'em slain to make a feast for them, and one sitting in one place envying another that sits at the same table because he gets money or because of an honorable title, and all the while having designs in his heart against him? Can you think that such sacraments are acceptable to God, and to the Lord Jesus Christ, the holy Lamb of God? No; they are abominable to him as the vomit of a dog![9]

7. MS: "Carrying on End Envious."
8. See *Self-Examination and the Lord's Supper*, below, for a sermon on this text.
9. Two announcements follow as a fitting postscript to the sermon: "Baptism" and "Fast."

HONEY FROM THE ROCK

THIS sermon, preached in the fall of 1730, is an extended meditation on what Edwards describes as the "elegant metaphor of sucking honey out of a rock." His text is from the Song of Moses. Placed immediately before the story of Israel's entrance into Canaan, the biblical poem memorializes God's miraculous provision for Israel in the wilderness, including the gifts of honey and oil from flinty rocks. Edwards does not pursue a typological association here between these images and corporate institutions like town or church. Rather, he dwells on the individual, spiritual significance of the metaphors: the lost and desperate soul who finds the honey of the Holy Spirit issuing from Christ the rock. *Honey from the Rock* is an illustration of how Edwards continues to preach on the inner spiritual life in the early 1730s even as he shows an increasing concern for public affairs.

An unusually complicated structure and repetitious formulation characterize the rhetorical flow of *Honey from the Rock.* It is a two-preaching-unit sermon, with what Edwards labels "Three Doctrines." We might designate these as three major propositions to the doctrinal portions of the sermon. Edwards does not give an Application to the doctrine as a whole, but gives separate Applications to the first and third propositions. At the start of the second preaching unit, immediately following the first Application, Edwards returns briefly to further explication of the text. Thus, instead of Edwards' usual tripartite divisions of Explication, Doctrine, and Application, the sermon has a concatenated structure.

Each of the three propositions incorporates a different approach to the text. Under the first, the most rhetorically effective of the sermon, Edwards discusses the meaning of the wilderness. It is a metaphor for sin. Edwards avoids a mere declamation on human viciousness, however, and instead describes the human condition in a series of visual images that evoke the frightening experience of living in the American wilderness: the feelings of being lost, surrounded by darkness, helpless, poor, and powerless. God finds the elect in this condition, Edwards argues, and provides for them out of grace. In the Application, Edwards encourages believers to praise God and unbelievers to continue to seek him even in the midst of their desolation. Under the second proposition, Edwards considers God's work of providing spiritual good out of afflictions in more general terms.

Under the third proposition, Edwards returns to his text and delves directly into the typological significance of the key images: rock and honey. He compiles scriptural uses of rock as a metaphor for outward meanness, inner weight, righteousness, strength, durability, and immutability, and draws a typological correspondence to Christ. Honey refers to divine blessings, conceived as peace, security, spiritual nourishment, or the Holy Spirit. In other typological writings, Edwards did not dwell on these images. He pursued the image of honey, however, in a subsequent sermon in this volume, *A Divine and Supernatural Light.*[1] In *Honey from the Rock* Edwards uses the image to encourage praise and spiritual determination. In *A Divine and Supernatural Light* he uses it to a remarkable effect to analyze the nature of spiritual perception, in defense of the doctrine of divine election.

* * *

The manuscript is a typical duodecimo booklet, consisting of sixteen leaves. Clearly written, it has few deletions, no marks for reorganization, and no indications of repreaching. Each of the sermon's two preaching units was written on a separate booklet. The booklets were then stitched together.

1. See also the sermon from 1723 that anticipates *Divine and Supernatural Light* and contains JE's first sermonic use of the honey analogy, *A Spiritual Understanding of Divine Things Denied to the Unregenerate,* in *Works, 14,* 67–96.

HONEY FROM THE ROCK

DEUTERONOMY 32:13.

And he made him to suck honey out of the rock,
and oil out of the flinty rock.

In this part of this song we have the great mercies of God to Israel recounted. In vv. 7–8 is declared how God had respect to them before they were, when he "divided to the nations their inheritance" and "separated the sons of Adam." He had respect to them in appointing them their bounds; he had respect to them as his own "portion" and "inheritance" [v. 9].

And then is declared what a forlorn condition God first found him in, and the grace of God magnified from thence: "He found him in a desert land, in a vast howling wilderness" [v. 10]. The more poor, necessitous, and wretched the condition of God's people is when he calls them to mercy, the more is his grace conspicuous in calling them.

And then we have the great mercy which God called them to declared in the four following verses: "As an eagle stirreth up her nest, fluttereth over her young, spreadeth abroad her wings, taketh them, beareth them on her wings; so the Lord alone did lead him, and there was no strange god with him. He made him ride on the high places of the earth, that he might eat the increase of the fields; and he made him to suck honey out of the rock, and oil out of the flinty rock; butter of kine, and milk of sheep, with fat of lambs, and rams of the breed of Bashan, and goats, with the fat of kidneys of wheat; and thou didst drink the pure blood of the grape."

There are several things signified by the words of our text. God causes his people to suck honey out of a rock; that is, he causes good to arise to them when they are in a state that is very remote from it, and one would think it impossible that they should receive it. He gives them oil and honey in the wilderness, where there is nothing but dry sands and barren rocks, which is represented, by the rocks yielding it to them, by an elegant metaphor and not unlike to other Scripture metaphors.

Thus it was, God did by Israel. God "found him in a desert land, in a waste howling wilderness," as it is said in v. 10. He found him in a wilderness where was nothing but sands and rocks for the supply of his necessities. But yet there God fed and nourished him with angels' food, so that he did, as it were, suck honey out of the dry sands or flinty rocks.

And another thing seems to be signified by it, and that is that God is wont to bring good to his people out of those things that seem the most unlikely to yield it, things that men are ready to imagine such good could not come from.

And particularly hereby is signified the great good [they] have from Christ, who is often called a rock and is so called in v. 4 of this chapter; "He is the Rock, his work is perfect: for all his ways are judgment: a God of truth and without iniquity, just and right is he"; and so in many other places in this song. It was Christ that was typified by that rock out of which the water gushed [at] Meribah, that quenched the thirst of the congregation in the wilderness; I Cor. 10:4, "They drank of that spiritual rock that followed them: and that rock was Christ."

THREE DOCTRINES.

I. *God causes good to arise to his elect people when they are in a state as that they are most remote from it.*

II. *God is wont to bring good to his people out of those things that seem most unlikely to yield it.*

III. *By causing his people to receive such great blessings from Jesus Christ, he does, as it were, cause them to suck honey out of the rock.*

I. The first doctrine [contains] two propositions.

First. God finds all his elect in a state wherein they are very remote from good.

He finds them all in a desert land, in a vast howling wilderness, as it is said of Israel in v. 10 of the context. The state that all God's elect are in at first, before God finds them or comes to them, is very fitly represented by that wilderness that the children of Israel were so long in, which we have described in Deut. 8:15–16: "Who led thee through that great and terrible wilderness, where were fiery serpents, and scorpions, and drought, where there was no water; who brought thee forth water out of the rock of flint; who fed thee in the wilderness with manna"; and Jer. 2:6, "Where is the Lord that brought us up out of the land of Egypt, that led us through the wilderness, through a land of deserts and of pits, through a land of drought, and of the shadow of death, through a land that no man passed through, and where no man dwelt?"

God did not find the children of Israel here in a literal sense. He found them in Egypt and led them into the wilderness, and therefore 'tis expressed thus in our context to signify rather how it is with God's spiritual Israel, who are found in a wilderness state when God comes to them and effectually calls them, a state much more remote from spiritual blessings than that wilderness was from the delights and blessings of Canaan. Here,

1. God finds his elect people all in a state wherein they are involved in great misery. The circumstances of the elect are naturally the same with the rest of fallen and lost mankind.

When God comes to his elect, he finds 'em in a very miserable state because he finds 'em in a state of guilt. Their souls are laden with guilt. They are greatly in debt to divine justice and wrath; there is a dreadful score stands against them; they owe ten thousand talents. There is justice stands against them, and there is the immutable law of God stands against them, and they are under obligation to eternal sufferings. They are heirs of hell and everlasting wrath.

They are found in a miserable condition in that they are separated from their chief good and only happiness: they are separated from God. They have wandered away from the "fountain of living waters" [Jer. 2:13]. All union that there was between God, the "Father of spirits" [Heb. 12:9] and the "Father of lights" [Jas. 1:17], is cut off, and God has left them there and they are lost. They wander alone in the wilderness. Without God in the world, they are as lost sheep.

Christ, when he finds those that God has given him, he finds 'em in a lost and a doleful condition. They wander desolate in a land of pits and of drought and fiery flying serpents, a land of darkness and the shadow of death. Christ finds his people poor, blind, and naked, poor creatures in rags, in the highways and hedges.

God finds them in a very miserable condition in that he finds 'em under the dominion of sin. They have lost all holiness which was their beauty and glory. They are become sordid and loathsome with the rags and filth of sin. They have lost their liberty and are become slaves to sin and Satan; they are "sold under sin" [Rom. 7:14]. They are sick of a most foul and mortal disease, with which they are blind and deaf and halt and maimed.

There is enough in their condition to contribute to their misery in this wilderness: there are fiery serpents, there are the scorching sunbeams. But there is nothing to yield them any good: there is nothing but dry heaths and barren rocks. They are in a pit wherein there is no water.

2. God finds his elect very remote from good in that they are in a very helpless condition; they are in an utter incapacity of helping themselves. God finds them as a forlorn, helpless infant wallowing in its blood; Ezek. 16:5–6, "Thou wast cast out into the open field, to the loathing of thy person, in the day that thou wast born. And when I passed by and saw thee polluted in thine own blood, I said unto thee when thou wast in thy blood, Live; yea, I said unto thee when thou wast in thy blood, Live."

They are not able to deliver themselves from guilt. They owe ten thousand talents, but they ben't able to pay a farthing. They can make nothing to satisfy divine justice; they can make no compensation for the contempt of divine majesty. They can work out no righteousness; they can do nothing but sin. They can't make themselves holy; they are "dead in trespasses" [Eph. 2:1]. And since they have no power to perform one act of faith in Christ, they can't put forth one act of love to God as one act of true and sincere obedience. They can do nothing that is good.

They have nothing in 'em from whence any goodness can be made to arise. They have no principle that good can be fetched from, strain it, turn it, model it how they will. You may as soon fetch oil out of the dry sands or water out of a rock. They are dead. Do what you will with a dead body, warm, rub, [or] chafe it, you can never get one act of life produced.

3. There is no creature can help them in the condition they are in. They not only can't help themselves, but they are found without help from any quarter. In vain would they look to any earthly friend; in vain would they call upon the angels. Alas, their case is beyond their help. They are as destitute of help from creatures as to their spiritual welfare, as a man would be as to his temporal if he were alone in vast deserts where no man was and that no men passed through.

4. No creature could help, if they were never so much stronger and wiser and better than they be. If you should add to their ability and goodness a thousandfold, and add to that another thousand, and add to that millions, yet their help would be insufficient for the delivering them out of their wretched case.

There is no finite power or merit that would be available for them, so that indeed they are, in a sense, at an infinite distance from help. They are further from that good that their souls stand in necessity of than the east is from the west. There is a vast separation, a wide distance, between them and their happiness, a great gulf fixed that nothing but infinite power and grace and merit can remove.

5. There is nothing in nature can be found from whence help can be obtained. Not only no created person can be found that can help, but there is nothing in the whole compass of nature that can, by anything in itself or by any improvement they can make of it, afford 'em any help.

"The depth saith, It is not in me; the sea saith, It is not in me" [Job 28:14]. If they turn to the right hand or to the left, there is nothing to be found to feed and support their perishing souls. If they dig into the bottoms of the mountains or bowels of the earth, there is not treasure to be found that will purchase help for them, that will procure food to nourish them and raiment to clothe them. If they look up to the heavens, they can afford them no relief, and if they wander to the ends of the earth or uttermost parts of the sea, they can find nothing.

Second. In this state and condition God finds his elect, and comes to 'em, and causes good to arise to them.

He finds 'em in this wilderness amongst those flinty rocks and causes such good to arise to them as they stand in need of. He finds them in this poor, famishing, perishing condition and causes waters to break out in the wilderness and streams in the desert; Is. 35:6, "Then shall the lame man leap as an hart, and the tongue of the dumb sing: for in the wilderness shall waters break out, and streams in the desert." God spreads a table for them in this wilderness, and from being in such an indigent and necessitous condition, he causes 'em to [be] encompassed about with blessings. Their souls are not only fed but feasted: the "rock pours" them "out rivers of oil" (Job 29:6). Here,

1. God meets them in his mercy and gives them grace in their hearts. He gives them his holiness. He cleanses them from their filth and puts his own beauty upon them. He infuses a principle of spiritual life into them. He opens their blind eyes and calls them out of their darkness and causes them to see the refreshing light of his glory, so that they no longer are in a land of darkness and the shadow of death.

By his grace he reunites them to himself, fills them with his Holy Spirit. Their natures are renewed and changed. And they have faith given them, whereby they are enabled to look to Jesus Christ and to feed on him, so that in him their souls, that were perishing with hunger, are nourished and strengthened; their souls, that were perishing with thirst, are refreshed and satisfied.

2. Their sins are all pardoned, and they are made to be partakers of God forever. The blood of Christ is given them to wash them from their

sins. They are justified freely through {the blood of Christ}, and there is no more condemnation to them. They are admitted into God's family to be his children. God now is reconciled to them; he is no more their enemy but their friend, and they are become heirs of eternal life.

3. God comes to them and gives them more comfort and peace. Till now they were without any true comfort. They were in a lonesome, doleful wilderness; it was a great and terrible wilderness; there were hideous mountains and rocks. But God causes there to arise to them comfort and joy that is sweeter than honey. The wilderness is turned into a fruitful and pleasant field to 'em.

Thus wonderfully does God work for his chosen. Who that saw them in such a doleful and forlorn condition as they were in would have thought to have seen such blessedness arising to them? Who would have thought to have seen such waters breaking out in the wilderness? Who would have thought to have seen honey dripping, and rivers of oil flowing, out of the flinty rock?

APPLICATION.

In the application of this doctrine,

I. I will direct myself to God's people that God hath dealt thus wonderfully with.

First. Let this doctrine put you upon comparing your present with your lost condition. Be often reflecting and considering what a miserable, lost condition you was in when God found you, when he came by his grace and called you to himself. Consider what a helpless condition you was in and how you must inevitably have perished if God had not here pitied you, if Christ so had not here sought you, and in his love and his pity redeemed you.

Remember how unable you were to do anything with your own heart to make yourself better and to work conversion in yourself. Remember how you wandered about seeking rest and finding none, and how God came to you in the midst of your distress and darkness. Remember how barren and desolate the wilderness appeared to you. Did you imagine then those barren rocks would ever yield you anything for your food and refreshment?

Second. Rejoice and praise God the more; the consideration of these things should have this effect upon you. A man that is perishing, and seems far from help, and it seems very unlikely he should have any, when he is delivered, it will affect him the more to consider how forlorn his case was. The greater the misery and the more helpless the condition, the greater the deliverance, and the greater will the joy be, if you are aright sensible both of the misery of your former and the happiness of your present state.

And you will be the more disposed to praise God, to admire his power that was able to bring forth such a flow of blessings to you in the wilderness and out of the rock. You will the more praise his grace, that he was pleased to make so great a difference and to cause such light to spring out of such darkness, that he should seek and save you when you was lost, that he should take you out of the miry clay and set your feet upon a rock, that he should take you when you was a beggar from the dunghill and set you {upon a rock}.

Third. By this you should learn not to be discouraged when you are in darkness afterwards: if God caused good to arise to you when you was in such a forlorn condition as you was in before your conversion, when you was so remote from it.

Don't be discouraged, though things seem to look dark again. You meet with difficulties, and God hides his face, and you have great temptations and an evil and corrupt heart; God is able to make you to suck honey out of the rock again. If it looks like a wilderness to you, he is able to cause waters to break forth in the desert again as he did before.

Therefore your faith and hope should be in God. You should learn both to hope and quietly to wait for the salvation of the Lord.

II. I would direct myself to awakened sinners.

First. Learn hereby not to be discouraged. Are you in a wilderness? Does it seem that there is nothing that can yield you any good: everything seems to conspire for your damnation? Do you see nothing but a wilderness in your own heart? Do you see no help on which side soever you turn? Do you see nothing but pits and rocks? Don't be discouraged. God is able to bring forth honey out of those rocks. However unlikely it seems to you that you should receive any spiritual and saving good (you are so wicked a creature, you have committed so much sin, and you see so much wilderness in your own hearts); as unlikely than that water or honey or oil should be fetched out of the flinty rock; yet God hath often done that.

Go on therefore seeking diligently and perseveringly for God's salvation. And O, that you could take encouragement from hence to look to Jesus Christ as one sufficient to supply all your wants and relieve your soul, however miserable a condition it is now in!

Second. Earnestly seek that you may be brought to see that you are in such a state thus remote from the good that you need. You must seek to see that you are in a wilderness, that you are thus remote from blessedness, that your state is thus miserable, and that you are thus helpless.

And then you will be in the likeliest way to be delivered. Don't flatter yourself that your condition is not so bad that you are able to help yourself, but beg of God that you may have your eyes opened to see that if ever your soul is fed, your food must be fetched out of the flinty {rock}.[2]

[DOCTRINE RESUMED.]

The words [of our text] do more immediately respect the children of Israel and, so far as they are intended, respect is had to God's feeding them in the wilderness, where there was nothing to yield them any food but dry sands and barren rocks. And his providing for 'em so well in such a desert with manna and water out of the rock is here represented by the elegant metaphor of sucking honey out of a rock.

It seems to have respect also to God's bringing of 'em out of their bondage in Egypt, and out of a barren wilderness to receive the blessings of Canaan, which are mentioned in the following verse: "Butter of kine, and milk of sheep, with fat of lambs, and rams of the breed of Bashan, and goats, with the fat of kidneys of wheat; and thou didst drink the pure blood of the grape" [Deut. 32:14]. Their being brought from so low and necessitous a condition to the enjoyment of such plenty is also implied in the metaphor of causing them to suck.

But the words have not only a respect to that nation, but they respect the spiritual Israel; as indeed most of those things that are said of that nation in parables, and songs, and prophecies have an ultimate and principal respect to the spiritual Israel. And so the spiritual blessings are signified: the honey and oil that were represented are typified by those temporal blessings of the children of Israel.

We observed from the words three doctrines which we supposed were implied in them.[3] We have already spoken [on the first of these].

II. *God is wont to bring good to his people out of those things that seem most unlikely to yield it.*

A rock is a thing that one would not expect to fetch honey from. The flinty rock is a thing that seems very unlikely to yield oil. They have

2. Here ends the first preaching unit. JE repeats the text to start the next preaching unit. In what immediately follows, he returns to an explication of the text before moving to the second doctrine.

3. Here JE reiterates the three doctrines.

naturally no such thing in them. So God is often wont to bring good to his people out of those things that naturally have no goodness in them, that in themselves are not good but evil.

So God brings spiritual good oftentimes to his people out of affliction. Afflictions in themselves are evil, and therefore man in a state of innocence had no affliction; and in heaven there will be none. The afflictions are evils in themselves, yet God brings good out of them to his people; Heb. 12:11, "No affliction for the present seemeth joyous, but grievous: nevertheless afterward it yieldeth the peaceable fruit of righteousness unto them which are exercised thereby."

So God often brings good to his people out of spiritual darkness they are under. When God hides his face from 'em and they are in the dark, they are exercised with doubts about their condition and with fears of wrath. He brings them into the wilderness amongst hideous rocks, but God turns it to their spiritual good; he makes them to suck honey out of those rocks. He causes light to arise out of this darkness.

Again, God often causes good to arise to God's people out of Satan's temptations. They are things evil in themselves and are designed by Satan to mischief those that are exercised by them; but God turns them to good. And so God brings to his people meat out of the eater, and sweetness out of the strong, as Samson got honey out of the carcass of the lion [Judg. 14:9]. So God makes his people to reap benefits by the sins of other men. Though this proves a snare to the wicked oftentimes, yet to the godly it is turned to good.

And again, God sometimes makes their own sins and falls an occasion of their good. When they have committed sin, they are more humble and place their confidence more in God and less in themselves. And when they have recovered themselves, they are more careful to avoid sin for the future, and more diligent to clear themselves of the remains of sin; II Cor. 7:11, "This selfsame thing, that ye sorrowed after a godly sort, what carefulness it wrought in you, yea, what clearing of yourselves." Peter, when he was converted after his fall, was stronger and more firmly fixed in grace and holiness than he was before. Therefore Christ bids him when he is converted to strengthen his brethren [John 21:15–17].

God oftentimes turns those things to his people's good that seem to them to tend only to their hurt. They can't see which way they can tend to any good. It seems to them that it only hinders the progress of grace in their souls and hinders them in their work; they can't serve God with that advantage that otherwise they might do. It seems to them as unlikely that any good should be got by it, it may be, as that they should get honey out of a rock. But yet God, that sees further than they do, knows how to turn it to their advantage. But not to insist upon this doctrine, I proceed to the [third].

III. *By causing his people to receive such great blessings from Jesus Christ, he does, as it were, cause them to suck honey out of a rock.*

As Christ was signified by that rock that the children of Israel drank water out of—as the Apostle himself tells us, "They drank of that spiritual rock that followed them: and that rock was Christ" (I Cor. 10:4)—we may also conclude that Christ is signified by the rock mentioned in the text, that God's people are said to suck honey and oil out of. The same thing is here signified by oil and honey as was typified by the water out of the rock, viz. the spiritual blessings which God's people do receive.

God several times in this very song is called a rock; Deut. 32:4, "He is the rock, his work is perfect: for all his ways are judgment: a God of truth and without iniquity, just and right is he"; v. 15; and again, v. 18; and again, in vv. 30–31. And it was the second person[4] more especially that was signified, for it was that person in which God was wont to appear to the children of Israel; and then he is called "the rock of salvation," in v. 15.

Therefore, we shall show, first, why Christ is fitly compared to a rock; [and] second, that the benefits which the godly receive from him are exceeding great and precious.

First. Christ is fitly compared to a rock.

1. Upon the account of his mean outward appearance, he appeared very unlikely to men's carnal eyes ever to yield such great blessings; a rock seems very unlikely. Christ was as a root out of a dry ground that seemed very unlikely to yield such excellent fruit and in such abundance; Is. 53:2, "For he shall grow up before him as a tender plant, and as a root out of the dry ground: he hath no form or comeliness."

He was born of a mean family, one that was so at that day at least, though they were of the royal line of David. His mother was a poor obscure virgin who dwelt in the city of Nazareth. The Jews looked upon both the family and the city as a dry ground. They did not expect any plant to spring from thence that should produce such excellent fruit; Matt. 13:55, "Is not this the carpenter's son?" say they; and John 1:46, "Can any good thing come out of Nazareth?"

He appeared in the form of a servant when he was here in the world. He made no great appearance; he did not appear with the glory of

4. I.e. the second person of the Trinity.

earthly princes, nor with that glory in which God was wont to appear sometimes under the Old Testament, nor yet with the glory of the angels. He was a man, and he appeared as ordinary men do when he was amongst men. There was [no] extraordinary pomp nor no shining brightness to distinguish him from anybody.

It seemed therefore an exceeding unlikely thing to the Jews that this was the Messiah. They could not believe it; they could not imagine that he that made no greater appearance was he in whom "all the families of the earth were to be blessed" [Gen. 12:3]; that he was to be the light of the world, the Savior of mankind, the fountain of everlasting blessedness and glory to all God's people. They could no more conceive of or expect any such thing, than they expected to see oil and honey flowing out of the flinty rock.

2. As a rock is solid and weighty, so Christ is perfect and without any defect. Sincerity, and uprightness, and true righteousness of heart is often represented in Scripture by solidity and soundness or weightiness; so God is said to ponder the hearts and to weigh the spirits to know whether they are truly righteous or no, and to ponder or weigh men's goings (Prov. 16:2, and other places). Belshazzar's wickedness is represented by his being light; Dan. 5:27, "Thou art weighed in the balances, and art found wanting." So the wicked are compared to chaff, that has no substance but is light, so that the wind drives it to and fro; and the righteous, to the wheat, which is more solid and weighty [Jer. 23:28; Hos. 13:3].

And so upon this account Christ is compared to a rock because he is perfect in righteousness and holiness, and there is no defect in him, as is evident by v. 4 of the context: "He is a rock, his work is perfect: for all his ways are judgment: a God of truth and without iniquity, just and right is he." There is no defect in Christ's nature. In his divine nature he is perfectly holy, perfectly just and right. It is impossible there should be anything in God contrary to holiness, righteousness, and truth. And there was no defect in his human nature. In him was no sin, neither was guile found in his mouth [I Pet. 2:22].

And again, there was no defect in him as mediator. When he was weighed in the balances, he was not found defective. His satisfaction was sufficient; what was paid to satisfy divine justice was of weight equal to our debt, which was ten thousand talents. And his righteousness is sufficient; it was a price that was looked upon by God as of weight sufficient to purchase heaven.

3. Christ is compared to a rock for his strength and ability to defend his people; Ps. 62:7, "In God is my salvation and my glory: the rock of my strength." Christ is a mighty redeemer; he is able to save unto the utter-

most all those that come to God through him. What Christ doth, there is none that can take from it or add to it. What God has decreed shall surely stand: there is no reversing of it. There is none ever hardened himself against God and prospered. 'Tis in vain to oppose, as it would be in vain for a man to fight with a rock. He would only bruise himself in so doing.

4. Christ is a rock for durableness. Christ is everlasting. He is the eternal God, who only hath immortality; Is. 26:4, "Trust ye in the Lord for ever: for in the Lord Jehovah is everlasting strength"; in the Hebrew it is "the Rock of Ages." Christ is everlasting in his righteousness and the fruits of it; Dan. 9:24, "Seventy weeks are determined to finish the transgression, and to make an end of sins, and to bring in everlasting righteousness."

His kingdom is an everlasting kingdom. The stone cut out of the mountains without hands is to grow great, and become a great rock like a mountain and fill the earth, and to abide forever [Dan. 2:45]. That is, the kingdom of Christ shall become great and stand forever, as Daniel interprets; Dan. 2:44, "And in the days of these kings shall the God of heaven set up a kingdom, which shall never be destroyed: and the kingdom shall not be left to other people, but it shall break in pieces and consume all these kingdoms, and shall stand for ever."

5. Christ is as a rock upon the account of his faithfulness and immutability. A rock is stable and immovable; Job 18:4, "Shall the rock be removed out of its place?" So Christ is the same yesterday, today, and forever (Heb. 13:8). He is unchangeable in his love to those whom God hath given him. He loved them before the foundation of the world; Jer. 31:3, "I have loved thee with an everlasting love: therefore with lovingkindness have I drawn thee." And as he loves them from everlasting, so he loves them to everlasting whom he loves to the end. And there is nothing, "neither height, nor depth, nor any other creature, shall separate" the saints from the love of God which is in Christ Jesus [Rom. 8:39].

Christ never departs from his promises; he may be depended upon. He don't repent, but is as immovable as a rock. He hath promised that those that come to him he will "no wise cast out" [John 6:37], and he will surely fulfill it. He has engaged to stand between such and all wrath. He has engaged by his power to bring all believers to eternal life and to raise them up at the last day. He hath said; and he will not repent.

With respect to the relation that Christ stands in to believers and the use he is of to them, he is a rock two ways.

(1) He is a rock for a foundation to build upon. He is a sure foundation; Matt. 7:24, "Whosoever heareth these sayings of mine, and doth

them, I will liken him unto a wise man, which built his house upon a rock." He is a strong, a durable, and [an] immutable foundation.

(2) He is a rock of defense. He is their strong rock and high tower. He is a fortress that will not fail them; Is. 33:15–16, "He that walketh righteously, and speaketh uprightly, he shall dwell on high: and his place of defense shall be the munitions of rocks."

Second. The blessings that the saints receive by Jesus Christ are exceeding sweet and precious. They may well be compared to honey and oil, and the best and sweetest of the blessings of the earthly Canaan.

1. The saints receive by Christ the most quiet and sure rest and peace. By his redemption they obtain or will obtain the most perfect rest and sweet repose of mind. They may lay themselves down and sleep and awake, the Lord sustaining of them. They may dwell quietly and without fear of evil. They may set their hearts at rest, and may enjoy undisturbed quietness without having anything to fear.

And that with good reason, for by Jesus Christ they enjoy the most perfect safety. They are thoroughly secured from all evil. He that is in Christ, he has the almighty God to be his defense. He is secured from all those evils and that misery he was exposed to while in a natural condition. He need not fear wrath; he need not fear those evils that the rest of the world are destroyed by. From the top of the highest mountain of God he may behold the dreadful work that storms make amongst miserable mankind below and himself be out of their reach, enjoying the most undisturbed tranquillity in Jesus Christ, his strong rock. They may enjoy peace, and freedom from fear of hell and death and from fear of what man or the devil can do unto him.

How rational a ground of peace have they that have their sins pardoned and that have God, who has all things in his hands, for their assured friend! What rest may such considerations well yield to the soul! It is "peace that passes all understanding" [Phil. 4:7]; Is. 32:17, "And the work of righteousness shall be peace; and the effect of righteousness quietness and assurance for ever."

2. The blessings the saints receive by Christ are most nourishing and perfective of their nature. The nature of man is exceedingly broken by sin in a most infirm, sickly, ruined state. The people of God do by Christ Jesus receive that grace whereby their natures are restored to a state of health and to their true excellency and perfection.

The Holy Spirit is given through Christ, whereby the soul is sanctified and a principle of spiritual life is infused, and the nature is renewed after the image of God.

Reason is restored to its government in the soul. And those spiritual principles which man had at first, wherein consisted his well-being, are restored, and man is raised to the heavenly life, so that he is enabled to live to God and to perform those actions that are for God's glory and for his own true happiness.

Jesus Christ is the true nourishment of the soul. It don't only preserve its life but it exalts its nature. It raises it above; and what is merely human, it exalts it to the angelic, yea, to a participation of the divine nature, and enables it to live an angelic and divine life.

3. [The blessings the saints receive by Christ are] most refreshing and delighting, "joy unspeakable" [I Pet. 1:8].

4. Christ yields that to the souls of his saints that is not only of a refreshing and nourishing, but of a satisfying, nature. The pleasure and joy that is in Christ Jesus is satisfying in two respects.

(1) As it is of such a nature that those that receive [it] desire no other kind of joy. When they have found this, they look no further; they desire no better sort. This is of a kind so suitable to the natures and to the needs of their souls that they can desire no better.

When Christ says to the woman of Samaria, "Whosoever shall drink of the water that I shall give him shall never thirst" [John 4:14], the meaning of it is not that he won't desire more of the same. Joy in Christ is of that nature, that he that has once tasted will long thirst earnestly for more of the same. The Psalmist says, "My soul breaketh for the longing it hath to thy statutes" (Ps. 119:20); and it is the character of godly man that he "hungers and thirsts after righteousness" (Matt. 5:6). But the meaning of it is that he shall never desire any other kind of joy; he will be satisfied in the kind he'll never desire any change from.

Now, it is not so with temporal enjoyments. After a man has enjoyed one kind a while, he is not satisfied with it. He desires change; he wants something new. But he that has found Christ never will desire any change. He'll never be weary in perpetually feeding on, enjoying, and delighting in him so as to desire any change.

(2) It is satisfying as there is enough in the fountain to satisfy in degree; the kind of joy is capable of being exalted to that degree as fully to satisfy. There is enough in Christ, the object and fountain, to equal the utmost strength of the desire. There is an ocean of it.

And therefore when the soul comes to have all obstacles removed and comes fully to enjoy, they shall be satisfied. Their happiness will be perfect and complete. The vessel shall be filled brimful, so that then it shall be satisfied both as to kind and also as to degree of blessedness.

APPLICATION.

I. This doctrine gives us argument of praise. 'Tis spoken of in this song as a glorious work of God, that he should make Israel "suck honey out of the rock, and oil out of the flinty rock." The expression denotes to us some strange and wonderful works, a peculiar effect of divine power.

It was a wonderful work of God in the wilderness when he caused water to gush out of the rock, upon Moses' smiting of it with his rod, in such abundance as to supply all the congregation, and is spoken of as such; Deut. 8:15, "Who led thee through that great and terrible wilderness, wherein were fiery serpents, and scorpions, and drought, where there was no water; who brought thee forth water out of the rock of flint." But this was but a little thing to this glorious work that is typified by it. It was a glorious work of God's power, as well as mercy, to provide such blessings for a lost world by Jesus Christ. It was wonderful that such blessings should be made to flow from this rock, whether we consider this similitude of a rock as denoting his outward meanness or his divine greatness.

Respect seems to be had to both in this metaphor. His meanness is hereby signified upon this account: it appeared to the carnal world very unlikely that such blessings should come from him, as we have already observed. And, indeed, it was a wonderful work of God to bring such exceeding great benefits to mankind from one of ourselves, from a man, from one that was born of a virgin, that had a frail mortal nature as we have, that was nursed and brought up as other children. He was supported by meat and drink as others of us are, and was subject to the common infirmities of the human nature. It was a wonderful work of God to make such an one the spring of such infinite blessings to the world, and is spoken of as such; Ezek. 17:22–23,

> Thus saith the Lord God; I will also take of the highest branch of the high cedar, and will set it; I will crop off from the top of his young twigs a tender one, and will plant it upon the high mountain and eminent: in the mountain of the height of Israel will I plant it: and it shall bring forth boughs, and bear fruit, and be a goodly cedar: and under it shall dwell all fowl of every wing; in the shadow of the branches thereof shall they dwell. And all the trees of the field shall know that I the Lord have brought down the high tree, have exalted the low tree, have dried up the green tree, have made the dry tree to flourish.

And 'tis wonderful also if we consider Christ's divine greatness, for this is also signified by this metaphor of a rock. As we have shown, it signifies his divine perfection and holiness, his omnipotence, his eternity, his immutability. Now, 'tis a wonderful work of God that such a glorious person should be made the head of influence and fountain of spiritual nourishment to lost mankind: that so great, so glorious a person should be given to us, to be to us a fountain of blessings to be enjoyed by us who are so mean and unworthy.

II. Here is encouragement to trust in Jesus Christ, both from the things signified in his being called a rock and from the rich and sweet blessings that flow therefrom.

We have shown that hereby is denoted that there is no defect in Christ as he is mediator. He is a perfect, a complete savior. His righteousness is perfect, both active and passive. He completely answers all our needs. This should move us to trust in him.

Hereby is also signified his strength, his ability to save and defend. He is a strong rock and high tower; let us therefore fly to him. They that are in Christ, their "place of defense is the munitions of rocks" [Is. 33:16].

Hereby is signified his everlastingness and unchangeableness. This should move us to trust in him, for he is an everlasting redeemer, and will be the everlasting portion of all that are his. His being, his glory, and his love will never fail. They that trust in Christ shall be like the "tree planted by the streams of living waters," whose leaf shall be always green and shall not see when drought comes nor cease to yield her fruit [Jer. 17:8].[5]

{Hereby is signified} his faithfulness. The rock shall sooner be removed out of its place, than Christ shall depart from anything that he has engaged. Christ invites us, and calls us, and engages [us], that if we will come to him, he will [be our rock].

He is a sure foundation to build upon. They that build their hope of heaven upon Christ Jesus, they build them upon the rock of ages; and whence they never will, nor can, fall. And the great and precious benefits which he yields to those that come to him should draw our hearts to him. We are in a needy state; we are often called to Jesus Christ. There we have honey out of the rock. And in him, whoever is weary and heavy laden may find sweet rest; [whoever is] sick [may be] healed.

5. See the paired sermons from mid-1729 on Jer. 17:7–8 (123), which considers the benefits of trusting in God, and on Jer. 17:5–6 (122), on the dangers of trusting in the creature.

GOD MAKES MEN SENSIBLE OF THEIR MISERY BEFORE HE REVEALS HIS MERCY AND LOVE

In this four-preaching-unit sermon dating from the fall of 1730, Edwards offers an extended analysis of the meaning and use of spiritual humiliation. According to Puritan teaching, an apprehension of one's sin, unworthiness, guilt, and condemnation is implied in, if not a logical antecedent to, conversion. Edwards frequently urged his auditors to seek such convictions. In this sermon, he also defends this sort of humiliation against objections that it places an undue moral burden on the unregenerate.

After a relatively lengthy explication of the context for his text—Hosea's warning that God would abandon Israel until the people became sensible of their guilt—Edwards draws the first major proposition of the Doctrine. God's way with his people is to bring them to an experience of misery before granting them mercy and deliverance. Edwards discusses the story of Israel from the patriarchs to the monarchy, reflecting in this the same comprehensive approach to biblical history he would later take in *The History of the Work of Redemption*. Whereas his focus in the latter work, however, is God's relation to historical collectivities, here he argues from corporate history to individual experience. The analogue to Israel's story is the soul who undergoes the torment of a sensible apprehension of guilt and fear of judgment as a prelude to the merciful experience of regeneration.

From this perspective, evangelical preaching leads people not only to apprehend their sinfulness—an uncontroversial point—but also to recognize their guilt and, therefore, to feel their vulnerability to the worst punishments of hell. Toward the end of the second major proposition of the Doctrine, Edwards raises the question of how the unconverted can properly seek anything, including a sense of shame and guilt, before they are enlightened by the Holy Spirit. God makes people sensible of their sin and guilt through common means: the pangs of natural conscience, a sense of divine majesty, the precepts of moral law, and an experience of one's inability to reform oneself. Even natural conscience, Edward maintains (anticipating later arguments in *The Nature of True Virtue*), reveals the supposed virtues of the unregenerate to be extensions of self-love and thus morally culpable.

In the third major head of the Doctrine, Edwards defends imprecatory preaching and other methods of inducing spiritual humiliation against charges that they deflect the sinner from an appreciation of God's love. His approach is both theological and christological. Sinners cannot apprehend the glory of God, he contends, without grasping the divine majesty that condemns sin and therefore threatens the sinner. Without such a sense, God's love appears as unworthy and the mediatorial work of Christ as unnecessary. But with such a sense, God's willingness to be merciful appears as an act of divine freedom, all the more loving in that it derives not from any virtue in the sinner but solely from sovereign grace. This truly glorifies God and points the sinner to Christ—an idea that Edwards developed at greater length in a subsequent, more widely known sermon in this volume, *God Glorified in Man's Dependence.*

In his discussion of natural conscience and divine majesty, Edwards drew directly from the "Miscellanies." He copied entry nos. 468 and 469 nearly verbatim under the first reason of the third major head of the Doctrine, and wrote nos. 470–475, which dealt with humiliation, mortification, conviction, conscience, and conversion, at about the same time he composed *God Makes Men Sensible of Their Misery.*[1] This integration of Edwards' private, more speculative meditations into the sermon, as well as his further explication of evangelical humiliation in *God Glorified in Man's Dependence,* illustrate the ongoing importance of the central theme of *God Makes Men Sensible of Their Misery.* As Edwards came to terms with life in Northampton, he searched for ways to prod people to recognize their moral failings and move beyond moralizing to spiritual renewal. Preaching the necessity of spiritual humiliation as a prelude to regeneration was one way to pursue this end.

* * *

The manuscript is a large duodecimo booklet, consisting of thirty well-preserved leaves. More than the usual amount of blank spaces, particularly at the end of major heads, indicate that Edwards gave some

1. For a close discussion of the "Miscellanies" used by JE in this sermon, and the "Miscellanies" cited, see *Works, 13,* 30–31, 440, 510–522.

thought to later revision or expansion at the time of original composition. A shorthand notation at the beginning of the sermon indicates a second delivery, and, later on, there is a marginal notation that Edwards repreached the sermon for the third time in 1750, "from the doctrine to the mark" at the end of the third part of the second head of the second proposition in the Doctrine.

In revising for repreaching, Edwards made a substantial number of revisions. These are mostly in the form of deletions, overwritten phrases, and additions. Later editors did not mark up the text itself, but at some point an amanuensis, for reasons now unknown, placed the number "26" at the top of manuscript p. 33 and the numbers "33" and "34" at the top of p. 43.

God Makes Men Sensible of Their Misery was first printed by Sereno Dwight (*8*, 44–69). Dwight's version omits several passages toward the end of the sermon, namely, the second through fifth subpoints under the first use, the final two subpoints of the third use, and the entirety of the fourth and fifth uses.

GOD MAKES MEN SENSIBLE OF THEIR MISERY BEFORE HE REVEALS HIS MERCY AND LOVE

HOSEA 5:15.

I will go and return to my place, till they acknowledge their offense, and seek my face: in their affliction they will seek me early.

In the foregoing part of the chapter is threatened the destruction of Ephraim. Now, by Ephraim in the Prophets is generally meant the ten tribes, or the kingdom of Israel as it is distinguished from the kingdom of Judah. When we read of Ephraim and Judah in the Prophets, thereby is meant the whole people of Israel of the twelve tribes, as here in this chapter, as in v. 12: "Therefore will I be unto Ephraim as a moth, and to the house of Judah as rottenness."

By Judah is meant the two tribes of Judah and Benjamin that were under the king of Judah, and by Ephraim is meant the ten tribes under the king of Israel. Ephraim is put for the whole kingdom of Israel because Samaria, the seat of the kingdom, the royal city, was in that tribe.

In the verse immediately going before the text is declared after what terrible manner God was about to deal with Ephraim: "For I will be unto Ephraim as a lion, and as young lion to the house of Judah: I, even I, will tear and go away; I will take away, and none shall rescue him."

In the text God declares how he would deal with them after he had torn as a lion {and gone away}. And here,

1. God declares how he would withdraw from them: "I will go and return to my place." When I have torn as a lion, I will go away. I'll leave them in this condition; I will depart from them, and they shall see no more of me.

2. What God will wait for in them, before he returns to them to show them mercy. There are three things here signified:

(1) That they should be sensible of their guilt till they acknowledge their offense. 'Tis in the original, "till they become guilty"; i.e. till they

become guilty in their own eyes, till they are sensible of their guilt, in the same sense as the same expression is used [in] Rom. 3:19, "that every mouth may be stopped, and all the world may become guilty before God," i.e. become guilty in their own eyes.

(2) That they should be sensible of their misery, implied in that expression, "in their affliction they shall seek me." Their calamity was brought upon them before God had tore them and left them, but in their pride and perverseness they were not well sensible of their own miserable condition, as this Prophet observes (Hos. 7:9).

(3) That they should be sensible of their need of God's help, which is implied in their seeking God's face and seeking him early, that is, with great care and earnestness. Before, they would not seek to God; they were not sensible of their helplessness in any other, as we have account in v. 13, the next verse but one before the text: "When Ephraim saw his sickness, and Judah his wound, then Ephraim went to the Assyrian, and sent to king Jareb" for help, but, as we are there told, he could not heal him nor cure his wound. And for all the help he could afford, God wounded him, tore him as a young lion and, as He here declares, would leave him till he should leave off going to any other, and should be sensible that no other could heal him, and should accordingly come to Him for healing.

DOCTRINE.

'Tis God's manner to make men sensible of their misery and unworthiness before he appears in his mercy and love to them.

I. 'Tis ordinarily thus with respect of the bestowment of great and signal mercies in general.

II. 'Tis particularly God's manner with respect to God's revealing his love and mercy to men's souls.

[III. Reasons.]

I. This is God's ordinary manner before any great and signal expression of his mercy and favor. He very commonly so orders it in his providence and so influences men by his Spirit, that they are brought to see their miserable condition as they are in themselves, and to despair of help from themselves or from an arm of flesh, before he appears for them, and also makes them sensible of their sin and unworthiness of God's help.

This appears by the accounts the Scriptures give us of God's dealings with his people all along. Joseph, before his great advancement in Egypt, must lie in the dungeon to humble him and prepare him for such honor and prosperity [Gen. 39:20].

The children of Jacob, before Joseph reveals himself to 'em and they receive that joy and honor and prosperity that was consequent thereupon, they pass through a train of difficulties and anxieties till at last they are reduced to distress, and were brought to reflect upon their guilt and to say that they were verily guilty concerning their brother. God humbled them in his providence, and then an end was put to all their difficulties, and their sorrow was turned into joy upon Joseph's revealing himself to them [Gen. 45:1].

Jacob, before he hears the joyful news of Joseph being yet alive, must be brought into great distress at the parting with Benjamin and the supposed loss of Simeon. He was reduced to great straits in his mind. He says, "All these things are against me" (Gen. 42:36). But soon after this, he had this gladsome tidings brought to him, that Joseph is yet alive and he is governor over all the land of Egypt, and to confirm it sees the wagons and the noble presents that Joseph sent to him. So that he was now brought to say, "It is enough; Joseph my son is yet alive: I will go and see him before I die" [Gen. 45:28].

And so the children of Israel in Egypt. Bondage must wax more and more extreme; their bondage had been very extreme, but yet Pharaoh gives commandment that more work should be laid upon them, and the taskmasters tell them they must get their straw where they can find it, and nothing of their work should be diminished [Ex. 5:11]. And quickly upon this was their deliverance.

So when the children of Israel were brought to the Red Sea. The Egyptians pursued them and were just at their heels, and they were reduced to the utmost distress. They see that they must assuredly perish unless God wrought a miracle for them, for they were shut up. The Red Sea was before 'em, and the army of the Egyptians encompassing 'em round behind, and they cried unto the Lord. And then God wonderfully appeared for their help, and made 'em pass through the Red Sea, and put songs of deliverance into their mouths.

So before God brought the children of Israel into Canaan. He led them about in a great and terrible wilderness through a train of difficulties and temptations for forty years together, that he might instruct them in their dependence on God and the sinfulness of their own hearts; Deut. 32:10, "He found him in a desert land, and in the waste howling wilderness; he led him about, he instructed him, he kept him as the apple of his eye."

God brought them into those trials and difficulties in the wilderness to humble them and let 'em see what was in their hearts, that [they] might be convinced of their own perverseness by the many discoveries of it under those temptations, and so that they might be sensible that it was not for their righteousness that God made them his people and gave them Canaan, seeing it was so evident that they were a stiffnecked people; Deut. 8:2–3, "And thou shalt remember all the way which the Lord thy God led thee these forty years in the wilderness, to humble thee, and to prove thee, to know what was in thine heart, whether thou wouldest keep his commandments, or no. And he humbled thee, and suffered thee to hunger, and fed thee manna, which thou knewest not, neither did thy fathers know; that he might make thee know that man doth not live by bread only, but by every word that proceedeth out of the mouth of the Lord doth man live." And vv. 15–17, "Who led thee through that great and terrible wilderness, wherein were fiery serpents, and scorpions, and drought, where there was no water; who brought thee forth water out of the rock of flint; who fed thee in the wilderness with manna, which thy fathers knew not, that he might humble thee, and that he might prove thee, to do thee good at thy latter end; and thou say in thine heart, My power and the might of mine hand hath gotten me this wealth."

And so we have from time to time examples of this in the history of the judges. When Israel revolted, God gave 'em into the hands of their enemies. He let them continue in their hands till they were reduced to great distress and see that they were in a helpless condition, and were brought to reflect upon themselves and to cry unto the Lord; and then God raised them up a deliverer. And when they cried unto God, he would not deliver 'em till he had humbled 'em, and brought 'em to own their unworthiness, and to own that they were in God's hands; Judg. 10:10–16,

> And the children of Israel cried unto the Lord, saying, We have sinned against thee, both because we have forsaken our God, and also served Baalim. And the Lord said unto the children of Israel, Did not I deliver you from the Egyptians, and from the Amorities . . . and from the Philistines? . . . Yet ye have forsaken me, and served other gods; wherefore I will deliver you no more. Go, and cry unto the gods, which ye have chosen; let them deliver you in the time of your tribulation. And the children of Israel said unto the Lord, We have sinned; do thou unto us whatsoever seemeth good unto thee; deliver us only, we pray thee, this day. And they put away the strange gods from

among them, and served the Lord; and his soul was grieved for the misery of Israel.

And this is the method that God declared from the beginning that he would proceed in with his people; Lev. 26:40–42, "If they shall confess their iniquity, and the iniquity of their fathers, with their trespass which they trespassed against me, and that also they have walked contrary unto me; and that I also have walked contrary unto them, and have brought them into the land of their enemies; if then their uncircumcised hearts be humbled, and they then accept of the punishment of their iniquity: then will I remember my covenant with Jacob, and also my covenant with Isaac, and also my covenant with Abraham will I remember; and I will remember the land."

'Tis God's manner, when he will bestow signal blessings in answer to prayer, to make men to seek them and pray for them with a sense of their sin and misery; I Kgs. 8:38–39, "What prayer and supplication soever be made by any man, or by all thy people Israel, which shall know every one the plague of his own heart, and spread forth his hands towards this house: then hear thou in heaven thy dwelling place, and forgive, and do, and give to every man according to his ways, whose heart thou knowest." By knowing the plague of their own hearts is meant both their sin and misery. A being sensible of their misery is included, as evident, by the manner of expressing the same petition of Solomon's prayer, as it is related in Chronicles; II Chron. 6:29, "Then what prayer or supplication soever shall be made of any man, or of all thy people Israel, when every one shall know his own sore and his own grief"; by which is probably meant his misery, and his sin which is the foundation of it.

Paul gives us an account how God brought him to have despair in himself before a great deliverance that he experienced; II Cor. 1:9–10, "But we had the sentence of death in ourselves, that we should not trust in ourselves, but in God which raiseth the dead: who delivered us from so great a death."

How did Christ humble the woman of Canaan, or bring her to the exercise and expression of a sense of her own unworthiness, before he answered her and healed her daughter! When she continued to cry after [him], he answered her not a word, seemed to take no notice of her, and his disciples desired him to send her away; and when she continued crying after him, he gave her a very humbling answer, saying, "It is not meet to take the children's bread, and cast it to dogs" [Matt. 15:26]. And when she took it well, as owning that then being called a dog was not too bad for her, and owning that she was therefore unworthy of children's bread and only sought the crumbs, then Christ answered her desire.

And the experience of God's people in all ages will answer to these instances. 'Tis God's usual method before remarkable discoveries of his mercy and love to them, especially by spiritual mercies, in a special manner to humble them and make them sensible of their misery and helplessness in themselves, and their vileness and unworthiness, either by some remarkable humbling dispensation of his providence or influence of his Spirit.

We are come now,

II. To show particularly that it is God's manner to make men sensible of their misery and unworthiness before he reveals his saving love and mercy to their souls. The mercy of God that he shows to a sinner when he brings him home to the Lord Jesus Christ is the greatest of all. 'Tis the most wonderful and most important mercy and love that [sinners] are ever the subject of. There are other things wherein God greatly expresses his mercy and goodness to men, many temporal favors. Those mercies that have been mentioned that God bestowed upon his people of old—his advancing of Joseph in Egypt, his deliverance of the children of Israel out of Egypt, his leading them through the Red Sea on dry feet, his bringing them into Canaan and driving out the heathen from before them, his delivering [them] from time to time from the hands of their enemies—they were great mercies; but they were not equal to this, of bringing his people from under the guilt and dominion of sin, and several of them were typical of it.

And as God would thus prepare men for the bestowment of these lesser mercies, by making of 'em sensible of their guilt and misery, so especially will he so do before he makes known to 'em this great love of his in Jesus Christ. When God has a design of mercy to a soul, 'tis his manner thus to begin with them; he first brings them to reflect upon themselves, and consider and be sensible what they are, and what a condition they are in.

What has been said already argues this. There is a harmony between God's dispensations; and as we see that this is God's manner of dealing with men when he gives them other great and remarkable mercies and manifestations of his favor, it is a confirmation that this is his method of proceeding with men's souls when about to reveal his mercy and love to them in Jesus Christ.

First. God makes men to consider and to be sensible what sin they are guilty of.

Before, it may be, they were very regardless of this. They went on sinning and never reflected upon what they did, never considered nor regarded what or how many sins they committed. They saw no cause why they should trouble their heads about it.

But when God convinces, he brings him to reflect upon himself. He sets his sins in order before his eyes, brings his old sins to his mind. They are fresh in his memory, things that he had almost forgotten. And many things that he used to look upon as light, that were not wont to be any burden to his conscience, that he did not think worthy to be taken notice, he now is made to reflect upon. And he sees what a multitude of transgressions he has been guilty of, which he has heaped up till they are grown to heaven. There are some sins especially that he has been guilty of [that] are ever before him. He can't get 'em out of his mind. Sometimes men's sins, when they are under conviction, do, as it were, follow 'em and haunt 'em like a specter.

God makes men sensible of the sin of their hearts, how corrupt and depraved their hearts [are]; and there are two ways that God doth this. One is by setting before 'em the sin of their lives. They are so set in order before 'em, they appear so many and so aggravated, that that convinces what a fountain of corruption there is in their hearts. Their sinful natures appear by their sinful lives. There is sin enough that every man has committed to convince him that his is like a viper, that he is sold under sin, that his heart is full of nothing but corruption, if God by his Spirit does lead him aright to consider it.

Another way that God sometimes makes use of is that he leaves men to such internal workings of corruption, under the temptation that they have in their terrors and fears of hell, that shows 'em what a corrupt and wicked heart they have. God sometimes brings this good out of this evil, to make men to see the corruption of their nature by the workings of it under the temptations they have in their terrors about damnation.

God leads them through the wilderness to prove them and let them know what is in their hearts, as he did the children of Israel, as we have already observed. By means of the trials that the children of Israel had in the wilderness, they might be made sensible what a murmuring, perverse, rebellious, unfaithful, and idolatrous people they were. So God sometimes makes sinners sensible what wicked hearts they have by their experience of the exercises of corruption while they are under convictions.

Not that this will in the least excuse men for allowing any such workings of corruptions in their hearts, because God sometimes leaves men to be wicked that he may afterwards turn it to their good, when he in infinite wisdom sees meet so to do. We must not go and be wicked on purpose, that we may get good by it. It will be very absurd and as well as horridly presumptuous for us so to do.

Though God sometimes in his sovereign mercy makes those workings of corruption and enmity against God a means of showing them the vileness of their own hearts and so to turn to their good, so also God oftentimes is provoked thereby utterly to withdraw and forsake them, after the example of those murmurers whose carcasses fell in the wilderness, of whom God swore in his wrath that they should never enter into his rest [Num. 14]. And those that allow themselves therein are the most likely so to provoke God.

But 'tis God's manner to show men the plague of their own hearts by some means or other before he reveals his redeeming love to their souls.

Sin, as it were, lies hid while sinners are unconvinced. They take no notice of it, but God makes the law effectual to bring man's own sins of heart and life to be reflected on and observed; Rom. 7:9, "I was alive without the law once: but when the commandment came, sin revived." Then sin appeared, came to light, which was not observed before. Joseph's revealing himself to his brethren is probably typical of Christ revealing himself to the soul of a sinner, a making known himself in his love and in his near relation of a brother and redeemer of his soul; but they, before Joseph revealed himself to 'em, were made to reflect upon themselves and say, "We are verily guilty" [Gen. 42:21].

Second. God convinces sinners of the dreadful danger they are in by reason of their sin. Having their sins themselves set before them, God makes 'em sensible of the relation that their sin has to misery. And here are two things that they are convinced of about their danger.

1. God makes 'em sensible that his displeasure is very dreadful. Before, they heard often about the anger of God and the fierceness of his wrath but they were not moved by it; but now they are made sensible that it is a dreadful thing to fall into the hands of the living God. They are made in some measure sensible of the dreadfulness of hell. They are led with fixedness and impression to think what a dismal thing it will be to have God an enraged enemy, setting himself to work the misery of a soul, and how dismal it will be to dwell in such torment forever without hope; Is. 33:14, "The sinners in Zion are afraid; fearfulness hath surprised the hypocrites. Who among us shall dwell with the devouring fire? who among us shall dwell with everlasting burnings?"

Other sinners are told of hell, but convinced sinners often have hell, as it were, in their view. They being impressed with a sense of the dreadfulness of its misery is the case why it works upon their imagination oftentimes, and it will seem as though they saw the dismal flames of hell. They saw God in implacable wrath executing his fury upon them, as though they heard the cries and shrieks of the damned.

2. They are made in some measure sensible of the connection there is between their sins and their will, or how their sin and guilt exposes them to that wrath which they have such a sense of the dreadfulness of. And so fears take hold of 'em. They are afraid that that will be their portion, and they are sensible that they are in a miserable and doleful condition by reason of sin.

There are many things in Scripture that make it evident that this is God's method. The account we have of our first parents confirms it [Gen. 3]. They had a sense of guilt and danger before Christ was revealed to them; they were guilty and were afraid of God's wrath and ran and hid themselves. They were terribly afraid when they heard God coming. And doubtless their sense of their guilt and fear, when they [were] brought before God and were called to an account, and God asked them what they had done and whether or not they had eaten of that tree whereof he commanded them that they should not eat, prepared 'em for a discovery of mercy.

God made them sensible of their guilt and danger before he revealed to 'em the covenant of grace. And 'tis probable that their reflecting upon what God had said about the seed of the woman's bruising the serpent's head soon wrought faith; that it was not long before that discovery, that God had made a merciful design towards them, was a means of true consolation and hope to them.

Joseph's brethren were brought into great distress for fear of their lives before Joseph reveals himself to 'em. Those that were converted by Peter's sermon, they were first "pricked in their heart," in a sense of their guilt and their danger (Acts 2:37). And Paul, before he had his first comfort, trembled and was astonished (Acts 9:6) and continued three days and three nights and neither ate nor drank, which expressed the distress that he was in (as v. 9). The jailer, before he was converted, he was in terror; Acts 16:29, "He called for a light, and sprang in, and came trembling, and fell down before Paul and Silas."

Christ's invitation is made more especially to the "weary and heavy laden" [Matt. 11:28], which doubtless has respect at least partly to the being laboring and being weary with a sense of guilt and danger. We read that when David was in the cave, then "every one that was in distress" was gathered unto him (I Sam. 22:2). This doubtless was written as typifying Jesus Christ and the resorting of those that were in fear and distress unto him. The expression of "flying for refuge," whereby coming to Christ is signified, implies that before they come they are in fear of some evil. They apprehend themselves in danger, which fear gives wings to their feet; Prov. 18:10, [a] "strong tower" [to] resort [to], as to a hiding place from the wind.

The voice of God to a sinner, when He gives him true comfort, is a still small voice. But this voice is preceded by a strong wind and a terrible earthquake and fire, like as it was in Horeb when Elijah was there; I Kgs. 19:11–12, "And, behold, the Lord passed by, and a great and strong wind rent the mountains, and break in pieces the rocks before the Lord; but the Lord was not in the wind: and after the wind an earthquake; but the Lord was not in the earthquake: and after the earthquake a fire; but the Lord was not in the fire: and after the fire a still small voice."

Another thing in Scripture that seems to evidence this is the frequent comparison made between the church's spiritually bringing forth Christ and a woman in travail, in pain to be delivered (John 16:21 and Rev. 12:2). The conversion of a sinner is represented by the same thing; 'tis a bringing forth Christ in the heart. Paul says he speaks of men's regeneration as of Christ being brought forth in them; Gal. 4:19, "My little children, of whom I travail in birth again until Christ be formed in you." And therefore Christ calls believers his mother; Matt. 12:49–50, "And he stretched forth his hand toward his disciples, and said, Behold my mother and my brethren! For whosoever shall do the will of my Father which is in heaven, the same is my brother, and sister, and mother."[2]

3. They are made sensible of the desert of their sin: that their sin deserves that wrath of God that their sin exposes them to.

They are not only sensible of the dreadfulness of God's wrath, how dreadful a thing it would be to fall into the hands of the living God, that it would be a dreadful thing to sustain the eternal expressions of his fierce wrath, and sensible of the connection between their sins and this wrath, or how their sins do expose 'em to it; but God also is wont, before he comforts them, to show them that their sins do deserve this wrath. By an approbation of the connection between their sin and God's wrath, they

2. JE here began a new illustration with the phrase "The very word gospel or glad tidings," but did not complete it. He ended the first preaching unit here, leaving the rest of the page blank. He began the next unit with a recapitulation of the text and doctrine, and mention of the major heads covered in the first unit.

are sensible of their danger of hell, which many are in a measure sensible of that ben't sensible of their desert of hell.

The threatenings of the law make them afraid, make them apprehend that [God] will punish their sins; and yet they have no thorough apprehension of their demerit of the punishment threatened and the effect. Many that are afraid do murmur against God; they charge him foolishly in their thoughts with being hard and cruel.

But 'tis God's manner, before he speaks peace to 'em [and] reveals his redeeming mercy and love in Jesus Christ, to make 'em sensible that they also deserve it; thus Matt. 18:24–26, "And when he had begun to reckon, one was brought unto him, which owed him ten thousand talents. But forasmuch as he had not to pay, his lord commanded him to be sold, and his wife, and children, and all that he had, and payment to be made. The servant therefore fell down, and worshipped him, saying, Lord, have patience with me, and I will pay thee all."

Very commonly when men first are made sensible of their dangers, their mouths are open against God and his dealings; that is, their hearts are full of murmurings. But 'tis God's manner, before he comforts and reveals his mercy and love to them, to stop their mouths and make 'em to own their guilt, and so to acknowledge their guilt as that they shall acknowledge their desert of the threatened punishment; Rom. 3:19–20, "Now we know that what things soever the law saith, it saith to them that are under the law: that every mouth may be stopped, and all the world may become guilty before God. Therefore by the deeds of the law there shall no flesh be justified in his sight: for by the law is the knowledge of sin."

God would convince men of their guilt before he reveals a pardon to 'em. Now, a man can't be said to be thoroughly sensible of his guilt till he is sensible of that he deserves hell. Man must be sensible that he is guilty of death or guilty of damnation, to use the Scriptures' manner of expression, before God will reveal to him his freedom from damnation.

A sense of guilt consists in two things, viz. in a sense of sin, and a sense of the relation that that sin has to punishment. Now, the relation that sin has to punishment is also twofold, viz. the connection it has with it whereby it exposes to punishment and brings it, and then, secondly, its desert of it. When a man is truly convinced of his desert of the punishment that his sin exposes him to, then may he be said to be thoroughly sensible of his guilt: that he is become guilty in the sense of our text and in the sense of Rom. 3:20.

Inq. How it is that a sinner is made sensible of his desert of God's wrath. A natural man may have a sense of this, [though] not a like sense that a person may have after conversion, because a natural man cannot have a true sight of sin and of the evil of it. A man cannot truly know the evil of sin as against God except it be by a discovery of the glory and excellency, and then he will be sensible how great an evil it is to sin against him.

And yet it cannot be denied that natural men are capable of a conviction of their desert of hell, and that a man's conscience may be convinced of it without a sight of God's glory. How else is it that wicked men's consciences will be convinced of the justice of their sentence and punishment at the day of judgment, as doubtless their consciences will echo to the sentence of the judge and will condemn them to the same punishment that the judge doth?

And therefore here we would inquire how it is that a natural man may be made sensible of this. We shall show, first, what is the principle assisted; second, how it is assisted; and, third, what are the principal outward means that are made use of in order to this.

(1) What principle in man is it that is assisted in convincing him of his desert of eternal punishment? For no new principle is infused; natural men have only natural principles, and therefore all that is done by the Spirit of God before regeneration is by assisting natural principles. Therefore, I answer to this inquiry:

Ans. That the principle that is assisted in making natural men sensible of their desert of wrath is natural conscience. Though man has lost a principle of love to God and all spiritual principles by the fall, yet natural conscience remains.

Now, there are three things that are the proper work of natural conscience:

1. To give man a sense of right and wrong. A natural man has no sense of the beauty and amiableness of virtue and the turpitude and odiousness of vice, but yet every man has that naturally within that testifies to him that some things are right and others wrong. Thus if a man steals or commits murder, there is something within that tells him that he has done wrong. He knows that he has not done well; Rom. 2:14–15, "For when the Gentiles, which have not the law, do by nature the things contained in the law, these, having not the law, are a law unto themselves: which show the work of the law written in their hearts, their conscience also bearing witness, and their thoughts the meanwhile accusing or else excusing one another."

2. To testify wherein right or wrong is to be ascribed to himself.

3. And then the other work of natural conscience is to suggest the relation there is between right or wrong and a retribution. Man has that in him that suggests to him, when he has done ill, a relation between that ill and punishment. If a man has done that which his conscience tells him is wrong, is unjust, his conscience tells him that he deserves to be punished for it. Thus natural conscience has a threefold power: a teaching, an accusing, and a condemning power.

The Spirit of God, therefore, assists natural conscience the more thoroughly to do its work and so convinces them of sin. Conscience naturally suggests to a man when he has done a known evil that he deserves punishment, and by being assisted to its work thoroughly a man is convinced that he deserves eternal punishment.

Though natural conscience does remain in man since the fall, yet it greatly needs assistance in order to the doing its work; it is greatly hindered in its doing its work by sin. Everything in man that is part of his perfection is hindered and impaired by sin. A faculty of reason remains since the fall, but it is greatly impaired and blinded. So natural conscience remains, but yet sin in a great degree stupefies it. It greatly clogs and hinders it in doing its work.

Now God, when he convinces a sinner, he assists it against the stupefaction of sin and helps it to do its work more freely and fully. The Spirit of God works immediately upon men's consciences in conviction. Their consciences are awakened. They are convinced in their consciences; their consciences smite 'em and condemn 'em.

(2) It may be inquired how it is that God assists natural conscience so as to convince of a desert of hell. I answer,

1. In the general, it is by light. The whole work of God is carried on in the heart of man from his first convictions to his conversion by light; 'tis by discoveries that are made to his soul. But, then, by what light is it that a sinner is made sensible that he deserves God's wrath? It is some discovery that he has that makes him sensible of the heinousness of disobeying and casting contempt upon God.

The light that gives evangelical humiliation and that makes men sensible of the hateful and odious nature of sin is a discovery of God's glory and excellency and grace. But what is it that a natural man sees of God that makes him sensible that sin against Him deserves His wrath, for they see nothing of God's lovely glory and grace? I answer,

2. Particularly, it seems to be a discovery of God's awful and terrible greatness. Natural men can't see anything of God's loveliness, his amiable and glorious grace, or anything in God that should attract their love; but they may see his terrible greatness to excite their terror.

Wicked men in another world, though they don't see his loveliness and grace of God, yet they see his awful greatness, and that makes 'em sensible of the heinousness of sin. The damned in hell, they are sensible of the heinousness of their sin. Their consciences declare it to 'em, and they are made sensible of it by this means by what they see: the awful greatness of that Being whom they have sinned against.

And wicked men in this world are capable of being made sensible of the heinousness of sin the same way. If a wicked soul is capable while wicked of receiving the discoveries of God's terrible majesty in another world, 'tis capable of it in this. God may, if he pleases, make 'em sensible of the same thing here.

And this way, natural men may be so made sensible of the heinousness of sin as to be convinced that they deserve hell, as is evident in that 'tis by this very means that wicked men will be made sensible of the justice of their punishment in another world and at the day of judgment. For then the wicked will see so much of the awful greatness of God the Judge that will convince their consciences what a heinous thing it was in them to disobey and contemn such a God, and will convince 'em that they therefore deserve his wrath, which shows that wicked men are capable of being convinced the same way. A wicked man, while a wicked man, is capable of hearing the thunders and seeing the devouring fire of Mt. Sinai; that is, he is capable of being made sensible of that terrible majesty and greatness of God that was discovered at the giving of the Law.

But this brings me to the third thing, viz. the principal outward means that the Spirit of God makes use of in this work of convincing men of their desert of hell.

3. And that is the law. The Spirit of God in all his work upon the souls of men works by his Word, and in this whole work of conviction of sin, that part of the Word is principally made use of, viz. the law.

'Tis the law that makes men sensible of their sin, and 'tis the law attended with its awful threatenings and curses that gives a sense of the awful greatness, the authority, the power, the jealousy of God. Wicked men are made sensible of the tremendous greatness of God, as it were, in the same manner that the children of Israel were, viz. by the thunders and earthquakes, and devouring fire, and sound of the trumpet, and terrible voice at Mt. Sinai; "All the people that was in the camp trembled" [Ex. 19:16]; and they said, "Let not God speak with us, lest we die" [Ex. 20:19].

So that 'tis the law that God makes use of in assisting natural conscience to do its work; Gal. 3:24, "wherefore the law was our schoolmaster to bring us to Christ." 'Tis the law God makes use of to make men sensible of their guilt and to stop their mouths; Rom. 3:19, "Now we know that whatsoever things the law saith, it saith to them that are under the law: that every mouth may be stopped, and all the world may become guilty before God." 'Tis the law that kills men as to trusting in their own righteousness; "For I was alive without the law once: but when the commandment came, sin revived and I died" [Rom. 7:9]; and Gal. 2:19, "For I through the law am dead to the law."

Conviction that precedes conversion is of sin and misery; but men are not thoroughly sensible of their sin or guilt till they are sensible they deserve hell, nor thoroughly sensible of their misery till they are sensible they are helpless.

4. And last, 'tis God's manner to make men sensible of their helplessness in their own strength. 'Tis usual with sinners when they are first made sensible of their danger of hell to go to work to try their own strength, hoping to help themselves; they in some measure see their danger, and they go about to work deliverance for themselves. They are striving to make themselves better.

They either strive to convert themselves. They strive to work their own hearts into a believing frame and are endeavoring, as it were, to force a trust in Christ. They have heard that if ever they believe, they must put their trust in Christ and in him alone for salvation. And they think they will trust in Christ; they will cast their souls upon him. And so they endeavor to do it in their own strength. This is very common with persons upon a sick bed. And when they are afraid that they shall die and go to hell, and are told that they must put their trust in Christ alone for salvation, they go about to do it in their own strength. So sinners will be striving without a sense of their insufficiency in themselves to bring their own hearts to love God and to choose him for their portions and to repent of their sins.

Or they strive to make themselves better that so God may be more willing to convert them and give them his grace, and enable them to believe in Christ and love God and repent of their sins.

But before God appears to 'em as their help and deliverer, 'tis his manner to make them sensible that they are utterly helpless in themselves; they are brought to despair of help from themselves. There is a death to all their hopes from themselves (Rom. 7:9).

Before God opens the prison doors, he makes 'em see that they are shut up, that they are closed prisoners, and that there is no way that they can get out. Christ tells us he was sent "to bind up the brokenhearted and proclaim liberty to captives, and the opening of the prison to them that are bound" (Luke 4:18). Christ was sent to open the prison to them that are not only really but sensibly bound; Gal. 3:23, "But before faith came, we were kept under the law, shut up unto the faith that should afterwards be revealed." God makes men sensible that they are in a forlorn condition, that they [are] wretched and miserable, before he comforts [them].

He makes 'em sensible that they are blind. Christ tells us, "For judgment I am come into the world, that they which see not might see; and that they which see might be made blind" (John 9:39), meaning partly at least by "those that see," those that think they see, having respect to the Pharisees, that were proud of their knowledge, and by the blind, those that are sensibly blind. This is emblematically represented by Paul's blindness before his first comfort. He was blind till Ananias came to him to open his eyes [Acts 9:17–18], probably designed to intimate to us that before God opens the eyes of men in conversion, he makes 'em sensibly blind.

God brings men to this despair in their own strength these ways:

a. God oftentimes makes use of men's own experience to convince that they are helpless in themselves. When they first set out in seeking salvation, it may be they thought it an easy thing to be converted. They thought they should presently bring themselves to repent of their sins and believe in Christ, and accordingly they strove in their own strength with hopes of success; but they were disappointed.

And so God suffers 'em to go on striving to open their own eyes and mend their own hearts, but they find no success. They have been striving to see this [a] long time, and they are as blind as ever. They can see nothing at all; it is all Egyptian darkness for all.

They have been striving to make themselves better, but they are as hard as ever. They have often strove to do something that is good, to be in the exercise of good affections that shall be acceptable to God, but they have no success. And it seems to them that instead of growing better they grow worse and worse; their hearts are fuller of wicked thoughts than they were at first. They see no more likelihood of their conversion than there was at first.

So God suffers 'em to strive in their own strength till they give out, till they come to despair of helping themselves. The prodigal son, he first strove to fill his belly with the husks which the swine did eat, but when he despaired of being helped that way, then he came to himself and entertained thoughts of returning to his father's house (Luke 15:16–17). Or,

b. God sometimes by a particular assistance of the understanding makes men to see so much of their own hearts as at once makes 'em despair of helping. God oftentimes convinces men by their own trials; he lets 'em try a long while till they are discouraged. But God can convince men without, if he pleases, and sometimes does, as it must be, in many speedy conversions that there are many instances of.

God assists men so to see their hearts that they see they are so remote from any love to God and from faith or any gracious exercise, so remote from spiritual light, that they despair of ever bringing themselves to it. They see they are blind; they see 'tis all darkness in their souls, as darkness itself and the shadow of death. And they see it is too big a thing for them to do to cause light. They see they are dead, dead to anything that is good, and therefore they despair of bringing themselves to the performance of gracious acts.

Thus we have shown that it is God's ordinary manner, before [he] reveals his redeeming mercy to men's souls, to make 'em sensible of their sinfulness and danger and desert of God's wrath and helplessness in themselves. This we have shown to be most agreeable to the holy Scriptures and agreeable and harmonious with God's methods of dealing with mankind in other things. And we have shown in an imperfect manner how and by what means is it that God thus convinces men.

This work is what Christ speaks of as one part of the work of the Holy Ghost; John 16:8, "When the Comforter is come, he will convince the world of sin, and of righteousness, and of judgment." 'Tis God's manner to convince men of sin before he convinces them of righteousness.[3]

III. Reasons.

The congruity of such a method of proceeding is very obvious. How very agreeable to divine wisdom does it seem, that the sinful soul should be brought to such a conviction of danger and misery as to see that it can't help itself by any strength or contrivance of its own, and that it is utterly unworthy of God's help and deserving of his wrath, and that they should be brought to an acknowledgment of the sovereignty of God, that he may do with him as he pleases: to own that it would be just with God so to do before he appears in his pardoning, redeeming mercy and love, and as his helper and friend.

A man that is converted is in two exceeding different states: first, a very miserable, wretched state, a state of condemnation, and then, in a blessed condition, a state of justification. Now, how agreeable does it seem to divine wisdom that men should be so sensibly first in a miserable,

3. For JE's sermon on John 16:8, see *The Threefold Work of the Holy Ghost*, in *Works*, *14*, 371–436. Here ends the second preaching unit; JE cites the text at the start of the third unit.

condemned state and then in a happy one, as he is really first guilty under an obligation and desert of hell before he is really pardoned and admitted to God's favor, so that he should be first sensibly guilty, and under obligation and desert of hell, before he is sensibly the object of pardoning and redeeming mercy and grace. But the congruity and wisdom of this God's manner of dealing with men's souls will appear perhaps better by considering the following reasons:

First. 'Tis the will of God that the discoveries of his terrible majesty, and awful holiness, and justice, should accompany the discoveries of his grace and love, and that he would glorify himself and make discoveries of himself as he is, and give to his creatures worthy and just apprehensions of himself.

'Tis the glory of God that those attributes are united in the divine nature, that as he is a Being of infinite mercy and love and grace, so he is a Being of infinite and tremendous majesty, and awful holiness and justice. These attributes being thus united in the divine nature and not interfering one with another is what is a great part of their glory: God's awful and terrible attributes, and his mild and gentle attributes. They reflect glory one on the other; and 'tis the glory of God that those attributes should always be exercised and expressed in a consistence and harmony one with the other.

If there were the mild and gentle attributes without the other, it would be no part of the glory of God. If there was love and mercy and grace in an inconsistence with God's sacred authority, and justice, and infinite hatred of sin, it would be no glory. If God's love and grace did not agree with his justice, and jealousy, and the honor of his majesty, his love and mercy would be so far from being an honor that it [would] be a dishonor to God.

Therefore, as God designs to glorify himself when he makes discoveries of the one, he will also make discoveries of the other. When he makes discoveries of his love and grace, it shall appear that they do harmonize with those other attributes. Otherwise, God's true glory would not be discovered.

If men were sensible of the love of God without a sense of those other attributes, they would be exposed to have improper and unworthy apprehensions of God, as though he were gracious to sinners and rebels in such a manner as did not become a Being of infinite majesty and infinite hatred of sin. And as it would expose to unworthy apprehensions of God, so it would expose the soul in some respects to behave unsuitably towards God. There will not be a due reverence with love and joy. Such discoveries of love without answerable discoveries of awful greatness will dispose the soul to come with an undue boldness to God.

The very nature and design of the gospel shows that this is the will of God, that those that have the discoveries of his love should also have the discoveries of those others. For this was the very end of Christ laying down his life and coming into the world: to render the glory of God's authority, holiness, and justice consistent with this grace of his in pardoning and justifying sinners; that while God thus manifested his mercy, we might not conceive any unworthy thoughts of God with respect to those other attributes.

Seeing, therefore, that this is the very end of Christ's coming into the world, we may conclude that those that are actually redeemed by Christ and have a true discovery of Christ made to their souls, they have a discovery of God's terribleness and justice to prepare them for the discoveries of his love and mercy.

God of old, before the death and suffering of Christ were so fully revealed, was evermore careful that the discoveries of both should be together, so that men might not apprehend God's mercy in pardoning sin and receiving sinners to the disparagement of his justice and terribleness. So when God proclaimed his name to Moses in answer to his desire that he might see God's glory, he proclaims his mercy; Ex. 34:6–7, "The Lord, the Lord God, great and merciful, longsuffering, and abundant in goodness and truth, keeping mercy for thousands, forgiving iniquity and transgression and sin." But he don't stop here, but also proclaims his holy justice and vengeance: "And that will by no means clear the guilty; visiting the iniquity of the fathers upon the children, and upon the children's children unto the third and fourth generation."

And so they are joined together again in the fourth commandment: "For I the Lord thy God am a jealous God, visiting the iniquity of the fathers upon the children unto the third and the fourth generation of them that hate me" [Ex. 20:5]. So in many other places we shall find 'em joined together, too many to be now mentioned. When God was about to speak to Elijah when he was in Horeb, he was first prepared for such a familiar conversing with God by awful manifestations of God's majesty. First there was a wind that rent the rocks and then an earthquake, and then a devouring fire (I Kgs. 19:11–12).

God is careful, even in heaven, where the discoveries of his love and grace are given in such an exalted degree, also to provide means for a proportionable sense of his terribleness, and the dreadfulness of his displeasure, by their beholding of it in the miseries and torments of the damned at the same time that they enjoy his love. And even the man Christ Jesus was first made sensible of the wrath of God before his exaltation to that transcendent height of enjoyment of the Father's love.

And this is one reason that God gives sinners a sense of his wrath against their sins, and of his justice, before he gives them the discoveries of his redeeming love.

Second. Unless a man be thus convinced of his sin and misery before God makes him sensible of his redeeming love and mercy, he can't be sensible of that love and mercy as it is, viz. free and sovereign.

When God reveals his redeeming grace to men and makes them truly sensible of it, he would make them sensible of it as it is. God's grace and love towards sinners is in itself very wonderful; as it is very great, it redeems from dreadful wrath. But men can't be sensible of this till they have something of a sense how dreadful God's wrath is.

God's redeeming grace and love in Christ is free and sovereign, as it is altogether without any worthiness in those that are the objects of it. But this men can't be sensible of till they are sensible of their own unworthiness.

The grace of God in Christ is glorious and wonderful, as it not only is without worthiness in the object but as the objects of it are so worthy of the contrary. They have deserved eternal death; they have deserved the everlasting wrath and displeasure of God. But this they can't be sensible of till they are made sensible that they have deserved God's eternal wrath.

The grace of God in Christ is wonderful, that it saves and redeems from so many and great sins and from the punishment they have deserved. But this they can't be sensible of till they are in some measure sensible of their sinfulness and brought to reflect upon the sin of their lives and to see the wickedness of their hearts.

'Tis the glory [of] God's grace in Christ that is so free and sovereign. And doubtless 'tis the will of God that when he reveals his grace to the soul, that it should be seen in its proper glory, though not perfectly. When men see God's grace aright, they see it with that glory of it being wonderful, free, and unmerited, and contrary to the demerit of our sins.

All that have a spiritual understanding of the grace of God in Christ have an understanding of the glory of that grace, but the glory of the grace consists mainly in its being bestowed after so exceeding miserable, extreme, necessitous conditions. So it conduces to the sensibleness of this glory that the man be first sensible of his misery and then sensible of mercy.

The heart of man is not prepared to receive the mercy of God in Christ as free and unmerited till he is sensible of his own demerits. Indeed, the soul is not capable of receiving a revelation or discovery of the redeeming grace of God in Christ, or redeeming grace, without being convinced of sin and misery. He must see his sin and misery before he can see the grace of God in redeeming of him from that sin and misery.

Third. Till the soul be convinced of sin and misery, 'tis not prepared to receive the redeeming mercy and grace of God as through a mediator.

Because the soul don't see its need of a mediator till it sees its sin and misery, if there was any such thing as absolute and immediate mercy of God to sinners bestowed without any satisfaction or purchase, the soul might possibly see that without a conviction of sin and misery; but there is no such thing. All God's mercy to sinners is through a savior: the redeeming mercy and grace of God is mercy and grace in Christ.

And when God discovers his mercy to a soul, he will discover it, as mercy, as a savior. And 'tis his will that the mercy should be received as, in, and through a savior, with a sensibleness of its being through his righteous satisfaction.

'Tis the will of God that as all the spiritual comforts his people receive are in and through Christ, so they should be sensible that they receive 'em through Christ, and could receive 'em no other way. 'Tis the will of God that his people should have their eyes to Christ and should depend upon him for mercy and favor, that whenever they receive comforts through his purchase that they should receive as from him.

And that because God would glorify his Son as mediator, as the glory of man's salvation belongs to Christ, so 'tis the will of God that all the people of Christ, all that are saved by him, should receive their salvation as of him, and should attribute the glory of it to him, and that none that won't give the glory of salvation to Christ should have the benefit of it.

Upon that account God insists upon it, and it is absolutely necessary that a soul's conviction of sin and misery, and helplessness, in and of itself should precede or accompany the revelation of the redeeming love and grace of God. I shall also mention two other ends that hereby are obtained.

Fourth. By this means the redeeming mercy and love of God is more highly prized and rejoiced in when discovered.

By the previous discoveries of danger, misery, and helplessness, and desert of wrath, the heart is prepared to embrace a discovery of mercy. When the poor soul stands trembling at the brink of the pit and despairs of any help from itself, it is prepared joyfully to receive tidings of deliverance. If God is pleased at such a time to make a soul to hear his still voice, his call to himself and to a savior, the soul is prepared to give joyful entertainment to it. The gospel, then, if it be heard spiritually, it will be glad tidings indeed. It will be the joyfulest sound that ever he heard.

The love of God and Jesus Christ to the world, and to him in particular, will be admired, and Christ will be most precious. He'll remember what danger he was in, what fears surrounded him; and to answer all his wants, it will cause the greater exultation of soul. God, in the method of his dealing with the souls of his elect, consults their happiness as well as his own glory, and it tends to their happiness for 'em to be first made sensible of their misery and unworthiness before God comforts them. For their comfort, when they receive it, is so much the sweeter.

Fifth. The heart is prepared and disposed to praise God for it. This follows from the reasons that have been already mentioned, viz. as they hereby have been made sensible how free and sovereign the mercy of God is to 'em that he manifests to their souls. And as they are made sensible how great the grace of God is in saving of 'em, and as they more highly prize the mercy and love of God made known to them, it will dispose them to magnify the name of God, to exalt the love of God the Father in giving his Son to them, and to exalt Jesus Christ by their praises, who laid down his life for them to redeem them from all iniquity.

They are ready to say, "O, how miserable should I have been had not God had pity upon me and provided me a savior! What a miserable a condition should I have been in had not Christ have loved me and given himself for me! I must have endured that dreadful wrath of God. I must have suffered the punishment that I had deserved by all that great sin and wickedness I have been guilty of."

APPLICATION.

Use I. In a word at this time to unawakened sinners. If it be so {that 'tis God's manner to make men sensible of their misery and unworthiness before he appears in his mercy and love}, then be exhorted to seek those convictions.

Though you are at present secure in your sins and have no terrifying sense of your danger of hell, yet I presume to say, concerning most of you at least, that you don't intend to go to hell when you happen to think about another world; you flatter yourself that some way or other you shall escape eternal misery, or at least you don't think of it with a willingness to be damned.

But if it be that you do not suffer eternal damnation, you have a great work to do before you die. It ordinarily is a very difficult work, especially to those that have gone on for a considerable time in ways of wickedness under means of grace. If ever you are truly comforted, you must be convinced of your misery and unworthiness. You must be guilty in your own sense. Therefore, set about your work and seek to be made sensible of your misery and unworthiness. And make haste and set about this work speedily. You may defer this work so long that it will be too late. [It] may be too late if you delay these two ways:

It may be too [late], as you may be overtaken with death before you set about it, as thousands and millions have been before you. And if you should not die before you begin, yet it may be too late, as you may never have opportunity to get through. Some persons are a long time under convictions before they are converted. There are some that God suffers to continue long while seeking salvation in their own strength before he makes them to despair of help from themselves. They continue many years, trusting in their own righteousness, as it were, wandering from mountain to hill, from one hold to another, seeking rest and safety. They are a long while a-building castles in the air. They sometimes flatter themselves from one consideration and sometimes from another. And if you should delay, there is danger that you may not have time. Some are many years under fears of damnation and are seeking salvation, and there are many that death is too quick for.

Here we will briefly consider what are the occasions of the stupidity and senselessness of sinners, and thence shall take occasion to direct those that would seek the convictions of God's Spirit.

First.[4] Natural stupidity, [the] general occasion.

Some provoke God to withhold the strivings and convincing influences of his Spirit. Some provoke God to give 'em up to hardness of heart. God lets 'em alone and intends to let 'em alone; Hos. 4:17, "Ephraim is joined to idols: let him alone"; Ps. 81:11–12, "But my people would not hearken to my voice; and Israel would none of me. So I leave 'em up to their own hearts' lust: and they walked in their own counsels."

[Some provoke God] especially by sins against great light; [they use] great means against strivings of the Spirit. [They commit] apostasy.

4. As JE neared the end of this preaching unit, he merely sketched the first through fifth occasions of the senselessness of sinners and briefly mentioned several subjects for consideration. Blank lines after each division may indicate his intention to expand on these points extemporaneously or in writing at another time. Bracketed phrases through the end of the first use, then, are editorial interpolations.

Therefore, be directed to take heed you don't provoke God. If some have been convinced and converted that have done as bad, that is no argument that God won't give you up; for God is sovereign in such things.

Second. Sensuality. Lusts of the flesh tend to harden and stupefy. If any lust [is] dear,[5] you must cut [it] off.

Third. A having the heart overcharged with the cares of this life (Luke 21:34).

Fourth. A keeping at a distance from God.

Fifth. Inconsiderateness.

Therefore, often consider [the occasions of your stupidity and senselessness]. Be often considering the dreadfulness of hell, of being there to eternity, upon all occasions. [Be often considering the] shortness and uncertainty of life.

Men have a degree of power over their own thoughts. Improve tender seasons to dwell upon such thoughts. Consider your sins.[6]

Use II. To exhort those that have some conviction of sin and danger, that they don't lose them.

If you have the strivings of God's Spirit [and] God has met with you, made you to reflect upon your sins and sensible that you are in danger of hell, and so made you concerned about your soul and put you upon seeking for salvation, take heed you don't lose your convictions and grow senseless of eternal things and negligent of your soul's concern, that you don't return to your former careless way of living, that you don't return to your former sins. Here consider,

First. That there is danger of it. It is not everyone that is under concern for their souls, and that by the strivings of God's Spirit is put upon seeking and striving for salvation, that holds out. There are many more that set out at the beginning of the race that don't hold out to the end. There are many things intervene between the beginning and the end of the race that divert and stop and turn back many that set out well. Many that seem to [be] under strong convictions and to be very earnest in seeking, yet their convictions are but short-lived; and some that seem to be much concerned about salvation for a considerable time, it may be for years together, yet by degrees grow careless and negligent.

There is much in your own heart that tends to stupefy you. 'Tis the natural tendency of sin and lust to stupefy the conscience, and as corrup-

5. MS: "if any dear lust."

6. Here ends the third preaching unit; several blank lines follow. The final unit begins with a recapitulation of the text and doctrine.

tion is reigning as yet in your heart, it will ever be ready to exert itself in such as will have a great tendency to drive away your convictions. And Satan is doubtless diligently watching over you, striving all ways to abate and to take off your convictions. He joins in with the sloth and lusts of your heart to persuade to negligence and to turn your mind to other things.

And the world is full of objects that take off your minds from soul concerns and are constantly, as it were, endeavoring to take possession of your minds and to drive out the concerns of another world.

Second. Consider, if you lose your convictions it will be no advantage to you that ever you had 'em as to any furtherance of your salvation. Whatever terrors you have been under about damnation, whatever reflections upon your sins you have been brought to, whatever strong desires you have had after deliverance, and whatever earnest prayers you have made, it will all be lost. What you have suffered of fear and concern will turn to no good account; and what you have done, the pains you have taken, will be utterly lost.

When you have strove against sin and labored in duty, have stemmed the stream, and have got a considerable way up the hill, and made some progress towards the kingdom of heaven, when once you have lost your convictions, you will be as far off from salvation as you was before you began. You'll lose all the ground you have gained; you'll go quite down to the bottom of the hill; the stream will immediately carry you back. All will be lost; you had as good never have had those convictions as to have had 'em and then to lose 'em.

Third. You don't know that ever you shall have such an opportunity again. God is now striving with you by his Spirit; if you should lose the strivings of his Spirit, it may be that God's Spirit never would return again.

If you are under convictions, you have a precious opportunity, which if you knew the worth of it, you would esteem it as better than any temporal advantages. You have a price in your hands to get wisdom that is more valuable than gold or silver. It is [a] great privilege to live under the means of grace, to enjoy the word and ordinances of God, and to know the way of salvation. It is a greater advantage still to live under a powerful dispensation of the means of grace under a very instructive, convincing ministry. But 'tis a much greater privilege still to be the subject of the convincing influences of the Spirit of God. If you have those, you have a precious advantage in your hands, and if you should lose it, 'tis questionable whether ever you will have the like advantage again.

We are counseled to "seek the Lord while he may be found" and to "call upon him while he is near" (Is. 55:6). A time wherein God's Spirit is striving with a man by convictions of his sin and danger is especially such a time that is a sinner's best opportunity. 'Tis especially a day of salvation. God may [be] said to be near when [he] pours out his Spirit upon many in the place where a person dwells. [It] is prudence for all, then, to be calling upon God as being near at such time; but especially is God near at a time when he is giving his Spirit in immediately convincing and awakening a man's own soul.

If God's Spirit, therefore, is now at work with you, you have a precious opportunity. Take heed you don't by any means let it slip. It may doubtless be said concerning a great many that they have missed their opportunity. Most men that live under the gospel have a special opportunity; there is a certain season that God appoints for 'em that is above all others a day of grace with them, when men have a very fair opportunity for the securing eternal salvation, if they did but know it and had a heart to it. But the misery of man is great upon him, for man knoweth not his time, the wise man tells us; Eccles. 8:6–7, "That to every purpose there is time and judgment, therefore the misery of man is great upon him. For he knoweth not that which shall be"; and again, 9:12, "Man knoweth not his time."

If the Spirit of God is now striving with [you], now, it may be, 'tis your time, and it may be your only time. Be wise, therefore, and understand the things that belong to your peace before they are hid from your eyes. You han't the influences of the Spirit of God in your own power. You can't have convictions and awakenings when you please; God is sovereign as to the bestowment of them. If you are ready to flatter yourself, that although you neglect now when you are young, yet you shall be awakened again, that is but a vain and groundless presumption.

It is a difficult thing for a man that has been going on in sinful course to reform. There are a great many difficulties in the way of thorough reformation. If you therefore have reformed and return again to your former sin, you will [have] all those difficulties to overcome again.

Fourth. If you lose your convictions and return again to a way of allowed sinning, there will be less likelihood of your salvation than there was before ever you had any convictions. Backsliding is a very dangerous and pernicious kind of thing to men's souls, and is often spoken of as such in God's Word, which was signified in that awful dispensation of God in turning Lot's wife into a pillar of salt [Gen. 19:26] to be a standing emblem of the dangerousness of looking back after one has set out in a way of religion.

Those that lose their convictions, the ill that they are subject to is not merely the loss of their convictions. Their convictions not only ben't a means of any good to 'em, but they turn to a great deal of ill. It would have been better for 'em that they never had had 'em, for they are now set remoter from salvation than they were before: for, having risen some considerable way towards heaven and falling back, they sink lower and further down towards hell than ever they were. The way to heaven is now blocked up with greater difficulties than ever it was.

Their hearts now are become harder for light, and convictions having once conquered, they evermore are an occasion of a greater hardness of heart than there was before. Yea, there is no one thing whatsoever that has so great a tendency to it. Man's heart is hardened by losing convictions, as iron is hardened being heated and quenched. If you are awakened and afterwards lose your convictions, it will be a harder thing to awaken you again.

If [it] were only that you are growing older, there would be less likelihood of your being awakened again, for as persons grow older they grow less and less susceptive of convictions. Evil habits grow stronger and more deeply rooted in the heart.

You greatly offend God by quenching of his Spirit and returning as a dog to his vomit and as a sow that was washed to be wallowing in the mire. And there is danger that God will say, concerning you, as he did concerning Jerusalem; Ezek. 24:13, "because I have purged thee, and thou wast not purged, thou shalt not be purged from thy filthiness any more, till I cause my fury to rest upon thee." If you return again to your wicked course, if you should go to hell, at last you will lament it that ever you have had any convictions. You will find your punishment so much the heavier.

And if you should hereafter be awakened and set about striving for salvation, yet you will probably find harder work on't. You do but make work for yourself by your backsliding. You won't only have all to do over again that you have done, and what you would have had to have done if you had gone on, but there will be new work for repentance. There probably must be greater and more dreadful terrors and, it may be, a much longer time spent in seeking and striving, [a] more difficult work with your own headstrong corruptions.

If you were but sensible of one half of the disadvantages of backsliding and the many woes and calamities it will involve you in, you would be careful not to lose your convictions.

Fifth. Consider the encouragement there is in Scripture, to hold on in a way of seeking conversion; Hos. 6:3, "Then shall we know, if we follow on to know the Lord." Thence we may gather that God usually gives success to those that diligently and constantly and perseveringly seek conversion.

And that you be the better directed in taking care not to lose your convictions, 'tis convenient that you should be aware of those things that are common occasions of persons losing their convictions. I shall, therefore, briefly mention some of them.

1. Persons' falling into sin [are] very often the occasion of their losing their convictions; some temptation prevails so that they are drawn into some sin. Some lust upon some occasion has been stirred up and they have been overcome by their sinful appetites and have provoked God to anger and so have quenched the Spirit. It may be they have been drawn into some criminal act of sensuality, or they are got into some quarrel with some person, or their spirits are raised and heated with malice and revenge and they have acted sinfully, or have sinfully expressed themselves and have driven away the Spirit of God, or by quarreling with God. These are the most ready ways to put an end to convictions.

2. Sometimes there happens some diverting occasion; there is some incident that for the present diverts their minds. Their minds are taken off from their business for a little while. They are drawn into company. It may be they see something that revives a desire of worldly enjoyments and entertainments, or they are engaged in some exercise of business and gives their minds a turn that way. And so afterwards they are more careless than they were before. They ben't so strict in attending private duties, and carelessness and stupidity by degrees steals upon them till they wholly lose their convictions.

3. Some change in their circumstances takes off their minds from the concerns of their souls. Their minds are diverted by the new circumstances they are attended with, or are taken up with new pleasures and enjoyments or with new cares and business that they are involved in.

It may be they grow richer. They prosper in the world and their worldly good things crowd in and take possession of their minds. Or worldly cares are increased upon them and they have so many things to look after that their minds are taken up and they han't time to look after their souls.[7]

4. Some grow discouraged.

5. Some lose their convictions by taking up a false hope. [They have] revealed some affections they call grace, have shed tears about their sins,

7. Here through the end of the second use, JE left several blank spaces after each sentence or phrase, possibly indicating his intention to expand on these points at a later time.

have had comfortable places of Scripture come to 'em, [and have had] some powerful imaginations they call saving discoveries.

Use III. To exhort those that are under convictions, to seek earnestly that their convictions may be thorough: that is, that you be brought to see your helplessness and that you deserve God's eternal wrath. Men are not thoroughly sensible of their misery till they see they are helpless, nor of their guilt.

The way to obtain the end of your convictions, that is, to have God appearing and manifesting himself to you in his redeeming love in Christ, is to have your convictions become thorough. When your convictions are thorough, then are you prepared for a sight of Christ as your redeemer.

Don't rest, therefore, till you have obtained thorough convictions or till you are sensible of your helplessness and your deserving of eternal misery, and that it would be just with God to inflict it upon you. And here, in order to this,

First Dir. Endeavor to be more sensible of your danger. Labor to be more sensible of the fearfulness of God's eternal wrath and of your great exposedness to it.

A great reason very many persons are so long under convictions, [and] they seem to be considerably concerned about another world and yet don't get through the work, is because their convictions are so slight. They never were made to bear the thunders of Mt. Sinai so as to give 'em a sufficient sense of the terrible anger of God; they want[8] to be more terrified with the apprehensions of God's wrath.

A seeing more of the terrible anger and jealousy of God would have a tendency to make you more thoroughly sensible of your guilt, and to bring you to own that you justly deserve to be damned. And it would have a tendency to impress upon your mind a sense of the awful greatness of God, and so make you sensible what dreadful presumption you have been guilty [of] in so disobeying of God as you have done, and what a horrid and heinous a thing it has been in you that you have so opposed and contemned God.

The anger of God as 'tis discovered by his law, it shows God's hatred of sin. It shows God's sacred authority and terrible majesty. When, therefore, the law is improved by God's Spirit and is set home upon the heart to make men sensible of God's fearful anger, it has a tendency to bring men to a sight of the heinousness of their sins and so of their desert of hell.

8. I.e. "they need."

And then, more of a sense of the dreadfulness of God's anger against your sins would have a tendency to bring you to see that God might justly cast you into hell another way, viz. as it would cause you to reflect more upon your sins. If you were more thoroughly sensible of the dreadfulness of God's displeasure against sin, it would make you think more of your sins than you do now. It would make you take notice of sins that are ready to escape your notice now; it would make you think more of your former sins. You could not help think of your sins if you was sensible how dreadful God's revenging wrath was. Your mind would dwell more intensely upon the aggravations of your sin. Your sins would be ever before you. You would often be thinking how you offended God at such a time and such a time, what convictions of conscience you went against. You would have all the aggravating circumstances come into your mind.

It would make you take more notice of the wickedness of your own heart. Your wicked thoughts and workings of heart would not pass through without your observation, and so you would be the sooner brought to know your own heart.

And the more sensible you are of your own wickedness of heart and life, the sooner will you see that God might justly cast you into hell. But this brings me to [the]

Second Dir. Labor to see your own wickedness. And to that end, be very much in self-reflections and confessions. As you have power in measure over your own thought, turn your thoughts often upon your own sins. And be very particular in setting your own sins in order before your own eyes. And be very particular and frequent in confessing them to God.

Keep a catalogue of your sins in your mind and be often reading of it and often spreading of it before God, for 'tis the greatness of your guilt that you want to be sensible of. And in order to [do] this, 'tis of necessity that you have your sins in your view.

Third Dir. That you may have thorough convictions, be directed very earnestly to strive in a way of religion. This is the direction Christ gives you; Luke 13:24, "Strive to enter in at the strait gate." Strive more earnestly in prayer to God. Strive more earnestly against your corruptions and resisting your sloth and all temptations. This will have a tendency to bring you to thorough convictions.

The more earnestly you strive the sooner will you be like to be convinced of your own helplessness. You will not find how little your strength is till you are brought to use your utmost strength or to lay out your strength to the utmost.

By earnestly striving against your corruptions, you'll find and, as it were, feel how strong and mighty your corruptions are and how that your soul is absolutely under the dominion of your corruptions.

Use IV is of *Self-Exam.*

First. All persons that think they have the discoveries of God's redeeming love and mercy to their souls, let them examine whether they have also had such a thorough conviction of their sin and misery as we have spoken of.

Have you been made sensible of the dreadfulness of God's anger and that you deserved it, that it would be a just and righteous thing with God to execute his eternal wrath upon you? Has such a sense preceded or accompanied that supposed discovery of God's mercy and love to you? And have you ever been made sensible what a poor, helpless creature you are in and of yourself, and so of the necessity you stand in of the sovereign mercy and grace of God in a savior? When you suppose God made known his grace to you, did you truly receive it as sovereign grace and was you sensible of your dependence on a mediator for it? Did you receive as through him and through him alone?

Was there a sense of the awful greatness and terrible majesty and justice of God accompanied your first comforts that you hope were true? We have shown that is one great reason why God convinces men of their sin and misery before he discovers to 'em his mercy, because 'tis his will that a sense of his awful and terrible attributes should accompany the discovery of more mild and attractive attributes.

The comforts of hypocrites, they very commonly have this defect: they think that God loves them and delights in them, but they have not a becoming sense of the awfulness, terribleness, and justice of God.

Second. Again, by this you may try not only your comforts you had at your supposed conversion but your comforts at other times. True comforts are commonly attended with a sense of [one's] own unworthiness, though the convictions of it that the saints have after conversion are not legal, as such as they have before conversion. Yet they have evangelical humiliation accompanying of them; and the greater the comforts and discoveries of God's grace and love the greater, the self-abasement in the sense of their own vileness.

The comfort and joys of hypocrites generally are otherwise. They have not that humiliation and that sense of the awful majesty and holiness of God attending of them.

STUPID AS STONES

ANOTHER sermon that was first written in late 1730 or early 1731, *Stupid as Stones* was as biting a condemnation of the people of Northampton as Edwards delivered until his more noted *Farewell Sermon* of 1750. We see here his disappointment with the congregation, a feeling that arose even before the disputes of the late 1740s that led to his dismissal. He turns his critique in *Stupid as Stones*, however, not to the issues that marked the later period—the vices of the rising generation or the sacramental controversy, for instance—but to something much more bothersome to a young preacher: indifference. What surfaces in this sermon is Edwards' nearly livid frustration with the churchgoer who has no enthusiasm for the preacher's message.

Edwards uses his text—God's instruction to Ezekiel to preach regardless of the response of the people—to address a problem of great import. What happens when God's messengers deliver his word and it has no effect? There are several indications in this sermon that Edwards had a difficult time in his approach to this unsettling question.[1] He revised the doctrine several times, changed his text twice at later repreachings, left room for extemporaneous expansion at rough spots, and lapsed into a stuttering diction at points. Yet there is a clear theme nonetheless. Such disappointments do not frustrate God's word; rather, they accomplish it another way from the one the preacher intended. If a people remain unmoved by the gospel message, then the word exacerbates their guilt and works to their damnation. God is glorified both by their belief and obedience and by their unbelief and punishment.

So Edwards argues that the preacher, as a latter-day figure in the tradition of the prophets or Christ himself, is called to continue to preach even though the people are "as senseless and stupid as stones." In criticizing people who would not be moved by the word, Edwards provides a vivid picture of how the people of Northampton behave in meetings on

1. For a discussion of sermons from the very earliest days of the Northampton period that address a similar problem, see *Works, 14*, 24–27.

Sunday mornings or Thursday evenings. He brings Christ to them, but what do they do? They daydream, doze, or gaze about, far more interested in local gossip, what their neighbors are wearing, business, or lusts than they are in their salvation.

* * *

The manuscript is a duodecimo booklet of eight well-preserved leaves. At the top, one notation indicates that Edwards repreached the sermon from Ezek. 2:4–5, which could well have served as a basis for the textual Exposition and Doctrine. A second notation, immediately above the statement of the doctrine, indicates that he preached the sermon yet again in June 1749—at the height of the sacramental controversy that ended in his dismissal—from that point, using Zeph. 1:6 as his text.

STUPID AS STONES

EZEKIEL 3:27.

But when I speak with thee, I will open thy mouth, and thou shalt say unto them, Thus saith the Lord God; He that heareth, let him hear; and he that forbeareth, let him forbear: for they are a rebellious house.

EZEKIEL was a prophet that God raised up in Chaldea amongst the captives there that were carried away with King Jehoiachin, to warn the people of the Jews, that were yet in Judea under King Zedekiah, of the approaching destruction that God would bring upon them if they did not turn from their evil ways.

The Jews at that time were so obstinate that, although God had of a long time been warning of 'em by his prophets, one and another of them, and particularly by the prophet Jeremiah, who prophesied many years before and continued in the time of the captivity, and though God had actually begun to fulfill his word by his prophets in Jehoiachin's captivity [1:2], wherein were carried away all the principal men of the land, and only the poor and baser sort were left, yet those that remained hardened their necks and refused to hear God's word by his prophets. They stubbornly continued in their wickedness.

God, nevertheless, besides the prophet Jeremiah, sends Ezekiel to them, and tells him how obstinate and rebellious a people he sent him to, how unlikely to hearken to him, as in [ch. 2], vv. 3–4 of the context. He forewarns him that the going and preaching the word of God to them would be like going amongst briars and thorns and scorpions. They would show themselves so perverse, so proud and spiteful (2:6).

Yea, he tells him plainly in 3:7 that they would not hearken to him: "But the house of Israel will not hearken unto thee; for the house of Israel are impudent and hardhearted." But yet he bids him go and speak to them whether they would hear or whether they would forbear. Here we have an account in the context of God's forewarning of Ezekiel of his being hindered for a while from speaking His words, and of God's afterwards opening his mouth again [3:25–27].

And now, beforehand, [God] gives him this message to deliver to 'em when his mouth shall be opened again, to introduce the word that God should then send him withal. He bids 'em say unto them, "Thus saith the Lord God; He that heareth, let him hear; and he that forbeareth, let him forbear: for they are a rebellious house" [3:27].

They, in their stubborn and proud opposition to God's prophets and to the word of God in their mouths, were not sensible that they hurt none but themselves by it. They seemed maliciously to oppose themselves to God and his prophets, as though they imagined that they were principally concerned in the word that was delivered, and as though God was an enemy within their reach. They were not sensible how by opposing him they were their own worst enemies.

These two propositions seem to be implied in the words.[2]

DOCTRINE.

When God sends his messengers to preach his word, his word shall not be in vain; or, God shall not be frustrated whether men hear or whether they forbear.

God won't be frustrated in sending them. He will obtain his end, let men treat his word how they will. If they cast it by, if they treat it with contempt and show never so little regard to it, yet God will take care and see that he don't miss of his end. He will see that his word does its work some way or other.

Though men may be regardless of his word, yet God is not nor will he be regardless of it. Though they are no way careful whether God's end be obtained or no, yet God himself will be careful of it. His word shall not be neglected by himself.

God himself hath declared that his word shall not return to him void; Is. 55:10–11, "For as the rain cometh down, and the snow from heaven, and returneth not thither, but watereth the earth, and maketh it bring forth [and] bud, that it may give seed to the sower, and bread to the eater: so shall my word be that goeth out of my mouth: it shall not return unto

2. I.e. the following doctrine contains two propositions: first, many refuse to hear God's word; second, yet God shall not be frustrated.

me void, but it shall accomplish that which I please, and it shall prosper in the thing whereto I sent it." Here,

I. There are many men that do refuse to hear God's word with which God sends his messengers to them.

First. Let 'em hear never so many calls and gospel invitations, they refuse to come to Christ and accept of him as a savior.

'Tis a thing that many will not be really convinced of: that there is a savior, that Jesus Christ is the Son of God and the Savior of the world. However light is set before [them], yet their hearts are so opposite to the light that they will not receive it; they "love darkness rather than light because their hearts and deeds are evil" [John 3:19].

And men's wills are opposite to the gospel. The gospel, the Savior, and his way of salvation don't suit with their natural inclination. The way of salvation is too holy for 'em; it ascribes too much to God and not enough to themselves. They can see no beauty in Christ wherefore they should desire, and it is impossible they should be persuaded to love Christ if they see no beauty in him. They see no excellency, no fitness in the way of salvation, but, on the contrary, 'tis a way contrary to the strongest bent and inclination of their souls.

They have many things in their hearts that keep 'em from closing with Jesus Christ. There is their worldly-mindedness. When God's messengers are sent forth to call them, they begin to make excuses. One has bought a piece of land, and another has bought cattle, and his heart is upon them, and another has married a wife and therefore cannot come [Luke 14:18–20]. And they go away, one to his farm and another to his merchandise.

There are many will not be persuaded to come off from their own righteousness. They are got into a way of trusting to themselves and their own works and so don't see their need of Christ. They will neither be persuaded to trust in Christ as their high priest to make satisfaction for 'em and recommendation to God by his righteousness, nor will they receive Christ's rule and government over 'em.

And telling men of their perishing necessity of a savior, their guilt, and setting forth the sufficiency of Christ's salvation; telling them what a complete redemption Christ has wrought and how fully his blood has satisfied divine justice, how acceptable Christ's obedience is to God, and how safe it is appearing in his righteousness, and how glorious the blessings are that he has purchased, and how amiable this person of Jesus Christ is, and how willing he is, how he has invited 'em to him: it all signifies nothing to persuade them.

There is such an opposition to their natures to Christ and the gospel that they will not come to him.

Thus it was with the Jews of old. They had abundant means used with them to persuade them to come to Christ. John the Baptist had borne witness of him, and God the Father had borne witness to him by a voice from heaven. His works, his many miracles, had been witness of him, and the Scriptures of the Old Testament abundantly bore witness of him. And yet they rejected him, obstinately refused to receive him as a savior; John 5:40, "And ye will not come to me, that ye might have life."

Second. There are many that will not be persuaded [by] God's word to seek their salvation and to be concerned for the general welfare of their precious and immortal souls, let the messengers of God use what arguments they will from the Word of God.

If they tell 'em of hell and set forth to 'em the terribleness of its torments, and how dreadful a thing it is to suffer to all eternity without any hope of ever being delivered, how unable they will be to bear the wrath of an Almighty Being; if they are told how uncertain they are of their lives, how uncertain the continuance of their opportunity to obtain salvation is, what a risk they run in delaying and putting off, how common it is for persons that do so to be surprised with death and driven away in their wickedness, hurried out of the world in an unprepared condition, how common it is for men to lament their sloth and neglect of their souls upon a death bed, what danger there is of God's giving of 'em up to hardness of heart, and the like; yet it don't move 'em. They are as stupid and senseless as stones.

They come to meeting from one sabbath to another and hear God's word, but all that can be said to 'em won't awaken 'em, won't persuade 'em to take pains they may be saved.

How many men are there that ben't persuaded, and won't be persuaded, so much as to pray in any constant way that they may be saved. Yea, they are so careless about the salvation of their souls that they seldom think of it with any seriousness or concern of mind.

Third. There are many that won't be persuaded by anything that can be said to 'em by the Word of God to forsake their vices and ways of known sin. They live in a way of gratifying some lust or other, and they know it to be a sin. They can't but have light enough to know it, and they will not forsake it.

If they are told of God's command, and have the heinousness of that particular sin set before 'em, and are told how dreadfully provoking it is to God obstinately to go on in a known wickedness against warnings, how great the danger is that God will be provoked to swear in his wrath that they shall never enter into his rest, yet they are bold to go on still. They'll go right from hearing the word to their old way of wickedness again; the word of God that they hear don't alter 'em at all.

Thus did the children of Israel before and in the time of the captivity: they would not forsake their idolatries and their other wickedness, for all that the prophets said to 'em. And when that remnant of 'em that fled into Egypt were warned by the prophet Jeremiah, they said to Jeremiah, "As to the word that thou hast spoken unto us in the name of the Lord, we will not hearken unto thee. But we will certainly do whatsoever thing goeth forth out of our own mouth, to burn incense to the queen of heaven, and to pour out the drink offerings unto her, as we have done, we, and our fathers, our kings, and our princes in the cities of Judah, and in the streets of Jerusalem: for then had we plenty of victuals, and were well, and saw no evil" (Jer. 44:16–17). There are many that do practically say after the same manner as those Jews did.

Fourth. There are many that take so little notice of God's word by his messengers, that 'tis not their aim to consider or lay up what is said. They come to meeting, but it is only in conformity to custom. 'Tis not what they aim at by coming to meeting that they may hear anything in order to their own practice and for their own souls' good. For they, when they come, take no sort of pains to attend to and to apply it to themselves. They hear the words, it may be, but it is without any reflection about 'em. They don't endeavor to remember 'em. They sit and hear as if what they heard was what did no way concern them. So do they treat the message of the Most High God to 'em.

Fifth. There are some take so little notice of the message that is delivered to 'em from God, that they don't so much as hear it so as to know what is spoken. Their thoughts are intent upon something else; their hearts are in the ends of the earth. They are gazing about the assembly minding this and the other person that is in it, or they are thinking of their worldly business. They are contriving how to do this or that piece of work and accomplish such and such a design, or they are thinking of this or that other occurrence that has lately passed, or of some business or diversion they have lately been engaged in, or they are feeding their lusts in their imaginations, so that they don't know what it is that the minister says. And it may be they are whispering with their companions or with them that sit next, or they are asleep and a-dreaming instead of hearing the word of God.

II. However men disregard his word, yet God will not be frustrated. He will see to it that his word shall not be in vain or without effect. God will make his word to obtain his ends one way or the other. If it ben't effectual upon men with respect to that which is the direct design of it, viz. convincing, reforming, and converting men, yet God will make it to take effect another way whereby he will glorify himself.

God's end in his word, as in his works, is to glorify himself. He had this end in inditing the Scriptures, and he hath this end in sending forth his messengers. And there is no doubt but God will see to it that that end be obtained, that his word shall be the occasion of glory to his name.

Here, first, we will show what effect the word will have upon such persons, or rather what it will be an occasion of in them as will not hear; and, secondly, how that effect will be to the glory of God.

First. The effects that the word of God will have upon such persons as won't hear it, or what the word will be an occasion of in 'em, will be twofold: there are effects in this world and in another.

1. The effects in this world are,

(1) The word of God will exceedingly enhance their guilt. It will enhance their guilt these two ways: both as they will have their obstinacy and rebellion of theirs to answer for, [and] their refusing to hear the word of God. They "add rebellion to their sin," as it is expressed [in] Job 34:37. This wickedness of refusing to hear warnings and counsels and gracious offers after their other wickedness shows the dreadful perverseness of their hearts and terribly provokes the wrath of God.

And then also their sins that they commit afterwards are exceedingly aggravated thereby. When they go on in sin after they have been so instructed and warned, their sin is looked upon by God as much more heinous, and contracts much more guilt. Thus if a person neglects prayer or is intemperate or unclean after he has [been] warned from the Word of God and in His name against it, his sin is the more exceedingly sinful for it.

(2) Another thing the word of God is the occasion of in this world in such persons is that it hardens their hearts to hear the word of God and the calls and warnings and threatenings of it; and to refuse them exceedingly establishes the power and dominion of sin in the heart, as a king's dominion is the more established by overcoming of his enemies.

After men have been used to hear the word of God and to contemn it, it is a harder thing to convince 'em or any way affect 'em with that which is good; sin and wickedness is sealed by it. What a message was Isaiah sent with to the people of Israel; Is. 6:9–10, "Go, and tell this people, Hear indeed, but understand not; see ye indeed, but perceive not. Make the heart of this people fat, and make their ears heavy; lest they should see with their eyes, and hear with their ears, and understand with their heart, and be converted, and be healed."[3]

2. As to the effects it will have upon 'em in another world.

(1) Their punishment will be the more dreadful. Thus we learn that those that have had the word of God preached to 'em and have refused to hearken to it, they have the most dreadful punishment in another world. What does Christ say of Bethsaida? "Woe unto thee, Bethsaida! for if the mighty works, which were done in you, had been done in Tyre and Sidon, they would have repented long ago in sackcloth and ashes" [Matt. 11:21]. And God tells the children of Israel, Amos 3:2, "You only have I known of all the families of the earth: therefore will I punish you for all your iniquities." They doubtless will have the heavier punishment if their guilt is enhanced and their hearts hardened, as we have shown.

Thus the word of God, as it will be a savor of life to some, so in others it will be a savor of death; II Cor. 2:15–16, "For we are unto God a sweet savor of Christ, in them that are saved, and in them that perish: to the one we are a savor of death unto death; to the other we are a savor of life unto life."

As it is of the personal, so it is of the revealed Word of God. It is to some for a stone of stumbling and rock of offense. Christ says, "For judgment I am come into the world, that they which see not might see; and that they which see might be made blind" (John 9:39).

(2) Those that thus refuse to hear the word that is preached to 'em in this world, they will regard it in another world. Now the word of God don't take any hold of 'em; it don't affect 'em. But then it will take hold of 'em. It will work up in 'em then, however it has been slighted by 'em now. Now they don't take the pains to consider it or reflect upon it, but then they will not be able to help reflecting on it. This is intimated in these words: "And [whether] they hear, or whether they will forbear, yet shall know that there has been a prophet among them" [Ezek. 2:5]. When the words of the Prophet come to be fulfilled, then they shall consider what has been said to 'em; as [Ezek.] 33:33, "And when this cometh to pass (lo, it will come), then shall they know that there has been a prophet among 'em." When wicked men come to be in hell, then they will believe that what God's messengers said to 'em was true, or rather they will know it to be so.

When they was told what a dreadful punishment God threatened, it did not seem to 'em a reality. They took little notice of it. But now it will be

3. JE's emendation of this passage from Isaiah follows Matt. 13:15.

brought to their minds how they were warned and what counsels they had [been] given, what offers and invitations were made them. And now they will be of another mind about them. They'll regard them now. They'll be sensible now of how great importance they were, when it will be too late to any other purpose to sharpen and envenom the sting of their consciences and augment their misery.

Second. How God would have his glory by these effects.

1. Hereby God will to a greater degree glorify the terribleness of his wrath. One design he has upon his heart is to {glorify his wrath}; God is willing to show his wrath and make the power of it known (Rom. 9:22). The word of God, when it is not regarded by men, it is an occasion of filling up the measure of their sin, and so of filling up the measure of their punishments. When it does men no good, it ripens the grapes for the winepress, it fits them for fuel for hellfire.

(2) It renders justice in their damnation the more conspicuous. And so God glorifies his justice the more in their destruction, for their guilt becomes greater and more notorious and they become more inexcusable; and their own consciences will condemn them the more and will justify the judge in the sentence he passes upon them. The iniquity of such men cries aloud for vengeance, and the justice of God in the destruction of such men as have refused his word will be especially clear and evident in the sight of men and angels.

Thus God is not frustrated. His word don't return to him void.

Two Reasons

1. God is infinitely wise and powerful and is able to obtain his end whether [men will hear, or whether men will forbear].

2. The word of God is too honorable and precious to be suffered to be in vain. 'Tis fit that the word of so great a God should take effect, should accomplish that. 'Tis the honor of the word; though men don't honor it, God will.

APPLICATION.

[*Use*] I. [Of *Encour.*] Ministers should not neglect faithfully to preach the word of God, however regardless men are of their message.[4]

'Tis a discouraging thing. Ministers are to aim at a people's good, but they don't know what God designs 'em for. They don't know whether

4. From here to the end of the sermon, JE merely sketched in phrases and a few sentences, leaving blank spaces after each. He may well have expanded upon these extemporaneously in preaching.

they are sent with Isaiah's message. God bid Ezekiel to speak his word whether they would hear or whether {they would forbear}.[5]

[*Use*] II. Of *Awak.* To ungodly men, seriously consider these things:

By so opposing God, you won't hinder him of [his word]. You do but fight against your own souls. God will be no loser by it; how great a loser will you be!

God's word you have, and it shall obtain its end. You may depend upon it, that one sermon that you hear, [however] regardless {you are of its message}, will [not] be lost as to God, though it be lost as to you.

If the word of God ben't as the dew and rain to you, it will at last be as fire to burn up your roots.

Consider the many sermons you have neglected and lost. They are all remembered; God will see that they ben't lost as to his ends proposed in them.

[*Use* III. Of] *Exh.* To hear the word of God {delivered by his messengers}. Fix that as your aim, and in hearing, that you may be profited for your spiritual good. Attend to and weigh [it]. Remember and apply it to yourself.

Let it be your constant endeavor to obey. Obey the commands of God; hearken to his counsels; accept of [his] calls; strive diligently with your own heart. Mix earnest and constant prayer with it.

Consider, first, [that] if you hear, God will attain his end in you, obtaining your own happiness; second, to how much greater advantage you may regard the word of God now than afterwards. You will regard it first or last.[6]

5. Here JE later added: "Ezek. 3.11, 'And go, get thee to them of the captivity, unto the children of thy people, and speak unto them, and tell them. Thus saith the Lord God; whether they will hear, or whether they will forbear'; vv. 26–27, 'And I will make thy tongue cleave to the roof of thy mouth, that thou shalt be dumb, and shalt not be to them a reprover: for they are a rebellious house. But when I speak with thee, I will open thy mouth, and thou shalt say unto them, Thus saith the Lord God; He that heareth let him hear; and he that forbeareth, let him forbear: for they are a rebellious house.'"

6. Here JE later added: "You have often had the books of Scripture opened. At the day of judgment the same books shall be opened, and then you will always seek the work of God. You never will make light of it any more."

BORN AGAIN

IN *Born Again*, Edwards reflects on new birth as a trope for conversion. Although part of John 3:3 served as his doctrine, Edwards omits his usual explication of the text. He may have done this extemporaneously. Along with the sometimes sketchy nature of the rest of the sermon, this omission indicates that the sermon may have been prepared for a private meeting and therefore did not warrant the completeness of a formal sermon. In any case, Edwards proceeds to a rather abstract meditation on the necessity of spiritual regeneration. *Born Again* has several focuses related, though somewhat disjointedly, to the central image. The result is rhetorically opaque; nonetheless, the sermon tells us much about Edwards' pastoral challenges and agenda.

The sermon's awkwardness also may have derived from the conceptual difficulties of Edwards' topic. He devotes the Doctrine to arguing that the usual measures for religious and moral socialization, including baptism, touch only the outer person, while the new birth implies a new nature, a new sense, a new disposition; it infuses the regenerate with a new principle of being, understanding, will, and inclination. And, as a parallel to physical birth, it comes to those who are imperfect and incapable of effecting it by natural efforts. It is therefore necessary to be born again, however much one participates in the ordinary course of religious and moral training. Yet Edwards also suggests, somewhat tenuously, that the image of birth implies a standard procedure or sequence for coming into existence. So he urges his auditors in the Application to pursue the customary means of spiritual awakening: self-examination, attendance on the Word, and participation in the divine ordinances.

Edwards clearly directed this sermon against what Puritans called carnal security—a false sense of spiritual confidence that affected individuals who were morally respectable but who had not undergone regeneration. Composed between the fall of 1730 and the spring of 1731, *Born Again* urges people to prepare for a conversion experience that would establish all their efforts as ineffective. In this sense, *Born Again* may have proved an important preparation for Edwards' duly celebrated treatment of the same topic, *A Divine and Supernatural Light.*[1]

* * *

The manuscript is a typical duodecimo booklet, consisting of ten well-preserved leaves. Many blank lines reflect an incomplete composition in parts. A notation indicates that Edwards repreached the sermon in 1753, undoubtedly the occasion for the insertions that are included in the footnotes to the sermon.

1. JE worked on the topic of preparation in the "Miscellanies" from this period, which also demonstrated some conceptual ambivalence. For example, see no. 481 and commentary in *Works, 13*, 37–38, 523–24.

BORN AGAIN

JOHN 3:3.

[*Jesus answered and said unto him, Verily, verily, I say unto thee, Except a man be born again, he cannot see the kingdom of God.*]

DOCTRINE.

Except a man be born again, he cannot see the kingdom of God.

I. EXPLAIN what is meant by being born again.
II. Show the necessity of it.

I. Explain how a man must be born again. [Negatively, hereby is] not [meant] baptism; baptism [is] useless without the thing signified. God looks at the heart. What is external [is] useless [unless there is a] circumcision of the heart (Jer. 9:26), of the soul, as explained by Christ in [John] 3:6. [This] plainly appears by v. 10;[2] baptism [is] not required till now.

But, affirmatively, hereby is meant that great change that is wrought in man by the mighty power of God, at his conversion from sin to God: his being changed from a wicked to a holy man. And we shall show how that man in this change is born again, whereby it will appear what kind of change it is that is wrought.

First. By birth is meant the whole progress of the formation of man according to a course of nature. In this change that is necessary in order to man's seeing the kingdom of God, man receives a new nature. In man's first conception and birth he receives his nature. 'Tis by that he comes to be a human creature; 'tis by that he receives the essential parts of man. The human soul is infused in the progress of this work of nature. Hereby he receives the parts and shape of a human body, with its senses

2. This sketchy sentence is difficult to reconstruct. The scriptural reference is unclear. The meaning of the following phrase is that baptism is required only after spiritual rebirth—not as the means of rebirth.

and principles of action. 'Tis by this that man becomes more than senseless, inactive dust. 'Tis by this that man receives life, that is, receives both its sensitive and rational nature.

So, in the same manner, man, in that change whereby he becomes holy, receives a new nature. When a man is changed from a sinner to a saint, the change is not a mere change of manners, a change in outward appearance; but 'tis a change of nature. In this change, a man receives a nature that is entirely diverse from the nature he had before or anything that he had in that nature. 'Tis as truly and entirely different as the nature of man is from the nature of mere clay or earth.

The change that is wrought is not such a change as may be wrought by education. A child may be mightily altered in many things by instruction, government, and example. There is a vast alteration in the outward behavior and in many qualifications of the child, but there is no proper change of nature. 'Tis not such a change as may be brought about by custom. Men may contract habits, may have many old habits eradicated and new ones enrooted, but yet there be no proper change of nature, as there is in conversion.

The change of man from a sinner to a saint is not a moral, but a physical change. A moral change is wrought by human instruction, and government, and example, and by a man in himself, by resolution and pains. But these changes don't reach to the nature of the soul so as to change that.

The nature of man consists in principles of perception and principles of action. The human nature whereby man differs from a beast or a tree consists in principles. Man's faculties are principles; the natural appetites are principles; a love of pleasure, and aversion to pain, and a love of honor are principles.

But man, when he is changed from a sinner to a saint, has new principles of perception and action, principles that are entirely diverse and not arising merely from [a] new disposition of the old, as contracted habits and those changes that are wrought by education do. They are principles that are vastly superior to those he had before, superior to 'em in such a manner that 'twould be as impossible that they should arise from them as that a principle of reason should arise from a power of sensation, and so that a brute could be changed into a rational creature without a physical change.

There is in conversion infused a principle of spiritual understanding and spiritual action that is as far above any principles that man had before, as the heaven is high above the earth. And this change of nature is such that he not only acts above what he did before, but contrary. The principles that were before, as they were ungoverned and inordinate, were most contrary to those supernatural principles that are infused. They are sinful, and these are mortified when spiritual principles are infused.

Second. The change is universal of the whole man. Man in his first birth or conception receives the beginnings of all that belongs to the human nature. Both soul and body are then begun, and all the faculties of the soul are then received, and all the members of the body, every vein, and sinew, and all the senses.

So when a man is changed from a sinner to a saint, the whole man is renewed or made new; Eph. 4:22, 24, "That ye put off concerning the former conversation the old man, which is corrupt according to the deceitful lusts . . . and that ye put on the new man, which after God is created in righteousness and true holiness." The whole man is sanctified; I Thess. 5:23, "And the very God of peace sanctify you wholly; and I pray God your whole spirit and soul and body be preserved blameless."

So, in conversion, there is a new principle of understanding, a principle whereby the soul knows God and understands his glory and excellency, and the truth and excellency of spiritual things: the great things of God's Word, the glorious doctrines of the gospel, and things pertaining to Christ the Savior, which the soul had no power to understand before. 'Tis as if there were added to the soul "eyes to see," which before was blind and had no eyes (Deut. 29:4).

There is a new principle of will and inclination. The man now loves God, and loves Christ, which he could not love before. He relishes holiness and holy and heavenly things, which he could not relish before. He could not find these things in his heart before, so that 'tis as if God gives man a new heart; Ezek. 36:26, "A new heart will I give unto you, and a new spirit will I put within you."

The body also in a sense is new: the whole spirit, soul, and body is renewed and sanctified. The members of the body are new, as [are] the purposes they are subservient to.

Third. In that change whereby a man is changed from a sinner to a saint, man doth, as it were, receive being.

Men, when they are conceived and born, receive their beings. So also in this change, there is that which is equivalent to a man's receiving being. Man, by the fall and corruption of his nature, is ruined, and is reduced to a state in many respects lower than when he was in his first dust. He was so spoiled and ruined that it was equivalent to a reduction to his first nothing, for everything that rendered his being either excellent or happy was lost, so that he had as good not be. Yea, he was brought to a state worse than his first nothing, not only having lost all that was good, but being plunged into all evil, both of sin and misery. He was spiritually dead, and was condemned to eternal death.

Therefore, when a man is converted, he doth, as it were, receive his being again. And therefore this change is called a creation, as well as new birth; Eph. 2:10, "For we are his workmanship, created in Christ Jesus."

Fourth. They come into a new world;[3] II Cor. 5:17, "Old things are done away, while all things are become new."

Fifth. This change is as a birth because 'tis brought to pass by stated means. It is the same as a birth, rather than an immediate creation. 'Tis God that makes man new, as truly as he made our first parents. But now, 'tis in a certain, stated way, according to a fixed law of nature. God could, if he pleased, convert man immediately without the use of any means at all; but he doth not so. But there are stated means which are appointed and fixed by the law of grace that are constantly made use of in producing this effect. Conversion is wrought by the Word and ordinances. There is an ordinary way of [the] Spirit's working: [it is] preparatory work.[4]

Sixth. [They are] born into a state like that of children (Matt. 18:3), into an imperfect state (I Pet. 1:23–25), [a] growing state; I Pet. 2:1–2, "Wherefore laying aside all malice, and all guile, and hypocrisies, and envies, and all evil speakings, as newborn babes, desire the sincere milk of the word, that ye may grow thereby." [They are] often called little children by Christ, John 13:33, "Little children, yet a little while I am with you"; by [the] apostle Paul, Gal. 4:19, "My little children, of whom I travail in birth till Christ be formed in you"; and [the] apostle John (I John 2:1 and other places).[5]

[II.] Reasons.

First. The end of man's being is not reached in the first birth. Man by his first birth receives being. That is attained by it, that he should be: that

3. Two blank lines follow. Here through the end of the first major head of the Doctrine, JE left one or two lines blank following most sentences, perhaps indicating his intention to expand on these points.

4. Four blank lines follow.

5. Two blank lines follow. JE later added, presumably for the 1753 repreaching of this sermon, the following passage: "*Seventh.* Hereby [they] become members of a family; Eph. 2:19, '[of the] household of God'; 3:15, '[the] whole family.' [They become] new relations. God is their father, Christ [their] elder brother; Heb. 2:11–12, 'For both he that sanctifieth and they who are sanctified are all of one: for which cause he is not ashamed to call them brethren, saying, I will declare thy name unto my brethren.' [Fellow] saints [are their] brethren; Matt. 23:8, 'But be ye not called Rabbi; for one is your Master, even Christ; and all ye are brethren.' "

he should have an existence in this world. But he don't attain the end of his being. And therefore there is need that he should be born again. By the first birth he is made, but the end for which he is made is not reached.

He comes into the world with those defects, with a want of those essential things that are as necessary in order to the obtaining the end of his being as his being itself, and his being without will as wholly and entirely frustrate the design of his being as if he wanted being itself. 'Tis not merely necessary that man should be, in order to his obtaining the end of his being; but he must be with such and such principles and qualifications, which if he wants, he will as certainly and entirely fail of reaching his end, as if he remained in his first nothing. To have a being is one step towards man's obtaining the end of his being. But if no other is taken, he entirely fails of reaching his end as if none was taken.

And it being thus, that man in his first birth is born [with] those defects, there is a necessity of a new birth, because a man had as good not be as not obtain the end of his being. But here, in order to the right understanding of what we mean when we say that the end of a man's being is not reached in his first birth, and that there is a necessity of a new birth in order to the end of his existence being obtained, it is not to be taken as though God were properly frustrated in his giving any man a being whether he is born again or not.

But when we speak of the end of man's being, it may be taken two ways. It may be taken either for that universal end which man hath in common with all other things, which is God's glory. This end, which is the most ultimate, must and shall be obtained whatsoever the defects of man's nature are, and whether a man be born again or no. God will so order and overrule things that this end shall be obtained. This, God takes for his own care; the obtaining of this end, he don't trust with any creature.

And then, by the end of man, in another sense, is to be understood the particular good which is the design of man's particular nature, which the human nature is capacitated for and adapted to particularly, which may be said to be the genuine design of this particular piece of workmanship.

There is a particular use which the nature of man seems evidently to be designed and capacitated [for], which may be said to be the proper use of the powers of the human nature. Thus the proper use of the human understanding is to know God, and the proper use of the human will and affections [is] to love God and enjoy him. That use which is the genuine design of human nature and powers may be said to be the proper end of man, as the proper end of an house is to dwell in, the proper end of a garment [is] to clothe man with, and the proper end of a vessel is to contain.

'Tis this proper end of man that man, in his first birth, fails of, as if a potter makes a vessel that is broken and leaky, the proper end of a vessel is not obtained, however he may turn [it] to some other use. If a man plants a fruit tree and it bears no fruit, the proper end is not obtained, however it may do to burn [it] [Matt. 7:19]. The proper end of a man is to glorify God in a way of knowing, and loving, and praising, and serving of him; but the end is not reached in the first birth. The vessel is broken: man is born with essential defects.

It is needful that man, in order to the obtaining the proper end of man, should not only have natural principles, or those principles which belong and are essential to the human nature, but supernatural principles, those principles which are superior to the natural, and were given to govern the natural principles, and which the natural principles were given to be subordinate to. The principles of spiritual life, of spiritual understanding, inclination, and action: these principles are absolutely necessary in man in order to his serving and glorifying God. But these principles, man in his first birth is born without; and the natural, inferior principles can be nothing without them, but evil. Therefore, there is need of a new birth in order to his being received and accepted of God and admitted into his kingdom, for 'tis not reasonable to suppose that those will be admitted and accepted as God's people in his kingdom and as his children in his family that don't answer the end of their beings. When a vessel is marred in the making so that it won't answer the end of a vessel, there is need of its being made over again by the potter; Jer. 18:3–4, "Then I went down to the potter's house, and, behold, he wrought a work on the wheels. And the vessel that he made of clay was marred in the hand of the potter: so he made it again another vessel."

Second. Man's proper excellency and perfection is not attained in the first birth. By the first birth man becomes man, but hath not those principles and endowments which are the excellency and glory of manhood. The true excellency of man consists in the image of God, but man by the fall has lost this image of God. He hath lost the divine nature, so that the nature of man is lost, a spoiled, ruined thing. And we all, as we come into the world, come with this defect of the image of God and are thus ruined.

And therefore we stand in need of another birth, that we may attain our proper perfection. God made man at first very good; Gen. 1:31, "God saw every thing that he had made, and, behold, it was very good." But this piece of God's workmanship, viz. man, as he now comes into the world in his first birth, is not so; but on the contrary, [is] very bad. And therefore men need to be born again, in order to their being owned and blessed of God as his people.

Third. Man by the first birth does not attain to a capacity of enjoying his proper happiness, and therefore 'tis necessary that he should be born again. Indeed, every man is capable of enjoying happiness remotely; that is, he is capable, without the addition of any new faculties, of receiving those principles whereby he shall be prepared and immediately capacitated for the enjoyment of his proper happiness. He is capable of obtaining to true happiness without the addition of any new faculties, but not without the addition of new principles.

Man's proper happiness consists in the enjoyment of God; but it is not possible that man should enjoy God with only those things in him which he receives by the first birth. So that there is this necessity of man's being born again in order to his obtaining the kingdom of God. 'Tis not possible in nature, that he should see the kingdom of [God] with only those principles of nature which he receives by his first birth. So that man still remains nothing, or as bad as nothing, [as], yea, was he.

Fourth. And then, it is necessary that man should be born again because those things that are wanting can't be attained by any modification whatsoever of anything that man receives by his first birth. Those natural principles which man has by his first birth, let them be turned and disposed and modified how they will, we never can attain by that means to those supernatural principles which are wanting, which are necessary in order to man's obtaining his proper end and his true excellency and in order to his being in a capacity to enjoy true happiness, the happiness of the kingdom of God.

Man by his first birth has natural faculties of understanding and will. He has self-love. He has a love to happiness and aversion to misery. And these principles may be so modified and directed that man may thereby attain to great learning, and human knowledge, and may excel in outward virtue and have a love to it. But man by this means can never come to the true knowledge of the glory of God, and the excellency of Christ, or come to a sincere and unfeigned love to God, or have a spiritual appetite, or be in a capacity for the reception of spiritual enjoyments. If any modifying of any principles that man has by his first birth could cause to arise those other principles that are wanting, there would be no need of their being new men. The nature of man might be mended without a new birth. If true love to God could by any means be made to arise from any modifications of self-love, a man need not be new born in order to his loving God. But it is not so.

APPLICATION.

I. If there is so great a change to be wrought, how unreasonable is the security of multitudes of men. Every man that shall not see the kingdom of heaven will feel the torments of hell to all eternity, so that, except he be born again, he cannot see the kingdom of God; so he cannot escape the damnation of hell. This is a rule that has no exceptions. 'Tis fixed and unalterable, as is intimated by the manner of expression in the text, "Verily, verily."

And yet, what a multitude of men are there that have experienced no such change, are most remote from it, that yet are careless and secure! They take little thought, they ben't inquiring and contriving, what they shall do that they may be born again, nor concerning themselves about [it]. They seem to live easy and undisturbed. Yea, and many of those that have been well instructed in this doctrine of the necessity of being born again, they ben't seeking such a change, nor doing anything towards it, but let time pass without taking any thought how it passes, how fast it slips away, and how soon it will all be gone, and their glass will be run, and their one opportunity slipped. And they don't know how soon it will be, but they don't trouble themselves about it. They have something else to mind: they mind the world, are concerned how to increase their estates, or mind their pleasures and their company, and let this matter of their being born again be as it will.

They are careless and secure, though there be no appearance of any such change nor anything towards [it]. 'Tis a very remote thing. There appears nothing in them that tends that way. There appears nothing in them that gives any reasonable prospect of any such a thing approaching, or renders it probable that it ever will be; nor, indeed, is there probability of it. And yet they are very secure, and their minds are very much taken up with other things.

How little likelihood is there that even so great a change as being born again will ever be obtained without striving and taking considerable pains. But yet they take no pains. They don't strive for it. Yea, many of them don't think of striving for it, and yet ben't terrified with that thought, that except they are born again before they die, they must certainly be damned forever. Yea, they not only [do] nothing towards such a change, but they are continually setting themselves at a greater and greater distance from [it]. They are as fast as they can laying blocks in the way, making of it more and more unlikely that ever they shall be the subjects of such a change. So that there is no likelihood of its being, and yet they are not concerned about it.

How wonderfully unreasonable is the security of those sinners that know the Bible, and hear such doctrine preached out of it!

II. Hence the great mistake of those who flatter themselves that they are converted that never experienced any remarkable, habitual change in their hearts. Being born again is surely a great and remarkable thing as we have described it; it appears to be so.

How unreasonable, then, is the mistake of those who, when they look back, can't return in their thoughts to any remarkable change that ever they experienced, and that ben't now any way remarkably different in their hearts, and tempers, and dispositions, from what they always have been, or from what they were before their supposed conversion; that are no way remarkably new in their sense and disposition about spiritual and heavenly things, never differing from what they used to be in their thoughts and sense about God and Jesus Christ, and about the gospel and way of salvation, about this world and the future; that are as worldly as ever {they were before};[6] whose change is not lasting; who have only superficial, transient affections;[7] whose change is chiefly outward, not in the principles and nature, but in the outward manners and customs.

There are many that think themselves born again, that they have been the subjects of this change which is so great, so wonderful, as it were, a coming out of nothing into being, that never have experienced any change of nature at all; that han't had one new principle added, nor one sinful disposition really mortified; that never saw one glimpse of divine light, never saw the least of God's or Christ's glory, nor ever put forth one act of love to God in their lives. They think themselves now made renewed in the whole man that never have had one finger renewed, if I may use such an expression.

[*First Dir.*] Examine whether or no you are new born.

1. Whether or no you are, "as little children," humble (Matt. 18:3–4).

2. Whether or no "as new born babes, you desire the sincere milk of the word," whether [you are] governed by spiritual appetites (I Pet. 2:2).[8]

6. Two blank lines follow, perhaps indicating JE's intention to extemporize.
7. Two blank lines follow, perhaps indicating JE's intention to extemporize.
8. See the sermon on I Pet. 2:2–3 (132), from late 1729.

3. Whether you are a "follower of God, as a dear child" (Eph. 5:1),[9] and "walk as a child of the light" and of the day [v. 8], [and] follow God: [a] child with a filial disposition, [with] love, reverence, [and] dependence as a little child on a father, imitating, obeying in everything.

[*Second*] *Dir.* Be in the steady and diligent use of appointed means.

Earnestly seek it of God, who is the Father.[1] Use the Word, which is as the seed; I Cor 4:15, "I have begotten you through the gospel." Use the law, which causes the pangs of the new birth.[2] Use the ordinances administered in the church, which is the mother. Believers are the children of the church; Is. 49:20–21, "The children which thou shalt have, after thou hast lost the other, shall say again in thine ears, The place is too strait for me: give place to me that I may dwell. Then shall thou say in thine heart, Who hath begotten me these, seeing I have lost my children, and am desolate, a captive, and removing to and fro? and who hath brought up these? Behold, I was left alone; these, where had they been?"; Is. 54:1, "Sing, O barren, thou that didst not bear; break forth into singing, and cry aloud, thou that didst not travail with child: for more are the children of the desolate than the children of the married wife, saith the Lord"; Gal. 4:26, "But Jerusalem which is above, which is the mother of us all."[3]

9. See the sermon on Eph. 5:1 (130), from late 1729.

1. Three blank lines follow, perhaps indicating JE's intention to extemporize.

2. Two blank lines follow, perhaps indicating JE's intention to extemporize.

3. JE added the following passage, with blank lines interspersed between sentences, at a later time, presumably for the 1753 reworking of this sermon: "Be speedy; don't halt; don't wait for a better time. Be earnest; don't spend time in contriving to spare yourself [the use of means]. Take heed you ben't undone through the deceitfulness of sin. Avoid temptation. Don't strive only in some duties. Don't flatter yourself that you are more likely to be saved than other sinners."

GOD GLORIFIED IN MAN'S DEPENDENCE

God Glorified in Man's Dependence was Edwards' first published work. He originally delivered the sermon in Northampton in the fall of 1730; on July 8, 1731, he preached it to a meeting of clergy in Boston, soon after which it appeared in print. One of his more noted efforts, the sermon was reprinted frequently in subsequent editions of his work, including the Dwight edition (*8*, 147–62).

Edwards here picks up many of the themes that he had been working on in his private notebooks and other sermons from the period and brings them together in an elegant, well-modulated statement in defense of the evangelical precept that human beings are so fallen that they are utterly dependent on God for spiritual good, especially salvation. Clearly, Edwards shaped his ideas to combat Arminianism and so carried forward the polemic he had begun with his Master's *Quæstio* in 1723.[1] To this extent, the sermon also reflected other efforts from this period, such as *God Makes Men Sensible of Their Misery*, to articulate the importance of evangelical humiliation.[2] *God Glorified*, however, adopts a different rhetorical strategy. Rather than stress the affective dimensions of humiliation, Edwards defends the Calvinist view of human nature by linking it to the doctrine of the Trinity.

In the Explication, Edwards contends that people depend on Christ for redemption, on God for Christ, and on the Holy Spirit for the faith that unites them with Christ. In the first major head of the Doctrine, he pursues this trinitarian structure. The redeemed have all of their good *of* (or from) God, which means that they, helpless in their sinful states, depend solely on God for the power to make them holy. The redeemed also have all their good *through* God's gift of the Mediator, Christ, who justifies them. The redeemed furthermore have all their good *in* God, who makes them morally excellent by the presence of the Holy Spirit.

1. Printed in *Works, 14*, 47–66.
2. The Doctrine of *God Glorified* reads as a near paraphrase of "Miscellanies" no. 486.

First page of the manuscript of *God Glorified in Man's Dependence.* Courtesy Beinecke Rare Book and Manuscript Library, Yale University.

These themes are also evident in Edwards' manuscript "Discourse on the Trinity" (also known as "Essay on the Trinity"), parts of which he composed during the same period in which he wrote *God Glorified.* Whereas his writing on the Trinity, however, was philosophically wide-ranging, covering such topics as the nature of God's being and revelation, *God Glorified* emphasizes more narrowly the Protestant doctrine of justification by faith alone. If human beings are so dependent on God, Edwards reasons in the sermon, then God redeems them out of "mere and arbitrary grace," which is to say, through the work of Christ and the

A

Divine and Supernatural

LIGHT,

Immediately imparted to the Soul by the

SPIRIT of *GOD*,

Shown to be both a

Scriptural, and *Rational* DOCTRINE;

In a SERMON

Preach'd at *Northampton*,

And Publiſhed at the Deſire of ſome of the Hearers.

By *Jonathan Edwards*, A. M.

Paſtor of the Church there.

Job 28. 20.——*Whence then cometh wiſdom ? and where is the place of underſtanding ?*
Prov. 2. 6. *The LORD giveth wiſdom.*
Iſa. 42. 18. *Look ye blind that ye may ſee.*
2 Pet. 1. 19. ——*Until the day dawn and the day-ſtar ariſe in your hearts.*

BOSTON:

Printed by S. KNEELAND and T. GREEN.

M,DCC,XXXIV.

Title page of *A Divine and Supernatural Light* (see pp. 405–26) presence of the Spirit. By implication, Arminian views on human nature, which deny humanity's complete dependence on God, effectively contradict the logic of the Trinity.

Edwards pursues this last point at greater length under the second proposition of the Doctrine. He argues that it is this very doctrine of human sin and dependence, rather than any supposition of human goodness or moral capability, that glorifies God. Here and in the Application, a call to faith, the sermon reaches its full rhetorical force. Edwards' theocentric vision of God as Redeemer leads him to a nearly doxological conclusion.

* * *

Printed in Boston in 1731 by Samuel Kneeland and Timothy Green, the published text is an octavo-sized pamphlet of twenty-eight pages. Its full title is *God Glorified in the Work of Redemption, By the Greatness of Man's Dependence upon Him, in the Whole of it. Preached on the Public Lecture in Boston, July 8, 1731.* An epigraph on the title page quotes Judg. 7:2. The short title at the head of the text is *God Gloried in Man's Dependence.* Preceding the text is a two-page preface, "To the Reader," by Thomas Prince and William Cooper, a recommendation of the sermon and its author. It is included as an appendix to the sermon in this volume.

The manuscript is a typical duodecimo booklet, consisting of fourteen well-preserved leaves. In preparing the sermon for publication, Edwards made a significant number of revisions, including emending of repeated phrases and expanding several points, most notably in the addition of the second proposition of the Doctrine and the second head of the Application, or Use. Some of these changes are marked on the manuscript; others are silent.[3]

3. Wilson H. Kimnach has provided a thorough description and analysis of changes from the MS to the printed version in *Works, 10*, 108–11, 148–53.

GOD GLORIFIED IN MAN'S DEPENDENCE

I CORINTHIANS 1:29–31.

That no flesh should glory in his presence. But of him are ye in Christ Jesus, who of God is made unto us wisdom, and righteousness, and sanctification, and redemption: that, according as it is written, He that glorieth, let him glory in the Lord.

THOSE Christians to whom the Apostle directed this epistle, dwelt in a part of the world where human wisdom was greatly in repute; and as the Apostle says in v. 22 of this chapter, "The Greeks seek after wisdom." Corinth was not far from Athens, that had been for many ages the most famous seat of philosophy and learning in the world.

The Apostle therefore observes to them how that God by the gospel destroyed, and brought to naught, their human wisdom. The learned Grecians, and their great philosophers, by all their wisdom did not know God; they were not able to find out the truth in divine things. But after they had done their utmost to no effect, it pleased God at length, to reveal himself by the gospel which they counted foolishness: he chose "the foolish things of the world to confound the wise, and the weak things of the world to confound the things which are mighty, and the base things of the world, and things that are despised, yea, and things that are not, to bring to naught the things that are" [vv. 27–28]. And the Apostle informs them why he thus did, in the verse of the text, "That no flesh should glory in his presence. But of him are ye in Christ Jesus, who of God is made unto us wisdom, and righteousness, and sanctification, and redemption: that, according as it is written, He that glorieth, let him glory in the Lord."

In which words may be observed,

1. What God aims at in the disposition of things in the affair of redemption, viz. that man should not glory in himself, but alone in God: "That no

flesh should glory in his presence; . . . that, according as it is written, He that glories, let him glory in the Lord."[4]

2. How this end is attained in the work of redemption, viz. by that absolute and immediate dependence which men have upon God in that work, for all their good. Inasmuch as,

(1) All the good that they have is in and through Christ; he "is made unto us wisdom, righteousness, sanctification, and redemption" [v. 30]. All the good of the fallen and redeemed creature is concerned in these four things, and can't be better distributed than into them; but Christ is each of them to us, and we have none of them otherwise than in him. "He is made of God unto us wisdom": in him are all the proper good, and true excellency of the understanding. Wisdom was a thing that the Greeks admired, but Christ is the true light of the world; 'tis through him alone that true wisdom is imparted to the mind. 'Tis in and by Christ that we have righteousness: 'tis by being in him that we are justified, have our sins pardoned, and are received as righteous into God's favor. 'Tis by Christ that we have sanctification: we have in him true excellency of heart, as well as of understanding; and he is made unto us inherent as well as imputed righteousness. 'Tis by Christ that we have redemption, or the actual deliverance from all misery, and the bestowment of all happiness and glory. Thus we have all our good by Christ who is God.

(2) Another instance wherein our dependence on God for all our good appears is this, that 'tis God that has given us Christ, that we might have those benefits through him; he "of God is made unto us wisdom, righteousness, sanctification, and redemption."

(3) 'Tis of him that we are in Christ Jesus, and come to have an interest in him, and so do receive those blessings which he is made unto us. 'Tis God that gives faith whereby we close with Christ.

So that in this verse is shown our dependence on each person in the Trinity for all our good. We are dependent on Christ the Son of God, as he is our wisdom, righteousness, sanctification, and redemption. We are dependent on the Father, who has given us Christ, and made him to be these things to us. We are dependent on the Holy Ghost, for 'tis of him that we are in Christ Jesus; 'tis the Spirit of God that gives us faith in him, whereby we receive him, and close with him.

4. In the MS, JE wrote "but" where the ellipsis appears in the printed version.

DOCTRINE.

God is glorified in the wisdom of redemption in this, that there appears in it so absolute and universal a dependence of the redeemed on him.

Here I propose to show,

I. That there is an absolute and universal dependence of the redeemed on God for all their good.

II. That God hereby is exalted and glorified in the work of redemption.

I. There is an absolute and universal dependence of the redeemed on God. The nature and contrivance of our redemption is such that the redeemed are in everything directly, immediately, and entirely dependent on God: they are dependent on him for all, and are dependent on him every way.

The several ways wherein the dependence of one being may be upon another for its good, and wherein the redeemed of Jesus Christ depend on God for all their good, are these, viz. that they have all their good *of* him, and that they have all *through* him, and that they have all *in* him: that he be the cause and original whence all our good comes, therein it is *of* him; and that he be the medium by which it is obtained and conveyed, therein they have it *through* him; and that he be that good itself that is given and conveyed, therein it is *in* him.

Now those that are redeemed by Jesus Christ do in all these respects very directly and entirely depend on God for their all.

First. The redeemed have all their good *of* God. God is the great author of it; he is the first cause of it, and not only so, but he is the only proper cause.

'Tis *of* God that we have our Redeemer. 'Tis God that has provided a Savior for us. Jesus Christ is not only of God in his person, as he is the only begotten Son of God; but he is from God as we are concerned in him, and in his office of mediator; he is the gift of God to us: God chose and anointed him, appointed him his work, and sent him into the world.

And as it is God that gives, so 'tis God that accepts the Savior. As it is God that provides and gives the Redeemer to buy salvation for us, so it is *of* God that that salvation is bought: he gives the purchaser, and he affords the thing purchased.

'Tis of God that Christ becomes ours, that we are brought to him, and are united unto him. 'Tis of God that we receive faith to close with him, that we may have an interest in him; Eph. 2:8, "For by grace are ye saved through faith; and that not of yourselves: it is the gift of God." 'Tis of God that we actually do receive all the benefits that Christ has purchased. 'Tis God that pardons and justifies and delivers from going down to hell, and 'tis his favor that the redeemed are received into, and are made the objects of, when they are justified. So it is God that delivers from the dominion of sin, and cleanses us from our filthiness, and changes us from our deformity. 'Tis of God that the redeemed do receive all their true excellency, wisdom and holiness; and that two ways, viz. as the Holy Ghost by whom these things are immediately wrought is from God, proceeds from him, and is sent by him; and also as the Holy Ghost himself is God, by whose operation and indwelling, the knowledge of God and divine things, and a holy disposition, and all grace is conferred and upheld.

And though means are made use of in conferring grace on men's souls, yet 'tis of God that we have these means of grace, and 'tis God that makes them effectual. 'Tis of God that we have the holy Scriptures; they are the Word of God. 'Tis of God that we have ordinances, and their efficacy depends on the immediate influence of the Spirit of God. The ministers of the gospel are sent of God, and all their sufficiency is of him; II Cor. 4:7, "We have this treasure in earthen vessels, that the excellency of the power may be of God, and not of us." Their success depends entirely and absolutely on the immediate blessing and influence of God.

The redeemed have all,

1. Of the grace of God. It was of mere grace that God gave us his only begotten Son. The grace is great in proportion to the dignity and excellency of what is given: the gift was infinitely precious, because it was of a person infinitely worthy, a person of infinite glory; and also because it was of a person infinitely near and dear to God. The grace is great in proportion to the benefit we have given us in him: the benefit is doubly infinite in that in him we have deliverance from an infinite, because an eternal, misery, and do also receive eternal joy and glory. The grace in bestowing this gift is great in proportion to our unworthiness to whom it is given; instead of deserving such a gift, we merited infinitely ill of God's hands. The grace is great according to the manner of giving, or in proportion to the humiliation and expense of the method and means by which way is made for our having the gift. He gave him to us dwelling amongst us; he gave him to us incarnate, or in our own nature; he gave him to us in our nature, in the like infirmities, in which we have it in our fallen state, and which in us do accompany, and are occasioned by, the sinful corruption of our nature. He gave him to us in a low and afflicted state; and not only so, but he gave him to us slain that he might be a feast for our souls.

The grace of God in bestowing this gift is most free. It was what God was under no obligation to bestow. He might have rejected fallen man, as he did the fallen angels. It was what we never did anything to merit: 'twas given while we were yet enemies, and before we had so much as repented. It was from the love of God that saw excellency in us to attract it; and it was without expectation of ever being requited for it.

And 'tis from mere grace that the benefits of Christ are applied to such and such particular persons. Those that are called and sanctified are to attribute it alone to the good pleasure of God's goodness, by which they are distinguished. He is sovereign and hath mercy on whom he will have mercy, and whom he will, he hardens.

Man hath now a greater dependence on the grace of God than he had before the fall. He depends on the free goodness of God for much more than he did then. Then he depended on God's goodness for conferring the reward of perfect obedience; for God was not obliged to promise and bestow that reward. But now we are dependent on the grace of God for much more. We stand in need of grace, not only to bestow glory upon us, but to deliver us from hell and eternal wrath. Under the first covenant we depended on God's goodness to give us the reward of righteousness; and so we do now. And not only so, but we stand in need of God's free and sovereign grace to give us that righteousness; and yet not only so, but we stand in need of his grace to pardon our sin and release us from the guilt and infinite demerit of it.

And as we are dependent on the goodness of God for more now than under the first covenant, so we are dependent on a much greater, more free and wonderful goodness. We are now more dependent on God's arbitrary and sovereign good pleasure. We were in our first estate dependent on God for holiness: we had our original righteousness from him; but then holiness was not bestowed in such a way of sovereign good pleasure as it is now. Man was created holy, and it became God to create holy all the reasonable creatures he created: it would have been a disparagement to the holiness of God's nature, if he had made an intelligent creature unholy. But now when man is made holy, it is from mere and arbitrary grace; God may forever deny holiness to the fallen creature if he pleases, without any disparagement to any of his perfections.

And we are not only indeed more dependent on the grace of God, but our dependence is much more conspicuous, because our own insufficiency and helplessness in ourselves is much more apparent, in our fallen and undone state, than it was before we were either sinful or miserable. We are more apparently dependent on God for holiness, because we are first sinful, and utterly polluted, and afterwards holy: so the production of the effect is sensible, and its derivation from God more obvious. If man was ever holy and always so, it would not be so apparent, that he had not holiness necessarily, as an inseparable qualification of human nature. So we are more apparently dependent on free grace for the favor of God, for we are first justly the objects of his displeasure, and afterwards are received into favor. We are more apparently dependent on God for happiness, being first miserable, and afterwards happy. 'Tis more apparently free and without merit in us, because we are actually without any kind of excellency to merit, if there could be any such thing as merit in creature excellency. And we are not only without any true excellency, but are full of, and wholly defiled with, that which is infinitely odious. All our good is more apparently from God, because we are first naked and wholly without any good, and afterwards are enriched with all good.

2. We receive all of the power of God. Man's redemption is often spoken of as a work of wonderful power as well as grace. The great power of God appears in bringing a sinner from his low state, from the depths of sin and misery, to such an exalted state of holiness and happiness; Eph. 1:19, "And what is the exceeding greatness of his power to us-ward who believe, according to the working of his mighty power."[5]

We are dependent on God's power through every step of our redemption. We are dependent on the power of God to convert us, and give faith in Jesus Christ, and the new nature. 'Tis a work of creation: "If any man be in Christ, he is a new creature" (II Cor. 5:17); "We are created in Christ Jesus" (Eph. 2:10). The fallen creature can't attain to true holiness, but by being created again; Eph. 4:24, "And that ye put on the new man, which after God is created in righteousness and true holiness." 'Tis a raising from the dead; Col. 2:12, "Wherein also ye are risen with him through the faith of the operation of God, who hath raised him from the dead." Yea, 'tis a more glorious work of power than mere creation, or raising a dead body to life, in that the effect attained is greater and more excellent. That holy and happy being, and spiritual life which is reached in the work of conversion, is a far greater, and more glorious, effect than mere being and life. And the state from whence the change is made, of such a death in sin, and total corruption of nature, and depth of misery, is far more remote from the state attained than mere death or nonentity.

5. Following this quotation there are dashes in the printed version, a reflection of the MS, where JE added here: "'Tis a new creation; 'tis a raising of the dead," suggesting Eph. 1:20.

'Tis by God's power also that we are preserved in a state of grace; I Pet. 1:5, "Who are kept by the power of God through faith unto salvation." As grace is at first from God, so 'tis continually from him, and is maintained by him, as much as light in the atmosphere is all day long from the sun, as well as at first dawning, or at sunrising.

Men are dependent on the power of God for every exercise of grace, and for carrying on the work of grace in the heart, for the subduing of sin and corruption, and increasing holy principles, and enabling to bring forth fruit in good works, and at last bringing grace to its perfection, in making the soul completely amiable in Christ's glorious likeness, and filling of it with satisfying joy and blessedness; and for the raising of the body to life, and to such a perfect state, that it shall be suitable for an habitation and organ for a soul so perfected and blessed. These are the most glorious effects of the power of God that are seen in the series of God's acts with respect to the creatures.

Man was dependent on the power of God in his first estate, but he is more dependent on that power now; he needs God's power to do more things for him, and he depends on a more wonderful exercise of his power. It was an effect of the power of God to make men holy at the first; but more remarkably so now, because there is a great deal of opposition and difficulty in the way. 'Tis a more glorious effect of power to make that holy that was so depraved and under the dominion of sin than to confer holiness on that which before had nothing of the contrary. 'Tis a more glorious work of power to rescue a soul out of the hands of the devil, and from the powers of darkness, and to bring it into a state of salvation, than to confer holiness where there was no prepossession or opposition; Luke 11:21–22, "When a strong man armed keepeth his palace, his goods are in peace; but when a stronger man than he shall come upon him, and overcome him, he taketh from him all his armor wherein he trusted, and divideth his spoils." So 'tis a more glorious work of power to uphold a soul in a state of grace and holiness, and to carry it on till it is brought to glory, when there is so much sin remaining in the heart, resisting, and Satan with all his might opposing, than it would have been to have kept man from falling at first, when Satan had nothing in man.

Thus we have shown how the redeemed are dependent on God for all their good as they have all *of* him.

Second. They are also dependent on God for all, as they have all *through* him. 'Tis God that is the medium of it as well as the author and fountain of it. All that we have, wisdom, and the pardon of sin, deliverance from hell, acceptance into God's favor, grace and holiness, true comfort and happiness, eternal life and glory, we have from God by a Mediator; and this Mediator is God, which Mediator we have an absolute dependence upon, as he *through* whom we receive all. So that here is another way wherein we have our dependence on God for all good. God not only gives us the Mediator, and accepts his mediation, and of his power and grace bestows the things purchased by the Mediator, but he is the Mediator.

Our blessings are what we have by purchase; and the purchase is made of God, the blessings are purchased of him, and God gives the purchaser; and not only so, but God is the purchaser. Yea, God is both the purchaser and the price; for Christ, who is God, purchased these blessings for us, by offering up himself as the price of our salvation. He purchased eternal life by the sacrifice of himself; Heb. 7:27, "He offered up himself"; and 9:26, "He hath appeared to take away sin by the sacrifice of himself." Indeed it was the human nature that was offered; but it was the same person with the divine, and therefore was looked upon as an infinite price: it was looked upon as if God had been offered in sacrifice.

As we thus have our good *through* God, we have a dependence on God in a respect that man in his first estate had not. Man was to have eternal life then through his own righteousness, so that he had partly a dependence upon what was in himself; for we have a dependence upon that *through* which we have our good, as well as that *from* which we have it. And though man's righteousness that he then depended on was indeed from God, yet it was his own; it was inherent in himself; so that his dependence was not so immediately on God. But now the righteousness that we are dependent on is not in ourselves but in God. We are saved through the righteousness of Christ: he "is made unto us righteousness"; and therefore is prophesied of under that name of "the Lord our righteousness" (Jer. 23:6). In that the righteousness we are justified by is the righteousness of Christ, it is the righteousness of God; II Cor. 5:21, "That we might be made the righteousness of God in him."

Thus in redemption, we han't only all things *of* God, but *by* and *through* him; I Cor. 8:6, "But to us there is but one God, the Father, of whom are all things, and we in him; and one Lord Jesus Christ, by whom are all things, and we by him."

Third. The redeemed have all their good *in* God. We not only have it *of* him and *through* him, but it consists *in* him; he *is* all our good.

The good of the redeemed is either objective or inherent. By their objective good I would mean, that extrinsic object, in the possession and enjoyment of which they are happy. Their inherent good is that excellency or pleasure which is in the soul itself. With respect to both of which the redeemed have all their good in God, or which is the same thing, God is all their good.

1. The redeemed have all their objective good in God. God himself is the great good which they are brought to the possession and enjoyment of by redemption. He is their highest good, and the sum of all that good which Christ purchased. God is the inheritance of the saints; he is the portion of their souls. God is their wealth and treasure, their food, their life, their dwelling place, their ornament and diadem, and their everlasting honor and glory. They have none in heaven but God; he is the great good which the redeemed are received to at death, and which they are to rise to at the end of the world. The Lord God, he is the light of the heavenly Jerusalem, and is the river of the water of life that runs, and the tree of life that grows, in the midst of the paradise of God [Rev. 21:23; 22:1–2]. The glorious excellencies and beauty of God will be what will forever entertain the minds of the saints, and the love of God will be their everlasting feast. The redeemed will indeed enjoy other things: they will enjoy the angels, and will enjoy one another; but that which they shall enjoy in the angels, or each other, or in anything else whatsoever, that will yield them delight and happiness, will be what will be seen of God in them.

2. The redeemed have all their inherent good in God. Inherent good is twofold: 'tis either excellency or pleasure. These the redeemed not only derive from God, as caused by him, but have them in him. They have spiritual excellency and joy by a kind of participation of God. They are made excellent by a communication of God's excellency: God puts his own beauty, i.e. his beautiful likeness, upon their souls. They are made "partakers of the divine nature," or moral image of God (II Pet. 1:4). They are holy by being made "partakers of God's holiness" (Heb. 12:10). The saints are beautiful and blessed by a communication of God's holiness and joy as the moon and planets are bright by the sun's light. The saint hath spiritual joy and pleasure by a kind of effusion of God on the soul. In these things the redeemed have communion with God; that is, they partake with him and of him.

The saints have both their spiritual excellency and blessedness by the gift of the Holy Ghost, or Spirit of God, and his dwelling in them. They are not only caused by the Holy Ghost, but are in the Holy Ghost as their principle. The Holy Spirit becoming an inhabitant is a vital principle in the soul. He acting in, upon, and with the soul, becomes a fountain of true holiness and joy, as a spring is of water, by the exertion and diffusion of itself; John 4:14, "But whosoever drinketh of the water that I shall give him shall never thirst; but the water that I shall give him shall be in him a well of water springing up into everlasting life"; compared with [John] 7:38–39, "He that believeth on me, as the Scripture hath said, out of his belly shall flow rivers of living water. (But this spake he of the Spirit, which they that believe on him should receive)." The sum of what Christ has purchased for us is that spring of water spoken of in the former of those places, and those rivers of living water spoken of in the latter. And the sum of the blessings, which the redeemed shall receive in heaven, is that "river of water of life" that proceeds from "the throne of God and the Lamb" (Rev. 22:1). Which doubtless signifies the same with those "rivers of living water," explained [in] John 7:38–39, which is elsewhere called the "river of God's pleasures" [Ps. 36:8]. Herein consists the fullness of good, which the saints receive of Christ. 'Tis by partaking of the Holy Spirit that they have communion with Christ in his fullness. God hath given the Spirit, not by measure unto him; and they do receive of his fullness, and grace for grace. This is the sum of the saints' inheritance: and therefore that little of the Holy Ghost which believers have in this world is said to be "the earnest of the inheritance"; II Cor. 1:22, "Who hath also sealed us, and given us the Spirit in our hearts"; and [II Cor.] 5:5, "Now he that hath wrought us for the selfsame thing is God, who also hath given unto us the earnest of the Spirit"; and Eph. 1:13–14, "Ye were sealed with that Holy Spirit of promise, which is the earnest of our inheritance until the redemption of the purchased possession."

The Holy Spirit and good things are spoken of in Scripture as the same, as if the Spirit of God communicated to the soul comprised all good things; Matt. 7:11, "How much more shall your heavenly Father give good things to them that ask him?" In Luke, it is ch. 11, v. 13: "How much more shall your heavenly Father give the Holy Spirit to them that ask him?" This is the sum of the blessings that Christ died to procure, and that are the subject of gospel promises; Gal. 3:13–14, "He was made a curse for us, that we might receive the promise of the Spirit through faith." The Spirit of God is the great promise of the Father; Luke 24:49, "Behold, I send the promise of my Father upon you." The Spirit of God therefore is called the "Spirit of promise" (Eph. 1:13). This promised thing Christ received, and had given into his hand, as soon as he had finished the work of our redemption, to bestow on all that he had redeemed; Acts 2:33, "Therefore being by the right hand of God exalted, and having received of the Father the promise of the Holy Ghost, he hath shed forth this, which ye now see and hear." So that all the holiness and happiness of the redeemed is *in* God. 'Tis in the communications, indwelling and acting of the Spirit of God. Holiness and happiness is in the fruit, here and hereafter, because God dwells in them, and they in God.

Thus 'tis God that has given us the Redeemer, and 'tis of him that our good is purchased; so 'tis God that is the Redeemer, and the price: and 'tis God also that is the good purchased. So that all that we have is *of* God, and *through* him, and *in* him; Rom. 11:36, "For of him, and through him, and to him," or "in him," "are all things." The same in the Greek, that is here rendered "to him," is rendered "in him" (I Cor. 8:6).[6]

II. God is glorified in the work of redemption by this means, viz. by there being so great and universal a dependence of the redeemed on him.

First. Man hath so much the greater occasion and obligation to take notice of and acknowledge God's perfections and all-sufficiency. The greater the creature's dependence is on God's perfections, and the greater concern he has with them, so much the greater occasion has he to take notice of them. So much the greater concern anyone has with and dependence upon the power and grace of God, so much the greater occasion has he to take notice of that power and grace. So much the greater and more immediate dependence there is on the divine holiness, so much the greater occasion to take notice of and acknowledge that. So much the greater and more absolute dependence we have on the divine perfections, as belonging to the several persons of the Trinity, so much the greater occasion have we to observe and own the divine glory of each of them. That which we are most concerned with is surely most in the way of our observation and notice; and this kind of concern with anything, viz. dependence, does especially tend to commend and oblige the attention and observation. Those things that we are not much dependent upon, 'tis easy to neglect; but we can scarce do any other than mind that which we have a great dependence on. By reason of our so great dependence on God, and his perfections, and in so many respects, he and his glory are the more directly set in our view, which way soever we turn our eyes.

We have the greater occasion to take notice of God's all-sufficiency, when all our sufficiency is thus every way of him. We have the more occasion to contemplate him as an infinite good, and as the fountain of all good. Such a dependence on God demonstrates God's all-sufficiency.

6. JE here deleted the following in the MS: "We have all of God the Father through the Son and in the Holy Ghost, so that God is the Alpha and Omega in this affair of Redemption." In the MS, the Application immediately follows, and JE's discussion of the second proposition is the final section of the sermon; the printed version reverses this order.

So much as the dependence of the creature is on God, so much the greater does the creature's emptiness in himself appear to be: and so much the greater the creature's emptiness, so much the greater must the fullness of the being be who supplies him. Our having all *of* God, shows the fullness of his power and grace: our having all *through* him, shows the fullness of his merit and worthiness; and our having all *in* him demonstrates his fullness of beauty, love and happiness.

And the redeemed by reason of the greatness of their dependence on God, han't only so much the greater occasion, but obligation to contemplate and acknowledge the glory and fullness of God. How unreasonable and ungrateful should we be, if we did not acknowledge that sufficiency and glory, that we do absolutely, immediately and universally depend upon?

Second. Hereby is demonstrated how great God's glory is considered comparatively, or as compared with the creature's. By the creature's being thus wholly and universally dependent on God, it appears that the creature is nothing, and that God is all. Hereby it appears that God is infinitely above us; that God's strength, and wisdom, and holiness are infinitely greater than ours. However great and glorious the creature apprehends God to be, yet if he be not sensible of the difference between God and him, so as to see that God's glory is great compared with his own, he will not be disposed to give God the glory due to His name. If the creature in any respects sets himself upon a level with God, or exalts himself to any competition with Him, however he may apprehend that great honor and profound respect may belong to God from those that are more inferior, and at a greater distance, [he] will not be so sensible of its being due from him. So much the more men exalt themselves, so much the less will they surely be disposed to exalt God. 'Tis certainly a thing that God aims at in the disposition of things in the affair of redemption, if we allow the Scriptures to be a revelation of God's mind, that God should appear full and man himself empty; that God should appear all and man nothing. 'Tis God's declared design that others should not "glory in his presence," which implies that 'tis his design to advance his own comparative glory. So much as man glories in God's presence, so much the less glory is ascribed to God.

Third. By its being thus ordered that the creature should have so absolute and universal a dependence on God, provision is made that God should have our whole souls, and should be the object of our undivided respect. If we had our dependence partly on God and partly on something else, man's respect would be divided to those different things on which he had dependence. Thus it would be if we depended on God only for a part of our good, and on ourselves, or some other being, for another part; or if we had our good only *from* God, and *through* another that was not God, and *in* something else distinct from both, our hearts would be divided between the good itself, and him *from* whom, and him *through* whom we received it. But now there is no occasion for this, God being not only he *from* or *of* whom we have all good, but also *through* whom, and one that is that good itself, that we have from him, and through him. So that whatsoever there is to attract our respect, the tendency is still directly towards God, all unites in him as the center.

USE.

I. We may here observe the marvelous wisdom of God in the work of redemption. God hath made man's emptiness and misery, his low, lost and ruined state into which he is sunk by the fall, an occasion of the greater advancement of his own glory, as in other ways so particularly in this, that there is now a much more universal and apparent dependence of man on God. Though God be pleased to lift man out of that dismal abyss of sin and woe into which he was fallen, and exceedingly to exalt him in excellency and honor, and to an high pitch of glory and blessedness, yet the creature has nothing in any respect to glory of; all the glory evidently belongs to God, all is in a mere, and most absolute and divine dependence on the Father, Son, and Holy Ghost.

And each person of the Trinity is equally glorified in this work. There is an absolute dependence of the creature on every one for all: all is *of* the Father, all *through* the Son, and all *in* the Holy Ghost. Thus God appears in the work of redemption, as all in all. 'Tis fit that he that "is, and there is none else" [Deut. 4:35], should be the "Alpha and Omega, the first and the last" [Rev. 1:11], the all and the only, in this work.

II. Hence those doctrines and schemes of divinity that are in any respects opposite to such an absolute and universal dependence on God, do derogate from God's glory, and thwart the design of the contrivance for our redemption. Those schemes that put the creature in God's stead, in any of the mentioned respects, that exalt man into the place of either Father, Son, or Holy Ghost, in anything pertaining to our redemption; that however they may allow of a dependence of the redeemed on God, yet deny a dependence that is so absolute and universal; that own an entire dependence on God for some things, but not for others; that own that we depend on God for the gift and acceptance of a redeemer, but deny so absolute a dependence on him for the obtaining of an interest in the Redeemer; that own an absolute dependence on the Father for giving his Son, and on the Son for working out redemption, but not so entire a dependence on the Holy Ghost for conversion, and a being in Christ, and so coming to a title to his benefits; that own a dependence on God for means of grace, but not absolutely for the benefit and success of those means; that own a partial dependence on the power of God, for the obtaining and exercising holiness, but not a mere dependence on the arbitrary and sovereign grace of God; that own a dependence on the free grace of God for a reception into his favor, so far that it is without any proper merit, but not as it is without being attracted, or moved with any excellency; that own a partial dependence on Christ, as he through whom we have life, as having purchased new terms of life, but still hold that the righteousness through which we have life is inherent in ourselves, as it was under the first covenant; and whatever other way any scheme is inconsistent with our entire dependence on God for all, and in each of those ways, of having all *of* him, *through* him, and *in* him, it is repugnant to the design and tenor of the gospel, and robs it of that which God accounts its luster and glory.

III. Hence we may learn a reason why faith is that by which we come to have an interest in this redemption; for there is included in the nature of faith, a sensibleness, and an acknowledgment of this absolute dependence on God in this affair. 'Tis very fit that it should be required of all, in order to their having the benefit of this redemption, that they should be sensible of, and acknowledge this dependence on God for it. 'Tis by this means that God contrived to glorify himself in redemption, and 'tis fit that God should at least have this glory of those that are the subjects of this redemption; and have the benefit of it.

Faith is a sensibleness of what is real in the work of redemption; and as we do wholly depend on God, so the soul that believes doth entirely depend on God for all salvation, in its own sense, and act. Faith abases men, and exalts God, it gives all the glory of redemption to God alone. It is necessary in order to saving faith, that man should be emptied of himself, that he should be sensible that he is "wretched, and miserable, and poor, and blind, and naked" [Rev. 3:17]. Humility is a great ingredient in true faith: he that truly receives redemption receives it "as a little child"; Mark 10:15, "Whosoever shall not receive the kingdom of heaven as a little child, he shall not enter therein." 'Tis the delight of a believing soul to abase itself and exalt God alone: that is the language of it; Ps. 115:1, "Not unto us, not unto us, O Lord, but to thy name give glory."[7]

IV. Let us be exhorted to exalt God alone, and ascribe to him all the glory of redemption. Let us endeavor to obtain, and to increase in, a sensibleness of our great dependence on God, to have our eye on him alone, to mortify a self-dependent, and self-righteous disposition. Man is naturally exceeding prone to be exalting himself, and depending on his own power or goodness, as though he were he from whom he must expect happiness, and to have respect to enjoyments alien from God and his Spirit, as those in which happiness is to be found.

And this doctrine should teach us to exalt God alone as by trust and reliance, so by praise. "Let him that glories glory in the Lord" [Jer. 9:24]. Hath any man hope that he is converted, and sanctified, and that his mind is endowed with true excellency and spiritual beauty, and his sins forgiven, and he received into God's favor, and exalted to the honor and blessedness of being his child, and heir of eternal life; let him give God all the glory, who alone makes him to differ from the worst of men in this world, or the miserablest of the damned in hell. Hath any man much comfort and strong hope of eternal life, let not his hope lift him up, but dispose him the more to abase himself, and reflect on his own exceeding unworthiness of such a favor, and to exalt God alone. Is any man eminent in holiness, and abundant in good works? Let him take nothing of the glory of it to himself, but ascribe it to him whose "workmanship we are, created in Christ Jesus unto good works" [Eph. 2:10].

Appendix to *God Gloried in Man's Dependence*[8]

TO THE READER

It was with no small difficulty that the author's youth and modesty were prevailed on to let him appear a preacher in our public lecture, and afterwards to give us a copy of his discourse, at the desire of divers, ministers and others, who heard it. But as we quickly found him a workman that needs not to be ashamed before his brethren, our satisfaction was the greater to see him pitching upon so noble a subject, and treating

7. For an interesting and formative sermonic precursor, see the sermon on Ps. 115:1 (25) from the fall of 1723.

8. This note to the reader from the sponsors of *God Glorified* prefaced the first edition.

it with so much strength and clearness, as the judicious reader will perceive in the following composure.

A subject which secures to God his great design in the work of fallen man's redemption by the Lord Jesus Christ, which is evidently so laid out as that the glory of the whole should return to him, the blessed ordainer, purchaser and applier. A subject which enters deep into practical religion, without the belief of which that must soon die in the hearts and lives of men.

For in proportion to the sense we have of our dependence on the sovereign God for all the good we want will be our value for him, our application to him, our trust in him, our fear to offend him, and our care to please him; as likewise our gratitude and love, our delight and praise, upon our sensible experience of his free benefits.

In short, it is the very soul of piety to apprehend and own, that all our springs are in him, the springs of our present grace and comfort, and of our future glory and blessedness, and that they all entirely flow through Christ by the efficacious influence of the Holy Spirit. By these things saints live, and in all these things is the life of our spirits.

Such doctrines as these, which by humbling the minds of men, prepare them for the exaltations of God. He has finally owned and prospered in the reformed world, and in our land especially in the days of our forefathers; and we hope they will never grow unfashionable among us. For, we are well assured, if these which we call the doctrines of grace ever come to be contemned or disrelished, vital piety will proportionably languish and wear away, as these doctrines always sink in the esteem of men, upon the decay of serious religion.

We cannot therefore but express our joy and thankfulness that the great head of the church is pleased still to raise up from among the children of his people, for the supply of his churches, those who assert and maintain these evangelical principles; and that our churches (notwithstanding all their degeneracies) have still high value for such principles, and for those who publicly own and teach them.

And as we cannot but wish and pray that the college in the neighboring colony (as well as our own) may be a fruitful mother of many such sons as the author, by the blessing of heaven on the care of their present worthy rector, so we heartily rejoice in the special favor of providence in bestowing such a rich gift on the happy church of Northampton, which has for so many lusters of years flourished under the influence of such pious doctrines, taught them in the excellent ministry of their late venerable pastor, whose gifts and spirit we hope will long live and shine in this his grandson, to the end that they may abound yet more in all the lovely fruits of evangelical humility and thankfulness, to the glory of God.

To his blessing we commit them all with this discourse, and every one that reads it, and are,

Your servants in the gospel,
T[homas] Prince
W[illiam] Cooper[9]

Boston, August 17, 1731

9. Thomas Prince (1687–1758) was a colleague of Joseph Sewall's at Boston's Old South Church from 1718 until his death; William Cooper (1694–1743) was a junior associate of Benjamin Colman's at Brattle Street Church, Boston. Both these ministers were to become close associates of JE's.

THE PERPETUITY AND CHANGE OF THE SABBATH

In *The Perpetuity and Change of the Sabbath,* Edwards deals with the basic premise of corporate Christian worship: the observance of Sunday as the Christian sabbath. Other sermons in this volume, including *Self-Examination and the Lord's Supper,* show Edwards' interest in sacramental issues and their relation to social practice. *The Perpetuity and Change of the Sabbath,* a three-preaching-unit lecture first delivered in late 1730 or early 1731, includes practical applications like exhortations to keep the sabbath holy, to provide a visible witness to the gospel, and to abstain from sins that divert the Christian from genuine worship, such as drunkenness, gossip, and preoccupation with business. Yet this sermon is not a typical New England jeremiad against immoral behavior on the sabbath. Rather, it is largely an exegetical and theological defense of Sunday worship.

There may have been several occasions for such an apologia, despite the universal acceptance of the Sunday sabbath (or Lord's day) in the Church of England and New England's congregational order. Strict observance of Sunday (that is, attendance at divine worship and abstinence from all secular business and public recreations) had become something of a badge of Puritanism in the Anglo-American world. It distinguished covenant-keepers from Anglicans and royalists who eschewed Puritan strictness, from rationalists and skeptics who dismissed such observance as superstitious, and from market-minded businessmen who would not forego the opportunity to conduct business on Sunday.

Edwards appears more directly concerned in this sermon, however, with historical and religious arguments against Sunday observance. Jeremiah Dummer, a son of a distinguished Boston family and celebrated graduate of Harvard, had scandalized New Englanders by producing a learned tome (*De Jure Judaeorum Sabbati* [Leyden, 1703]) that cast the scriptural and historical bases for Sunday worship into question. Dummer's work was symptomatic of a debate that ranged beyond the sabbath to the historical legitimacy of much of traditional Christianity. A defense of the Lord's day against the likes of Dummer was, to some extent, a defense of orthodox readings of Scripture. Furthermore, New England had become home in Edwards' day to several free-church sects, such as the Seventh-Day Baptists (largely settled in Rhode Island but scattered also in Massachusetts) and the Rogerenes (in Connecticut), who worshiped on Saturday. Arguing that the only true sabbath as instituted in the fourth commandment was the last day of the week, they rejected laws that required Sunday worship as part of a corrupt and tyrannical church-state order.[1]

In explanation of the doctrine, Edwards offers two propositions: one day ought to be set aside for worship; and Sunday, for Christians, is that day. In defense of the first proposition he begins with an argument from nature, providing commonsense reasons for having one day set aside by a whole society. He then moves to scriptural evidence that the observance of such a day was not a mere ceremonial precept for ancient Israel. In a complex exegesis, he attempts to show that a day of observance was a universal and perpetual moral law.

In defense of the second proposition, Edwards offers fourteen points of scriptural evidence. He argues that the fourth commandment mandated one day to be kept holy but did not specify which day. Focusing on the theme of the new creation, he discusses a standard compilation of texts that were read as evidence for the day of Christ's resurrection as the new sabbath. Edwards also gives a particularly ingenious reading of the Exodus as a type of redemption and therefore of the resurrection. Because a recollection of Israel's deliverance from Egypt prefaces the command to keep the sabbath, Edwards reasons, Christians' deliverance from sin through the resurrection of Christ (on Sunday) should provide the chronological location for the Christian sabbath.

Edwards draws much of his exegetical commentary in the sermon from his private notebooks. Indeed, *The Perpetuity and Change of the Sabbath* is one of the more striking instances of how Edwards brought his historical, philological, and theological studies to bear on his preaching. He writes on the sabbath as integral to the order of creation in "Miscellanies" no. 45 and "Notes on the Apocalypse" no. 16. Edwards also addresses the question of the sabbath in several "Miscellanies" from the early 1730s (e.g., nos. 464, 466, 495, and 500) and, later, during the mid-1730s (nos. 531, 536, 551, 691, and especially 693). His discussion of the Exodus reflects contemporaneous entry nos. 204 and 211 from

1. See Solberg, *Redeem the Time*, 264–81.

"Notes on Scripture," and entry nos. 52 and 53 from "Images of Divine Things." "Notes on the Apocalypse" no. 77, a meditation from the mid-1730s on the Exodus and its meaning for the sabbath, shows that Edwards drew from Arthur Bedford's *The Scripture Chronology Demonstrated by Astronomical Calculations* (London, 1730). Edwards cites Bedford in his "Notes on the Apocalypse" and in this sermon may have used Bedford for historical evidence of the shift from the last to the first day of the week as the day of worship in the ancient church.[2]

It is difficult to surmise whether the people of Northampton appreciated Edwards' exegetical discussions and display of erudition. *The Perpetuity and Change of the Sabbath* tells us at least that he believed that a reasoned defense of orthodox Christian practice was an important task of the preacher. At times he was content simply to address theological issues in scholarly terms and to expand on the affective and moral implications of them at another occasion.

* * *

The manuscript is a large duodecimo booklet, consisting of thirty-two leaves. Extensive revisions and additions by Edwards at or closely after the time of composition suggest that he worked over this manuscript carefully. Several inserted leaves written by him considerably later are evidence of at least one repreaching. These inserted leaves (15–18) contain three exegetical excurses, which are printed in the notes. The first, for inclusion under the third subhead of the second proposition of the Doctrine, provides a philological study of "sabbath rest" in Heb. 4. The second insertion, in the seventh subhead of the second proposition, amplifies Edwards' interpretation of the Exodus as a type of Christ's resurrection. The third insertion, under the twelfth subhead, addresses additional references in the Bible to the Lord's day.

Jonathan Edwards, Jr., first published *The Perpetuity and Change of the Sabbath* as Sermons XIII–XV in his edition of his father's works, *Sermons on the Following Subjects* (Hartford, 1780). In preparing the manuscript for transcription, he wrote brief directions in the inserted leaves and at the corresponding points in the original to indicate where the passages belonged.

2. See *Works, 14*, 226, 506–08, 538. On Bedford and the "Notes on the Apocalpyse," see *Works, 5*, 64–65, 129–30, 179–82.

THE PERPETUITY AND CHANGE OF THE SABBATH

I CORINTHIANS 16:1–2.

Now concerning the collection for the saints, upon the first day of the week let every one of you lay by him in store, as God has prospered him.[3]

We find in the New Testament often mentioned a certain collection that was made by the Grecian churches for their brethren in Judea, who were reduced to pinching want by a dearth that then prevailed, which was the heavier upon them by reason of the circumstances of the Christians, who were from the beginning greatly oppressed and persecuted by unbelieving Jews.

We have this contribution twice mentioned in Acts, as in 11:28–30, 24:17. So it is taken notice of in several of the epistles: in the Epistle to the Romans (15:26); and again in the Epistle to the Galatians (2:10). But 'tis most largely insisted on in these two epistles to the Corinthians: in this First Epistle in this sixteenth chapter, and in the Second Epistle in the eighth and ninth chapters. The Apostle begins his directions in this place with the words of our text, wherein we may observe,

1. What is the thing to be done about which the Apostle gives them direction: and that is the making a collection for the saints.[4] The exercising and manifesting their charity towards their brethren by communicating to them for the supply of their wants, which was by Christ and

3. JE amended the text here, but referred to the whole of it in the Explication and transcribed the complete text to begin the second preaching unit: "'Now concerning the collection for the saints, as I have given order to the churches of Galatia, even so do ye. Upon the first day of the week let every one of you lay by him in store, as God hath prospered him, that there be no gatherings when I come.'"

4. The Explication to this sermon anticipates the larger treatment of almsgiving in a subsequent sermon in this volume, *The Duty of Charity to the Poor.*

his apostles often spoken of and insisted on, [is] one main duty of the Christian religion, and is expressly so declared to be by the apostle James; Jas. 1:27, "Pure religion and undefiled before God and the Father is this, to visit the fatherless and widows in their affliction, and to keep himself unspotted from the world."

2. We may observe the time in which the Apostle directed that this should be done, viz. on the first day of the week. The Apostle by the inspiration of the Holy Ghost insists upon it, that it be done on such a particular day of the week, as if no other day would do so well as that or were proper and fit a time for such work. Thus, although the inspired Apostle was not for making that distinction of days in gospel times as the Jews did—Gal. 4:10–11, "Ye observe days, and months, and times, and years. I am afraid of you, lest I have bestowed upon you my labor in vain"—yet here the Apostle gives the preference to one day of the week before any other for the performance of a certain great duty of Christianity.

3. It may be observed that this is the direction that the Apostle had given to other churches that were concerned in the same duty upon this occasion. He had given direction to them also to do it on the first day of the week: "as I have given order to the churches of Galatia, even so do ye." Whence we may learn that it was not anything peculiar in the circumstances of the Christians at Corinth that was the reason why the Holy Ghost insisted on its being done on this day of the week by them. The Apostle had given the like order to the churches of Galatia. Now, Galatia was far distant from Corinth; there was the sea that parted 'em, and besides that there were several other countries between 'em.

Therefore it cannot be thought that the Holy Ghost directs 'em to this time upon any secular account, having respect to some particular circumstances of the people in that city, but upon a religious account, something he has respect to that reached all Christians throughout the wide world, upon the account of which he gives a preference to this day, for such work, before any other day.

And we learn by other passages of the New Testament that the case was the same with respect to other exercises of religion, that the first day of the week was the day preferred before any other amongst the primitive Christians in the age of the apostles in the churches immediately under the apostles' care; Acts 20:7, "Upon the first day of the week, when the disciples came together to break bread, Paul preached unto them."

It seems by those things to have been amongst the primitive Christians in the apostles' days with respect to the first day of the week as it was amongst the Jews with respect to the seventh. The doing of alms, showing mercy, we are taught by Christ, is proper work for a sabbath day. When the Pharisees found fault with Christ suffering the disciples to pluck the ears of corn and eat on the sabbath day, Christ corrects them with that: "I will have mercy, and not sacrifice" (Matt. 12:7). And Christ teaches that works of mercy are proper on the sabbath in Luke 13:15–16, 14:5. 'Tis work that used to be done on sacred festivals and days of rejoicing under the old testament, as it was in Nehemiah's and Esther's time (Neh. 8:10; Esther 9:19, 22). And Josephus and Philo, two very learned and noted Jews that wrote not long after Christ's time, give that account, that it was the manner amongst the Jews on the sabbath to make collections for sacred and pious uses on the sabbath day.

DOCTRINE.

'Tis the mind and will of God that the first day of the week should be the day that should be especially set apart for religious exercises and duties amongst Christians.

That this was the doctrine that the Holy Ghost intended to teach us by this and some other passages of the New Testament, I hope will appear more plainly by the sequel.

'Tis a doctrine that we have been generally brought up in by the institutions and examples of our ancestors, and 'tis and has been the general profession of the Christian world that this day ought to be observed and religiously distinguished from other days of the week.

However, there are some that do deny it. There are some that refuse to take any notice of the day or any way difference it from other days. There are others that own that 'tis a laudable custom of the Christian church, that they fell into by agreement and by the appointment of her ordinary rulers to set apart this day for public worship, but deny any other original to such observation of the day besides prudential human appointment. There are others that religiously observe the Jewish sabbath, suppose the institution of that to be of perpetual obligation, and that we want foundation for determining that that is abrogated and another day of the week appointed in its room.

All those kinds say that there is no clear revelation of its being the mind and will of God that the first day of the week should be observed as a day to be set apart for religious exercises in the room of the ancient sabbath, which there ought to be in order [to] the Christian churches' observing of it as a divine institution. They say that we ought not to go upon the tradition of past ages, and uncertain and farfetched inferences from some passages of the history of the New Testament or obscure and uncertain hints in the apostles' writings; but we ought to expect a plain institution, which, they say, we may conclude God would have given us if he designed that the whole Christian church in all ages should observe another day of the week for a holy sabbath besides what was appointed by plain and positive institution of old. And so far is undoubtedly true: that if this be the mind and will of God, [then] he has not left the matter to human tradition but has so revealed his mind about it in his Word that there is there to be found good and substantial evidences that it is his mind, and that the revelation is plain enough for them that have ears to hear, that is, for them that will justly exercise their understandings about what God says to them.

And no Christian should rest till he has satisfactorily discovered the mind of God in this matter. If the Christian sabbath be of divine institution, it is doubtless a thing of great importance to religion whether it be well kept or no, and therefore that every Christian should be well acquainted with the institution of it.

If persons only take it upon trust, keep the first day of the week only because their parents taught 'em so and they see other folks do so, and so take it for certain that it is right, they will never be like to keep it so conscientiously and strictly as if they had seen with their own eyes and had been convinced by themselves, seeing good grounds in the Word of God to go upon. And when they are negligent in sanctifying the sabbath or are guilty of profaning it, their consciences won't have that advantage to smite them for it.

And those that have a sincere desire to obey God in all things, they'll keep the sabbath more carefully and more cheerfully if they have seen and been convinced that they therein do what is according to God's will and commandment, and what is acceptable to him. A person will have a great deal more of comfort, in the reflection, upon his having carefully and painfully kept the sabbath.[5]

I design now, therefore, by the help of God, to show that it is sufficiently revealed in the Scriptures that it is the mind and will of God that the first day of the week should be distinguished in the Christian church from other days of the week as a sabbath to be devoted to religious

5. JE here deletes: "There is need at this day of inquiring into the Scripture grounds of this practice of keeping the first day of the week as a sabbath, when there are rising up those that do oppose it and many begin to call it in question." See the headnote to this sermon for possible references.

exercises. In order to this, I would here, in the first place, premise that the mind and will of God may be sufficiently revealed in his Word concerning any duty to be performed by us without a particular precept in so many express terms.

The human understanding is the ear to which the Word of God speaks, and if it be but so spoken as that that ear may plainly hear it, it is enough. God is sovereign as to the manner of revealing his mind, whether he will reveal it by saying it in express terms or whether we can perceive it by laying several things that he has said together. If his mind be but revealed, it is sufficient for us if there be but sufficient means for the communication of his mind to our minds, whether we hear so many express words with our ears or see them with our eyes or see by the eye of reason and understanding the thing that he would signify to us.

Who can say that if that had been the mind of God that we should keep the first day of the week, he would have commanded it in express terms, as he did the keeping the seventh day of old? Indeed, if God had so made our faculties that we were not capable of receiving a revelation of God's mind in any other way, then there would be some reason to say so. But God has given such understanding that we are capable of receiving a revelation when made in another manner. And if God deals with [us] agreeably to our natures and in a way proportionable to our capacities, it is enough.

And if God any way whatsoever discovers his mind in a way proportionable to our faculties, we are obliged to obedience, and God may expect our notice and observance [of] his revelation in the same manner as if he had revealed it in express terms.

Two Propositions[6]

Prop. I. 'Tis sufficiently clear that 'tis the mind and will of God that one day of the week, or one day in seven, should be devoted to rest and religious exercises throughout all ages and nations, and not only amongst the Israelites till Christ came, but even in these gospel times and amongst all nations professing Christianity. Here,

First. 'Tis most consonant and agreeable to human reason from the consideration of the nature and state of mankind in this world, that certain fixed parts of time should be set apart to be spent by the church wholly in religious exercises and duties of God's worship.

It is the duty incumbent upon all mankind in all ages alike to worship and serve God, and his service should be our great business. And it

6. In revising for repreaching, JE added: "I. One day of the week. II. This day."

becomes us to worship him with the greatest devotion and engagedness of mind, and therefore to put ourselves at times under such circumstances as shall most contribute to our having our minds entirely devoted to this work without being diverted or interrupted by other things.

And the state of mankind in this world is such that we are called to concern ourselves in secular business and affairs that will necessarily in a considerable degree take up the thoughts and exercise the attention of the mind. And however some particular persons may be in such circumstances as to be more free and disengaged, yet the state of mankind is such that the bulk of 'em in all ages and nations are called ordinarily [to] exercise their thoughts about secular affairs and to follow worldly business that is in its own nature remote from the solemn duties of religion.

It is therefore most meet and suitable that certain times should be set apart wherein men should be required to throw by all other concerns, that their minds may the more freely and entirely be engaged in spiritual exercises, and duties of religion, and God's more immediate worship, so that religion may not be mixed and the mind may be disengaged; and that those times should be fixed and settled, that the church may agree therein, that they should be the same for all, that men mayn't interrupt one another but may rather assist one another by each other's example. For example has a great influence in such cases. If there be a time set apart for public rejoicings and there be generally manifestations of joy given, the general example seems to inspire men with a spirit of joy and mirth: one kindles another. So if it be a time of mourning and there be general appearances and manifestations of sorrow, it naturally affects the mind: it disposes it to depression, it casts a gloom upon the mind, and does, as it were, dull and deaden the spirits. So if a certain time be set apart as holy time for general devotion and solemn religious exercises, a general example tends to solemnize the spirit.

Second. Without doubt one proportion of time is better and fitter for this purpose than another. One proportion [is] more suitable to the state of mankind and has a greater tendency to answer the ends of such times than another. The times may be too far asunder. Thus I think human reason is sufficient to discover that it would be too seldom for the purposes of such solemn times that they should be but once a year. And so, I conclude, nobody will deny but that such times might be too near together to agree with the state and necessary affairs of mankind.

And therefore there can be no difficulty in allowing that some certain proportion of time, whether we can exactly discover it or no, is really fittest and best, and considering all things, considering the end for which such times are kept and the condition and circumstances of men and their necessary affairs, and considering what this state of man is, taking one nation and age with another, that one proportion of time would be more convenient and suitable than any other, which God may know and exactly determine, though we cannot by reason of the scantiness of our understanding.

And as there is a certain frequency of the returns of these times [that] may be more suitable than any other, so one length or continuance of the times themselves may be fitter than another to answer the purposes of such times. Thus if such times, when they come, were to last but an hour, it would not well answer the design of such times, for then worldly things would crowd too near upon sacred exercises, and that would not be the opportunity to get the mind so thoroughly freed and disengaged from other things. But the times being so short, they would be, as it were, mixed together.

There is therefore a certain distance between those times, and a certain continuance of them when they come, that is more meet than others, which God knows and is able to determine, though perhaps we may not be.

Third. 'Tis unreasonable to suppose any other than that God's working six days and resting the seventh, and blessing and hallowing [it], was to be of general use in determining this matter, and that it is written that the practice of mankind in general might some way or other be regulated by it. Or else, what should be the meaning of God's resting the seventh day and hallowing and blessing it, which he did before the giving the fourth commandment [Ex. 20:8–11; Deut. 5:13–15],[7] except he hallowed and blessed it with respect to mankind? For he did not bless and sanctify it with respect to himself, or that he himself and within himself might observe it as holy; that is most absurd. And 'tis unreasonable to suppose that he hallowed and blessed it only with respect to the Jews, a particular nation that rose up above two thousand years after.

So much, therefore, must be intended by it, that it was his mind that mankind should, after his example, work six days and then rest, and hallow and sanctify the next after, or that they should rest and sanctify every seventh day, or that the space between rest and rest or one hallowed time and another amongst his creatures here upon earth should be six days. And so that 'tis the mind and will of God that not only the Jews but men in all nations and ages should sanctify one day in seven, which is the thing we are endeavoring to prove. But,

7. The fourth commandment according to Reformed numbering.

Fourth. God's mind in this matter is clearly revealed in the fourth commandment; i.e. God's will is not only there revealed that the Israelitish nation, but all nations, should keep every seventh day holy or, which is the same thing, one day after every six.

This commandment, as well as that rest, is doubtless everlasting and of perpetual obligation, at least as to the substance of it, as is intimated by its being engraven in tables of stone. And 'tis not to be thought that Christ ever abolished any commandment of the ten, but that there is the complete number ten yet, and will be to the end of the world.

Some say that the fourth commandment is perpetual but not in its literal sense, not designing any particular proportion of time to be set apart and devoted [to] literal rest and religious exercises. They say that 'tis abolished in that sense, and stands in force only in a mystical sense, viz. as that weekly rest of the Jews typified spiritual rest in the Christian church. And so they say that we under the gospel ben't to make any distinction of one day from another, but are to keep all time holy, doing everything in a spiritual manner.

But this is an absurd way of interpreting the commandment as it refers to Christians. For if the commandment be so far abolished, it [is] entirely abolished; for that is the very design of the commandment, to fix the time of worship. The first commandment fixes the object, the second the means, the third the manner, the fourth the time. And if it only stands in force now as signifying a spiritual Christian rest and holy behavior in all times, it don't remain as one of the commandments but as a summary of all the commandments.

[*Obj.*] The main objection against the perpetuity of this commandment is that the duty required is not moral.

Those laws whose obligation arises from [the] nature of things and the general state and nature of mankind, as well as from God's positive revealed will, are called moral laws; and there are others, whose obligation depends merely upon God's positive and arbitrary institution, not moral, such as the ceremonial laws and the gospel precepts about the two sacraments. Now, the objectors say that they will allow all that is moral in the Decalogue to be of perpetual obligation; but this commandment, they say, is not so.

[*Ans.*] But this objection is weak and insufficient for the purpose it is brought forth, or to argue that the fourth commandment as to the substance of it is not of perpetual obligation. For,

[1.] In the first place, if it should be allowed that there was no morality [that] belonged to the commandment but that the duty required is founded merely upon arbitrary institution, it can't therefore be certainly concluded that the commandment is not perpetual. We know there may be commandments in force under the gospel and to the end of the world that are not moral: such are the institutions of the two sacraments. And why may there not be a positive commandment in force in all ages of the church? If positive, arbitrary institutions [were] in force in gospel times, what is there that concludes that there can be no positive precept before gospel times that shall yet continue? But,

2. As we have observed already, the thing in the general—that there should be certain fixed parts of time set apart to be devoted to religious exercises—is founded in the fitness of the thing, arising from the nature of things and the nature and universal state of mankind; and therefore, there is as much reason that there should be a commandment about it that should be perpetual and universal as about any other duty whatsoever. For if the thing in general be founded in the nature of things, that there should be a time fixed, there is consequent upon it a necessity that the time should be limited by a commandment, for there must be a proportion of time fixed, or else that general moral duty can't be observed.

3. The particular determination of the proportion of time in the fourth commandment is also founded in the nature of things, only our understandings are not sufficient absolutely to determine it of themselves. We have observed already that without doubt no proportion of time is in itself fitter than another, and a certain continuance of time fitter than any other, considering the universal state and nature of mankind, which God may see, though our understandings are not perfect enough absolutely to determine which was the fittest of themselves. So that the difference in this commandment from other commandments don't lie here, that other commandments are founded in [the] fitness of the things themselves arising from the universal state and nature of mankind, and this not; but only in this, that the fitness of other commandments were more obvious to men's understandings, and they might have seen it of themselves, but this could not be precisely discovered and positively determined without the assistance of revelation.

So that the commandment of God that every seventh day should be devoted {to religious exercises and duties is} founded in the universal state and nature of mankind as well as other commandments, only man's reason is not sufficient without divine direction so exactly to determine, though perhaps man's reason is sufficient to determine that it ought not to be much seldomer or much oftener than once in seven days.

Fifth. It further confirms it, that it is the mind and will of God that such a weekly sabbath should forever be kept, viz. that God appears in his Word as laying abundantly more weight upon this precept about the sabbath than any of the ceremonial laws, not only by inserting of it into the Decalogue, and making of it one commandment of the ten that was delivered by God with an audible voice, and writing of it with the finger of God in the tables of stone that were the work of God in the mount [Deut. 5:22], and appointing them afterwards to be written in the tables that Moses made; but the keeping the weekly sabbath is spoken of by the prophets as that wherein consisted [a] great part of holiness of life and inserted amongst moral duties, as particularly in Is. 58:13–14, "If thou turn away thy foot from the sabbath, from doing thy pleasure on my holy day; and call the sabbath a delight, the holy of the Lord, honorable; and shalt honor him, not doing thine own ways, nor finding thine own pleasure, nor speaking thine own words: then shalt thou delight thyself in the Lord; and I will cause thee to ride upon the high places of the earth, and feed thee with the heritage of Jacob thy father: for the mouth of the Lord hath spoken it."

Sixth. It was foretold that this commandment should be observed in gospel times. And in Is. 56, at the beginning, there it is spoken of as a great part of holiness of life and amongst moral duties, and also as a duty that should be most acceptable to God from his people, even where the Prophet is speaking of gospel times as in the foregoing chapter [Is. 55:11–15] and in the first verses of this chapter, and of the abolishing of the ceremonial law: "Thus saith the Lord, Keep ye judgment, and do justice: for my salvation is near to come, and my righteousness to be revealed. Blessed is the man that doeth this . . . that keepeth the sabbath from polluting it" [Is. 56:1–2].

Here in the third and fourth verses, the Prophet is speaking of the abolishing of ceremonial law in gospel times, as particularly of that law that forbids eunuchs coming into the congregation of the Lord [Deut. 23:1], and yet here the man is pronounced blessed that keeps the sabbath from polluting of it. And even in the very same sentence where the eunuchs are spoken of as being free from the ceremonial law, they are spoken of as being yet under obligation to keep the sabbath, and their doing of it being that which God lays great weight upon: "Thus saith the Lord to the eunuchs that keep my sabbaths, and choose the things that please me, and take hold of my covenant" [Is. 56:4]. And the strangers that are spoken of in the sixth and seventh verses, they are the Gentiles that should be called in gospel times, as is evident by the last clause in v. 7 and v. 8; but yet 'tis represented here as their duty to keep the sabbath.

Thus 'tis the mind and will of God that every seventh day, or one day in seven, [should be set apart for religious exercises amongst Christians].[8]

Prop. II. That 'tis the will of God that this day should be the first day of the week now, under the gospel dispensation or in the Christian church. In order to the making this clear, let the following things be considered:

First. The words of the fourth commandment afford no objection against this being the day that should be the sabbath any more than against any other day. That this day, which according to the Jewish reckoning is the first of the week, should be kept as a sabbath is no more opposite to any sentence or word of the fourth commandment than that the seventh of the week should be the day.

And that, because the words of the fourth commandment do not determine which day of that week. They determine this, that we shall rest and keep as a sabbath every seventh day, or one day after every sixth; it says, "Six days thou shalt labor and the seventh thou shalt rest," which implies no more than that after six days of labor we shall rest the next to the sixth and keep it holy. And so, to be sure, we are obliged to do forever. But the words no way determine where those six days shall begin, and so where the rest or sabbath shall fall. There is no direction in the fourth commandment how to reckon the time, that is, where to begin and end it. That is not meddled with in the fourth commandment but is supposed by it to be determined otherwise. The Jews did not know where to begin their six days and which particular day to rest by the fourth commandment. That was determined elsewhere by another precept.

The fourth commandment does suppose a particular day appointed, but it don't appoint any. It requires us to rest and keep holy a seventh day, one after every six of labor, which particular day God either had or should appoint. The particular day was designed for that nation in another place; it was determined in that place, in Ex. 16:23, 25–26, "And he said unto them, This is that which the Lord hath said, Tomorrow is the rest of the holy sabbath unto the Lord: bake that which ye will bake today, and seethe that ye will seethe; and that which remaineth over lay up for

8. Here ends the first preaching unit; JE recites the text in full and reiterates the doctrine to begin the next unit. In revising for repreaching, he deleted this paragraph and added, on the verso of the blank tenth leaf, another head: "*Seventh.* Pray that your flight be not in the winter, nor on the sabbath day (Matt. 24:20). Speaking of flying out of Jerusalem (vv. 16–19). Thus I have shown that 'tis the mind and will of God [that every seventh day, or one day in seven, should be set apart for religious exercises amongst Christians]."

you to be kept until the morning. . . . And Moses said, Eat that today; for today is a sabbath unto the Lord: today ye shall not find it in the field. Six days shall ye gather it; but on the seventh day, which is the sabbath, in it there shall be none." There is the first place that we have any mention of the sabbath from the first sabbath on which God rested.

It seems that the Israelites in the time of their bondage in Egypt had lost the reckoning of time, the days of the week, reckoning from the first day of the creation, if it had been kept up till that time. They were slaves and in cruel bondage, and had in a great measure forgotten the true religion; for we are told that they served the gods of Egypt. And 'tis not to be supposed that the Egyptians would suffer their slaves to rest from their work every seventh day. And they continuing in bondage for so long a time had probably lost the weekly reckoning. And therefore when God had brought them out of Egypt into the wilderness, then he made known the sabbath to 'em here in this place. Therefore, we read in Nehemiah that when God led the children of Israel out of Egypt {into the wilderness}, he made known unto them the holy sabbath (Neh. 9:14 and Ezek. 20:12).

But they never would have known where the particular day would have fallen by the fourth commandment. Indeed, the fourth commandment, as it was spoken to the Jews, did refer to their Jewish sabbath, but that don't argue that that day was determined and appointed by it. The precept in the fourth commandment is to be taken generally of a seventh day, such a seventh day as God should appoint. And because such a particular day had been already appointed for the Jewish church, therefore, as it was spoken to them, it did refer to that particular day. But this don't argue but that the same words do refer to another appointed seventh day now in the Christian church. The words of the fourth commandment may oblige the church under different dispensations to observe different appointed seventh days, as well as the fifth commandment obliges different persons to honor different fathers and mothers.

The Christian sabbath, in the sense of the fourth commandment, is as much the seventh day as the Jewish, because 'tis kept every seventh day as much as theirs. 'Tis kept after six days of labor as well as theirs; 'tis the seventh, reckoning from the beginning of our first working day, as well as theirs was the seventh from the beginning of their first working day. All the difference is the seven days formerly began from the day after God's rest from creation, and now the days [begin on the day after that]. 'Tis no matter by what names the days are called, [as] if our nation called Wednesday the first day. Therefore by the institution of the Christian sabbath, there is no change from the fourth commandment, but the change is from another law that determined the beginning and ending of their working days.

So that those words of the fourth commandment, viz. "Six days shalt thou labor, and do all thy work: but the seventh day is the sabbath of the Lord thy God" [Ex. 20:9–10], afford no objection against that that is called the Christian sabbath, for those words remain in their full force still; neither do these words following, viz. "For in six days the Lord made heaven and earth, the sea, and all that in them is, and rested the seventh day: wherefore the Lord blessed the sabbath day, and hallowed it" [Ex. 20:11]. These words ben't made insignificant words as to Christians by the institution of the Christian sabbath. They remain in their full force as to that which is principally intended by 'em still. These words are to give us a reason why we are to work but six days at a time and then rest the seventh: because God has set us the example. And taken so, they remain still in as much force as ever they were. This is the reason still, as much as ever it was, why we work but six days at a time. What is the reason that Christians rest every seventh day and not every sixth or eighth or ninth or tenth day? 'Tis because God worked six days and rested the seventh.

'Tis true these words did carry something further in their meaning as they were spoken to the Jews and the church before Christ's coming; it was also intended by 'em that the seventh day was to be kept in commemoration of the work of creation. But this need be no difficulty, that the words as they relate to us should not import all that they did as they related to the Jews. For there are other words that were written upon those tables of stone with the Ten Commandments that are known and allowed not to be of the same import, as they relate to us, as they were of as they related to the Jews, viz. these words in the preface to the Ten Commandments: "I am the Lord thy God, which brought thee out of the house of bondage" [Ex. 20:2]. These words were written in tables of stone with the rest, and these words are spoken to us as well as to the Jews. They are spoken to all that the commandments themselves are spoken to, for they are spoken as an enforcement of the commandments. But they don't remain now in all the signification they had as they respected the Jews; for we never were brought out of Egypt, out of the house of bondage, as [in] those words in the commandments themselves (Deut. 5:15) [but] only in a mystical sense.

So that all the arguments of those that are against the Christian sabbath taken from the fourth commandment, which is all their strength, come to nothing.

Second. The ancient churches, being commanded to keep a seventh day in commemoration of the work of creation, is an argument for the keeping a weekly sabbath in commemoration of the work of redemption, and not an objection against it.

We read in Scripture of two creations, the old and the new, and these words of the fourth commandment are to be taken as of the same force to those that belong to the new creation, with respect to that new creation, as they were to them that belonged to the old creation, with respect to that old creation. We read that God in the beginning "created the heavens and the earth" [Gen. 1:1], and the church of old was to commemorate that. But when God creates "a new heaven and a new earth" [Rev. 21:1], those that belong to that new heaven and new earth by a like reason are to commemorate the creation of their heaven and earth.

The Scriptures teach us to look upon the old creation as destroyed and, as it were, annihilated by sin, or as being reduced to a chaos again, without form and void, as it was at first; Jer. 4:22–23, "They are wise to do evil, but to do good they have no knowledge. I beheld the earth, and, lo, it was without form, and void; and the heavens, and they had no light." I.e. they were reduced to same state they were in at first: "the earth was without form, and void," and there was no light, but "darkness was upon the face of the deep" [Gen. 1:2].

And the Scriptures teach us to call the gospel restoration and redemption, a creation of a new heaven and a new earth; Is. 65:17–18, "For, behold, I create new heavens and a new earth: and the former shall not be remembered, nor come into mind. But be you glad and rejoice forever in that which I create: for, behold, I create Jerusalem a rejoicing, and her people a joy"; and Is. 51:16, "And I have put my words in thy mouth, and have covered thee in the shadow of mine hand, that I may plant the heavens, and lay the foundation of the earth, and say unto Zion, Thou art my people"; and Is. 66:22, "For as the new heavens and the new earth, which I shall make, shall remain before me, saith the Lord, so shall your seed and your name remain." We in these places are not only told of the creation of new heavens and new earth, but we are told what is meant by it, viz. the gospel renovation, the making Jerusalem a rejoicing and her people a joy, saying unto Zion, "Thou art my people." The Prophet in all these places is prophesying of the gospel redemption.

The gospel state is everywhere spoken of as a renewed state of things, wherein "old things are done away and all things are become new" [II Cor. 5:17]; we are said to be created anew in Christ Jesus. All things are restored and reconciled whether in heaven or in earth, and God has "caused the light to shine out of darkness" [II Cor. 4:6], as he did at the beginning. And the dissolution of the Jewish state was often spoken of in the Old Testament as the end of the world. Now, we that belong to the gospel church belong to the new creation.

Third. There is another thing that confirms that the fourth commandment will reach[9] God's resting from the new creation as well as the old, because the Scripture does expressly speak of one as parallel with the other; i.e. Christ resting from the work of redemption is expressly spoken of as being parallel with God's resting from the work of creation; and that, in Heb. 4:10, "For he that is entered into his rest, he also hath ceased from his own works, as God did from his." Now, Christ rested from his works when he rose from the dead on the first day of the week. When he rose from the dead, then he finished his work of redemption;[1] his humiliation was at an end. He rested from his labors and was refreshed.

Fourth. The Holy Ghost has implicitly told us that the sabbath that was instituted in commemoration of the old creation shall not be kept in gospel times. In Is. 65:17, there we are told that when God should "create

9. I.e. extend to in terms of influence.

1. At this point L. 14v. of the MS ends. In revising for repreaching, JE deleted the remainder of the sentence at the top of what was originally L. 15r. and rewrote it on the bottom of L. 14v., along with a new catchword, "when," cueing him to the first of four pages inserted into the manuscript. The insert contains three exegetical excurses that were incorporated by JE, Jr., into his printed version of this sermon. See above, p. 219.

The first insert, located here, reads: "When it is said in this place, 'there remaineth a rest to the people of God,' in the original it is 'a sabbatism,' or the keeping of a sabbath. And this reason is given for it: 'For he that is entered into his rest, he also ceased from his own works, as God did from his.' These three things at least we are taught by these words: 1. We are taught by 'em to look on Christ's rest from his work of redemption as parallel with God's rest from the work of creation, for they are expressly compared together as parallel one with another. 2. They are spoken of as a parallel particularly in this respect, viz. the relation they both have to the keeping of a sabbath amongst God's people, or with respect to the influence these two rests have as to sabbatizing in the church of God: for 'tis expressly with respect to this that they are compared together. Here is an evident reference: God's blessing and hallowing the day of his rest from the creation to be a sabbath, and appointing a sabbath of rest in imitation of him. For the Apostle is speaking of this, v. 4, 'For he spake in a certain place of the seventh day on this wise, And God did rest the seventh day from all his works.' Thus far is evident, whatsoever the Apostle has respect to by this keeping of a sabbath by the people of God, whether it be a weekly sabbatizing on earth or a sabbatizing in heaven. 3. It is evident in the words that the preference is given to the latter rest, viz. the rest of our Savior from his works, with respect to this influence it has, [or] should have, or relation it bears to the sabbatizing of the people of God now under the gospel, evidently implied in the expression, 'There *remaineth* therefore a sabbatism to the people of God. For he that entered into his rest.' For in this expression, 'There remaineth,' is intimated that the old sabbatism, appointed in remembrance of God's rest from the work of creation, don't remain but ceases, and this new rest in commemoration of Christ's resting {from the work of redemption} remains in the room of it."

a new heavens and a new earth: the former should not be remembered, nor come into mind." And if that be so, 'tis not to be supposed that we are to keep a seventh part of time on purpose, to remember it and call it to mind. Let us understand this which way we will, it will not be well consistent with the keeping one day in seven in the gospel church principally for the remembering and calling to mind the old creation.

If the meaning of the place be only this, that the old creation shall not be remembered or come into mind in comparison of the new, [that] the new will be so much more remarkable, and glorious, and so much more nearly concerning us that so much more notice shall be taken of it, and it shall be thought so much more worthy to be remembered and commemorated that the other shall be forgotten, shall not be remembered nor come into mind: if we understand it thus, it is impossible it should be more to our purpose. For then, hereby the Holy Ghost teaches us that the Christian church has a great deal more reason to commemorate the new creation than the old, insomuch that the old is worthy to be forgotten in comparison of it.

And we are taught in the following verse that as the old creation shall no more be remembered nor come into mind, so the church is directed forever to commemorate the new: "But be you glad and rejoice forever in that which I create: for, behold, I create Jerusalem a rejoicing, and her people a joy" [Is. 65:18]. I.e. though you forget the old, yet forever to the end of the world keep a joyful remembrance of the new.

Fifth. It is an argument that the Jewish sabbath is not to be perpetual, that the Jews were commanded to keep it in remembrance of their deliverance out of Egypt. And one reason why it was instituted was because God thus delivered them, as we are expressly told in the Decalogue itself in one of the places where we have it recorded in the books of Moses; Deut. 5:15, "And remember that thou wast a servant in the land of Egypt, and that the Lord thy God brought thee out thence through a mighty hand and by a stretched out arm: therefore the Lord thy God commanded thee to keep the sabbath day." Now, can anybody think that God would have all nations under the gospel, and to the end of the world, keep a day every week that was instituted in remembrance of the Jews' deliverance out of Egypt? But,

Sixth. The Holy Ghost has implicitly told us that instituted memorials of the Jews' deliverance from Egypt shall no longer be upheld in gospel times in that place of Scripture, Jer. 16:14–15, speaking there of gospel times: "Therefore, behold, the days come, saith the Lord, that it shall no more be said, The Lord liveth, that brought up the children of Israel out

[of] Egypt; but, the Lord liveth, that brought up the children of Israel from the land of the north, and from all the lands whither he had driven them: and I will bring them again into their own land"; and 23:7, "they shall no more say, The Lord liveth, that brought up the children of Israel out of the land of Egypt"; i.e. at least they shall no more keep up any public memorials of it.

And if there be a sabbath kept up in gospel times, as we have shown there must be, 'tis more just from these words to suppose that it will be as a memorial of that which is spoken of in the latter verse, the bringing out of the north, etc., that is, the redemption of Christ and his bringing home the elect, not only in Judea but from the north and from all quarters of the world. See Is. 43:16–19.

Seventh. 'Tis no more than just to suppose that God intended to intimate to us that the sabbath ought by Christians to be kept in commemoration of Christ's redemption, in that the Israelites were commanded to keep it in remembrance of their deliverance out of Egypt, because that deliverance out of Egypt is an evident and known and allowed type of it. It was contrived and ordered of God on purpose to represent it; everything about it was typical of it and much is made of it principally for that reason, because it was so remarkable a type of it.

And it was but a shadow; the work in itself was nothing in comparison of the work of redemption. What is a petty redemption of one nation from a temporal bondage to the eternal salvation of the whole church of the elect, in all ages and nations, from eternal damnation, and bringing them not into a temporal Canaan but into heaven to eternal glory and blessedness? Was that shadow so much to be commemorated as to keep a day once a week for it? And shall we not much more commemorate that great and glorious work that it was designed on purpose to be a shadow of?

And, besides, these words in the fourth commandment can be of no significancy unto us unless they are to be interpreted of the gospel redemption. But the words of the Decalogue are spoken to all nations and ages. Therefore, as the words were spoken to the Jews, they referred to the type and shadow; as they are spoken to us, they are to be interpreted of the antitype and substance. For the Egypt that we are redeemed from under the gospel is the spiritual Egypt; the house of bondage we are redeemed from is of spiritual bondage. Therefore the words as spoken to us are to be thus interpreted: "And remember thou wast a servant to sin and Satan, and the Lord, the Lord thy God, delivered thee from this bondage with a mighty hand and outstretched arm; therefore the Lord thy God commanded thee to keep the sabbath day."

And as the words in the preface to the Ten Commandments about the bringing out of Egypt are interpreted in our catechism, and must be interpreted, as they have respect to us of our spiritual redemption, so by an exact identity of reason must those words in Deuteronomy annexed to the fourth commandment be interpreted of the same gospel redemption.[2]

2. This is the point at which JE, Jr., placed a second later addition by JE from L. 17r. through L. 18v. At the top of L. 17r., JE, Jr., wrote that "This belongs to argument 7." The insert reads: "The Jewish sabbath was kept on the day of the children of Israel's coming up out of the Red Sea. For we are told in Deut. 5:15 that this holy rest of the sabbath was appointed in commemoration of that coming up out of Egypt. But the day of their going through the Red Sea was the day of their coming up out of Egypt; for till then, they were in the land of Egypt. The Red Sea was the boundary of the land of Egypt. The Scripture itself tells us that that day, when they sung of Moses, was the day of their coming up out of the land of Egypt; Hos. 2:15, 'and she shall sing there, as in the days of her youth, as in the day when she came up out of the land of Egypt,' referring plainly to her triumphant song that Moses and the children of Israel sang when they came up out of the Red Sea.

"The Scripture tells us that God appointed the Jewish sabbath in commemoration of the children of Israel's deliverance from their taskmasters, the Egyptians, and their rest from their hard bondage and slavery under them. Deut. 5:14–15, that thy man servant and maid servant 'may rest as well as thou. And remember that thou wast a servant in the land of Egypt, and that the Lord thy God brought thee out thence with a mighty hand and a stretched out arm: therefore the Lord thy God commanded thee to keep the sabbath day.' But the day that the children of Israel were delivered from their taskmaster and had rest from them was the day when {they came up out of the Red Sea}; they had no rest from 'em till then, for though they were come forth from their journey to go out {of Egypt}, yet they were pursued by 'em till then, and were exceedingly perplexed and distressed. But that morning, when they came up {out of the Red Sea}, they had complete and final deliverance; then they had full rest. God said to 'em, 'the Egyptians which ye have seen this day, ye shall see no more forever' (Ex. 14:13). Then they enjoyed rest, a joyful day, a day of refreshment; then they sung the song of Moses, and on that day was their sabbath of rest.

"But this coming up of the children of Israel out of the Red Sea was only a type of Christ's resurrection. That people was the mystical body of Christ, and Moses was a great type of Christ; and then, on that day, Christ went before the children of Israel in the pillar of cloud and fire as their savior and redeemer; on that morning, Christ in this pillar of cloud and fire rose out of the Red Sea as out of great waters, which was a type of Christ's rising from a state of death and that great humiliation that he had suffered. Christ's resurrection from the dead in Scripture is represented by his coming up out of deep water; so it is in Christ's resurrection, by Jonah's coming forth out of the sea (Matt. 12:40).

"Christ's resurrection is expressly compared to a being delivered out of deep water, in Ps. 69:1–3, 14–15. These things are said of Christ, as is evident, because many things in this psalm are in the New Testament expressly applied to Christ, as in abundance of places, as you may see by comparing v. 4 with John 15:25; and v. 9 and John 2:17; and v. 2 and Matt. 27:34, 48 and Mark 15:23 and John 19:29; v. 22 and Rom. 11:9–10; v. 25 and Acts 1:20.

"So that it being so, that the Jewish sabbath being appointed on the day of the rising of the

Eighth. I would argue from that place, Ps. 118:22–24. There we are taught that the day of Christ's resurrection is to be celebrated with holy joy by the church: "The stone which the builders refused is become the head stone of the corner. This is the Lord's doing, it is marvelous in our eyes. This is the day which the Lord hath made; we will rejoice and be glad of it."

The stone spoken of is Christ. He was refused and rejected by the builders, especially when he was put to death. That making of him the head of the corner spoken of, which is the Lord's doing and so marvelous in our eyes, is Christ's exaltation, which began with his resurrection. While Christ lay in the grave, then he lay as a stone cast by the builders; but when God raised him from the dead, then he became the head of the corner. Thus it is evident the Apostle interprets it; Acts 4:10–11, "Be it known unto you all, and to all the people of Israel, that by the name of Jesus Christ of Nazareth, whom ye crucified, whom God raised from the dead, even by him doth this man stand here before you whole. This was the stone which was set at naught by you builders, which is become the head of the corner." And the day on which this was done, we are here taught that God hath made to be the day of the rejoicing of the church.

Ninth. The abolition of the Jewish sabbath seems to be intimated by Christ. The Lord of the sabbath lying buried on that day, Christ, he is the creator of the world. It was he that was the author of that work of creation that the Jewish sabbath was a memorial of. It was he that worked six days and rested the seventh day from all his works and was refreshed. He now is held in the chains of death on that day. God that created the world now in his second work of creation did follow his own example, if I may so speak. He did not rest on the same day but remained imprisoned in the grave on that day and took another day to rest in.

The sabbath was a day of rejoicing, for it was in commemoration of the glorious and gracious works of God, of creation and redemption out of Egypt. We are directed to call the sabbath a delight. But it [is] not a proper day for the church, Christ's spouse, to rejoice in when Christ the bridegroom lies buried, as Christ says; Matt. 9:15, "the children of the bride chamber cannot mourn while the bridegroom is with them, but the

---

pillar of cloud {and fire}, and Moses and the church, the mystical body of Christ, which was the type, it is a great confirmation that the Christian sabbath should be kept on the day of the rising of the real body of Christ from the grave, which is the antitype. For surely the Scripture has taught us that the type should give way to the antitype, and the shadow should give way to the substance."

time will come, when the bridegroom shall be taken from them, then shall they mourn." While Christ was held under the chains of death, then the bridegroom was taken from them; then it was a proper time for the spouse to mourn and not rejoice. But when Christ rose again, then it was a day of joy, because we are "begotten again to a living hope by the resurrection of Jesus Christ from the dead" [I Pet. 1:3].

Tenth. Christ has evidently, upon purpose and design, peculiarly honored the first day of the week, the day on which he rose from the dead, by taking this day of the week from time to time to appear to the apostles in, and by taking this day to pour out the Holy Ghost on the apostles, which we read of in Acts 2. For this was on the first day of the week, being on Pentecost, which was on the first day of the week, as you may see by Lev. 23:15–16. And by pouring his Spirit on John, and giving him his visions on this day [Rev 1:10], now doubtless Christ had his meaning in his thus distinguishingly honoring this day.

Eleventh. 'Tis evident by the New Testament that this especially was the day of the public worship of the primitive Christian church by the direction of the apostles. We are told that this was the day that they were wont to come together to break bread with the apostles' approbation, in that they preached to 'em on that day and, therefore, doubtless by their direction; Acts 20:7, "Upon the first day of the week, when the disciples came together to break bread, Paul preached unto them." And so the Holy Ghost was careful that the public contributions should be on this day in all the churches rather than any other day, as appears by our text.

Twelfth. This first day of the week is called the Lord's day in the New Testament (Rev. 1:10). Some say, "How do we know that that was the first day of the week? Every day is the Lord's day." But 'tis ridiculous so to talk, for John's design is to tell us when he had those visions. And if by Lord's day is meant any day, how can that inform us when?

But what is meant by this expression we know just the same way as we know what is the meaning of any word in the original of the New Testament, or the meaning of any expression in any ancient language, viz. by what we find to be the universal intent and signification of the expression in ancient times. This expression of "the Lord's day" is found by the ancient use of the whole Christian church, by what appears by all the writings of ancient times, even from the apostles' days, to signify the first day of the week. And the expression implies in it the holiness of the day, for doubtless the day is called the Lord's day as the sacred supper is called the Lord's Supper, which is so called because 'tis a holy supper to be celebrated in remembrance of the Lord Christ and his redemption. So this is a holy day to be kept in remembrance of the Lord Christ and his redemption.[3]

Thirteenth. The tradition of the church from age to age, though it be no rule, yet may be a great confirmation of the truth in such a case as this is. We find by all accounts, that it has been the universal custom of the Christian church in all ages, even from the age of the apostles [to keep this day]. We read in the writings that remain of the first and second and third centuries of the Christians keeping the Lord's day, and so in all succeeding centuries; and there are no accounts that contradict them. This day has all along been kept by Christians in all countries throughout the world, and by almost all that have borne the name of Christians of all denominations, however different in their opinions as to other things.

Now, though this ben't sufficient of itself without a foundation in Scripture, yet it may be a confirmation of it, because here is really matter of conviction to our reason in it. Reason may greatly confirm truths revealed in Scripture. The universality of the custom through all Christian countries, in all ages, by what account we have of 'em, is a good argument that the church had it from the apostles. And 'tis difficult to conceive how all should come to agree to set up such a custom through the world, of different sects and opinions, and we have no account of any such thing.

3. Here JE, Jr., directs the insertion of JE's later passage written on L. 16 with a hash mark and the note, "See next page but two." At the top of L. 16r. is an identical hash mark by JE, Jr. The addition reads: "The first day of the week being called in Scripture 'the Lord's day' sufficiently marks it out to be the day of the week that is to be kept holy unto God. For God has been pleased to call it by his own name. God's putting his name upon anything, or anything's being called by God's name, in Scripture denotes the holiness of that thing, and it appropriates honor to God. Thus God put his name upon his people of Israel of old; Num. 6:27, 'And they shall put my name upon the children of Israel.' They were called by God's name, as 'tis said, II Chron. 7:14; i.e. they were called God's people or the Lord's people. This denoted that they were a holy peculiar people above all other. Deut. 7:6, 'Thou art an holy people unto the Lord'; and so v. 14, and many others. So the city Jerusalem was a city that was called by God's name. Jer. 25:29, 'upon the city that is called by my name'; Dan. 9:18–19, 'and the city which is called by my name.' This denoted that that was a holy city, a city chosen of God above all other cities for holy uses, as it's often called 'the holy city' very often in Scripture; Neh. 11:1, 'to dwell in Jerusalem, the holy city,' and many other places. So the temple is said to be an house that was called by God's name; I Kgs. 8:43, 'This house that is called by my name,' and often elsewhere. That is, it was called God's house, or the Lord's house. This denoted that it was a holy place, an house devoted to holy uses above all others. So also we find that the first day of the week is called by God's name, being called in Scripture 'God's day,' 'the Lord's day,' which denotes that 'tis an holy day, a day appropriated to holy uses above all others in the week."

Fourteenth. 'Tis no ways weakening unto these arguments, that there is nothing more plainly said about it in the New Testament till John wrote his Revelation, because there is a sufficient reason to be given for it.

In all probability it was purposely avoided by the Holy Spirit in the first settling of Christian churches in the world, both amongst heathen and Jews, but especially for the sake of the Jews, out of tenderness to the Jewish Christians. For it is evident that Christ and the apostles declared one thing after another to 'em gradually as they could bear it. The Jews had a regard for their sabbath above almost anything in the law of Moses, and there was that in the Old Testament which tended to uphold them in the observance of this much more strongly than anything else that was Jewish: God had made so much of it, so solemnly, frequently, and carefully commanded it, and often so dreadfully punished the breach of it, that there was more color[4] for their retaining this custom.

And therefore Christ dealt very tenderly with them in this point. Other things of this nature we find very gradually revealed. Christ had many things to say, as we are informed, which yet he said not because they could not bear them yet [John 16:12], and gave that reason for it, because it was like putting "new wine into old bottles" [Matt. 9:17]. They were so contrary to their old customs that Christ was gradual in revealing them, here a little and there a little, as they could bear. 'Twas a long time before he told 'em plainly the principal doctrines of the kingdom of heaven. He took such opportunities to tell 'em of his death and sufferings when they were full of admiration for some signal miracle, and were confirmed in it that he was the Messiah. He told 'em much more plainly after his resurrection than before; but he did not tell them all yet, but left more to be revealed by the Holy Ghost at Pentecost. They therefore were much more enlightened after this than before. But he did not reveal all yet; the abolishing of the ceremonial law about meats or drinks was not fully known till after this.

The apostles were in the same manner careful and tender of those they preached and wrote to. 'Twas very gradually that they ventured to teach them the cessation of the ceremonial laws of circumcision and abstinence from unclean meats. How tender is the apostle Paul with such as scrupled in Rom. 14. He directs those that had knowledge to keep it to themselves for the sake of their weak brethren (Rom. 14:22). But I need to say no more to evince this.

4. I.e. pretext, justification.

But I will say this, that it was very possible that the apostles themselves at first might not have had this change of the day of the sabbath fully revealed to them. The Holy Ghost at his descent revealed much to them, yet there was much of the gospel doctrine they were ignorant of after that. Yea, a great while after they did the part of apostles by preaching, baptizing and governing the church, Peter was surprised when he was commanded to eat legally unclean meats [Acts 10:9–16], and so were the apostles in general when Peter was commanded to go to the Gentiles to preach to them [Acts 10:45].

Thus tender was Christ of the church while an infant. He did not feed 'em with strong meat, but was careful to bring in the observation of the Lord's day by degrees, and therefore took all occasions to honor it by appearing from time to time upon choice on that day, sending down his Spirit on this day in that remarkable manner at Pentecost, ordering Christians to meet to break bread on this day, ordering their contributions and other duties of worship on this [day], thus working of it in by degrees. And though the Holy Ghost did not speak very plainly about it yet, yet God took special care that there might be sufficient evidences of his will to be more fully found out by the Christian church, when it should be more established, and settled, and come to the strength of a man.

And thus I leave it with everyone to judge whether there ben't sufficient evidences that 'tis the mind and will of God that the first day of the week should be kept by the Christian church as a sabbath.[5]

APPLICATION.

Use of *Exh.*

First. Let us be thankful for the institution of the Christian sabbath. 'Tis a thing wherein God hath greatly shown his mercy to us, and his care for our souls. He has shown that he, by his infinite wisdom, is contriving for our good. As Christ teaches us, the sabbath was made for man; Mark 2:27, "The sabbath was made for man, and not man for the sabbath." It was made for the profit and for the comfort of our souls.

The sabbath is a day of rest. God hath appointed that we should every seventh day rest from all our worldly labors. Instead of that, he might have appointed the hardest labors for us to go through, some severe hardships for us to endure. 'Tis a day of outward, but especially of spiri-

5. Here ends the second preaching unit. At the start of the final unit, JE reiterates the text and doctrine, and writes "two propositions."

tual, rest. 'Tis a day appointed by God that his people therein might find rest unto their souls, that the souls of believers might rest and be refreshed in their Savior.

'Tis a day of rejoicing. God made it to be a joyful day to the church; Ps. 118:24, "This is the day which the Lord hath made; we will rejoice and be glad in it." They that might receive and improve sabbaths, they call it a delight, and honorable; 'tis a pleasant and joyful day to 'em. 'Tis an image of the future heavenly rest of the church; Heb. 4:9–11, "There remaineth therefore a rest," or sabbatism, as it is in the original, "to the people of God. For he that has entered into his rest, he also hath ceased from his own works, as God did from his. Let us labor therefore to enter into that rest."

The Christian sabbath is one of the most precious enjoyments of the visible church. Christ showed his love to his church in instituting of it, and it becomes the Christian church to be thankful to her Lord for it. The name of this day, the Lord's day or Jesus' day, should endear it to Christians, as it intimates the special relation it has to Christ, and the design of it, which is the commemoration of our dear Savior, and his love to his church in redeeming of it.

Second. Be exhorted to keep holy this day. You can't justly say that there is not sufficient evidence that 'tis the mind and will of God that you should sanctify this day. Seeing, therefore, God has sufficiently declared his mind in this, take heed that you do according to it.

God has given such evidences of this being his mind, that he will surely require it of you if you do not strictly and conscientiously observe it. And if you do so, you may have this comfort in the reflection upon [it], that you have not been superstitious in it, but have done as God has revealed it to be his mind and will in his Word that you should do, and that in so doing you are in the way of God's acceptance and reward.

Motives

1. A strict keeping of the sabbath is a thing whereby the name of God is honored. God looks upon himself as honored hereby, and it is in such a way as is very acceptable to him; Is. 58:13, "if thou call the sabbath a delight, the holy of the Lord, honorable, and shalt honor him."

God is honored by it, as it is a visible showing of respect to God's holy law and a reverencing that which has a peculiar relation to himself, and that, more in some respects than the observation of many other commandments. A man may be just, and may be generous, and yet not so plainly show respect to the revealed mind and will of God, as many of heathens have been so. But if a person with evident strictness and care observes the sabbath, it is a visible manifestation of a conscientious regard to God's declaration of his mind and so is a visible honor done to his authority.

A strictly keeping the sabbath is that by which the face of religion is kept up in the world. If it were not for the sabbath, there would be but little public and visible appearance of serving, worshipping, and reverencing the supreme and invisible Being. The sabbath seems to have been appointed much for this end, viz. the upholding the visibility of religion in the public or amongst professing societies of men. And the greater strictness the sabbath is observed with, and the more solemnity the duties of it are attended with amongst a people, the more is there of the appearance and manifestation of respect to the divine Being amongst them.

This should be a powerful motive with us to the keeping the sabbath. It should be our study above all things to honor and glorify God. It should be the great thing with all that bear the name of Christians, how they shall do what shall be [to] the honor of their great God and king, and, I hope, is a great thing with many that hear me at this time. And if this be your inquiry, if this be your desire, hereby you are directed to one way whereby you may do much that way, viz. by honoring the sabbath, and by showing a careful and strict observance of that.

2. That which is the business of the sabbath is the greatest business of our lives, viz. the business of religion. A serving and worshipping God is that for which we were principally made, for which we had our beings given us. Other business that is of a secular nature, that we are wont to attend on weekdays, is but subordinate, to be subservient to the higher purposes and ends of religion. Therefore we surely should not think it much to devote one seventh part of our time to be wholly spent in this business, and set it apart to exercise ourselves in the immediate duties of religion.

3. Let it be considered that all our time is God's; and therefore, when he challenges of us one day in seven, he challenges his own. He don't exceed his right; he would not have exceeded his right if he had challenged a far greater proportion of our time to be spent in his immediate service. But he hath mercifully considered our state and our necessities here. And as he hath consulted the good of our souls in appointing a seventh day for immediate duties of religion, so he hath considered our outward necessities and hath allowed us six days for attendance on our temporal affairs. What unworthy treatment therefore will it be of God, if we refuse to allow him even the seventh day.

4. As the sabbath is a day which we are especially to set apart for religious exercises, so 'tis a day wherein God especially confers his grace and blessing.

As God hath commanded us to set it apart to have to do with him, so God hath set it apart for himself to have to do with us. As God has commanded us to observe the sabbath, so God observes the sabbath, too. It is with respect to the sabbath, as Solomon prayed, that it might be with respect to the temple; II Chron. 6:20, his eyes are "open upon it." He stands ready then especially to hear prayers, to accept of religious services, to meet his people, to manifest himself to 'em on this day, to give his Holy Spirit and blessing to those that diligently and conscientiously sanctify it.

That men should sanctify the sabbath, as we have observed, is according to God's institution. God, in a sense, observes his own institutions; that is, he is wont to cause them to be attended with his blessings. God's institutions are his appointed means of grace. He has promised his blessing with his institutions; Ex. 20:24, "In all places where I record my name I will come unto thee, and I will bless thee."[6] And for the same reason may we conclude that God will meet his people and bless them, waiting upon him not only in appointed places but times and in all his appointed ways. Christ has promised that where "two or three are gathered together" in his "name, there am I in the midst of them" (Matt. 18:20). One thing included in the expression "in his name," is by his appointment, according to his institution.

God hath made it our duty by his institution to set apart this day for an especial seeking of his grace and blessing, from which we may argue that he will be especially ready to confer it upon those that thus seek it. If it be the day wherein God requires us especially to seek him, we may argue that 'tis a day wherein especially he will be found. That God is ready on this day especially to bestow his blessing on them that keep it aright is implied in that expression of God's blessing the sabbath day [Ex. 20:11]. God has not only hallowed the sabbath day but blessed it, he hath given his blessing to it, and will confer his blessing upon all the due observers of it. He hath hallowed it, or appointed that it be kept holy by us, and hath blessed it. He hath determined to give his blessing upon it. So that here is great encouragement to us to keep holy the sabbath day, as we would seek God's grace and our own spiritual good. The sabbath day is an accepted time. 'Tis a day of salvation; 'tis a time wherein God especially loves to be sought and loves to be found.

6. See the sermon on this text (97) from the fall of 1729 dealing with the means of grace.

The Lord Christ Jesus takes delight in his own day. He delights to honor it. He delights to meet with and manifest himself to his disciples on it, as he showed before his ascension by appearing to them from time to time on this day. He delights to give his Holy Spirit on this day, as he intimated by choosing of it to pour it out on the primitive church in so remarkable a manner upon it, and by giving his Spirit to the apostle John on this day.

God blessed the seventh day of old, or appointed it to be a day wherein he especially would bestow blessings on his people as an expression, as it were, of his own joyful remembrance of that day and of the rest and refreshment he had on it; Ex. 31:16–17, "Wherefore the children of Israel shall keep the sabbath. . . . for in six days the Lord made heaven and earth, and on the seventh day he rested, and was refreshed," as princes give gifts on their birthday, on their marriage days, and the like.

But how much more reason has Christ to bless the day of his resurrection, and to delight to honor it, and to be conferring his graces and blessed gifts on his people on this day. It was a day wherein Christ rested and was refreshed in a literal sense. It was a day of great refreshment and joy to Christ, being the day of his deliverance from the chains of death, the day of his finishing that great and difficult work of redemption that had been upon his heart from all eternity, the day of his justification of the Father, the day of the beginning of his exaltation and the fulfillment of the promises of his Father, the day when he had eternal life, which he had purchased, put into his hands. And Christ does delight to distribute gifts and blessings and joy and happiness on this day, and will to the end of the world.

O, therefore, how well is it worth our while to improve this day, to call upon God and seek Jesus Christ on it!

Let awakened sinners be stirred up by these things to improve the sabbath day, as they would lay themselves most in the way of the Spirit of God. Improve the sabbath day to call upon God, for then he is near. Improve the sabbath day for reading the holy Scriptures and diligently attending his Word preached, for then is the likeliest time to have the Spirit accompanying of it. Let the saints that are desirous of growing in grace and enjoying communion with Christ improve the sabbath in order to it.

5. [Fifth,] and last motive, is the experience of the influence that strictly keeping the sabbath has upon the whole of religion. It may be observed that in those places where the sabbath is well kept, religion in general will be most flourishing; and that in those places where the

sabbath is not much taken notice of, much is not made of it, there is no great matter of religion any way.

Directions in answer to this inquiry, viz. How ought we to keep the sabbath?

1. We ought to be exceeding careful on this day to abstain from sin. Indeed, all breaches of the sabbath are sinful; but we speak now of those things that are in themselves sinful, or sinful upon other accounts besides their being done upon the sabbath.

The sabbath being holy time, it is especially defiled by the commission of sin upon this day. Sin, by being committed on this day, becomes the more exceeding sinful. We are required to abstain from sin at all times but especially on holy times. The commission of immoralities on the sabbath is the worst way of profaning of it, that which most provokes God and brings most guilt upon men's souls. How provoking must it be to God when men do those things on that day, which God has sanctified and set apart to spend the immediate exercises of religion, that ben't fit to be done on common days, are impure and wicked whenever they are done.

Therefore, if any persons are guilty of wicked actions on the sabbath, as intemperance, or of any unclean actions, [or] profaneness in worship, they do in a very horrid manner profane the sabbath. Or if they are guilty of wickedness in speech, of talking profanely or after an unclean and lascivious manner, of talking against their neighbors, they do in a dreadful manner profane the sabbath.

Very commonly those that are used to such things on weekdays han't a conscience to restrain 'em on the sabbath. Those that live in the indulgence [of] their lusts of uncleanness on weekdays, 'tis well if it ben't a common thing for 'em to be some way or other unclean on the sabbath. They'll be indulging the same lusts then; they'll be indulging their impure flames in their imaginations at least, and 'tis well if they keep clear while at meeting and pretend to be a-worshipping God. The unclean young man gives this account of himself; Prov. 5:14, "I was almost in all evil in the midst of the congregation and the assembly." So those that are addicted to an impure way of talking in the weektime, they have nothing to keep 'em from the same upon the sabbath when they get together. But dreadfully is God provoked by such things.

We ought carefully to watch over our own hearts and to avoid all sinful thoughts on the sabbath day, and we ought to maintain such a reverence for the sabbath as to have a peculiar dread of sin such as shall awaken us to a very careful watch over ourselves.

2. By abstaining from all worldly concerns. This is the reason, as we have showed, why it is needful and proper that certain stated parts of time should be set apart to be devoted to religious exercises, because the state of mankind is such in this world that they are necessitated to exercise their minds and employ their thoughts about secular matters. 'Tis therefore convenient that there should be stated times wherein all should be obliged to throw by all other concerns, that their minds might the more freely and with less entanglement be engaged in religious and spiritual exercises.

We are therefore to do thus, or else we frustrate the very design of the institution of a sabbath. We are strictly to abstain from being outwardly engaged in any worldly thing, either in our actions in worldly business, or recreations; we are told to rest in remembrance [of the Lord Jesus Christ and his redemption].

We should be careful that we don't encroach upon the sabbath at its beginning by busying ourselves about the world after the sabbath is begun. We should avoid talking about worldly matters and thinking about them. For whether we are outwardly concerning ourselves with the world or no, yet if our minds are upon it, we frustrate the end of the sabbath. The design of its separation from other days was that our minds might be disengaged from worldly things, and we are to avoid being outwardly concerned with the world only for this reason, because that can't be without taking up our minds.

We ought therefore to give the world no place in our thoughts on the sabbath, but to abstract ourselves from all worldly concernment and maintain a watch over ourselves that the world does not encroach, as it is very apt to do; Is. 58:13, "if thou turn away thy foot from the sabbath, from doing thy pleasure on my holy day; and call the sabbath a delight, the holy of the Lord, honorable; and shalt honor him, not doing thine own ways, nor finding thine own pleasure, nor speaking thine own words."

3. By spending the time in religious exercises. This is the more ultimate design of the sabbath. We are to keep our minds separate from the world principally for this end: that [we] might [be] the more free for religious exercise.

Though it be a day of rest, yet it was not designed that it should be a day of idleness. To rest from worldly employments without employing ourselves about anything is but to lay ourselves so much the more in the devil's way. The mind will be employed some way or other and therefore, doubtless, the end for which we separate our minds from worldly things on the sabbath day [is] that we may employ 'em about those things that are better.

We are to attend spiritual exercises with the greatest diligence; it being a day of rest don't hinder that, for we are to look upon spiritual exercises but as the rest and refreshment of the soul. In heaven, where the people of God have the most perfect rest, they are not idle but are employed in spiritual and heavenly exercises.[7]

We should take care, therefore, to employ our minds on a sabbath day on spiritual objects, by holy meditation, improving for our help therein the holy Scriptures and other books that are according [to] the Word of God. We should also employ ourselves outwardly on this day in the duties of God's worship in private and public. It is proper to [be] more frequent and abundant in secret duties on this day than on other days, as we have time and opportunity, as well as to attend on public ordinances on this day.

It is proper not only on this day to be especially promoting the exercises of religion in ourselves, but also in others: to be assisting them and endeavoring to promote their spiritual good on this day by religious conversation and conference. And especially those that have the care of others ought on this day especially to endeavor to promote their spiritual good. Heads of families should be instructing and counseling their children, and quickening them in the ways of religion, and should see to it that the sabbath be strictly kept in their houses. A peculiar blessing may be expected upon those families where there is due care taken that the sabbath be strictly and devoutly observed.

4. We are especially to meditate upon and celebrate the work of redemption. We are especially joyfully to remember the resurrection of Christ, because that was Christ finishing the work of redemption; that was the day wherein he rested and was refreshed after he had endured those extreme labors that he underwent for our perishing souls. This was the day of the gladness of Christ's heart. It was the day of his deliverance from the chains of death, and of our deliverance; for we are delivered in him who is our head. He, as it were, rose with his elect; he is the "firstfruits"; those that are Christ's will follow [I Cor. 15:20, 23]. Christ, when he rose, was justified as a public person, and we are justified in him. This is the day of our deliverance out of Egypt.

We should therefore meditate on this with joy. We should have a sympathy with Christ in his joy. He was refreshed on this day; we should be

7. For a further exploration of this theme, see *Serving God in Heaven*, below.

refreshed, as those whose hearts are united with his. When Christ rejoices, it becomes all his church everywhere to rejoice. We are to say of this day, "this is the day that the Lord hath made" [Ps. 118:24].

But we are not only to commemorate the resurrection, but the whole work of redemption, of which this was the finishing. We keep the day on which the work [was] finished, because 'tis in remembrance of the whole work. We should on this day contemplate the wonderful love and {work of redemption}, and our remembrance of these things should be accompanied with suitable exercises of soul with respect to them. When we call to mind Christ's love, it should be with the exercise of mutual love. When we commemorate this work, it should be with faith in the Savior. And we should praise God and the Lamb for this work, for his glory and his love manifested in it, in our private and public prayers, in talking of God's wondrous works and singing divine songs.

Hence 'tis proper that Christ's disciples should choose this day to come together to break bread, to celebrate the ordinance [of the] Lord's Supper (Acts 20:7), because 'tis an ordinance instituted in remembrance of the work of redemption.

5. And lastly, works of mercy and charity are very proper and acceptable to Christ on this day. They were proper with [the] ancient sabbath. Christ was wont to do such works on the sabbath day; but they are especially becoming the Christian sabbath, because 'tis a day kept in commemoration of the greatest work of mercy and love of God towards us that ever [was].

What can be more proper, than that on such a day we should be expressing our mercy and love to our fellow creatures, and especially fellow Christians? Christ loves to see us show our thankfulness. Therefore, we find that the Holy Ghost was especially careful that such works should be performed on the first day of the week in the primitive church, as we learn by our text.

SERVING GOD IN HEAVEN

In *Serving God in Heaven,* first delivered on March 14, 1731,[1] Edwards contrasts a heavenly life of active service to God with the earthly temptations of religious apathy and inactivity. Edwards pursues the doctrine on the Aristotelian premise that human beings fulfill their nature by realizing their potency in activity. He also draws on contemporary Anglo-American ethical theory, which held that people became happy when they acted according to their powers. So, according to Edwards, "the happiness of the reasonable creature don't consist in idleness but rather in action." Because serving God was the most excellent end of humanity, acting in such service led to the most delightful happiness.

In the second proposition of the Doctrine, Edwards reinforces this conclusion with reference to the activity of the saints in heaven. Their service to God makes them happy because they find therein a delight in the justice of serving the One who was fit to rule and who redeemed them. They also delight in the rightness of seeing God's will done, in imitating the service of Jesus Christ, and in finding an expression of their love for God. In the Application, Edwards reproves the "dullness, sluggishness, and coldness" of so much that passed for religion among his people. He exhorts his congregation to a fervent service of God on earth, which provides an opportunity to experience at least some of the joy of heavenly service.

Serving God in Heaven displays a typically Calvinist emphasis on activism and antipathy to idleness. The Reformed ideal of sanctification implied worldly effort. There were temporal, which is to say political and economic, implications to this ideal. By focusing on the image of the saints in heaven, however, Edwards directs the activity of the godly explicitly to the theocentric, perhaps even otherworldly, dimensions of piety. From the perspective of this sermon, worldly activity is but the effect of a higher calling of service shaped to transcendent ends.

1. *Works, 13,* 109.

This sermon anticipated some of the approaches that Edwards later would take in such well-known texts as *Heaven Is a World of Love,* the last sermon in the series on I Corinthians 13 from 1738, known as *Charity and Its Fruits*; and in *The End for Which God Created the World,* published posthumously in 1765. Here, for instance, are partial developments of the ideas that all creation served to glorify God and that it was the design of rational agents to participate actively in that glorification and so find their true happiness. In *Serving God in Heaven,* Edwards paid less attention to theoretical issues than to a remarkable juxtaposition of images from heaven—dynamic, joyful, and active—with the commonplace realities of religious life on earth, which was often torpid, resentful, and listless.

* * *

The manuscript is a typical duodecimo booklet of eight well-preserved leaves. There are few marks of revision or reworking. One notation indicates that Edwards repreached the sermon "the second time from Ps. 115:17–18," a text that urges praise of God.

SERVING GOD IN HEAVEN

REVELATION 22:3.

And there shall be no more curse: but the throne of God and of the Lamb shall be in it; and his servants shall serve him.

THIS [is the] first part of the description which John gives us of the glory and blessedness of the new Jerusalem, or of the church in her happy state. And respect seems to be had in those things that are said of it both to the happy state of the Christian church here on earth after the destruction of Antichrist and the other public enemies of the church, and also to the triumphant state of the church in heaven and after the resurrection. Some expressions seem best to suit the former, such as its being built upon twelve foundations which have the names of the twelve apostles of the Lamb, which signifies the churches being built upon their doctrine; as in 21:14, "And the wall of the city had twelve foundations, and in them the names of the twelve apostles of the Lamb"; and nations walking in the light of it, and kings bringing their honor and glory into it (v. 24); and leaves of the tree being for the healing [22:2]. But many things that are here said of this city are too great to be understood of any other state of the church than its triumphant, sinless, and immortal state. And especial respect seems to be had to the state of the church after the resurrection.

After the description of the glory of the city itself in the foregoing chapter, here in this chapter he gives an account of the rich supplies of it and the blessedness of the inhabitants. The supplies of the city are two things, viz. the "pure river of water of life, clear as crystal, proceeding out of the throne of God and of the Lamb" [for] drink; and "the tree of life, which bare twelve manner of fruits, and yielded her fruit every month" for food.

The description of the blessedness of the inhabitants begins with this. We shall read the whole description which is in this and the two following verses: "And there shall be no more curse: but the throne of God and of the Lamb shall be in it; and his servants shall serve him. And they shall see his face; and his name shall be in their foreheads. And there shall be no night there; and they need no candle, neither light of the sun; for the Lord God giveth them light: and they shall reign for ever and ever" [22:3–5].

This is a part of the description: that his servants shall serve. The saints in their glorified state, though they are advanced to such a pitch of honor and blessedness, yet they are the servants of God. The throne of God and the Lamb shall be in the heavenly Jerusalem, and all the inhabitants of that world shall be in subjection, and shall serve God and Christ. And this is mentioned as part of the description of the glory and blessedness of that state.

DOCTRINE.

The happiness of the saints in heaven consists partly in that they there serve God.

I. Show how the happiness of man consists [in serving God].

II. Particularly, how 'tis a part of [the happiness of the saints in heaven].

[I. The happiness of man consists in serving God.]

First. The happiness of the reasonable creature don't consist in idleness but rather in action. The perfection and excellency of man consists in his faculties and principles. God hath endowed man with noble and excellent faculties and powers far above the beasts, wherein consists the natural image of God. The excellency of man above the brute creatures consists in that, that he is capable of a more noble sort of acts.

But man's powers of action were given him for action. God aimed at action, in giving man such capacities of action. And therefore when the reasonable creature is in action, or in the exercise of those powers of action which God hath given it, then 'tis in its more perfect state if its acts are suitable to the rational nature, and consequently is more happy than in a state of idleness.

When the creature is in that state that is most agreeable to the proper perfection of its nature, then is it in its most happy state. The well being, or happy being, of the creature, and its perfect and excellent being, evermore go together. But 'tis more excellent in the creature to be in action than in a state of inactivity. While men's powers of action lie dormant and inactive, they are useless; they are as if men had them not. Thus, for instance, if a man has a power of reason and don't exercise his reason, he is as if he had not the power. It is a natural excellency in man to have reason in power, but 'tis a greater excellency for him to have reason in action, for the end of power is action. If it were not for the relation that power has to action, power would be no excellency at all. If it were not for the relation that a power of reasoning and contemplating has to actual reasoning and contemplation, it would be no perfection at all.

God evermore so orders it that the creature should be most happy when it is most according to his design in creating of it. But God created man for action, as is evident by his giving of him those powers of action which he hath. By his giving of him such noble and excellent powers of action as he hath done, it is evident that he made him for action.

Second. A serving of God is that sort of action that man, by the faculties that God has endowed him, is most fitted for. God gave man higher powers than he did the beasts for this end, that he might be capable of those exercises wherein the service of God consists.

He was made capable of reasoning, that he might be capable by his reason to see God in his works, and capable of rational actions, that he might be capable of serving God; God seeks of us a "rational service" [Rom. 12:1]. A creature is not capable of serving God without understanding and reason. A creature may be capable of serving that has no reason, as the brute creatures are capable of serving men; but God can be served only by rational creatures.

Therefore, when man serves God, he acts most according to his nature. He is employed in that sort of action that is most distinguishing of him from the beasts. He acts then in a way most according to the end of his formation, and most agreeable to his make and formation of the human nature itself. A man never acts so rationally as when he serves God. No actions [are] so agreeable to reason, and all that are contrary to God's service are contrary to reason. And therefore, doubtless, his happiness consists in serving God.

Third. The serving of God is the most excellent kind of action that man is capable of. If man's happiness consists in action, doubtless it consists chiefly in that kind of action which is most excellent.

'Tis the most excellent kind of action that man is capable of, because 'tis not only the action that man by his noble powers was most fitted for, but as 'tis the exercise of the most excellent principles of the heart. That principle of heart that is the greatest beauty of man is holiness, a principle of love to God. This principle was that wherein man's primitive excellency consisted, which he lost by the fall. And this principle is that wherein consists the beauty of the angels in heaven.

By a principle of holiness men are conformed to God and have the image of God. But such a principle is exercised in the creature in serving of God. There is no exercise of holiness in the creature any other way.

II. Particularly, how 'tis a great part of the happiness of the saints in heaven.

First. The saints in heaven will take great delight in serving of [God], as they delight in doing that which is just and right. Justice is what they delight in; if anything is right and equal, it is sufficient to make those spirits that are made perfect to love it and take pleasure [in] it. They will see those charms in equity that will cause them to have a perfect love to it. Saints' love to equity and justice in this world is not perfect. Sometimes a love to other things prevails over it. A saint here may be drawn to do those things that are contrary to it, but it will not be so in heaven, where the soul shall be brought to its perfect rectitude of nature.

It is a most equal and reasonable thing that all other beings should be subject to God, who is so infinitely exalted in the perfection and glory of his nature above all other beings. They will see how worthy he is to govern, and to be the lawgiver and absolute sovereign of the world. They will see how fit God is to rule, and order, and give directions to all other beings by reason of his infinite wisdom, justice, and holiness. And they will rejoice in it, that God reigns, that he that is so worthy to rule has the government in his hands. They will see that it is most just and equal that he that is the first being and the fountain of all, and upon whom all are dependent, should rule all. They will see that 'tis most equal that he of whom, and through whom, and to whom, are all things should be supreme Lord: how just it is, that he that created them and keeps them in being every moment should govern them.

They will be sensible that 'tis most reasonable that God should be their ruler, in that he has redeemed them. They will see that all the service which they can render to him is but a small recompense for that great redemption. They will be sensible then how great the redemption was, much more sensible than they are now; for then, they will be sensible how terrible the destruction is that they were redeemed from, and shall know by experience how glorious the happiness which was purchased for them.

They will see how just it is that they should serve him upon whom they live, and from whom they continually receive such great glory and happiness. They will be much more sensible how reasonable it is than the saints do in this world, and they will take great delight in it upon this account, as they will take delight in doing that which [is] so right and equal, see that God's authority is rightful, and they will love to be subject to it.

Second. They will take delight in doing God's will because they will know that what [he] wills them to do is best to be done. They will choose to be directed and ordered of God, rather than to be entirely left to themselves, for they will know that God perfectly knows what is best to be done, what will be most for his glory and the good of the blessed society. They will know that God is infinitely wise and holy and that he always wills that which is best.

It will be a great pleasure to the saints to see God accomplishing his own glorious purposes, fulfilling his own will. They will rejoice in seeing God's will done, and it will be a pleasure to them to be made use of as the instruments of it, as it is to the angels. The angels in heaven are blessed, and doubtless 'tis a part of their blessedness that they are continually employed as God's emissaries to accomplish his purposes and to bring to pass those events which God designs. So 'tis a part of the happiness of the saints to fulfill God's will, to fulfill that which is determined by an infinitely wise and holy God.

Third. They will take delight in serving God because they therein become conformed unto God. The thing which God requires of his creatures is to be holy, to do holy actions, to be holy as he is holy; but the saints in heaven will have such an high esteem and admiration of God that they will greatly delight in conforming to him. It will be a great pleasure to 'em to be conformed to him whose beauty they constantly behold with exaltation and ecstasy of soul, and whose glory they cease not day nor night to extol. To see the same beauty in their dispositions and actions will be what they will esteem a great part of their honor and happiness.

And herein especially they will imitate the Lord Jesus Christ. The service of God is an imitation of God, as it is the exercise of holiness; but 'tis an imitation of Jesus Christ, as it is a subjecting to God's authority. Christ, when he was in this world, he obeyed God perfectly; he was obedient even unto death. He delighted to do God's will, as it was written; Ps. 40:8, "I delight to do thy will, O my God: yea, thy law is within my heart."[2] And in heaven, Christ will be subject to the Father; I Cor. 15:28, "And when all things shall be subdued unto him, then shall the Son

2. See *The Sacrifice of Christ Acceptable*, in *Works, 14*, 437–57.

himself be subject unto him that put all things under him, that God may be all in all." It will be a great pleasure to 'em to be conformed to, and to imitate, the Lord Jesus Christ.

Fourth. They will know what they do in God's service is what is pleasing and acceptable to God, and that consideration will cause them to take great delight in it. It will be what they will greatly rejoice in, that they may do anything that is pleasing and acceptable to God. 'Tis a great honor done to them and testimony of God's favor that he will delight in anything that they do. And it will maintain their pleasure in doing God's will that they have the constant assurance and continual testimonies of God's acceptance of and complacence in their service. It will be as a sweet smelling savor unto God.

Fifth. They will take delight in it as they will have the honor of glorifying God therein. The glory of God is what the saints in heaven will exceedingly value. They will see that 'tis more worthy to be sought than any other end, and above all things worthy to be rejoiced in when accomplished. And they will esteem it a great honor and happiness that they may be the instruments of glorifying God. Therefore they will take pleasure in praising God, and they will take pleasure in serving and obeying of him.

Sixth. Herein they will have an opportunity to express their love to God. Strong love is a thing that seeks vent. He that has a great love to another, he necessarily desires to express that love and is not satisfied without an opportunity. The saints in heaven therefore will greatly delight in serving of God, as that service will be a service of love. It will be the pure exercise of an unfeigned and perfect love to God. True love is an active principle; it desires to show itself not only in words, but in deeds, by doing something for the beloved.

The saints in heaven have no opportunity to express their love by doing anything for the proper benefit [of God], but they have an opportunity another way, viz. by showing their cheerful subjection to his authority, and obedience to his commands, and by doing what shall be pleasing and acceptable to him and to his praise and glory.

Therefore the saints in heaven are much happier in a subjection to God's authority and in his service than if they were not in such a state.

APPLICATION.

I. Hence we may learn something of the nature of the heavenly state. They are not idle but active. 'Tis true the heavenly state is a state of rest:

they that enter into heaven, they enter into Christ's rest. And 'tis also a state of reward for what they have done: when those that are in the Lord die, "they shall rest from their labors; and their works do follow them" [Rev. 14:13].[3]

But this don't hinder but that their state will be a state of action and employment. We need not suppose that they spend their time in doing nothing: no, the saints never are so active as in heaven. As it is said of the angels, that they are as a flame to signify their activity in serving of God, so may it be said of the glorified saints (Luke 20:36). They will forever be employed in heavenly works, and shall be diligent in it. They shall not cease day nor night.

They shall rest from their labors, for although they will still be employed in the service, yet it will be no labor to them. It won't then be as 'tis now. Now, by reason of the infirmity of our flesh and by reason of the corruption of our hearts, it requires a great deal of labor and striving to serve God aright; there are many difficulties in the way. There is labor that causes weariness.

There shall be nothing of this in the other world, for though the saints won't cease to serve God in heaven, yea, though they will be vastly more active in his service than they are now, yet 'twill be rest to 'em. There will be no difficulty or no need of labor and striving, no weariness. They will be active in holiness easily, freely, and naturally as the sun shines. They will have no need of ceasing, to take their rest; it will be all rest. It will be refreshment to them, and not labor, to do the will of God.

The heavenly state will be a state of reward for their works. But yet that don't argue but that they will still continue to act and still to serve. They shall enjoy God in that time. They shall perpetually behold God's glory and perpetually enjoy his love. But they shall not remain in a state of inactivity, merely receiving from God; but they return to him and shall enjoy him in a way of serving and glorifying him.

Every faculty of the soul will be employed and exercised, and will be employed in vastly more lively, more exalted exercises than they are now, though without any labor or weariness. That for which God has given us power of action, as we have observed already, is action. And 'tis not only that those powers may be used a little while, but they shall be used forevermore. And these powers will be perfected in heaven. They will be

3. See JE's MS funeral sermon from Feb. 1736 for his grandmother Rebecca Warham Mather Stoddard, which is on this text and treats the idea that the good works of the saints follow them to heaven.

more fitted for action then than they are now, that the saints may act to a greater degree. The souls of the saints, instead of acting less, act a great deal more in heaven than here. Here the faculties are benumbed and stupefied and clogged with flesh and sin; but there they will be as "a flame of fire" [Heb. 1:7].

A man, when he is converted, he begins that work that he is not only to spend all his life in, but to spend his eternity in.

II. Hence idleness is greatly to be blamed and reproved in those that hope to go to heaven. We in general do hope to spend our eternity in heaven, and to [be] employed after the same manner as the blessed inhabitants of that world are. Therefore idleness, especially in things of religion, is very unbecoming any of us.

But there are some that do especially entertain hopes of heaven that think they have actually a title to the happiness of that state; and in them especially is idleness in God's service unbecoming. If you hope that you belong to that active company above, why don't you imitate [them]? Is not the consideration of their incessant activity in God's service sufficient to make you ashamed of your dullness and sluggishness in God's service, your drowsiness in God's worship, your coldness in prayer and on attendance on ordinances, and sleepiness in hearing of sermons, and that you are no more watchful against sin and diligent in doing good in your day? If you think that you are one that is to spend your eternity in heaven, it becomes you now to endeavor more and more to behave yourself as you will do then, if ever you do come to heaven.

III. Hence those are reproved that esteem the service of God as a hard bondage. There are many that seem to account [it] a misery faithfully and diligently to obey God's commands, because they abridge their liberty of satisfying their lusts and require mortification of irregular appetites. They don't look upon such as live a holy life [as] happy, but account themselves much better on, in that [they] ben't so precise and straitlaced but that they allow themselves to enjoy the pleasures of the world.

But they are greatly mistaken. The service of God is not a slavery as they imagine. They are [not] the worst and most miserable slaves that are the servants of him; but they enjoy the best and most desirable liberty that are holy; they have the "liberty of the children of God" [Rom. 8:21]. They are free indeed; John 8:36, "If the Son therefore shall make you free, ye shall be free indeed." God's law is a perfect law of liberty; Jas. 1:25, "But whoso looketh into the perfect law of liberty, and continueth therein, he being not a forgetful hearer, but a doer of the work, this man shall be blessed in his deed."

It is because wicked men have not right notions of happiness and misery. They are blinded and deluded by Satan, and their lusts. That makes them look upon the service of God as a bondage.

IV. [We are] exhorted to devote ourselves to the service of God. There are not only such motives as these to excite us to it. The authority that requires it is the authority of God; the Majesty of heaven and earth challenges of us, that we devote ourselves to the service of God. And if we do not, we shall expose ourselves to his eternal displeasure; and if we do faithfully serve him, he will eternally reward us. But our happiness does very much consist in this very thing, insomuch that 'tis [the] great part of the glory and blessedness of the inhabitants of heaven.

The heavenly state is that which God's infinite wisdom has contrived for happiness. God knows wherein the happiness of his own creatures does consist; and the blessedness of that state which his infinite wisdom has contrived for the perfection of happiness consists very much in serving of God. And doubtless, that which is a part of the happiness of heaven is pleasant and delightful here in this world. A life of fervent serving of God is a pleasant life. Wisdom's "ways are ways of pleasantness, and all her paths are peace" [Prov. 3:17]. He, therefore, that desireth "life, and would see good days, let him eschew evil, and speak no guile" [I Pet. 3:10].

This doctrine should encourage those that have chosen God's service, to serve him with the greater cheerfulness. It should endear the service of God to you, to consider that your future and eternal blessedness so much consists in it.

Hereby you may be directed how to live a pleasant life here in this world and inform you what is the likeliest way for you to enjoy much comfort, viz. to be watchful, diligent, and fervent in spirit, serving {of God}.

SELF-EXAMINATION AND THE LORD'S SUPPER

In *Self-Examination and the Lord's Supper*, first delivered on Mar. 21, 1731,[1] Edwards uses a sacramental occasion to bring the theme of self-examination to bear on religious complacency and social faction. He applies a pungent New Testament text—Paul's warning that those who partake of the Lord's Supper in an unworthy fashion endanger their souls—to the Northampton church in a straightforward manner. Although Edwards' heightened interest in such sacramental issues as qualifications for church membership lies behind *Self-Examination and the Lord's Supper*, he does not address those controversies directly here. Instead, he focuses on the individual's responsibility to undergo intense self-scrutiny before participating in the Lord's Supper.

Edwards alerts hypocrites to the damage they do their souls in partaking unworthily of the sacrament. Like many New England pastors, he wrestles with the problem of parishioners who could have applied for admission to full communion but who feared to do so out of overly tender consciences and self-scrupulosity. At the beginning of the first proposition to this sermon, Edwards offers a passing word of encouragement to such hesitant ones. Yet in most of this sermon he addresses the underscrupulous. Arguing that people should not neglect self-examination before partaking of the Lord's Supper, Edwards gives a trenchant critique of those who assume the covenantal prerogatives of admission to the sacrament on the basis of church membership alone. All people, he urged, should examine whether they are engaged in sin and are resolute to forsake it before they partake of the Lord's Supper. Edwards directs himself here to social affairs in the town, as he had in the previous sacramental sermon in this volume, *Envious Men*. He admonishes his people to think about whether they came to the Lord's table in a state of envy or contention with neighbors. He emphasizes in addition that there must be a proper motivation for attendance. Those who come merely to enhance their social image or to assume the rights of church member-

1. For dating, see *Works, 13*, 75, n. 8.

ship and qualify their children for baptism, for instance, violate the true design of the ordinance.

Edwards does not here explain what that true design is, but he does give a warning against church members in good standing who, having been admitted to the sacraments, presume that the ordinances are an established right. Although the brunt of this sermon falls on conscious sinners, Edwards also admonishes those who wrongly absent themselves from communion because of overscrupulous consciences (a frequent problem in western Massachusetts churches). He urges these people to distinguish between a general apprehension of their sinfulness and unworthiness, which was no bar to partaking, and a recognition of a specific sin in which they were currently engaged. Participating in the Supper while engaged in a sin, in a dispute with others, or motivated by other than a sincere desire to obey the Lord amounts to a crime. Such contempt is akin to the hatred of those who crucified Christ; it implicates the insincere communicant in Christ's murder. This betrayal of the covenantal oath, which premised sacramental privileges on true repentance, amounts to a mockery of Christ. Thus, even long-standing church members show a damnable spiritual disposition if they approach the Lord's table in an unworthy manner. So, Edwards concludes in the Application, self-examination is an urgent task before approaching the Lord's Supper.

This sermon joins several writings in which Edwards struggles to define the proper use of the sacraments. Elsewhere, he addresses the right administration of the sacraments, qualifications for communion, and the prerogatives of the church to excommunicate wayward members. "Miscellanies" nos. 462, 464, 466, and 485, all from this period, deal with some aspects of these sacramental or disciplinary issues, as do entries written after *Self-Examination and the Lord's Supper*, such as nos. 610 and 612.[2] In January 1733, Edwards preached on I Cor. 11:29 (270), again stressing the necessity for respect and esteem at the communion table.

* * *

The manuscript is a typical duodecimo booklet, consisting of eight well-preserved leaves. One note indicates that Edwards repreached the sermon in October 1756, undoubtedly the occasion for three or four additions after the original composition. Otherwise, the manuscript shows few signs of significant revision.

2. *Ibid.*, 36–37, 503–08, 527.

SELF-EXAMINATION AND THE LORD'S SUPPER

I CORINTHIANS 11:28–29.

But let a man examine himself, and so let him eat of that bread, and drink of that cup. For he that eateth and drinketh unworthily, eateth and drinketh damnation to himself, not discerning the Lord's body.

THE Apostle in the context is reproving of the disorders the Corinthians were guilty of in their public assemblies; v. 17, "Now in this that I declare unto you I praise you not, that ye come together not for the better, but for the worse." And he first puts them in mind that there were contentions and divisions among them, and that they brought their schismatical spirit into their public assemblies with them, and manifested [it] in their behavior [vv. 18–19].

And particularly he reproves them for their unbecoming, unworthy attendance on the Lord's Supper. They partook after such a manner as made void the ordinance; vv. 20–21, "When ye come together therefore into one place, this is not to eat the Lord's Supper. For in eating every one taketh before other his own supper: and one is hungry, and another is drunken." They did not come to the ordinance in a religious manner and for the commemoration of Christ's death so much as to satisfy their appetites and to make use of the bread and wine of this ordinance for the same purposes as they eat and drank in their own houses.

They were wont to have the sacrament of the Lord's Supper in the primitive church very often, by all accounts of ecclesiastical history. And it seems by the account of holy Scripture that they were at first wont to celebrate this ordinance daily, as Acts 2:46, "and they, continuing daily with one accord in the temple, and in breaking bread from house to house"; afterwards weekly, every sabbath day, Acts 20:7, "and upon the first day of the week, when the disciples came together to break bread."

And it coming so frequently, the Corinthians it seems were wont to improve it for a profane use, viz. for the same end as they did their meals in their own houses, viz. to satisfy their hunger and thirst and to nourish their bodies. And therefore the Apostle says, "What? have ye not houses to eat and to drink in?" (v. 22). Your own houses and not the house of God is the place where you ought to eat and drink for bodily refreshment and nourishment.

And then it seems they did not merely profane this ordinance by making use of the elements of it as ordinary meat and drink, but they profaned it by intemperance, especially in drinking, as the Apostle intimates in v. 21. They did not profane it by gluttony or in being intemperate in eating that bread, for there is scarcely any room for a temptation to be gluttonous in eating bread simply. They were excessive in their drinking wine.

Another abuse the Apostle hints at is that they would not suffer any to partake that were poor and were not able to help bear the charge of the sacrament, or at least they contrived the matter so that they should not; v. 22, "despise ye the church of God, and shame them that have not?" i. e. "Send home them that are poor, and han't houses of their own to eat and drink in, ashamed and disappointed, being denied the privilege of other Christians?" Everyone came to take "his own supper," that which he had been at the cost of providing, so that "one was hungry"—that is, the poor were sent away without anything—and "another was drunken"—that is, those that were rich, that made the provision, by drinking all that was provided [11:21].

So that they did not attend this ordinance in that solemn manner and as seriously aiming at those purposes which were the design of the institution, the doing of it in remembrance of Christ's death; so that they did not eat the bread with a respect to it as representing Christ's body, or drink of the cup as representing his blood, but as common food. And that seems to be what the Apostle means in v. 29, of their "not discerning the Lord's body"; that is, they did not distinguish the bread and wine from common meat and drink, from the relation that they had to Christ's body and blood as representing of them.

He therefore puts them in mind of the institution and the end of it which Christ expressed (vv. 23–26) and tells them how dreadfully they make themselves guilty; v. 27, "Wherefore whosoever shall eat this bread, and drink this cup of the Lord, unworthily, shall be guilty of the body and the blood of the Lord."

By showing such contempt of those sacred things that represented Christ's body and blood, and the bruising that body and shedding that blood by his death, they did by their interpretation show a contempt of Christ himself like to that which those showed that killed [him]. And by no more regarding the death of Christ exhibited in so solemn a manner in these sensible signs, they showed an unaffectedness at his death itself, and thereby a kind of consent to the act of the murderers.

In our text we have, first, the Apostle's direction how to avoid eating and drinking unworthily; second, the enforcement of it. Unworthiness is meant unfitly, as it is often used; Rev. 3:4; Matt. 10:37, "he that loveth father or mother"; Luke 20:35, "they which shall be accounted worthy to obtain that world."

DOCTRINE.

Persons ought to examine themselves of their fitness before they presume to partake of the Lord's Supper, lest by their unworthy partaking, they eat and drink damnation to themselves.

I. What is that fitness or unfitness here spoken of.

II. What things he ought particularly to examine himself about as rendering of him in this sense unfit.

III. How it behooves him thus to examine himself: because if he comes with such an unfitness, he will eat and drink judgment to himself.

[I. What is that fitness or unfitness here spoken of.]

First. The fitness or unfitness here spoken of is not that of desert or undeserving. There is no man upon earth that deserves such a blessing and privilege. If God had dealt with us according to our deservings, he never would have appointed us any means of grace at all; he never would have appointed such a signification and seal of his infinite mercy and grace. Here are in this ordinance the exhibitions of [the] dying love of Christ and the offer made of the benefits of it. Now, we are all far from being worthy of such an offer.

As we are unworthy of these gospel blessings themselves, so we are unworthy of the means, the signs, and the offers of them. As we are unworthy of real communion with God, so we are unworthy of such a visible signification of it.

They are not those to whom this ordinance is due, that are invited to these or those,[3] who have purchased such a blessing with money. They ben't the rich and the worthy but the poor, the maimed, the halt and the blind, the naked, the filthy, the miserable, the undone.

3. I.e. invited to the gospel blessings or to the means, signs, or offers of them.

Second. [It is] not every unfitness that renders the attendance defective and sinful in that manner. A man's having so much sin in his heart that he can no other than attend the Lord's Supper in a very defective manner is not the unfitness we speak of. In this sense, all men are also unworthy of any gospel privilege and unfit for an attendance on any gospel duty. If a man's being so sinful that he can expect no other, if he partakes of the Lord's Supper, than to partake with very great and sinful defects, viz. what would be sufficient to render his partaking an eating and drinking judgment to themselves, all would eat and drink judgment.

All may confess that in this respect they are unworthy of an attendance on the Lord's Supper; and when they have partook that they have partook in a very unworthy manner. In the sense that this makes us unfit to partake of the Lord's Supper, so it renders [us] unfit to pray to God or come into his presence in any duty of worship. Indeed, men offend God and might justly be condemned by him for all sinful defects in an attendance on this duty, and so they might justly be condemned for the sinful defects of their prayers. But,

Third. 'Tis such an unfitness as it renders the ordinance void. A man may be evangelically fit for the ordinance and yet be very unworthy of such an approach to God. He may be qualified so as to have a right to come by the gospel, and so as to have ground of encouragement of benefit in coming from God's Word, and yet attend the ordinance in a very defective manner.

But then there are some qualifications that make a man so unfit that there is no encouragement in the Word of God of any benefit to such an attendant. It is utterly against the mind and will of God that such should come bringing these unfitnesses with them.[4] Therefore,

II. A man before he comes to this ordinance ought to examine himself with respect to these following things:

First. Whether or no he lives in any known sin. Those persons that live immoral lives, whatever immorality it is that is their practice, that live in the customary indulgence of any lust whatsoever, they are utterly unfit to come to the holy ordinance of the Lord. Whether the sin that he lives in be of commission or omission, if it be allowed and known, if he comes he comes unworthily, it makes him unfit.

Whether the sin that he lives in be lesser or greater, yet if against the habitual light of his conscience he comes to the Lord's table before he

4. JE here deleted: "They are not so unfit that the ordinance was not designed nor appointed for such, and that for that reason the sacrament of the Lord's Supper was not appointed for all because they ben't fit for it; they are not evangelically qualified."

forsakes it, he is an unfit and unworthy partaker, and such persons had a thousand times better stay away than come. For such persons to come to the Lord's Supper is an abominable profanation of the ordinance; it is a defiling of the temple of God and the sacred things of it.

[Persons should examine themselves before they come to the Lord's Supper] whether they don't live in some former sin, some injury to their neighbor.[5]

As of old, those that were legally unclean were not allowed to come to the Passover or to eat of the sacrifices, so neither are men that live in wicked practices of any kind allowed to come near to the holy ordinance of the Lord's Supper. God doubtless has as much care that this sacrament of the New Testament should not be defiled as he had that the temple and altar and sacrifices and feasts of old should be kept pure. Unclean persons were very strictly forbidden of old to come near; so those that are thus unclean by allowed wickedness are no less strictly to approach to the ordained sacred signs of the body and blood of Christ.

Second. Persons ought to examine whether or no it be their serious resolution to avoid all sin and live in obedience to all known commands as long as he lives. Whether he now be in the practice of any known ways of sinning or no, yet if he has a design of sinning hereafter, or, if he don't explicitly design it, yet if he stands ready to commit sin as occasions offer, not having any resolutions against [it], having never come to any determination of mind of truly endeavoring to do everything that he ought to do and of avoiding whatever he ought not to do, he is not fit to come to the sacrament, as will evidently appear presently.

Therefore persons before they presume to come to the sacrament of the Lord's Supper ought to examine themselves strictly as to this matter, whether that be their determination, to avoid as long as they live all known sins and to set themselves to walk in a way of obedience. But,

Third. Persons should particularly examine themselves before they come to the Lord's Supper whether or no they don't entertain a spirit of hatred or envy or revenge towards their neighbor. If a man has such a spirit towards any of his brethren and don't disallow it, but from time to time acts upon it, maintains such a spirit and disposition towards him, and gives vent to it, it renders him unfit to attend the sacrament of the Lord's Supper. And if he don't first draw up a resolution to lay it by and no more to allow it, he eats and drinks unworthily.

5. This sentence is sketched as an interlineation; bracketed phrases are interpolations based on JE's phraseology elsewhere in the sermon.

Such a spirit in a man renders a man unfit and makes the ordinance void as to him in the same manner as the having leaven in a house rendered the Passover void. Leaven typified any wickedness, but especially malice and hatred. It fitly represented this by reason of its sourness; and the Apostle calls malice leaven, and directs us to keep the Christian feast without this leaven, as they formerly kept the Passover without leaven; I Cor. 5:8, "Therefore let us keep the feast, not with old leaven, neither with the leaven of malice and wickedness." Here both wickedness in general or any wicked practice and malice in particular are mentioned as being in the Christian feast as malice was of old in the Jewish feast of the Passover.

Persons, therefore, should particularly examine themselves whether or no they have forgiven their enemies, those that have done them any hurt, so as to allow of no wishing of any hurt to them and especially so as never to design to do anything to gratify a revengeful disposition towards them.

If men have quarrels one with another, they should see to it to put an end to 'em before they come to the Lord's Supper. If they come together to the table of the Lord maintaining their quarrels one with another and indulging a contentious spirit, a spirit of hatred, they eat and drink unworthily. [Persons should particularly examine themselves] whether they have any sincere disposition and desire to these things that are the main designs, and ends, and benefits [of their] profession.[6]

Fourth. Persons ought to examine themselves what it is they aim at in coming to the Lord's Supper: whether any of those ends for which the ordinance was appointed be what they aim at in coming, or whether it be only and altogether something else that Christ had no respect to in appointing of it. The ordinance was appointed for [the] spiritual good of the partakers; if those, therefore, that come don't seek that in it, and 'tis not [from] any desire of their spiritual good or from any conscientious regard to God's command that they come, but only for some end, some temporal advantage or credit, or merely that their children mayn't lie under the disgrace of being unbaptized, they eat and drink unworthily.

Thus did the Corinthians of whom the Apostle speaks in the text. What moved them to come to the sacrament was not that they might commemorate Christ's death according to his institution, or that they might obtain spiritual good, but to nourish their bodies and gratify their sensitive appetite, not discerning the Lord's body.

6. This sentence is sketched as an interlineation; bracketed phrases are interpolations based on JE's previous phraseology.

III. Persons should examine themselves with respect to those things, that they may not eat and drink damnation to themselves. They that come with this unfitness or in this unworthy manner, all the while living in known sins or having never truly resolved against living in such sins and harboring a spirit of hatred, ill will to their brethren, or aiming at nothing else but only some end perfectly [alien][7] from the design of the ordinance, they eat and drink judgment to themselves. That is to say, their eating and drinking does but much the more expose them to eternal damnation and seals that damnation.

Those that worthily partake, they eat and drink eternal life; that is, their eating and drinking will be profitable to their souls and tend to their salvation, and the promise of eternal life is sealed to them. But those that eat and drink unworthily, eat and drink their own damnation; that is, by their eating and drinking, they do greatly expose themselves to damnation and seal their own damnation.

Reasons

1. Because coming after such a manner is horrid contempt of the ordinance and the things signified in it. To come and pretend to eat Christ's body and blood, and to dare allowedly in the meantime to continue in their wicked practices and to bring them into the presence of Christ, to the communion of his body and blood, shows a great contempt of it. If a person should be invited to a prince's table and should willfully and allowedly come with his garments all over defiled with ordure, it would show a great contempt of the prince and what he was invited to.

So it shows a great contempt of the ordinance and of Jesus Christ and his body and blood to improve it only for some temporal design and aim. Such persons are guilty of the body and blood of the Lord; they make themselves mere murderers of Christ. Those that stood by when Christ was crucified, and showed that they made a light matter of it, and had treated the body of Christ, when dying or dead, contemptuously and with indignity, it might justly be imputed to 'em as partaking in his murder. So those that contemptuously treat those symbols of the body of Christ slain and his blood shed, why, they make themselves guilty of the body and blood of the Lord, that is, of murdering of it.

There are two ways of eating and drinking the body and blood of Christ. One is eating and drinking for spiritual food and nourishment as the worthy partakers do. And another is eating the body and drinking the

7. MS: indecipherable. The deleted phrase, "temporal advantage," after "some" and replaced with "end perfectly," may indicate JE's meaning here.

blood of Christ as a wild beast eats his prey: they do, as it were, drink the blood of Christ out of a murderous bloodthirstiness. They eat his flesh as Job says the men of his tabernacle said of him, that they longed to be revenged on; Job 31:31, "O that we had of his flesh!" And this is to eat and drink as the murderers of Christ might be metaphorically said to eat the flesh and drink the blood of Christ, that is, a prey to their malice. Unworthy partakers, they are partakers with those murderers. They are guilty of the body and blood of the Lord.

They eat and drink their own damnation because they therein expressed such a contempt of that which is their only remedy from damnation, viz. the body and blood of Jesus Christ. They that in eating and drinking do receive and embrace Jesus Christ, they eat and drink their salvation because they receive the Savior. But they which in eating and drinking do but trample on Christ and, as it were, spit in his face, they eat and drink their damnation because they cast this indignity upon the only means of their salvation.

2. There is the most horrid dissimulation and mockery. Persons, when they come into the church, they promise [to own the covenant].[8] And every participation in this ordinance is the most solemn renewal and sealing of those promises possible, for this ordinance is a seal on both parts. Christ sets to his seal by the institution and by the action of the minister, his representative at this ordinance; and men set to their seal.

And what a horrible piece of mockery is it to engage and promise themselves explicitly at owning the covenant, and so exceeding solemnly at the partaking, and the while never so much as seriously to purpose any such thing and, much more, when they actually at the same time do live allowedly in things directly contrary: contrary to the gospel, contrary to the holy religion of Christ! They go on in known wickedness, things that they know Christ hates and has forbidden. They go on in the indulgences of their filthy lusts and come away from them, and pretend, like saints, to commemorate Christ's death and to eat his flesh and drink his blood and give up themselves to Christ, and then go from the table of God to their old courses again.

So to come with malice and envy [is a horrible piece of mockery].[9] [Those that come, they] pretend to have great respect to the dying love of Christ to us; [but they are] the enemies, bruising his body, shedding

8. A blank line follows "promise"; bracketed phrase is an editorial interpolation.

9. JE only sketched in phrases from here to the end of sermon, leaving blank spaces or lines for later completion or extemporaneous expansion. Bracketed phrases are editorial interpolations.

his blood for the remission of our sins. [They] pretend to love and friendship [and] family; [but come in malice and envy]. If any eat the Passover with leaven, they eat and drink condemnation to themselves.

[APPLICATION.]

[The] *Use* of this doctrine [is] to warn all persons carefully to examine themselves before they come to the Lord's Supper, that they don't seal their own damnation. If you would [not], as it were, consign yourself over to Satan, be careful {to examine yourself before you come to the Lord's Supper}. And if there be any that belong to this church that have hitherto neglected this duty of self-examination before they come, let them no more neglect it. And if there be any that have not taken up a resolution, any that live in any {wickedness}, let them by no means approach till they have. If upon self-examination, you find yourself unfit in these respects, it won't excuse you from coming. One wickedness don't excuse [you], though, 'tis true, if [you] will continue, you had much better stay away than come. But the end of examination is that you may amend before you come.

If there be any now about to approach that are in any of these mentioned ways {of wickedness}, I forewarn them in the name of Jesus Christ not to presume to touch till they have taken up a resolution. If you live in any known way of wickedness, don't come here to eat and drink damnation to yourselves.

CHRISTIANS A CHOSEN GENERATION

In *Christians a Chosen Generation*, first preached in May 1731,[1] Edwards delivers a major statement on the nature of Christian existence. Although a lengthy, six-preaching-unit performance, it is relatively straightforward in organization. Edwards derives two doctrines from the text and develops each with a compilation of scriptural references. Under the first, which takes up the five units included in the Dwight edition, he gives four propositions that follow the text. Christians were a chosen generation, a royal priesthood, a holy nation, and a peculiar people. Under the second doctrine he dwells on the theme of being called from darkness into light: the means, as it were, of entry into the select company of saints whose corporate character occupies the first doctrine.

From one perspective the sermon represents the ideal character of a Christian community in contrast to the state of public affairs. The image of a royal priesthood gives Edwards occasion to speak of the spiritual riches and self-sacrificial demeanor of life in Christ—antitheses to the competitive toil and trouble of earthly societies. In the phrase "holy nation," Edwards finds parallels between the church and "a body politic," with the notable difference that Christians are united as "subject to the same king, Jesus Christ," who gave perfect laws and provided perfect freedom. Likewise, the trope of a peculiar people represents God's love for believers and protection of them against all enemies, including political adversaries and religious hypocrites.

This disjunction between divine society and worldly institutions leads Edwards nonetheless beyond corporate affairs to address the spiritual response of individuals. In the seven applications or improvements interspersed throughout the sermon, Edwards contends that the doctrine should motivate individuals to seek their own conversions or devote themselves to one another and to Christ. So Edwards moves from historical analysis of the nature of the church to an evangelistic appeal to individuals.

1. *Works, 13*, 109.

Edwards reinforces this approach with a distinctly Pauline emphasis. The doctrine of election brackets the discussion of the character of Christian life in *Christians a Chosen Generation.* The sermon begins with a lengthy description of the origin of the "chosen generation" in the "electing love of God" apart from moral or social qualities. It closes with a compelling discussion of the natural ignorance of unbelievers, who can be brought to see the truth of Christianity only by the gift of divine light. Edwards develops this last theme to great effectiveness in a subsequent sermon from this period, *A Divine and Supernatural Light.*

Edwards' lengthy appeal both to corporate chosenness and individual holiness may have arisen from a specific case in Northampton, evidence of which he incorporated into the manuscript of the sermon itself. He wrote part of the sermon on a slip of paper containing a note signed by Hampshire County ministers Isaac Chauncy and William Rand. The note reads: "We the subscribers are of opinion y^t in Case a married Cople has a Child born at seven months after marriage and there be no other evidence against them, this is not alone a sufficient evidence to Convict y^m before a Church of ye sin of fornication." This was surely in reply to a question from the Northampton church. In spite of the negative answer, Edwards, who as time went on would show increasing impatience with "licentiousness," nonetheless used this sermon to construct a solemn call to moral behavior. But here, rather than specifically mention the situation about which everyone in the church was doubtless informed, he indirectly referred to it, warning, for example, against "lascivious impurities." Here, then, is a classic instance of how an elaborate, significant sermon often arose from a single socially troublesome occasion.

* * *

The manuscript, in duodecimo booklets, consists of fifty leaves. Edwards used several salvaged pieces of paper that had writing on them, including part of a letter addressed to him, some financial accounts, and the response to the church's question about discipline in regard to premarital pregnancy, mentioned above. The manuscript shows only minor signs of revision, and little reorganization. Edwards did, however, leave several blank areas, possibly indicating his intention to return to the sermon after its original composition.

Five notations on repreaching confirm this. Each refers to a "second" repreaching, but the number and spacing of them indicate several repreachings. The notations suggest that Edwards repreached discrete sections of the sermon as follows: from the second head of the second proposition of the first doctrine, using Rev. 1:6 as the text (presumably through the improvement that immediately follows); from the start of the third proposition of the first doctrine "to the improvement" that immediately follows; from the start of the fourth proposition of the first doctrine, taking the second use of improvement that immediately follows; "from hence [the second use of improvement] three pages the second time" (presumably a reiteration of the previous note); and from the second proposition of the second doctrine to the end, using Acts 26:18 as the text.

Sereno Dwight first published this sermon under the title *Christians a Chosen Generation, a Royal Priesthood, a Holy Nation, a Peculiar People* (*8*, 379–417). He did not significantly deviate from the manuscript but did omit the sixth and final preaching unit, consisting of the second doctrine and its application.

CHRISTIANS A CHOSEN GENERATION

I PETER 2:9.

But ye are a chosen generation, a royal priesthood, an holy nation, a peculiar people; that ye should show forth the praises of him who hath called you out of darkness into marvelous light.

THE Apostle in the preceding verses had observed the great difference between Christians and unbelievers in regard of their diverse and opposite relation and respect to Jesus Christ. The former had Christ for their foundation. They came to Christ as to a living stone, a stone chosen of God and precious, and they, also as living stones, were built up a spiritual house. The Christian church is the temple of God, and particular believers are the stones of which that temple is built. The stones of Solomon's temple, which were so curiously polished and well fitted for their places in that building, were a type of believers. Christ is the foundation of this building or as the chief cornerstone.

On the contrary, to the latter, to unbelievers, Christ, instead of being a foundation on which they rest and depend, is "a stone of stumbling, and rock of offense" [2:8]. Instead of being a foundation to support them and keep them from falling, he is an occasion of their stumbling and falling.

And again, to believers Christ is a precious stone: "unto you therefore which believe he is precious" [2:7]. But to unbelievers he is a stone that is "disallowed," and rejected, and set at naught [2:4]. They set light by him, as by the stones of the street. They make no account of him; they disallow him; when they come to build, they cast this stone away as being of no use, not fit for a foundation, not fit for a place in their building.

In v. 8 the Apostle tells the Christians he writes to that those unbelievers that thus reject Christ and to whom he is "a stone of stumbling and rock of offense" were appointed to this: "and a stone of stumbling, and a rock of offense, even to them which stumble at the word, being disobedient, whereunto also they were appointed." It was appointed that they should stumble at this word, that Christ should be an occasion not of their salvation [but] of their deeper damnation.

And then in our text he puts the Christians in mind how far otherwise God had dealt with them than with those reprobates. They were a chosen generation. God rejected them[2] in his eternal decree and appointed them to stumbling and falling, but them[3] he had chosen from eternity. They were "a chosen generation, a royal priesthood, a peculiar people."

As God distinguished the people of Israel of old from all other nations, so he distinguishes true Christians. 'Tis probable the Apostle had in his mind some expressions that were used in the Old Testament concerning the people of Israel. Christians are said here to be "a chosen generation," according as it was said of Israel of old; Deut. 10:15, "Only the Lord thy God had a delight in thy fathers to love them, and he chose their seed after them, even you above all people, as it is this day." Christians are here said to be "a royal priesthood, an holy nation, a peculiar people," agreeable to what was said of old of Israel; Ex. 19:5–6, "Now therefore, if ye will obey my voice indeed, and keep my covenant, then ye shall be a peculiar treasure unto me above all people: for all the earth is mine; and ye shall be unto me a kingdom of priests and an holy nation."

But there is something further said here of Christians than there of Israel. There it is promised to Israel that if they obey, they shall be "a kingdom of priests." But here Christians are said to be a priesthood of kings or "a royal priesthood," which is the same thing; they were a priesthood, and not only so, but kings and priests too.

[TWO DOCTRINES.]

[I. *True Christians are a chosen generation, a royal priesthood, an holy nation, a peculiar people.*

II. *Persons, when they are converted, are called out of darkness into marvelous light.*]

[I.] I propose to insist distinctly upon the several propositions contained in the words.

First Prop. True Christians are a chosen generation. Here are two things contained. First, that true Christians are chosen by God out of the rest of

2. I.e. unbelievers.

3. I.e. believers.

the world to be his. Second, that God's people are of a peculiar descent and pedigree, different from all the world besides.

1. True Christians [are chosen by God out of the rest of the world to be his].

God han't utterly cast off the world of mankind. Though they are fallen and corrupted and there is a curse brought upon the world, yet God entertained a design of appropriating a certain number to himself. Indeed, all men and all creatures are his. They are his since, as well as before, the fall. Whether they are elected or no, they are his. God don't lose his right to them by the fall. Neither doth he lose his power to dispose of them: they are still in his hands. Neither doth he lose his end in creating them: God "hath made all things for himself: and even the wicked for the day of evil" (Prov. 16:4). It possibly was Satan's design, in endeavoring the fall of man, to cause that God should lose the creature that he had made by getting of him away from God into his own possession, and to frustrate God of his end in creating man. But this, Satan hath not obtained.

But yet in a sense the wicked may be said not to be God's. God don't own them. He hath rejected them and cast them away. They are not God's portion; they are Satan's portion. God hath left them and they are lost. When man fell, God left and cast off the bulk of mankind. But only he was pleased, notwithstanding the universal fall, to choose out a number of them to be his whom he would fit appropriate to himself, notwithstanding the fall. Though the world be a fallen, lost world, yet 'twas the will of God still to have a portion in it, and therefore he chose out some and "set them apart" for himself (Ps. 4:3). God's "portion is his people; and Jacob is the lot of his inheritance" (Deut. 32:9). Those that are God's enemies and whom he is an enemy to, they are his; but those are his friends that are his children, that are his jewels, that compose his treasure, are his in a very different manner.

God has chosen those that are godly out of the rest of the world to be nearly related to him, to stand in the relation of children, to have a propriety in him, that they might not only be his people but that he might be their God. He has chosen those to bestow himself upon them.

He hath chosen them from amongst others to be gracious to them, to show them his favor. He has chosen them to enjoy him, to see his glory, and to dwell with him forever. He hath chosen them as his treasures, as a man picks and chooses out gems from a heap of stones, only that with this difference: that man finds gems very different from other stones and therefore chooses. But God chooses them, and therefore they become gems and very different from others; Mal. 3:17, "in the day that I make up my jewels"; Ps. 135:4, "The Lord hath chosen Jacob unto himself, and Israel for his peculiar treasure."

God hath chosen them for his most noble and excellent use, and therefore they are called "vessels unto honor" [Rom. 9:21] and elect vessels. God has different uses for different men. Some are destined to a baser use as vessels unto dishonor; others are chosen for the most noble use, viz. the serving and glorifying of God, and that God may show the glory of divine grace upon them. Here are several things [that] may be observed concerning this election of God, whereby God chooses truly godly persons.

(1) This election supposes that the persons chosen are found amongst others. The word "election" denotes this; it signifies a choosing out. The elect are found by cleansing grace amongst the rest of mankind. They were of the company from amongst whom they are chosen. They were found amongst them not only as they dwell amongst them—elect and reprobate are found mixed together, as tares and wheat—and not only as they are of the same human nature: they are descended of the same first parents and are in the same outward condition.

But they are found amongst them in the same sinfulness and in the same misery. They are alike partakers of original corruption. They are amongst them in the guilt of the first transgression. They are amongst them in being destitute of anything in them that is good. They are amongst them in enmity against God in serving Satan and being in bondage to him. They are amongst them in condemnation to eternal destruction. They are amongst them in being without righteousness. And they are amongst them every way, so that there is no distinction between them prior to the distinction that election makes. There is no respect wherein the elect are not amongst the common multitude of mankind. 'Tis [that] they are chosen from amongst them, and election makes a distinction; I Cor. 4:7, "Who maketh thee to differ?"; I Cor. 6:11, "Such were some of you." And therefore,

(2) Nothing foreseen, foreseen excellency or endeavors of the elected, is the motive that influences God to choose them; but election is only from his good pleasure. God's election being the first thing that causes any distinction, it can be no distinction that is already the foresight of which is to [be] considered as prior, that it influences God to choose them.

It is not the seeing of any amiableness in these above the rest that causes God to choose them rather than the rest. God don't choose men because they are excellent, but he makes them excellent because he has chosen them. 'Tis not because God considers them as holy that he chooses them; he chooses them that they might be holy; Eph. 1:4–5, "According as he hath chosen us in him before the foundation of the world, that we should be holy and without blame before him in love: having predestinated us unto the adoption of children by Jesus Christ to himself, according to the good pleasure of his will."

God don't choose them from any foresight of any respect they will have to him more than others. God don't choose men and set his love upon them because they love him, for he hath first loved us; I John 4:10, "not that we loved him, but that he loved us"; and v. 19, "because he first loved us."

'Tis not from any foresight of good works, either any good works that men do before or after conversion. But, on the contrary, men do good works because God hath chosen them; John 15:16, "Ye have not chosen me, but I have chosen you, and ordained you, that you should go and bring forth much fruit, and that your fruit should remain."

Nor did God choose men because he foresaw that they would believe and come to Christ. Faith is the fruit of election and not the cause of it; Acts 13:48, "As many as were ordained to eternal life believed." 'Tis because God hath chosen men that he calls them to Christ and causes them to come to him. To suppose that election is from the foresight of faith is to place calling before election, which is contrary to the order in which the Scriptures represents things; Rom. 8:30, "Whom he did predestinate, them he also called."

'Tis not from the foresight of any, neither moral nor natural qualifications, or any circumstances, that God chooses men: not because he sees that some men are of a more amiable make, a better natural temper, or genius, not because he foresees that some men will have better abilities and will have more wisdom than others and so will be able to do more service for God than others that he chooses, or because he foresees that they will be great and rich and so under greater advantages to do service for him; I Cor. 1:27–28, "God hath chosen the foolish things of this world to confound the wise; and God hath chosen the weak things of the world to confound the things which are mighty; and base things of the world, and things which are despised, hath God chosen, yea, and things which are not, to bring to naught things that are." Nor is it from any foresight of men's endeavors after conversion, because he sees that some will do much more than others to obtain heaven, that he chooses. But God chooses them and therefore awakens them and stirs them up to strive for conversion; Rom. 9:16, "not of him that willeth, but of God that showeth mercy."

Election in Scripture is everywhere referred to [as] God's mere good pleasure; Matt. 11:26, "Even so, Father: for so it seemed good in thy sight"; II Tim. 1:9, "not according to our works, but according to his own purpose and grace, which was given us in Christ before the world began."

(3) True Christians are chosen of God from all eternity, not only before they were born but before the world was created. They were foreknown of God and chosen by him out of the world; Eph. 1:4, "according as he hath chosen us in him before the foundation of the world"; and II Tim. 1:9, "according to his own purpose and grace, which was given us in Christ before the world began."

(4) God in election set his love upon those that he elected; Rom. 9:13, "Jacob have I loved, and Esau have I hated"; Jer. 31:3, "I have loved thee with an everlasting love: therefore with lovingkindness have I drawn thee"; and, in the forementioned place, I John 4:19, "We love him, because he first loved us." God of infinite goodness and benevolence can love those that have no excellency to merit or attract it. The love of man is consequent upon some loveliness in the object, but the love of God is enticed out to it and the cause of it.

Believers were from all eternity beloved both by the Father and the Son. The eternal love of the Father appears in that, that he from all eternity contrived a way for their salvation and chose Jesus Christ to be their redeemer, and laid help upon him. 'Tis a fruit of this electing love that God sent his Son into the world to die. It was to redeem that certain number that were his chosen; he so loved the chosen; I John 4:10, "Herein is love, not that we loved him, but that he loved us, and sent his Son to be a propitiation for our sins." It is a fruit of the eternal electing love of Jesus Christ that he was willing to come into the world and die for sinners, and that he actually came and died; Gal. 2:20, "who loved me, and gave himself for me."

And so conversion, and glorification, and all that is done for a believer from the first to the last is a fruit of electing love.

(5) This electing love of God is singly of every particular person. Some deny a particular election and say that there is no election; there [is] only a general determination that all that believe and obey shall be saved. Some own no more than an absolute election of nations. But God did from all eternally and singly and distinctly choose and set his love upon every particular person that ever believes, as is evident by that place in Gal. 2:20, "who loved me, and gave himself for me."

God set his love from eternity upon this and that believer as particularly as if there were no others chosen but he. And therefore 'tis represented as though they were mentioned by name. Their names are written in the book of life; Luke 10:20, "Rejoice, that your names are written in heaven"; Rev. 13:8, "And all that dwell upon earth shall worship him, whose names are not written in the book of life of the Lamb slain from the foundation of the world."

(6) In election, believers were from all eternity given to Jesus Christ. As believers were chosen from all eternity, so Christ was from eternity chosen and appointed to be their redeemer, and he undertook the work of redeeming them. But there was a covenant about it between the Father and Son. Christ, as we have already observed, loved them. This is the account he gives of himself, how it was with him before the world, and one thing is that then he rejoiced in the habitable parts of God's earth and his delights were with the sons of men [Prov. 8:31]. And when he undertook for them, he knew what success he should have. God promised him a certain number, and he had their names, as it were, written in a book; and therefore the book of life is called the Lamb's book; Rev. 21:27, "but they that are written in the Lamb's book of life." And he bears their names upon his heart, as the high priest of old did the names of the tribes of the children of Israel on his breastplate [Ex. 28:29]. Christ often calls the elect those that God had given him; John 17:2, "As thou hast given him power over all flesh, that he should give eternal life to as many as thou hast given him"; and again, in v. 9, "I pray not for the world, but for them which thou hast given me"; v. 11, "Keep through thy name those whom thou hast given me." By way of

IMPROVEMENT.

I. I would first observe that God's thus from all eternity electing a certain definite number from amongst fallen men shows the glory of God.

It shows the glory of the divine sovereignty. God hereby shows us himself the absolute disposer of the creature. He shows how far his sovereignty and dominion extends. In eternally electing some and passing by others and leaving them to perish, God appears in a majesty that is unparalleled. This is a God-like act of sovereignty. Those that can see no glory of dominion in this act, 'tis because they han't attained to right apprehensions of God and never have been made sensible of the glorious greatness of God.

And here is especially shown the glory of divine grace. God's having chosen his people to blessedness and glory long before they are born, his choosing them out of the mass of mankind from whom they were not distinguished, and his love to them being prior to all that they have or do, being not influenced by any excellency of theirs, by the sight of any labors or endeavors of theirs or any respect of theirs to God, it shows the freeness and greatness of God's grace.

The doctrine of election shows that if those that are converted have earnestly sought grace and holiness and in that way have obtained, their obtaining is not owing to their endeavors; but that it was from the grace and mercy of God that God caused them earnestly to seek conversion that they might obtain. And it shows that faith itself is the gift of [God], and that the godly's persevering in a way of holiness unto glory is also from a fruit of electing love. Believers' love to God is a gift that is the fruit of God's love to them, and it shows that the giving of Christ, and preaching the gospel, and appointing ordinances are fruits of the grace of election. All grace that is shown to any of mankind, either in this world or the world to come, is comprised in the electing love of God.

This doctrine shows the glory of God's grace because it shows the freedom and sovereignty of it. God's choosing only a certain number and leaving others of like qualifications and condition shows that God is not obliged to show mercy to those that he doth show mercy to, for he refuses mercy to others as deserving as they: "God hath mercy on whom he will have mercy" [Ex. 33:19].

II. If believers are the chosen of God, here is a great argument for their love and gratitude to God. The consolation of the miserableness of the condition in which God found them, and in which he left others, should stir you up. How wonderful that God should take such thought for a poor little worm from all eternity, undeserving!

God might have reprobated you as well as any other, but it pleased the Lord to set his love upon you. What cause have you of love and thankfulness that God should choose you when there were so few chosen, that he should make choice of you and set you apart for himself rather than so many thousands of others, that God hath chosen you not merely to be his subjects and servants but to be his children, to be his peculiar treasure! He has chosen you to be blessed forever in the enjoyment of himself, chosen you to dwell with him in his glory, given you from all eternity to his Son to be united unto him to become the spouse of Christ, chosen you that you might be holy and without blame, that you might have your filth taken away, and that you might have the image of God put upon you, and that your soul might be adorned to be the bride of his glorious and dear Son; that God has chosen you for such glorious purposes as the manifestation of his glorious grace upon you and chosen you for such glorious work as the eternal praising of him.

III. If believers are a chosen generation, let all labor earnestly to make their election sure. If those that are true Christians are chosen ones of God, this should stir all up earnestly to inquire whether they are true Christians or no. But here,

Let us see to it that we are called. Calling is a kind of temporal [matter].[4] Those [that] are elected, them he also called. Them that are chosen out from eternity are called out in time. Therefore inquire whether you ever heard the inward call of the gospel. Have you ever by the calls and invitation of Christ had your heart powerfully bent to a compliance, irresistibly inclined to Christ, an attracting of your heart to close with him?

You have often been outwardly called, been invited to come and put your trust {in him}, to give up yourself. Have you ever chosen God [as] your chosen above all others: [your] chosen friend, chosen treasure, chosen happiness? Have you ever set apart yourself for God?

Are you careful to reserve yourself alone for him, jealous over your own heart, look upon yourself and behave as having no right to yourself in observance of his commands, his will, rather than your own inclinations? Are you for Christ and not for your lusts? Are you strict to God's covenant, not prostituting your soul to other lovers?

Are God's chosen your chosen, friends, companions, and associates? [Do you] love the brethren? "I am a companion of all them that fear" (Ps. 119:63); "[the] excellent, in whom is all his delight" (Ps. 16:3).[5]

[DOCTRINE I RESUMED.]

We now come to the consideration of this:

2. What their being called a generation imports.[6]

There are three things signified when the Scriptures speaks of a generation.

4. Here through the end of this preaching unit, JE left several blank spaces or lines after short phrases, perhaps indicating an intention to expand extemporaneously. This and following bracketed phrases are editorial conjectures.

5. Twelve blank lines follow, ending the first preaching unit. On the next leaf, JE begins the second preaching unit with a citation of the text and a summary of the major heads covered.

6. Here JE refers to the first proposition, second part, of the first doctrine, which he recapitulates in the summary immediately above as follows: "God's people are a distinct race of men, or those that are of a peculiar descent or pedigree different from the rest of the world."

[(1)] Sometimes thereby is meant, or is now commonly meant by it, a set of persons amongst a people in the world that are born together [or] so nearly together, as the time of their being in the different stages of the age of man is together; they shall be young persons, middle-aged, and old together. Or at least their being together upon the stage of action: all that are together upon the face of the earth on the stage of action are very often accounted as one generation. Thus when God threatened that not one of that "generation" should see the good land [Deut. 1:35], it is meant all from twenty years old. Thus by generation is sometimes meant all whose generation or birth agrees as to time, being alike included within a certain space of time.

(2) Or, those that are born at the same remove from a common progenitor: "in the fourth generation came hither" [Gen. 15:16]; "a bastard [shall] not enter [the congregation of the Lord] till his tenth generation" (Deut. 23:2).

(3) But then, at other times by generation in Scripture is meant a certain race of mankind whose generation and birth agrees not as to time but as to descent and pedigree, or as to those persons whom they originally proceeded from. So it is to be understood; Matt. 1:1, "This is the book of the generation of Jesus Christ"; that is, this is the book that gives an account of his pedigree.

And by a generation is meant those that are of the same race and descent. Thus it must be understood in the text. The righteous are often spoken of in Scripture as being a different generation; Ps. 14:5, "The Lord is in the generation of the righteous"; Ps. 24:6, "This is the generation of them that seek thee, that seek thy face, O Jacob"; Ps. 73:15, "If I say, I will speak thus; I should offend against the generation of thy children."

That the godly are a different race appears as, inasmuch as they are descended from God, they are a heavenly race; they are derived from above. The heathen were wont to feign that their heroes and great men were descended from the gods, but God's people are descended from the true and living God without a fiction; Ps. 22:30, "A seed shall serve him; and it shall be accounted to the Lord for a generation." That is, a seed or a posterity shall serve him, and it shall be accounted to the Lord for his posterity or offspring.

Now, the people of God may be considered as descending from God and being his posterity either remotely or immediately.

1. They are remotely descended from God. The church is a distinct race that originally came from God. Other men are of the earth; they are of earthly derivation. They are the posterity of men, but the church is the posterity of God. Thus 'tis said, in Gen. 6:2, "that the sons of God saw the daughters of men that they were fair; and they took them wives of all that they chose." The sons of God were the children of the church, of the posterity of Seth. The daughters of men were those that were born out of the church and of the posterity of Cain and those that adhered to them. It was God that set up the church in the world. Those that were the first founders of the church, they were of God and were called by way of specialty, the sons of God. Seth was the seed that God appointed; Gen. 4:25, "And Adam knew his wife again; and she bare a son, and called his name Seth: For God, said she, hath appointed me another seed instead of Abel."

Adam, in Luke's genealogy of Christ, is called the son of God (Luke 3:38), possibly not only because he was immediately created by God, but also because he was from God and was begotten by him, as he was a good man and was the founder of the church of which Christ himself became a son. He was the first in the line of the church, and as such he was from God.

When the church was almost extinct, God called Abraham; he called him out of Ur of the Chaldees and afterwards out of Haran. Abraham was one immediately from God, and all God's people in all succeeding ages are accounted as the children of Abraham. God promised Abraham that his seed should be as the stars of heaven and as the sand on the seashore [Gen. 22:17], meaning not so much his posterity according to the flesh; John the Baptist says, "God is able of stones to raise up children unto Abraham" [Matt. 3:9]. Those are of the seed of Abraham, as we are taught in the New Testament, that are of the faith of Abraham. Christians as well as Jews are the seed of Abraham: if Christ's, then "Abraham's seed" (Gal. 3:29). So the church is the seed of Jacob, who is called God's. So all God's people are called Israel (Hos. 11:1), not only his posterity according to the flesh, but proselytes of old and Gentile Christians now under the gospel. The sincerely godly, and they only, are the true Israel.

So the people of God, they are descended from God the Father originally as they are descended from Christ the Son of God. Christians are called the seed of Christ (Gal. 3:29); they are, as it were, his posterity. Christ calls them his children; Heb. 2:13,[7] "Behold I and the children which thou hast given me."

So that if we trace the pedigree of God's people up to the original, they will be found to be descended from God. They are of heaven; they are not of this world. Other men are of the earth and are earthly, but these are

7. JE miscites the text as Gal. 2:19.

heavenly and are of heaven. Thus the wicked are called the "men of this world" (Ps. 17:14). The first beginnings of the church were from God, the great founder of the church. Jesus Christ is the Son of God, and those men that under him have been founders were of God, were of him. God chose them, called them, begot them, created them for this purpose.

Since which God's people are descended one from another, the church is continued and propagated, as it were, by generation. If there were no ordinary and stated means made use of for the continuing and propagating the church, it would not be so. But God's people are made the instruments of each other's conversion, begetting one another's. The church is continued by itself instrumentally through all generations. The people of God are begotten through the education, instructions, and endeavors of those that were of God's people before. Therefore the church is represented in Scripture as being the mother of its members; Gal. 4:26, "Jerusalem which is above, which is the mother of us all." Believers are the children of the church, as they are often called: Is. 49:20; 54:1; and many other places.

God's people are often through their education and instruction the spiritual parents of those of whom they are the natural parents. The ministers of the Word and ordinances, they are the spiritual fathers; the Apostle tells the Christian Corinthians that he had begotten them through the gospel [I Cor. 4:15].

2. God's people are immediately begotten of God. When they become saints, are made holy, they are born again. They have new natures given them; they have a new life begun. They are renewed in the whole man by a new generation and birth, wherein they are born of God; John 1:12–13, "But as many as received him, to them gave he power to become the sons of God, even to them that believe his name: which were born, not of blood, nor of the will of the flesh, nor of the will of man, but of God." They are born of the Spirit of God; John 3:8, "The wind bloweth where it listeth, and thou hearest the sound thereof, and canst not tell whence it cometh, and whither it goeth: so is every one that is born of the Spirit." God is said to have formed the church from the womb; Is. 44:2, "Thus saith the Lord that made thee, and formed thee from the womb."

IMPROVEMENT.

Hence,

I. Christians ought to love one another, being of the same race. It appears from this that they are all of one kindred. There is a relation that

Christians have to other Christians that they have not to the rest of the world, being of a distinct race from them. But they are of the same race one with another. They are descended all along from the same progenitors; they are the children of the same universal church of God. They are all the children of Abraham; they are the seed of Jesus Christ; they are the offspring of God.

And they are yet much more akin than a being of the same race originally argues them to be. They are also immediately the children of the same Father. God hath begotten all by the same word and spirit. They are all of one family and should therefore love as brethren; I Pet. 3:8, "Finally, be ye all of one mind, having compassion one of another, love as brethren, be pitiful, be courteous."

'Tis very unbecoming those that are God's offspring to entertain a spirit of hatred and ill will one towards another. 'Tis very unbecoming thus to be backward in helping and assisting one another and supplying each other's wants, much more to contrive and seek one another's hurt, to be revengeful one towards another.

II. Let Christians take heed so to walk that they mayn't dishonor their pedigree. You are of a very honorable race, more honorable by far than if you were of the offspring of kings and had royal blood in your veins. You are a heavenly offspring, the seed of Jesus Christ, the children of God.

They that are of noble race are wont to insist greatly upon the honor of their families. They value the ensigns of the honor of their families, the coat of arms, and the like. How much more careful should you be of the honor of your descent, to see to it that you in nothing behave yourself unworthy of the great God, the eternal and omnipotent king of heaven and earth whose offspring you are.

There are many things that are very base and too mean for such, as a giving way to earthly-mindedness, a groveling like swine or moles in the earth, a suffering your soul to cleave to those earthly things, to be fastened to them which ought to be neglected and despised by those who are of heavenly descent. A giving way to the lusts of the flesh, suffering the soul to be immersed in filth, a being taken up with mean and unworthy delights common to the beasts, a being intemperate in the gratification of any carnal appetites whatsoever, a being overmuch concerned about earthly honor: 'tis surely a disgrace to them that are accounted to God for a seed or a generation much to care whether or no they are accounted great upon this dunghill. So 'tis unworthy of your noble descent for you to be governed by your passions. Such as you shall be guided by higher principles of reason and virtue and an unbiased respect to the glory and honor of God.

But Christians should seek after those things which will be to the honor of their birth. They should seek spiritual wisdom, a knowledge of the most worthy and noble truths. They should seek more and more of an acquaintance with God. They should seek to be assimilated to God, their great progenitor and their immediate Father, that they may have the image of his excellent and divine perfections. They should endeavor to act like God, wherein they are capable of imitation of him. They should seek heavenly-mindedness, those noble appetites after heavenly and spiritual enjoyments, a noble ambition after heavenly glory, a contempt of the trifles and mean things of this world. They should seek after those noble delights and satisfactions that can be enjoyed by none but heavenly minds. They should exercise a spirit of free, universal, and disinterested love and beneficence and Christian charity, which is a noble disposition. They should be much in devotion and divine contemplation, which are excellent and noble exercises.

III. Hence a reason why Christians are of so different a nature and temper from the rest of the world: the truly godly are very different in their dispositions from the rest of the world. They hate those things that the rest of the world love, and love those things which the rest of the world have no relish of, insomuch that the rest of the world are ready to wonder at it. They wonder they should place any happiness in a strict observance of the self-denying duties of religion. They wonder what delight they can take in spending so much time in meditation and prayer, and that they don't place happiness in those things which they do. They wonder that "you run not to the same excess of riot with themselves" (I Pet. 4:4).

But the reason is they are of a different race, and so derive different dispositions from those they are descended from. 'Tis ordinary to see that those that are of different families are of a different temper. The natural tempers of parents are commonly in some degree derived down to their posterity. Indeed, all agree in many things, for all are of the same blood originally; all are descended from the same Adam and the same stock. But Christians are born again of another stock, different from all the rest of the world, and therefore they are of a temper by themselves, wherein none of the rest of the world agree with them.

[DOCTRINE I RESUMED.]

We are come now to consider the second part of the text and shall now proceed to show,

Second [*Prop.*] How Christians are a royal priesthood.

The two offices of king and priest were accounted very honorable both among Jews and heathens. But it was a thing not known under the law of Moses, that the same man should sustain both these offices in a stated manner. Moses himself is said to be king in Jeshurun [Deut. 33:5], yet his brother Aaron was the high priest. Those that were kings by divine appointment in Israel were of another tribe, viz. of the tribe of Judah.

Before the giving the law we have an instance of one that was king and priest both, viz. Melchizedek; Gen. 14:18, "And Melchizedek king of Salem brought forth bread and wine: and he was priest of the most high God." Therefore in prophecies of Christ it is spoken of as a remarkable thing of him that he should be a priest after the order of Melchizedek; Ps. 110:4, "The Lord hath sworn, and will not repent, Thou art a priest forever after the order of Melchizedek." The same again is prophesied of as a wonderful thing by Zechariah, that he should be a priest upon a throne; Zech. 6:13, "He shall sit and rule upon his throne."

Herein the gospel dispensation differs from the legal, that is, reveals the compatibleness of the two offices. One person, Jesus Christ, is antitype of both kings and priests under the law.

And as 'tis the will of Christ, who became in all things like unto us that his disciples should in many things become like unto him, so in this, amongst others. As Christ is the Son of God, so those that are Christ's are the children of God. As Christ is the heir of God, so {those that are Christ's are the heirs of God}. As Christ liveth, so 'tis his will that they should live also. As Christ rose from the dead, so 'tis the will of Christ {that they should rise also}. As Christ is herein in glory, so 'tis the will of Christ that they should be with him where he is. As Christ bore the cross, {so 'tis the will of Christ that they should bear the cross}. So as Christ is both king and priest, so shall believers be made kings and priests.

What is said in the text is either with respect to what they now are or what change shall be hereafter. The Apostle says, "Ye are a royal priesthood"; that is, ye have these honors in reversion. Christians are kings here as a king that is in his minority, who, though the crown is his right, is not yet come actually to reign. They are indeed in an exalted state whilst here, but not as they will be hereafter.

Christians while here indeed are priests, but not as they will be. Christians are called kings and priests here in this world; Rev. 1:6, "and hath made us kings and priests unto God and his Father." But in the fifth chapter of Revelation the saints in heaven speak of this as what they are brought to by their glory and exaltation; Rev. 5:9–10, "And they sung a new song, saying, Thou art worthy to take the book, and to open the seals thereof: for thou wast slain, and hast redeemed us to God by thy blood out of every kindred, and tongue, and people, and nation; and hast made us unto our God kings and priests."

Therefore we shall show,

1. That Christians are as kings, including both what they actually have in this world and what they have in a future state.

The reward which our Lord Jesus promised to his disciples was a kingdom; Luke 22:29, "I appoint unto you a kingdom, as my Father appointed unto me." Christians having this promise are therefore heirs of a kingdom here, which they are hereafter to receive (Jas. 2:5). The reward of the saints is represented as a kingdom because the possession of a kingdom is the top of human advancement here in this world, and 'tis the common opinion that those that have a kingdom have the greatest earthly happiness.

The happiness of a kingdom or royal state, for which 'tis so much admired by mankind, consists in these things, viz. first, the honor of a kingdom; second, the wealth that kings possess; and lastly, [the] government or the opportunity they have of having things done according to their own wills. Now, with respect to each of these, the happiness of the saints is far greater than that of the kings and greatest potentates in the world.

(1) True Christians shall be advanced to honor far above that of earthly kings. They will have a vastly higher dignity, as to what in them is honorable, as anything that belongs to their persons they will be much above. Princes, if they are nobly descended, that is not so great an honor as to be the sons of God. If they are nobly educated and have their minds formed for government and have princely qualifications, those qualifications are not so honorable as those with which God endows his saints, whose minds he fills with divine knowledge and gives them true and perfect holiness.

Princes appear honorable by reason of their outward ensigns of honor and dignity: their royal robes and their stately palace, splendid equipage and the like. But these are not so honorable as those white robes, those inherent ornaments with which the saints shall appear in heaven [Rev. 7:9], with which they "shine forth as the sun in the kingdom of their Father" [Matt. 13:43]. What is a king's palace to these mansions in heaven that Christ prepares for his saints?

The honor of the creature consists in likeness and nearness to the divine Being. In heaven the saints shall be like him, for they shall see him as he is. They shall be most near to him, shall be admitted to a most near approach to him and intimate fellowship.

(2) The saints shall have greater and more extensive possessions than any earthly monarch. One thing for which a kingly state is admired is their wealth; they have the most precious things amassed in their treasures. We read of the peculiar treasure of kings; Eccles. 2:8, "I gathered me also silver and gold, and the peculiar treasure of kings," that is, the peculiar treasure of other kings. His father David conquered and subdued many kings and spoiled their peculiar treasures, which fell to his son Solomon.

But the precious things that are in kings' treasures, they are not to be compared to those precious things which Christ will give his saints in another world: that gold tried in the fire that Christ has purchased with his own blood, those precious jewels, those graces and joys of his spirit and ornaments of mind, with which he will endow them.

Kings' possessions are very extensive. Especially were they so anciently when kings were generally absolute and their whole dominions, their subjects, and their fortunes were looked upon as their possessions. But this falls short of the extensiveness of the possessions of the saints who possess all things. They are the heirs of God, and all that is God's is theirs so far as it can contribute to their happiness; Rev. 21:7, "He that overcometh shall inherit all things"; I Cor. 3:21–22, "All things are yours; whether Paul, or Apollos, or Cephas, or the world, or life, or death, or things present, or things to come; all are yours."

(3) The saints shall also be advanced to the state of kings with respect to government. Christ has appointed to them a kingdom and they in that kingdom shall reign. It is promised concerning the saints that they shall reign; Rev. 5:10, "hath made us kings and priests: and we shall reign on earth"; Rev. 22:5, "And they shall reign for ever and ever." 'Tis evident that they shall have a kingdom with respect to rule and government, as appears by Rev. 2:26–27, "And he that overcometh, and keepeth my works unto the end, to him will I give power over the nations: and he shall rule them with a rod of iron."

But we must see that we rightly understand this. They shall not be appointed by God as sovereigns of the world without any superior to direct. Neither shall they be properly deputies or viceroys, as King Agrippa and some other kings were the Roman emperor's deputy. But they shall reign in fellowship with Christ [as] joint heirs.[8] [They shall] reign in the same kingdom with him, shall have that happiness of having things done

8. From here to the end of this preaching unit, JE sketched in phrases followed by blank spaces or lines, perhaps indicating his intention to expand extemporaneously. Brackets indicate editorial interpolations where necessary.

according to their will as much as if superiors. Christ wills their will, disposed for them for their happiness. [They shall reign] rather as the queen than as viceroy, who reigns in communion and as partaking with her royal husband; [the] church [is] called "queen" (Ps. 45:9); [the] church [is called] "bride, the Lamb's wife" [Rev. 21:9]; [she will] sit down with Christ "in his throne" (Rev. 3:21).

Reigning as governing consists partly in judging. In this respect the saints shall reign: they shall judge the world, angels, and men, with Christ; Matt. 19:28, "sit upon twelve thrones, judging the twelve tribes of Israel"; I Cor. 6:2, "Saints shall judge the world"; [and] v. 3, "judge angels."

[IMPROVEMENT.]

Exhortation to the practice of true Christianity. How earnestly do men seek a kingdom: what fatigues, what dangers [do they] run through, [what] bloodshed! In seeking conversion you seek a kingdom. You that are but in ordinary circumstances, you that are children, you have opportunity to obtain a kingdom. You have opportunity to be advanced higher to a nobler dignity, greater honor, a more precious treasure; clothed with more beautiful, glorious robes; [to have] dainties, [a] palace, greater possessions, more extensive rule. 'Tis a crown that you are to run for, [an] incorruptible crown. Earthly kings can enjoy [theirs] but a little while.[9]

Encouragement to the saints under straits and reproaches. What are they to the wealth and honors of a heavenly kingdom?[1] They will work out for you a far more exceeding and eternal weight of glory. When once you have got your crown of glory on your head and are seated on Christ's throne and shine forth in robes of light and are set down at his royal banquet, then you'll suffer no more difficulties forever. All trouble, all reproach shall be driven away. You'll be too high to be reached by the spite of men and devils. And then you'll soon forget all your sorrow.[2]

[DOCTRINE I RESUMED.]

We have shown how they are kings; it now remains,

2. To show how that true Christians are priests of God.

The priesthood under the law was very honorable and sacred. It was a very great honor that Aaron and his sons were called to; 'tis spoken of as

9. Two blank lines follow.
1. Five blank lines follow.
2. Here ends the second preaching unit; JE begins the next unit with a citation of the text.

such; Heb. 5:4, "No man taketh this honor to himself." It was for this that those proud men, Korah and their company, envied Aaron [Num. 16], and God asserted and vindicated Aaron's right to it by causing his rod to bud [Num. 17:8].

It was an honor, before the giving of the law, when every particular family used to offer sacrifices for themselves, that the first born used to claim; and therefore the birthright was so much esteemed and valued. Therefore Jacob had such a desire of having the birthright of his brother Esau, and Esau's despising of it is spoken of as a great instance of his profaneness [Gen. 25:34]. A priest is said to be "a chief man among his people" (Lev. 21:4). Because that the office of the priesthood was so honorable, 'tis therefore taken notice of as a wicked contempt of it in several wicked kings, that they made of the meanest of the people priests [I Kgs. 12:31].

The office was so honorable that a king coveted the honor of it, viz. King Uzziah, and 'tis mentioned as an instance of his pride that he did so; II Chron. 26:16, "But when he was strong, his heart was lifted up to his destruction: for he transgressed against the Lord his God, and went into the temple of the Lord to burn incense upon the altar of incense."

And it was a very sacred office, and that above all other offices. And therefore those things were forbidden the priests that were lawful for all others, such as being defiled for the dead, or take to wife one that is put away from her husband, and the reason is given; Lev. 21:6, "They shall be holy unto their God, and not profane the name of their God: for the offerings of the Lord made by fire, and the bread of their God, they do offer: therefore they shall be holy"; and v. 7, "For he is holy unto his God"; v. 8, "Thou shalt sanctify him therefore; for he offereth the bread of thy God: he shall be holy unto thee: for I the Lord, which sanctify you, am holy."

Jesus Christ is the only proper priest that is to offer sacrifice and make atonement for sin under the New Testament. He was the priest of which all the priests of old were typical. But yet all believers are herein in a measure conformed to their head and assimilated to him. The priesthood now is no longer confined to one family in Israel, to Aaron and his sons. But all the true Israel are priests. Every true Christian hath a work and office that is as sacred as that of the priests was under the law, and everyone is advanced to a like honor and indeed to a greater. But how every true Christian is a priest of God will appear in the following things:

(1) Every Christian is allowed as near an access to God and as free a use of sacred things as the priests were of old. God under the law dwelt in the

tabernacle and temple; they were the symbols of his presence, and these places were holy. They might go into the holy place to minister before the Lord, but if any other that was not of the seed of Abraham came nigh, they were to be put to death; Num. 3:10, "And thou shalt appoint Aaron and his sons, and they shall wait upon their priest's office: and the stranger that cometh nigh shall be put to death."

But now all are allowed to come nigh. We are all allowed a free access to God to come with boldness and confidence. God's people are not kept at such a distance now as they were under the law. The church then was in its minority; and "the heir, while a child, differs nothing from a servant" [Gal. 4:1]. The servant is not allowed that free access as a child. They were kept more off with awe and dread, agreeable to the nature of that dispensation. There were not those several discoveries of the grace and love of God that there are now which invite to, rather than forbid, near access.

When God was wont to appear to the children of Israel of old, it was more with terror and manifestations of awful majesty and not so much with the discoveries of grace as now. We know how God appeared when he appeared on Mt. Sinai. It was in flaming fire and with thunder and lightning and earthquakes. But in how different a manner did he appear, when he appeared in the person of Christ, with mildness and gentleness and love.

There is much the same difference between us and them with respect to the liberty of access to God as there was between the liberty [of] approach of the children of Israel at Mt. Sinai and the liberty that Christ's disciples had of approach to him when he was upon earth. At Mt. Sinai only Moses and Aaron and Nadab and Abihu were allowed to come up into the mount, and none but Moses was to approach nigh (Ex. 24:1–2). But if any other presumed to touch the mount, God would break forth upon him. But Christ's disciples used daily to converse with him as an intimate friend; Heb. 12:18, "For ye are not come to the mount that might not be touched, nor unto blackness, and darkness, and tempest."

Yea, Christians are now allowed as near an approach unto God as the high priest himself. The high priest was allowed a much nearer approach than any of the other priests. God's dwelling place was the temple, but more especially was it in the holy of holies, on the mercy seat between the cherubim. There was a veil that separated that part of the temple from the rest, and no one ever might enter that veil but the high priest, and that but once a year, not oftener upon pain of death; Lev. 16:2, "And the Lord said unto Moses, Speak unto Aaron thy brother, that he come not at all times into the holy place within the veil before the mercy seat; that he die not: for I will appear in the cloud upon the mercy seat." The way into the holiest of all was not as yet made manifest, but now it is; Heb. 9:7–8, "But into the second went the high priest alone once every year, not without blood, which he offered for himself, and for the errors of the people: the Holy Ghost this signifying, that the way into the holiest of all was not yet made manifest, while as the first tabernacle was yet standing."

But now we are all allowed as near an access to God as the high priest only was under the law, and more free, for he might approach but once a year, but Christians at all times through the blood of Christ without any danger of dying. We may come boldly; Heb. 4:16, "Let us therefore come boldly to the throne of grace"—the throne of grace and the mercy seat are the same thing—and 10:19–22, "Having therefore, brethren, boldness to enter into the holiest by the blood of Jesus, by a new and living way, which he hath consecrated for us, through the veil, that is to say, his flesh; and having an high priest over the house of God; let us draw near with a true heart in full assurance of faith, having our hearts sprinkled from an evil conscience, and our bodies washed with pure water."

That access into the holiest of all was allowed for all under the gospel, and at any time, [and] was signified by the rending of the veil upon the death of Christ; for then was that blood shed by which we have access; Matt. 27:50–51, "And Jesus, when he had cried again with a loud voice, gave up the ghost. And, behold, the veil of the temple was rent in twain from the top to the bottom."

But especially will the access of saints in another world be much more near and familiar than that of the high priest. They shall not only enter into [the] holy of holies but shall dwell with God in it, for heaven is the holiest of all. They shall then dwell in God's presence. They shall see his face which no man can see and live. Now, in this world, though there is greater liberty of access than there was of old, yet still Christians are kept at a great distance from God in comparison of what they will be in heaven, where they shall be admitted even to a higher privilege than Moses in the mount. When he beseeched God to show him his glory, he passed by him and covered him with his hand, and he saw only his back parts [Ex. 33:23]. For then God will not cover them with his hand; they shall see with open face and shall know as they are known.

Thus true Christians are as a priesthood with respect to the access which they are allowed to God.

(2) They are a priesthood with respect to what they offer to God. The principal part of the work of the priests of old was to offer sacrifice and to

burn incense. As the priests of old offered sacrifice, so the work of Christians is to offer up spiritual sacrifices to God; I Pet. 2:5 (v. 5 of the context), "Ye also, as lively stones, are built up a spiritual house, an holy priesthood, to offer up spiritual sacrifices, acceptable to God by Jesus Christ." And here,

1. Christians offer up their own hearts to God in sacrifice. They dedicate themselves to God; Rom. 6:13, "Yield yourselves to God, as those that are alive from the dead." The Christian gives himself to God freely as of mere choice. He doth it heartily; he desires to be God's and to belong to no other. He gives all the faculties of his soul to God. He gives God his heart, and 'tis offered to God as a sacrifice upon two accounts:

a. As 'tis broken for sin. A sacrifice, before it can be offered, must be wounded and slain. The heart of a true Christian is first wounded by a sense of sin, of the great evil and danger of it, and is slain with godly sorrow and true repentance. When the heart truly repents, it dies unto sin. Repentance is compared unto a death in the Word of God; Rom. 6:6–8, "Knowing this, that our old man is crucified with him. For he that is dead is freed from sin. Now, if we be dead with Christ, we believe that we shall also live with him"; 6:11, "Likewise ye also reckon yourselves to be dead indeed unto sin, but alive unto God through Jesus our Lord"; and Gal. 2:20. As Christ, when he was offered, he was offered broken upon the cross, so there is some likeness to this when a soul is converted. The heart is offered to God slain and broken; Ps. 51:17, "The sacrifices of God are a broken heart: a broken and a contrite spirit."

b. A Christian offers his heart to God flaming with love. The sacrifice of old was not only to be slain but to be burnt upon the altar. It was to ascend in flame and smoke and so to be a sweet savor to God.

That fire upon the altar was a type of two things. It was a type of the fire of the wrath of God, and it was also a type of the fire of the Spirit of God or of divine love. The Holy Ghost is often compared to fire. With respect to the former, Christ alone is the sacrifice offered in the flame of God's wrath. But with regard to the latter, the hearts of the children of men are offered in the flame of divine love and ascend up to God in that flame.

This divine love is fire from heaven, as the fire upon the altar of old was. When a soul is drawn to God in true conversion, fire comes down from God out of heaven in which the heart is offered in sacrifice. The soul is baptized with the Holy Ghost and with fire. In many of the sacrifices that were offered only the fat about the inwards was burnt upon the altar [Ex. 29:13], which fat of the inwards signified the soul. 'Tis that which God looks at; 'tis that which must be offered in sacrifice to God.

Especially hereafter, when the saints will be made priests in a more glorious manner than at present, will they offer up their hearts wholly to God in the flame of love. They shall, as it were, all be transformed into love, as fat or oil is transformed into flame, and so in that flame shall they ascend up to God. Their souls will be as the angels who are as a flame of fire, not only for activity in God's service but in love, too. They shall be a flame ever burning, which shall burn longer than the fire upon the altar in Israel, which never went out from the time that fire came down out of heaven in the wilderness till the carrying away into Babylon.

2. This spiritual priesthood offers up to God the sacrifice of praise. Many of their sacrifices under the law were sacrifices of peace offerings, which were mostly for thanksgiving and praise. But the spiritual sacrifice of hearty and sincere praises of a saint are more acceptable to God than all their bulls and rams and he-goats that they offered. The hearty praises of one true Christian are of more account with God than all those "two and twenty thousand oxen, and an hundred and twenty thousand sheep" which Solomon offered to God at the dedication of the temple as a sacrifice of peace offerings [I Kgs. 8:63].

Praise is called a sacrifice; Heb. 13:15, "By him also let us offer the sacrifice of praise to God continually, that is, the fruit of our lips giving thanks to his name"; Ps. 50:13–14, "Will I eat the flesh of bulls, or drink the blood of goats? Offer unto God thanksgiving"; and v. 23, "Whoso offereth praise glorifieth me"; and Ps. 69:30–31, "I will praise the name of God with a song, and will magnify him with thanksgiving. This also shall please the Lord better than an ox or bullock that hath horns and hoofs." Praises are therefore in Hosea called "calves of our lips" because they are like calves offered in sacrifice; Hos. 14:2, "Take with you words, and turn to the Lord: say unto him, Take away all iniquity, and receive us graciously: so will we render the calves of our lips."

Only true Christians offer these sacrifices. However hypocrites pretend to praise God, to offer thanksgiving to him, yet they being insincere, they are not sacrifices with which God is well pleased. They ben't spiritual sacrifices, and therefore they are not of the spiritual priesthood.

In heaven especially are the saints a holy priesthood upon this account, whose work it is forever to offer these sacrifices to God, who cease not day nor night to praise God and sing forth their ardent, joyful hallelujahs. They sing a new song, a song that never will end and never will grow old.

3. The next sacrifice which is offered by this spiritual priesthood is obedience: sincere obedience. The sacrifices under the law did not only represent Christ's satisfying for sin by suffering, but they also represent

Christ's obeying in suffering. For the sacrifices under the law were not only for propitiation, but they were for purchasing of benefits, and so typified not only the satisfaction but merit of Christ, which was by obedience; Ps. 40:6–8, "Sacrifice and offering thou didst not desire; mine ears hast thou opened: burnt offering and sin offering thou hast not required. Then said I, Lo, I come: in the volume of the book it is written of me, I delight to do thy will, O my God: yea, thy law is within my heart."[3] And though the obedience of saints don't merit, yet 'tis pleasing and acceptable to God. 'Tis as a sweet-smelling savor and is compared to their sacrifices, though preferred before them; I Sam. 15:22, "To obey is better than sacrifice, and to hearken than the fat of rams."

Christians, by offering obedience to God in their lives and conversation, they do what the Apostle calls, in Rom. 12:1, offering their bodies to God "a living sacrifice, holy, and acceptable to God," as their "rational service." They offer their bodies; that is, they dedicate their bodies to holy uses and purposes. They yield their members as instruments of righteousness unto holiness. The soul, while here, acts by the body as to the external conversation, but in this Christians do serve God. They yield their eyes, their ears, their tongues, their hands and feet as servants to God, to be obedient to the dictates of his Word and of his Holy Spirit in the soul.

4. Another sacrifice which we shall mention as offered by this spiritual priesthood is charity or expressions of Christian love in gifts to others, to any fellow Christian. Whatsoever is given from a spirit of Christian love, if it be but a cup of cold water [Matt. 10:42], it is an acceptable sacrifice to God. As, indeed, whatsoever is given for a good and pious use, if it be to promote religion and uphold the public worship of God or to benefit a particular person, if it be done from a good spirit, 'tis a Christian sacrifice; Heb. 13:16, "But to do good and communicate forget not: for with such sacrifices God is well pleased." But sacrifices of this kind may principally be ranked under two heads.

a. Liberality to ministers of the gospel. The priests of old lived upon the sacrifices that were offered to God. And still what is offered to ministers for their comfortable and honorable support, Christ looks upon as offered to himself; for, says Christ, "He that receiveth you receiveth me" (Matt. 10:40). Thus Paul says of those things that were sent him by his hearers, that it was a sacrifice acceptable and well pleasing to God; Phil.

3. For a sermon on this text and theme, see *The Sacrifice of Christ Acceptable*, in *Works*, *14*, 437–57.

4:14–18, "Notwithstanding ye have well done, that ye did communicate with my affliction. Now ye Philippians know also, that in the beginning of the gospel . . . no church communicated with me as concerning giving and receiving, but ye only. For even in Thessalonica ye sent once and again unto my necessity. . . . But I have all, and abound: I am full, having received of Epaphroditus the things which were sent from you, an odor of a sweet smell, a sacrifice acceptable, well-pleasing to God."

b. Bounty to the poor. Christ accepts what is done to them as being done to himself; Matt. 25:40, "Inasmuch as ye did it to one of the least of these my brethren, you did it unto me." This God prefers before the legal sacrifices; Hos. 6:6, "I will have mercy, and not sacrifice."[4]

[5.] Again, another [sacrifice] I may mention which the spiritual priesthood offers to God, and that is the prayer of faith. Though this be rather compared to incense in Scripture than a sacrifice, yet that is equally an evidence of their priesthood. Incense was that sweet confection that we read of in Ex. 30:34, made of sweet spices, stacte, and onycha, and galbanum, and frankincense, which they were wont to burn upon the censer or altar of incense as they offered it, which made a most fragrant smell. That incense is a type of the merits of Jesus Christ, and seems also to be a type of the prayers of God's people in faith of those merits. It was the custom when the priest in the temple was burning incense for the people to be praying without (Luke 1:10). And gracious prayer is compared to incense; Ps. 141:2, "Let my prayer be set forth before thee as incense." The prayer of faith is as a fragrant savor to God through the merits of him in whom that faith is.

APPLICATION.

I. Here is great motive for all earnestly to seek that they may become true Christians. 'Tis a great honor to be priests of God. It was a great honor of old to be a priest under the law, as we have already observed. It was greater in some respects than to be a king, because they were nearer to God, and they in their work were more immediately concerned with him. It was a more holy and divine office.

But more honorable is it to be of the spiritual priesthood. The access to God is nearer. And an infinitely greater privilege especially is the access to God which they will have in another world, where they shall see God and shall converse with Christ as a man with his friend. If even a king was

4. See *The Duty of Charity to the Poor*, below.

ambitious of the honor of the legal priesthood, surely you may well desire the spiritual, which is an eternal priesthood.

First. Consider you are capable of this priesthood. Of old, none that were not of the posterity of Aaron were capable of the priesthood; it would be in vain for them to seek it. But it is not in vain for you to seek this spiritual priesthood.

Second. Consider that you have a call to it; you have warrant sufficient. It would be a dreadful profanation for you to seek this honor if you had not a call to it; Heb. 5:4, "No man taketh this honor to himself, but he that is called of God, and is Aaron." But you are called, and now it would be presumption and profane contempt in you to refuse it, to refuse such an honor as God offers you.

Take heed therefore that there be not any among you that is a "profane person, as Esau, who for a morsel of meat sold his birthright" [Heb. 12:16], and sold the priesthood that belonged to it. Take heed that you don't sell this spiritual priesthood for a morsel of meat or for the trifles of this world, that you ben't more concerned about a little worldly pelf or vain glory: that you are about that which is so sacred and honorable.

For direction, that you may be one of this spiritual priesthood: seek of God his holy anointing, that is, that God would pour out his Spirit in his sanctifying influences upon you. The priests of old were consecrated by the holy anointing oil; Ex. 29:7, "Then shalt thou take the anointing oil, and pour it upon his head, and anoint him"; and 30:30, "And thou shalt anoint Aaron and his sons, and consecrate them, that they may minister unto me in the priest's office." If you are ever separated for this holy station and service, you must have that holy anointing of the Spirit of God, typified by the oil that was poured upon Aaron's head. The holy anointing oil of God must be upon you.

II. Let all that profess themselves Christian take heed that they don't defile themselves and profane their sacred character. There was a great strictness required of old of the priests, lest they should defile themselves and profane their office. And it was looked upon [as] a dreadful thing to profane that which [was] so holy. And God hath threatened in the New Testament that if any man defile the temple of God, him will God destroy; I Cor. 3:17, "If any man defile the temple of God, him will God destroy, which temple ye are"; the same as is said in v. 5 of the context [I Pet. 2], ye are "a spiritual house, a holy priesthood."

Avoid the commission of all immoralities, as things that have a horrid filthiness in them, things that will dreadfully profane the sacred name by which you are called and the sacred station wherein you are set. Take heed especially of lascivious impurities. Such things as these were looked upon as dreadful, defiling the holy office of the priesthood of old, insomuch that if but a daughter of a priest was guilty of whoredom, she was to be burnt [Lev. 21:9]. Remember Hophni and Phinehas, how severely God dealt with them for their profaning their office by their impurities [I Sam. 4:11], and with good Eli, that he was no more thorough to restrain them. God brought a curse upon the whole family which never was removed. God took away the priesthood from him, and took away the ark of the covenant from him and from Israel, and delivered it into captivity, and fulfilled his threatening that there should not be an old man of his house forever [I Sam. 3:12–14]. Take heed of every sin. An allowing any sin whatever is a dreadful profanation of your holy character.

III. And lastly, see that you will execute your office. Get and keep a new access to God; come with boldness. Offer up your heart in sacrifice; get it broken for sin, and more and more so. Offer it up flaming with love to God.

Offer praise to God. Praise God for his glorious excellency, for his love and mercy. Consider what great things you have to praise God for: the redemption of Jesus Christ, [his] obedience, all [his] commands, [his] sincere [love].[5]

Be ready to distribute [charity], willing to communicate and do good. Consider 'tis part of your office thus to do, to which you are called and anointed, [for it is] well pleasing to God. Pity others in want. Be ready to help one another. God will have mercy and not sacrifice.

And be much in offering up your prayers to God and see that all your offerings be offered upon the right altar, otherwise they will be abominable to God. [Offer] your hearts to God through Jesus Christ, [and your] praise, obedience, [and] charity; [offer] prayers on the golden altar perfumed with the incense of Christ's merits.

Your reward will be to have this honor in heaven: to be exalted to that glorious priesthood, to be made a priest unto God forever and ever.[6]

[DOCTRINE I RESUMED.]

[*Third Prop.*] We are now come to the third part of the character of a true Christian in the text, viz. a holy nation.

5. Four blank lines follow. From the beginning of this paragraph to the end of this preaching unit, JE sketched incomplete sentences and phrases, leaving blank spaces after each as an indication of his intention to expand extemporaneously. Bracketed phrases are editorial interpolations.

6. Here ends the third preaching unit. JE begins the next unit with a citation of the text.

And, first, we shall briefly show how they are as a distinct nation; and, second, how they are holy.

1. [As a] distinct nation.

(1) The saints are all of the same native country. Heaven is the native country of the church; they are born from above. Their Father of whom they are begotten is in heaven. The new nature and those principles that are infused, they are, as it were, sent down from heaven in that the Holy Ghost, whose immediate fruits those principles are, is from heaven. The Word of God, which is the seed by which they are begotten, is from heaven. The Bible is a book, as it were, sent down from heaven.

The saints here in this world ben't in their native country but are pilgrims and strangers in the earth.[7] They are near akin to the inhabitants of the heavenly world and are properly of that society (Heb. 12:22–23). Heaven is a country that much better suits their natures than this earth because 'tis their native climate; when they are in heaven, they breathe their native air. In heaven is their inheritance. Heaven is the proper country of the church: where the greater part of the church is, and where they all will be, and where is their settled abode. From thence all that are now upon earth are derived, and thither they will return again. Though they are for a little while itinerant, at a distance from their native country, yet they are of the same nation with those that do now dwell there.

(2) All speak the same language. They all profess the same fundamental doctrines. They "hold fast the form of sound words" (II Tim. 1:13) that "was once delivered to the saints" [Jude 3]. They all in like manner use their tongues to the same purposes.

They have the same language to God in prayer and praise: expressing the same humility and repentance in confessing their sins, expressing the same adoration and admiring sense of God's glory and excellency, expressing the same humble submission and resignation, the same thankfulness, in like manner showing forth God's praises, expressing the same faith and humble dependence on the mercy and all-sufficiency of God, expressing the same love and longing desires after God. The saints in all ages speak the same language, that [of] David and the saints of old, which we have an account of in the Word of God. The Spirit of God teaches the saints the same language in their prayers; their prayers are the breathings of the same Spirit.

So they have the same language one to another in things pertaining to God and Christ, and things of a spiritual nature. They in like manner use

7. For a fuller treatment of the topic of this paragraph, see *The True Christian's Life a Journey Towards Heaven*, below.

their tongues religiously, and to promote religion one in another. They express the same sense of spiritual things, savoring of the same experience. They have the same language in general to the rest of the world in instructing, counseling, reproving.

And as they have the same language as it savors of the same religion, so they have the same kind of language as their speech expresses the same meekness and charity. Indeed, the saints while here in this world, they are but learners of the heavenly language and therefore speak it but imperfectly, and with a stammering tongue, and with a pronunciation that in many things savors of their old language.

The tongues of the saints are renewed in their conversion. Thus the conversion of the Gentiles is represented by their having a new language given them; Zeph. 3:9, "For then will I turn to the people a pure language, that they may all call upon the name of the Lord, to serve him with one consent." And in this sense is that also to be understood; Is. 19:18, "In that day shall five cities in the land of Egypt speak the language of Canaan." As it is said of the "new song" which the saints sing, that "no man could learn that song but" those that are "redeemed from the earth" [Rev. 14:3],[8] so no man can learn that language but those that are of this holy nation.

(3) They are under the same government. They are one society, one body politic, and therefore as here the church is represented by a nation, so oftentimes [it] is called a city. They are subject to the same king, Jesus Christ. He is the head of the church; he is the head of this body politic. Indeed, all men are subject to the power and providence of this king, but these are in his kingdom of grace. They all acknowledge the same king, own his rightful sovereignty over them. They are willing to be subject to him, to submit to his will and yield obedience to his commands; Ps. 110:3, "Thy people shall be willing in the day of thy power."

They are all governed by the same laws. There is the same rule for everyone, and all subject themselves to the same rules. The commands of God that are obeyed by the saints are the same all over the world.

There is the same method of government that all are subject to; there are the same means of government. [There are] the same outward and visible means: the same kinds [of] officers, angels, and gospel ministers, in like manner appointed and sent forth by the head of the church, the same visible order and discipline appointed for all. And there are the

8. For an application of this text in a later, revivalistic context (Nov. 1740), see *The Redeemed Sing a New Song*, in *Works of Jonathan Edwards, Sermons and Discourses, 1739–1742*, ed. Harry S. Stout and Nathan O. Hatch (New Haven, Yale Univ. Press, forthcoming).

same inward and spiritual means of government. Christ governs his people after a manner differing from all other kings. He immediately influences their wills and inclinations and powerfully brings them to a compliance with God's commands and rules. He influences all by the same spirit, and in the manner of influencing them in the main is the same.

(4) And lastly, they are a society united in the same public interest and concerns. It is by the same covenant and promises that they have their inheritance, and that they hold their title to their enjoyments as a people of the same nation, hold their temporal rights by the same rules, and [as] citizens hold their rights by the same municipal laws.

The flourishing and prosperity of the society will be to the advantage and advancement of the interests of the particular parts. A Christian has the same reason to be concerned for the flourishing of the church and the advancement of religion as a particular subject has for the flourishing of the nation or kingdom. When the church is in flourishing circumstances, the souls of particular saints are like to be flourishing, and when the church is in low, languishing circumstances, particular souls are generally so. When iniquity abounds, the love of many waxes cold. As 'tis the interest of every subject to have the nation flourish, so 'tis the interest of every Christian to have the church flourish.

So Christians have the same common enemies that seek their hurt and overthrow. He that is an enemy to one saint as a saint is an enemy to all. They are jointly called to resist the same powers of darkness. The church here upon earth is as an army that goes forth under Jesus Christ, the captain of their salvation, to resist the common adversary.

IMPROVEMENT.

[*Use*] I. [Of] *Exh.* To join yourself to this nation. As it was of old, those that were of other nations, if they were proselytized to the acknowledgment of the God of Israel and to the true religion and were circumcised, they were received as being of the nation of Israel and were accounted as those that were descended from Abraham and Jacob. So now is there free liberty to any to come and join themselves to this nation, and they shall be received and admitted to the same rights and privileges and be in all respects treated as some of the same people.

And especially now under the gospel are all called to come, let them be who they will. They may come and join to this people, and welcome. There is no wall of partition to separate this people from others, and to exclude those of other nations that are wished to come and join themselves to them. The gates of the new Jerusalem are always open to receive all whose hearts inclined them to come.

Here, for motives, consider,

First. There is no nation under such a happy government as this nation; there is no nation so happy in their king as this nation. The Lord Jesus Christ is their king, as we have said, and he is a most glorious king. He is the eternal, infinitely glorious Son of God. Solomon says, "Blessed art thou, O Lord: teach me thy statutes" [Ps. 119:12]. How much more blessed is that nation whose king is the Son of God.

He is a most wise prince. He knows how to govern; he perfectly understands how best to promote the interests of his people. He understands how to govern in peace and war. He has that wisdom that infallibly guides him to a right judgment and discerning in all cases. He is infinitely wise.

He is a most merciful and gracious king, that greatly loves his people, most earnestly and faithfully seeks their interest. His people are a people that he has redeemed; he has purchased [them] with his own blood and therefore will surely seek their welfare. His government is a most mild and gracious government.

And thus he is a very powerful prince. He is able to defend his people against all their enemies. If anything needs to be done for the promotion of the good of the nation, it cannot be too hard for him to accomplish it.

This nation is governed by most wise and righteous laws, as it was said of Israel of old; Deut. 4:8, "What nation is there so great, that hath statutes and judgments so righteous as all this law, which I set before you this day?" So, and more eminent, is it true of the spiritual Israel, since the law of God has been set forth thus in abundantly more clearly and in a more lovely light by the rules and precepts of the gospel. The manner of Christ's government in the kingdom of his grace is most excellent and different from that of all other kings, for he governs by the powerful influence of his upon the heart, whereby he sweetly inclines them to a willing and chosen subjection to him.

This nation is a free people. The happy government they are under is most consistent with freedom. It don't in the least infringe upon the liberty of the subject but promotes it. There is nothing like slavery in the kingdom of grace; the law of this nation is a law of liberty. There are none that enjoy such a blessed liberty as those that are subject to the king of the church. Those that are sinners, they are slaves. They are slaves to their lusts, slaves to Satan, slaves to the worst and cruelest of masters. But they that the Son makes free are free indeed (John 8:36). The subjects of the heavenly king, they are all as free under his government as a man's children are in their father's house. The government is a paternal government; the king looks upon all his subjects as his children.

Under so happy a government are this nation. Be persuaded therefore to join yourself to them and be of them; Ps. 144:15, "Happy is that people, that is in such a case: yea, happy is that people, whose God is the Lord"; and Ps. 33:12, "Blessed is the nation whose God is the Lord; and the people whom he hath chosen for his own inheritance."

Second. There is no nation that dwell in that love and peace that this holy nation doth. The happiness of a people or kingdom very much consists in the peace; a nation is never more miserable than when it is rent by civil wars or disturbed by intestine broils. Nothing tends more to the happiness of the people than when they are all united as brethren and do with one heart seek the good of one another and the community.

But there is no nation that enjoys so much happiness of this kind as this holy nation. The Lord Jesus Christ, who is the king of this people, is the Prince of Peace; his kingdom is a kingdom of peace. Every member of this society has reigning in his heart a principle of peace and love. These are all the marks that are of the kingdom of God. Love is the bond of perfectness that unites the members of this society together. They all have a disposition heartily to seek and promote each other's good.

Third. And lastly, this nation have for their settled abode a most glorious land. The heavenly Canaan is their land, flowing with milk and honey, a land that God hath desired and that he hath blessed above all lands. There is no land so fertile of excellent fruits. 'Tis a land that is full of delights. There grows the tree of life in plenty. There flows the river of the water of life. There is no curse, nothing that hurts or offends. This is a delightful garden. This is the paradise of God.

Hearken therefore; consider of the blessedness of this people. Is it not well worth your while to be one of this people? I would now invite you, in the name of Christ, as Moses invited his father-in-law to join himself to that nation; Num. 10:29, "And Moses said unto Hobab, the son of Raguel the Midianite, Moses' father-in-law, We are journeying to the place of which the Lord God said, I will give it you: come thou with us, and we will do thee good: for the Lord hath spoken good concerning Israel."

Use [II. Of] *Dir.*

First. Labor to be sensible of the misery of that people that you are now one of. You are of a very different company; you are one of those that are in slavish subjection to Satan, the prince of darkness, one of the seed of the serpent. Ye are some of those that are from beneath, are the offspring of the devil; John 8:23, "Ye are from beneath"; v. 44, "Ye are of your father the devil, and the lusts of your father ye will do."[9]

Second. Do but heartily yield yourself to Christ, the king of this people, to be subject to his government. Nothing else [is] required of you, nothing inclined. [Be] heartily desirous. See the gloriousness of this king. [Be] sensible of the happiness of his government. Choose him for your Lord; choose his laws and commands. Perform the obedience of love.

The king makes this offer, that all that will willingly and heartily [yield] shall enjoy all the rights and privileges he gives. [He] will become engaged by covenant; his faithfulness is engaged.[1]

Third. You must choose your inheritance in their land, not in this world.

Fourth. See that you come up to the distinguishing character of those that are of this nation: that they are holy.

Let those that are of this nation, [first],[2] be more mindful of their native country, the land where their inheritance is; second, seek more and better to learn the heavenly language; third, be more subject to [their King]; [and] fourth, more to seek the interests of the community to which they belong.

[DOCTRINE I RESUMED.]

2.[3] This nation is an holy nation by a twofold holiness: a relative, and an inherent holiness.

(1) They are a holy nation by a relative holiness, as they are set apart by God for a divine and holy use. So things are often called holy in Scripture. The utensils of the tabernacle and temple are in this sense called holy. The priests' garments, they are called holy. The places of worship appointed of God in the Old Testament are called holy because they were set apart by him for a holy use and service.

Things in being thus set apart are said to be sanctified. Thus Jeremiah is said to have been sanctified before he came forth out of the womb; Jer. 1:5, "Before I formed thee in the belly I knew thee; and before thou camest forth out of the womb I sanctified thee, and ordained thee a prophet unto the nations." God sanctified; that is, God set him apart for this holy use and service to be a prophet to the nations, as Paul says of

9. Six blank lines follow. Here through the end of this preaching unit, JE again relies on partial sentences and phrases, followed by blank spaces or lines to indicate his intention to expand extemporaneously. Brackets mark editorial interpolations.

1. Two blank lines follow this and next two directions.

2. Two blank lines follow this and each of the three directions in this paragraph.

3. I.e. the second subhead of the third proposition of the first doctrine.

himself; Gal. 1:15, "when it pleased God, who separated me from my mother's womb." So the people of Israel of old seem to be called an holy nation; Deut. 7:6, "Thou art an holy people to the Lord." Not that they were a holy people by inherent holiness, for God often tells them that they are a stiff-necked people. But God had called and separated them from other nations to a divine [use], to be the keepers of the sacred oracles.

So the saints are a nation that God has set apart for a sacred use. He hath set them apart to serve and glorify him and to show forth his praise: as is said in the verse of the text, to be vessels for their master's use, to see the manifestations of God's glory and eternally to ascribe the glory due to his name.

(2) They are holy by inherent holiness. With respect to this kind of holiness, they are holy two ways: holiness of heart and life (Ps. 24:4),[4] viz.

1. By holiness of heart. Holiness may be considered either as a purity from sin or as something positive.[5]

They are holy in heart as to what is positive, as their hearts are endowed with spiritual excellency in their dispositions. There are dispositions that are in some kind excellent that have nothing [of] spiritual excellency.[6] By holiness is meant the spiritual beauty of any heart. The divine nature is the standard of excellency; [and their holiness is] conformed to that divine nature. Their love is to such excellencies, their appetites often [are in] compliance in such things, [their] dispositions to such actions. Their happiness is in the beholding and enjoying that which is thus spiritually excellent.[7]

[2.] They are holy in life, acting excellently; their beauty appears in action. [Their] purity [appears in] clearness from allowed known sins, in general imitation of God, seeking and following of God, obedience to God with care, diligence, tenderness, universality; glorifying God, doing good to men, conforming to Christian rules of the royal law of meekness [and] charity.[8]

4. Two blank lines follow.

5. Here JE leaves the rest of the leaf, some seventeen lines, blank.

6. Three blank lines follow.

7. Here the MS contains an unusually personal reflection by JE that does not appear to be part of the preached text. He may have used a salvaged piece of paper at this point on which he had written previously: "I at length determined, if ever I had opportunity, to make it known to some person of whom I could have confidence, that he was a person of thorough judgment in things of such a nature." Seven blank lines follow.

8. Here ends the fourth preaching unit. Leaving one and a half leaves blank, JE begins the next preaching unit with a citation of the text.

[*Fourth Prop.*] [We] shall briefly show how Christians are God's peculiar people in the following respects: first, in the value God set upon them; second, in the mercy he bestows upon them; third, in the interest he has in them; fourth, in what they do for God.

First. True Christians are God's peculiar people with respect to the value God sets upon them, in that he sets a higher value upon one true Christian than upon all the wicked in the world. God sets a high value upon his saints. They are his "jewels," as they are called [Mal. 3:17]. God's high value of them appears in all the ways wherein persons are wont to show a great value that they set upon any possession. God keeps them as the apple of his eye [Deut. 32:10]. He will by no means lose one of his saints; not one of all the number shall fail. He by no means will suffer any to do them harm. His almighty power is thoroughly engaged for them to defend them.

The life, the happiness, and welfare of the saints is precious in God's sight. God values one saint more than thousands of ungodly men, yea, more than all the ungodly in the world. God shows the higher value that he sets upon the godly than others by giving the wicked for them, making them subservient to them, and destroying them when they stand in the way of the welfare of the godly; Prov. 21:18, "The wicked shall be a ransom for the righteous, and the transgressor for the upright."

This is to show how much more highly God values the righteous than the wicked, as if a man had a child in the hand of an enemy and should be willing to give a hundred slaves to redeem that one child. This would show that he set a higher value upon that child than upon all those slaves. So God, whenever the life or welfare of the wicked stands in the way of the welfare of the righteous, God is wont to procure the welfare of his people, though it be at the expense of the lives or welfares of never so many of them; so Prov. 11:8, "The righteous is delivered out of trouble, and the wicked cometh in his stead."

Thus God sets forth the value that he set upon the patriarchs. Though there were but very few of them, yet even kings were rebuked for their sakes; Ps. 105:12–15, "When they were but a few men in number; yea, very few, and strangers in it; when they went from one nation to another, from one kingdom to another people; he suffered no man to do them wrong: yea, he reproved kings for their sakes; saying, Touch not mine anointed and do my prophets no harm." So he sets forth the value he sets upon the children of Israel by that, that he gave nations for them; Is. 43:3–4, "For I am the Lord thy God, the Holy One of Israel, thy Savior: I gave Egypt for thy ransom, Ethiopia and Sheba for thee. Since thou wast precious in my sight, thou hast been honorable, and I have loved thee: therefore will I give men for thee, and people for thy life."

When the Egyptians stood in the way of the welfare of the church, God brought plagues upon them one after another where he sorely distressed them. When their lives stood in the way, God destroyed all the first born of Egypt; and when Pharaoh and his host sought their destruction, he drowned them in the Red Sea. And when the nations of Canaan stood in their way, God destroyed them, destroyed many of them miraculously by sending hailstones from heaven upon them [Josh. 10:11]. God will sooner at one blow destroy all the wicked of the world than that one of his saints should be lost.

There are many great men of the world, noble men and kings and men of great power and policy, men of noble blood and honorable descent, men of great wealth, men of vast learning and knowledge in the world, that are greatly honored and make a great figure, and great account is made of 'em in the world, that are wicked men and reprobates; and they all ben't of so great value in God's sight as one poor saint.

God has shown the great value that he has for his saints and how much he sets by them by several remarkable providences. He has changed or interrupted the course of nature for their sakes many a time, as in the miracles that were wrought for them in dividing the Red Sea, but especially in causing the sun to stand still [Josh. 10:13]. God don't change or stop the course of nature upon slight occasions. Nothing except God himself is more constant and unchangeable than the course and laws of nature. But yet so great a value doth God set upon his saints, that the procuring of their welfare he did not look upon as too slight an occasion for stopping the sun in his course.

But above all, hath God shown how great a value he sets upon his saints by the great price which he has paid for them: the price with which he bought them was the blood of his own Son. 'Tis very fair arguing from hence, as we may fairly argue how greatly a man values that which he buys by the price that he pays for it. God values every saint so highly that he bought him with the blood of his own dear Son. God doubtless values the blood of his Son more than the lives of all ungodly [men] and reprobates. There is no price of gold or silver that can be equaled with the price of the blood of Christ.

Second. They are his peculiar people with respect to the mercy that he bestows upon them, in that he bestows more mercy upon one godly man than upon all the world of ungodly men. God bestows abundance of mercy upon ungodly men; he bestows great temporal mercies upon them. God is kind to the evil and the good, to the just and the unjust. God is good to wicked men in preserving their lives, in providing for their subsistence, in giving them many things that are for their comfort in the world. Wicked men receive a great deal of goodness from God that they have cause to admire and be thankful for every day, and [there are] but few that live any considerable time but what are the subjects of special instances of God's goodness and mercy to them in deliverances from trouble, and danger, and otherwise. Ungodly men especially receive great kindness from God. God heaps temporal good things upon them; he gives them wealth, and ease, and honor, and great temporal prosperity. God distributes the world amongst them. And they show their great ingratitude in that they, notwithstanding all God's bounty to them, will not learn righteousness; Is. 26:10, "Let favor be showed to the wicked, yet will he not learn righteousness." Thus Samuel reproves Saul for his great ingratitude, that he took no more notice of the great kindness of God to him; I Sam. 15:17, "When thou wast little in thine own sight, wast thou not made the head of the tribes of Israel, and the Lord anointed thee king over Israel?" So there are many other wicked men that are advanced to the state of princes and nobles.

But God bestows more goodness upon one godly man than upon all the ungodly in the world. Put all their preservations, all their deliverances, all their wealth, all their comforts that have been heaped upon them by providence together: these things are but trifles that God bestows on ungodly men. But they are peculiar blessings which he bestows on the righteous; they are precious things that God has in reserve for his own favorites, in comparison of which all earthly treasure is but dirt and dung.

As for the saints, Christ has died for them. They have all their sins pardoned. They are delivered from a hell of eternal misery. They have a title to eternal life bestowed upon them. They have God's own image conferred on them. They are received into favor and everlastingly to enjoy God's love.

Third. They are God's peculiar people with respect to the interest God has in them. God has a peculiar interest in a godly man. As we have observed already in a former discourse, they are God's peculiar propriety; they are God's as they are redeemed by him and as they have given themselves to him. God has an interest in a godly man's heart. They have a true love and respect to God. They have true honor to God. God has a greater interest in their hearts than anything else, greater than the dearest friend on earth, greater than the world or any earthly enjoyment.

They are of a spirit to prefer God before all other things. They reserve the throne of their hearts for God. They are of a spirit to exalt him as the greatest and highest, to love him as the most excellent, to praise him as the most gracious and merciful.

God has no interest in the hearts of natural men. There are many of them that seem to show respect to God outwardly. The Pharisees of old pretended to an extraordinary devotion, to a great love to God. And so many hypocrites in these times, they come before God as God's people come. They seem as though they delighted to draw near to God, and many make a high profession of respect to God and religion. But God has indeed no interest in their hearts. They give God the outward appearance; they give God the words of their lips; but their hearts are far from him. The show which they make is from a principle of self-love; 'tis from respect to something else and not from respect to God. They have not one jot of love to God.

But God has an interest in the hearts of true Christians. However small it is, and inconsiderable in comparison of what it ought to be, yet they are of a spirit to prefer God above all. And God has an interest in them as they offer up their bodies a living sacrifice to him. They do serve God and actively glorify him with their bodies and with their spirits.

God is glorified in wicked men as they are occasions of the manifestations of God's glory, or as God glorifies himself in them; but these do devote themselves to serve and glorify God. Though 'tis but a small interest that God has in the hearts of the Christians in this world in comparison of what ought to be, yet he hath a greater interest in one godly man than in all the ungodly and hypocrites that are in the world.

Fourth. They are God's peculiar people with respect to the complacence God hath in them. God takes delight in his saints; Ps. 11:7, "For the righteous Lord loveth righteousness; and his countenance doth behold the upright." God doth, as it were, rejoice over a convert. He delights in beholding that beauty and those ornaments of mind which he hath given them. God takes delight in the graces of a godly man's heart, and he delights in the good works and religion of the Christian; Ps. 37:23, "The steps of a good man are ordered by the Lord: and he delighteth in his way." God takes delight in the godly man's prayers; Prov. 15:8, "The prayer of the upright is his delight." God takes more delight in the sincere, humble devotion of one true saint than in all the moral virtue and outward religion of all the natural men in the world.

If wicked [men] that are rich should offer to God ten thousand sacrifices, or if they should devote never so much of their substance to religious uses, if they should give all their goods to feed the poor, it would not be so acceptable to God as one cup of cold water given by a saint with a spirit of true charity [Matt. 10:42]. Ungodly kings may do a great deal in many respects for religion. They may build stately churches for the worship of God. They may encourage religion in their dominions by their power and influence. Cyrus, a heathen prince, he restored the people of God from captivity and restored the state of the Jews [Ezra 1:1–4]. But [God] has a greater delight in the sincere, secret devotion of a poor, obscure Christian than in all this.

Thus they are God's peculiar people.

IMPROVEMENT.

Hence it may well be expected of such as profess hopes of their being true Christians, that they should live after a peculiar manner as being devoted unto God for his use. There should be a great difference between their way of living and other men's, the way that men commonly live. Godly men should not be carried away with general example. If any evil practice is become a common custom, it may well be expected of those who profess themselves godly, that they should stem the stream of common custom and example though they are despised for it.

Men are ready oftentimes to plead for their neglect of such duties and the commission of such evils, that 'tis a common custom. "Who is there," say they, "but what does so? I shall be singular if I did otherwise." But if ill things are common, God may well expect of them that their way and manner should be singular and peculiar, for Christians are a peculiar people. There should be a difference, and a great difference, between them and the generality of the world. If their neighbors and relations and companions fall in with the common custom that is evil, yet they should be peculiar and stand alone.

It may well be expected that they should go further than other men in doing their duty and practicing Christian rules. As for instance, 'tis a common thing for men, when they are affronted or injured by their neighbors, to entertain a spirit of revenge, to drink in a spirit of ill will against their neighbors and wish them hurt. But Christians should be peculiar and there should be a difference between them and others. They should not do so, but they should forgive those that injure them and not entertain any spirit of ill will to them upon that account.

'Tis common for men when injured to endeavor to come up with him that injures them some way or other, either by acting or talking against them. But those that call themselves godly should tolerate no kind of revenge; Matt. 5:38–39, "Ye have heard that it hath been said, An eye for an eye, a tooth for a tooth: but I say unto you, That ye resist not evil: but whosoever shall smite thee on thy right cheek, turn to him the other also." The generality of men will love their friends that are kind and friendly to them and hate their enemies. 'Tis very rare that 'tis otherwise. Men pretend that they don't hate their enemies, but they really do in their hearts. But Christians should be peculiar in this matter. Their way should be different from the way of the world, for they are a peculiar people. They should love their enemies from their hearts and do good to them that hate them and do evil to them. However rare it is that there is any such thing, yet such a rare thing very well becomes God's peculiar people; Matt. 5:43–44, "Ye have heard that it hath been said, Thou shalt love thy neighbor, and hate thine enemy. But I say unto you, Love your enemies, bless them that curse you, do good to them that hate you, and pray for them that despitefully use you, and persecute you."

'Tis a rare thing for persons to accustom themselves to great self-denial. Many will indeed deny themselves something for the sake of their duty, but if it very much crosses with their interest, they are few that will be steadfast to their duty notwithstanding. But it may well be expected of you [that you] should greatly deny yourself for God's and Christ's sake, and so be peculiar in this matter. Self-interest is the thing that governs the generality of men. They will mind their own interest rather than anything else. But it may well be expected of those that profess godliness, that they should show themselves peculiar in this matter, and that they should sacrifice their private, separate interest to the glory and honor of God and to the public good.

Most men will content themselves and quiet their consciences by an avoiding the more gross acts of sin, by avoiding an outward gratification of lusts. But it becomes Christians to distinguish themselves here and avoid sinning, so much as in their thoughts not to indulge any lust, so much as in their imaginations.

'Tis a shame to professors of godliness that their lights shine no brighter before men, that there is no more appearing in them of an amiable Christian spirit, that they don't seem to shine any brighter in their outward conversations than many other men that don't make the profession that they do. Many such seem to be as exact and as careful to avoid sin and to deny themselves as they; yea, many perhaps that for the outward practice of some particular virtues shine brighter than they. They are more liberal and kind, more courteous and obliging in their behavior. It is expected of those that are of this peculiar people that they should do more than others; Matt. 5:46–47, "For if ye love them that love you, what reward have ye? do not even the publicans the same? And if ye salute your brethren only, what do you more than others? do not even the publicans so?"

I. Here is argument and motive to become godly: that if you will forsake your sins and with all your heart turn to God, you shall become some of God's peculiar people. You shall have the same privileges with those that have been mentioned. You will immediately upon your conversion become one of those that God sets such an high value upon. If you are assured of your conversion, you may withal be assured that God, the supreme Lord of heaven and earth, sets a higher value upon you than upon all the reprobates in the world, that God has set so high a value upon you that he has given the blood of his own Son for your ransom.

If you do savingly turn to God, you will receive from God greater mercies and blessings than all the wealth and outward prosperity of all ungodly men in the world comes to. Put all the honor, all the wealth of the great men of the world together; put all that the kings of the earth possess, their treasures and revenues, their dominions and power, their robes, their stately seats and palaces, their robes and their dainties together; and they will not amount to so great things as God will bestow upon you.

If you will turn from your sin and come to Christ, the great God will accept of you and delight in you. You then will have those spiritual ornaments that will be more amiable in the sight of God than all the learning and knowledge and morality of all the ungodly men in the world.

If you continue in a natural condition, God will make no account of you. God will not value you at all. Instead of being as God's jewels, you will be esteemed by God as vile and refuse and fit for nothing but to be trampled underfoot. Instead of being gold, you will be esteemed by God as dross; Jer. 6:30, "Reprobate silver shall men call them, because the Lord hath rejected them." Hereafter you will be thrown away as being good for nothing. You will be esteemed worth nothing, as is represented in that parable; Matt. 13:47–49, "Again, the kingdom of heaven is like unto a net, that was cast into the sea, and gathered of every kind: which, when it was full, they drew to the shore, and sat down, and gathered the good into vessels, and cast the bad away. So shall it be at the end of the world: the angels shall come forth, and sever the wicked from among the just."

Yea, you shall not only be cast away as good for nothing, but shall be cast out as filth into the great receptacle of the filth of the world, viz. hell. You will be cast into a furnace of fire as barren branches are gathered up and burnt (John 15:6); or as barren trees are cut down and cast into the fire (Matt. 3:10); as the tares were gathered together in bundles and burnt [Matt. 13:30]. You will be looked upon as fit for nothing but to be destroyed; II Pet. 2:12, "but these, as natural brute beasts, made to be taken and destroyed."

Instead of bestowing such peculiar mercies upon you, you in a little time will be stripped of all mercy. God will not have mercy on you, but your miseries will be as dreadful as those mercies that God bestows on his saints are valuable. They are but poor things, but trifles, that wicked men have bestowed upon them while in this world in comparison of what the righteous shall have. The blessings of one righteous is more worth than the enjoyments of all the wicked. But hereafter wicked men won't have those; they will have nothing but the fiery wrath and indignation of God for their portion.

While you are in a natural condition, instead of your being God's peculiar ones with respect to the interest God hath in your heart, the devil has the greatest interest in your heart. He has the government and possession there, and therefore you are and will be the devil's people, those that he claims and those that will fall to his share at last, if you continue in such a condition.

Instead of being one in whom God has peculiar complacence, you are detested by God as an abominable thing. He has no pleasure in you when you pretend to worship him. He has no delight in your hypocritical prayers and services, but they are an abomination to him.

II. If [you are] true Christians, then let God be peculiar with you, as,

First, let God be your peculiar portion. If you are of one of his peculiar people, he is so. All that are God's people, they have chosen him for their God and portion, but do so more and more and more. Let all other things be rightly set by and treated by you with neglect in comparison of God.

Let God be the object of your peculiar value and esteem. If God has made you one of those in whom he sets a peculiar value who are a poor worthless worm, if he has set such a value upon you as to purchase you with the price of the blood of his Son who are in yourself a filthy despicable creature, how much more reason is there that you should peculiarly value God who is so great and glorious. 'Tis fitting that this value should be mutual, and 'tis fitting that it should be in answerable degree.

It will be but a little thing for you to esteem God above all in comparison of what it [is] for God so to prize his saints. See to it therefore that there be nothing that stands in any competition with God in your esteem. Value him more than all riches. Value his honor and glory more than all the world. Be ready at all times to part with all things else and cleave to God.

Let God be your peculiar friend. Value his friendship more than the respect and love of all the world. When you lose other enjoyments, when you lose earthly friends, let this be a supporting, satisfying comfort to you, that you have God left. You han't lost God.

Second. Let God be your peculiar confidence. There is great encouragement in this doctrine for you to make him so, and reason to enforce it as your duty. God expects that those that are his peculiar people should put their trust in him, and well they may do so. For God has a peculiar favor for them, is peculiarly careful and tender of them.

Be sensible therefore that 'tis unbecoming any, but especially those that are so near to God and so favored by him, to trust in their own righteousness or in any arm of flesh. The peculiar people of God should not trust in themselves. They should not trust in friends. They should [not] trust in great men. They should not trust in their estates or in any worldly enjoyment, as expecting happiness from it, but alone in the Lord God. He ought to be their refuge and hiding place. In time of trouble they should "hide themselves under the shadow of his wings" [Ps. 17:8].

Third. Make God the peculiar object of your praises. The doctrine shows what great reason you have so to do. If God so values you, sets so much by you, has bestowed greater mercies upon you than on all the ungodly in the world, is it too little a requital for you to make God the peculiar object of your praise and thankfulness? If God so distinguishes you with his mercies, you ought to distinguish yourself in his praises. You should make it your great care and study how to glorify that God who has been so peculiarly merciful to you. And this, rather, because there was nothing peculiar in you differing from any other person that moved God thus to deal thus peculiarly by you: you was as unworthy to be set by as thousands of others that are not regarded of God, and are cast away by him forever as worthless and filthy.[9]

9. Dwight's published version of this sermon ends at this point. In a later repreaching, JE here added the following three brief exhortations under the second major head of the application: "*Fourth.* Let the word of God be treated by you as men are wont to treat the precious portion they depend on for life. *Fifth.* Devote yourself to God and reserve yourself for him as one that is his portion. *Sixth.* It is expected that you should do more than others in the service of

II. *Persons, when they are converted, are called out of darkness into marvelous light.*

[There are] four propositions. First, natural men [are] in darkness. Second, when they are converted [they are] brought out of darkness into light. Third, this is marvelous light. Fourth, when they thus come out of darkness {into marvelous light}, 'tis God calls them.

First Prop. Natural men are in darkness. By this metaphorical expression, of wicked men's being in darkness, is intimated the doleful state that men are in before conversion in these following respects:

1. Natural men are blind to spiritual objects. He that walks in darkness seeth not the objects that are round about him. Though the world be full of objects that would be very delighting to the sight if they were seen, though there are objects on every side he is encompassed about with, though many of them are very near him, yet he sees them not. So natural men see not spiritual objects. The spiritual world is all invisible to him, as the natural world is to him that is stone blind or that walks in perfect darkness.

A natural man is ignorant of the being of spiritual objects. He knows not whether there are any such things. They don't know whether there be a God or no. They are ignorant of the being of a Savior. They are at a loss whether there be any such thing as a future invisible and spiritual world, whether there be a heaven or a hell or any state of rewards and punishments.

They are ignorant of those things that we are informed of in the Word of God. They don't know but that all that the Scriptures gives account [of] is fabulous. They don't know whether there ever were such things transacted as God's creating the world according to the account of Scripture, whether there ever was any such thing as the flood, and the calling of Abraham, and bringing the children of Israel out of Egypt, whether there ever were any such things as we have there an account of concerning Jesus Christ, and what he did and suffered, and his rising again from the dead and his ascending up {into heaven}.

They are ignorant of the being of those things because they don't see them and never have seen them, as a man that walks in darkness. There are many things round about him, but he don't know it; he is ignorant

God." This ends the fifth preaching unit. After reciting the second part of the text, JE gives the second doctrine as a head to the sixth and final preaching unit.

that there are any such things in being. He may wander hither and thither and is ignorant of the being of those objects that he is surrounded with. Natural men may have a sort of belief of the being of spiritual things. They may suspect that such and such things are, but they don't know that they are, neither have they right notions about them, as he that walks in gross darkness and never saw the light, though he supposes and guesses that such and such things are round about him, but knows it not.

So natural men are ignorant of the manner of spiritual things' existence. They han't right notions of them. They call evil good, and good evil. Many suspect that there is a God, but they are ignorant of his glory. They don't know what an excellent Being he is: how full of majesty, how holy a God, how he hates sin, how opposite sin is to his nature, how merciful and gracious a God he is, how all-sufficient, how full he is of blessedness, and what a fountain of happiness he is for all that trust in him. They are ignorant of the excellency of the Lord Jesus Christ. They don't see any beauty in him any more than a man that has no eyes can see the glory of the sun. They are ignorant of the sufficiency of Christ, his wonderful love, his readiness to receive and embrace sinners.

They are ignorant of the excellency of spiritual enjoyment. They see no more beauty in holiness, and a way of Christian walk and behavior, or the excellency of heaven and heavenly enjoyments, the happiness of those that are in the presence of God and behold his glory and enjoy his love; they see no more of these things than a man that is in perfect darkness sees the beauty of the fields, trees, herbs, and flowers. As a man in perfect darkness, if he should be placed in the midst of the garden of Eden, would see no more pleasant objects than if he were in the hideous desert, so natural men see no beauty or excellency in spiritual objects, that is, any ways taken with them.

2. Natural men are lost and in a most doubtful and uncertain state. They are like a man that wanders in perfect darkness, who knows not where he is, nor where he is going nor what dangers he is encompassed by. He may be just ready to fall into the mouths of wild beasts, but he knows not that any mischief is near him. He may be treading upon snares, but he sees nothing. He is not aware but that he stands safe enough. He may be going into a pit that his enemies have digged for him, or may be walking directly towards a precipice, or going to step into deep water or mire, but knows not but that 'tis all firm ground. He may be ready to stumble upon steep mountains or dash himself against rocks, but he is not aware of anything that is in his way.

A man that wanders in perfect darkness knows not which way to turn himself nor how to extricate himself. He knows not where to find the sure road nor which is the way home. Thus it is with a man in a natural condition. They are in a lost condition; they are as lost sheep. They know not whither they go; John 12:35, "For he that walketh in darkness knoweth not whither he goeth."

Natural men ben't sensible, till God is pleased to awaken them, where they are, nor in what state and condition they are in. They are in a very doleful state, but they don't know it. They are encompassed with dangers on every side, but they are secure. There are roaring lions round them ready to devour them, but they see nothing of them. They are going directly towards the pit of hell, towards the dismal precipice from whence the fall is into the bottomless gulf of woe and misery, but they know it not.

And they know not the way of deliverance; the way of salvation is hidden from them. Christ is the way, but they see him not; II Cor. 4:3–4, "But if our gospel be hid, it is hid to them that are lost: in whom the god of this world hath blinded the minds of them that believe not, lest the light of the glorious gospel of Christ, who is the image of God, should shine unto them."

3. They are in a state wherein they are destitute of all true comfort. It is uncomfortable dwelling in darkness; "the light is sweet, and a pleasant thing it is to behold the sun" [Eccles. 11:7]. One of the plagues of Egypt was perfect darkness, which was doubtless very uncomfortable [Ex. 10:22]. So those that are in a natural condition, they are void of all true comfort. They never had the experience of anything of true happiness.

And ordinarily they are sensibly, for some time, in a very uncomfortable state; before they are converted, they are wounded by convictions of God's spirit. They are made sensible of their evil which lies as a heavy load upon their souls. They are sensible that God is angry with them and that they are in a condemned state and condition. They are sensible that they lie under the curse of the law. They are brought into an uneasy and afflicted, wounded condition. They are sensible of their doleful state. Not that they are really in any greater darkness than they were before, but it pleases God to make them sensible of it. They are sensible that they are encompassed with danger, and their minds are filled with the darkness of fear and trouble.

Second Prop. When they are converted, they are brought out of darkness into light.

They are brought to the discovery of spiritual objects; God reveals them to them. Sometimes the change is represented in Scripture as the opening of the eyes of the blind. Christ several times wrought this miracle upon men's bodies while he was here upon earth; he opened the eyes of the blind, and sometimes the eyes of those that were born blind, which miracles were only a figure of his opening the eyes of men's souls.

Here in the text, this change is represented by his bringing men from a dark and obscure region into a region of light. Believers do, as it were, dwell in a different region from the wicked and unbelieving; they dwell in a land of light. It is with the church as it was with Israel in the land of Goshen: the Egyptians, they dwelt in thick darkness but "the children of Israel had light in their dwellings" [Ex. 10:23]. And when men are converted, they are, as it were, called out of one region into the other, out of a region of darkness into the land of light.

The wicked and the godly, they dwell in two very different kingdoms. The wicked dwell in a kingdom of darkness. And when anyone is converted, he is translated out of that kingdom into the kingdom of Christ where there is light; Col. 1:13, "who hath delivered us from the power of darkness, and translated us into the kingdom of his dear Son." Natural men are as those that are shut up in a dark dungeon, out of which dungeon Christ came to deliver men; Is. 42:7, "to open the blind eyes, to bring out the prisoners from the prison, and them that sit in darkness out of the prison house."

In conversion they are brought to see spiritual objects. Those things which before they only heard of by the hearing of the ear, they now are brought to a sight of: a sight of God, and a sight of Christ, and a sight of sin and holiness, a sight of the way of salvation, a sight of the spiritual and invisible world, a sight of the happiness of the enjoyment of God and his favor, and a sight of the dreadfulness of his anger.

They now see the truth of spiritual things which before they were uncertain about. They see that those things that the Word of God treats about are real things. They are now convinced of the being of God, after another manner than ever they were before. They are now convinced that Jesus Christ is the Savior of the world, and the only Savior, and a sufficient and glorious Savior, and that he indeed satisfied for sin, and rose again from the dead, and ascended up into heaven, and that he is now at the right hand of God the Father in glory; and that the Scripture is the Word of God. 'Tis not merely by ratiocination that those things are confirmed to them; but they are convinced that they are, because that they see them to be. A man that looks on visible objects, on the sun or earth and fields, is not convinced by ratiocination of their being, but by sight; the light that shines shows these things to be. So there is a spiritual light that shines into men's hearts that shows spiritual objects to have a being.

So likewise it shows the excellency and glory of them. God is seen to be, and he is seen to be a glorious God. Christ is seen to be, and he is seen to be a most excellent Redeemer. Heaven is seen to be, and it is seen to be a world of exceeding bliss and happiness. The Scripture is seen to be the Word of God, and it is seen to be a holy, a wise, and gracious word beyond all parallel. The Word of God is not a dead letter; there is seen to be more in it than in the word of men. When the Word of God is read, especially at some times, there is a light shines from the sacred pages of it into the heart. The soul is irradiated by it, that before was read without seeing anything in it but a dull, lifeless, insipid parcel of words.

There is a world of new objects that is discovered, a spiritual world, a great variety of beautiful and glorious objects that were till now altogether hidden. And there is a light that shines from outward objects that before did not; the visible world has a light shining in it that before was not seen. There is a light shines from God's works of creation and providence. The face of the earth, the fields and trees, they have a spiritual light shining from them that discovers the glory of the Creator. And the sun, moon, and stars shine with a new kind of light, even spiritual light. The sun shone bright with outward light before, but it shines brighter now with discoveries of the glory of its Creator. Though this spiritual light indeed is but dim here, and often interrupted, a true saint can see this light from the Word of God or the works of God at all times.

Third Prop. This is marvelous light.

1. As 'tis altogether new and very different from anything that ever was seen before. If a man had dwelt all his days in darkness, supposing he had been shut up in a dungeon and never had seen the light and should be afterwards brought out to behold the world with all its variety of objects enlightened by the light of the sun, or if one should have his eyes opened that had been blind from his birth, doubtless the light would be very marvelous to him. The variety of objects that are to be seen by the light would affect such an one after a very different manner from others. Thus it is in conversion: a soul that is brought out of darkness in a region of light that never before was seen, their eyes are opened that till then were blind. Objects are discovered that till then were altogether unseen. There is a marvelous change wrought in them.

2. But this light is marvelous as the things discovered by it are in themselves very marvelous. They are not only marvelous because they are new, but they are such things as will be eternally admired and won-

dered at. They won't only appear marvelous upon first discovery, but will appear so after they have been beheld many years, yea, many ages. They never will cease to appear wonderful, and the more they are thought of and understood, the more and more marvelous will they appear to all eternity, and that because they are so wonderful in themselves. The greatness and glory of those spiritual objects will ever more appear wonderful.

And particularly the glory of God that this light discovers is a marvelous glory. There is such a majesty and excellency and beauty so divine, so peculiar, so vastly beyond all parallel, that the more of it is understood, the more wonderful [it will appear]. 'Tis so with the wisdom of God, and so 'tis the grace of God, particularly the wisdom of God in the work of redemption. The contrivance is wonderful, and is wondered at by angels, and never will cease to be wondered at by them.

And the grace of God in the work of redemption, when it is seen in its true light discovered by divine and spiritual light to the soul, will evermore appear wonderful. It will appear a wonderful thing that God should so pity, and that Christ should so love, such sinful worms of the dust, to come into the world and take on him the human nature, and lay down his life, and suffer such a cruel death for them. Thinking much of this, and conversing much of it, and continuing to praise God for it, will never make it grow old; but it will seem wonderful and surprising. There is wonderfulness and glory enough in it to keep the souls of saints and angels forever in admiration and rapture.

Such things as these are they that are discovered by this light, which persons are brought into at conversion, which the unconverted see no wonderfulness in. They see no wonderful glory in God, no wonderful beauty and excellency in the Lord Jesus Christ, no wonderfulness in the love of Christ in coming into the world and dying for sinners.

3. The manner of discovery of these things is marvelous. This light is caused to shine into the soul by the immediate and almighty power of God; it don't shine into the heart but at his command. The shining of this light into the heart is a wonderful work of God, a work of wonderful power, a greater work than Christ's miracle of opening the eyes of one that was born blind, which yet was deservedly much wondered at; John 9:32, "Since the world began was it not heard that any man opened the eyes of one born blind."

It is a wonderful thing that such light should be made to shine into those hearts that are naturally under the power of darkness, in whom sin has had dominion. 'Tis a marvelous thing that light should be upheld in a heart in which there is still so much corruption, as there in the heart of every saint here in this world.

4. [This light is] marvelous [in its] sweetness; [it is] pleasant "to behold the sun" [Eccles. 11:7].[1]

5. This light is marvelous as to the effect of it upon the soul. 'Tis an exceeding powerful light. It with an irresistible power wins and inclines the perverse, wicked hearts of the children of men to God. It has a transforming virtue and efficacy with it, changes the nature of the soul. It changes the heart, which till now was loathsome, having the image of Satan, into a conformity unto God, to be in his image and likeness. He changes the heart into a likeness to God's glory; II Cor. 3:18, "But we all, with open face beholding as in a glass the glory of the Lord, are changed into the same image from glory to glory, even as by the Spirit of the Lord."

Fourth Prop. 'Tis by the call of God that sinners are brought thus out of darkness into marvelous {light}. While they are wandering in that gross and worse-than-Egyptian darkness [Ex. 10:21], they are lost and never would be able to extricate themselves out of that darkness and out of their lost condition, nor would they ever come out of it, did not God call, were they not directed, as it were, by the voice of God where to go. Though they know not how to deliver themselves, yet God knows how to deliver them. And God mercifully seeks them and calls to them, as it were, and tells them which is the way. So by his call, [he] both directs them and inclines them how to come out of that darkness. God in sovereign mercy hath pity on some poor souls and calls them out of their doleful darkness.

Ques. How doth God call them?

Ans. God calls them by the inward and immediate influence of his Spirit on the heart, making use of the calls of the gospel. Here are two things:

1. There is the inward and immediate influence of the Spirit of God on the heart, changing the heart and so disposing of it that it shall be receptive of divine light. The heart is drawn and inclined and fashioned and renewed by the mighty power of God's Spirit.

The Spirit of God immediately brings them out of their darkness into light. When God calls a sinner out of darkness, he speaks to the heart; he causes the sinner to hear him inwardly and spiritually.

2. But herein the Spirit of God makes use of the call of the gospel. The outward call of the gospel is the instrument that the Spirit of God makes use of. The outward call of the gospel will do nothing of itself, but when it

1. JE briefly sketched the outline of this fourth head; bracketed phrases are conjectures.

is made use of by the Spirit of God, it is effectual. The words that the Spirit of God makes use of in his call are the words of Christ in the gospel, his gracious invitations there. The Spirit of God opens the heart to receive and entertain this gospel call. That call that we hear from time to time, that is the call, which, being made use by the Spirit of God, brings men out of darkness into marvelous light.

APPLICATION.

Use [I. Of *Conviction*] By this doctrine the unconverted may be made sensible of their doleful condition. They walk in darkness and are under the power of darkness, and are lost and know not whither they go; those that walk in outward darkness, they are in danger of stumbling and falling. But you are in danger of falling and never rising more. You, if you ben't called out of darkness into light before long, your "feet will stumble upon the dark mountain of death" (Jer. 13:16). You walk, as it were, on a mountain where there is a precipice on every side, from whence you are in continual danger of falling into the depths of hell. You walk blindfold amongst snares and pits that the devil hath made to catch souls. And if you are taken by him, you will be devoured by him. He'll carry you to his den where you will be meat for those poison and carnal serpents [of] the devil. The jaws of the great dragon will trickle down with your blood [Rev. 20:2].

A man that is lost in a wilderness may be in danger of perishing by wild beasts or by famine. But you are [in] such a lost condition that you are exposed to a death and destruction infinitely more dreadful than any temporal perishing. You now perhaps are not sensible of your misery, but that is a part of that misery that we speak of, that like a man in darkness, you don't know whither you go nor what dangers you are encompassed by. You are just upon the brink of the pit of hell and ben't sensible of it.

You ben't sensible of your misery in being destitute of the true light. As a man that has been blind from his birth is not sensible of his misery in wanting sight, because he never knew what it was to see, never was sensible of the pleasant entertainments that those have that have sight more than they that are blind, so you think yourself happy. It may be in darkness, but 'tis because you never knew what true comfort and happiness were. Consider this for your awakening, that if you continue in your present darkness, there is reserved for you the blackness of darkness forever.

[*Use*] II. [Of *Exh.*] Therefore be exhorted earnestly to seek of God, that [he] would call you out of darkness into marvelous [light]. You are one to whom the call of the gospel is directed to come out of darkness into this marvelous light. There is a possibility of your being brought into the spiritual Goshen and dwelling all your lifetime and to all eternity in this glorious light. Of those glorious, spiritual objects that others who have their eyes open do see, you may see the glory of Christ, and the wonderfulness of his love and grace, which are the most glorious objects in the universe.

And if you see this light here, it will be your portion to dwell in the regions of everlasting and glorious lights in heaven, where you see these most clearly which now you see but in part. You shall see; that light which is dim now, will shine with an incredible luster.

And be sure to seek this light of God and him alone, for 'tis by his [call, and][2] his only, that any are brought out of darkness into light. Except God be pleased to call you, you will still continue wandering in darkness. It is a thing that is dependent on the mere and sovereign grace of God, whereby "he hath mercy on whom he will have mercy" [Ex. 33:19].

[*Use*] III. *Exhort* God's people to:

[*First.*] "Have no fellowship with the works of darkness, but rather reprove them," as the Apostle exhorts (Eph. 5:11). Those that God has called into marvelous light, they should have done with darkness. It becomes the children of light to abhor the works of darkness, that is, to abhor all those practices of men which the shamefulness of them men are wont to do in the dark to conceal from the eye of the [Lord]. You should most strictly avoid having anything to do in such practices, and not only so, but take all opportunities to reprove them in others so far as you know of them.

Second. Walk as children of the light; Eph. 5:8, "For ye were sometimes darkness, but now are ye light in the Lord: walk as children of light."

1. Watch and be sober; I Thess. 5:4–6, "But ye, brethren, are not in darkness, that that day should overtake you as a thief. Ye are all the children of light, and the children of the day: we are not of the night, nor of the darkness. Therefore let us not sleep, as do others; but let us watch and be sober."

2. Be constant and diligent at work. Men work in the day; [at] night they are wont to rest.

3. Let your walk be such as will bear to be examined in the light, such as will bear to be examined by the power of God's word. Frequently try them

2. MS: damaged. Editorial conjecture.

by the light yourself; [this is][3] the character that Christ gives of those that do; John 3:21, "But he that doeth truth cometh to the light."

Do such things only as if they were known and published in the light, [and] would appear honorable and worthy. Never allow of things that you would have cause to be ashamed of, if they should be declared in the light. Practice such as would be honorable in the light. This seems to be what the Apostle means by "walking as children of light" (Eph. 5:8); for it follows in the next verse, "For the fruit of the Spirit is in all goodness and righteousness and truth." Do that which appears honorable when things come to be brought to light at the day of judgment. Christ tells us, "Whatsoever [ye have] spoken in darkness shall be heard in the light" [Luke 12:3].

3. MS: damaged. Editorial conjecture.

EAST OF EDEN

THE third chapter of Genesis, which Edwards here calls "the most sorrowful and melancholy chapter that we have in the whole Bible," recounts humanity's fall from innocence. Edwards uses his text, on the subsequent expulsion of Adam and Eve from the garden and the placing of a flaming sword to guard the tree of life, for a meditation on the debilitating effects of the fall. Edwards offers a theological analysis of the fall by way of contrast with life in Edenic paradise, not unlike a previous sermon in this volume, *Serving God in Heaven*, which contrasted life in this sinful world with eschatological paradise.

East of Eden, preached in the summer of 1731, was long on doctrine and might have been a lecture. Yet Edwards enlivens his doctrinal discussion through the use of concrete visual imagery to convey the import of the loss of Eden. In the first doctrine, he presents a point-by-point contrast between the physical bounty, natural harmony, social concord, and religious felicity of life before the fall and the state of humanity after it: subject to death, wracked by toil, beset by discord, and, worst of all, separated from God. Our knowledge of this contrast deepens the sadness occasioned by sin.

In the second doctrine, Edwards contends with the image of the flaming sword, which, by his account, represents the hopelessness of the human predicament: the inability of us all to recover our previous state. Asserting that the permanent alienation of humanity from paradise was a just sentence, Edwards anticipates arguments that he would later use in *Original Sin*. An offense against God's justice, holiness, and majesty, Adam's disobedience merited a condemnation so great that humans can never through their own powers reverse the effects of the fall. Edwards' portrait of the human inability that followed such judgment, especially the loss of natural moral faculties and the corruption of conscience, parallels several of his other writings from the period, including *God Glorified in Man's Dependence*, "Miscellanies" nos. 472 and 501, and no. 60 in the notebook on "Faith." Edwards clearly directed such reflections against the Arminian tendencies of a people who had grown accustomed to thinking of religion as a work of moral training and covenantal performance. In the closing of the sermon he reiterates his warning against a dependence on natural moral powers.

In the Application, Edwards extends an invitation to faith. He matches the rhetorical power of the first part of the sermon with a dense and fast-paced description of the joy of salvation, when "the world shall again smile upon us." After some exhortations to faith in Christ, he turns to a discussion of the atonement by which God reversed the fall. Here Edwards offers one of the more striking images in the sermon: God ultimately wielded the flaming sword to slay his own Son. Through Christ's death, believers experience the joy of holiness and obedience in a measure even fuller than that enjoyed by Adam in paradise.

* * *

The manuscript has some peculiarities. The length of a typical two-preaching-unit sermon (eighteen leaves), it has no indication that Edwards did divide the sermon into preaching units—a further indication, beyond the lengthy Doctrine, that this was a lecture. There are no significant revisions nor any indication that he repreached the sermon. For the last two leaves, Edwards used paper from a discarded Scripture index, on which were written lists of chapter numbers from several books of the Bible; the sermon was composed around these numbers. Alexander B. Grosart, a nineteenth-century editor, scribbled on the manuscript when visiting Tryon Edwards in New London, Connecticut, making a few interlineations and signing at the end "Copied by Alex. B. Grosart, New London, April 1854."

EAST OF EDEN

GENESIS 3:24.

So he drove out the man; and he placed at the east of the garden of Eden cherubims, and a flaming sword which turned every way, to keep the way of the tree of life.

THIS chapter is the most sorrowful and melancholy chapter that we have in the whole Bible. Herein we have an account of the fall of man, and of the curses which God pronounced, first upon the serpent and then upon the woman and then the man. In v. 22, what a miserable change man had made; and how much he was accursed by eating the forbidden fruit is represented in God's ironical speech concerning it. One of the persons of the Trinity is represented as speaking to the rest: "And the Lord said, Behold, the man is become as one of us, to know good and evil."

Our first parents were not contented with the honor and happiness they as mere man had. They had a mind to be like God, as Satan promised them, knowing good and evil [Gen. 3:5]. They knew what good was before the fall, but they did not know what evil was; having never had any experience of it, they knew not what kind of thing it was. God knew they both had a mind to be like God in this respect. They imagined it would be a great exaltation of their nature. When they fell they knew both good and evil to their cost, which is the occasion of God's thus speaking ironically concerning it: "Behold, the man is become as one of us, to know good and evil."

In these last two verses, we have an account of the beginning of the execution of the curse upon our first parents: "Therefore the Lord God cast him forth from the garden of Eden, to till the ground whence he was taken" [v. 23]. God told Adam, when he pronounced the curse upon him, that "in the sweat of his face he should eat bread" [v. 19]. And here is the beginning of the accomplishment of this. While he lived in Eden, he had no need of labor in order to the providing of food to sustain his nature. The trees of the garden of Eden yielded him a great variety of most delicious food for his support and delight.

This is further amplified in the verse of the text, wherein we

1. Have an account of our first parents' loss of their former blessedness: "So he drove out the man." He drove him out of paradise, by which we may understand that he not only lost the outward enjoyments and delights of the garden but that he by the fall was deprived of all the blessings, whether spiritual or outward, which he enjoyed in paradise. He lost paradise, and not only [that] but all the blessings of it, or all the blessings he had been wont to enjoy in it.

2. We here have an account of the irrecoverable loss (that is, irrecoverable by them) of eternal life and those blessings, by their fall, which otherwise they would have obtained. If man had stood, and had not eat of the forbidden fruit, and had kept the law, he was to have eat of the tree of life and so to live forever. If man had stood out his time of trial, which was to be as long as divine wisdom should determine, he was then, after that due time, to have eaten of the tree of life as a seal of his reward. As soon as ever he had finished his obedience, God would have given him the fruit of that tree as a seal of eternal life, as a token that now he should live forever.

Not that the fruit of the tree of life had any such virtue in it to make man immortal, but it was an established sign and seal of it, which he was to have of God as a sign and token that now he, having performed obedience, should surely live forever.

While man kept in obedience, he was in the way to come to eat of this tree; but when he fell, God took effectual care that he should never come at it. As it is said, "And now, lest he put forth his hand, and take also of the tree of life, and eat, and live for ever, he sent him forth from the garden of Eden, to till the ground from whence he was taken. He drove him out, and placed at the east of the garden of Eden cherubims, and a flaming sword which turned every way, to keep the way of the tree of life" [vv. 22–24].

TWO DOCTRINES.

I. *When man fell, God drove him away from all his former blessedness.*[1]

II. *When we fell, we so procured the displeasure of God that there was no hope by anything that we could do of ever attaining that life and eternal blessedness which otherwise we should [have] attained.*

1. In this initial statement of the first doctrine, or proposition, JE adds here "from the former clause," i.e. "so he drove out the man." He does not give this reference in other statements of the first doctrine or proposition.

I. [The first] doctrine [has] several propositions.

First Prop. Man, when he fell, lost all his former blessedness. When God first created man, he made [him] in happy circumstances. 'Tis not to be supposed that his happiness was equal to what it would have been if he had stood after he had eaten of the tree of life, but yet his blessedness was very great.

He was in a state wherein he enjoyed a perfect freedom from all trouble. He knew what good was, but he did not know what evil was. There was nothing in the earth below or in the heaven above that offended him. The earth brought forth no hurtful thing; amongst all of the creatures that God made on the earth, there was nothing that was hurtful to him. The air had nothing in its temperature at any time any way noxious or unpleasant. The influences of the sun and heavenly bodies had nothing but what were sweet and rejoicing. He had no diseases, infirmities, or disorders in his own body any way the least uneasy or burdensome. There was nothing that fell out in the course of things, as in providence, that interrupted his quiet. He had no uneasy principles in his own mind to disturb the calm and peace of that or bring any dark clouds upon it.

He never saw any frown of heaven upon him to beget any troublesome concern in his mind. God did not frown but only smiled; he enjoyed the uninterrupted light of God's countenance. He did not want anything. He was not obliged from his necessities to troublesome labor to supply his want. Nature yielded a great plenty of her own accord into his hand and for his outward supply, and he had all needed supplies of God for the wants of his soul.

He was outwardly in the most delightful circumstances. The ground was not then cursed. And what a delightful place then was the face of this earth to what it is now! All nature smiled and seemed to rejoice. The heavenly bodies constantly shed down their most benign and sweet influences. The air was most refreshing and enlivening. Man was placed in a garden that God had planted, a place that the skill of the Maker of all things had contrived for delight and plenty. Man was rich in a fullness of outward blessings. Everything around him poured in delight and gladness into his soul. The visible world and all the fullness of it was contrived to cheer and delight his senses. And the senses themselves and all the organs of the body were without doubt in a perfect vigor and sprightliness, and the form of the body exquisitely beautiful.

And his soul was in a very perfect state, the faculties of it in full strength, not broken, impaired, and weakened and ruined, as they are now. The soul of man with regard to the quickness and clearness of its faculties was then like the heavenly intelligences—as a flame of fire. The natural image of God that consists in reason and understanding was then complete.

And man then had excellent endowments. His mind shone with the perfect spiritual image of God, being without any defect in its holiness and righteousness, or any spot or wrinkle to mar its spiritual beauty. God had put his own beauty upon it; it shone with the communication of his glory. And man enjoyed uninterrupted spiritual peace and joy that hence arose. His mind was full of spiritual light and peace as the atmosphere in a clear and calm day.

Man enjoyed the favor of God and smiles of heaven; there were smiles without any frowns. He had communion with God; God was wont to come to him and converse as a friend and father. How sweet was it thus to have the smiles and fellowship of the glorious Creator!

And as God was man's friend, so were the angels. And man, besides, enjoyed the pleasure of human society: our first parents mutually in each other in perfect love, without anything to interrupt or spoil their joy, no unloveliness, no unbecoming passions or unsuitable behavior in each of them, but the contrary, in that perfection that the perfectness of their faculties, the excellency of their endowment, and pleasantness of their circumstances, and the smiles of heaven upon them, allowed and caused.

All this happiness was lost when man sinned against God. He was no longer free from what was troublesome. He immediately began to know what sorrow and affliction were.

The earth lost its beauty and pleasantness. There was a curse brought upon it; there was, as it were, a deathly darkness brought upon things here below. The tokens of the presence and blessing of God were taken away. His smiles were gone and the tokens of his anger were everywhere seen. That bloom and beauty and joy that all nature seemed to [be] clothed with was gone.

Man lost the soundness and vigor and luster of his own body; he then saw that he was naked (v. 7 of the context). Corruption and death began to take hold of his frame from that day. Man's body, which before appeared like something heavenly, began now to look earthly, being about to return to the dust from whence he was taken. He lost the vigor and strength of his faculties. His understanding was clouded and broken, and the whole man in all its faculties was but the ruins of what it before was.

And man lost that which was his highest excellency and the proper glory of human nature, viz. his original righteousness and the spiritual image of God. And herein he lost his spiritual peace and comfort. This ceased to shine; there was a total eclipse of it in his mind, and the gloom of a guilty conscience and the darkness of sin began to fill his mind.

And his communion with God was lost; he lost God's favor and smiles. God ascended and forsook the earth, and instead of smiling and blessing, as he was wont to, now pronounces a curse on man. Instead of delighting in God's love and friendship, he had now the anger of the great God to think of, and his own folly in procuring it. The angels, they were no longer man's friends, and that happiness of their smiles and society which before was so great began now to be spoiled.

And in this miserable condition man lost paradise. He was suffered no longer to dwell there; he lost all the delights of that garden. He lost that delicious food that the trees were wont to yield to him in great plenty, and was sent forth to get his bread by the sweat of his face.

Thus man was left a poor, forsaken, disconsolate, and undone creature. It was a doleful change. How great was the difference of his state now from what it was before!

Second [*Prop.*] After man had sinned, there was a necessity of his parting with all his former blessedness, however loath and unwilling he was. This is implied in the expression of his being "driven away." Man was greatly disappointed when he hearkened to Satan's temptation. Satan promised a higher degree of happiness, and our first parents expected it. But they found it otherwise.

Indeed, our first parents lost the relish of their former spiritual happiness when they fell. Their natures were corrupted and their hearts full of enmity against God. Having lost the love of God, they lost the love of holiness and the relish of that pleasure and happiness that consisted in the exercise of holiness and the enjoyment of communion with God, till his hatred was removed by grace. But yet he in the general might remember that he was very happy, and so from self-love might wish that he could relish and enjoy the same happiness that he used to. He found himself how very miserable in suffering the uneasiness of a guilty conscience, and seeing the tokens of God's displeasure and a cause of his being His enemy.

And he yet retained his love of his former, outward happiness. It was therefore surely against his will that he was deprived of them. O, how loath was he forever to leave that delightful paradise! How doleful and melancholic was the thought that he must now, for his sin and folly, leave and no more see that pleasant dwelling place; he must no more taste of those delicious fruits, no more live in that ease, no more breathe that sweet, refreshing air, no more drink of the pure streams of paradise; that he must go forth with his infirm, deformed, and hoary body into the world that was cursed, that brought forth briars and thorns instead of the flowers and fruits of paradise; and instead of his receiving his dainty food from Eden's trees ready prepared by nature, he must get his bread by moiling and toiling in the earth, till he turned to earth, and he should die and his body rot in the dark and silent grave. O, what reluctance was there! But thus it must be. He has been so foolish as to disobey his bountiful Creator; he must therefore be deprived of all this blessedness.

Third [*Prop.*] When man fell, God in his displeasure separated between man and his former blessedness. It was because he provoked and offended God that he was driven away from paradise and all the blessings of it. It was God that bestowed man's primitive blessedness upon him; He planted the garden for him and placed him in it. From Him were all his outward and spiritual delights. The same God that gave them now took them away.

Immediately upon our first parents eating the forbidden [fruit], God took away his Holy Spirit from him, which left him destitute of original righteousness and all that moral excellency of mind which before he was endowed with, and left him under the dominion of sin.

And God [took] away all comfortable intercourse and communion. He hid his face from him, and he drove him away from paradise; which expression denotes:

1. That he was odious and abominable to God now he had sinned against, and He could not bear to have one so hateful so near to Him, or in a place where there were such manifestations of his presence and goodness as there was in paradise. Paradise was a place that God had prepared for his favorites and not for rebels. It was a place for the holy and pure, not for the sinful and loathsome.

The delights and blessings of paradise were tokens of the love and favor of God, unsuitable to be enjoyed by such an one as fallen man. God saw it utterly unfit that such should any longer enjoy such blessings. Paradise was made for a place of God's special presence, a place, as it was said of Canaan, which the Lord "careth for" and his "eyes were always upon it" [Deut. 11:12].

2. That he was separated from the blessings of paradise. In anger God drove him; he in indignation thrust him forth. He forced him to go out of paradise. He would by no means suffer him to continue any longer there. He would not suffer him any longer to enjoy his former happiness.

This made the loss of paradise and its blessings much more doleful, that he was driven from it from the loathing and wrath of God.

II. *When we fell, we so incurred the displeasure of God towards us that there was no hope of our ever obtaining that eternal life and blessedness*[2] *which otherwise we should have obtained.*

First Prop. If we had fulfilled the conditions of the first covenant, we should, by what we did, have obtained eternal life and blessedness.

Man was not made naturally immortal or incapable of death. Every creature is capable of death, and therefore we are told that God only hath immortality (I Tim. 6:16). Indeed, man when he was first created had no seeds of corruption and death in his nature, no principle of decay that tended gradually to bring him again to the dust, but yet he was not incapable of dying. He was capable of both temporal and eternal death.

This matter therefore must be as God should dispose, whether he should die or live forever. God was not pleased absolutely to promise this to man when he first created him, but he gave him a trial for it. He promised implicitly that if he would approve himself perfectly obedient to Him, after a due time he should have eternal life and blessedness made sure to him. Though his living forever as yet was not certain to him, yet God gave him a fair opportunity to have it made sure to him afterwards. It depended only on his own fidelity to his Creator. He had a fair opportunity after a while of being called to the tree of life, and so having everlasting life sealed to him, and be put out of all possibility of ever dying either eternally or temporally and, withal, of receiving a great addition of happiness.

Man in the state wherein he was created was in a very happy condition in paradise, as we have already shown. But doubtless, if he had stood, he would have been advanced to a much greater happiness. 'Tis most reasonable to suppose that the blessedness he enjoyed even while in a state of trial shouldn't be so great as after he had done his work and come to receive his reward. He now enjoyed life, but if he had stood he would have been called to the tree of life to eat of that, and his life should not only have been ascertained to him forever, but he would have advanced to a higher degree of life.

Eternal life was then, as it is now, the great promise of God. It was the promise of the covenant of works as well as the covenant of grace. And as eternal life don't now, so it did not then, only denote a continuance of man's life forever so that he should never die, but it denotes a most glorious and blessed life.

2. JE here deleted: "by anything that we could do."

If Adam had stood, the tree of life would have been a tree of life to him these two ways, viz. as upon the eating of it after his trial he was to have a living forever ascertained to him, and was also to be exalted to a more glorious and blessed life.

His time of trial would not have lasted always. After a due time, if man had stood, he was to be confirmed then, and man would have [been] put beyond all possibility of falling. Not beyond a natural possibility—no creature ever was or ever will be naturally impeccable or naturally incapable of sinning—but God would have become engaged for his never sinning or dying, as we have all reason now to conclude that it is with the angels. They had a time of probation as well as man, as is evident because some of 'em fell. But the angels of light are now past their probation and are in a state of confirmed holiness and blessedness.

We have no account how long man was to have been tried before he was to be confirmed, and 'tis not probable that God revealed that to man. But if he proved obedient, after a due time he was to have eat of the tree of life.

The tree of life was a tree that God planted with the rest of the garden, that man might be the more assured of his reward in case of his obedience, and that this consideration might engage his spirit the more earnestly to seek that he might come to taste of it. 'Tis probable that God told Adam of this tree to encourage his obedience. He might tell him in earnest that man had an opportunity of obtaining the fruit of this tree, and that eternal life and blessedness of which it was a seal, by what he himself did; an obtaining of this blessed reward was in his power.

It was in man's own power perfectly to obey the law of God, which is not in our power now since the fall, as it was more in man's power perfectly to obey the law and persevere in it then, than it is for fallen man to perform one act of sincere obedience. And that, upon two accounts, viz.

1. As he had no sin then that he was under the power and dominion of. We can't obey now because we are dead in trespasses; Eph. 2:1, "and you hath he quickened, who were dead in trespasses and sins." We are stones; our hands are pinioned by strong lusts. But our first parents, they were free, not under any such bondage.

2. Adam had a sufficient assistance of God always present with him to have enabled him to have obeyed if he had used his natural abilities in endeavoring it, as he might do, though the assistance was not such as it would have been after he was confirmed to render it impossible for him to sin. Man might be deceived so that he should not be disposed to use his endeavors to persevere, but if he did use his endeavors, there was a

sufficient assistance always with him to enable him to persevere. So that man had a very fair opportunity of obtaining eternal life and blessedness under the first covenant, and it was in his power to obtain it by what he did himself.

Second Prop. There was no hope of our ever obtaining for ourselves this eternal life and blessedness after we had fallen. When we fell we not only were driven away from all that blessedness that we did enjoy, but lost all that which we had so fair an opportunity of obtaining.

This eternal life would have been a most glorious reward if we had obtained it; it was a blessing of inestimable value. A blessed opportunity was that which man had of being made [happy] to all eternity. In a little time he might have been adjudged to the reward of a never-ending, holy, and happy life, as the angels of light now are.

But when man fell, this was all lost. The opportunity that he had was irrecoverably gone; he might think of it, and lament his loss, and wish that he had the like opportunity again, but he could not obtain it. There was no coming at the tree of life. He had his loss to lament without any manner of hope of getting what he had lost. As soon as ever he fell, eternal life and blessedness, which [was] within his reach before, was put out of his reach as far as the stars of heaven. He could as soon climb up to the third heaven as get eternal life by anything he could do.

Third Prop. There was no possibility of it upon this account: that we had by the fall so incurred God's displeasure. This reward was entirely in God's hands and at his disposal, and it was of His goodness that God had promised such a reward to Adam upon his perfect obedience. But man by his apostasy had lost all friendship with God. There was entirely a breach between God and man; they were no longer friends but enemies. And therefore there was no hope of God's suffering of him to have that eternal life and blessedness which before He gave him opportunity to get. But that there was no hope of obtaining this blessedness by anything he could do will appear if we consider the properties of that anger of God which man had incurred.

1. If we consider how great it was. Sin is a thing which God has an infinite abhorrence of, as it is contrary to his nature, which is infinitely holy, and also as it is rebellion against his authority. The anger of God against all sin is such that it burns to the lowest hell. God has an implacable hatred of sin. It is impossible that he should be at peace with it.

This sin of our first parents was peculiarly provoking to God. God had dealt very bountifully with man in giving of him the blessings of paradise, conferring on him such a fullness of temporal and spiritual benefits. And it was very provoking to God that man should notwithstanding hearken rather to the devil and, for the sake of the gratifying a sensual appetite and an ambition of being like God, rebel against him; that man should thus heedless disobey God's commands when, though he might freely eat as God told him of all the trees in the garden but this, that yet he would not be contented with all this; that he should thus cast off his subjection to Him who made him, and made him the most excellent of all creatures here below, that had made the earth and all the fullness of it, and put all things under his feet, and made him lord and king of this lower creation, that had endowed [him] with those excellent faculties, had light upon divine light in His soul, and bestowed His own image upon and had offered and promised him eternal life, which He was not obliged to offer: well might God be exceeding angry with man for such a foolish, needless, unreasonable, ungrateful apostatizing from him. The anger of God for the apostasy of man was not the anger of a father but of an enemy. God before was as a father to man and loved him as a child. He had communion with him as a friend. But now God became man's enemy. He was angry with him with a displeasure infinitely dreadful, an anger that would surely appear in a punishment; this was so. This terrible anger of God towards fallen man is well represented by the emblem of a flaming sword in our text, and it being such would effectually prevent man's any way coming at the tree of life.

2. It will appear to have been utterly impossible for man by anything that he could do to have gained eternal life if we consider that His anger was the anger of a just judge. As God was man's lawgiver, so He was his judge. It belonged to Him as the Supreme Being to avenge all iniquity.

When man had sinned, he deserved eternal death. It was what justice called for. It was most fit that justice should be executed and that sin should be revenged. It was no ways meet that that which was so infinitely unjust and unreasonable should be let pass without being taken notice of with due resentment and with due vengeance by the Supreme Lord of the universe; so that justice would not allow of man's eating of the tree of life after he had sinned.

The anger of God was the anger of One to whom it belonged to execute the law. The law of God is a fixed, unalterable rule for God's proceeding with the creature. The law threatened death, and it must be fulfilled. And as God was judge of the law, justice required that he should judge according to law.

And it was a thing utterly impossible that man should do anything, that the law should not stand in the way of his having eternal life. The law could not be fulfilled and satisfied by him any other way than by his suffering its penalty. Therefore vindictive justice was as a flaming sword that turned every way to keep the way of the tree of life, that would effectually prevent his putting forth his hand and eating and living forever.

3. If we consider this anger of God as a holy anger. God, being an infinitely holy being, could do no other than be implacably displeased with sin. God could not be an infinitely holy God and not have loathing and abhorrence of sin and of those that are under the guilt of it. God being so holy a God, therefore he would by no means admit a guilty and filthy creature to the possession and enjoyment of eternal life. It would have been a disparagement to the holiness of God if he had so.

So that it was impossible upon this account for man after the fall, by anything that he could do, [to] come to the enjoyment of that life and blessedness which he fell short of. The holiness of God would render Him as a consuming fire to such a filthy creature if he presumed to approach to take of the fruit of [the] tree of life.

There could be no way that man could obtain eternal life by anything he could do unless he could do something or offer something that was not due from him to God: that merited His love and favor as much as his sin had His abhorrence. But this was impossible for man to do because, if he had never so holy a principle in him and were able to act never so holily, he could not offer any more than was God's due before. But then consider this: he had lost all holy principles, and instead of offering something that make compensation for his offense, he could offer nothing at all. He could not do one holy action.

4. God's anger towards man after the fall was the resentment of an affronted infinite majesty. Our sin was what cast contempt upon God's majesty. God and his holy and sacred authority and infinite majesty, in the eating the forbidden fruit, was set below the gratification of the taste and man's desire of his own honor. God will surely vindicate his own majesty. That greatness of his, which is thought so light and made so little of, God will show to be great in the punishment of such contempt.

If men deny God's authority, God will cause it to take place one way or other. God will appear as man's supreme Lord either in having his law obeyed or in having it executed; the law of God must some way or other take place with respect to him who is the subject of it. Now, there was no way whereby this might be by anything that man could do. There was no way that God's awful and glorious majesty could be vindicated by anything in man but by his eternal death. God therefore could as soon deny himself and quit the honor of His own majesty, as He could suffer man for anything that he could do to taste of the fruit of the tree of life.

Thus man, when he fell, he lost his opportunity of getting eternal life, that blessed reward which he had before offered him upon condition of his obedience. He lost it fatally and irrecoverably as to anything that he could do; the flaming sword turned every way. There was no way therefore that he could come at this blessedness. He could not rush through without being slain by the sword, for it was a flaming sword. It was the sword of God's dreadful wrath, the sword of divine justice wielded by his infinite power, flaming with holy abhorrence of the filthiness of sin and sharpened by a divine resentment of the affront to his holy majesty.

These two doctrines may give us something of an idea of the melancholy and doleful loss that man sustained by the fall.

APPLICATION.

I shall make improvement of both these doctrines under one.

I. How joyful then is the tidings that is proclaimed to us in the gospel! The gospel proclaims those glad tidings to us that are sufficient to dispel all this melancholy darkness. We have the joyful tidings of the reparation of all this loss; we have tidings of deliverance from this misery. But the joyfulness of the tidings that we have in the gospel may appear by the following considerations:

First. We have the tidings of willingness to restore us to our first state of happiness that we were wrath-driven from when we fell, of being restored to a like innocency and holiness and the image of God, to have our naked, deformed, loathsome souls covered and made to shine with the communication of God's glory (II Cor. 3:18). After we have despoiled ourselves of all our primitive excellency and loveliness and become odious and in the image of Satan, we may have God's beauty put on us again; yea, we may be brought to perfect holiness as spotless as that which we lost. God is willing to restore our whole man, to exalt our faculties to a like strength and vigor with that which we had before, and our bodies to the like beauty and life. This corruptible may put on incorruption and this mortal immortality.

'Tis proclaimed in the gospel that God is willing again to receive us into his favor, to pardon all our sins, to quit all enmity, to bury all former difference and to be our friend and our father; that he is willing again to admit us to sweet communion with him, and that he will converse with us as friendly and intimately as he did before the fall; and that God is willing to receive us to paradise again, to a like freedom from all grief and trouble; that he will wipe away all tears from our eyes, and that sorrow and sighing shall flee away; that he will make us to forget our former melancholic, forsaken, and doleful state; that we may be again admitted to as great a fullness of blessings, to as pleasant and delightful a dwelling place as the garden of Eden, as full of those things which tend the delight of life, to pleasures as refreshing and satisfying; and we shall be as free from want. The curse shall be removed, and all frowns and tokens of displeasure. The world shall again smile upon us and congratulate us. God will be our friend and the angels shall be our friends, and all things shall be at peace with us, and we shall enjoy as great and uninterrupted a pleasure in mutual society.

The wrath of God drove us out of paradise, but the grace of God invites us to return. The Son of God in the name of his Father comes and calls to us to return from our banishment; he ceases not to call us. He beseeches us to return again. He is come forth on purpose to make known those joyful tidings to us. Christ calls us away from this cursed ground, that brings forth briars and thorns, to a better country. Our first parents were driven away very loath and unwilling to go, but we are invited back again.

Second. In the gospel we have the joyful tidings of another opportunity to obtain eternal life and blessedness that we missed of by the fall. We han't only the tidings that we may return again to that blessedness which we were already in possession of before we fell, but of obtaining that further blessedness and eternal life which man would have had sealed to him by his eating of the fruit of the tree of life, if he had persevered in his perfect obedience.

We had brought ourselves into a doleful condition when we fell because there was no possibility of obtaining it by anything that we could do; but yet we have the news that we may obtain it. We may yet attain to it, to live forever. We may yet attain to such a state wherein we shall have life ascertained and confirmed to us, to a state wherein we shall be impeccable and immortal, shall be in this respect as the angels are in heaven. However the way to the tree of life was guarded and defended by a flaming sword, the sword of God's wrath and vindication, yet now there is no such thing. We have it proclaimed to us that the way to the tree of life is open and free. There is nothing that will hurt us in our coming to it.

Third. There is proclaimed to us in the gospel not only such an opportunity as Adam had of eating of the tree, if we will first obey, but we are invited to come to the tree of life immediately without any conditions. Adam had a glorious opportunity of obtaining eternal life if he would persist in perfectly obeying the law and performed righteousness, which he had power to do. He was then to be invited by God to eat of the tree of life and so was to live forever.

But the gospel don't merely offer to us such an opportunity as Adam had before the fall; we have the same offer made to us as Adam would have had after he should have finished his obedience. Then the condition would have been already performed, and he would have been immediately invited to the tree of life; and so we are now. So that we han't merely the glad tidings of a restoration to that state that we were in before the fall. It is not merely the privilege of being tried once more to see whether we won't obey and so obtain eternal life in that way; but all is done already that needs to be done. The obedience is performed already by another.

Christ himself now stands instead of that tree of life that grew in the midst of the garden of Eden. 'Tis Christ that is meant by "the tree of life, that grows in the midst of the paradise of God" (Rev. 2:7). And we are immediately invited and called to Christ to eat of the fruit of this tree without any sort of terms, but only to come and take and eat. The condition of righteousness is fulfilled already by our surety. God shows us which is the tree of life and where it grows, which Adam probably did not know, nor was to know, till he had finished his obedience. We are as immediately invited now as Adam would have been if he had stood and had finished his obedience.

Fourth. The tidings of the gospel are very joyful because the eternal blessedness itself that is offered is in many respects greater than what was offered in the first covenant, though eternal life, indeed, in the substance of it, would have been the same: it would have consisted in perfect holiness and the enjoyment of God, beholding his glory and enjoying his love.

But there are many things that greatly contribute to the happiness of those that are saved that Adam, if he had stood, would not have had. The saints that are saved by Jesus Christ, they shall have happiness of most intimate union and relation to Jesus Christ as being his members, his spouse, his brethren, etc., which Adam would not have had. And through Christ they stand in a nearer relation to God the Father, and are partakers of a greater love of the Father, as partaking with Christ of his relation and love and partaking with him in the rewards of his obedience. Christ's obedience is a more glorious obedience than Adam's would have been, and rewarded with a better reward. Believers sitting with Christ in his throne are partakers with him in his exaltation, which was the reward of his mediatorial righteousness.

They have a greater advantage intimately to enjoy God in that God is incarnate, has taken upon him the human nature and so is nearer to them. God has given himself to them in a manner that he would not then. He has given himself to them in their own nature.

God had now manifested his love to them in a higher and more wonderful manner, in giving his Son in Christ's incarnation and in his dying for their sakes, and so they are under greater advantages to be happy in the enjoyment of that love. It would not have been known that there was such love in the heart of God as was manifested in the death of Christ. This will make all their enjoyments and blessedness the sweeter, the consideration of their being the fruits of such a wonderful love and grace.

And they will have a greater manifestation of the glory of God, God having taken occasion from the fall of man to make a more wonderful display of his glory in the work of redemption. And the more is seen of the glory of God, the greater advantage is there for happiness in the contemplation of it.

But then, here a question will very naturally arise, viz.

Ques. How came there to be way made for man's receiving such joyful tidings as these after the fall? We have been informed how that man, when he fell, was by an angry God driven from all his former happiness, and that He placed cherubims and a flaming sword to prevent his eating of the tree of life; that there was no hopes of man's coming to attain life by anything that he could do; there was no possibility of it; that the dreadful anger and vindictive justice of God and holy resentment of God would not suffer it. How then came those obstacles to be removed out of the way? How came it to pass that the flaming sword is taken away and that God, who is still as implacable a hater and dreadful revenger of sin as ever he was, now, instead of driving away and keeping off with a flaming sword, calls and invites?

And before I make answer to this question, I will observe,

1. That no less than divine wisdom could find out a way for the accomplishing this. It is not to be supposed that any such thing would ever have entered into the thought of any creature. Without doubt, when Adam was driven out of paradise and the flaming sword was placed by the tree of life, all that beheld it looked upon [it] as utterly a desperate case, and that it was impossible for man to be restored.

2. No less than a divine person could accomplish it. It was the greatest work that ever was undertaken in this world; there [was] needed infinite strength, and infinite merit, and infinite love and grace to accomplish

[it]. All the angels in heaven would have been but vain things for any such undertaking as this. Therefore, to this question I [answer]:

Ans. 1. The Son of God himself was pleased to take our guilt upon him, and in our name has suffered and so satisfied the justice and wrath of God. The eternal and infinitely dear Son of God, when he beheld us fallen, beheld us driven by justice from the blessings of paradise, and beheld us excluded from eternal life, he had a pity and love to us, and was pleased to undertake for us and take our guilt upon him and place himself in our stead, and stand before the Father for us as being ready to bear what we deserved that we might be free. And he came and suffered our deserved wrath, so that wrath and justice was satisfied.

Christ undertook to lead us to the tree of life, and he went before us. Christ himself was slain by that flaming [sword]; and this sword, having slain the Son of God appearing in our name, who was a person of infinite worthiness, that sword did full execution in that. And when it had shed the blood of Christ, it had done all its work, and so after that was removed. And Christ arising from the dead, being a divine person himself, went before us; and now the sword is removed, having done its execution, already having nothing more to do there, having slain Christ. There is no sword now, and the way is open and clear to eternal life for those that are in Christ.

2. Christ did the work which Adam should have done and performed, that perfect obedience which he failed of; he is the second Adam (I Cor. 15:45). He became our representative and surety, as Adam did, and did that honor to the authority and law of God which is the stated price of eternal life. He has not merely wrought out as good a righteousness, but immensely better. It was not sufficient that Christ should merely work out as good an obedience, for that obedience had no merit in it; it was only what was naturally due from man to God. But man can't by paying a debt make up for a past robbery.

We have observed already that man could not attain to eternal life by anything that he could do unless he could do something, offer something, that was not due from him to God, that merited His love and favor as much as his sin merited His displeasure and abhorrence. This, an obedience no better than what is naturally due from man, could not do, for it can't merit at all. Therefore it was needful that Christ should work out a righteousness infinitely worthy, as he did, as it was of such a person with such love.

Thus we see how the infinite wisdom and grace of God hath made way for our eternal happiness and glory after our doleful fall. Let us therefore, who are all partakers of that misery of the fall, embrace the glad tidings. As you have heard, the offer is free: nothing required now but going and taking of the fruit of the tree of life. If the tidings be joyful tidings to us, and we believe them and receive with our hearts, our love, and confidence the Redeemer, we shall be restored to the blessings of paradise, and shall have eternal life, and be advanced to a more glorious state than Adam would have been if he had stood.

II. Hence how vain and dangerous are their attempts that are attempting to get eternal life themselves. There are many that, notwithstanding the flaming sword of God's justice and vindictive wrath that turns every [way], are endeavoring to find out ways to come at the tree of life. Many are bold to come in their own names and in their own righteousness. [There is] no sword for them that come in Christ's name, but a flaming sword still for them that come in their own names.

Men are exceeding apt to seek eternal life through their own righteousness though in a fallen state. And the holiness, majesty, justice, wrath, and power of God be engaged to prevent it, and to slay and consume all such that come thus in their own righteousness. Men are exceeding prone to do thus for the following reasons:

First. They are exceeding loath to perish. Destruction is terrible to nature; all men hate misery. Eternal death is frightful to an awakened conscience, [and] puts the soul into distress.[3]

Second. The light of nature seems to suggest that the favor of God and his reward must be obtained by righteousness. Or, if it don't suggest it of itself, yet when it is taught as it is in the Word of God, it falls in with the light of nature.[4]

Third. A being saved by another's righteousness is a thing that men naturally can have no conception of the propriety of. [They are] ignorant of God's righteousness, can't see how they can be saved any other way. They have no faith, ben't taught by the spirit of God. They think right in thinking that it must be by righteousness, and they, being not enlightened, can't see any other righteousness [but their own]. And this makes them keep striving to get a righteousness of their own; Rom. 10:3, "[they] being ignorant of God's righteousness, and going about to establish their own righteousness, have not submitted themselves unto the righteousness of God."

3. From here to the end of the sermon, JE wrote several partial sentences, leaving blank spaces or lines after each. Eight blank lines follow here, indicating perhaps his intention to expand at a later time.

4. Four blank lines follow.

Fourth. They have that proud conceit of their own goodness that they are ready to think it sufficient. [They have a] high opinion of their own worthiness, excellency, good deeds, prayer, [and] religion, [but are] ignorant what a distance [is] between God and them: ignorant of the holiness and glorious majesty of God, and therefore ignorant of the heinousness of their offense against such a God. [They] think this makes compensation, and think there is a proportion between [their goodness and God's righteousness]. These seem to be their true reasons.[5]

But a consideration of the doctrine will teach us how vain all such attempts are. Let those therefore that are going about to seek the fruit of the tree of life consider, that if they continue so to do they never will be able to attain to it, and not only so, but will be slain by the flaming sword of God's vengeance.

5. Bracketed phrases are editorial interpolations.

THE STATE OF PUBLIC AFFAIRS

THE *State of Public Affairs* is one of Edwards' most explicitly political orations—a clear and direct discussion of the ideal civic order, the problem with politics in Massachusetts in the early 1730s, and the relation between religion and political leadership. Delivered sometime between August 1731 and December 1732, a period of great political turmoil in Massachusetts, this two-preaching-unit sermon appears to have been occasioned by a fast day or the death of a civic leader. As Edwards notes, there is an obvious "application" to "the circumstances of this land."

Edwards took the sermon's text, Prov. 28:2, as a commentary on "politics," which he defines as "the art of government" whose end is securing "the welfare of the community." In the first proposition he contends that the commonweal prospers under orderly and stable government. Conversely, the public good suffers under an unstable or changing government. When political rule changes rapidly or frequently, politics degenerates into factions and power struggles. Contention, corruption, ambition, intrigue, and avarice replace harmony and public-spiritedness. An unsettled state, Edwards reasons, is a judgment of God on a community for its sins.

However oblique at points, Edwards' references evoke contemporary struggles between the elected legislature of Massachusetts and the royal governorship, as well as unusually strongly contested elections in the early 1730s and disputes between court and country factions in the assembly (not to mention within Northampton itself). Controversy came to the crisis point in 1731 and 1732 when Gov. Jonathan Belcher, under directives from London and supported by court partisans, demanded that the colony reform its deflated currency and fix an annual budget for the royal administration (i.e., Belcher's salary and other expenses). Opponents feared that fiscal reform would result in a scarcity of money and economic collapse. They also resented the governor's demands on an already empty treasury. Rumors of an impending war with Spain further alarmed colonists, for Massachusetts was unable to fund a strong militia.

Both sides of the political contest raised questions of political rights, charter obligations, and self-determination, producing an ominous tone. To Edwards, who assumed that godliness and civic solidarity were mutually dependent, the news of contention and the prospect of disorder were shocking.[1]

His discussion of the threat of ambitious men to the rights and privileges of the people sounds certain notes of republican ideology, which often fostered opposition to sitting authorities. Edwards nonetheless leaves such a critique implicit only. In the Application to the first Proposition, he urges people to forsake contention, discontinue criticism of political leaders, and examine themselves for the underlying moral cause of their troubles: the general sin of the community. In the second Proposition, he argues that the community's privileges will be secured only by the righteousness, prayers, and piety of its citizens and, more important, of its elected magistrates, whose example could influence others and induce God's blessings. In the final Application, Edwards laments the death of godly men (the reference here is unclear) and calls on people to repent and seek the pouring out of the Spirit of God.

As in other sermons from the early 1730s, *The State of Public Affairs* bears certain evidence of Edwards' experimentation with sermon structure. He improved on the simple Explication-Doctrine-Application format by setting up two major doctrinal propositions and labeling them doctrines. The first unit contains Explication, Proposition, and Application; the second unit returns to Explication followed by the second Proposition and a second Application.

* * *

The manuscript is a duodecimo booklet of eighteen leaves. The last leaf is blank. For a sermon that shows no indications of being repreached, it has an unusually large number of crossings out and reorganization marks. These changes, along with Edwards' contorted syntax and incomplete sentences, are signs of a nervous composition—perhaps a reflection of Edwards' state of mind as he addressed such troublesome and divisive issues.

1. See Pencak, *War, Politics, and Revolution in Provincial Massachusetts*, 91–113; and Spencer, *Constitutional Conflicts in Provincial Massachusetts*. For further information and citations, see above, pp. 17–28.

THE STATE OF PUBLIC AFFAIRS

PROVERBS 28:2.

For the transgression of a land many are the princes thereof: but by a man of understanding and knowledge shall the state thereof be prolonged.

ORDINARILY, great men [are] men of great understanding. Their greatness lies chiefly in eminency in some particular kind of knowledge. Some great men are great philosophers, others are great divines, others great statesmen. Solomon, of whom it is said that God gave him "wisdom and understanding exceeding much, and largeness of heart, even as the sand that is on the sea shore" (I Kgs. 4:29), he excelled in all kinds of knowledge. He was eminent for his knowledge in divinity, as is evident by the improvement which the Holy Ghost made of his wisdom in those divine writings of his that we have in our hands.

He excelled greatly in philosophy as knowledge of nature, as appears by I Kgs. 4:33, "And he spake of trees, from the cedar tree that is in Lebanon even to the hyssop that springeth out of the wall: he spake also of beasts, and of fowl, and of creeping things, and of fishes." He greatly excelled in his knowledge of the nature of the human soul. He excelled in his prudential knowledge of things as related to man's good and happiness. He excelled in a knowledge of men and manners, as appears by his books of Proverbs and Ecclesiastes. He excelled in a practical genius, because it is spoken of as one thing wherein he showed his wisdom, that he made so many songs; I Kgs. 4:32, "His songs were a thousand and five."

But yet if there was any one part of wisdom wherein we can say he chiefly excelled, it must be politics, or his skill in the art of government. For this was especially that wisdom which Solomon asked of God when God bid him ask what he should give him; he asked [for] a wise and understanding heart, that he might judge the people and know how to "go out and come in" before them [II Chron. 1:10]. He excelled in knowledge of things wherein the welfare of a community consisted, and in a discerning of the means for obtaining it. He knew what tended to the mischief and misery of a people, and what to their prosperity, which he discovered by many passages relating to these things in his books of Proverbs [and] of Ecclesiastes, among which is our text: "For the transgression of a land many are the princes thereof: but by a man of understanding and knowledge the state thereof shall be prolonged."

One part of this verse explains the other. We may observe in the verse,

1. A public calamity here mentioned in the former part, and the public blessing opposite thereto in the latter part. The calamity of a land here mentioned is the having many princes. We may understand what is meant by it by the opposite blessing mentioned, of having the state thereof prolonged; by which it appears that the wise man, by a land's "having many princes," don't mean its having many [at] once, but its often changing its princes, often changing the persons governing and the forms of government that it is under.

In short, the public good here mentioned is a settled, the calamity is an unsettled, state of the public affairs. While public affairs are in an unsettled posture, they are continually liable to be shifting and altering; and this is a great calamity to a land. But when the public state is settled and prolonged, and remains unshaken and undisturbed, this is a great blessing to any people.

2. We may observe the opposite procuring causes of those opposite conditions of a community, viz. the wickedness or righteousness of the members thereof. The changing unsettled state of public affairs of a people is from their transgression, but the prolonging of their state is from their understanding and knowledge, which words are commonly used to signify righteousness, especially in the book of Proverbs.

Here it is observable that the procuring cause of the public calamity mentioned is the transgression of the land, but the procuring cause of the public good mentioned is the understanding {and knowledge} of a particular person, by a man of understanding, which is because God is more ready to take notice of it, if there be any righteousness among a people, than to take notice of their wickedness. He is not wont to bring judgments on a people unless it be for a general corruption; but he often bestows blessings for the righteousness of particular persons.

TWO DOCTRINES.

I. *An unsettled state of people's public affairs is a token of God's anger against them for their sins.*

II. *The privileges of a community are prolonged and established by the wisdom and righteousness of its members.*

[I.] In some instances, first represent an unsettled state of the public affairs of a people. Second, show that such a state is a token of God's anger {against them for their sins}.

First. Represent in some instances how the public affairs of a people or land may be in an unsettled state.

1. When the circumstances of a people are such that the continuance of a present establishment and of the rights and privileges which they thereby enjoy is doubtful, whether a people are threatened with this by the invasion of a foreign enemy, or are threatened with it by the supreme authority which they are under, or prove their own enemies and their privileges are in danger of being lost through their own imprudence and mismanagement.

This is the calamity that is directly spoken of in the text: the state of public affairs of a land being in a changeable posture, whereby a people are exposed to lose those rights, privileges, and public blessings which they enjoy by virtue of the present establishment; when a people are threatened with being deprived of their ancient privileges either in whole or in part and put under a new form of government; when the case is such that it is doubtful what of their civil enjoyments shall be continued to them, whether they ben't about to lose all their privileges or, if not, what they shall not lose; when there are powerful enemies abroad that seek the eversion of the state or enemies in a people's own bowels that are carrying on plots and designs against the present establishment, that they may have the better opportunity to advance their private interest or the interest of a party that they are attached to, or do it out of spite to any person or parties that they are enemies to.

2. When the persons in whose hands the government is often changed, this often arises from the unsettled state of public affairs; and if it don't arise from it, it has a tendency to it.

If persons that are governors are often changing, it naturally will tend to a frequent change of the methods and manner of government. Different persons have different judgments and opinions of things, different tempers and different designs and views to carry on. To have many princes or frequently to have new ones tends to unhinge things, and keeps them unsettled, and frequently causes great convulsions in a state. The tendency is the same in degree whether the change be in higher or inferior officers. 'Tis no part of public prudence to be often changing the persons in whose hands is the administration of government, and 'tis a calamity to have them often changed. Indeed, if the persons in power are not fit for their places, 'tis best they should be removed; but then the imprudence or calamity was in putting of them in at first, so as to make a change necessary.

The long continuance of the same persons in power, if they are fit for their places, tends much to the strength and stability of the affairs of [a] community. Old and experienced rulers have a vast advantage in the management of public [affairs] through their experience: knowledge of the state of a land, knowledge of the manner, and tempers, and ways of the subject, and the methods of managing them, a comprehensive view of the circumstances of the community both past and present, a facility and expediteness in the management of business which use gives.

We may conceive of the reason of the thing sometimes by considering what confusion it would make in a family to have the heads and governors of it changed once in two or three years. It would be the way utterly to ruin the children and servants of a family. A land's often changing its princes or having many princes tends to its mischief no less than for a family often to be changing its heads.

3. When it is a matter undetermined and unsettled where the power of administration lies, then are the public affairs of a land in an unsettled state. When there are debates long maintained about privilege and prerogative, and matters of great importance to the government are long held in suspense because it is not determined who has powers of administration: in such a case the public affairs of a country are not settled on any foundation, because it is a thing as yet remains in suspense, on what foundation they ought to be settled upon.

4. When there is strife between different persons and parties for the power of government.

When there are many that would be princes and are contending together for the power; when the principal men of a country are designing men, are carrying designs one against another, each one to advance himself and to depress others; when the main struggle amongst the great men is who shall be uppermost and keep down the rest; when there is a spirit of jealousy amongst rulers one of another, [and] each one is suspicious of another lest he should have the most honor and influence in the government and accordingly are plotting to prevent him and to advance themselves; when the principal men don't make the public good but their own advancement their principal aim, and each one is striving to bring others into a dependence on him, and are for that end industriously insinuating themselves into the favor of the supreme power or striving for the favor and esteem of the people; when there are opposite parties among rulers each laboring to weaken the other and, as much as may be, to engross the power themselves; when the different orders of those who have the management of public business are not cemented, but one are jealous of another, [and] the lower orders are jealous lest the superior should take too much upon them and so should strive[2] to keep them down, to get the power more into their hands; and the superiors, on the other hand, are jealous of the inferiors encroaching upon them and so are striving to get from them their privilege; when the people are striving with rulers, and rulers with people, and power becomes a bone of contention among them: [then are the public affairs of a land in an unsettled state].

We come now,

Second, [to show] that such an unsettled state of the public affairs of a people is a token of God's anger towards them for their sins. Here,

1. When a people's public affairs are thus in an unsettled state, it shows that God don't take care of 'em. Not but that God's providence is over all things: God don't neglect any part of the creation, but orders all affairs of heaven and earth. But when I say God don't take care of them, my meaning is that he don't take care of them as concerning himself for their welfare. He don't take care of their affairs as concerning himself in them, or providing for a people, taking care that things go right, that they are managed so as shall be for a people's good. God don't interest himself in their affairs, or himself presiding over them, taking it upon himself to be their ruler. He don't take the concern of the public weal into his own hands.

When a people are in favor with God, he himself will be their king and will take care of their affairs; Is. 33:22, "The Lord is our judge, the Lord is our lawgiver, the Lord is our king; he will save us." God is amongst such a people. He holds the helm of government in his own hand. When their rulers meet together about public affairs, he presides amongst them and invisibly influences and guides and orders all that is done according to his infinite wisdom and in mercy to a people and for their good.

2. MS: "are striving."

But when the affairs of a people are in such an unsettled state, 'tis a sign that God has in a measure forsaken a people, and that he don't take care of their affairs: that [he] has let go the helm of the ship and suffers it to be driven at random by the winds and seas.

And this will appear by two considerations:

(1) It will appear if we consider the nature of divine government; it is not unsettled and confused but in established and regular order. Where God is king, the government must be stable and things must needs proceed in a most established order. If it were otherwise, it would reflect on his glorious perfection, as though he were fallible and mutable, or weak and not always able to order things as he would have 'em. When an almighty and an infinitely wise and unchangeable Being is the governor, the government can't be unsettled.

And so we find it actually is. For instance, God rules the natural world, and how settled and established is the method of things proceeding according to certain and immutable laws which the Creator has fixed. God rules in the rest of the visible heavens, the sun, moon, and stars, and how settled is their order and how regular their motions from age to age, never clashing and running into any confusion. The sun nor moon nor any star ever forgets its appointed course or becomes exorbitant in its motion. God rules in the highest heavens amongst the angels. He takes care of their affairs, and there is no such thing as an unsettled state of government.

So when God graciously takes care of the public affairs of any people here on earth and takes the management of 'em into his own hands, government will be settled on a firm base, and things will proceed in regular and established order. When God steers the ship, it will be true and steady in its course. But when things are at loose ends and government is upon no settled foundation, when the public state is often changing and shifting and always in confusion, this is a sign that God has forsaken them and don't take care of them.

(2) Such an unsettled state {of the public affairs of a people} argues that God don't take care of them, as 'tis a vast calamity to a people. If God took care of a people's public affairs, they would be preserved from such a calamity.

The mischiefs of such a state of the affairs of a land are innumerable. It tends to bring all things into confusion and to defeat the design and end of men's uniting in communities. Unsettledness and instability is an unhappiness in any concern, but in nothing more than in [the] government [of] public affairs. 'Tis unhappy to have an house not to stand strong, not to be well-settled on its foundation, to be liable ever and anon to move and jog out of place. It rocks the whole frame and tends to its ruin; it makes it unsafe living in such an house. But how much more unhappy is it for the frame of the public state not to be well settled on some basis, to have its foundation loose and often moving and giving way.

The very excellency of a public state is its stability. The very end of men's uniting in a community is strength and firmness. This is the foundation on which we stand and on which our particular rights and privileges are built. And if this foundation be loose and unsettled, how miserable are we.

The unsettled state of public affairs commonly greatly interrupts the proceeding of public business. Things that need to be done are neglected, and the public in the meantime greatly suffers. The minds of those who have the care of public business are diverted by the changes, overturnings, and tumults there in public affairs. Rulers' minds are very much taken off from public business, and their time spent in those disputes and debates that arise.

Rulers are not so deeply engaged in seeking the public good. They don't act with that strength and resolution, their own circumstances being unsettled and uncertain. And rulers, not being united among themselves, don't assist and strengthen one another, but rather weaken one another's hands.

Such an unsettled state is commonly attended with abundance of strife and contention, with jealousies [and] envyings. Rulers are divided into parties, and so the whole land with them. The distemper becomes general, so that the devil hereby gets a great advantage to promote his kingdom amongst them. Abundance of sin is committed by this means, and people are enemies, and very uncomfortable one to another. And while all are engaged in contention, justice and righteousness is neglected. The suppressing of vice and wickedness is neglected, and they take advantage and prevail without restraint. Rulers, instead of discouraging and suppressing vice, do rather encourage it by their own unchristian behavior in their heats and debates. And commonly at such a time the wealth of a people is greatly wasted and consumed. While a state is unsettled, its strength and wealth consumes, as the health of the body natural under a sore disease.

And such an unsettled state, if continued, tends to a people's ruin. It tends to its ruin from within and from without. The commonwealth is exposed, to become a prey to the ambition and avarice of men in its own bowels, of those that should be its fathers. The enemies of people that desire its overthrow have a great advantage given 'em hereby. It stirs up the public enemies; it awakens them to seek for an opportunity to make a prey of the country. They wish for its fall, and when they see it tottering they will be sure to put their shoulders to to throw it down.

A people in such circumstances are weak and not so well able to resist a public enemy. A house whose foundation is loose and unsettled is easily blown down when the wind arises. Such a calamitous state of a people is a sign that God has in a great measure forsaken them, and don't take care of 'em.

2. God don't forsake a people and neglect their public welfare unless he is provoked to it by their sins.

As God takes notice of particular persons, how they behave themselves, and deals with them accordingly, so he doth also of a people. And God has often promised that if a people are obedient to his voice, he will not forsake them; Deut. 4:31, "The Lord thy God is a merciful God; he will not forsake thee nor destroy thee."

And this is manifest by the instances we have in the holy Scriptures from the state of Israel while they walked in God's ways. He was the king in their midst and ordered their affairs for them. And when he forsook and left their affairs in an unsettled state, it was always a time of degenerating and corruption with them.

This was remarkably exemplified in the kingdom of Israel or the ten tribes. They departed from God in the days of Jeroboam, and set up the calves of Bethel and Dan [I Kings 12:28–29], and never reformed of their apostasy. And in how unsettled a state were their affairs; how many were their princes! The crown often shifted from one family to another. First, Jeroboam and his son reigned, and then Baasha that was of another family conspired against Nadab and took the crown [I Kgs. 15:27]. And then Zimri slew his son and all his posterity and took the crown and he reigned but seven days [16:9–15]. And then they slew him and made Omri king, one of another family, whose son was Ahab [16:16]. And then Jehu slew all his posterity and took the crown [II Kgs. 9:3]. And then Shallum, of another family, took the crown [II Kgs. 15:10]. And then Menahem, of another family, slew him and reigned in his stead [15:14]. And then Pekah, of another family, slew his son and reigned in his stead [15:25]. And then Hoshea, of another family, took the crown [17:1]. They had forsaken God, and God took not care of their affairs, and so {he left their affairs in an unsettled state}. So the public affairs of Judah were in a most unsettled posture a little before their destruction, as might be shown.

But I hasten to a conclusion with a brief

APPLICATION.

I. This doctrine may give us occasion to conclude that very often when a people are in such circumstances, there is too much done at inveighing against instruments and too little at reflecting on themselves. As there is commonly among a people at such a time much of a spirit of contention, so it appears in finding fault very much one with another.

All will own the calamitousness of the circumstances of the public, and there is much fault found with these and those; all find fault. Rulers themselves will find fault and be full of invectives one against another, all clearing themselves. One will lay blame to another that he dislikes and that is of an opposite party. The people, they find fault with rulers and charge them with folly or treachery and falseness to their trust. One party will find fault with rulers on one side, and another with another. There is much done at finding fault with real or supposed public enemies.

But how little is there of self-reflection! How little is it considered that the unsettled and calamitous circumstances of the land is the judgment of God upon it for general corruption and [the] abounding wickedness of it. When we get into this humor of finding fault, 'tis fit that [we] should begin with ourselves, for here is the beginning of all our calamities. What instruments soever are made use of, we should strike at the root.

If we would but reform our own evil ways and doings, we should soon find an end to our calamities. Whatever instruments have a hand in bringing [it], 'tis God, who is angry with us for our sins, that has all second causes in his hands. Let it be considered what God says; Is. 45:7, "I form light, I create darkness: I make peace, I create evil: I the Lord do all these things"; Amos 3:6, "Is there any evil in the city, and the Lord hath not done it?"

In such circumstances a people look too much abroad for the root of calamity; they don't look enough at home. And so [the] generality of the people find fault, and the generality clear them; and yet 'tis general corruption and wickedness [that] is the very thing that make all the mischief.

II. Hence wicked men are the actors or troublers of a land. 'Tis for the transgression of such persons that the land is left of God, and its affairs are left in such disorder and confusion.

Men that are vicious persons, especially such as are otherwise men of influence, considerable men for natural ability or estate or public improvement, if they are such as han't the fear of God before their eyes and don't govern themselves by the rules of his Word, but are immoral persons, they are public enemies. They do, as it were, undermine the foundations of a state and weaken the whole frame.

III. Hence how much we should, all in our places and as God gives us opportunity, labor to suppress prevailing wickedness, for herein we establish the land. Every man, so much as he does towards suppressing of vice and wickedness, so much good doth he do for his country.

IV. Hence we may learn how much a people may wrong their posterity by their wickedness. The transgression of a people unsettles the state of a land and often puts an end to it, overthrows the privileges and rights which they enjoyed by virtue of a former establishment, which when lost are not easily recovered; so that not only the present, but future generations reap the bitter fruits of it. Their children and children's children may have cause to rue the transgressions of their fathers, whereby they are deprived of precious privileges which the land formerly enjoyed and which, had it not been for their forefathers' provocations, might have been handed down to them.

V. And lastly, hence we may infer that [God] has of late been, and now is, giving tokens of his anger for the transgressions of this land.

It would be needless for me to say how unsettled a state the public affairs of this land have lately been, and now are in. When I described in some instances an unsettled state {of public affairs}, the application was easy to the circumstances of this land; and such as every attentive hearer could not but make as I went along.

What will be the issue and how affairs will settle at last, we are yet ignorant. Whether the state of the land will be prolonged or not is a thing that yet remains in suspense. We have reason to fear because we are grown so very corrupt. And God has been warning and threatening of us so long, and seems loath to execute what he threatened, but is waiting to be gracious, to see whether there will be any amendment; and there being so little appearance of any such thing, we have reason greatly to fear what God will do with [us], and earnestly to deprecate the strokes of his hand.[3]

[DOCTRINE II.]

[We come now to the] latter part of the verse: "but by a man of understanding and knowledge shall the state thereof be prolonged." In these words may be observed,

3. Here ends the first preaching unit. JE begins the next unit by reciting the text and returning to explication of it. What immediately follows, then, is explication before the second doctrine.

1. A public benefit or blessing mentioned, viz. the prolonging the state of a land, as opposite to the calamity mentioned in the former part of the verse: its having many princes, or having its princes or its government or public state unsettled and unsteady. To have the state of the land prolonged is a blessing upon two accounts:

(1) The state of the land that the wise man here speaks of must be understood as containing some privilege. The case may be so, that it may be a blessing to have an end put to the state of a land; it may be so miserable that it may be a calamity to have it continued, as if a land is conquered by a foreign enemy and is in bondage under a cruel tyrant. We read in the book of Judges how the children of Israel were one [such case] while ruled over by the king of Mesopotamia [Judg. 3:8], and another while by the king of Moab [Judg. 3:14], and another while by Jabin, king of Canaan [Judg. 4:2], and another while by the Midianites [Judg. 6:1], etc.; they were for their sins delivered into the hands of their enemies. Now, the continuance of such a state as this was not what the wise man meant by the state of a land's being prolonged, for such a state as this contains nothing of privilege in it. But by "the state of a land," 'tis evident the wise man intends a constitution whereby it has its power of government that it has within itself, and management of its own public affairs in a freedom from those whose interest is not united with theirs.

And the prolongation of the state of a land in this sense is spoken of in opposition to two things, viz. first, to a final end's being put to it by their land's being deprived of all its privileges it has as free from foreign power; second, in opposition to the often changing [of] its own form, [of] its being stable and settled in one certain regular order and method, or its often changing princes, though those princes are all in, and of, itself. And therefore,

(2) For a land to have its state prolonged is a blessing as it preserves from the mischiefs which are the natural fruit of change.

2. We may observe how this blessing is obtained: by a man of understanding and knowledge. By which the wise [man] don't mean only a subtile, cunning man; by understanding and knowledge is not meant merely state policy, for it is designing, crafty, political men that ordinarily are the instruments of overthrowing the state of a land, and their cunning will either tend to the prolonging of it or the overthrow of it according as they are well or ill inclined. But by a man of understanding and knowledge seems to be intended a man of righteousness [or] piety, though not exclusive of natural and moral wisdom and prudence, for these terms, wisdom [or] understanding, are generally so to be understood in this book for righteousness or piety. And this does more univer-

sally tend to the establishment of a people's public weal than cunning and policy.

And then this best agrees with the former part of the verse. If we understand it in this sense, then the procuring cause of this benefit will be opposite to the procuring cause of the opposite calamity here mentioned. As 'tis the transgression of a people that renders their state unsettled, not durable, so 'tis their righteousness that prolongs it.

II. *The privileges of any community are established and prolonged by the righteousness of its members; or, the righteousness of the members of a community tends to the establishing and prolonging of its privileges.*

Here,

First. The righteousness of private members of a community tends to this. However mean and obscure a man may be, however little known and taken notice of, yet he may be a public blessing. The man don't know, yet God knows him and observes. And such men may bring down showers of blessing on all around them. The wickedness of private persons helps to pull down God's judgments on the land where he dwells; so much more doth the piety of {a righteous man bring down blessings}. Christ teaches us that the godly are "the salt of the earth" (Matt. 5:13); so are they the salt of the land, or particular community to which they belong, that preserve it [from] spoiling and coming to ruin. But,

Second. Especially doth the righteousness of men in public places tend to this. Men in public places have more public influence than others, both with God and with men. These, when they are men of integrity and piety, are the props and pillars of a state. Public men have the same places in the body politic that the head and heart and more noble and vital parts have in the body natural, on which the whole body in all its members depend, and the place that the foundation has in a building. In Ps. 82:5, rulers are called "the foundations of the earth."

But the reason of this may appear more fully in what may [follow]. I proceed therefore particularly to show how the righteousness of the members of a community tends to the establishing and prolonging of its privileges.

1. It tends to it from the respect that God hath to such. Such men as we speak of are very dear to God, and they have his blessing accompanying them. His blessing is not only upon them, but it surrounds them, so that oftentimes it falls on those that [are] round about them and that they are concerned with. Their presence brings down God's blessing on those with whom they are present. Thus God blessed Laban's affairs because of

Jacob [Gen. 30:27]; thus God blessed the house of Potiphar and all that he had for Joseph's [sake]; and again, God blessed the prison keeper for his sake when he was no otherwise concerned with him than only that he was a prisoner under his care [Gen. 39:5].

The blessing of God that is with the godly is very diffusive, so their presence in a land, it has a tendency to bring down God's blessing upon the land. Where the righteous are, there God [is] graciously present; and therefore the presence of such has a tendency to keep the presence of God in a land. God delights to be, and graciously to work and show himself, amongst the godly. If there are many godly ones in a land, therefore, this will have a tendency to prevent God's leaving them; and if he don't leave them, and if God don't forsake a land, there is no danger of its state being overthrown.

When the godly are members of a community, their interest and the interest of their families is involved with the interest of the community, and God has a great respect to the interest of his saints. When there are many such therefore in a land, there is hope that God will preserve its privileges out of respect to their concern in them and for the sake of their posterity. For God hath respect to the posterity of the godly; Ps. 112:2, "The generation of the upright shall be blessed."

God hath respect to those that are dear to the godly for their sakes. Now, the community that the godly man belongs to is dear to him. He is a lover of his country; godliness tends to make men public-spirited. And they are lovers of the privileges of the people that they are of, and God therefore will have respect to the same for their sakes. God told Abraham that if there had been ten righteous men in Sodom, he would not have destroyed it for the ten's sake (Gen. 18:32). So when God was about to destroy Jerusalem, he saith, as Jer. 5:1, "Run ye to and fro through the streets of Jerusalem, and see now, and know, and seek in the broad places thereof, if ye can find a man, if there be any that executeth judgments, that seeketh the truth, and I will pardon it."

The godly are among a people in the time of God's anger like Aaron in the congregation, who, when the plague was begun, ran and stood in the breach between the dead and the living, and the plague was stayed (Num. 16:47). Thus God said, when he was about to destroy the land of Israel; Ezek. 22:30, "I sought for a man among them, that should make up the hedge, and stand in the gap before me for the land, that I should not destroy it: but I found none." The godly are the blessing in a land for whose sake God says, "Destroy it not"; Is. 65:8, "Thus said the Lord, As the new wine is found in the cluster, and one saith, Destroy it not; for a blessing is in it: so will I do for my servants' sakes, that I may not destroy them all."

2. The righteous prolong the privileges of a land by their prayers. Their prayers are not only for themselves; they won't forget the people and land to which they belong when they make their addresses to God. They will deprecate the public calamities.

And the godly are powerful with God in their prayers; Jas. 5:16, "The effectual fervent prayer of a righteous man availeth much." This is represented by a lively emblem, by Jacob's wrestling with God and prevailing when he had his name Israel, because as a prince he had power with God and prevailed (Gen. 32:28). A poor man in a cottage that walks with God and loves the prosperity of Zion, that can do but little towards preserving or advancing the public good himself, yet may do much by his fervent prayers and more, it may be, than some of the great men with their power and policy.

But when men in public places are true fearers of God, their prayers especially will have a tendency to preserve the peace and privileges of a land, because, as they stand in the place of fathers, so 'tis part of their work that is expected of them that they should be intercessors. As they are public persons, so they should represent the people toward God. And when they are holy men and do the part of intercessors, God has respect to them as public representatives and men who stand in the place of intercessors.

We have many instances in Scripture of the great power of the prayer of pious men in public places for the averting of public judgments and procuring public blessings. How often did Moses by his intercessions turn away God's anger from the congregation of Israel. And when Joshua their captain prayed, the sun stood still to give 'em opportunity to destroy their enemies [Josh. 10:12–13]. When Samuel the judge of Israel prayed, God thundered on the Philistines [I Sam. 7:10]. When David the king of Israel prayed, the plague was stayed [II Sam. 24:25]. Upon the prayer of Daniel, who was a prophet and prince, Israel was restored from captivity [Dan. 9:16–19]. At the prayers of Nehemiah and Ezra, the people were preserved and their state restored [Neh. 2:4; Ezra 10:1].

3. The piety of the members of a community has a natural tendency to establish and preserve the state and privileges thereof. It is the prevailing of sin and wickedness that ordinarily not only provokes God, and so procures the unsettledness and overthrow of the state of a people, but 'tis also the means by which 'tis effected. All history verifies this. While virtue has prevailed in a state, it has been strong and stable; but when vice has prevailed, it has hastened their ruin.

When piety prevails among a people, it prevents the prevailing of ambition, and avarice, and self-seeking, and treachery among rulers that is very commonly the means by which the state of a land is unsettled and destroyed. When men have the fear of God before their eyes, they won't be governed by an aim to advance or enrich themselves more than the public good. They won't betray the public weal for private ends; they'll sincerely and conscientiously seek every one the good of the public. Their country may depend upon them. If they are wise and seeing and politic men, they will improve their policy to establish and advance the good of the land, and not to advance themselves and supplant others. The securing of the public peace will be their first care.

A spirit of true piety would prevent the prevailing of a spirit of contention which divides a kingdom against itself and therefore tends to its overthrow. The spirit of piety is a spirit of peace and love, a spirit that disposes men to look every one not at his own things but every one also at the things of others. Godliness will dispose every one in whatever station to be faithful in doing the duty of his place. It tends to make rulers just and faithful, and to do their duty to the people, and tends to make the people quiet and submissive to government. It unites all parts of the community and strongly cements them together.

When the case is so with a land, the state of it is like to be firm and won't be liable easily to be disturbed, much less to be overthrown.

APPLICATION.

Use I. [Of] *Inf.* Hence learn that when God threatens a people with a being deprived of their public privileges, 'tis a loud call to reformation and repentance.

When things are unsettled, and providence makes the continuance of privilege to be doubtful, the matter remains in suspense. From whatever second causes this is from, it is a call of God to a land to turn to him and obey his voice. 'Tis a call to all ranks and degrees, every one to examine himself, to search his own heart and ways, and to turn unto the Lord.

'Tis a call to rulers and those who are set in eminent stations carefully to purge themselves from all iniquity, and to set bright examples of holiness of life and conversation, and to rule in the fear of God, that they may be such as may "stand in the gap" and "make up the hedge" that the hedge may not be utterly broken down [Ezek. 22:30].

'Tis a call to ministers to "shine as lights in the world," and faithfully and zealously to endeavor to promote piety amongst their hearers [Phil.

2:15]. 'Tis a call to heads of families to train up their families "in the nurture and admonition of the Lord" [Eph. 6:4], to use their example, instruction, and powers to restrain and suppress whatever is vicious or disorderly, to maintain the practice of virtue and religion in their families.

Use II. Hence learn how much the death of those that are eminently godly is to be lamented, especially those that are in public places. When such are taken away, there is so much of the presence of God is taken away from a people. Those are taken away for whose sakes God had respect to the land and withheld his judgments, and by whom, in God, our tranquillity was prolonged.

We have no longer the advantage of the blessing of God which surrounded [them], and which others, while they lived, were partakers of with them. We have them no more to be concerned for the continuance of public blessings and to pray for it. We have now no more of their intercessions for the public weal. They were very dear to God, and he was tender of their interest, but their interest now is no longer connected with ours or comprehended in the good of the land. They now no longer stand related to any civil society.

When the righteous are taken away, especially in public, civil, or ecclesiastical stations, there are, as it were, so many breaches made in the walls of the city, so many props or pillars of the building broken, which, if God don't place others in their stead, threaten our downfall. Therefore the death of such persons is greatly to be lamented by us. It is spoken of in Scripture as instance of the stupidity and desperate depravedness of a people that they don't lay to heart such losses, and that upon this account that it so threatens the future calamity of a people; Is. 57:1, "The righteous perisheth, and no man layeth it to heart: and merciful men are taken away, none considering that the righteous is taken away from the evil to come."

Use III. Hence learn how much it concerns a state to countenance and encourage virtue and piety, as it would seek its own preservation. As God hath given to every creature a principle of self-preservation, and nature has furnished them with a faculty and means in order to it, any creature therefore would be monstrous and unnatural that should not seek its own preservation. And it is no less monstrous, and of much more dreadful consequence, in a people not to seek the preservation of their state and public enjoyments.

By the doctrine we learn the likeliest method in order thereto: to make this very much their concern, to promote religion and virtue in the land.

Rulers should make this their study; this should be a thing that they should look upon very much [as] their business. This should be a thing lying upon the hearts of all that are improved in the government. It concerns a state not only to suppress vice and immorality by suitable penalties but to be also encouraging virtue with rewards.

And great respect ought to be had to virtue and piety in the improvement that is made of persons in public business. Hereby they give them the greater advantage to improve their piety, in establishing and prolonging the public tranquillity;[4] for, as we have shown, the doctrine is true especially of godly men in public places, that their piety tends to the prolonging the privileges of a land. It should be the study and delight of both rulers and people to be putting honor upon such persons. This, the Apostle tells us, is one end of civil government, not only to be a terror to evildoers but to reward with honor them that do that which is good; Rom. 13:3, "For rulers are not a terror to good works, but to the evil. Wilt thou then not be afraid of the power? Do that which is good, and thou shalt have praise of the same." So the apostle Peter to the same purpose; I Pet. 2:14, "or unto governors, as unto them that are sent by him for the punishment of evildoers, and for the praise of them that do well."

Use IV. Hence learn that when the affairs of a people are in an unsettled and doubtful posture, the best method they can take in order to the prolonging their tranquillity is to turn from sin to God. Let the circumstances of a land [be what] they will, this is the best method that can be taken. It is a method that suits all possible cases. This method has the advantage of all other methods that can be taken in difficult and doubtful circumstances of a people, upon every account.

'Tis the readiest, directest method. If we would forsake our sins and turn to God, if we would hear the call of providence to us and generally agree in it, that we would turn and seek and serve the Lord, we should soon see an alteration. Providence would soon remove public calamities; Ps. 81:13–14, "O that my people had hearkened unto me, and Israel had walked in my ways! I should soon have subdued their enemies, and turned my hand against their adversaries."

It is the surest way. If we use our own policy and trust to that to preserve and secure us, that may fail us. We may be disappointed innumerable ways. Not but that our utmost prudence is to be used, but if we have nothing else to trust to, our success will be very uncertain. But if we turn

4. I. e. respect to virtuous rulers gives them opportunity to improve the piety of the people, thereby promoting the public tranquillity.

to God and walk in his ways, God will do the thing for us. He will use his own wisdom, which can't be frustrated, and power, that can't be controlled, in our behalf. Let the difficulties be what they will, they shall be removed. Though those that are wiser and more politic than we seek to deprive us of our privileges, it will signify nothing; God will defend us. Whatever instruments are at work against [us], God has those instruments in his hand and can dispose of 'em just as he pleases. Is the supreme power of the nation against us? Still, we shall be safe; God is able to "turn the hearts of kings whithersoever he will" (Prov. 21:1).

This is the best method because there is no danger of erring in it. If we trust to our policy, we may commit blunders and overthrow ourselves; but if God's wisdom be for us, that can't blunder. If we trust to our own wisdom, we may be overpowered by those that have us in their hands; but if we take this method, there is no danger, for then he will be for us that has us, and them too, in his hands. This way we may have our tranquillity lengthened out, if we will but agree to it. But there is no certainty in any other way.

This is the properest method, for here our mischief began, and 'tis proper that here our remedy should begin. Our sins were the cause of our state's becoming so unsettled and doubtful, and therefore it must be our righteousness that must settle and establish them again.

And there is no other method will do. If we don't reform our sins, do what else we will (we may cast what policy we can) we shall always be confounded. Our wisdom will be turned into foolishness. We shall not enjoy settled prosperity so long as we are so corrupt. If we should seem to get by the present threatening appearance, it won't be long before we shall have another, if we don't reform and turn to God. Our calamities are from God, and he'll continue 'em till we amend our ways.

Use V. And lastly, hence 'tis a blessing that we should seek above all other public blessings that he would pour out his Spirit upon us. For 'tis by this that God gives a people knowledge and understanding; 'tis by this that God gives that blessing which lays a foundation for all other blessings. By this means we shall be reformed and religion and righteousness will be promoted amongst us. And this will procure for us, and secure to us, all manner of prosperity.

THE DUTY OF CHARITY TO THE POOR

Delivered in January 1733, *The Duty of Charity to the Poor* is a lengthy sermon devoted to almsgiving. Edwards spends little effort here in development of the doctrine. The biblical text, he avers, clearly commands the people of God to supply the wants of the needy in bountiful measure and with free and willing dispositions. Giving to the poor is a duty, as necessary to religious practice as worship, and as important for salvation as prayer. This rather striking claim shows the concrete and practical side of Edwards' ethics. Indeed, in this sermon his insistence on social action almost overwhelms his evangelical theology.

According to Edwards, few people doubt that giving to the poor is a Christian obligation, but New Englanders obtusely fail to do so. "We in this land have a high conceit of ourselves for religion, but do not many other countries shame us? Do not the Papists and Quakers, that we abhor, shame us" in their giving to the poor? So Edwards devotes most of the sermon—some 80 percent—to application. He first urges self-examination, calling on his people to determine whether they have the brotherly affection and kindness called for in the text. Second, he exhorts them with seven motives to give to the needy. Here he criticizes those who look upon their property as privately owned, when it really belongs to the God who commanded charity. He emphasizes Christ's teaching that kindness to the poor will be a criterion for the final judgment. Edwards also draws heavily on Eccles. 11:1 ("Cast thy bread upon the waters, for thou shalt find it after many days") to maintain that providence so ordered earthly affairs that those who give to the poor find rewards in this life as well. Compassion to those in need is an investment, a prudential virtue that might well benefit the giver in some future calamity.

Third, Edwards answers what he deems to be eleven common objections for refusing to help the poor. He deals with questions about proper motives, the dangers of legalism, and the apparent lack of worldly rewards for almsgiving. More poignantly, he attempts also to unmask the viciousness of those who excuse their unwillingness to relieve those in need. Those who claim that few people are so indigent that they require the aid of others in order to live, Edwards contends, lack sympathy for neighbors who are needy but not yet desperate. Those who refuse to give to a poor person because of past offenses are unforgiving. Those who demand further information before giving to a poor person disobey the command to give to strangers. Those who claim that poverty is self-inflicted, and therefore just, lack compassion. Those who claim that civil law provides poor relief do not appreciate how people's needs often fall outside the legal definition of poverty.

The Duty of Charity to the Poor thus portrays something of the day-to-day tensions of social life in Northampton. The town's economic growth in the early eighteenth century heightened the appearance, if not the reality, of class division and poverty.[1] Northampton's pastor gave his attention in this sermon not to systemic economic issues, however, but to the strains on human relationships. Even as Edwards developed a theology of evangelical revival, such social changes moved him to assert the concrete ethical demands of Christianity as integral to religious practice.

* * *

The manuscript is a duodecimo booklet of thirty-nine well-preserved leaves. The last page is blank. The hand is clear, and there are relatively few deletions, additions, or other editorial changes. There are no indications of repreaching. This was the first sermon that Edwards dated, noting "Jan. 1732/33" at the beginning (1733 by the modern calendar). Jonathan Edwards, Jr., prepared the sermon for its first publication as "*The Duty of* Charity *to the Poor, explained and enforced*," in *Practical Sermons, never before Published* (Edinburgh, 1788), pp. 343–85. This version was reprinted in the Dwight edition (*6*, 536–68).

1. For discussions of the economy and social affairs in Northampton, see Tracy, *Jonathan Edwards, Pastor*. For JE's preaching on the economy, see Valeri, "The Economic Thought of Jonathan Edwards." Further discussion and citations are provided in the Preface to the Period, above, pp. 17–28.

THE DUTY OF CHARITY TO THE POOR

DEUTERONOMY 15:7–11.

If there be among you a poor man of one of thy brethren within any of thy gates in thy land which the Lord thy God giveth thee, thou shalt not harden thy heart, nor shut thine hand from thy poor brother: but thou shalt open thine hand wide unto him, and shalt surely lend him sufficient for his need, in that which he wanteth.
Beware that there be not a thought in thy wicked heart, saying, The seventh year, the year of release, is at hand; and thine eye be evil against thy poor brother, and thou givest him naught; and he cry unto the Lord against thee, and it be sin unto thee. Thou shalt surely give him, and thine heart shall not be grieved when thou givest unto him: because that for this thing the Lord thy God shall bless thee in all thy works, and in all that thou puttest thine hand unto.
For the poor shall never cease out of the land: therefore I command thee, saying, Thou shalt open thine hand wide unto thy brother, to thy poor, and to thy needy, in thy land.

[We shall] observe in the words,

1. The duty here enjoined, viz. giving to the poor: "If there be among you a poor man of one of thy brethren . . . thou shalt open thine hand wide unto him." Whereby "thy poor brother" is to be understood the same as in other places is meant by neighbor: not only those of their own country, as 'tis explained; Lev. 25:35, "And if thy brother be waxen poor, and fallen in decay with thee; then thou shalt relieve him: yea, though he be a stranger, or a sojourner." The Pharisees interpreted it to signify only one of their own nation, but Christ removes this interpretation; Luke 10:29–37.[2] Christ there teaches, contrary to their opinion, that the rules of charity in the law of Moses are to be extended to the Samaritans, that were not of their nation, and between whom and the Jews there was the most bitter enmity, and were a people that were very troublesome to the Jews.

2. The parable of the good Samaritan.

2. God gives us direction how we are to give in such a case in two things:

(1) That we should give bountifully and sufficient for the supply of his needs; vv. 7–8, "thou shalt not shut up thine hand from thy poor brother: but thou shalt open thine hand wide unto him, and lend him sufficient for his need, in which he wanteth"; and v. 11, "thou shalt open thine hand wide unto thy brother, to thy poor, and thy needy, in thy land."

(2) The second direction God gives about the manner of giving is to give willingly and without grudging; v. 7, "thou shalt not harden thine heart against thy poor brother"; and v. 10, "and thine heart shall not be grieved when thou givest him."

3. We may observe how peremptorily this duty is enjoined and how much insisted on. 'Tis repeated over and over again, and enjoined in the strongest terms; in v. 7, "thou shalt not harden thine heart, nor shut thine hand from thy poor brother"; v. 8, "but thou shalt open thine hand wide unto him, and shalt surely lend him"; v. 10, "thou shalt sure give him"; and v. 11, "I command thee, saying, thou shalt open thine hand wide unto thy brother, to thy poor, and thy needy."

4. God strictly warns against objections, as v. 9: "Beware that there be not a thought in thy wicked heart, saying, The seventh year, the year of release, is at hand; and thine eye be evil against thy poor brother, and thou givest him naught; and he cry unto the Lord against thee, and it be sin unto thee." The matter concerning the seventh year, or year of release, was thus: God had given Israel a law in the beginning of the chapter that every seventh year should be a year of release, and that if any man had lent anything to any of his poor neighbors, if he had not been able to repay him before that year, he should release it and should not exact it of him, but give it to him.

God therefore warns the children of Israel against making an objection against helping their poor neighbors of that, that the year of release was near at hand and it was not likely that he would be able to pay him again before that, and then he should lose it wholly because he should be obliged then to release it. God foresaw that the wickedness of their hearts would be very ready to make such an objection.

But God very strictly warns them against it, that they should not be the more backward to supply the wants of the needy for that, but be willing to give him: "thou shalt be willing to lend expecting nothing again." Men are exceeding ready to make objections against such duties, which God speaks of here as a manifestation of the wickedness of the heart: "Beware that there be not a thought in thy wicked heart."

The warning is exceeding strict. God don't only say, "Beware that thou don't refuse to give him," but "Beware that thou han't one objecting thought against it arising from a backwardness to liberality." God warns against those beginnings of uncharitableness in the heart, or what tend to his forbearing to give: "And thou givest him naught, and he cry unto the Lord against thee, and it be a sin unto thee." God warns them from the guilt they will be likely to bring upon themselves hereby.

5. We may observe here several enforcements of this duty. There is a reason of the duty implied in that, in God's calling him that is needy "our brother": "thou shalt not shut thine hand from thy poor brother"; and v. 9, "beware that thine eye be not evil against thy poor brother"; and v. 11, "thou shalt open thine hand wide to thy brother." We are to look upon ourselves as related to all mankind, but especially to those that are of the visible people of God. We are to look upon 'em as brethren and to treat them accordingly. We shall be base indeed if we are not willing to help a brother in want.

Another enforcement is God's promise that for this thing God will bless us in all our works and in all that we put our hands unto: a promise that we shall not lose but be gainers by it (as v. 10).

Another is that we shall never want proper objects of our charity and bounty; v. 11, "for the poor shall never cease out of the land." This, God says to the Jewish church; and the like, Christ says to the Christian church; Matt. 26:11, "the poor ye have always with you." This is to cut off an excuse that uncharitable persons would be ready to make for their not giving, that they could find nobody to give to, that they saw none that needed. God here, and in that other place in Matthew, cuts off such an excuse by telling of us that he would so order it in his providence that his people everywhere and in all ages shall have occasion for the exercise of that virtue.

DOCTRINE

'Tis the most absolute and indispensable duty of a people of God to give bountifully and willingly for the supply of the wants of the needy.

[There are] three propositions.

Prop. I. 'Tis the duty of a people of God to give bountifully. 'Tis commanded once and again in the text, "thou shalt open thine hand wide unto him." A merely giving something is not sufficient; it don't answer the rule or come up to God's holy command. But we must open our hand wide.

What we give, considering our neighbor's wants and our ability, should be such as may be called truly a liberal gift. It is explained in the text, what is meant by opening our hand wide in a people that are able, in v. 8: "thou shalt open thine hand wide unto him, and shall surely lend him sufficient for his want in that which he needeth." By lending here, as is evident by the two following verses, and as we have just now shown, is not only meant lending to receive again; the word "lend" in the Scriptures is sometimes used for giving, as in Luke 6:35: "Do good and lend, hoping for nothing again."

We are commanded therefore to give our poor neighbor what is sufficient for his need. There ought to be none suffered to live in pinching want, among a visible people of God that are able to cause it to be otherwise, unless persons are idle, or spendthrifts, or some such case that the Word of God excepts.

It is said in the beginning of the chapter wherein is the text that the children of Israel should lend to the poor, and in the year of release should release what he had lent, save when there shall be no poor among them [Deut. 15:1–4]. It is rendered in the margin,[3] "to the end there be no poor among you"; you should so supply the wants of the needy that there may be none that may be in pinching want among you; which translation seems the more likely because God says in v. 11 that there shall be no such time when there shall be no poor so as to be proper objects of charity.

When persons give very sparingly, it is no manifestation of charity, but of a contrary spirit; II Cor. 9:5, "Therefore I thought it necessary to exhort the brethren, that they would go before unto you, and make up beforehand your bounty, whereof ye had notice before, that the same might be ready, as a matter of bounty, and not as of covetousness." The Apostle calls a very sparing contribution, a matter of "covetousness."

Prop. II. 'Tis the duty of a visible people of God to give for the supply of the needy freely, and without grudging. It don't at all answer the rule before God if it be done with an inward grudging; if the heart is grieved, and inwardly it hurts a man to give what he gives. "Thou shalt surely give," says God, "and thine heart shall not be grieved." God looks at the heart, and the hand is not accepted without it; II Cor. 9:7, "Every man according as he hath purposed in his heart, so let him give, not grudgingly, or of necessity; for God loveth a cheerful giver."

3. The text of the King James Bible included marginal commentary, variant translations, and cross-references.

Prop. III. This is a duty that a people of God are under very strict and indispensable obligations to. 'Tis not merely a commendable thing for a man to be kind and bountiful to the poor, but our bounden duty, as much a duty as 'tis to pray or go to meeting, or anything else whatsoever; and the neglect of it brings great guilt upon any person. I shall mention [two] reasons.

First. Upon the account of its being so absolutely commanded and so much insisted on in the Word of God. Where have we any command in the Bible laid down in stronger terms, and in a more preemptory, urgent manner, than the command of giving to the poor in the text? And we have the same law again in a positive manner laid down in Lev. 25:35, "And if thy brother be waxen poor, and fallen in decay with thee; then thou shalt relieve him: yea, though he be a stranger, or a sojourner; that he may live with thee." And at the conclusion, in v. 38, God enforced it with this: "I am the Lord thy God."

'Tis mentioned in Scripture not only as a duty, but as a great duty. 'Tis generally acknowledged to be a duty to be kind to the needy, but by many seems not to be looked upon as a duty of very great importance. But 'tis mentioned in Scripture as one of the greater and more essential duties of religion; Mic. 6:8, "He hath showed thee, O man, what is good; and what doth the Lord thy God require of thee, but to do justly, and to love mercy, and to walk humbly with thy God?" Here, to love mercy is mentioned as one of the three great things that are the sum of all religion. So 'tis mentioned by the apostle James as one of the two things wherein pure and undefiled religion consists; Jas. 1:27, "Pure religion and undefiled before God and the Father is this."

So Christ tells us it is one of the weightier matters of the law; Matt. 23:23, "ye have omitted the weightier matters of the law, judgment, mercy, and faith." And the Scripture teaches us again and again that 'tis a more weighty and essential thing than attending the outward ordinances of worship; Hos. 6:6, "I desired mercy, and not sacrifice"; and Matt. 9:13; and 12:7.

And I know of scarce any particular duty that is so much insisted upon, so pressed and urged upon us, both in the Old Testament and New, as this duty of charity to the poor.

Second. The reason of the thing strongly obliges to it. 'Tis not only very positively and frequently insisted upon by God, but 'tis most reasonable in itself; and so, upon this account, there is reason why God should much insist upon it. Here,

1. 'Tis most reasonable considering the general state and nature of mankind. This is such as renders it most reasonable that we should love our neighbor as ourselves. For men are made in the image of God, and are worthy of our love upon this account. And then, we are all nearly allied one to another by nature: we have all the same nature, like faculties, like dispositions, like desires of good, like needs, like aversion to misery, and are made of one blood. And we are made to subsist by society and union, one with another, and God has made us with such a nature that we can't subsist without the help one of another.

Mankind in this respect are as the members of the natural body, are one, can't subsist alone without an union with and the help of the rest. Now, this state of mankind shows how reasonable and suitable it is that men should love their neighbors, and that we should not look every one at his own things, but "every man also on the things of others" (Phil. 2:4).

A selfish spirit is very unsuitable to the nature and state of mankind. He that is all for himself and none for his neighbors deserves to be cut off from the benefit of human society, and to be turned out among wild beasts, to subsist as well as he can. A private, niggardly spirit is more suitable for wolves and beasts of prey than for human beings.

Loving our neighbor as ourselves is the sum of the moral law respecting our fellow creatures, and helping of them and contributing to their relief is the most natural expression of this love. It is vain to pretend to a spirit of love to our neighbor when it grieves us to part with anything for their help when under calamity. They that love only in word and in tongue, and not in deeds, have no love in truth; any profession without it is a vain pretense.

To refuse to give to them that are needy is unreasonable, because we therein do by others contrary to what we would have them do to us in like circumstances. We are very sensible of our own calamities, and when we suffer are ready enough to think that our state requires others' compassion and help, and are ready enough to think hard if others won't deny themselves to help us when in straits.

2. 'Tis especially reasonable considering our circumstances under such a dispensation of grace: considering how much God hath done for us, how greatly he hath loved us, and what he hath given us when we were so unworthy, and when he could have no addition to his happiness by us; considering that silver and gold and earthly crowns were but mean things to give us in his esteem, and hath therefore given his own Son; considering how Christ hath loved us and pitied when we were poor, and how he has laid out himself to help us, and shed his precious blood for us without

grudging, did not think much to deny himself and be at such great cost for us vile miscreants, not merely to relieve us in some measure, and deliver us from the extremity of want, but to make rich, to clothe with kingly robes when we were naked, to feast us at his own table with dainties infinitely costly when we were starving, to advance us from the dunghill and set us among princes, and make us to inherit the throne of his glory, and so to give us the enjoyment of the greatest wealth and plenty to all eternity; II Cor. 8:9, "For ye know the grace of our Lord Jesus Christ, that, though he was rich, yet for our sakes he became poor, that ye through his poverty might be rich."

Now, what a poor business will it be for them that hope to have the benefit of this, that yet can't give something for the relief of a poor neighbor without grudging: if it grieves them to part with a small matter to help a fellow servant in calamity, when Christ did not grudge to shed his blood!

How unsuitable will it be for us that live wholly by kindness to be unkind! What should we have done, if Christ had been so choice and saving of his blood, and loath to bestow it, as many men are of their money or goods: if he had been as ready to excuse himself from dying for us, as many men are to excuse themselves from charity to their neighbor? If Christ would have made objections of such things, as men commonly do against charity for their neighbor, he would have found enough of them.

And then, Christ by his redemption has brought us into a more near relation one to another, hath made us children of God, children in the same family. We are all brethren, having God for our common Father, which is much more than to be brethren in any other family. He has made us all one body; therefore, we ought to be united, and subserve to one another's good, and bear one another's burdens, as members of the same body in the natural body. If one of the members suffers, all the other members bear the burden with it (I Cor. 12:26). If one member be diseased or wounded, the other members of the body will minister to it and help it. And so surely it should be in the body of Christ; Gal. 6:2, "Bear ye one another's burdens, and so fulfill the law of Christ."

APPLICATION.

Use I. Of *Self-Exam.* Whether or no you don't lie under guilt upon the account of a neglect of this duty, in withholding that charity that God has required of you towards the needy. You have often been put upon examining yourself whether or no you don't live in some way displeasing to God; it may be, at such times, this never came into your mind, whether or no you did not lie under guilt upon this account.

But this neglect is a thing that brings great guilt upon the soul in the sight of God, as is evident by the text; Deut. 15:9, "beware that thine eye be not evil against thy poor brother, and thou givest him naught; and he cry unto the Lord against thee, and it be sin unto thee." 'Tis often mentioned as one of the sins of Judah and Jerusalem, for which God was about to bring such terrible judgments upon them. And it was one of the sins of Sodom, for which that was destroyed, that she did not give to supply the poor or needy; Ezek. 16:49, "This was the iniquity of thy sister Sodom, pride, fullness of bread, and abundance of idleness in her, and in her daughters; neither did she strengthen the hand of the poor and needy."

And han't we reason to fear that much guilt lies upon this land upon this very account? We in this land have a high conceit of ourselves for religion, but do not many other countries shame us? Do not the Papists and Quakers, that we abhor, shame us in this respect? So far as I can understand the tenor of the Christian religion, and the rules of God's Word, the same are in no measure answered by the general practice of most places in this land, in this respect. There be many that make a high profession of religion; but do not many of 'em want[4] to have the apostle James tell them what true religion is?

Let everyone examine himself, whether he don't lie under guilt with respect to this matter. Han't you forborne to give, when you have seen your brother in want? Han't you shut up the bowels of your compassion towards him, forborne to deny yourself a little for his relief? Or, when you have given, have [you not] done it very grudgingly? Han't it inwardly hurt and grieved you: you have looked upon what you have given as lost, as it were, so that what you have given has been, as the Apostle expresses, a matter of covetousness rather than of bounty [II Cor. 9:5]? Han't occasions of giving been unwelcome to you; han't you been uneasy under them? Han't you felt considerable backwardness, and loatheness? Han't you, from a grudging backward spirit, been apt to raise objections against giving, and to excuse yourself? Such things as these bring guilt upon the soul, and oftentimes bring down God's curse upon persons, as we may show more fully hereafter.[5]

4. I.e. need.

5. Here ends the first preaching unit. JE begins the second unit by reciting the text and repeating the doctrine.

Use II. Of *Exh.* to this duty. We are professors of Christianity, pretend to be the followers of Jesus, pretend to make the gospel our rule. We have the Bible in our houses; let us not behave ourselves in this particular as if we had never seen the Bible, and were ignorant of Christianity, and did not know what kind of religion it was. What will it signify to pretend to be Christians, and at the same time live in the neglect of the rules of Christianity that are mainly insisted on in the institution of it? But there are several things that I would here particularly propose to your consideration:

First [*Motive*]. Consider that what you have is not your own, i.e. you have no absolute right to it, have only a subordinate right. Your goods are only lent to you of God to be improved by you in such ways as God directs you. You yourselves are not your own; I Cor. 6:19–20, "Ye are not your own, for ye are bought with a price; your body and your spirit are his." And if you yourself are not your own, so then neither are your possessions your own. You have by covenant given up yourself and all you have to God; you have disclaimed and renounced any right in yourself, as in anything that you have, and given God all the absolute right. And if you are a true Christian, you have done it from your heart.

Your money and your goods are not your own. They are only committed to you as stewards, to be improved for him who committed 'em to you; I Pet. 4:9–10, "Use hospitality one to another without grudging. As every man hath received the gift, even so minister the same one to another, as good stewards of the manifold grace." A steward has no business with his master's goods to use 'em any other wise than for the benefit of his master's family or according to his master's direction. He has no business to make use of them as if he were the proprietor of 'em, or had anything to do with them, only as he is to use them for his master. He is to give everyone of his master's family their portion of meat in due season [Luke 12:42].

But if, instead of that, he hoards up his master's goods for himself, and withholds them from those of the household, so that some of the family are pinched for want of food and clothing, he is therein guilty of robbing his master and embezzling his substance. And would any householder endure such a steward? If he discovered him in such a practice, would he not take his goods out of his hands and commit 'em to the care of some other steward, that shall give everyone of his family their portion of meat in due season?

We must remember that we must, all of us, give account of our stewardship, and how we have disposed of those goods that our Master has put into our hands. And if it be found, when our Master comes to reckon with us, that we have denied some of his family their proper provision, while we have hoarded up for ourselves as if we had been the proprietors of our Master's goods, what account shall we give of this?

Second [*Mot.*] Consider that God tells us that he shall look upon what is done in charity to our neighbor that is in want as done unto Him, and what is denied unto them as denied unto Him; Prov. 19:17, "He that hath pity upon the poor lendeth to the Lord." God has been pleased to make our needy neighbors his receivers. He, in his infinite mercy, hath so interested himself in their case that he looks upon what is given in charity to them, given to himself; and he looks upon it when we deny them what their circumstances require of us as that we therein rob him of his right.

So Christ teaches that we are to look upon our fellow Christians in this case as himself, and that our giving to or withholding from them shall be so taken as if we so behaved ourselves towards him. In Matt. 25:40, there Christ says to the righteous on his right hand, who had supplied the wants of the needy, "in that ye have done it to one of the least of these my brethren, ye have done it unto me." In like manner, he says to the wicked, who had not shown mercy to the poor, "inasmuch as ye did it not to one of the least of these, ye did it not to me" (v. 45).

Now what stronger enforcement of this duty can be conceived, or is possible, than this, that Jesus Christ looks upon our kind and bountiful, or unkind and uncharitable, treatment of our needy neighbors as such a treatment of himself. If Christ himself was here upon earth and dwelt amongst us in a frail body, as he once did, and was in calamitous and needy circumstances, should not we be willing to supply him? Should we be apt to excuse ourselves from helping him? Should we not be willing to supply him, so that he might live free of distressing poverty? And if we did otherwise, should we not bring great guilt upon ourselves; might it not justly be very highly resented by God? Christ once was here in a frail body and stood in need of peoples' charity, and was maintained by it; Luke 8:2–3, "And certain women which had been healed of evil spirits and infirmities, Mary called Magdalene, out of whom went seven devils, and Joanna the wife of Chuza, Herod's steward, and Susanna and many others, which ministered unto him out of their substance." And so he still, in many of his members, needs the charity of others.

Third [*Mot.*] Consider that there is an absolute necessity of our complying with the difficult duties of religion. A giving to the poor in the manner and measure that the gospel prescribes is a difficult duty; i.e. 'tis very contrary to corrupt nature, and that covetousness and selfishness of which there is so much in the wicked heart of man. Man is naturally governed only by a principle of self-love, and 'tis a difficult thing, to corrupt nature, for us men, to deny themselves of their present interest, trusting in God to make it up to them.[6]

But how often has Christ told us the necessity of our doing difficult duties of religion: if we will be his disciples, then we must sell all, and take up our cross daily, to deny ourselves, to deny our own worldly profit and interest [Luke 16:24]. And if this duty seems hard and difficult to you, let not that be an objection with you against your doing of it; for you have taken up a quite a notion of things, if you expected to go to heaven without performing difficult duties, if you expected any other than to find the way to life a narrow way.

Fourth [*Mot.*] The Scripture teaches us that this very particular duty is necessary.[7] The Scripture teaches us this three ways.

1. In that the Scripture teaches that God will deal by us as we do by our fellow creatures in this particular; that with what measure we mete to others in this respect, God will measure to us again. This, the Scripture asserts both ways. It asserts that if we are of a merciful spirit, God will be merciful unto us; Matt. 5:7, "Blessed are the merciful, for they shall obtain mercy"; Ps. 18:25, "With the merciful thou wilt show thyself merciful." On the other hand, it tells us that if we ben't merciful, God will not be merciful unto us, and that all our pretenses to faith and a work of conversion won't avail us to obtain mercy unless we are merciful to them that are in want; Jas. 2:13–16, "For he shall have judgment without mercy, that hath showed no mercy; and mercy rejoiceth against judgment. What doth it profit, my brethren, though a man say he hath faith, and have not works? can faith save him? If a brother or sister be naked, and destitute of daily food, and one of you say unto them, Depart in peace, be you warmed and filled; notwithstanding ye give them not those things that are needful to the body; what doth it profit?"

2. This very thing is often mentioned in Scripture as an essential part of the character of a godly man; Ps. 37:21, "the righteous showeth mercy, and giveth"; and again, v. 26, "He is ever merciful, and lendeth"; and Ps. 112:5, "A good man showeth favor and lendeth"; and again, v. 9, "He hath dispersed, and given to the poor." So Prov. 14:31, "he that honoreth" God "hath mercy on the poor"; so Prov. 21:26; so in Is. 57:1, a

6. JE here excised: "Many find it a matter of great difficulty to trust God with a small matter of their estates."

7. JE here deletes: "to salvation."

righteous man and a merciful man are used as synonymous terms: "The righteous perisheth . . . the merciful men are taken away." So 'tis mentioned in the New Testament as a thing so essential that the contrary can't consist with a sincere love to God; I John 3:17–19, "But whoso hath this world's good, and seeth his brother have need, and shutteth up his bowels of compassion from him, how dwelleth the love of God in him? My little children, let us not love in word and in tongue; but in deed and in truth. And hereby we know that we are of the truth, and shall assure our hearts before him." So the apostle Paul, when he writes to the Corinthians and proposes their contributing for the supply of the poor saints, he tells 'em that he does it for a trial of their sincerity; II Cor. 8:8, "I speak to prove the sincerity of your love."

3. Another thing whereby the Scripture teaches us the necessity of this duty in order to salvation is that Christ teaches that judgment will be passed at the great day according to men's works in this respect. This, Christ teaches us in the account that he gives us of the day of judgment in Matt. 25, which is the most particular account of the proceedings of that day that we have in the whole Bible; Matt. 25:34–46,

> Then shall the King say unto them on his right hand, Come, ye blessed of my Father, inherit the kingdom prepared for you from the foundation of the world: for I was an hungered, and ye gave me meat: I was thirsty, and ye gave me drink: I was a stranger, and ye took me in. . . . Then shall the righteous answer him, saying, Lord, when saw we thee an hungered, and fed thee? or thirsty, and gave thee drink? . . . And the King shall answer and say unto them . . . Inasmuch as ye have done it unto one of the least of these my brethren, ye have done it unto me. Then shall he say also unto them on the left hand, Depart from me, ye cursed, into everlasting fire . . . for I was an hungered, and ye gave me no meat: I was thirsty, and ye gave me no drink: I was stranger, and ye took me not in. . . . Then shall they also answer him, saying, Lord, when saw we thee an hungered, or athirst, or a stranger . . . ? Then shall he answer them, saying, Verily I say unto you, Inasmuch as ye did it not to one of the least of these, ye did it not to me. And these shall go away into everlasting punishment: but the righteous into life eternal.

'Tis evident that Jesus Christ thus represented the proceedings and determinations of this great day, as turning upon this one point, of purpose and on design to lead us into this notion, and to fix it in us, that a charitable spirit and practice towards our brethren is necessary to salvation. Consider, in the

Fifth [*Mot.*]. [Fifth] place, what abundant encouragement the Word of God gives you, that you shall be no loser by your charity and bounty to them that are in want. As we have already observed, that there is scarce any one particular duty that is prescribed in the whole Bible so much insisted on as this, so there is scarce any that there is so many promises of reward made to it as to this duty. We could not desire more and greater promises; this virtue especially has the promises of this life, and that which is to come.

If we may believe the Scripture, when a man charitably gives to his neighbors in want, it is the giver that has the greatest advantage by it, greater than the receiver; Acts 20:35, "I have showed you all things, how that so laboring ye ought to support the weak, and to remember the words of the Lord Jesus, how he said, It is more blessed to give than to receive." He that gives bountifully is a happier man than he that receives bountifully; Prov. 14:21, "He that hath mercy on the poor, happy is he."

Many persons are ready to look upon what is bestowed to charitable uses as lost, but we ought not so to esteem it. We ought not to look upon it as lost, because it benefits those to whom it is given, whom we ought to love as ourselves; and not only so, but 'tis not lost to us if we give any credit to the gospel. See the advice that Solomon gives; Eccles. 11:1, "Cast thy bread upon the waters," says he, "for thou shalt find it after many days." By casting our bread upon the waters, Solomon means giving of it to the poor, as appears by the next words: "give a portion to seven and also to eight." Waters are sometimes in Scripture put for peoples and multitudes.

What strange advice would this seem to many, to cast their bread upon the waters, which would seem to them like throwing of it away! What more direct method to lose our bread, than to go to throw it into the sea? But the wise man tells us, "No, 'tis not lost; you shall find again after many days." It is not sunk, but you commit it to providence; you commit it to the winds and the waves, but, however, it will come about to you, and you shall find it again. Though it should be many days first, yet you shall find it at last, at a time when you most need it.

He that gives to the poor, lends to God, and God is not one of them that won't pay again what is lent to him. If you lend to God, you commit it into faithful hands; Prov. 19:17, "He that hath pity on the poor lendeth to the Lord, and that which he hath given will he pay him again." And God won't only pay you again, but he'll pay you with great increase; Luke 6:38,

"Give and it shall be given you in good measure, pressed down, and shaken together, and running over."

Men don't account that lost that they let out to use; but what is bestowed in charity is lent to the Lord, and he pays with great increase; Is. 32:8, "The liberal deviseth liberal things, and by liberal things shall he stand." Here,

1. If you give what you bestow with a spirit of true charity, you shall be rewarded in what is infinitely more valuable than what you give. For parting with a small part of your earthly substance, you shall be rewarded with eternal riches in heaven; Matt. 10:42, "whosoever shall give to drink unto one of these little ones a cup of cold water only in the name of a disciple, verily I say unto you, he shall in no wise lose his reward."

A giving to our needy brethren is in Scripture called a laying up treasure in heaven in bags that wax not old; Luke 12:33, "Sell what ye have, and give alms; provide yourselves bags that wax not old, a treasure in the heavens that faileth not, where no thief approacheth, nor moth corrupteth." Men, when they have laid up their money in their chests, don't look upon it that they have thrown it away; but on the contrary, it is laid up safe. Much less is treasure thrown away when it is laid up in heaven. What is laid up there is laid up much safer than what is locked up in cabinets. You can't lay up treasure so on earth but that it may be liable to be stolen or otherwise to fail; but there, no thief approacheth nor moth corrupteth. It is committed to God's care, and he'll keep it safe for you; and when you die, then you shall receive it with infinite increase. For a part of your earthly substance thus bestowed, you shall receive heavenly riches in which you may live in the greatest fullness, honor, and happiness to all eternity, and shall never be in want of anything. For feeding with some of your bread those that cannot recompense you, you shall be rewarded at the resurrection, and eat bread in the kingdom of God; Luke 14:13–15, "when thou makest a feast, call the poor, the maimed, the lame, and the blind: and thou shalt be blessed; for they cannot recompense thee: for thou shalt be recompensed at the resurrection of the just. And when one of them that sat at meat with him heard these things, he said unto him, Blessed is he that shall eat bread in the kingdom of God."

2. If you give to the needy only in the exercise of a moral virtue, you won't be in the way to lose by it, but greatly to gain in your temporal interest. They that give in the exercise of a gracious charity, they are in the way to be gainers both here and hereafter; and those that give, in the exercise of a moral bounty and liberality, they have many temporal promises made to them. We learn by the Word of God that they are in the way

to be prospered in their outward affairs. Ordinarily, such don't lose by it; but there is such a blessing attends their concerns, that they are paid double for it; Prov. 11:24–25, "There is that scattereth, and yet increaseth; there is that withholdeth more than is meet, and it tendeth to poverty. The liberal soul shall be made fat; and he that watereth, shall be watered also himself"; Prov. 28:27, "He that giveth to the poor shall not lack."

When men give to the needy, they do, as it were, sow seed for a crop. Men, when they sow their seed, they seem to throw it away; but they don't look upon it [as] thrown away, because, though they don't expect the same again, yet they expect a great deal more as the fruit of it. And though it ben't certain that they shall have a crop, yet they are willing to run the venture of it; for that is the ordinary way wherein men obtain increase. So it is when persons give to the poor. Though the promises of gaining in our outward affairs are not absolute, yet 'tis as much the ordinary consequence of it as men's having increase for their sowing their seed. 'Tis compared to sowing seed in this respect in Eccles. 11:6, "In the morning sow thy seed, in the evening withhold not thine hand: thou knowest not whether shall prosper, either this or that, or whether they shall both be alike good." By "withholding thine hand," the wise man means from giving to the poor, for he was speaking of that in vv. 1–2: "Thou knowest not whether shall prosper, either this or that, or whether they shall both be alike good," which intimates that giving to the poor is as likely a way to obtain prosperity and increase, as sowing seed in a field.

The husbandman don't look upon his seed [as] lost that he sows in his field, but is glad that he has opportunity to sow. It don't grieve him that he has land to be sowed; but [he] rejoices in it. For the like reason, we should not be grieved that we find needy people to bestow our charity upon; for this is as much an opportunity for the obtaining increase as the other. Some may think this a strange doctrine, and 'tis to be said that not many will so far believe as to give to the poor with as much cheerfulness as they sow their ground. But, however, 'tis the very doctrine of the Word of God; 'tis easy with God; II Cor. 9:6–8, "He which soweth sparingly shall reap also sparingly; and he which soweth bountifully shall reap also bountifully. Every man according as he purposeth in his heart, so let him give; not grudgingly, or of necessity: for God loveth a cheerful giver. And God is able to make all grace abound toward you; that ye, always having all sufficiency in all things, may abound to every good work."

Many men but do but little consider how their prosperity in their outward affairs, on the contrary, depends upon providence. There are a thousand turns of providence that their affairs are liable to, whereby God may either add to their outward substance, or diminish from it: a great deal more than they are ordinarily called to give to their neighbors.

How easy is it with God to diminish what they possess by sickness in their families, or by drought, or frost, or mildew, or vermin, or unfortunate accidents, or by entanglement in their affairs, or disappointments in their business. And how easy to increase them by suitable season or health and strength, giving them fair opportunities for promoting their interest in their dealings with men, by conducting them by his providence so that they may attain their design, and innumerable other ways that might be mentioned. How often is it that only one turn of providence in a man's affairs either adds to him or diminishes from him, more than he would need to give to the poor in a whole year! And God has told us that this is the way to have his blessing attending our affairs; thus in the text, v. 10: "Thou shalt surely give him, and thine heart shall not be grieved, when thou givest unto him, because that for this thing the Lord thy God shall bless thee in all thy works, and in all that thou puttest thine hand unto"; and Prov. 22:9, "He that hath a bountiful eye, shall be blessed."

It is a remarkable evidence how little many men realize the things of religion, whatever they pretend: either how little they realize that the Scripture is the Word of God, or, if it be, that he speaks true, that notwithstanding all the promises made to bounty to the poor in his Word, yet men are so backward to such duties, and are so afraid to trust God with a little of their estates. But observation may confirm the same thing that the Word of God teaches in this. It may be that God in his providence generally smiles upon and prospers those men that are of a liberal, charitable, bountiful spirit.[8]

Sixth Mot. God has threatened to follow them with his curse that are uncharitable to the poor; as Prov 28:27, "He that giveth to the poor shall not lack: but he that hideth his eyes shall have many a curse." 'Tis said that [he] "hideth his eyes" because this is the way of uncharitable persons: they hide their eyes from seeing the wants of their neighbor. A charitable person, whose heart disposes him to bounty and liberality, will be quicksighted to discern the needs of others. They won't be at any

8. The next sentence reads, "I propose to assert some further motives, and to answer those objections that are common against this duty, at another time, if God gives the opportunity." Fourteen blank lines follow. This ends the second preaching unit; JE begins the third unit with a recitation of the text, a recapitulation of the doctrine, a brief mention of the three propositions, and a reminder that he is now engaged in an exhortation from the doctrine.

difficulty to find out who is in want; they'll see objects enough of their charity, let 'em go where they will.

But, on the contrary, he that is of a niggardly spirit, so that it goes against the grain to give anything, they'll be always at a loss for objects for their charity. They'll excuse themselves with that, that they don't find anyone to give to; they hide their eyes and won't see their neighbor's wants. And if a particular object presents [himself], they won't very readily see his circumstances; they are a long while a-being convinced that he is an object of charity. He hides his eyes, and 'tis not an easy thing to make him sensible of the distresses and necessities of his neighbor, or at least that they are such that he ought to give him any great matter. Another man, that is of a more bountiful spirit, sees 'em very easily. They are very unapt to see their obligations to this duty; 'tis because they are of that sort spoken of here by the wise man: "he hides his eyes." Men will readily see where they are willing to see, but where they hate to see, they will hide their eyes.

God says such an one as hides his eyes in this case shall have many a curse. Such an one is in the way to be cursed in soul and body, in both his spiritual and temporal affairs. We have shown already how those that are charitable to the poor are in the way of being blessed; there are so many promises of God's blessing, that we may look upon it as much the way to be blessed in our outward concerns as sowing seed in a field is the way to have increase. A being closed and uncharitable is as much the way to be followed with a curse as a being charitable is to be followed with a blessing. Withholding more than is meet tends as much to poverty, as scattering tends to increasing (Prov. 11:24).

Therefore, if you withhold more than is meet, you will cross your own disposition, and will frustrate your own end. What you seek by withholding from your neighbor is your own temporal interest and outward estate. But if you ben't atheistical, so as not to believe the Scripture to be the Word of God, you must believe that you can't take a more direct course to lose and be crossed and cursed in your temporal interest than this. Consider,

Seventh [*Mot.*], you know not what calamitous and necessitous circumstances you yourself or your children may be in. It may be you are ready to bless yourself in your heart, as though there was no danger of your being brought into calamitous and distressing circumstances; there is at present no prospect of it, and you hope you shall be well able to provide for your children. But then, you little consider what a shifting, changing, uncertain world you live in, and how often it has been so upon earth, that men have been reduced from the greatest prosperity to the greatest extremity, and how often the children of the rich have been reduced to pinching want. This is the advice that the wise man gives us; Eccles. 11:1–2, "Cast thy bread upon the waters. . . . Give a portion to seven, and also to eight; for thou knowest not what evil shall be upon the earth." Thou knowest not what calamitous circumstances thou mayest be in thyself, here on earth, in this changeable, uncertain world.

You know not what circumstances you or your children may be brought into by captivity or other unthought of providences. Providence governs all things. You may trust, it may be, to your own wisdom to uphold your prosperity, but you can't alter what God determines and orders in providence, as in the words immediately following the forementioned text; Eccles. 11:2–3, "Give a portion to seven, and also to eight; for thou knowest not what evil shall be upon the earth. If the clouds be full of rain, they empty themselves upon the earth: and if the tree fall toward the south, or toward the north, in the place where the tree falleth, there it shall be." I.e. you can't alter the determinations of providence. You may trust to your own wisdom {to uphold your prosperity}, but if God has ordered adversity, it shall come. Like when the clouds are full {of rain}, so what is in the womb of providence shall surely come to pass. And as providence casts the tree, whether toward the south or toward the north, whether for prosperity or adversity, there it shall be, for all that you can do, agreeable to what the wise man observes; [Eccles.] 7:13, "Consider the work of God: for who can make that straight, which he hath made crooked?"

This consideration, that you don't know what calamity and necessity you may be in yourself, or your children, tends very powerfully to enforce this duty several ways.

1. This may put you upon considering how your heart would be if it should be so. If it should be so that you or some of your children should be brought into such circumstances as these and those your neighbors are in, how grievous it would be to you! Now, it may be you say of this and the other poor neighbors that they can do well enough; if they do pinch a little, they can live. You can now make light of their difficulties. But if providence should so order it that you or your child should be brought into the same circumstances, would you make light of 'em then? Would you not use another sort of language about it? Would you not think that your case was such as needed your neighbor's being kind to you; would you not think that they ought to be ready to help you, and would you not take it hard if you saw a contrary spirit among them, and saw that they made light of your difficulties?

If one of your own children should be brought to poverty, by captivity or otherwise, how would your heart have stood affected in such a case? If you should hear that some should take pity on it and be very liberal and bountiful to it, would you not think they did very well in so doing? Should you be at all ready to accuse 'em of folly, or lavishness and profuseness, that they should go to give so much to it?

2. If there ever should be such a time, your kindness to others now will be but a laying up against such a time. If you yourself should be brought to calamity and necessity, then you will find what you have given in charity to others laying ready in store for you. "Cast thy bread upon the waters, and you shall find it after many days," says the wise man [Eccles. 11:1]. But when shall we find it, he tells us in the next verse: "Give a portion to seven, and also to eight; for thou knowest not what evil shall be upon the earth." Then is the time when you shall find it: when the day of evil comes, you shall find your bread again, that you have cast upon the waters. When you want it most and stand in the greatest necessity of it, God will keep it for you against such a time. When other bread fails them, God will bring to you the bread that you formerly have cast upon the waters, so that you shall not famish. "He that gives to the poor shall not lack" [Prov. 28:27].

A giving to the needy is like laying up against winter, against a time of calamity. 'Tis the best way of laying up for themselves, and laying up for their children. Children in a time of need very often find their father's bread that they have cast upon the waters; Ps. 37:25, "I have been young and now am old, yet have I not seen the righteous forsaken, nor his seed begging bread." Why? What is the reason of it? It follows in the next verse: "He is ever merciful, and lendeth; and his seed is blessed."

Whether the time will ever come or not that we or our children shall be in pinching and distressing want of bread, yet, doubtless, evil will be on the earth. We shall have our times of calamity, wherein we shall stand in great need of God's pity and help, if not that of our fellow creatures. And God has promised that at such a time, he that has been of a charitable spirit and practice shall find help; Ps. 41:1–2, "Blessed is he that considereth the poor: the Lord will deliver him in time of trouble. The Lord will preserve him, and keep him alive; and he shall be blessed upon the earth: and thou wilt not deliver him unto the will of his enemies." Such as have been merciful and liberal to others in their distress, God won't forget it, but will so order it that they shall have help when they are in distress; yea, their children shall reap the fruit of it in the day of trouble.

3. God hath threatened uncharitable persons, that if ever they come to be in calamity and distress they shall be left helpless; Prov. 21:13, "Whoso

stoppeth his ears at the cry of the poor, he shall cry himself, and not be heard."

[III.] I proceed now to answer some objections that are sometimes made against this duty.

First Obj. I am in a natural condition, and if I should give considerable to the poor, I should not do it with a right spirit, and so should get nothing by it.

Ans. 1. We have already shown that a temporal blessing is promised to a moral bounty and liberality. This is the way to be prospered and blessed in your affairs, as much as sowing seed is the way to increase. We find many promises of temporal blessings to moral virtues in Scripture, as to diligence in our business, justice in our dealings, faithfulness, temperance. So there are many blessings promised to bounty and liberality.

[*Ans.*] 2. You may as well make the same objection against any other duty of religion. You may as well make the same objection against keeping the sabbath, against prayer, or going to meeting, or against doing anything at all in religion; for you, while in a natural condition, don't do it with a right spirit. If you say you do these duties because God has commanded and required them of you, and you shall sin greatly if you neglect them, you shall increase your guilt, and so expose yourself the more to damnation and to a greater punishment, the same may be said of the neglect of this duty as those. It is as much required and commanded as those, and the neglect of it as provoking to God.

If you say that you read, and pray, and come to meeting because that is the appointed way for you to seek conversion in; so is bounty to the poor, as much as that. The appointed way for us to seek God's grace, it is a way of the performance of all known duties, of which giving to the poor is one, as much known and as necessary as reading, and {praying, and coming to meeting}. Showing mercy to the poor does as much belong to the appointed way of seeking salvation as any other duty whatever. And, therefore, this is the way that Daniel directed Nebuchadnezzar to seek mercy; Dan. 4:27, "Wherefore, O king, let my counsel be acceptable to thee, and break off thy sins by righteousness, and thine iniquities by showing mercy to the poor."

Second Obj. If I am liberal and bountiful, I shall only make a righteousness of it, and so it will do me more hurt than good. To this I say,

[*Ans.*] 1. The same answer may be made to this as to the last objection, viz. that you may as well make the same objection against doing any religious or moral duty at all. If this be a sufficient objection against deeds of charity, then 'tis a sufficient objection against your ever praying to

God; for nothing is more common than for persons to make a righteousness of their prayers. And so 'tis a good objection against your keeping the sabbath, or attending any public worship, or ever reading in the Bible; for all these things, you are in danger of making a righteousness of. Yea, if the objection be good against deeds of charity, then 'tis as good against acts of justice. And you may neglect to speak the truth, and may neglect to pay your debts, may neglect acts of common humanity; for all these things, you are in danger of making a righteousness of.

So that if the objection be good, you may throw up all religion, and live like a heathen or atheist, and may be a thief, and a robber, a fornicator, and adulterer, and murderer, and commit all the sins that you can think of, lest if you should do otherwise, you should make a righteousness of it.

[*Ans.*] 2. Your objection carries it thus, that it is not best for you to do as God commands and counsels you to do. We find many commands in Scripture to be charitable to the poor; the Bible is full of 'em; and you ben't excepted from those commands. God don't make any exception of any particular kinds of persons that are especially in danger of making a righteousness of what they do; and God often counsels and directs persons to this duty. Now, will you presume to say that God has not directed you to the best way? He has advised you to do thus, but you don't think it is best for you but would do you more hurt than good if you should do it. You think there is other counsel better than God's, and that 'tis the best way for you to go contrary to God's command.

Third Obj. I have given to the poor in times past and never found myself the better for it. I have heard ministers preach that giving to the poor was the way to be blessed and prospered, but I don't perceive that I have any more prospered than I was before; yea, I have met with many misfortunes and crosses and disappointments in my affairs since. Yea, it may be, some will say, that very year or soon after the very time I had been giving to the poor, hoping to be blessed for it, I met with great losses, and things went hardly with me. And therefore I don't find what I hear preached, about giving to the poor being the way to be blessed and prospered, agreeable to my experience.

To this objection, I would answer several things.

[*Ans.*] 1. It may be you looked out for the fulfillment of the promise too soon, before you had fulfilled the condition. As, particularly,

(1) It may be, you have been so sparing and grudging in your kindness to the poor as that what you have done has been rather a discovery of a covetous, niggardly spirit than of any bounty or liberality.

The promises ben't made to every man that gives anything at all to the poor, let it be never so little, and let it be after what manner soever given. You mistook the promises if you understood 'em so. A man may give something to the poor and yet be entitled to no promise, either temporal or spiritual. The promises are made to mercy, and bounty, and liberality; it is to this that the promises are made, in the text and everywhere throughout the Bible. A man may give something and yet be so niggardly and grudging in it that what he gives may be, as the Apostle calls it, a matter of covetousness [II Cor. 9:5]. What he does may be more a manifestation of the man's covetousness and closeness than anything else. Now, there are no promises made to men's expressing their covetousness.

[(2)] It may be, what you gave was not freely, but, as it were, of necessity. It was grudgingly; your heart was grieved when you gave. And if you gave once or twice what was considerable, yet that don't answer the rule. It may be, for all that, in the general course of your life it has been very far from being true of you that you have been a person that has been kind and liberal to your neighbors. You thought perhaps that because you once or twice gave a few shillings to the poor that you then stood entitled to the promises of being blessed in all your concerns, and increasing, and being established by liberal things, though in the general you have lived in a very faulty neglect of that duty.

You make objections from experience before you have made any trial. To give once or twice or thrice, though you give considerably, is not to make trial. You can't make any trial unless you become a liberal person, or so as that you may truly be said to be of a liberal, bountiful practice. Let one that is truly such an one, and has been in the course of his life, tell what he has found.

[*Ans.* 2.] If you have been liberal to the poor and have met with calamities since, yet how can you tell how much greater calamities and losses you might have met with if you had been other wise? You say you have met with crosses, and disappointments, and frowns. You mistook the matter if you expected to meet with no trouble in the world because you have given to the poor. Though there be many and great promises made to the liberal, yet God has nowhere promised that they shall not find this world a world of trouble. It will be so to all; man is born to sorrow, and must expect no other than to meet with sorrow here.

But how can you tell how much greater sorrow you might have met with if you had been closed and unmerciful to the poor? How can you tell how much greater losses you might have met, and how much more vexation and trouble you might have been followed with? Has never none met with greater frowns in their outward affairs than you have done?

[*Ans.*] 3. How can you tell what blessings God has yet in reserve for you if you do but continue in well-doing? Though God has promised great blessings to liberality to the poor, yet he has not limited himself as to the time of bestowment. If you han't yet seen any evident fruit of your kindness to the poor, yet the time may come when you may see it remarkably, at a time when you most stand in need of it. You cast your bread upon the waters, and looked for it, and expected to find it again presently. And sometimes, it is so; but this is not promised. 'Tis promised, thou shalt find [it] again after many days.

God knows how to choose a time for you better than you yourself. You should wait his time. If you go on in well-doing, God may bring it to you when you stand most in need. It may be there is some winter a-coming, some day of trouble, and God keeps your bread for you against that time; and then, God may give you good measure, and pressed down, and shaken together, and running over. We must trust in God's word for the bestowment of the promised reward, whether we can see in what manner it is done or no. Pertinent to the present purpose are those words of the wise man in Eccles. 11:4, "He that observeth the winds shall not sow; and he that regardeth the clouds shall not reap." The wise man is there in the context speaking of charity to the poor and comparing of it to sowing seed, and advises us to trust providence for success in that, as we do in sowing seed. He that regards the wind and clouds, to prognosticate from thence to prosper his seed, and won't trust providence with his seed, is not like to sow, nor to have breadcorn; so he that will not trust providence for the reward of his charity to the poor is like to go without the blessing. And then follows his[9] advice in v. 6: "In the morning sow thy seed, and in the evening withhold not thine hand: for thou knowest not whether shall prosper, either this or that, or whether they both shall be alike good."

I conclude with the words of the Apostle; Gal. 6:9, "And let us not be weary in well-doing: for in due season we shall reap, if we faint not." Then think you have not reaped yet; but whether you have or no, go on still in giving and doing good, and if you do so you shall reap in due time. God only knows the due time, the best time, for you to reap in.[1]

9. I.e. the wise man's.

1. Here ends the third preaching unit. Ten blank lines follow. JE recapitulates the text, doctrine, and major heads covered, including the three objections and answers, at the start of the fourth and final unit.

Fourth [*Obj.*] Again, some may object against charity to such or such particular persons, that they are not obliged to give 'em [charity], for though they are [in] need yet they ben't in extremity. 'Tis true, they meet with difficulty, but yet not so but that they can live, though they suffer some hardships.

Ans. It don't answer [the] rules of Christian charity only to relieve those that are in extremity, as might be abundantly shown. But I shall at this time mention but two things as an evidence of it.

1. We are commanded to love and treat one another as brethren; I Pet. 3:8, "have compassion one of another, love as brethren, be pitiful." Now is it a brotherly part for brethren to refuse to help one another, and to do anything for each other's comfort and for the relief of each other's difficulties, only when they are in extremity? Does it not become brothers and sisters to have a more friendly disposition one towards another than this comes to, and to be ready to be compassionate to one another under difficulties, though they ben't extreme?

The rule of the gospel is that when we see our brother under any difficulty or burden we should be ready to bear the burden with him; Gal. 6:2, "Bear ye one another's burdens, and so fulfill the law of Christ." So we are commanded, "by love" to "serve one another" (Gal. 5:13).

The Christian spirit will make us apt to sympathize with our neighbor when we see him under any difficulty; Rom. 12:15, "Rejoice with them that do rejoice, and weep with them that weep." When our neighbor is under difficulty, he is afflicted; and we ought to have such a spirit of love to him that we should be afflicted with him in his affliction. And if we ought to be afflicted, then it will follow that we ought to be ready to relieve, because if we are afflicted with him, we relieve ourselves in relieving him; his relief is so far our relief as his affliction is our affliction. Christianity teaches [us] to be afflicted in our neighbor's affliction; and nature teaches us to relieve ourselves when afflicted.

We should behave ourselves one towards another as brethren that are fellow-travelers, for we are pilgrims and strangers here on earth, and are on a journey. Now, if brethren are on a journey together, if one meets with difficulty in the way, does it not become the rest to help him not only in the extremity of broken bones or the like? If the provision for the journey falls short, it becomes his fellow-travelers to afford him supply out of their stores, and not to be over nice, and exact, and fearful, lest they should give him too much; for 'tis but provision for a journey, and it makes no odds when they get to their journey's end.

2. That we should only relieve our neighbor when in extremity is not agreeable to that rule of loving our neighbor as ourselves. Though that rule don't imply that we should love our neighbor to the same degree as we love ourselves, yet it implies that our love towards our neighbor should work in the same manner and express itself in the ways as our love to ourselves. We are very sensible of our own difficulties; we should also be ready to be sensible of their difficulties. We, from our love to ourselves, when we are under difficulties and suffer hardships, are apt to be concerned for our relief, to seek relief, and lay ourselves out for it. And, as we would love our neighbor {as ourselves}, we ought in like manner to be concerned when our neighbor is under difficulty and seek their relief.

Fifth Obj. Some may object against charity to a particular object, that he is an ill sort of person and has been injurious to them. He don't deserve that people should be kind to him; he is of a very ill temper; he is of an ungrateful spirit and is an ill sort of man upon other accounts; and, particularly, he had not deserved well of me, but has treated me ill, has been injurious, and has a spirit against me.

Ans. We are obliged to relieve persons in want, notwithstanding those things, both by the general and particular rules of God's Word.

1. We are obliged to do so by general rules. I shall mention two.

(1) That of loving our neighbors as ourselves. A man may be our neighbor, though an ill sort of man and our enemy, as Christ himself teaches us by his discourse with the lawyer (Luke 10:25–37). A certain lawyer came to Christ, and asked him what he should do to inherit eternal life. Christ asked him how it was "written in the law." He answers, "Thou shalt love the Lord thy God with all thy heart, and with all thy soul, and with all thy strength, and with all thy mind; and thy neighbor as thyself" [10:27]. Christ tells him, if he does thus, he shall live. But then the lawyer asks him who is his neighbor, because it was a received doctrine among the Pharisees that no man was their neighbor but their friends and those of the same people and religion. Christ answers him by parable, or story, of "a certain man" who "went down from Jerusalem to Jericho, and fell among thieves, which stripped him of his raiment, and wounded him, and departed, leaving him half dead" [10:30]. {After a priest and a Levite passed by the man on the other side,} "a certain Samaritan . . . came where he was: and when he saw him, he had compassion on him, and went to him . . . and brought him to an inn, and took care of him" [10:33–34]. And then Christ asks him, "Who was neighbor unto him that fell among the thieves?" [10:36].

Christ proposed in such a manner that the lawyer could not help owning that the Samaritan did well in relieving the poor Jew: that he did the duty of a neighbor to him. Now there was an inveterate enmity between the Jews and the Samaritans. They hated one another more than any nation in the world; and the Samaritans were a people exceeding troublesome to the Jews.

But yet, we see, Christ teaches us that the Jews ought to do that part of neighbors to the Samaritans, i.e. to love 'em as themselves, for it was that Christ was speaking of. And the consequence was plain: if the Samaritans were neighbors to the distressed Jew, then the Jews by a parity of reason are {neighbors to the distressed Samaritan}. If the Samaritan did well, did as he ought to, in relieving a Jew that was his enemy, then the Jews would do well and as they ought to do in relieving the Samaritans, their enemies.

That which I particularly observe is that Christ here plainly teaches that our enemies, those that abuse and injure us, are our neighbors, and therefore come under that rule of loving our neighbor as ourselves.

[(2)] Another general rule that obliges us to it is that wherein we are commanded to love one another as Christ has loved us; we have it [in] John 13:34, "A new commandment I give unto you, That ye love one another; as I have loved you, that ye also love one another." Christ calls it a new commandment with respect to that old commandment of the Lord, of loving our neighbor as ourselves. This, of loving our neighbor as Christ has loved us, implies something further in it than that. And 'tis, with respect to that, a new commandment, as it opens our duty to us in a new manner and in a further degree than that did. We must not only love our neighbor as ourselves, but as Christ hath loved us. We have the same again [in] John 15:12, "This is my commandment, That ye love one another, as I have loved you."

Now the meaning of this is not that we should love one another to the same degree that Christ {loved us}, though there ought to be a proportion, considering our nature and capacity, but that we should exercise our love one to another in like manner. As, for instance, Christ has loved us so as to be willing to deny himself and to suffer greatly for our help, so should we be willing to deny {ourselves, and to suffer greatly to help others}. Christ loved us, and showed us great kindness, though we were far below him; so should {we be willing to love others, and show them kindness, though they be below us}. Christ denied himself to help us, though we are not able to recompense him; so we should be willing to lay out ourselves to help our neighbor freely, expecting nothing again.

Christ loved us, and was kind to us, and was willing to relieve us, though we were very hateful persons, of an evil disposition, not deserving any good, but deserving only to be hated, and treated with indignation; so we should be willing to be kind to those that are an ill sort of person, of a hateful disposition, and that are very undeserving. Christ loved us, and laid himself out to relieve us, though we were his enemies, hated him, had an ill spirit towards him, had treated him ill; so, as we would love Christ as he hath loved us, should {we love those who are our enemies, hate us, have an ill spirit toward us, and have treated us ill}.

2. We are obliged to by many particular rules. We are particularly required to be kind to the unthankful and to the evil, therein to follow the example of our heavenly Father, who causes his sun to rise {on the just and the unjust [Matt. 5:45]}: not only to be kind to them that are so to us, but to them that abuse us, to love our enemies, [and] do good to them that hate and that despitefully use us. I need not mention the particular places [where it is said that] we should relieve wicked men, [such as] Ezek. 16:49, [where] Sodom is condemned, and Dan. 4:27, [where Daniel advises] Nebuchadnezzar.[2]

Not but that when persons are virtuous and pious persons, and of a grateful and thankful disposition, and are friendly to us, they are the more the objects for our charity for it; and our obligation to kindness to 'em is the greater. But yet if they are the contrary, that don't make 'em not fit objects of our charity or set us free from obligations to kindness to 'em.

Sixth [*Obj.*] Some may object from their own circumstances, that they have nothing to spare; they han't more than enough for themselves. To this, I say,

[*Ans.*] 1. That it must doubtless be allowed to be so in some cases that persons by reason of their own circumstances are not obliged to give to others. As, for instance, if there be a contribution for the poor, if those that are the poor themselves, are as much in need as those that [the contribution is to be] given to, it savors of a ridiculous pride [and] vanity in them to contribute with others, to give to those that are not more needy than they. It savors of a proud desire to conceal their own circumstances and an affectation of having them accounted above what in truth they are. But,

[*Ans.*] 2. There is scarce anybody but what may make this objection, as they may mean by it. There is nobody but what may say he has not more than enough for himself, as he may mean by enough. He may mean that

2. JE only sketched in key words for this last sentence; bracketed phrases are interpolations.

he has not more that he desires, or more than he can dispose of to his own advantage, or not so much but that if he had anything less he should look upon himself worse out than he is now. He'll own that he could live if he had less, but then he'll say he could not live so well.

Rich men may say they han't more than enough for themselves, as they may mean by it. They need it all, they may say, to support their honor and dignity proper for the place and degree they stand in. Those that are poor, [to] be sure, will say they han't too much for themselves. And those that are the middle sort will say they han't too much for themselves. The rich, they'll say {they han't too much for themselves}. And so there will be none found to give to the poor.

[*Ans.*] 3. We in many cases may, by the rule of the gospel, be obliged to give to others when we can't without suffering ourselves: as if our neighbor's difficulties and necessities are much greater than ours and we see that they are not otherwise like to be relieved, we should be willing to suffer with 'em and to take part of their burden upon ourselves. Or else, how is that rule fulfilled of bearing one another's burdens? If we are never obliged to relieve others' burdens but only when we can do it without burdening ourselves, then how do we bear our neighbor's burdens, when we bear no burden at all? Though we han't a superfluity, yet the case may be so that we may be obliged to give for the relief of others that are in much greater necessity, as appears by that rule; Luke 3:11, "He that hath two coats, let him impart to him that hath none; and he that hath meat, let him do likewise."

Yea, the case might be so that they that are very poor might be obliged to give to the relief of others in much greater distress than they. If there was no other way of their relief, those that have the lightest burden might be obliged still to take some of his neighbor's burden, to make his burden more supportable. A brother may be obliged to help a brother in extremity, though they are both very much in want. The Apostle commends the Macedonian Christians, that they were liberal to their brethren, though they were in deep poverty themselves; II Cor. 8:1–2, "Moreover, brethren, we do you to wit of the grace of God bestowed on the churches of Macedonia: how that in a great trial of affliction, the abundance of their joy, and their deep poverty, abounded to the riches of their liberality."

[*Ans.*] 4. Those that han't too much for themselves are willing to spare seed to sow that they may have some hereafter. They, it may be, need that which they scatter on the field and seem to throw away. They need it for bread for their families, but yet they will spare seed to sow that they may provide for the future and may have increase. But we have already shown that giving to the poor is in Scripture compared {to sowing seed}, and is as much the way to increase. It don't tend to poverty, but the contrary. It is not indeed the way to diminish our substance, but to increase it. All the difficulties in this matter is in trusting God with what we give, in trusting his promises; if men could but trust his faithfulness to his promises, they would give freely.

Seventh [*Obj.*] Some may object, concerning a particular person, that they don't certainly know whether he be an object of charity or no. They ben't perfectly acquainted with his circumstances; they don't know what sort of man he is; they don't know whether he be in want, as he pretends, or, if he be, they don't know how he came to be in want, whether it was not by his own idleness, or whether he was not a spendthrift. They argue that they ben't obliged till they certainly know.

Ans. 1. This is Nabal's objection, for which he was greatly condemned in Scripture. In I Sam. 25, David in his exiled state came and begged relief of Nabal. Nabal objected, as in vv. 10–11: "Who is David? and who is the son of Jesse? there be many servants nowadays that break away every man from his master. Shall I then take my bread, and my water, and my flesh that I have killed for my shearers, and give it unto men, whom I know not whence they be?" His objection was that David was a stranger to him. He did not know who he was nor what his circumstances were. He did not know but he was a runaway; and he was not obliged to go to support and harbor a runaway: "shall I then take my bread, and my water, and my flesh that I have killed for my shearers, and give it unto men, whom I know not whence they be?" He objected [that] he did not know that he was a proper object of charity; he did not know but he was very much the contrary.

But Abigail no way countenanced his behavior herein, but greatly condemned it. She calls him a man of Belial, and [says] that he was as his name was: "Nabal was his name, and folly was with him" [v. 25]. Her behavior was very contrary to his, and she is greatly commended for it; the Holy Ghost tells us in that chapter, v. 3, that "she was a woman of a good understanding." And God exceedingly frowned on Nabal's behavior here, as we are informed; we are told that about "ten days after God smote Nabal," that "he died" (25:38).

This story is doubtless told us partly for that end, to discountenance an over-scrupulousness as to the object on whom we bestow our charity, and a making merely that an objection against kindness to, and charity to, others, that we don't certainly know their circumstances.

'Tis true, when we have opportunity to come to be certainly acquainted with their circumstances, 'tis well to improve [it]; and to be influenced in a measure by probability in such cases is not to be condemned. But yet 'tis better to give to several that are not objects of charity, than to send away empty one that is.

Ans. 2. We are commanded to be kind to strangers, whom we know not nor their circumstances. It is commanded in many places, but I shall mention but one at this time; and that is that in Heb. 13:2, "Be not forgetful to entertain strangers; for thereby some have entertained angels unawares." By strangers there, the Apostle means one that we don't know and whose circumstances we don't know, as is evident by these words: "for thereby some have entertained angels unawares." Those that entertained angels unawares did not know the persons they entertained, nor their circumstances; else how could it be unawares?

Eighth [*Obj.*] Some may say they ben't obliged to give to the poor till they ask: "If any man is in necessity, let him come and make known his straits to me, and it will be time enough for me to give then. Or if he needs a contribution let him come and ask; I don't know that the congregation or church are obliged to relieve persons till they ask relief."

Ans. 1. 'Tis surely most charitable to relieve the needy in that way wherein we shall do them the greatest kindness. Now 'tis certain that we shall do 'em a greater kindness by inquiring into their circumstances and relieving of 'em without putting of 'em upon begging. There is none of us all, but that if it were our case, we would look upon it so. We should think it more kind in our neighbors to inquire into our circumstances and help us of their own accord.

To put upon begging in order to relief is, as the times are, a real difficulty; and we should, any of us, look upon it so. It is more charitable, more brotherly, more becoming Christians and the disciples of Jesus, to do it without. I think it is self-evident, and needs no proof.

[*Ans.*] 2. This is not agreeable to the character of the liberal man given us in Scripture, viz. that he devises liberal things; Is. 32:8, "But the liberal man deviseth liberal things." That is not to devise liberal things: to neglect all liberality till the poor come a-begging to us. But to inquire and contrive to find out who stand in need of our charity, and to contrive to relieve 'em in that way that shall do 'em the greatest kindness: that is to devise liberal things.

[*Ans.*] 3. We should not commend a man for doing so to his own brother. If a man had an own brother and sister in want, under great straits, and he was well able to supply him, but should say, "If he or she wants anything, let 'em come and ask, and I will give him," we should hardly think such an one behaved like a brother. But, as I observed before, Christians are commanded to love as brethren: to look upon one another as brethren in Christ, and to treat one another as such.

[*Ans.*] 4. We should commend any other people for taking the contrary method. If we should hear or read of any people that were so charitable, and took such care of the poor, and were so concerned that none that might suffer among 'em that were proper objects of charity, that they were wont diligently to inquire into the circumstances of others, to find out who [were in] need, and liberally supplied them of their own accord: I say, if one should hear or read of such a people, would it not appear well to us? Should not we commend 'em? Should we not have the better thought of that people, upon that account?

Ninth Obj. He has brought himself to want by his own fault.

Ans. It must be considered what you mean by "his fault."

1. If you mean a want of a natural faculty to manage affairs to advantage, that is to be considered as his calamity. Such a faculty is a gift that God bestows on some and not on others, and 'tis not owing to themselves. You ought to be thankful that God has given you such a gift that he has denied to him. And it will be a very suitable way for you to show your thankfulness to help them to whom that gift is denied and let them share of the benefit of it, which [is] as reasonable as that he to whom providence had imparted sight should be willing to help him to whom sight is denied, and that he should have the benefit of his sight, who has none of his own, or as he that God has given wisdom should be willing that the ignorant should have the benefit of his knowledge, or that he that has sound feet should be willing to lead the lame.

2. If they have been reduced to want by some oversight and are to be blamed that they did not consider themselves better, yet that don't free us from all obligation of charity to 'em. If we should forever refuse to help a man because of that, that would be for us to make his inconsiderateness and imprudent act an unpardonable crime, quite contrary to the rules of the gospel, which insist so much upon forgiveness. We should not be disposed so highly to resent such an oversight in any that we have a dear affection for, as our children or near friends, so as to refuse to help 'em in that necessity and distress which they have brought upon themselves by their own inconsiderateness; but we ought to have a dear affection and concern for the welfare of all our fellow Christians, whom we should love as brethren, as Christ has loved us.

3. If they are come to want by a vicious idleness or prodigality, yet we ben't thereby excused from all obligation to relieve 'em unless they continue in it. If they don't continue in it, the rules of the gospel direct us

to forgive 'em; and if their fault be forgiven 'em, then it won't remain to be any bar in the way of our charitably relieving of 'em. If we do otherwise, we shall act very contrary to that rule of loving {one another} as Christ hath {loved us}: as we observed, not in degree, but [in the] manner of our expressing {love}. Now, Christ has loved us, pitied us, and greatly laid out himself to relieve us from that want and misery that we brought on ourselves by our own folly and wickedness. We foolishly and perversely threw away those riches that we were provided with, upon which we might have lived and been happy to all eternity.

4. If they continue in the same courses still, yet that don't excuse us from charity to their families that are innocent. If we can't relieve those of their families without them having something of it, yet that ought not to be a bar in the way of our charity; and that, because 'tis supposed that those of their families are proper objects of charity. And those that are so, we are bound to relieve; the command is positive and absolute. If we look upon that which the heads of the families have of it[3] as entirely lost, yet we had better lose something of our estates than suffer those who are really proper objects of charity to remain without relief.

Tenth [*Obj.*] Some may object and say others don't do their duty. If others did their duty, the poor would be sufficiently supplied; if others did as much as they in proportion to their ability and obligation, they would have enough to help 'em out of their straits. Or, some may say, it belongs to others more than it does to me. They have relations that ought to help 'em, or there are others that it more properly belongs to than to me.

Ans. We ought to relieve others that are in want through others' fault. If our neighbor is poor and in necessity, though others are to blame that it is so, yet that don't excuse us from helping them.

If it belongs to others more than to us, yet if those to whom it properly belongs will neglect their duty, and our neighbor therefore continues in want, we may be obliged to relieve him. If a man is brought into straits through others' injustice—supposing he be brought into distress by thieves or robbers, as the poor Jew that the Samaritan relieved—yet we may be obliged to relieve him, though it was not through our fault that he is in want but through other men's. And whether that fault be a commission or a neglect, that alters not the case. The poor Jew that fell among thieves between Jerusalem and Jericho, it properly belonged to those thieves that brought him into that distress to relieve him more than any other. But yet, seeing they would not do it, others were not excused; and

3. I.e. our charitable gift.

the Samaritan did no more than his duty in relieving of him as he did though it more properly belonged to others. So if a man has children or other relatives to whom it most properly belongs to relieve him, yet if they won't do it {we may be obliged to relieve him}.

So we should do the more by the same reason for the relief of the poor, because others don't do their proportion or what belongs to them, and because, by reason of others' failing of doing their proportion, they need more; their necessity is greater.

Eleventh Obj. The law makes provision for the poor and obliges the town to provide for them. And therefore some argue that there is no occasion for particular persons to exercise any charity this way. They say the case is not the same with us now as it was in the primitive church; for then Christians were under a heathen government. And therefore, however the charity of Christians in those times is much to commended, yet now, by reason of our different circumstances, there is no occasion for private charity. In the state that Christians are now in, provision is made for the poor otherwise.

Ans. This objection is built upon these two suppositions, both of which I suppose are false.

1. That the towns are obliged by law to relieve everyone that otherwise would be an object of charity. This, I suppose to be false, unless it be supposed that none are proper objects of charity but only those that have no estate left to live upon, which is very unreasonable, and what I have already shown the falseness of, in answer to the fourth objection, where I have already shown that it don't answer the rules of Christian charity to relieve only those that are reduced to extremity.

Nor do I suppose it was ever the design of the law to cut off all occasion for Christian charity; nor is it fit there should be any such law. 'Tis fit the law should make provision for those that have no estates of their own; 'tis not fit that persons that are reduced to that extremity should be left to anything so precarious as a voluntary charity. They are in necessity of being relieved, and, therefore, 'tis fit that there should be something sure for 'em to depend upon. But a voluntary charity in this corrupt world is an uncertain thing; and therefore the wisdom of legislators did not think fit to leave those that are so reduced upon such a precarious foundation for a subsistence. But I don't suppose it was ever the design of the law to make such a provision for all that are in want, as to leave no room for Christian charity. But then,

2. This objection is built upon another supposition that is equally false, viz. that there are in fact none that are objects of charity but those that are relieved by the town.

Let the design of the law be what it will, yet if there are in fact persons that are in want, so as to stand in need of our charity, notwithstanding that [law], that don't free us from obligation to relieve 'em by our charity. For, as we have just now shown in answer to the last objection, if it more properly belongs to others to relieve them than we, yet if they don't do it, we ben't free. So that if that be true, that it belongs to the town to relieve all that are in want, so as otherwise to be proper objects of charity, yet if they in fact don't do it, we are not excused. If one of our neighbors suffers through the fault of a particular person, a thief or a robber, or of a town, it alters not the case; but if he suffers and is without relief, 'tis an act of Christian charity in us to relieve him. Now, 'tis too obvious to be denied that there are in fact those that are in want, so that it would be a charitable act in us to help them, notwithstanding all that is done by the town as a town. A man must hide his eyes to think otherwise.

A DIVINE AND SUPERNATURAL LIGHT

In *A Divine and Supernatural Light,* Edwards condensed much of a decade of preaching, rumination, and private writing on the nature of spiritual knowledge into a single, remarkable effort. First delivered in Northampton in August 1733 and printed in Boston the following year, it enhanced his reputation as a spokesman for experimental Calvinism and set forth many of the themes that undergirded his preaching through the Great Awakening.

Edwards draws heavily on eighteenth-century faculty psychology to argue that a saving knowledge of God is far beyond the faculty of understanding. The text (Matt. 16:17), he contends, reveals that Peter's confession of Christ's messianic nature derived not from speculative knowledge or a purely rational recognition of an objective fact; it was an affective and moral response to the presence of divine light in Peter's soul. As Edwards develops the Doctrine in three propositions, he argues that true revelation evokes love, esteem, and trust—responses of the faculty of the will (which, by Edwards' use here, includes moral judgment) rather than of the understanding. As such, it implies an experience of God, a sensation of God's moral character, and a new vital principle within the believer. God, that is, must bestow the Holy Spirit by his own sovereign initiative before individuals can have a right perception of him. Because revelation comes only from God's self-disclosure to the elect, natural reason or any other human means alone cannot be said to convey spiritual knowledge. In the short but quite powerful Application, Edwards asks his auditors to decide whether they have received divine light and exhorts them with reminders that this light is not only morally pleasing and joyful but the means of conversion and salvation.[1]

These were important themes to Edwards, developed in other writings in bits and pieces. The image of light served him several times in his

1. For further discussion of the argument of this sermon, see the Preface to the Period, pp. 40–44.

notebooks as a type for spiritual life, or beauty, or Christ. As early as 1723, he devoted a sermon to reflection on Christ, revelation, and light.[2] In the printed version of *A Divine and Supernatural Light*, he incorporated "Miscellanies" no. 489, on spiritual knowledge; several subsequent entries in the notebooks reflect a continuing interest in clarifying the relation between heart or spiritual knowledge and reason, the understanding and the will, affective judgment and faith. His treatise on *Religious Affections* picks up many of the ideas from *A Divine and Supernatural Light*. In sum, his expression of the nature of spiritual knowledge in this 1733 lecture became an integral part of his theology.[3]

In the preface to the first printed version of *A Divine and Supernatural Light*, Edwards claimed that his subject was "unfashionable" and "out of mode." Although he includes some warnings against enthusiasm in the lecture, his reference here appears more pertinent to religious rationalism. Certainly his comments could be construed as a critique of the implicit Arminianism of New Englanders who assent to the creed but who, in Edwards' terms, have only a notional knowledge of God. They deny—or simply ignore—the possibilities of a conversion experience initiated by the infusion of the divine and supernatural light of the Spirit. To this extent, the lecture on Matt. 16:17 gave Edwards a theoretical basis from which to promote evangelical revival.

* * *

The first edition, printed by Samuel Kneeland and Timothy Green in Boston in 1734, is an octavo pamphlet with a preface of two pages (printed here as an appendix to the sermon) and a main text of thirty-one pages. The full title reads: *A Divine and Supernatural* LIGHT, *Immediately imparted to the Soul by the* SPIRIT *of* GOD, *Shown to be both a* Scriptural, *and* Rational DOCTRINE, *In a* SERMON *Preach'd at* Northampton, *And Published at the Desire of some of the Hearers.* Under the title appear quotes from Job 28:20, Prov. 2:6, Is. 42:18, and II Pet. 1:19. The sermon proper is headed by the short title "The Reality of Spiritual Light."

The manuscript, a duodecimo booklet of thirteen leaves, shows several small editorial changes but does not indicate many of the major reorgani-

2. See *A Spiritual Understanding of Divine Things Denied to the Unregenerate*, in *Works, 14*, 67–96.

3. See "Images" nos. 52, 58, and 185, in *Works, 11*, 65, 67–69, 120; *Christ, the Light of the World*, in *Works, 10*, 287, 533–46; "Miscellanies" no. 498, in *Works, 13*, 533; and "Miscellanies" nos. 540, 628, and 630 in the forthcoming volume of *"Miscellanies," 501–832* in the Yale edition.

zations or additions made from manuscript to printed version.[4] The date "August 1733" appears at the front. There are no marks of a unit division, unusual for a sermon of this length. This suggests that Edwards intended it as a major statement even at the time of composition.

4. For a detailed discussion of the changes, see *Works, 10*, 111–15.

A DIVINE AND SUPERNATURAL LIGHT

MATTHEW 16:17.

And Jesus answered and said unto him, Blessed art thou, Simon Barjona: for flesh and blood hath not revealed it unto thee, but my Father which is in heaven.

CHRIST says these words to Peter, upon occasion of his professing his faith in him as the Son of God. Our Lord was inquiring of his disciples, who men said he was; not that he needed to be informed, but only to introduce and give occasion to what follows. They answer, that some said he was "John the Baptist, and some Elias, and others Jeremias, or one of the prophets" [16:14]. When they had thus given an account, who others said he was, Christ asks them, who they said he was. Simon Peter, whom we find always zealous and forward, was the first to answer; he readily replied to the question, "Thou art Christ, the Son of the living God" [16:16].

Upon this occasion Christ says as he does *to* him and *of* him in the text: in which we may observe,

1. That Peter is pronounced blessed on this account. "Blessed art thou. . . ." "Thou art an happy man, that thou art not ignorant of this, that I am Christ, the Son of the living God. Thou art distinguishingly happy. Others are blinded, and have dark and deluded apprehensions, as you have now given an account, some thinking that I am Elias, and some that I am Jeremias, and some one thing, and some another; but none of them thinking right, all of them misled. Happy art thou, that art so distinguished as to know the truth in this matter."

2. The evidence of this his happiness declared; viz. that God, and he only, had revealed it to him. This is an evidence of his being blessed,

(1) As it shows how peculiarly favored he was of God, above others, *q.d.* "How highly favored art thou, that others that are wise and great men, the scribes, Pharisees, and rulers, and the nation in general, are left in

darkness, to follow their own misguided apprehensions, and that thou should'st be singled out, as it were by name, that my heavenly Father should thus set his love on thee, Simon Barjona. This argues thee blessed, that thou should'st thus be the object of God's distinguishing love."

(2) It evidences his blessedness also, as it intimates that this knowledge is above any that flesh and blood can reveal. "This is such knowledge as my Father which [is] in heaven only can give. It is too high and excellent to be communicated by such means as other knowledge is. Thou art blessed, that thou knowest that which God alone can teach thee."

The original of this knowledge is here declared, both negatively and positively. Positively, as God is here declared the author of it. Negatively, as 'tis declared that flesh and blood had not revealed it. God is the author of all knowledge and understanding whatsoever: he is the author of the knowledge that is obtained by human learning; he is the author of all moral prudence, and of the knowledge and skill that men have in their secular business. Thus it is said of all in Israel that were wise-hearted, and skilled in embroidering, that God had filled them with the spirit of wisdom (Ex. 28:3).

God is the author of such knowledge; but yet not so but that flesh and blood reveals it. Mortal men are capable of imparting the knowledge of human arts and sciences, and skill in temporal affairs. God is the author of such knowledge by those means: flesh and blood is made use of by God as the mediate or second cause of it; he conveys it by the power and influence of natural means. But this spiritual knowledge, spoken of in the text, is what God is the author of, and none else: he reveals it, and flesh and blood reveals it not. He imparts this knowledge immediately, not making use of any intermediate natural causes, as he does in other knowledge.

What had passed in the preceding discourse, naturally occasioned Christ to observe this; because the disciples had been telling, how others did not know him, but were generally mistaken about him, and divided and confounded in their opinions of him: but Peter had declared his assured faith that he was the Son of God. Now it was natural to observe, how it was not flesh and blood, that had revealed it to him, but God; for if this knowledge were dependent on natural causes or means, how came it to pass that they, a company of poor fishermen, illiterate men, and persons of low education, attained to the knowledge of the truth; while the scribes and Pharisees, men of vastly higher advantages, and greater knowledge and sagacity in other matters, remained in ignorance? This could be owing only to the gracious distinguishing influence and revelation of the Spirit of God. Hence, what I would make the subject of my present discourse from these words, is this

DOCTRINE.

There is such a thing, as a spiritual and divine light, immediately imparted to the soul by God, of a different nature from any that is obtained by natural means.

In what I say on this subject at this time, I would

I. Show what this divine light is.

II. How it is given immediately by God, and not obtained by natural means.

III. Show the truth of the doctrine.

And then conclude with a brief improvement.

I. I would show what this spiritual and divine light is. And in order to it would show,

First, in a few things what it is not. And here,

1. Those convictions that natural men may have of their sin and misery is not this spiritual and divine light. Men in a natural condition may have convictions of the guilt that lies upon them, and of the anger of God, and their danger of divine vengeance. Such convictions are from light or sensibleness of truth: that some sinners have a greater conviction of their guilt and misery than others, is because some have more light, or more of an apprehension of truth, than others. And this light and conviction may be from the Spirit of God; the Spirit convinces men of sin: but yet nature is much more concerned in it than in the communication of that spiritual and divine light, that is spoken of in the doctrine; 'tis from the Spirit of God only as assisting natural principles, and not as infusing any new principles. Common grace differs from special, in that it influences only by assisting of nature, and not by imparting grace, or bestowing anything above nature. The light that is obtained, is wholly natural, or of no superior kind to what mere nature attains to; though more of that kind be obtained, than would be obtained if men were left wholly to themselves. Or in other words, common grace only assists the faculties of the soul to do that more fully, which they do by nature; as natural conscience, or reason, will by mere nature make a man sensible of guilt, and will accuse and condemn him when he has done amiss. Conscience is a principle natural to men; and the work that it doth naturally, or of itself, is to give an apprehension of right and wrong; and to suggest to the mind

the relation that there is between right and wrong, and a retribution. The Spirit of God, in those convictions which unregenerate men sometimes have, assists conscience to do this work in a further degree, than it would do if they were left to themselves: he helps it against those things that tend to stupefy it, and obstruct its exercise. But in the renewing and sanctifying work of the Holy Ghost, those things are wrought in the soul that are above nature, and of which there is nothing of the like kind in the soul by nature; and they are caused to exist in the soul habitually, and according to such a stated constitution or law, that lays such a foundation for exercises in a continued course, as is called a principle of nature. Not only are remaining principles assisted to do their work more freely and fully, but those principles are restored that were utterly destroyed by the fall; and the mind thenceforward habitually exerts those acts that the dominion of sin had made it as wholly destitute of, as a dead body is of vital acts.

The Spirit of God acts in a very different manner in the one case, from what he doth in the other. He may indeed act upon the mind of a natural man; but he acts in the mind of a saint as an indwelling vital principle. He acts upon the mind of an unregenerate person as an extrinsic occasional agent; for in acting upon them he doth not unite himself to them; for notwithstanding all his influences that they may be the subjects of, they are still "sensual, having not the Spirit" (Jude 19). But he unites himself with the mind of a saint, takes him for his temple, actuates and influences him as a new, supernatural principle of life and action. There is this difference; that the Spirit of God in acting in the soul of a godly man, exerts and communicates himself there in his own proper nature. Holiness is the proper nature of the Spirit of God. The Holy Spirit operates in the minds of the godly, by uniting himself to them, and living in them, and exerting his own nature in the exercise of their faculties. The Spirit of God may act upon a creature, and yet not in acting communicate himself. The Spirit of God may act upon inanimate creatures; as "The Spirit moved upon the face of the waters," in the beginning of the creation [Gen. 1:2]: so the Spirit of God may act upon the minds of men, many ways, and communicate himself no more than when he acts upon an inanimate creature. For instance, he may excite thoughts in them, may assist their natural reason and understanding, or may assist other natural principles, and this without any union with the soul, but may act, as it were, as upon an external object. But as he acts in his holy influences, and spiritual operations, he acts in a way of peculiar communication of himself; so that the subject is thence denominated "spiritual."

2. This spiritual and divine light don't consist in any impression made upon the imagination. 'Tis no impression upon the mind, as though one saw anything with the bodily eyes: 'tis no imagination or idea of an outward light or glory, or any beauty of form or countenance, or a visible luster or brightness of any object. The imagination may be strongly impressed with such things; but this is not spiritual light. Indeed when the mind has a lively discovery of spiritual things, and is greatly affected by the power of divine light, it may, and probably very commonly doth, much affect the imagination: so that impressions of an outward beauty or brightness, may accompany those spiritual discoveries. But spiritual light is not that impression upon the imagination, but an exceeding different thing from it. Natural men may have lively impressions on their imaginations; and we can't determine but that the devil, who transforms himself into an angel of light, may cause imaginations of an outward beauty, or visible glory, and of sounds and speeches, and other such things; but these are things of a vastly inferior nature to spiritual light.

3. This spiritual light is not the suggesting of any new truths, or propositions not contained in the Word of God. This suggesting of new truths or doctrines to the mind, independent of any antecedent revelation of those propositions, either in word or writing, is inspiration; such as the prophets and apostles had, and such as some enthusiasts pretend to. But this spiritual light that I am speaking of, is quite a different thing from inspiration: it reveals no new doctrine, it suggests no new proposition to the mind, it teaches no new thing of God, or Christ, or another world, not taught in the Bible; but only gives a due apprehension of those things that are taught in the Word of God.

4. 'Tis not every affecting view that men have of the things of religion, that is this spiritual and divine light. Men by mere principles of nature are capable of being affected with things that have a special relation to religion, as well as other things. A person by mere nature, for instance, may be liable to be affected with the story of Jesus Christ, and the sufferings he underwent, as well as by any other tragical story: he may be the more affected with it from the interest he conceives mankind to have in it. Yea, he may be affected with it without believing it; as well as a man may be affected with what he reads in a romance, or sees acted in a stage play. He may be affected with a lively and eloquent description of many pleasant things that attend the state of the blessed in heaven; as well as his imagination be entertained by a romantic description of the pleasantness of fairyland, or the like. And that common belief of the truth of the things of religion, that persons may have from education, or otherwise,

may help forward their affection. We read in Scripture of many that were greatly affected with things of a religious nature, who yet are there represented as wholly graceless, and many of them very ill men. A person therefore may have affecting views of the things of religion, and yet be very destitute of spiritual light. Flesh and blood may be the author of this: one man may give another an affecting view of divine things with but common assistance; but God alone can give a spiritual discovery of them.

But I proceed to show,

Second. Positively, what this spiritual and divine light is.

And it may be thus described: a true sense of the divine excellency of the things revealed in the Word of God, and a conviction of the truth and reality of them, thence arising.

This spiritual light primarily consists in the former of these, viz. a real sense and apprehension of the divine excellency of things revealed in the Word of God. A spiritual and saving conviction of the truth and reality of these things, arises from such a sight of their divine excellency and glory; so that this conviction of their truth is an effect and natural consequence of this sight of their divine glory. There is therefore in this spiritual light,

1. A true sense of the divine and superlative excellency of the things of religion; a real sense of the excellency of God, and Jesus Christ, and of the work of redemption, and the ways and works of God revealed in the gospel. There is a divine and superlative glory in these things; an excellency that is of a vastly higher kind, and more sublime nature, than in other things; a glory greatly distinguishing them from all that is earthly and temporal. He that is spiritually enlightened truly apprehends and sees it, or has a sense of it. He don't merely rationally believe that God is glorious, but he has a sense of the gloriousness of God in his heart. There is not only a rational belief that God is holy, and that holiness is a good thing; but there is a sense of the loveliness of God's holiness. There is not only a speculatively judging that God is gracious, but a sense how amiable God is upon that account; or a sense of the beauty of this divine attribute.

There is a twofold understanding or knowledge of good, that God has made the mind of man capable of. The first, that which is merely speculative or notional: as when a person only speculatively judges, that anything is, which by the agreement of mankind, is called good or excellent, viz. that which is most to general advantage, and between which and a reward there is a suitableness; and the like. And the other is that which consists in the sense of the heart: as when there is a sense of the beauty, amiableness, or sweetness of a thing; so that the heart is sensible of pleasure and delight in the presence of the idea of it. In the former is exercised merely the speculative faculty, or the understanding strictly so-called, or as spoken of in distinction from the will or disposition of the soul. In the latter the will, or inclination, or heart, are mainly concerned.

Thus there is a difference between having an opinion that God is holy and gracious, and having a sense of the loveliness and beauty of that holiness and grace. There is a difference between having a rational judgment that honey is sweet, and having a sense of its sweetness. A man may have the former, that knows not how honey tastes; but a man can't have the latter, unless he has an idea of the taste of honey in his mind. So there is a difference between believing that a person is beautiful, and having a sense of his beauty. The former may be obtained by hearsay, but the latter only by seeing the countenance. There is a wide difference between mere speculative, rational judging anything to be excellent, and having a sense of its sweetness, and beauty. The former rests only in the head, speculation only is concerned in it; but the heart is concerned in the latter. When the heart is sensible of the beauty and amiableness of a thing, it necessarily feels pleasure in the apprehension. It is implied in a person's being heartily sensible of the loveliness of a thing, that the idea of it is sweet and pleasant to his soul; which is a far different thing from having a rational opinion that it is excellent.

2. There arises from this sense of divine excellency of things contained in the Word of God, a conviction of the truth and reality of them: and that either indirectly, or directly.

(1) Indirectly, and that, two ways.

1. As the prejudices that are in the heart, against the truth of divine things, are hereby removed; so that the mind becomes susceptive of the due force of rational arguments for their truth. The mind of man is naturally full of prejudices against the truth of divine things: it is full of enmity against the doctrines of the gospel; which is a disadvantage to those arguments that prove their truth, and causes them to lose their force upon the mind. But when a person has discovered to him the divine excellency of Christian doctrines, this destroys the enmity, removes those prejudices, and sanctifies the reason, and causes it to lie open to the force of arguments for their truth.

Hence was the different effect that Christ's miracles had to convince the disciples, from what they had to convince the scribes and Pharisees. Not that they had a stronger reason, or had their reason more improved; but their reason was sanctified, and those blinding prejudices, that the scribes and Pharisees were under, were removed by the sense they had of the excellency of Christ, and his doctrine.

2. It not only removes the hindrances of reason, but positively helps reason. It makes even the speculative notions the more lively. It engages the attention of the mind, with the more fixedness and intenseness to that kind of objects; which causes it to have a clearer view of them, and enables it more clearly to see their mutual relations, and occasions it to take more notice of them. The ideas themselves that otherwise are dim, and obscure, are by this means impressed with the greater strength, and have a light cast upon them; so that the mind can better judge of them. As he that beholds the objects on the face of the earth, when the light of the sun is cast upon them, is under greater advantage to discern them in their true forms, and mutual relations, than he that sees them in a dim starlight or twilight.

The mind having a sensibleness of the excellency of divine objects, dwells upon them with delight; and the powers of the soul are more awakened, and enlivened to employ themselves in the contemplation of them, and exert themselves more fully and much more to purpose. The beauty and sweetness of the objects draws on the faculties, and draws forth their exercises: so that reason itself is under far greater advantages for its proper and free exercises, and to attain its proper end, free of darkness and delusion. But,

(2) A true sense of the divine excellency of the things of God's Word doth more directly and immediately convince of the truth of them; and that because the excellency of these things is so superlative. There is a beauty in them that is so divine and godlike, that is greatly and evidently distinguishing of them from things merely human, or that men are the inventors and authors of; a glory that is so high and great, that when clearly seen, commands assent to their divinity, and reality. When there is an actual and lively discovery of this beauty and excellency, it won't allow of any such thought as that it is an human work, or the fruit of men's invention. This evidence, that they, that are spiritually enlightened, have of the truth of the things of religion, is a kind of intuitive and immediate evidence. They believe the doctrines of God's Word to be divine, because they see divinity in them, i.e. they see a divine, and transcendent, and most evidently distinguishing glory in them; such a glory as, if clearly seen, don't leave room to doubt of their being of God, and not of men.

Such a conviction of the truth of religion as this, arising, these ways, from a sense of the divine excellency of them, is that true spiritual conviction, that there is in saving faith. And this original of it, is that by which it is most essentially distinguished from that common assent, which unregenerate men are capable of.

II. I proceed now to the second thing proposed, viz. to show how this light is immediately given by God, and not obtained by natural means. And here,

First. 'Tis not intended that the natural faculties are not made use of in it. The natural faculties are the subject of this light: and they are the subject in such a manner, that they are not merely passive, but active in it; the acts and exercises of man's understanding are concerned and made use of in it. God in letting in this light into the soul, deals with man according to his nature, or as a rational creature; and makes use of his human faculties. But yet this light is not the less immediately from God for that; though the faculties are made use of, 'tis as the subject and not as the cause; and that acting of the faculties in it, is not the cause, but is either implied in the thing itself (in the light that is imparted), or is the consequence of it. As the use that we make of our eyes in beholding various objects, when the sun arises, is not the cause of the light that discovers those objects to us.

Second. 'Tis not intended that outward means have no concern in this affair. As I have observed already, 'tis not in this affair, as it is in inspiration, where new truths are suggested: for here is by this light only given a due apprehension of the same truths that are revealed in the Word of God; and therefore it is not given without the Word. The gospel is made use of in this affair: this light is "the light of the glorious gospel of Christ" (II Cor. 4:4). The gospel is as a glass, by which this light is conveyed to us; I Cor. 13:12, "Now we see through a glass. . . ." But,

Third. When it is said that this light is given immediately by God, and not obtained by natural means, hereby is intended, that 'tis given by God without making use of any means that operate by their own power, or a natural force. God makes use of means; but 'tis not as mediate causes to produce this effect. There are not truly any second causes of it; but it is produced by God immediately. The Word of God is no proper cause of this effect: it don't operate by any natural force in it. The Word of God is only made use of to convey to the mind the subject matter of this saving instruction: and this indeed it doth convey to us by natural force or influence. It conveys to our minds these and those doctrines; it is the cause of the notion of them in our heads, but not of the sense of the divine excellency of them in our hearts. Indeed a person can't have spiritual light without the Word. But that don't argue, that the Word properly causes that light. The mind can't see the excellency of any doctrine, unless that doctrine be first in the mind; but the seeing the excellency of the doctrine may be immediately from the Spirit of God;

though the conveying of the doctrine or proposition itself may be by the Word. So that the notions that are the subject matter of this light, are conveyed to the mind by the Word of God; but that due sense of the heart, wherein this light formally consists, is immediately by the Spirit of God. As for instance, that notion that there is a Christ, and that Christ is holy and gracious, is conveyed to the mind by the Word of God: but the sense of the excellency of Christ by reason of that holiness and grace, is nevertheless immediately the work of the Holy Spirit. I come now,

III. To show the truth of the doctrine; that is, to show that there is such a thing as that spiritual light that has been described, thus immediately let into the mind by God. And here I would show briefly, that this doctrine is both scriptural, and rational.

First, 'tis scriptural. My text is not only full to the purpose, but 'tis a doctrine that the Scripture abounds in. We are there abundantly taught, that the saints differ from the ungodly in this, that they have the knowledge of God, and a sight of God, and of Jesus Christ. I shall mention but few texts of many; I John 3:6, "Whosoever sinneth hath not seen him, nor known him"; III John 11, "He that doth good, is of God: but he that doth evil, hath not seen God"; John 14:19, "The world seeth me no more; but ye see me"; John 17:3, "And this is eternal life, that they might know thee, the only true God, and Jesus Christ whom thou hast sent." This knowledge, or sight of God and Christ, can't be a mere speculative knowledge; because it is spoken of as a seeing and knowing, wherein they differ from the ungodly. And by these scriptures it must not only be a different knowledge in degree and circumstances, and different in its effects; but it must be entirely different in nature and kind.

And this light and knowledge is always spoken of as immediately given of God; Matt. 11:25–27, "At that time Jesus answered and said, I thank thee, O Father, Lord of heaven and earth, because thou hast hid these things from the wise and prudent, and hast revealed them unto babes: even so Father; for so it seemed good in thy sight. All things are delivered unto me of my Father; and no man knoweth the Son, but the Father, neither knoweth any man the Father, save the Son, and he to whomsoever the Son will reveal him." Here this effect is ascribed alone to the arbitrary operation, and gift of God, bestowing this knowledge on whom he will, and distinguishing those with it, that have the least natural advantage or means for knowledge, even babes, when it is denied to the wise and prudent. And the imparting the knowledge of God is here appropriated to the Son of God, as his sole prerogative. And again, II Cor. 4:6, "For God, who commanded the light to shine out of darkness, hath shined in our hearts, to give the light of the knowledge of the glory of God in the face of Jesus Christ." This plainly shows, that there is such a thing as a discovery of the divine superlative glory and excellency of God and Christ; and that peculiar to the saints; and also that 'tis as immediately from God, as light from the sun: and that 'tis the immediate effect of his power and will; for 'tis compared to God's creating the light by his powerful word in the beginning of the creation; and is said to be "by the Spirit of the Lord," in the eighteenth verse of the preceding chapter [I Cor. 3:18]. God is spoken of as giving the knowledge of Christ in conversion, as of what before was hidden and unseen, in that [place], Gal. 1:15–16, "But when it pleased God, who separated me from my mother's womb, and called me by his grace, to reveal his Son in me . . ." The Scripture also speaks plainly of such a knowledge of the Word of God, as has been described, as the immediate gift of God; Ps. 119:18, "Open thou mine eyes, that I may behold wondrous things out of thy law." What could the Psalmist mean, when he begged of God to "open his eyes"? Was he ever blind? Might he not have resort to the law and see every word and sentence in it when he pleased? And what could he mean by those "wondrous things"? Was it the wonderful stories of the creation, and deluge, and Israel's passing through the Red Sea, and the like? Were not his eyes open to read these strange things when he would? Doubtless by "wondrous things" in God's law, he had respect to those distinguishing and wonderful excellencies, and marvelous manifestations of the divine perfections, and glory, that there was in the commands and doctrines of the Word, and those works and counsels of God that were there revealed. So the Scripture speaks of a knowledge of God's dispensation, and covenant of mercy, and way of grace towards his people, as peculiar to the saints, and given only by God; Ps. 25:14, "The secret of the Lord is with them that fear him; and he will show them his covenant."

And that a true and saving belief of the truth of religion is that which arises from such a discovery, is also what the Scripture teaches. As John 6:40, "And this is the will of him that sent me, that every one that seeth the Son, and believeth on him, may have everlasting life." Where it is plain that a true faith is what arises from a spiritual sight of Christ. And John 17:6–8, "I have manifested thy name unto the men which thou gavest me out of the world. . . . Now they have known that all things whatsoever thou hast given me are of thee; for I have given unto them the words which thou gavest me, and they have received them, and known surely that I came out from thee, and they have believed that thou didst send me." Where Christ's manifesting God's name to the disciples, or giving them the knowledge of God, was that whereby they knew that Christ's doctrine was of God, and that Christ himself was of him, proceeded from him, and was sent by him. Again, John 12:44–46, "Jesus cried and said, He that believeth on me, believeth not on me, but on him that sent me; and he that seeth me seeth him that sent me. I am come a light into the world, that whosoever believeth on me should not abide in darkness." Their believing in Christ and spiritually seeing him, are spoken of as running parallel.

Christ condemns the Jews, that they did not know that he was the Messiah, and that his doctrine was true, from an inward distinguishing taste and relish of what was divine, in Luke 12:56–57. He having there blamed the Jews, that though they could "discern the face of the sky and of the earth," and signs of the weather, that yet they could not "discern" those "times"; or as 'tis expressed in Matthew, "the signs of" those "times" [Matt. 16:3]; he adds, "Yea, and why even of your own selves judge ye not what is right?" i.e. without extrinsic signs. "Why have ye not that sense of true excellency, whereby ye may distinguish that which is holy and divine? Why have ye not that savor of the things of God, by which you may see the distinguishing glory, and evident divinity of me and my doctrine?"

The apostle Peter mentions it as what gave them (the apostles) good and well-grounded assurance of the truth of the gospel, that they had seen the divine glory of Christ; II Pet. 1:16, "For we have not followed cunningly devised fables, when we made known unto you the power and coming of our Lord Jesus Christ, but were eyewitnesses of his majesty." The Apostle has respect to that visible glory of Christ which they saw in his transfiguration [Matt. 17:1–9]: that glory was so divine, having such an ineffable appearance and semblance of divine holiness, majesty, and grace, that it evidently denoted him to be a divine person. But if a sight of Christ's outward glory might give a rational assurance of his divinity, why may not an apprehension of his spiritual glory do so too? Doubtless Christ's spiritual glory is in itself as distinguishing, and as plainly showing his divinity, as his outward glory; and a great deal more: for his spiritual glory is that wherein his divinity consists; and the outward glory of his transfiguration showed him to be divine, only as it was a remarkable image or representation of that spiritual glory. Doubtless therefore he that has had a clear sight of the spiritual glory of Christ, may say, "I have not followed cunningly devised fables, but have been an eyewitness of his majesty," upon as good grounds as the Apostle, when he had respect to the outward glory of Christ, that he had seen. But this brings me to what was proposed next, viz. to show that,

Second, this doctrine is rational.

1. 'Tis rational to suppose that there is really such an excellency in divine things, that is so transcendent and exceedingly different from what is in other things, that if it were seen would most evidently distinguish them. We can't rationally doubt but that things that are divine, that appertain to the supreme Being, are vastly different from things that are human; that there is that godlike, high, and glorious excellency in them, that does most remarkably difference them from the things that are of men; insomuch that if the difference were but seen, it would have a convincing, satisfying influence upon anyone, that they are what they are, viz. divine. What reason can be offered against it? Unless we would argue that God is not remarkably distinguished in glory from men.

If Christ should now appear to anyone, as he did on the mount at his transfiguration; or if he should appear to the world in the glory that he now appears in in heaven, as he will do at the day of judgment; without doubt, the glory and majesty that he would appear in, would be such as would satisfy everyone, that he was a divine person, and that religion was true: and it would be a most reasonable, and well-grounded conviction too. And why may there not be that stamp of divinity, or divine glory on the Word of God, on the scheme and doctrine of the gospel, that may be in like manner distinguishing and as rationally convincing, provided it be but seen? 'Tis rational to suppose, that when God speaks to the world, there should be something in his word or speech vastly different from men's word. Supposing that God never had spoken to the world, but we had notice that he was about to do it; that he was about to reveal himself from heaven, and speak to us immediately himself, in divine speeches or discourses, as it were from his own mouth; or that he should give us a book of his own inditing; after what manner should we expect that he would speak? Would it not be rational to suppose, that his speech would be exceeding different from men's speech, that he should speak like a God; that is, that there should be such an excellency and sublimity in his speech or word, such a stamp of wisdom, holiness, majesty, and other divine perfections, that the word of men, yea of the wisest of men, should appear mean and base in comparison of it? Doubtless it would be thought rational to expect this, and unreasonable to think otherwise. When a wise man speaks in the exercise of his wisdom, there is something in everything he says, that is very distinguishable from the talk of a little child. So, without doubt, and much more, is the speech of God (if there be any such thing as the speech of God) to be distinguished from that of the wisest of men; agreeable to Jer. 23:28–29. God having there been reproving the false prophets that prophesied in his name, and pretended that what they spake was his word, when indeed it was their own word, says, "The prophet that hath a dream, let him tell a dream; and he that hath my word, let him speak my word faithfully. What is the chaff to the wheat? saith the Lord. Is not my word like as a fire? saith the Lord; and like a hammer that breaketh the rock in pieces?"

2. If there be such a distinguishing excellency in divine things, 'tis rational to suppose that there may be such a thing as seeing it. What should hinder but that it may be seen? 'Tis no argument that there is no such thing as such a distinguishing excellency, or that, if there be, that it can't be seen, that some don't see it; though they may be discerning men in temporal matters. It is not rational to suppose, if there be any such excellency in divine things, that wicked men should see it. 'Tis not rational to suppose, that those whose minds are full of spiritual pollution, and under the power of filthy lusts, should have any relish or sense of divine beauty, or excellency; or that their minds should be susceptive of that light that is in its own nature so pure and heavenly. It need not seem at all strange, that sin should so blind the mind, seeing that men's particular natural tempers and dispositions will so much blind them in secular matters; as when men's natural temper is melancholy, jealous, fearful, proud, or the like.

3. 'Tis rational to suppose that this knowledge should be given immediately by God, and not be obtained by natural means. Upon what account should it seem unreasonable, that there should be any immediate communication between God and the creature? 'Tis strange that men should make any matter of difficulty of it. Why should not he that made all things, still have something immediately to do with the things that he has made? Where lies the great difficulty, if we own the being of a God, and that he created all things out of nothing, of allowing some immediate influence of God on the creation still? And if it be reasonable to suppose it with respect to any part of the creation, 'tis especially so with respect to reasonable intelligent creatures; who are next to God in the gradation of the different orders of beings, and whose business is most immediately with God; who were made on purpose for those exercises that do respect God, and wherein they have nextly to do with God: for reason teaches that man was made to serve and glorify his Creator. And if it be rational to suppose that God immediately communicates himself to man in any affair, it is in this. 'Tis rational to suppose that God would reserve that knowledge and wisdom, that is of such a divine and excellent nature, to be bestowed immediately by himself, and that it should not be

left in the power of second causes. Spiritual wisdom and grace is the highest and most excellent gift that ever God bestows on any creature: in this the highest excellency and perfection of a rational creature consists. 'Tis also immensely the most important of all divine gifts: 'tis that wherein man's happiness consists, and on which his everlasting welfare depends. How rational is it to suppose that God, however he has left meaner goods and lower gifts to second causes, and in some sort in their power, yet should reserve this most excellent, divine, and important of all divine communications, in his own hands, to be bestowed immediately by himself, as a thing too great for second causes to be concerned in? 'Tis rational to suppose that this blessing should be immediately from God; for there is no gift or benefit that is in itself so nearly related to the divine nature, there is nothing the creature receives that is so much of God, of his nature, so much a participation of the Deity: 'tis a kind of emanation of God's beauty, and is related to God as the light is to the sun. 'Tis therefore congruous and fit, that when it is given of God, it should be nextly from himself, and by himself, according to his own sovereign will.

'Tis rational to suppose, that it should be beyond a man's power to obtain this knowledge, and light, by the mere strength of natural reason; for 'tis not a thing that belongs to reason, to see the beauty and loveliness of spiritual things; it is not a speculative thing, but depends on the sense of the heart. Reason indeed is necessary in order to it, as 'tis by reason only that we are become the subjects of the means of it; which means I have already shown to be necessary in order to it, though they have no proper causal influence in the affair. 'Tis by reason, that we become possessed of a notion of those doctrines that are the subject matter of this divine light; and reason may many ways be indirectly, and remotely an advantage to it. And reason has also to do in the acts that are immediately consequent on this discovery: a seeing the truth of religion from hence, is by reason; though it be but by one step, and the inference be immediate. So reason has to do in that accepting of, and trusting in Christ, that is consequent on it. But if we take reason strictly, not for the faculty of mental perception in general, but for ratiocination, or a power of inferring by arguments; I say if we take reason thus, the perceiving of spiritual beauty and excellency no more belongs to reason, than it belongs to the sense of feeling to perceive colors, or to the power of seeing to perceive the sweetness of food. It is out of reason's province to perceive the beauty or loveliness of anything: such a perception don't belong to that faculty. Reason's work is to perceive truth, and not excellency. 'Tis not ratiocination that gives men the perception of the beauty and amiableness of a countenance; though it may be many ways indirectly an advantage to it; yet 'tis no more reason that immediately perceives it, than it is reason that perceives the sweetness of honey: it depends on the sense of the heart. Reason may determine that a countenance is beautiful to others; it may determine that honey is sweet to others; but it will never give me a perception of its sweetness.

I will conclude with a very brief improvement of what has been said.

[IMPROVEMENT.]

I. This doctrine may lead us to reflect on the goodness of God, that has so ordered it, that a saving evidence of the truth of the gospel is such, as is attainable by persons of mean capacities, and advantages, as well as those that are of the greatest parts and learning. If the evidence of the gospel depended only on history, and such reasonings as learned men only are capable of, it would be above the reach of far the greatest part of mankind. But persons, with but an ordinary degree of knowledge, are capable, without a long and subtile train of reasoning, to see the divine excellency of the things of religion: they are capable of being taught by the Spirit of God, as well as learned men. The evidence that is this way obtained, is vastly better and more satisfying, than all that can be obtained by the arguings of those that are most learned, and greatest masters of reason. And babes are as capable of knowing these things, as the wise and prudent; and they are often hid from these, when they are revealed to those; I Cor. 1:26–27, "For ye see your calling, brethren, how that not many wise men, after the flesh, not many mighty, not many noble, are called. But God hath chosen the foolish things of the world . . ."

II. This doctrine may well put us upon examining ourselves, whether we have ever had his divine light, that has been described, let into our souls. If there be such a thing indeed, and it ben't only a notion, or whimsy of persons of weak and distempered brains, then doubtless 'tis a thing of great importance, whether we have thus been taught by the Spirit of God; whether the light of the glorious gospel of Christ, who is the image of God, hath shined into us, giving us the light of the knowledge of the glory of God in the face of Jesus Christ; whether we have seen the Son, and believed on him, or have that faith of gospel doctrines that arises from a spiritual sight of Christ.

III. All may hence be exhorted, earnestly to seek this spiritual light. To influence and move to it, the following things may be considered.

First. This is the most excellent and divine wisdom, that any creature is capable of. 'Tis more excellent than any human learning; 'tis far more excellent, than all the knowledge of the greatest philosophers, or statesmen. Yea, the least glimpse of the glory of God in the face of Christ doth more exalt and ennoble the soul, than all the knowledge of those that have the greatest speculative understanding in divinity, without grace. This knowledge has the most noble object that is, or can be, viz. the divine glory, and excellency of God, and Christ. The knowledge of these objects is that wherein consists the most excellent knowledge of the angels, yea, of God himself.

Second. This knowledge is that which is above all others sweet and joyful. Men have a great deal of pleasure in human knowledge, in studies of natural things; but this is nothing to that joy which arises from this divine light shining into the soul. This light gives a view of those things that are immensely the most exquisitely beautiful, and capable of delighting the eye of the understanding. This spiritual light is the dawning of the light of glory in the heart. There is nothing so powerful as this to support persons in affliction, and to give the mind peace and brightness, in this stormy and dark world.

Third. This light is such as effectually influences the inclination, and changes the nature of the soul. It assimilates the nature to the divine nature, and changes the soul into an image of the same glory that is beheld; II Cor. 3:18, "But we all with open face beholding as in a glass the glory of the Lord, are changed into the same image, from glory to glory, even as by the Spirit of the Lord." This knowledge will wean from the world, and raise the inclination to heavenly things. It will turn the heart to God as the fountain of good, and to choose him for the only portion. This light, and this only, will bring the soul to a saving close with Christ. It conforms the heart to the gospel, mortifies its enmity and opposition against the scheme of salvation therein revealed: it causes the heart to embrace the joyful tidings, and entirely to adhere to, and acquiesce in the revelation of Christ as our Savior; it causes the whole soul to accord and symphonize with it, admitting it with entire credit and respect, cleaving to it with full inclination and affection. And it effectually disposes the soul to give up itself entirely to Christ.

Fourth. This light, and this only, has its fruit in an universal holiness of life. No merely notional or speculative understanding of the doctrines of religion, will ever bring to this. But this light, as it reaches the bottom of the heart, and changes the nature, so it will effectually dispose to an universal obedience. It shows God's worthiness to be obeyed and served.

It draws forth the heart in a sincere love to God, which is the only principle of a true, gracious and universal obedience. And it convinces of the reality of those glorious rewards that God has promised to them that obey him.

Appendix to *A Divine and Supernatural Light*

THE PREFACE

I am sensible that my consenting that the following discourse of mine should be published needs excuse; but yet don't think it worth the while for me, here, to excuse myself by declaring how backward I was to it, and how much I was urged, and that I was prevailed with to do it, more to gratify others, and from an aim at promoting the interest of religion, and the good of souls, than by any thought I had of any honor that I should get by it. For such things, I apprehend, ordinarily make less impression upon the readers, to alter their thought of the author and his design, than the authors generally think for. They at whose desire, and upon whose account chiefly, this sermon is printed, are already acquainted with the circumstances of the matter; and if any others should happen to see it, and should think it worth their while to read it, I shall only desire of them, that they would put as favorable a construction upon my herein appearing in print as they can, and that they would read the following discourse with candor and without prejudice against it, either from an idea of the author's forwardness and ostentation, or the unfashionableness of the subject.

As to you, that are the people of the flock, of which Christ hath called me to the oversight, I have no reason to be jealous that you will have any prejudice against this discourse, upon either of those mentioned accounts, to stand in the way of your duly weighing, and considering, and suitably entertaining the things treated of in it. I have reason to bless God, that there is a more happy union between us than that you should be prejudiced against anything of mine, because 'tis mine. And however the subject is out of mode in the world, 'tis doubtless your peculiar happiness that you have been so thoroughly instructed in such like doctrines, even from your beginning. And I rejoice in it, that providence, in this day of corruption and confusion, has cast my lot where such doctrines, that I look upon so much the life and glory of the gospel, are not only owned, but where there are so many in whom the truth of them is so apparently manifest in their experience, that anyone who has had the opportunity of acquaintance with them in such matters, that I have had, must be very unreasonable to doubt of it. It is pleasant to me to read discourses on such subjects, and to see such doctrines well treated of in books, but much more pleasant to see them clearly exemplified. If what is here offered to you shall be a means further to establish you in such truths, and to make those among you that yet remain in spiritual darkness and blindness sensible of their misery and stir them up earnestly to seek after this spiritual and divine illumination, and shall be for the comfort and edification of those that have experienced it, I shall have great reason to rejoice and be thankful.

And I desire your earnest and continual prayers for me, that I may be the instrument of much such good to you, and glory to God therein.

J. E.

THE TRUE CHRISTIAN'S LIFE A JOURNEY TOWARDS HEAVEN

In this sermon, Edwards gently exhorts his listeners to forsake worldly attachments in pursuit of heaven. First delivered in September 1733, it may have been a funeral sermon, for it bears all the marks of that genre. It has a distinctly pastoral tone. The death of pious persons, Edwards preaches, should occasion not undue grief but rather reflection on the brevity of life in this world and the importance of self-sacrificial obedience in preparation for the afterlife.

The central metaphor of the sermon—life as a journey to heaven—was commonplace in Christian preaching. Edwards sustains this motif with simple organization and direct argument. The first of two units contains the Doctrine, the second the Application. Under the Doctrine, Edwards draws a parallel between wise travelers, who sacrifice all temporary pleasures in pursuit of their final destination, and Christians, who subordinate all earthly enjoyments—wealth and family included—in pursuit of heaven. In the Application, Edwards instructs people to forsake worldly preoccupations and sins like so much unnecessary baggage, exhorts them to labor for holiness, holds out the joys of heaven and the misery of hell as motives, and directs them to meditate on the true end of life's journey. He repeatedly draws on aspects of travel—toil and weariness, lodging and rest, perseverance and anticipation, homecoming and joy—to encourage a life of discipleship.

The True Christian's Life a Journey Towards Heaven also contains some of the most pietistic, even mystical, passages in all of Edwards' sermons. We should pursue knowledge of God, Edwards writes, to "come nearer and nearer to the beatific vision"; and we should grow in divine love "till our hearts ascend wholly in this flame." Saints' sight of heaven distances them from all temporal loyalties. This devotional language nearly overshadows Edwards' concern for theological precision (not to mention his concern for issues of social reform). He calls on the unregenerate to labor and strive to be obedient in order to reach heaven. He urges the regenerate to gain a larger measure of grace and secure heaven through their efforts. Yet he also reminds his auditors that heaven is a free gift offered only on the merits of Christ. Edwards does not bother to explain here the apparent incongruities between heaven as a reward and as a gift or to include a discussion of evangelical humiliation—that is, this sermon was not meant as a full statement of evangelical doctrine. Rather, it is a pastoral exhortation, given for rhetorical effect rather than for theological accuracy. As such, it may provide an inkling of the "flexibleness" (or interest in spiritual matters) that began toward the end of 1733 among Northampton's young people, and which shortly would erupt into full-blown revival.

* * *

The manuscript is a duodecimo booklet of eighteen leaves. The date of its first preaching, September 1733, is noted on the first page. Three subsequent preachings are also noted: at New Haven, at Boston in October 1753, and at Stockbridge to the Indian congregation on an unspecified date. There are also six "decibel" symbols near the top of the page, presumably Edwards' indication of popular reception. The manuscript bears many editorial marks, chiefly notations for repreaching. Following the statement of the doctrine is a shorthand notation: "Preached the parts marked in the margin the second time." Substantial portions of the first proposition are marked with vertical lines in the left margins. Later changes, most of them made in a black ink for the Boston repreaching, are supplied in the notes.

Samuel Hopkins edited the first printed version of the sermon for his *Life and Character of the late Reverend Mr. Jonathan Edwards . . . with . . . a Number of his Sermons* (Boston, 1765), pp. 253–79. Hopkins significantly condensed several sections, eliminating what he judged to be questionable formulations, repetitious sentences, and problematic prose.

THE TRUE CHRISTIAN'S LIFE A JOURNEY TOWARDS HEAVEN

HEBREWS 11:13–14.

And confessed that they were pilgrims and strangers on the earth. For they that say such things declare plainly that they seek a country.

THE Apostle is here setting forth the excellencies of the grace of faith by the glorious effects and happy issue of it in the saints of the Old Testament. He had spoken in the preceding part of the chapter particularly of Abel, Enoch, Noah, Abraham and Sarah.[1] Having enumerated these instances, he takes notice that these "all died in faith, not having received the promises, but having seen them afar off, were persuaded of them, and embraced them, and confessed that they were strangers and pilgrims on earth" [Heb. 11:13].

In these words the Apostle seems to have a more particular respect to Abraham and Sarah and their kindred that came with them from Haran out of Ur of the Chaldees, by v. 15, where the Apostle says, "and truly if they had been mindful of that country from whence they came out, they might have had opportunity to have returned." It was they that, upon God's call, left their own country. Two things may be observed in the text.

1. What these saints confessed of themselves, viz. that they were "strangers and pilgrims on earth." Thus, we have a particular account concerning Abraham; Gen. 23:4, "I am a stranger and sojourner with you." And it seems to have been the general sense of the Patriarchs, by what Jacob says to Pharaoh; Gen. 47:9, "And Jacob said to Pharaoh, The days of the years of my pilgrimage are an hundred and thirty years: few and evil have the days of the years of my life been, and have not attained to the days of the years of the life of my fathers in the days of their

1. For the Boston repreaching, JE added "Isaac and Jacob."

pilgrimage"; and Ps. 39:12,[2] "I am a stranger and sojourner with thee, as were all my fathers."

2. The inference that the Apostle draws from hence, viz. that they sought another country as their home: "for they that say such things declare plainly that they seek a country." In confessing that they were strangers, they plainly declared that this is not their country: that this is not the country where they are at home. And in confessing themselves to be pilgrims, they declared plainly that this is not their settled abode; but they have respect to some other country that they seek and are traveling to as their home.

DOCTRINE.

This life ought so to be spent by us, as to be only a journey toward heaven.

I. Explain the doctrine.[3]

First. We ought not to rest in this world and its enjoyments, but should desire heaven. This, our hearts should be chiefly concerned and engaged about; we should "seek first the kingdom of God" (Matt. 6:33). He that is on a journey, he seeks the place that he is journeying to. Thus, he is not content with the accommodations that he meets with upon the road, to rest in them. We ought above all things to desire a heavenly happiness: to go to heaven, and there to be with God and dwell with Jesus Christ.

We ought not to be content with this world, or so to set our hearts on any enjoyments we have here as to rest in them. No, we ought to seek a better happiness.[4] If we are surrounded with many outward enjoyments and things are comfortable to us; if we are settled in families and have those friends and relatives that are very desirable; if we have companions whose society is delightful to us; if we have children that are pleasant and likely,[5] and in whom we see many promising qualifications, and live by good neighbors, and have much of the respect of others, have a good name and are generally beloved where we are known, and have comfortable and pleasant accommodations: yet we ought not to take up our rest in these things. We should not be willing to have these things for our portion, but should seek happiness in another world.

2. JE mistakenly cites Ps. 119:12.

3. JE interlineated, but then deleted, the following outline here: "I. Explain the doctrine. II. Give the reasons." These headings have been restored for structural clarity.

4. In revising for repreaching at Boston, JE excised the foregoing part of the paragraph with a diagonal line.

5. In revising for repreaching at Boston, JE changed "likely" to "hopeful."

We should not merely seek something else in addition to them,[6] but should be so far from resting in them that we should choose and desire to leave these things for heaven, to go to God and Christ there. We should not be willing to live here in the enjoyment of these things always, if we could, in the same strength and vigor of body and mind, as when in youth or in the midst of our days, and always enjoy the same pleasant and dear friends and other earthly comforts. We should choose to leave 'em all in God's due time, that we might go to heaven, and there have the enjoyment of God.

We ought to desire that there may be an end to our living here in this world, when God shall choose. We should desire our journey's end, that we may arrive at our heavenly home. And whenever we are called to leave things, however pleasant to us, we ought so much to seek and desire heaven that we should be willing to part with them to go [to] heaven.[7] We ought to possess them and enjoy and make use of them with no other view or aim but readily to quit them whenever we are called to it, and to change them for heaven. And when we are called away from them, we should go cheerfully and willingly.

He that is going on a journey, he is not wont to rest in what he meets with, that is comfortable and pleasing, on the road. If he passes along through pleasant places, flowery meadows or shady groves, he don't take up his content in those things, he is not willing to sit down and stop here. He don't desire to stay here, no,[8] but he is content only to take a transient view of these pleasant objects as he goes along. He is not enticed by these fair appearances to stop[9] his journey and leave off the thoughts of proceeding; no, but his journey's end is in his mind. That is the great thing that he aims at. So, if he meets with comfortable and pleasant accommodations on the road, at an inn, yet he don't rest there. He won't take up his abode there in the inn.[1] He entertains no thoughts of settling there. He considers that these things are not his own but his landlord's,[2] and that this is not allotted for his home, that he is but a stranger. And when he has refreshed himself, or tarried but for a night, he is for leaving these accommodations, and going forward, and getting onwards towards his journey's end.

6. For the Boston version, JE changed "them" to read "these things."

7. For the Boston version, JE excised the preceding part of the paragraph with a vertical line.

8. For the Boston version, JE struck out the passage beginning "he is not willing to sit down" and ending here.

9. For the Boston version, JE replaced "to stop" with "to put an end to."

1. JE deleted this sentence in revising the sermon for Boston.

2. JE deleted "but his landlord's" in revising the sermon for Boston.

Though he has been comfortably entertained there, yet it is not at all grievous to him when he goes away. He goes from thence cheerfully, with the thoughts of getting to his own home, where he desires to be. And the thoughts of coming to his journey's end is not at all grievous to him. He don't desire to be traveling always, and never come to his journey's end; the thought of that would be discouraging to him. But it is pleasant to him to think that there is so much of the way is gone, that he is now near home, and that he shall presently be there, and the toil and fatigue of his journey will be over.

So, we should so desire heaven so much more than the comforts and enjoyments of this life that we should long to change these things for heaven. We should wait with earnest desire for the time when we shall arrive to our journey's end. The Apostle mentions it as an encouraging, comfortable consideration to Christians, when they draw nigh their happiness; Rom. 13:11, "now is our salvation nearer than when we believed."

Our hearts ought to be loose to these things, as it is with a man that is in a journey; however comfortable enjoyments are, yet we ought to keep our hearts so loose from them as cheerfully to part with them whenever God calls; I Cor. 7:29–31, "But this I say, brethren, the time is short: it remaineth, that both they that have wives be as though they had none; and they that weep as though they wept not; and they that rejoice, as though they rejoiced not; and they that buy, as though they possessed not; and they that use this world, as not abusing it: for the fashion of this world passeth away." But heavenly happiness should be all our salvation. We ought to look upon these things as only lent to us for a little while, to serve a present turn; but we should set our hearts on heaven as our inheritance forever.

When persons have dear companions, or children that are dear to them and need their care of them, yet they should enjoy them with no other view or aim but to quit and leave them to go to heaven whenever God calls them. Or when they have a comfortable subsistence or the credit and esteem of others, they should enjoy [them] with no other thought but, only in a little time, in God's time, to leave them for heaven without discontent or any anxiety. They should consider and use all these things only as the accommodation of a journey.

Second. We ought to seek heaven by traveling in the way that leads thither. The way that leads to heaven is a way of holiness; we should choose and desire to travel thither in this way, and in no other.

We should part with all those sins, those carnal appetites, that are as weights that will tend to hinder us in our traveling towards heaven; Heb.

12:1, "let us lay aside every weight, and the sin that doth so easily beset us, and let us run with patience the race that is set before us." However pleasant any practice or the gratification of any appetite may be, we must lay it aside, cast it away, if it be any hindrance, any stumbling block, in the way to heaven.

We should travel on as a way of obedience to all God's commands, even the difficult, as well as the easy, commands. We should travel on in a way of self-denial, denying all our sinful inclinations and interests. The way to heaven is ascending; we must be content to travel up hill, though it be hard, and tiresome, and contrary to the natural tendency and bias of our flesh, that tends downward to the earth. We should follow Christ in the path that he has gone; the way that he traveled in was the right way to heaven. We should take up our cross and follow him. We should travel along in the same way of meekness and lowliness of heart, in the same way of obedience, and charity, and diligence to do good, and patience under afflictions.

The way to heaven is an heavenly life. We must be traveling towards heaven in a way of imitation of those that are in heaven, in imitation of the saints or angels therein, in their holy employments, in their way of spending their time in loving, adoring, serving, and praising God and the Lamb.

This is the path that we prefer before all others. If we could have any other that we might choose, if we could go to heaven in a way of carnal living, the way of the enjoyment and gratification of our lusts, we should rather prefer a way of holiness, and conformity to the spiritual, self-denying rules of the gospel.

Third. We should travel on in this way in a laborious manner. The going of long journeys is attended with toil and fatigue, especially if the journey be through a wilderness. Persons in such a case expect no other than to suffer hardship and weariness, in traveling over mountains and through bad places.

So we should travel in this way of holiness in a laborious manner, improving our time and strength to surmount the difficulties and obstacles that are in the way. The land that we have to travel through is a wilderness; there are many mountains, and rocks, and rough places that we must go over in the way, and there is a necessity that we should lay out our strength.

Fourth. Our whole lives ought to be spent in traveling this road.

1. We ought to begin early. This should be the first concern and business that persons engage in when they come to be capable of acting, or

doing any business. When they first set out in the world, they should set out on this journey.

2. And we ought to travel on in this way with assiduity. It ought to be the work of every day to travel on towards heaven. We should often be thinking of our journey's end; and not only thinking of it, but it should be our daily work to travel on in the way that leads to it.

He that is on a journey, he is often thinking of the place that he is going to, and 'tis his care and business every day to get along, to improve his time to get towards his journey's end. He spends the day in it; 'tis the work of the day whilst the sun serves him, and when he has rested in the night he gets up in the morning and sets out again on his journey. And so, from day to day, till he has got to his journey's end. Thus should heaven be continually in our thought; and the immediate entrance or passage to it, viz. death, should be present with us, and it should be a thing that we familiarize to ourselves. And so it should be our work every day to be preparing for death and traveling heavenward.

3. We ought to persevere in this way as long as we live. We should hold out in it to the end; Heb. 12:1, "let us run with patience the race that is set before us." Though the road be difficult, and it be a toilsome thing to travel it, we must hold out with patience and be content to endure the hardships of it. If the journey be long, yet we must not stop short; we should not give out in discouragement, but hold on till we are arrived to the place we seek. We ought not to be discouraged with the length and difficulties of the way, as the children of Israel were, and be for turning back again. All our thought and design should be to get along; we should be engaged and resolved to press forward till we arrive.

Fifth. We ought to be continually growing in holiness and, in that respect, coming nearer and nearer to heaven. He that [is] traveling towards a place, he comes nearer and nearer to it continually; so we should be endeavoring to come nearer to heaven, in being more heavenly, becoming more and more like to the inhabitants of heaven, and more and more as we shall be when we are arrived there, if ever that be.

We should endeavor continually to be more and more as we hope to be in heaven, in respect of holiness and conformity to God. We should endeavor to be more & more {as we hope to be in heaven},[3] with respect to light and knowledge, should labor to be continually growing in knowledge of God and Christ, and divine things,[4] clear views of the glorious-

3. In revising for Boston, JE deleted the preceding part of the sentence and added "and" before "with respect."

4. In revising for Boston, JE deleted "and divine things."

ness[5] and excellency of divine things, that we come nearer and nearer to the beatific vision.

We should labor to {be continually growing} in divine love, that this may be an increasing flame in our hearts, till our hearts ascend wholly in this flame. {We should labor to be continually growing} in obedience, and an heavenly conversation, that we may do the will of God on earth, as the angels do in heaven.

{We should labor to be continually growing} in comfort and spiritual joy, in sensible communion with God and Jesus Christ. Our path should be as "the shining light, that shines more and more to the perfect day" (Prov. 4:18).

We ought to be hungering and thirsting after righteousness, after an increase of righteousness; I Pet. 2:2, "As newborn babes, desire the sincere milk of the word, that ye may grow thereby." And we should make the perfection of heaven our mark. We should rest in nothing short of this, but be pressing towards this mark, and laboring continually to be coming nearer and nearer to it; Phil. 3:13–14, "this one thing I do, forgetting those things which are behind, and reaching forth unto those things which are before, I press toward the mark for the prize of the high calling of God in Christ Jesus."

Sixth. And lastly, all other concerns of life ought to be entirely subordinated to this. As when a man is on a journey, all the steps that he takes are in order to further him in his journey and subordinated to that aim of getting to his journey's end; and if he carries money or provision with him, 'tis to supply him in his journey.

So we ought wholly to subordinate all our other business and all our temporal enjoyments to this affair, of traveling to heaven. Journeying towards heaven ought to be our only work and business, so that all that we have and do should be in order to that. When we have worldly enjoyments, we should be ready to part with them whenever they are in the way of our going towards heaven; we should sell all this world for heaven. When once anything that we have becomes a clog and hindrance to us in the way heavenward, we should quit it immediately. When we use our worldly enjoyments and possessions, it should be with such [a] view and in such a manner as to further us in our way heavenward: thus we should eat, and drink, and clothe ourselves, and thus we should improve the conversation and enjoyment of friends.

5. In revising for Boston, JE changed "gloriousness" to "glory" and interjected "of God, the beauty of Christ."

And whatever business we are setting about, whatever design we are engaging, we should inquire with ourselves whether this business or undertaking will forward us in our way to heaven; and if not, to quit our design. We ought to make use of worldly enjoyments and to pursue worldly business in such a degree and manner as shall have the best tendency to forward us in our journey heavenwards, and no otherwise.

[II.] Reasons.

First. This world is not our abiding place. Our continuance in this world is but very short: man's "days on earth are as a shadow" [I Chron. 29:15].

It was never designed by God that this world should be our home. We were not born into this world for that end; neither did God give us these temporal things that we are accommodated with for that end. If God has given us good estates, if we are settled in families and God has given us children, or other friends that are very pleasant to us, 'tis with no such view or design that we should be furnished or provided for here as for a settled abode. It was with that design, that we should use them for the present, but leave them again in a very little time.

If we are called to any secular business, or if we are charged with the care of a family, with the instruction or education of children, we are called to these things with that design, that we shall soon be called off from them again: [they are] not to be our everlasting employment.

So that if we improve our lives to any other purpose than as a journey towards heaven, all our labor will be lost. If we spend our lives in the pursuit of a temporal happiness; if we set our hearts on riches and seek happiness in them; if we seek to be happy in sensual pleasures; if we spend our lives to seek the credit and esteem of men, the good will and respect of others; if we set our hearts on our children and look to be happy in the enjoyment of them, in seeing them well brought up, and well settled, etc.,[6] all these things will be of little significancy to us. Death will blow up all our hopes and expectations, and will put an end to our enjoyment of these things. The places that have known us will know us no more, and the eye that hath seen us shall see us no more. We must be taken away forever from all these things. And 'tis uncertain when. It may be soon after we have received them and are put into the possession of them; it may be in the midst of our days, and from the midst of our enjoyments. Where will be all our worldly employments and enjoyments

6. A dash in the MS here perhaps indicates JE's intention to provide further examples.

when we are laid in the silent grave? For "man lieth down, and riseth not again: till the heavens be no more" (Job 14:12).

Second. The future world was designed to be our settled and everlasting abode. Here it was intended that we should be fixed, and here alone is a lasting habitation, and a lasting inheritance, and enjoyments to be had. We are designed for this future world. We are to be in two states: one in this world, which is our present state, the other in the world to come. The present state, in this world, is short, and transitory; our state in the other world is everlasting.

When we go into another world, there we must be to all eternity; and as we are there at first, so we must be, without change. Our state in the future world, therefore being eternal, is so exceedingly of greater importance than our state in this world, that it is worthy that our state here and all our concerns in this world should be wholly subordinated to it.

Third. Heaven is that place alone where is to [be] obtained our highest end, and highest good. God hath made us for himself: "of God, and through God, and to God are all things" (Rom. 11:36). Therefore then do we attain to our highest end, when we are brought to God. But that is by being brought to heaven, for that is God's throne; that is the place of his special presence, and of his glorious residence. There is but a very imperfect union with God to be had in this world: a very imperfect knowledge of God in the midst of abundance of darkness, a very imperfect conformity to God, mingled with abundance of enmity and estrangement. Here we can serve and glorify God but in an exceeding imperfect manner, our service being mingled with much sin and dishonoring to God.

But when we get to heaven, if ever that be, there we shall be brought to a perfect union with God. There we shall have the clear views of God's glory: we shall see face to face, and know as we are known [I Cor. 13:12]. There we shall be fully conformed to God, without any remains of sin: "we shall be like him; for we shall see him as he is" [I John 3:2]. There we shall serve God perfectly. We shall glorify him in an exalted manner, and to the utmost of the powers and capacity of our nature. Then we shall perfectly give up ourselves to God; then will our hearts be wholly a pure and holy offering to God, offered all in the flame of divine love.

In heaven alone is attainment of our highest good. God is the highest good of the reasonable creature. The enjoyment of him is our proper happiness, and is the only happiness with which our souls can be satisfied. To go to heaven, fully to enjoy God, is infinitely better than the most pleasant accommodations here: better than fathers and mothers, husbands, wives, or children, or the company of any or all earthly friends. These are but shadows; but God is the substance. These are but scattered beams; but God is the sun. These are but streams; but God is the fountain. These are but drops; but God is the ocean.

Therefore, it becomes us to spend this life only as a journey towards heaven, as it becomes us to make the seeking of our highest end, and proper good, the whole work of our lives; and we should subordinate all the other concerns of life to it. Why should we labor for anything else, or set our hearts on anything else, but that which is our proper end, and true happiness?

Fourth. Our present state, and all that belongs [to it], is designed by him that made all things to be wholly in order to another world. This world was made for a place of preparation for another world. Man's mortal life was given him here only that he might here be prepared for his fixed state. And all that God has here given us is given us to this purpose. The sun shines upon us, the rain falls, the earth yields her increase to us, civil affairs, ecclesiastical affairs, family affairs, all our personal concerns, are designed and ordered in a subordination to a future world by the maker and disposer of all things. They therefore ought to be subordinated by us.[7]

APPLICATION.

Use I is of *Instr.*

First. This doctrine may teach us moderation in our mourning for the death of such dear friends that, while they lived, improved their lives to right purposes. If they lived a holy life, then their lives were a journey towards heaven. And why should we be immoderate in mourning, when they are got to their journey's end?

Death to them, though it appears to us with a frightful aspect, is a great blessing to them. Their end is happy and better than their beginning: the "day of their death" is better to them than "the day of their birth" (Eccles. 7:1). While they lived, they desired heaven and chose it above this world or any of the enjoyments of it. They earnestly sought and longed for heaven. And why should we grieve that they have obtained heaven that they so desired and so earnestly sought?[8]

7. Here ends the first preaching unit. JE began the second unit by reciting the text and doctrine.

8. In revising the sermon for repreaching at New Haven, JE deleted the words "that they so desired and so earnestly sought."

Now they are got to heaven; they are got home; they never were at home before. They are got to their Father's house. They find more comfort, a thousand times, now they are got home, than they did on their journey. While they were on their journey, they underwent much labor and toil. It was a wilderness that they traveled through, a difficult road; there were abundance of difficulties in the way, mountains and rough places. It was a laborious, fatiguing thing to travel the road: they were forced to lay out themselves to get along and had many wearisome days and nights. But now they have got through; they have got to the place they sought. They are got home, got to their everlasting rest. They need travel no more, nor labor any more, nor endure any more toil and difficulty, but enjoy perfect rest and peace, and will, forever; Rev. 14:13, "And I heard a voice from heaven saying unto me, Write, Blessed are the dead which die in the Lord from henceforth: Yea, saith the Spirit, for they rest from their labors; and their works do follow them." They don't mourn that they are got home, but greatly rejoice. They look back upon the difficulties, and sorrows, and dangers of this life rejoicing that they have got through them all.

We are ready to look upon death as though it was a calamity to them. We are ready to mourn over them with tears of pity, to think that these that were so dear to us should be in the dark, rotting grave, that they should there turn to corruption and worms, that they should be taken away from their dear children, and other pleasant enjoyments, and that they should never more have any part in anything under the sun. Our bowels are ready to yearn over them, and to look upon it as though some sorrowful thing had befallen them, and as though they were in awful circumstances.

But this is owing to our infirmity, that we are ready thus to look upon it. They are in an happy condition; they are inconceivably blessed. They don't mourn, but rejoice with exceeding joy; their mouths are filled with joyful songs. They drink at rivers of pleasures. They find no mixture of grief at all that they have changed their earthly houses, and earthly enjoyments, and earthly friends, and the company of moral mankind, for heaven. They think of it without any degree of regret.

This is an evil world in comparison of that they are now in. Their life here, if attended with the best circumstances that ever any earthly life was, was attended with abundance that was adverse and afflictive. But now there is an end to all adversity; Rev. 7:16–17, "They shall hunger no more, nor thirst any more; neither shall the sun light on them, nor any heat. For the Lamb which is in the midst of the throne shall feed them, and lead them unto living fountains of waters: and God shall wipe away all tears from their eyes."

'Tis true, we shall see them no more while we are here in this world; yet we ought not immoderately to mourn for that, though it used to be pleasant to us to see them and though their company was sweet. For we should consider ourselves as but on a journey too: we should be traveling towards the same place that they are gone to. And why should we break our hearts with that, that they are got there before us, when we are following after them as fast as we can and hope, as soon as ever we get to our journey's end, to be with them again, to be with them in better circumstances than ever we were with them while here?

A degree of mourning for near relations, when departed, is not inconsistent with Christianity, but very agreeable to it; for as long as we are flesh and blood, no other can be expected than that we shall have animal properties and affections. But we have not just reason to be overborne, and sunk in spirit. When the death of near friends is attended with these circumstances,[9] we should be glad that they are got to heaven. Our mourning should be mingled with joy; I Thess. 4:13, "But I [would not] have you to be ignorant, brethren, concerning them which are asleep, that ye sorrow not, even as others which have no hope"—i.e. that they should not sorrow as the heathen that had no knowledge of a future happiness nor any certain hope of anything for themselves or their friends after they were once dead. This appears by the following verse: "For if we believe that Jesus died and rose again, even so them also which sleep in Jesus will God bring with him."

Second. If it be so, that our lives ought so {to be spent by us, as to be only a journey toward heaven}, how ill do they improve their lives that spend them in traveling towards hell. Some men spend their whole lives, from their infancy to their dying day, in going down the broad way to destruction. They don't only draw nearer to hell in[1] time, but they every day grow more and more ripe for destruction; they are more assimilated to the inhabitants of the infernal world. While others press forward in the straight and narrow way to life, towards Zion, and laboriously travel up the hill against the inclination and tendency of the flesh, these run with a swift career down towards the valley of eternal death, towards the lake of fire, towards the bottomless pit.

This is the employment of every day with all wicked men; the whole day is spent in it. As soon as ever they awake in the morning, they set out anew

9. I.e. with heavenly felicity.

1. In revising for Boston, JE added "length of."

towards hell, and spend every waking moment in it. They are constant in it; it is a work that they are very assiduous in. They are earnestly engaged in it.[2] They begin in early days, before they begin to speak; Ps. 58:3, "The wicked are estranged from the womb: they go astray as soon as they be born, speaking lies." They hold onto it with perseverance. Many of them that live to be old are never weary of it; if they live to be an hundred years old, they won't give out traveling in the ways to hell till they arrive there.

And all the concerns of life are subordinated to this employment. A wicked man is a servant of sin: his powers and faculties are all employed in the service of sin, and in fitting [them] for hell. And all his possessions are so used by him as to be subservient to the same purpose. Some men spend their time in "treasuring up wrath against the day of wrath" (Rom. 2:5). Thus do all unclean persons, that live in lascivious practices in secret. Thus do all malicious persons. Thus do all profane persons, that neglect duties of religion. Thus do all unjust persons, and those that are fraudulent or oppressive in their dealings. Thus do all backbiters and revilers. Thus do all covetous persons, that set their hearts chiefly on the riches of this world. Thus do tavern-haunters, and frequenters of evil company; and many other kinds of persons that might be mentioned.

Thus do far the greater part of man. The bulk of mankind are hastening onward in the broad way to destruction. The way, as broad as it is, is, as it were, filled up with the multitudes that are going with one accord this way. And they are every day flowing[3] into hell out of this broad way by thousands. Multitudes are continually flowing into the great lake of fire and brimstone out of this broad way, as some mighty river constantly disembogues its waters into the ocean.

Third. Hence, when persons are converted they do but begin their work, and set out on the way they have to go. They never, till then, do anything of that work which their whole lives ought to be spent in, which we have now shown to be traveling towards heaven. Persons before conversion never take a step that way. Then does a man first set out on this journey, when he is brought home to Christ. And he is but just set out in it; so far is he from having done his work, that he only begins first to set his face towards heaven. His journey is not finished; he is only then first-brought to be willing to go to and begins to look that way. So that his care and labor in his Christian work and business is then but begun, which he must spend the remaining part of his life in.

2. In revising for Boston, JE deleted the previous two sentences.

3. In revising for Boston, JE changed "flowing" to "going."

Those persons do ill who, when they are converted and have obtained hope of their being in a good condition, don't strive as earnestly as they did before, while they were under awakening. They ought henceforward, as long as they live, to be as earnest and laborious as ever, as watchful and careful as ever; yea, they should increase more and more.

It is no just objection or excuse from this, that now they han't the same to strive for: before, they strove that they might be converted, but that, they have obtained. Is there nothing else that persons have as much reason to strive, and lay out their strength for, as their own safety? We should will to be diligent and laborious that we may serve and glorify God, as that we ourselves may be happy. And if we have obtained grace, yet that is not all obtained that may be obtained. 'Tis but a very little grace that we have obtained; we ought to strive, that we may obtain more. We ought to strive as much as that we may [obtain] the other degrees that are before as we did to obtain that small degree that is behind. The Apostle tells that he forgot "what was behind," and "reached forth towards what was before" (Phil. 3:13).

Yea, those that have converted have now a further reason to strive for grace than they had before, for now they have tasted and seen something of the sweetness and excellence of it. A man that has once tasted the blessings of Canaan has more reason to press forward towards Canaan than he had before.

And then, those that are converted should strive that they may make their calling {and election sure}.[4] All those that are converted are not sure of it, don't know that they shall be always so. Still seeking and serving God with the utmost diligence is the way to have assurance, and to have it maintained.

Use II may be of *Exh.* So to spend the present life that it may only be a journey towards heaven. Labor to be converted, and sanctified, and to obtain such a disposition of mind that you may choose heaven for your inheritance and home, and may earnestly long for it, and be willing and desirous to change this world and all the enjoyment of it for heaven. Labor to have your heart so much taken up about heaven and heavenly enjoyments, as that you may rejoice at any time when God calls you to leave your best earthly friends and those things that are most comfortable to you here to go to heaven, there to enjoy God and Christ.

Be persuaded to travel in the way that leads to heaven, viz. in a way of holiness, in a way of self-denial and mortification, in a way of obedience

4. JE originally drew a dash to finish the sentence, but in revising for Boston he interlineated the final words.

to all the commands of God, in a way of following Christ's example, in the way of a heavenly life, an imitation of the saints and angels that live in heaven. Be content to travel on in this way in a laborious manner, to endure all the fatigues of it. Begin to travel it without delay, if you have not already begun it. And travel on it with assiduity; let it be your daily work, from morning to night, and hold out in it to the end. Let there be nothing that shall stop or discourage you, or turn you aside from this road. Labor to be growing in holiness, to be coming nearer and nearer to heaven, in that you are more and more as you shall be when you get to heaven, if ever that be. And let all other concerns be subordinated to this great concern of getting forwards towards heaven.

Consider the reasons that have been mentioned why you should thus spend your life. Consider that the world is not your abiding place and was never so intended of God. Consider how little a while you are to be here, and how little worth your while it is to spend your life to any other purpose. Consider that the future world is to be your everlasting abode, and that the enjoyments and concerns of this world have their being only and entirely in order to another world.

And consider further, for motive,

First. How worthy is heaven, that your life should be wholly spent as a journey towards it. To what better purpose can you spend your life, whether you respect your duty or your interest? What better end can you propose to your journey than[5] heaven?

Here you are placed in this world, in this wilderness, and have you your choice given you, that you travel which way you please; and there is one way that leads to heaven. Now where can you direct your course better, than this way? What can you choose better for your journey's end? All men have some aim or other in living. Some mainly seek worldly things; they spend their days in the pursuit of those things. But is not heaven, where is fullness of joy, forever and ever, much more worthy to be sought by you? How can you better apply your strength, and use your means, and spend your days, than in travelling in the road that leads to the everlasting enjoyment of God, to his glorious presence, to the city of the new Jerusalem, to the heavenly Mount Zion, where all your desires will be filled and [there is] no danger of ever losing your happiness?

No man is at home in this world. Whether he chooses heaven or no, yet here he is but a transient person. Where can you choose your home better than in heaven? The rest and glory of heaven is so great that 'tis worthy that we should desire it above riches, above our fathers' houses or

5. In revising for Boston, JE added "to obtain."

our own, above husbands, or wives, or children, or all earthly friends. It is worthy that we should subordinate these things to it, and that we should be ready cheerfully to part with them for heaven whenever God calls.

Second. This is the way to have death comfortable [to] us: if we spend our lives so as to be only a journey towards heaven. This will be the way to have death, that is the end of the journey and entrance into heaven, not terrible, but comfortable.

This is the way to [be] free from bondage through the fear of death, and to have the prospect and forethought of death comfortable. Does the traveler think of the journey's end with fear and terror? Especially when he has been many days traveling, it being a long and tiresome journey, is it terrible to him to think that he has almost got to his journey's end; are not men, rather, wont to rejoice at it? Were the children of Israel sorry, after forty years travel in the wilderness, when they had almost got to Canaan? This is the way to have death not terrible when it comes. 'Tis the way to be able to part with the world without grief. Does it grieve the traveler when he has got home to quit his staff and load of provisions that he had to sustain him by the way?

Third. No more of your life will be pleasant to think of, when you come to die, than has been spent after this manner. All of your past life that has been spent on a journey {to heaven} will be comfortable to think of on a death bed, and no more.

If you have spent none of your life [after this manner], your whole life will be terrible to you to think of unless you die under some great delusion. You will see then how that all of your life that has been spent otherwise is lost. You will then see the vanity of other aims you may have proposed to yourself. The thought of what you have possessed and enjoyed in the world will not be pleasant to you unless you can think, withal, that you have subordinated them to this purpose.

Fourth. Consider that those that are willing thus to spend their lives as a journey {to heaven} may have heaven. Heaven, as high as it is, and as glorious as it is, is attainable. It is attainable for such poor, worthless creatures as we are. Even such as we may have for our home that glorious region that is the habitation of the glorious angels: yea, the dwelling place of the glorified Son of God, and where is the glorious presence of the great Jehovah.

And we may have it freely. There is no high price that is demanded of us for this privilege. We may have it without money or price, if we are but willing to set out and go on towards it, are but willing to travel the road that leads to it, and bend our course that way as long as we live. We may, and shall, have heaven for our eternal resting place.

Fifth. Let it be considered that if our lives ben't a journey to heaven, they will be a journey to hell. We can't continue here always, but we must go somewhere else. All mankind, after they have been in this wilderness a little while, they go out of it. And there is but two places that they go to: the two great receptacles of all that depart out of this world. The one is heaven, whither a few, a small number in comparison, travel; the way hither is but thinly occupied with travelers. And the other is hell, wither the bulk of mankind do throng. And one or other of these must be our journey's end, the issue of our course in this world.

[III.] Directions.

First. Labor to get a sense of the vanity of this world: of the vanity of it upon the account of the little satisfaction [that] is to be enjoyed here, and upon the account of its short continuance and unserviceableness when we must stand in need of help, viz. on a death bed.

All men that live any considerable time in the world see abundance that might convince 'em of the vanity of the world, if they would but consider. Be persuaded to exercise consideration when you see and hear, from time to time, of the death of others. Labor to turn your thoughts this way; see if you can't see the vanity of the world in such a glass. If you were sensible how vain a thing this world is, you would see that it is not worthy that your life should be spent to the purpose thereof, and that all is lost that is not some way aimed at heaven.

Second. Labor to be much acquainted with heaven. If you are not acquainted with it, you will not to be like to spend your life as a journey thither; you won't be sensible of the worth of it, won't long for it. Unless you are much conversant in your mind with a better good, it will be exceeding difficult to you to have your hearts loosed from these things, and to use them only in subordination to something else, and to be ready to part with them for the sake of the better good. Labor to obtain a realizing sense of the heavenly world, to get a firm belief of the reality of it, and to be very much conversant with it in your thoughts.

Third. Seek heaven only by Jesus Christ. Christ tells us that he is "the way, the truth, and the life" (John 14:6). He tells us that he is the door of the sheep; John 10:9, "I am the door: by me if any man enter in, he shall be saved, and go in and out, and find pasture." If we therefore would improve our lives as a journey towards heaven, we must seek it by him and not by our own righteousness: as expecting to obtain [it] only for his sake, looking to him, having our dependence on him only for the purchase of heaven, and procuring it for us by his merit. And expect strength to walk in a way of holiness, the way that leads to heaven, only from him.

Fourth. And lastly, let Christians help one another in going this journey. There are many ways that Christians might greatly help and forward one another in their way to heaven: by religious conference and otherwise. And persons greatly need help in this way, which is, as I have often observed, a difficult way. Let Christians be exhorted to go this journey, as it were, in company, conversing together about their journey's end and assisting one another. Company is very desirable in a journey, but in no journey so much as this. Let Christians go united, and not fall out by the way, which will be the way to hinder one another, but use all means they can to help one another. This is the way to be more successful in traveling and to have the more joyful meeting at their Father's house in glory.

APPENDIX: DATED BATCHES OF SERMONS, 1730–1732, AND DATED SERMONS, JANUARY–DECEMBER 1733
DATING BY THOMAS A. SCHAFER

THE following list records the extant undated sermons that Edwards preached from January 1730 through December 1732, as well as sermons preached from January 1733, when he began dating his sermons, to December 1733, the end of the period covered by this volume. Undated sermons are listed according to approximate date of composition and the original Schafer number, followed by the title, if printed, or by the Scripture text, a statement of the doctrine, and any other relevant information, if unpublished. Within period groups, sermons are listed in canonical order. In some cases, more precise dating of a sermon consequent to its original numbering may be noted in its description. Sermon texts followed by an asterisk are printed in previous editions. Unless stated otherwise, the manuscript is in the Beinecke Rare Book and Manuscript Library, Yale University.

Winter–Summer 1730[1]

139. Num. 14:22–23. "There is such a thing as men's going on to provoke God by their sins, till they have committed the last sin that God will bear with, before he as it were takes up a resolution that they never shall be saved."
140. Deut. 32:35(b). "Vengeance for sin properly belongs to God."
141. II Sam. 22:26–27. "God will deal with all men according to their own temper and practice."
142. I Kgs. 8:35–36. "If a people in a time of sore drought acknowledge God, and turn from their sins which procure this judgment, and go to God through Christ by prayer and supplication; 'tis the way for them both to obtain the temporal blessing they need, and also to

1. Seven sermons (nos. 140, 147, 149, 152–54, and 158) are linked together by ink and are probably the earliest sermons in this group.

obtain great spiritual blessings that are far better." Doctrine from a later preaching.[2] Probably a fast sermon.

143. Job 36:22. "There is none teaches like God."
144. Ps. 10:6. "Wicked men ben't apt to be sensible but that it will always be with them as it is now."[3]
145. *Practical Atheism* (Ps. 14:1 [a]).
146. Ps. 119:2. "The way to receive the blessed fruits of religion, is to practice it with our whole hearts."
147. Is. 5:20. "The putting evil for good and good for evil in affairs of religion and the concerns of our souls, is a thing of a very fatal tendency."
148. Is. 33:14(a). "Wicked men cannot bear the misery of damnation."
149. Hab. 2:4. "The saints do live by faith."
150. *The Pure in Heart Blessed* (Matt. 5:8[a]).* Dwight ed., *8*, 280–304.
151. Matt. 5:13. "The church of God is in this depraved and corrupted world as the salt that preserves it from utter ruin."
152. Mark 9:44. "The torments of hell will be eternal."
153. Rom. 4:16. "The grace of God in the new covenant eminently appears in that, that it proposes justification only by faith."
154. Rom. 7:14. "Men as they are by nature are perfect slaves to corruption; or, they are entirely under the dominion of sin."
155. Rom. 9:22(a). "It is one design that God has upon his heart, to show how terrible his wrath is."
156. I Cor. 10:16(a). "The thing designed in the sacrament of the Lord's Supper, is the communion of Christians in the body and blood of Christ. Sacrament sermon.
157. I Cor. 10:22. "They that are so daring as to provoke God to jealousy, would do well to consider whether their strength be sufficient to oppose to his."
158. Phil. 3:11. "'Tis no matter what we go through in order to get salvation, so that we do but obtain it at last."
159. *Envious Men* (Jas. 3:16). Sacrament sermon, probably Aug. 9, 1730.
160. *The Dangers of Decline* (Rev. 2:4–5). Election sermon, probably May 27, 1730.

2. There are no watermarks in this sermon, but chain line spacing, ink, and hand require its location here. As the sermon was originally written, the text functioned as the doctrine, on which JE made eight observations. When he preached the sermon again in 1749, he attached a slip of paper with a doctrine summarizing the observations.

3. This sermon lacks a cm but has been distinguished from the London / GR sermons by the chain line positions.

Fall 1730[4]

161. *Honey from the Rock* (Deut. 32:13).
162. *God Makes Men Sensible of Their Misery Before He Reveals His Mercy and Love* (Hos. 5:15[a]).* Dwight ed., *8*, 44–63.[5]
163. John 1:14(a). "Our Lord Jesus Christ is full of grace and truth." Two sermons in separate booklets; the first on "truth," the second on "grace."
164. I Pet. 5:8. "The devil is exceeding great in his endeavors for the destruction of men's souls." MS at Franklin Trask Library, Andover Newton Theological School, Newton Centre, Massachusetts.

Fall 1730–Spring 1731[6]

165. Num. 14:21. "The glory and honor of God requires that his displeasure be manifested against sin." Fast day, Mar. 25, 1731 (according to auditor's notes, Hawley Papers, New York Public Library).
166. II Chron. 32:35. "God expects of us, that we should show our thankfulness for our mercies by our deeds." Thanksgiving sermon, Nov. 12, 1730.
167. Job 33:6–7. "'Tis a most desirable thing in our circumstances, to have a Mediator between God and us in our own nature, <one that is flesh, that is formed out of the clay as we are>."[7]
168. Ps. 73:18–19. "Those that are in a natural condition have reason to be always in fear of being destroyed."
169. Prov. 19:21. "However men may project about many things, yet there is never nothing cometh to pass but what God determines." Not extant; probably preached Mar. 21 (p.m.), according to auditor's notes.
170. Eccles. 2:26. "1. 'Tis to the godly alone that God gives wisdom and understanding to know how to use the worldly good things they possess, and ['tis the godly alone] that he enables truly to enjoy the comfort of them. 2. God gives wicked men the travail and vexation

4. Sermons in this batch are written on paper with either a London/IV or an English/GR[WT] watermark.

5. This sermon contains three double leaves constituting a half sheet bearing a London Wm. Though the mark is not identical with that on the rest of the London/IV paper, the sheet may have come with that batch, and the ink is compatible with this location of the sermon. But the possibility must be kept open that JE wrote it later, in fall 1730 or spring 1731.

6. Sermons in this batch are written on paper with an English/GR[WT] watermark.

7. JE added the words in angle brackets to the doctrine while writing the second sub-head under the third division of the doctrinal section; the earlier parts of the sermon presuppose the shorter form of the doctrine.

of gathering and heaping [up] worldly good things, but 'tis not for their own but the godly's benefit." Trask Library.

171. Eccles. 12:7.† "When a man dies, his soul goes to God who gave it."[8]
172. Jer. 17:9. "The heart of man is exceeding deceitful." Probably Mar. 28, 1731 (auditor's notes).
173. *Stupid as Stones* (Ezek. 3:27).†
174. Mic. 3:11. "A pretense of trusting Christ is a vain pretense, as long as men live wicked lives."
175. Zech. 11:8. "There is a mutual loathing and abhorrence between God and wicked men."
176. Matt. 7:21. "1. Not everyone that saith unto Christ, Lord, Lord, shall enter {into the kingdom of heaven}. 2. He that doth the will of God, he shall enter into the kingdom of heaven; or, he that keeps God's commandments ('tis the preceptive will of God that is spoken of)."
177. Matt. 11:12(a). "They that go to heaven are those that are set to obtain the kingdom of heaven." Preached May 2, 1731 (auditor's notes).
178. Matt. 11:29(a). "They that do truly come to Christ, they at the same time take Christ's yoke upon them."
179. Luke 6:24. "All the pleasure or comfort that ever wicked men are to have, they have in this life." Probably early Apr. 1731 (auditor's notes).
180. John 1:16. "1. Believers do receive of Christ, of the benefits he himself hath, and do partake with him therein. 2. There is every grace in the heart of a believer, which there is in Jesus Christ himself."
181. *Born Again* (John 3:3).
182. Acts 8:22. "Particular repentance is necessary to salvation."
183. Rom. 9:31–32. "It's of fatal consequence to men's souls, for 'em to trust in their own righteousness."
184. *God Glorified in Man's Dependence* (I Cor. 1:29–31).* Preached in Northampton in the fall of 1730; delivered with revisions at Boston on July 8, 1731, and published there the same year. Worcester rev. ed., *4*, 169–78.
185. *Self-Examination and the Lord's Supper* (I Cor. 11:28–29). Sacrament sermon, probably Mar. 21, 1731 (auditor's notes).

8. Sermons in this group marked with a dagger have no cm but have been distinguished from the following English/GR group by the spacing of the chain lines in the paper.

186. *The Perpetuity and Change of the Sabbath* (I Cor. 16:1–2).* Jonathan Edwards, Jr., *Sermons on the Following Subjects* (Hartford, 1780); Worcester rev. ed., *4*, 616–37.
187. *Serving God in Heaven* (Rev. 22:3). Mar. 14, 1731 (auditor's notes).

May–June 1731[9]

188. Eccles. 7:8. "'Tis what is more to be regarded how things will be in their end and issue, than how they begin."
189. Luke 11:27–28. "The hearing and keeping the word of God renders a person more blessed than any other privilege that ever God bestowed on any of the children of men." Octavo.
190. John 15:10. "Jesus Christ kept all his Father's commandments."
191. Rom 5:7–8. "There never was any love that could be paralleled with the dying love of Christ." Edwards removed the Application and incorporated it into the May 1737 sermon on II Cor. 9:15.
192. *Christians a Chosen Generation* (I Pet. 2:9).* Dwight ed., *8*, 379–417.
193. I John 3:9. "Grace is in the hearts of the saints, in this world, as a seed."

July–August 1731[1]

194. *East of Eden* (Gen. 3:24). Possibly a lecture.
195. Ps. 108:4. "God is a Being of transcendent mercy."
196. Luke 10:38–42. "1. The way to receive spiritual knowledge and wisdom, is to sit at Jesus' feet and hear his word. 2. The most acceptable way of showing respect to Christ, is to give hearty entertainment to his word. 3. Anxiousness and fullness of cares about the things of this world, is inconsistent with our minding the great concern of our souls as we ought to do." Three sermons.
197. Rev. 17:14. "1. Those that are Christ's and belonging to him, 'tis of God that they are so. 2. They that belong to Jesus Christ, they are faithful to Christ."
198. Rev. 22:17. "Nothing is required in order to having all the blessings of the gospel, but willingly receiving." Incomplete as extant; possibly uncompleted.

9. Paper in sermons from this period are English/GR^{WT}, Maid of Dort/CAW, and odd pieces.

1. Of the sermons in this batch, no. 198 is composed wholly of a discarded "Notes on Scripture" index (three double leaves), the much longer no. 197 is mostly from the index, no. 196 contains two double leaves of index paper to eleven of English/GR, and nos. 194 and 195 are wholly English/GR except for a piece of index paper at the end of each.

August 1731–December 1732[2]

199. Gen. 4:7.† "Wicked men's sins lie at their door."[3]
200. Gen. 32:26–29. "The way to obtain the blessing of God, is not to let God go except he bless us."
201. Ex. 19:4. "God carries his people along through the world towards glory far above the reach of all their enemies, or anything that might hinder their blessedness."
202. Ex. 33:18–19. "God's goodness is that wherein his glory doth eminently appear to the children of men." Possibly a thanksgiving sermon.
203. II Kgs. 20:1–3. "When persons look death in the face, they stand in great need of clear evidences of their being at good terms with God."
204. Job 11:12. "Man is naturally a proud creature."
205. Job 18:15. "The wrath and curse of God attends all the concerns of some men."
206. Ps. 78:25. "Those that spiritually partake of Christ, they eat angels' food." Probably a sacrament sermon.
207. Ps. 94:12(a). "He is a happy man, though an afflicted one, whom God chastens and teaches out of his Word." Edwards titled this "For bid lecture."
208. Prov. 8:34. "The way to obtain grace, is daily to wait upon God for it in the use [of] the means of his appointment."
209. Prov. 14:14. "They that set out in religion and go back again, shall have enough of the fruits of it to make them bitterly repent it."
210. Prov. 16:4.† "Wicked men answer the end of their creation no other way but in their suffering."
211. Prov. 26:11. "Wicked men, though for a while they may seem to forsake their sins; yet if their natures are not changed, they will be very liable to return to them again."
212. *The State of Public Affairs* (Prov. 28:2). Possibly for an election or for a fast day to commemorate the death of a public leader.
213. Prov. 28:13. "God stands ready to forgive every sinner, upon his heartily confessing and forsaking his sin."
214. Eccles. 12:1(a).† "The time of youth is the best time to be improved to religious purposes."

2. Sermons in this batch are written on paper with an English/GR watermark.

3. Sermons in this batch marked with a dagger have no cm but are distinguished from the preceding English/GR^{WT} by the spacing of the chain lines.

215. Is. 1:5. "There are some men that, whatever means are used with them, will only grow worse and worse."
216. Is. 53:10(a). "That Christ should see sinners converted and saved, was part of the reward that God promised him for his sufferings."
217. Jer. 5:31. "They that are going on in sin would do well to consider, what they shall do in the end thereof."
218. Jer. 6:4. "'Tis very sorrowful when 'tis late in the day with persons, and a work of great importance and difficulty remains undone, that must be done before the day be past."
219. Jer. 10:16. "1. God is his people's portion. 2. God's people are God's portion." Two sermons.
220. Ezek. 7:10. Not extant; cited in "Miscellanies" no. 588 on the "eternity of hell punishment, the justice and suitableness of it."
221. Ezek. 16:5–6. "Man never would have had any pity from anyone, in the miserable state into which he fell, if God had not pitied him."
222. Ezek. 23:37–39.* "When they that attend ordinances of divine worship allow themselves in known wickedness, they are guilty of dreadfully profaning and polluting those ordinances." Probably a sacrament sermon. Worcester rev. ed., *4*, 525–39.
223. Dan. 5:5–6. "Guilt is a thing that is sufficient to ruin sensual pleasures."
224. Hos. 11:9. "'Tis well for us, that God is not as we are."
225. Zech. 7:5–6. "No religion is acceptable to God but that which is done from a true respect to him."
226. Zech. 8:23. "It is what may well make us willing and desirous to go with God's people, that God is with them."
227. Matt. 5:4(a).† "Mourning is the way to true comfort."
228. Matt. 5:29. "Wicked men shall go to hell."
229. Matt. 5:44. "Men ought to love their enemies."
230. Matt. 10:17. "The nature of man is so corrupted, that he is become a very evil and hurtful creature."
231. Matt. 11:6. "They are blessed persons, that hear the gospel of Christ and are not offended in him."
232. Matt. 11:21. "Sinners under means of grace are ordinarily more hardened in sin than the heathen."
233. Matt. 11:29(b). "We ought to follow Christ's example."
234. Matt. 16:21–23. "It was a thing exceeding offensive to Christ, to hear anything said against enduring those great sufferings which he came into the world to undergo."

235. Matt. 22:14. "There are but few, even of those that live under the calls of the gospel, that shall be saved." Only the first double leaf is extant.
236. Matt. 25:8. "1. The religion of hypocrites is not of a durable nature. 2. When Christ comes, wicked men's hopes of salvation, and seeming evidences of conviction, will at once totally vanish and disappear."
237. Luke 6:35. "God is kind to the unthankful and to the evil."
238. Luke 9:18. "True Christians differ from all the world in their thoughts of Jesus Christ."
239. Luke 10:2. "1. The character under which God is here spoken of, viz. the Lord of the harvest. 2. The duty here directed to, viz. to pray that God would send forth laborers into his harvest." Preached to a congregation without a pastor.
240. Luke 10:42(a). "1. Grace is the one thing needful. 2. True grace is the good part . . . 3. Grace differs from all worldly enjoyments in this, that it is a portion that never shall be taken away from those that do possess [it]."
241. Luke 12:4–5. "1. The worst evils that the power of men can inflict, are as nothing in comparison of damnation. 2. 'Tis a thing of great importance, that persons be thoroughly possessed with a dread of the wrath and vengeance of God."
242. Luke 13:7. Not extant; the Application is cited in "Miscellanies" no. 564 as giving "reasons why hell is the fittest place for wicked men."
243. Luke 13:28–29. "Wicked men will hereafter have this to aggravate their woe, that they shall see many of all kinds and nations admitted into glory, when they themselves are thrust out."
244. Luke 16:25(a). "Wicked men in hell will remember how things were with them here in this world."
245. Luke 16:25(b). "The wicked in hell will be sensible what a happy state the saints are in in heaven." This and no. 244 are now in separate booklets but were preached on the same day.
246. Luke 22:31. "Christ's intercession is that which will effectually secure believers from ever totally and finally falling away from grace."
247. Acts 8:8.† "'Tis a blessed time amongst a people, when it is a time of the pouring out of God's Spirit upon them."
248. Rom. 2:5(a). "Unawakened and impenitent sinners do heap up to themselves wrath against the day of wrath, as men are wont to heap up treasures."
249. Rom. 3:13–18. "The nature of man in his fallen state is utterly and universally corrupt."

250. Rom. 9:18.* "God doth exercise his sovereignty in the affair of men's eternal salvation." Dwight ed., *8*, 105–22.
251. I Cor. 8:13. "We ought to be exceeding careful that we don't lead others into sin."
252. I Cor. 10:8–11. "Those awful temporal destructions that we have an account of God's bringing on wicked men of old, are types and shadows of God's eternal judgments."
253. I Cor. 15:34. "It is a matter of awful note and consideration, that there are some men that have not the knowledge of God."
254. Gal. 2:17. "The gospel is no encouragement to sin."
255. Col. 2:13–15. "When a sinner is converted, then Jesus Christ triumphs over his enemy the devil."
256. Heb. 12:2–3. "The redeeming love of Christ held out under great difficulties and discouragements."
257. Heb. 12:29(a). "God is a consuming fire."
258. Jas. 1:26. "Bridling the tongue is a great and essential part of religion."
259. Jas. 2:19(a).† "The devils tremble at the thoughts of the wrath of God."
260. I Pet. 1:13. "When persons are seeking God's grace and blessing in the way of his appointment, they ought to hope to the end for the bestowment of it."
261. I Pet. 2:5. "The good works of the godly can't be accepted any other way, than in and through Christ."
262. Rev. 3:5(a). "He that overcomes in the spiritual warfare, Christ will confess his name before his Father and before his angels."
263. Rev. 5:12. "Christ was worthy of his exaltation upon the account of his being slain."
264. Rev. 6:15–16. "Wicked men will hereafter earnestly wish to be turned to nothing and forever cease to be, that they may escape the wrath of God."
265. Rev. 19:2–3. "'Tis not inconsistent with the attributes of God, to punish ungodly men with a misery that is eternal."

Undated Sermons: Printed Text Only

266. "Great Guilt No Obstacle to the Pardon of the Returning Sinner" (Ps. 25:11).* Worcester rev. ed., *4*, 422–28.
267. "The Vain Self-Flatteries of the Sinner" (Ps. 36:2).* Worcester rev. ed., *4*, 322–29.
268. "The Warnings of Scripture are in the Best Manner Adapted to the Awakening and Conversion of Sinners" (Luke 16:31).* Worcester rev. ed., *4*, 330–37.

Dated Sermons

269. *The Duty of Charity to the Poor* (Deut. 15:7–11).* Jan. 1733. Possibly a contribution lecture. [John Erskine, ed.,] *Practical Sermons* (Edinburgh, 1788), 343–85; Dwight ed., *6*, 536–68.
270. I Cor. 11:29. "The sacrament of the Lord's Supper is a very sacred ordinance." Jan. 1733. Two sermons.
271. I Sam. 1:27–28. "'Tis a reasonable and becoming thing that we should give those things to God and devote 'em to his service that we receive from him as the fruit of his goodness." Feb. 1733.
272. I Sam. 28:15. "Saul was a remarkable instance of the awful and doleful circumstances a man is in when left of God." Feb. 1733.
273. Eccles. 4:5. "Many persons suffer the most extreme misery through slothful neglecting to seek their own good." Feb. 1733. Trask Library.
274. Job 20:11. "Many persons never get rid of the guilt of the sins of their youth, but it attends them to their graves and goes with them into eternity." Mar. 1733, to young people at a private meeting.
275. Ps. 51:17. "A broken heart is an acceptable sacrifice to God." Mar. 1733. Fast sermon.
276. Eph. 3:10. "The wisdom appearing in the way of salvation by Jesus Christ is far above the wisdom of the angels." Mar. 1733.
277. Rev. 18:20. "When the saints in glory shall see the wrath of God executed on ungodly men, it will be no occasion of grief to 'em, but of rejoicing." Mar. 1733.
278. Matt. 5:27–28. "The law of God is exceedingly strict." Apr. 1733.
279. Matt. 13:22(b). "The world is commonly a great snare to the souls of men." Apr. 1733.
280. Eph. 2:12. "When men are in a natural condition, they are without Christ and are alien from the commonwealth of Israel, and strangers from the covenant of promise, having [no] good ground of hope, and without God in the world." Apr. 1733.
281. Jas. 1:13. "'Tis impossible that God should be under any temptation to do anything that is evil." Apr. 1733. Lecture.
282. Ps. 110:2. "Christ will rule in the midst of his enemies." May 1733. Lecture.
283. Cant. 2:3(a). "The true believer hath rest in Christ." May 1733.
284. Matt. 13:41–42. "The wicked hereafter will be cast into a furnace of fire." May 1733.
285. Heb. 12:14. "None will ever be admitted to see Christ but only holy persons." May 1733.

286. John 5:43. "Man's heart is naturally wholly opposite to the gospel." June 1733.
287. Luke 22:30. "The saints shall hereafter as it were eat and drink with Christ at his table in his kingdom of glory." June 1733. Sacrament. Trask Library.
288. Cant. 1:3. "That Jesus Christ is a person transcendently excellent and lovely." June 1733, at Boston. Octavo.
289. Ps. 39:4. "It would be a thing that would tend much to men's spiritual profit and advantage if they would be much in considering their own mortality." July 1733.
290. Rom. 12:17. "It becomes Christians in all things relating to their outward estates to live honestly with their neighbors." July 1733.
291. II Cor. 4:18(a). "The things of the unseen world are eternal things." July 1733. Edwards noted that "This may be preached at new place."
292. John 14:23. "They that love and obey Christ, God and Christ will come to them and dwell with them." Aug. 1733.
293. Eph. 4:19. "Some men's consciences are in a great measure past feeling." Aug. 1733.
294. I Cor. 5:7. "Christ was represented by the lamb that was sacrificed at the Passover." Aug. 1733. Sacrament.
295. *A Divine and Supernatural Light* (Matt. 16:17).* Aug. 1733. Published in Boston, 1734. Worcester rev. ed., *4*, 438–50.
296. I Pet. 2:8. "It would have been better for some persons if Christ never had come into the world to save sinners." Aug. 1733.
297. Ps. 139:23–24. "Persons should be much concerned to know, whether they do not live in some way of sin." Sept. 1733.
298. Dan. 6:23. "Faith renders those things that are most terrible in their own nature harmless to believers." Sept. 1733.
299. *The True Christian's Life a Journey Towards Heaven* (Heb. 11:13–14).* Sept. 1733. Hopkins, *Life and Character of the late Reverend Mr. Jonathan Edwards* (Boston, 1765), 253–79; Worcester rev. ed., *4*, 579–84.
300. Jer. 8:11. "'Tis greatly to be desired that we should have a thorough and not only a slight and deceitful cure of our spiritual wound." Oct. 1733.
301. Matt. 28:9. "We ought to exercise the most dear, humble and adoring respect to the Lord Jesus Christ." Oct. 1733.
302. II Tim. 2:26. "Wicked men are the devil's captives." Oct. 1733.
303. Prov. 27:22. "Folly is naturally so rooted and confirmed in men that

if God leaves them to themselves, let what will be done with them, they will not learn wisdom." Nov. 1733.

304. Micah 2:11. "If the business of ministers was the further gratification of men's lusts, they would be much better received by many than they are now." Nov. 1733.

305. Mark 6:17–20. "There are many persons that would feign have salvation and do many things for it, and yet there are some particular sins that they will not part with." Nov. 1733.

305a. Phil. 4:19. "All the mercy that we receive of God is by Jesus Christ." N. d. [c. Nov.-Dec. 1733].

306. Deut. 10:13. "There is much of the goodness and mercy of God appears in the commands that he has given us." Dec. 1733.

307. Eccles. 9:10(b). "Persons ought to do what they can for their salvation." Dec. 1733. Originally stitched together with no. 311.

308. John 15:15. "When Christ was upon earth, he did not keep at an awful distance from his disciples, but was intimate with them as friends." Dec. 1733.

309. John 1:41–42. "When persons have truly come to Christ themselves, they naturally desire to bring others also to him." Dec. 1733.

310. Phil. 3:13. "There is one affair that we would be so taken up about and so devoted to that all others things should be nothing with us in comparison of it." Dec. 1733, at a private meeting in Windsor.

GENERAL INDEX

In this index the abbreviation JE has been used for Jonathan Edwards. All works are by Edwards unless otherwise indicated.

INDEX OF BIBLICAL PASSAGES

OLD TESTAMENT

NEW TESTAMENT